Subject
and
Information
Analysis

BOOKS IN LIBRARY AND INFORMATION SCIENCE
A Series of Monographs and Textbooks
EDITOR
ALLEN KENT
School of Library and Information Science
University of Pittsburgh
Pittsburgh, Pennsylvania

ADVISORY BOARD

C. David Batty
University of Maryland

Julie H. Bichteler
The University of Texas at Austin

Anindya Bose
University of Denver

Scott Bruntjen
Pittsburgh Regional Library Center

Eric de Grolier
Paris, France

Tom Featheringham
New Jersey Institute of Technology

Maurice J. Freedman
Columbia University

Thomas J. Galvin
University of Pittsburgh

Edward J. Kazlauskas
University of Southern California

Chai Kim
University of Rhode Island

Irving M. Klempner
State University of New York at Albany

Boaz Lazinger
Jerusalem, Israel

John A. McCrossan
University of South Florida

Paul E. Peters
Columbia University

Allan D. Pratt
The University of Arizona

Gary R. Purcell
The University of Tennessee

Tefko Saracevic
Case Western Reserve University

Thomas P. Slavens
The University of Michigan

Roy B. Stokes
The University of British Columbia

K. Subramanyam
Drexel University

Jean M. Tague
The University of Western Ontario

Vol. 1   Classified Library of Congress Subject Headings, Volume 1—Classified List, *edited by James G. Williams, Martha L. Manheimer, and Jay E. Daily* (out of print; see Vol. 39, Part A)
Vol. 2   Classified Library of Congress Subject Headings, Volume 2—Alphabetic List, *edited by James G. Williams, Martha L. Manheimer, and Jay E. Daily* (out of print; see Vol. 39, Part B)
Vol. 3   Organizing Nonprint Materials, *by Jay E. Daily*
Vol. 4   Computer-Based Chemical Information, *edited by Edward McC. Arnett and Allen Kent*
Vol. 5   Style Manual: A Guide for the Preparation of Reports and Dissertations, *by Martha L. Manheimer*
Vol. 6   The Anatomy of Censorship, *by Jay E. Daily*
Vol. 7   Information Science: Search for Identity, *edited by Anthony Debons* (out of print)
Vol. 8   Resource Sharing in Libraries: Why • How • When • Next Action Steps, *edited by Allen Kent* (out of print)
Vol. 9   Reading the Russian Language: A Guide for Librarians and Other Professionals, *by Rosalind Kent*
Vol. 10 Statewide Computing Systems: Coordinating Academic Computer Planning, *edited by Charles Mosmann* (out of print)
Vol. 11 Using the Chemical Literature: A Practical Guide, *by Henry M. Woodburn*
Vol. 12 Cataloging and Classification: A Workbook, *by Martha L. Manheimer* (out of print; see Vol. 30)
Vol. 13 Multi-media Indexes, Lists, and Review Sources: A Bibliographic Guide, *by Thomas L. Hart, Mary Alice Hunt, and Blanche Woolls*
Vol. 14 Document Retrieval Systems: Factors Affecting Search Time, *by K. Leon Montgomery*
Vol. 15 Library Automation Systems, *by Stephen R. Salmon*
Vol. 16 Black Literature Resources: Analysis and Organization, *by Doris H. Clack*
Vol. 17 Copyright—Information Technology—Public Policy: Part I—Copyright—Public Policies; Part II—Public Policies—Information Technology, *by Nicholas Henry* (out of print)
Vol. 18 Crisis in Copyright, *by William Z. Nasri*
Vol. 19 Mental Health Information Systems: Design and Implementation, *by David J. Kupfer, Michael S. Levine, and John A. Nelson*
Vol. 20 Handbook of Library Regulations, *by Marcy Murphy and Claude J. Johns, Jr.* (out of print)
Vol. 21 Library Resource Sharing, *by Allen Kent and Thomas J. Galvin*
Vol. 22 Computers in Newspaper Publishing: User-Oriented Systems, *by Dineh Moghdam*
Vol. 23 The On-Line Revolution in Libraries, *edited by Allen Kent and Thomas J. Galvin*
Vol. 24 The Library as a Learning Service Center, *by Patrick R. Penland and Aleyamma Mathai*
Vol. 25 Using the Mathematical Literature: A Practical Guide, *by Barbara Kirsch Schaefer*
Vol. 26 Use of Library Materials: The University of Pittsburgh Study, *by Allen Kent et al.*
Vol. 27 The Structure and Governance of Library Networks, *edited by Allen Kent and Thomas J. Galvin*
Vol. 28 The Development of Library Collections of Sound Recordings, *by Frank W. Hoffmann*
Vol. 29 Furnishing the Library Interior, *by William S. Pierce*
Vol. 30 Cataloging and Classification: A Workbook Second Edition, Revised and Expanded, *by Martha L. Manheimer*

Vol. 31 Handbook of Computer-Aided Composition, *by Arthur H. Phillips*
Vol. 32 OCLC: Its Governance, Function, Financing, and Technology, *by Albert F. Maruskin*
Vol. 33 Scientific and Technical Information Resources, *by Krishna Subramanyam*
Vol. 34 An Author Index to Library of Congress Classification, Class P, Subclasses PN, PR, PS, PZ, General Literature, English and American Literature, Fiction in English, and Juvenile Belles Lettres, *by Alan M. Greenberg*
Vol. 35 Using the Biological Literature: A Practical Guide, *by Elisabeth B. Davis*
Vol. 36 An Introduction to Automated Literature Searching, *by Elizabeth P. Hartner*
Vol. 37 The Retrieval of Information in the Humanities and the Social Sciences: Problems as Aids to Learning, *edited by Thomas P. Slavens*
Vol. 38 The Information Professional: Survey of an Emerging Field, *by Anthony Debons, Donald W. King, Una Mansfield, and Donald L. Shirey*
Vol. 39 Classified Library of Congress Subject Headings, Second Edition: Part A—Classified List; Part B—Alphabetic List, *edited by James G. Williams, Martha L. Manheimer, and Jay E. Daily*
Vol. 40 Information Technology: Critical Choices for Library Decision-Makers, *edited by Allen Kent and Thomas J. Galvin*
Vol. 41 Structure and Subject Interaction: Toward a Sociology of Knowledge in the Social Sciences, *by Stephen Bulick*
Vol. 42 World Librarianship: A Comparative Study, *by Richard Krzys and Gaston Litton*
Vol. 43 Guide to the Successful Thesis and Dissertation: Conception to Publication: A Handbook for Students and Faculty, *by James E. Mauch and Jack W. Birch*
Vol. 44 Physical Disability: An Annotated Literature Guide, *edited by Phyllis C. Self*
Vol. 45 Effective Online Searching: A Basic Text, *by Christine L. Borgman, Dineh Moghdam, and Patti K. Corbett*
Vol. 46 Easy Access to DIALOG, ORBIT, and BRS, *by Patricia J. Klingensmith and Elizabeth E. Duncan*
Vol. 47 Subject and Information Analysis, *edited by Eleanor D. Dym*

Additional Volumes in Preparation

Subject and Information Analysis

Edited by
Eleanor D. Dym
SCHOOL OF LIBRARY AND INFORMATION SCIENCE
UNIVERSITY OF PITTSBURGH
PITTSBURGH, PENNSYLVANIA

MARCEL DEKKER, INC.　　　　　　　　　New York and Basel

Library of Congress Cataloging in Publication Data

Main entry under title:

Subject and information analysis.

(Books in library and information science ; vol. 47)
1. Content analysis (Communication) 2. Information storage and retrieval systems. 3. Information retrieval.
I. Dym, Eleanor D. II. Series: Books in library and information science ; v. 47.
P93.S9   1985   025.3   84-28611
ISBN 0-8247-7354-3

SMU LIBRARY

Copyright © 1985 by Marcel Dekker, Inc.   All Rights Reserved

Neither this book nor any part may be reproduced or transmitted in any form or by any means, electronic or mechanical, including photocopying, microfilming, and recording, or by any information storage and retrieval system, without permission in writing from the publisher.

Marcel Dekker, Inc.
270 Madison Avenue, New York, New York 10016

Current printing (last digit):
10 9 8 7 6 5 4 3 2 1

PRINTED IN THE UNITED STATES OF AMERICA

Preface

Document description for information storage and retrieval (ISR) systems may entail a variety of methods ranging from descriptive cataloging to natural language text processing or any combination in between. The type(s) of analysis performed has been dependent upon the philosophical, organizational, and material orientations of a particular ISR system. As a result, it becomes important for individuals designing, developing, or operating ISR systems to understand all of the analysis (objective and subjective) techniques.

The Subject Analysis Methodologies course offered through the Interdisciplinary Department of Information Science (IDIS), School of Library and Information Science (SLIS) of the University of Pittsburgh is concerned with all types of analyses (objective and descriptive) that may be utilized in describing a document.

The available textbooks in this area tend to be limited to single types of subject analysis (e.g., indexing, classifying, abstracting), and descriptive cataloging is either discussed separately or as a part of classifying. There has been an urgent need for a publication containing readings for all of the analysis types. To facilitate the development of such a publication, Marcel Dekker, Inc. has permitted the extraction of portions from three of their publications.

>   ENCYCLOPEDIA OF COMPUTER SCIENCE AND TECHNOLOGY. Edited by Jack Belzer, Albert G. Holzman, and Allen Kent. New York, Marcel Dekker, Inc., c1975-c1980. vol. 1-14.
>   ENCYCLOPEDIA OF LIBRARY AND INFORMATION SCIENCE. Edited by Allen Kent and Harold Lancour. Assistant Editor, William Z. Nasri. New York, Marcel Dekker, Inc., c1968-c1972. vol. 1-8.
>   ENCYCLOPEDIA OF LIBRARY AND INFORMATION SCIENCE. Edited by Allen Kent, Harold Lancour, and Jay E. Daily. Assistant Editor, William Z. Nasri. New York, Marcel Dekker, Inc., c1973-c1982. vol. 9-33.
>   Manheimer, Martha L. CATALOGING AND CLASSIFICATION: A WORKBOOK, 2nd ed. New York, Marcel Dekker, Inc., c1980. 148 p.

In addition, the article "Relevance Predictability in Information Retrieval Systems," by Allen Kent et al., published in *Methods of Information in Medicine,* 6, no.2 (April 1967), pages 45-51, has been included.

The texts that have been selected for these readings represent an introductory approach to document analysis. Since all areas associated with information science have been, by nature, dynamic, it will always be necessary to augment any volume with an awareness of currently published material. Research, technology development, and new systems design reported through the literature will add to or alter the information contained in the various selections. As a result, this compilation should be considered only as a starting point in the study of document analysis.

These readings have been developed to complement a course offered at the University of Pittsburgh, and the selections have been organized by the topics associated with the course: *Overview, Descriptive Cataloging, Natural Language Text Processing, Indexing, Terminology Control, Classifying, Abstracting,* and *Extracting.* Within a topical area, the selections have been listed alphabetically by author or title. Because of this arrangement, a specific discussion may precede a generic review.

Complete bibliographic citations for each selection appear as a footnote on the first page of the selection in the readings. In general, the selections have been reproduced as contained in the original publication. In a few instances, it has been necessary to alter the original presentation for purposes of clarity or space economy.

Eleanor D. Dym

Contributors

Susan Artandi* Associate Professor, Graduate School of Library Service Rutgers University, New Brunswick, New Jersey

Jack Belzer* Professor, School of Library and Information Science, University of Pittsburgh, Pittsburgh, Pennsylvania

Charles L. Bernier* Professor, School of Information and Library Studies, State University of New York at Buffalo, Buffalo, New York

Anindya Bose† Research Associate, School of Library and Information Science, University of Pittsburgh, Pittsburgh, Pennsylvania

Jay E. Daily Professor, School of Library and Information Science, University of Pittsburgh, Pittsburgh, Pennsylvania

Eleanor D. Dym Professor, School of Library and Information Science, University of Pittsburgh, Pittsburgh, Pennsylvania

Douglas J. Foskett Director of Central Library Services, DCLS and Goldsmiths' Librarian, University of London Library, London, England

Carol E. Hicks Computer Science Department, Cleveland State University, Cleveland, Ohio

Karen Sparck Jones Computer Laboratory, University of Cambridge, Cambridge, England

---

*Presently retired
†Presently Professor, Kent State Graduate School of Library Science, Kent State University, Kent State, Ohio

Allen Kent Distinguished Service Professor of Information Science, School of Library and Information Science, University of Pittsburgh, Pittsburgh, Pennsylvania

Marvin Kurfeerst[†] Professor, School of Library and Information Science, University of Pittsburgh, Pittsburgh, Pennsylvania

Bertrand C. Landry Martin Marietta Corporation, Denver, Colorado

William N. Locke[†] Foreign Study Office, Massachusetts Institute of Technology, Cambridge, Massachusetts

Winfred Lehmann Department of Linguistics and Germanic Languages, University of Texas, Austin, Texas

Martha L. Manheimer Professor, School of Library and Information Science, University of Pittsburgh, Pittsburgh, Pennsylvania

Betty A. Mathis Computer Science Department, The Ohio College Library Center, Columbus, Ohio

A. Neelameghan Indian Statistical Institute, Documentation Research and Training Centre, Bangalore, India

James E. Rush James E. Rush Associates, Powell, Ohio

Naomi Sager Linguistic String Project, New York University, New York, New York

Donald L. Shirey Associate Professor, School of Library and Information Science, University of Pittsburgh, Pittsburgh, Pennsylvania

Mary Elizabeth Stevens[‡] Center for Computer Sciences and Technology, National Bureau of Standards, Gaithersburg, Maryland

Suzanne M. Strong The Ohio College Library Center, Columbus, Ohio

B. C. Vickery Head of Research Department, ASLIB, London, England

---

[†] Deceased
[‡] Presently retired

Contents

Preface   iii
Contributors   v

OVERVIEW

1. Automatic Analysis   3
   Mary Elizabeth Stevens
2. Analysis of Information   6
   B. C. Vickery

DESCRIPTIVE CATALOGING

3. Descriptive Cataloging   39
   Jay E. Daily

NATURAL LANGUAGE TEXT PROCESSING

4. Content Analysis   57
   Carol E. Hicks, James E. Rush, and Suzanne M. Strong
5. Machine Translation   110
   Winfred Lehmann
6. Machine Translation   124
   William N. Locke
7. Natural Language Analysis and Processing   154
   Naomi Sager
8. Automatic Analysis   169
   Mary Elizabeth Stevens

INDEXING

9. Coordinate Indexing — 181
   Susan Artandi
10. Subject Indexes — 185
    Charles L. Bernier
11. Automatic Indexing: Progress and Prospects — 198
    Bertrand C. Landry and James E. Rush
12. Automatic Analysis — 241
    Mary Elizabeth Stevens

TERMINOLOGY CONTROL

13. Authority Files — 249
    Jay E. Daily
14. Subject Headings — 256
    Jay E. Daily
15. Thesaurus — 270
    Douglas J. Foskett
16. Subject Headings — 317
    Martha L. Manheimer

CLASSIFYING

17. Abstract Classification — 323
    Jay E. Daily
18. Classification and Categorization — 327
    Jay E. Daily
19. Natural Classification — 350
    Jay E. Daily
20. Clumps, Theory of — 370
    Karen Sparck Jones
21. Dewey Decimal Classification — 385
    Martha L. Manheimer
22. Techniques Used in Library of Congress Classification — 387
    Martha L. Manheimer
23. Classification, Theory of — 391
    A. Neelameghan
24. Automatic Analysis — 418
    Mary Elizabeth Stevens

ABSTRACTING

25. Abstracts and Abstracting — 423
    Charles L. Bernier
26. Abstracting — 445
    Betty A. Mathis and James E. Rush

EXTRACTING

27. Relevance Predictability in Information Retrieval Systems 487
    Allen Kent, Jack Belzer, Marvin Kurfeerst, Eleanor D. Dym, Donald L. Shirey, and Anindya Bose

OVERVIEW

1

Automatic Analysis

Mary Elizabeth Stevens* / National Bureau of Standards, Gaithersburg, Maryland

The area of "automatic analysis" is important to the information and library sciences in a number of different ways. "Automatic analysis" implies the detection by machine of significant patterns. These patterns may be (1) punched in cards to represent the encoding of administrative, statistical, bibliographic, and subject-content-indicating data; (2) in the form of printed characters and other pictorial or photographic data; (3) in the sounds of human speech; or (4) in the form of the words that occur frequently enough (but not too frequently or too rarely) to be indicative of the probable subject contents of a given text. The subject broadly includes punched-card or computer processing of various types of recorded data, such as library loan records or subscription renewals at one extreme and question-answering by machine in a conversational interaction with a user at the other end of a spectrum of potential applications. This area includes the automatic recognition of printed or typed characters on a page or report form; the automatic recognition of other patterns such as spoken words or the records of electrocardiograph measurements; the selective display of keywords in text (as in Keyword-in-Context, or KWIC, indexing); or the selective display of attributes or features of objects, photographs, and drawings. Also included is the display of previously observed associational relationships between words in text, between words in one document by comparison with those in other documents, and between words in texts and subject headings or classification codes or descriptors or other types of content-indicating and indexing terms. Furthermore, display of relationships among the documents in a particular collection (or in a subject-oriented subset of a collec-

---

From Stevens, Mary Elizabeth. *Automatic Analysis*. ENCYCLOPEDIA OF LIBRARY AND INFORMATION SCIENCE. Vol. 2. Edited by Allen Kent and Harold Lancour. Assistant Editor, William Z. Nasri. New York, Marcel Dekker, Inc., c1969. pp. 144-147.
Any opinions expressed in this article are those of the author alone and do not represent the official views of the National Bureau of Standards. This article, however, is a contribution of the National Bureau of Standards and, therefore, not subject to copyright.
*Presently retired

tion) and of document-to-other-document relationships specifically including the sets of documents, all of which cite some other particular document as a reference, and those which are all cited by some particular document (as in Citation Indexing), are included.

Historically the techniques of automatic analysis have had an intimate association with the information and library sciences. For example, it was apparently the result of informal discussions between John Shaw Billings, the first head of the Army Medical Library, and Herman Hollerith, of the U.S. Census Bureau, that the concepts of punched-card machine processing of information-carrying data were first advanced.

The first and most obvious area of automatic analysis is that of tabulation and summarization of detail data recorded in machine-useful form. Thus, for example, a suitable combination of arithmetic operations on, e.g., census data as recorded in punched cards will produce tabulations, summaries, and tables of statistics of various kinds. In libraries such techniques have been applied to circulation records, subscription renewals, loan recalls, and a variety of other record-keeping operations for which mechanized analysis and control procedures are desired. With the advent of computers and automatic data-processing systems, these and far more sophisticated operations, including the experimental demonstration of automatic classification and indexing techniques, can be applied.

More specifically, the techniques of automatic analysis that have been developed over the past two decades have been applied to library and documentation operations in such areas as the following:

> First, the compilation of periodic accession lists and bulletins, the listing and announcement of holdings, and the preparation of card and book catalogs.
>
> Second, the compilation of a variety of indexes such as author, subject, corporate author, citation index, and the like, and the reassembly of a given index into another one ordered differently, as in the case of converting by machine procedures an alphabetically ordered index of subject headings to a classified subject order. A pioneering example is that of an index of subject headings classified by the use of punched-card equipment in the Welch Medical Library research project for the Army Medical Library in the period 1948–1954.
>
> Third, the machine preparation of concordances to the Bible, the Dead Sea Scrolls, the complete works of St. Thomas Aquinas, and other important literary works.
>
> Fourth, the preparation of permuted-keyword-from-title indexes such as KWIC with the index entry keyword surrounded by the adjacent words of the title or KWOC (Keyword-out-of-Context) with the separated index entry keyword accompanied by all or part of the title in natural order. An example of the differences which also illustrates certain difficulties imposed by machine line-length restrictions is as follows:
> KWIC: EROTIC TENDENCIES AMONG . . . TRAPPIST MONKS. AN INV
> KWOC: TRAPPIST . . . AN INVESTIGATION OF ATHEROSCL
>
> Fifth, the automatic normalization of index entries by lookup in a computer-based thesaurus.

In each of these areas of application, fully mechanized procedures of automatic analysis had come into regular productive operation in at least some installations by the mid-1960s. In addition, by this same time, pilot production and experimental applications of the techniques of automatic analysis had been successfully demonstrated in the following areas:

> First, sample publications of keyword indexes that are computer-generated by means of the automatic extraction of words from text in accordance with pre-established selection formulas such as relative word frequency determinations or by means of automatic extraction of words occurring in certain syntactic structures, and, similarly, of key sentence extractions which, it has been suggested, can serve as a substitute for conventional abstracts.
>
> Second, machine compilation and use of statistics of co-occurrences of words in documents, of words with index terms, and of terms with other terms for purposes of suggesting additional terms to an indexer and of expanding or modifying the terms of a search request.
>
> Third, automatic assignment of descriptors, subject headings, and/or subject classification codes to documents.

The techniques of automatic analysis can be exemplified next in the case of character recognition, whether of the odd-looking numbers that appear on bank checks, of those on a printed page such as this, or of those that have been hand-printed or handwritten. For library automation and mechanized documentation systems, in general, the need for multifont automatic character readers is a probable requirement because of disadvantages of other methods of preparing machine-useful material. The present high cost of keystroking is illustrated by the fact that the information on Library of Congress catalog cards alone (much less the texts that they represent) has been estimated as having a price tag of more than $3 million.

The future applicability of automatic analysis techniques will also include questions of machine sensing and input of recorded data, whether of remotely collected data acquisition systems or of source data automation such as mark-sensed inventory control records.

When remote data-sensing and laboratory measurement automation techniques are coupled to automatic report generation capabilities, a new type of processing of scientific and technical information is promised—one which, it may be reasonably predicted, will sharply increase in importance in the future.

Finally, there are prospects for automatic indexing, abstracting, and other types of linguistic data processing, for automatic classification or categorization and for automatic content analysis. These and related techniques may in the future be applied not only for purposes of generation by machine of condensed representations for documentary items but also for direct use in one-line analytic information retrieval and question-answering systems.

2

Analysis of Information

B. C. Vickery / ASLIB, London, England

"Analysis of information" here means deriving from a document a set of words that serves as a condensed representation of it. This representation may be used to identify the document, to provide access points in literature search, to indicate its content, or as a substitute for the document. It may take the form of, for example, an extract, a summary, an abstract, a catalog entry, an alphabetic or classified index entry, or a punch-card coding.

In a wider sense analysis is a functional unit involved in the transfer of information from source to user. We can regard the whole transfer process as involving four intermediate functions:

$$\begin{array}{c} \text{Source} \rightarrow \text{Publishing} \rightarrow \text{Storage} \rightarrow \text{User} \\ \uparrow \\ \text{Analysis} \rightarrow \text{Search} \end{array}$$

Information is recorded and multiplied by publishing units. They distribute it to storage units (libraries and other depositories) and to analysis units, which may or may not be associated with the stores. The analysis units prepare catalogs, abstracts, indexes, bibliographies, and other guides to the literature. In these guides documents are identified by search units (who may be individual users) and are subsequently obtained from the stores on demand.

As used in this article, however, the analysis of information covers a somewhat narrower field. Kent (1) separated the whole analysis function into three operations:

From Vickery, B.C. *Analysis of Information.* ENCYCLOPEDIA OF LIBRARY AND INFORMATION SCIENCE. Vol. 1. Edited by Allen Kent and Harold Lancour. Assistant Editor, William Z. Nasri. New York, Marcel Dekker, Inc., c1968. pp. 355-384.

1. Analysis of documents, involving their perusal and selection from them of "analytics," characteristic words that are representative of them
2. Control of the terminology in which the analytics are expressed
3. Recording of the results of analysis on a searchable medium, such as catalog card, printed index, a punched tape, magnetic tape, film

This article will deal only with the first two operations.

"Analysis of information" is a general term covering many traditional library techniques such as cataloging, indexing, classifying, and abstracting, as well as experimental techniques such as automatic indexing, classification, and abstracting. All such analysis is an aid to the selection of documents from a collection. The need for it arises as soon as any collection becomes too large to be scanned directly. It is not easy to select a particular book from an unsorted collection of even a few hundred volumes. We must select characteristic analytics for each book (such as author and title), record these on some medium (e.g., the spines of the books), and arrange the spines in a sequence that can be easily scanned. Analytics are condensed representations of documents and are used to simplify and accelerate information search.

The traditional techniques of analysis have a long history, which has not yet been adequately documented. There is fragmentary evidence of a catalog of the Alexandrian library (the *Pinakes* of Callimachos, 250 B.C.). There are a number of extant medieval library catalogs—casual and unorganized inventories of manuscripts. The invention of printing led to a rapid increase in the supply of and demand for books, and so to a much greater need for lists of them for various purposes. Bibliographic analysis begins with the Renaissance.

The idea of an entry word for each book, as an access point in the information search, appeared in 1545 in the *Bibliotheca Universalis* of Konrad Gesner. This listed books in the alphabetic order of author's forenames, with a supplementary cross-reference index of surnames. In 1548 Gesner published a second volume listing the same volume in a coded subject classified order, with an alphabetic subject index to the class codes.

This is not the place to describe the subsequent history of cataloging (2). Even at this early stage the main problems of analysis can be seen. Two sets of words can be derived from documents. One set relates to the origin of the document (the author, issuing authority, publisher, place of publication, and so forth) and the other to its information content (subject matter). The title of a document has always occupied an ambiguous intermediate position. It can certainly be an indication of the contents, but it is often used as no more than a convenient label to identify the document. (In the case of untitled manuscripts or poems, the first line of text may serve the same purpose.)

Corresponding to this division, bibliographic analysis has been split into two traditional techniques: (1) author/title cataloging, concerned with the choice as entries of words relating to the origin of the document, and (1a), linked with this, descriptive cataloging, concerned with the choice of other words—including the title—that will serve uniquely to identify the document; (2) subject analysis, concerned with the information content of the document. It is convenient to treat (1) and (1a) separately from and more briefly than (2), as articles on cataloging will be found elsewhere in the encyclopedia.

Author/Title and Descriptive Cataloging (3)

Many people contribute to the origination of a book. As well as one or more personal authors, there may be an issuing authority (e.g., an institution employing the author), a publisher, a printer, an editor, a translator, an illustrator, and so forth. The place, date, and language of publication are also marks of origin. All these elements may, on occasion, be used as entry words in a catalog, so that documents by a certain author, or produced by a certain printer, or issued in a certain year, and so forth, may be readily located. A choice must be made as to which of these possible indications of origin are to be used as entry words accessible to search. This choice will depend (1) on cataloging policy—what user needs the catalog is designed to meet—and (2) on available resources—what labor can be expended on the work.

Usually information about all these bibliographic elements can be derived by inspection of the early pages (the "prelims") of a document, although sometimes the information may have to be amplified by a search of other sources (for example, if a publisher fails to record the name of a translator). If a catalog or bibliography is to bring together all the works of a certain author, or all from a certain issuing authority, then names must be cast into a standard form. This problem was already apparent in Gesner's time: Should authors be entered under forenames (the medieval practice that Gesner followed in the body of his list) or surnames (which did not become standard practice until the seventeenth century)?

By the nineteenth century the need to standardize names in catalogs led to the first lengthy set of rules, prepared in 1841 for the British Museum by Anthony Panizzi. Many other codes have since been published. In the English-speaking world the most important are the Anglo-American or Joint Code (1908), issued in revised form in 1967; The American Library Association Code (1949); and the Library of Congress Rules for Descriptive Cataloging (1949).

The standardized rendering of an English personal name very often presents no difficulties: the surname becomes the leading word, followed by forenames (e.g., Whitehill, Walter Allan). But a hyphenated name needs a decision: Is Baring-Gould entered under B or G? Similarly surnames with prefixes: Does De Quincey go under D or Q? And is the rule the same for de Gaulle? Each code gives rules for such decisions. Once we step outside Europe and the Americas, name patterns differ from those familiar in our culture, and for these the Western codes (says the Indian librarian, Ranganathan) "are as shapeless as liquid."

However, a greater immediate problem facing Western catalogers is the rendering of "corporate authors" (i.e., institutions responsible for issuing documents of multiple or anonymous personal authorship). This type of material appears in ever-increasing quantity: government publications of all kinds, reports from institutions, conference proceedings, periodicals, and so forth.

An extensive literature has grown up around this problem, which may be illustrated by a single complex example. There is a report on "Nonconventional Retrieval Systems," issued by:

Analysis of Information

>Center for Documentation Research,
>School of Library Science,
>Western Reserve University,
>Report AFOSR TN 58-575,
>Directorate of Research Communication,
>Air Force Office of Scientific Research,
>Air Research and Development Command,
>U.S. Air Force

Which one or more of these names is to be taken as the corporate author of the report? How is the corporate name to be rendered? Each code of cataloging rules gives different answers. The essence of current practice is to use as entries only distinctive and self-sufficient names. For example, there may be many "centers for documentation research." This one must be identified as Western Reserve University, Center for Documentation Research.

Periodicals, journals, and serials of all kinds may be cataloged as publications of their corporate issuing body, but it is more usual to use the title as an entry. This may be distinctive (e.g., *American Documentation*), or it may itself include a corporate name (such as *Bulletin of the Medical Library Association*). Particularly in science and technology, standardization of periodical titles has taken the form of standard abbreviations.

The abridged form usually drops articles, conjunctions, prepositions, and the like. A long title may be abbreviated by dropping later words. Individual words are usually abbreviated by dropping terminal letters, although sometimes internal letters are also omitted. Examples are as follows:

>Journal → J.
>Annals, Annalen, Annales, Annali, Annaes → Ann.
>Report, Reports → Rep.
>Biology, Biologia, Biologie, Biologiya → Biol.
>Engineering → Eng.
>Manufacturing → Mfg.
>*Journal of the American Chemical Society* → *J. Am. Chem. Soc.*
>*Archives des maladies professionelles de medicine du travail et de securite social*
> → *Arch. mal. prof.*

A still shorter form of standard abbreviation has been developed: the coden (*4*). This reduces each title to a unique and partly mnemonic four-letter code, e.g.,

>*J. Am. Chem. Soc.* → JACS
>*Arch. mal. prof.* → AMPM
>*Am. Doc.* → AMDO

After this brief survey of the standardization of names, it will be well to summarize what marks of origin are commonly used as entry words. For books, access is usually provided via personal author(s) and/or corporate author(s), and sometimes via title and any series to which the book belongs. For reports issued by institutions, access via report number may also be provided.

Next comes the further problem of descriptive cataloging: What other bibliographic elements should be incorporated in the representation of a document to help identify it and indicate its nature? For books it is common to include in an author entry: the title and any series title, the edition, the publisher, the place and date of publication, the collation (number of volumes, pages, illustrations, and so forth), a note if the book is or contains a bibliography, and sometimes a statement of the language in which the text is written. For reports there may also be statements of contract number, source of acquisition (if different from the corporate author or publisher), and security classification.

For articles in periodicals, further search access points have been provided in some recent analytical guides. Earlier documents that an author says he has consulted may also be regarded as characteristics of origin. There are occasions when it is useful, for example, to discover what writings have been influenced by Newton's *Principia* by finding who claims to have consulted this work. Answers to questions of this type are provided by citation indexes, which list cited books and papers and show which documents have cited them.

All author/title and descriptive cataloging is at present carried out by human operators. Faced with the title page of a document—or even a machine-readable transcript of it—no machine can select the author, title, publisher, and so forth, unless these elements have already been tagged as such by an analyst. Only when documents are published with these marks of origin already distinctively tagged will automatic descriptive cataloging be possible. Once a catalog entry has been humanly made and recorded in machine-readable form, it can of course be manipulated by data-processing machines for many purposes, and this aspect of "computerized cataloging" is already common.

Subject Analysis

The bibliographic elements that can serve as indications of the origin of a document are relatively few and relatively easily identifiable. By contrast only one possible indication of information content—the title— is readily identifiable, and the whole remaining text of the document is available as a source of subject information. The task of subject analysis is therefore in principle far less straightforward than descriptive cataloging, although it can in practice be made to look much easier by simply choosing the title of a document as a subject entry.

Indexing by title relies on the author naming the subject of his document. More extended indexing often continues this reliance, by choosing as further entries the chapter headings or section headings of the document. But subject analysis differs in purpose from descriptive cataloging. Characteristics of origin are innate to a document; its author, publisher, and so forth, are unique. But the subject aspects of a document that are of interest will vary from one user to another. While descriptive cataloging of a given document is relatively invariable, its subject analysis may vary from one index to another.

One reader will find George Bernard Shaw's *Prefaces* valuable for their autobiographic information, another for the light they throw on his plays, another for their social criticism, another for their comments on other writers, and so forth.

Each interest represents a point of view from which a subject analysis of the *Prefaces* might be made. In fact, the subject analysis we make will depend on the users we expect to serve. There is no guarantee that the title and headings supplied by an author will be appropriate for a particular user group. Consequently subject analysis in principle requires a study of the whole text to select a set of words that indicates those aspects of its information content that are likely to interest the users of the resulting subject index.

The product of subject analysis may be an extract from the document (e.g., its title), one or more verbal index entries (commonly called subject headings), the same in some coded form (as in library class numbers), or a more extended abstract or summary. An instance of each of these is shown in the following example:

Title: Collective Electron Ferromagnetism III. Nickel and Nickel-Copper Alloys
Wohlfarth, E. P., *Proc. Roy. Soc. (London)*, **A195**, 434–462 (1949)
Subject headings: Nickel Alloys: Ferromagnetism
Nickel-Copper Alloys: Ferromagnetism
Magnetic Susceptibility: Temperature variation
Class number: 538.114:669.245

Abstract: The theoretical implication of the overlap of the d and a electronic bands are considered. The dependence of the electron distribution on temp. is discussed. Calcns. are carried out for the transfer effect and the influence of thermal expansion is considered. The theory is applied to the temp. variation of susceptibility above the Curie point. For Ni-rich alloys satis. agreement with expt. is obtained. For Cu-rich alloys the high-temp. variation is accounted for, but the low-temp. is discussed also. Its variation with compn. is satis. accounted for with the Ni-rich regions, but again discrepancies appear at the low-temp. range of the Cu-rich alloys.

The operation of subject analysis can be divided into four stages: (1) selecting from a document certain words, phrases, or sentences that may suitably represent its information content; (2) if necessary, transforming these sets of words into a standard terminology and casting them into standard form; (3) if necessary translating the text words or standard terms into a code; (4) choosing certain of these words, terms, or codes as access points for the information search. The first and last of these stages are obligatory: They occur in all forms of subject analysis. The second is usual, although not universal. The third is needed only in certain information systems, and it will be convenient to treat coded analysis as a whole after the other three stages have been discussed.

Identifying Subjects of Interest

Scanning a document to decide what it is about is the key operation in subject analysis, yet it is the least discussed and the least reducible to rule. Logically we can distinguish two phases to the operation: (1) scanning to select a set of words, phrases, or sentences that collectively represent the information content; and (2) deciding which of these are worth recording as being relevant to the interests of those who are expected to use the information system. In practice subject analysts (indexers) perform these two phases concurrently: They select only such words as are relevant to the purpose of the system.

How do we select indexing words? Some indexers can read a text and "understand" it—their understanding being shown, perhaps, by their ability to formulate its subject in words that differ from those used by the author. We have very little knowledge of the mental processes involved in such human understanding. Other indexers cannot understand a text in this full sense, but they are adept at picking out from it words, phrases, and sentences that the author has emphasized as important: the title and section headings, introduction, conclusions, summary, and so forth. Some indexing systems deliberately restrict the selected phrase to the title alone to minimize the skill and effort needed at this stage of subject analysis.

In some specialist systems the analyst is guided by the system designer in his choice of indexing words. For example, an indexer of scientific and technical articles may be instructed to select the following:

> The leading subject of the text, normally taken from the title
> The type of study (experimental, survey, product development, theoretical, and so forth)
> The problems investigated
> Direct conclusions
> Supporting results that answer problems
> Methods of investigation

The journal *Chemical Abstracts* regards as suitable for index entries: "every measurement, observation, method, apparatus, suggestion and theory that is presented as new and of value in itself; all new chemical compounds, and all elements, compounds and other substances for which new data are given" (5). The journal *Biological Abstracts* asks analysts of biological articles to include in their selections the nature of the investigation (descriptive, experimental, theoretical), the nature of the report (research, review, bibliography), the organisms and/or substances investigated, the techniques used, and the locality of the investigation.

Only the most general-purpose of information systems work on the assumption that every subject in every analyzed document is of potential relevance to the users of the system. Otherwise, the subject field and viewpoint of the system are usually delimited. A document dealing mainly with subjects falling outside the limits may be indexed only for its minor references to subjects within the field. In general, the selection of indexing words is influenced by what is already in the index, so that repetition of references to the same information in different documents is minimized.

How many indexing words should be selected from a document? This will in practice be a policy decision, based on the purpose of the system and on the amount of indexing labor that is available. Working information systems show a very wide variation in this respect. Some may average only 2 indexing words per document; others may average 50 or 60; while the index to a book (another example of subject analysis) may have hundreds of entries. In general, there is a trend to increase the number of indexing words. This is due, first, to an increase in the number of documents analyzed—requiring more detailed analysis if the specific information content of each document is to be represented; and second, to a greater urgency in the use of documents—requiring specific information lying within a document to be more precisely located.

Analysis of Information

One typical product of this stage of subject analysis is a set of phrases, such as might be used for titles, each phrase representing a subject theme or topic selected from the document as worth recording. These phrases form the raw material for subsequent stages of subject analysis.

A second product of analysis may be an abstract, such as has already been illustrated, either briefly indicative of the information content, or more fully informative on the detail of the document. A third product may be extracts from the document, either key sections of the text or selected data such as the physical properties of materials or the biological effects of chemical substances.

But before discussing the next stage in analysis, an interpolation is necessary.

Automatic Indexing

Thus far we have considered only the human analyst. Can he (or she) be replaced by machine? The phrase "automatic indexing" (6) is used to cover the performance by mechanical means of any or all of the four stages of subject analysis. Only the selection of index entries from text will be considered here.

Machine indexing in this sense requires (1) that the text of documents be in a form that can be "read" by a machine, (2) that the machine can "recognize" individual words, and (3) that we can provide the machine with rules for selecting certain words and phrases as index entries. Machine-readable text can be produced in the form of codes on punched cards, punched tape, or magnetic tape, and the problems of preparing these are discussed elsewhere in the encyclopedia. Such coded text can be "read" and manipulated by digital computers.

Two types of rules have been used in experiments on machine indexing. In the first a human analyst compiles a list of key words of potential interest to future users of the index; this list is compared by the computer with each word in the text of a document; if a key word appears, the fact is recorded, and these selected words make up the index entry for the document.

The second type of machine indexing works on an opposite principle: a human analyst compiles a list of words that are *not* to be selected for indexing. These include all the common "little" words such as "the," "of," "on," "an," "a," "that," "are," "not," "to," "be," "for," and so forth, and also "general" words that have little specific meaning (e.g., in scientific texts the words "report," "theory," "conclusions," and so forth, are too common to be useful as index entries). There still remain in each text hundreds or thousands of other words, and they cannot all be selected for the index. Computer techniques have been developed to count the number of times each different word occurs in the document. The most frequently occurring words are selected. As an example, in a one-page article entitled "Experiments Suggest a New Approach to the Treatment of Heart Attacks," the most frequent noncommon words were "hormones" (occurring 14 times), "female" (11), "effect" (8), "animal" (7), "cholesterol" (7), "heart" (7), "physics" (7), and "reticuloendothelial" (7).

Choosing Access Points

It is convenient now to skip to the fourth stage of subject analysis, an obligatory step: the choice of certain of the selected subject words as access points for the information search. In principle one would like to use all of them in this way: All have been selected as suitably representing the information content of the document. The only restriction is an economic one: The more access points provided, the more the index will cost to construct. On the other hand, providing fewer access points will make the index less easy and so more costly to use, and the trend is toward increasing access points.

The problem may be illustrated as follows. Suppose that the first stage of analysis has isolated as a subject theme of a document "The Control of Plant Disease by Antibiotics." Different users might expect this topic to be indexed in different ways, e.g.,

Control of plant disease by antibiotics
Control by antibiotics of plant disease
Plant disease, control by antibiotics
Disease of plants, control by antibiotics
Disease control, by antibiotics, in plants
Antibiotic control of plant disease

Each of these is a potential access point. If we express the topic by linking four nouns, "plants:disease:control:antibiotics," and use every possible permutation, we could make 24 entries. How many would be useful? How many are essential?

Many indexes provide only one entry per topic. In this case, if there is to be consistency in the choice of this one access point, some rules are needed to indicate which entry word to choose whenever the topic is expressed by more than a single word. Should we index "town planning" under "Planning" or "Towns?" "The casting of aluminum" under "Casting" or "Aluminum?" "The strength of concrete" under "Strength" or "Concrete?" "Bicycle wheels" under "Bicycles" or "Wheels?" "Suspension bridges" under "Suspension" or "Bridges?" One of the first to become aware of this problem was Charles Ami Cutter (7), but his rule, "enter a compound subject name by its first word, inverting the phrase only where some other word is decidedly more significant," does not give sufficient help. Would all indexers and users agree on the most significant word in "Control of Plant Disease by Antibiotics?"

The librarian J. Kaiser (8) proposed that the words in subject phrases be considered as either *concretes* or *processes*. Among concretes he included things, places, and abstract terms not signifying actions or processes, e.g., boats, paint, towns, aluminum, concrete, bicycles, bridges, France, heat. His rule was to make an entry under "The Concrete." So we would make entries such as the following:

Towns: Planning
Aluminum: Casting
Concrete: Strength
Boats: Painting
Liver: Injury

Analysis of Information

This rule would not cover the topics "Bicycle wheels" and "Suspension bridges," where two concretes appear. Kaiser would enter them under "Bicycle" and "Suspension," respectively. His rule cannot help us to index "Control of Plant Disease by Antibiotics," where two concretes (plants and antibiotics) and two processes (control and disease) appear. More complex rules have been developed and are discussed by Eric Coates (9).

In moving toward the provision of more access points, subject analysis has next developed standard techniques for deriving further entries from the first chosen entry. One way is to "rotate" the entry: to index both "Towns:Planning" and "Planning:Towns," and to provide four entries:

Plants:Disease:Control:Antibiotics
Antibiotics:Plants:Disease:Control
Control:Antibiotics:Plants:Disease
Disease:Control:Antibiotics:Plants

This technique has been applied mechanically by computer to produce so-called KWIC (Key Word in Context) indexes (6). Each subject phrase—in practice it is usually the title of the document—is rotated to bring each significant word in turn into an entry position, thus:

	Entry word
plant disease by	antibiotics, the control
by antibiotics, the	control of plant disease
control of plant	disease by antibiotics
biotics, the control of	plant disease by anti

The final step toward increasing access has been taken by "postcoordinate" indexing systems. In these every word chosen by subject analysis is available as an access point. There are many ways in which the results of analysis can be recorded so as to achieve this object—on Uniterm cards, in dual dictionaries, on punched cards, magnetic tape, or film—and these methods are described elsewhere in the encyclopedia.

Standardizing Terminology

We may now return to what is logically the second possible stage of subject analysis: to transform the subject words and phrases selected from a document into a standard terminology. This stage is usual but not universal—the most outstanding examples of indexes using words extracted from documents without modification being those that are mechanically compiled: the machine indexes and KWIC indexes based on titles. In nearly all other indexes there is some control of terminology.

The basic reason for applying this control is the immense variety of natural language. Suppose that an index user desires to find documents dealing with oscillating motion, movement to and fro, and searches the index for entries under "Oscillation." Authors may have discussed this concept under many other names:

vibration, undulation, pulsation, nutation, swing, beat, rolling, pitching, and so forth. If each index entry uses each author's own word and no links are made between them, the searcher will miss all these entries. He can be helped in two ways: (1) at the time of indexing, all the varied terms for this concept, used by authors, can be represented by a standard entry, "Oscillation"; (2) at the time of searching, from each term used as an entry the searcher can be guided to all the other terms used, so that he can, if he wishes, cover all possibilities. In practice most systems rely on both methods: some degree of term standardization at "input" and some guiding at "output." In either case the terminology of the field covered by the system will be controlled and organized (10).

Some forms of this control have already been suggested. In machine indexing a standard list of key words for which a text is examined sets a limit to what terms will be used as index entries. Again, in the Kaiser system to define terms as either concretes or processes already limits their use. An even more elementary form of control is to decide on a standard word form. For example, many systems use nouns whenever possible ("heat" rather than "hot," "roughness" instead of "rough," "pouring" and not "pour"). The names of specific materials (such as urea, beeswax), qualities (roughness, purity), and processes (constructing, installing) are used in the singular, but types of material (solvents, dyes) and equipment (pumps, bicycles) are used in the plural.

The next step is to bar the introduction of synonyms (words having the same meaning). There are perhaps rather few exact synonyms in most fields of knowledge—each word has its own shade of meaning and usage—and it is better to define synonyms as words that in a particular information system are represented by the same index term. An example has already been given of the group of terms related to oscillation. Depending on the purpose of the system, these may or may not be treated as synonymous. The analyst must consider whether potential users will want to distinguish between these concepts or will prefer them to be treated as equivalent. When the latter choice is made, the analyst may treat as synonymous closely related words such as "lighting" and "illumination," or "duration" and "time"; he may treat "smoothness" as only another way of looking at "roughness" and may represent all specific amino compounds by the general term "amines."

Proceeding in this way, the analyst makes a series of decisions. Some are general, relating to the use of nouns, singulars and plurals. Many are specific and may be embodied in a standard word list:

    amines: *use for* specific amines
    beat: *use* Oscillation
    beeswax
    bicycles
    constructing
    duration: *use* Time
    dyes
    ethylamine: *use* Amines
    heat
    hot: *use* Heat
    illumination: *use* Lighting
    installing
    lighting: *use for* Illumination

Analysis of Information

nutation: *use* Oscillation
oscillation: *use for* Vibration, Undulation, Pulsation, Nutation, Swing, Beat, Rolling, Pitching
pitching: *use* Oscillation
pour: *use* Pouring
pouring: *use for* Pour
pulsation: *use* Oscillation
pumps
purity
rolling: *use* Oscillation
rough: *use* Roughness
roughness: *use for* Rough, Smoothness
smoothness: *use* Roughness
solvents
swing: *use* Oscillation
time: *use for* Duration
undulation: *use* Oscillation
urea
vibration: *use* Oscillation

As indexing continues and the list grows, other relations become apparent among the words chosen as index entries. For example, some specific amines may be of particular interest to potential users and worthy of specific entry: urea is one of them, and so are hydrazine and melamine. It may be worthwhile amplifying the word list to show these relations. In what follows, NT means "narrower terms" and BT "broader terms."

amines: *see also* NT Hydrazine, Melamine, Urea
hydrazine: *see also* BT Amines
melamine: *see also* BT Amines
urea: *see also* BT Amines

In another case certain specific dyes may be judged not worthy of specific entry, but worth adding to the list as a guide to indexers and users:

gentian violet: *use* Dyes
sulfur colors: *use* Dyes
vat colors: *use* Dyes

Many particular kinds of lighting may deserve specific entry, so that the list is amplified to read as follows:

lighting: *see also* NT Commercial lighting (henceforth abbreviated to L),
Electric L, Exterior L, Flood L, Industrial L, Interior L, Residential L, Street L

Experience with the ways of index users lead to the recognition that one seeking information on purity or solvents may find helpful documents indexed under related terms (RT), and guidance such as the following may be introduced:

purity: *see also* RT Cleaning, Contamination, Pollution, Purification, Quality
solvents: *see also* RT Cleaning compounds, Dispersants, Extenders, Extraction, Leaching, Solubility, Solutions

The linking of broader, narrower, and related terms eventually develops into a network in which a whole group of terms may be concerned. For example, all the following terms on "lighting" may be connected by BT, NT, or RT links:

    Lighting   Lamps
        commercial light   carbon arc light
        electric light   flash light
        exterior light   glow light
        flood light   incandescent light
        industrial light   infrared light
        interior light   mercury light
        residential light   neon light
        street light   xenon light
    Optical properties   Signal lights
        brightness   indicator light
        colors   identification light
        diffraction   approach light
        distortion   beacon light
        reflection   navigation light
        refraction
        visibility

When this has occurred, the analyst is only one step away from casting the whole collection of indexing terms into the form of a classification. This step is taken in a number of information systems.

The outcome of terminology control is thus some form of standard word list showing the terms that are available for indexing and searching, their relations to words that are not to be used, and their relations among themselves. There are two basic forms to these lists: the terms may be arranged either alphabetically or systematically. These forms will be discussed in the next two sections.

Alphabetic Word List

Standard terminologies for indexing came into use toward the end of the nineteenth century. One of the earliest alphabetic lists was published in 1895 by the ALA; one of its compilers was C. A. Cutter. Since then many subject-heading lists have appeared (*11*). A typical recent example is devoted to aviation (*12*). Entries may appear in the following forms:

    a. Single words, e.g., Aeronautics
    b. Phrases of two or three words, e.g., Naval aviation, Airport buildings, Traffic control centers
    c. Inverted phrases, e.g., Airplanes, experimental; inversion is used when the grouping of a related set of entries is considered desirable, thus
        Airplanes
        Airplanes, cargo
        Airplanes, convertible
        Airplanes, experimental
        Airplanes, light
        etc.

Analysis of Information

    d. Words followed by a note in parentheses to distinguish between terms with the same spelling but different meanings, e.g., Pitch (frequency), Pitch (inclination), Pitch (material), Mercury (metal), Mercury (planet), Inflation (swelling), Inflation (economic)
    e. Words linked by "and," expressing overlapping concepts, e.g., Maps and Charts, Maintenance and Repair
    f. Compound phrases such as Electronics in aeronautics, Packing for shipment
    g. Corporate and personal names

Many entries may be subdivided, for example,

    Airlines
      certification
      depreciation (×)
      economics (×)
      employees
      fares
      flying equipment
      ground equipment
      history (×)
      management
      officials
      regulation
      schedules

In some cases (those marked "×" above) there is a cross-reference entry under the subheading, so that the user gains access from it as well, but this is not always so.

There are entries for some words not used as index entries, e.g.,

    Aviators, *see* Pilots
    Mileages, *see* Distances
    Stewardesses, *see* Flight attendants

and the reverse relation is also shown:

    Pilots: *use for* Aviators
    Distances: *use for* Mileages
    Flight attendants: *use for* Hostesses, Pursers, Stewards, Stewardesses

All the relationships distinguished as BT, NT, and RT in the last section are expressed in the words "see also" and its reverse "××," thus

    Accidents: *see also* Collisions, Hazards, Safety, Survival
    Collisions: ×× Accidents

Hazards: ×× Accidents, *see also* Altitude effects, Fatigue, Fires, Fog, Ice formation, Lightning
Lightning: ×× Hazards
Safety: ×× Accidents, *see also* Industrial safety, Public safety
Survival: ×× Accidents, *see also* Rescue, Search.

During the last few years a new form of alphabetic listing of standard indexing terms has been developed; it is called the thesaurus (*13*). It differs from the older subject heading list in five ways:

a. Thesauruses sometimes contain more detailed terms.
b. They avoid inverted phrases, making only direct entries such as Cargo airplanes, Convertible airplanes.
c. There are no subdivided entries: Each word or phrase used is an independent entry.
d. Cross references ("see" or "use," "use for" or "UF," "see also") are much more extensive.
e. Among the "see also" cross references, links between narrower (NT) and broader terms (BT) are distinguished from other links (RT).

This last point needs a little more elucidation. When one term represents a species or kind of another term (as "steel" is a kind of "metal"), the two are linked as follows:

Steel: BT Metal
Metal: NT Steel

In other cases, when two terms are not in this generic relation to one another but it is considered helpful to guide indexer and user from one to the other, they are linked as follows:

Food: RT Carbohydrates, Fats, Proteins, Flavor, Nutrition, Seasonings, Vitamin

A typical extract from an engineering thesaurus is illustrated in Figure 1.

Corresponding to their difference in structure, subject-heading lists and thesauruses are used in different ways. Subject headings are derived directly from the list. A document dealing with the topic "The Control of Fuel Mixing and Flow" could be indexed by the standard subject headings

Fuel: Flow meters
Fuel: Mixture controls, *see also* Carburetors

with a cross reference only from "Mixture controls." With the thesaurus the topic could be indexed with the following independent terms, which would be coordinated (brought together to represent a topic) during a search:

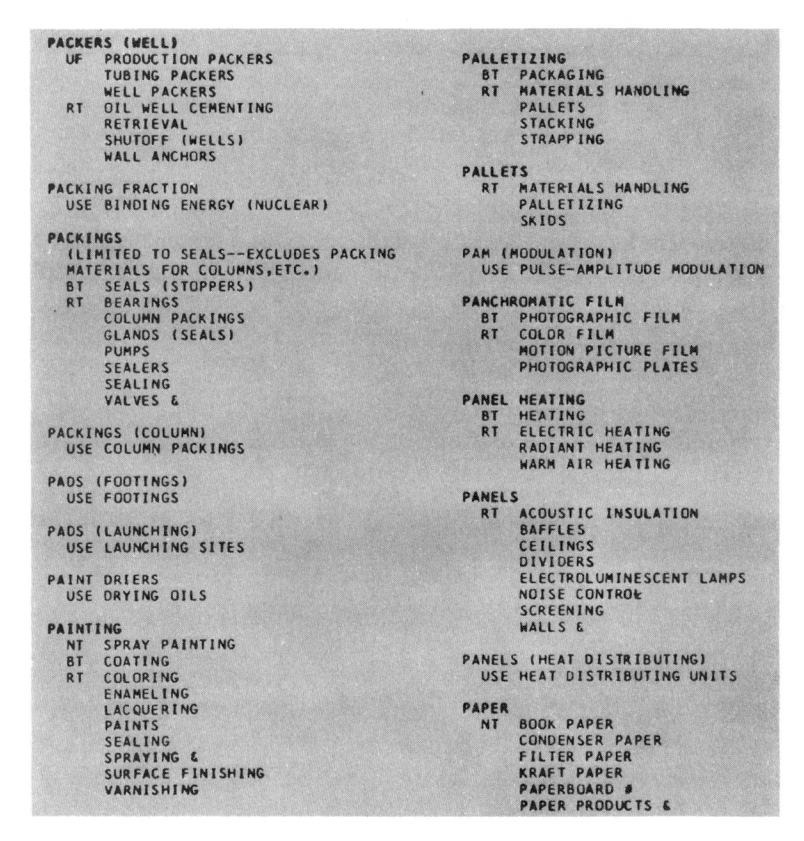

```
PACKERS (WELL)
    UF  PRODUCTION PACKERS
        TUBING PACKERS
        WELL PACKERS
    RT  OIL WELL CEMENTING
        RETRIEVAL
        SHUTOFF (WELLS)
        WALL ANCHORS

PACKING FRACTION
    USE BINDING ENERGY (NUCLEAR)

PACKINGS
    (LIMITED TO SEALS--EXCLUDES PACKING
    MATERIALS FOR COLUMNS,ETC.)
    BT  SEALS (STOPPERS)
    RT  BEARINGS
        COLUMN PACKINGS
        GLANDS (SEALS)
        PUMPS
        SEALERS
        SEALING
        VALVES &

PACKINGS (COLUMN)
    USE COLUMN PACKINGS

PADS (FOOTINGS)
    USE FOOTINGS

PADS (LAUNCHING)
    USE LAUNCHING SITES

PAINT DRIERS
    USE DRYING OILS

PAINTING
    NT  SPRAY PAINTING
    BT  COATING
    RT  COLORING
        ENAMELING
        LACQUERING
        PAINTS
        SEALING
        SPRAYING &
        SURFACE FINISHING
        VARNISHING

PALLETIZING
    BT  PACKAGING
    RT  MATERIALS HANDLING
        PALLETS
        STACKING
        STRAPPING

PALLETS
    RT  MATERIALS HANDLING
        PALLETIZING
        SKIDS

PAM (MODULATION)
    USE PULSE-AMPLITUDE MODULATION

PANCHROMATIC FILM
    BT  PHOTOGRAPHIC FILM
    RT  COLOR FILM
        MOTION PICTURE FILM
        PHOTOGRAPHIC PLATES

PANEL HEATING
    BT  HEATING
    RT  ELECTRIC HEATING
        RADIANT HEATING
        WARM AIR HEATING

PANELS
    RT  ACOUSTIC INSULATION
        BAFFLES
        CEILINGS
        DIVIDERS
        ELECTROLUMINESCENT LAMPS
        NOISE CONTROL
        SCREENING
        WALLS &

PANELS (HEAT DISTRIBUTING)
    USE HEAT DISTRIBUTING UNITS

PAPER
    NT  BOOK PAPER
        CONDENSER PAPER
        FILTER PAPER
        KRAFT PAPER
        PAPERBOARD &
        PAPER PRODUCTS &
```

FIGURE 1. *Extract from an engineering thesaurus. Here "UF" means "use for."*

Controllers: RT Combustion control, Flow control
Fuel systems: RT Carburetors
Mixing: NT Carburetion
Flowmeters

In the first case there are four possible access points to the topic (including cross references). In the second there are eight.

The thesaurus thus provides more access points for the information search. This feature is particularly apparent when the number of index entry terms is restricted, and the thesaurus lists a whole group of words that each term is "used for." In one industrial system the thesaurus directs that the term "flow" be used whenever any of the following concepts are selected from text for indexing:

air bubbles
bubbles
coalescence
compressibility of liquids
drainage of liquids
fluid mechanics
gas flow
hydraulic fluids
jets

laminar boundary layer
pour point
pressure drop
rheology
swirl
transport properties
viscoelasticity
vortices
wetting

Starting with any one of these words in mind, the searcher is led by "use" references to index entries under "Flow."

One further aspect of terminology control may be noted here. Some postcoordinate information systems, in which each index entry term is independently recorded, find it useful to identify the "role" which each term is playing in the topic indexed. For example, in the topic "The Production of Alcohol from Wood," "alcohol" is a product; in "The Use of Alcohol to Make Formaldehyde," it is a raw material; in "The Solubility of Hydrocarbons in Alcohol," it is a medium. To separate a search for methods of producing alcohol from one for derivatives of alcohol, or from one for uses of alcohol, the index term "alcohol" can in each case be tagged with a different "role indicator." A set of roles developed by the Engineers Joint Council is shown in Figure 2.

Systematic Word Lists

As previously explained, developing BT, NT, and RT links in an alphabetic list is only one step away from constructing a systematic classification. In fact, at the back of some alphabetic lists, such as the M.I.T. *Thesaurus of Textile Engineering Terms,* will be found systematic charts linking related terms (see Figure 3).

If *all* the indexing terms used are brought together and arranged hierarchically, we have a systematic thesaurus or classification schedule. The aviation subject-heading list previously discussed (*12*) includes an aeronautics classification schedule, based on a Library of Congress scheme. The terms in this schedule do not wholly coincide with those in the alphabetic list, but offer an alternative organization of aviation terminology. Two extracts may be compared:

535	Airlines, scheduled
535.1	Traffic (passenger and cargo)
535.12	Traffic potential
535.2	Finance: economic aspects
535.21	Accounting
535.3	Operations
535.4	Equipment
535.5	Statistics
535.6	Regulations
535.7	Rates and fares
535.8	Miscellaneous
535.8.A8	Associations
535.8.C3	Certification
535.8.C8	Competition
720	Accidents, safety
720.1	Safety programs, codes, rescue facilities
720.3	Collisions, near misses
720.4	Accident reports
720.5	Accident prevention, air safety, investigations, hazards, safety devices (see 697.53, Parachutes)
720.6	Safety procedures, search and rescue
720.61	Firefighting
720.7	Survival
720.8	Adventures and narratives

Analysis of Information

8

The primary topic of consideration is; the principal subject of discussion is; the subject reported is; the major topic under discussion is; there is a description of

1

Input; raw material; material of construction; reactant; base metal (for alloys); components to be combined; constituents to be combined; ingredients to be combined; material to be shaped; material to be formed; ore to be refined; subassemblies to be assembled; energy input (only in an energy conversion); data and types of data (only when inputs to mathematical processings); a material being corroded

2

Output; product, by-product, coproduct; outcome, resultant; intermediate product; alloy produced; resulting material; resulting mixture or formulation; material manufactured; mixture manufactured; device shaped or formed; metal or substance refined; device, equipment, or apparatus made, assembled, built, fabricated, constructed, created; energy output (only in an energy conversion); data and types of data (only as mathematical processing outputs)

3

Undesirable component; waste; scrap; rejects (manufactured devices); contaminant; impurity, pollutant, adulterant, or poison in inputs, environments, and materials passively receiving actions; undesirable material present; unnecessary material present; undesirable product, by-product, coproduct

4

Indicated, possible, intended present or later uses or applications. The use or application to which the term has been, is now, or will later be put. To be used as, in, on, for, or with; for use as, in, on, for, or with; used as, in, on, for, or with; for later use as, in, on, for, or with

5

Environment; medium; atmosphere; solvent; carrier (material); support (in a process or operation); vehicle (material); host; absorbent, adsorbent

6

Cause; independent or controlled variable; influencing factor; "X" as a factor affecting or influencing "Y," the "X" in "Y" is a function of "X"

7

Effect; dependent variable; influenced factor; "Y" as a factor affected or influenced by "X"; the "Y" in "Y" is a function of "X"

9

Passively receiving an operation or process with no change in identity, composition, configuration, molecular structure, physical state, or physical form; possession such as when preceded by the preposition *of, in,* or *on* meaning possession; location such as when preceded by the prepositions *in, on, at, to,* or *from* meaning location; used with months and years when they locate information (not bibliographic data) on a time continuum

10

Means to accomplish the primary topic of consideration or other objective

0

Bibliographic data, personal names of authors, corporate authors and sources, types of documents, dates of publication, names of journals and other publications, other source-identifying data, and adjectives

FIGURE 2. *Role indicators as developed by Engineers Joint Council.*

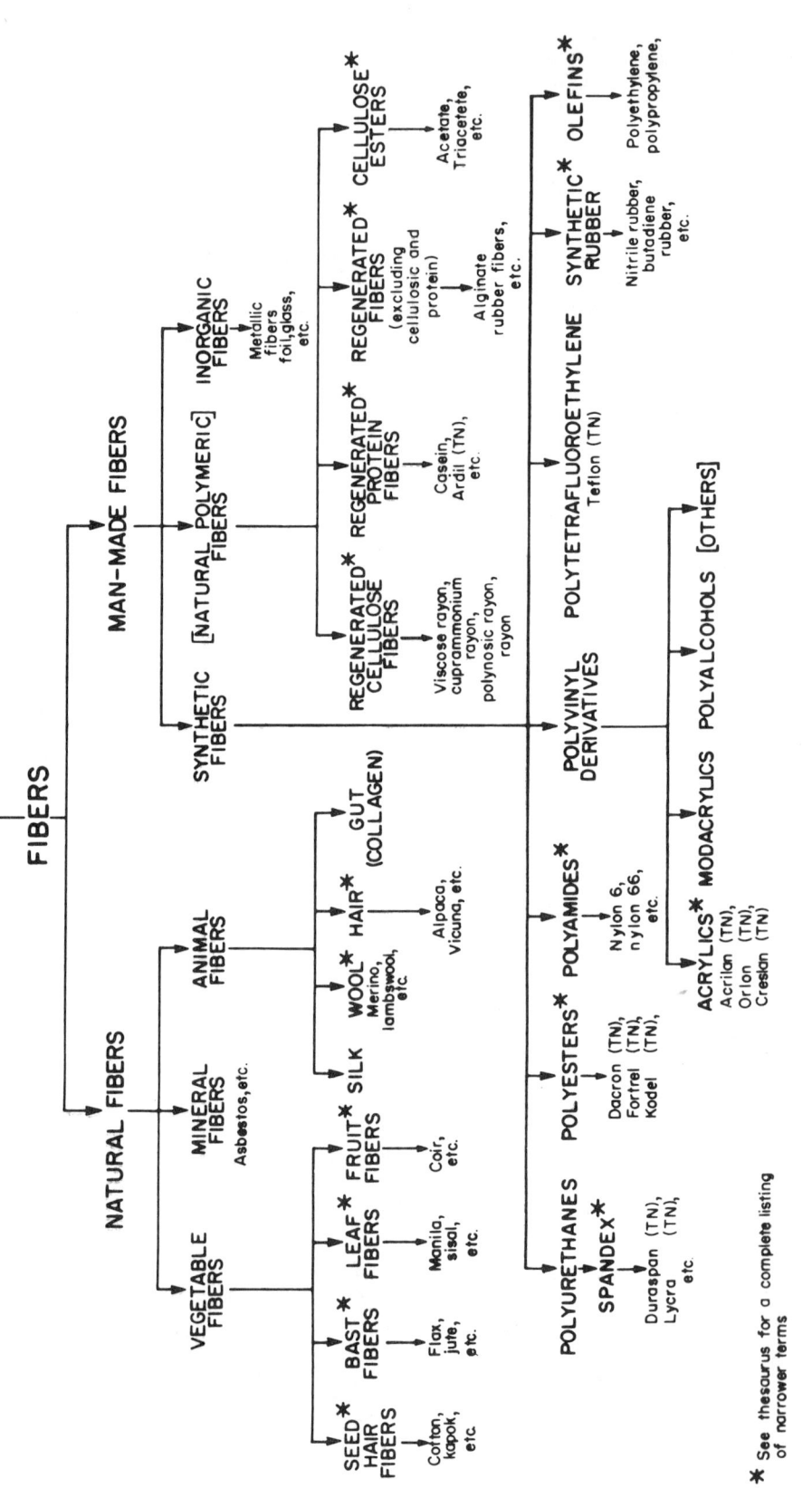

FIGURE 3. Systematic chart linking related terms developed by M.I.T. Thesaurus of Textile Engineering Terms.

Analysis of Information

The essential features of a classified, systematic list are (1) the arrangement of entries according to nearness in meaning, (2) little regularity in the form of verbal headings, (3) some cross references (such as the one above to "Parachutes") but not many, and (4) usually a serial code—such as the decimal numbers—to aid filing in subject sequence.

This aviation schedule contains about 800 coded entries. To gain access to the entry for "hazards," it is necessary to identify its position in the general structure of the classification, which is as follows:

533 to 544	Civil aviation
545 to 567	Aeronautics in general
568 to 569	Special report series
570 to 578	Mechanics of flight, aerodynamics, aeroelasticity
586 to 588	Air navigation
589	Instruments
600 to 697	Aircraft
698 to 699	Materials of construction
701 to 704	Motors, engines
705 to 707	Propellers, air screws
708	Nuclear power plants
709	Jet propulsion
710 to 713	Operation of airplanes, flying
714	Other types of aircraft
720	Accidents, safety
724	Aircraft industry and trade
725 to 740	Airports
741 to 745	Airways
750 to 758	Parachutes
759	Kites
760 to 769	Gliders
770 to 777	Models
780 to 785	Rocket propulsion
787 to 798	Astronautics

Having hit on 720 as a possible place for "hazards," the detailed schedule already cited must be scanned to locate this word at 720.5. All the indexing words at this code have only one entry point. The cross-reference structure of the alphabetic list is replaced in the systematic list by the grouping together of related entries, through which analyst and user can browse to identify appropriate entries for indexing and searching.

Classified word lists for indexing have been used in bibliographies and libraries for many centuries; Konrad Gesner has already been mentioned as an example. Once again, their history cannot detain us here (*14*). The most well known of library schemes is undoubtedly the decimal classification of Melvil Dewey (*15*), described elsewhere in the encyclopedia. In this article we shall pay attention to the development of systems for detailed subject analysis.

The Dewey system essentially aims to provide a single coded entry for each topic isolated by subject analysis. Based on its fifth edition, the Universal decimal classification (UDC) was first published in 1905 by two Belgians, Paul Otlet and Henri La Fontaine. It has since been developed into a much more detailed scheme than Dewey's (*16*). Like his, its schedules cover all subject fields, but from its early days the scheme has expressed specific topics by combining terms. The schedules consist mainly of coded subject headings in systematic order, similar to the aviation classification already illustrated. Thus we have the following:

669	Metallurgy
669.1	Ferrous metals
669.14	Steel
669.18	Production of steel
669.183	By reverberatory processes
669.183.2	Open hearth processes
669.183.21	Furnaces
669.183.211.2	Hearths
669.183.211.3	Walls
669.183.216	Cooling
669.183.217	Firing
669.183.218	Operation

The topic "Firing the Open Hearth Furnace in Steel Production" is expressed by the single index entry at 669.183.217. More detailed subjects may sometimes be expressed by combining terms. Thus the terms 669.14, "Steel," and 620.194.8, "Sea-water corrosion," can be linked by a colon to form 669.14:620.194.8, representing "The Corrosion of Steel by Sea Water." At other points in the schedules instructions are given for forming briefer compound entries. So we have the following:

669	Metallurgy
669-4	Shape of metal object
669-46	Hollow
669-462	Tubular, pipe
669.01	Behavior of metal
669.018	Physical properties
669.018.2	Mechanical
669.3	Copper
669.35	Alloys

The topic "Mechanical Properties of Copper Alloy Pipes" can be expressed by the compressed number 669.35-462.018.2.

The UDC thus provides a very detailed systematic list of terms, with devices to express even more detailed topics by the combination of terms. To gain access to the schedules and to index entries, an alphabetic index is provided, of which the following is an extract, showing many of the occurrences of the concept "metal":

Metal(s)	546.2, 669
ferrous	669.1
light	669.7
nonferrous	669.2
Metal articles	672
building materials	691.7
cleaning	621.7.02
household	648.55

Analysis of Information

coating of	669.86
coating with	669.81
(see also Metallization)	
compounds	661.8
(see also Organometallic)	
construction work	693.8
(see also Steel-framed)	
Metal-base paints	667.633.42
Metal-cutting (art)	736
(presswork)	655.35
Metallic pigments	667.622.2
Metalliferous ores	553.3
mining	622.34
Metallization	621.793
(see also Metal coatings)	
Metallography	620.18
(see also Physical Metallurgy)	
Metalloids	546.1
Metallurgy	669

The development of systematic lists of terms, that are combined or coordinated in indexing, has gone further in recent years. A general classification of this kind, the colon classification of S. R. Ranganathan (17), considerably stimulated this development, and many special schedules have been prepared. The name given to combinatory lists of this kind is "faceted classification" (18). In these, terms within a given field of knowledge are first of all sorted into homogeneous groups called "facets." In science and technology, facets are often groups of things, products, their parts, constituents and attributes, and operations on them, as in the following examples:

Facet	Examples
Things, entities	
Naturally occurring	Minerals, animals, plants, soils
Products	Bridges, engines, fibers
Mental constructs	Equations, rectangles
Parts, components, structure	Beam, wheel, wing
Organs	Heart, seed
Materials, constituents	Metal, glass, nitrogen
Attributes	
Qualities, properties	Cohesion, color, solubility
Processes, behavior	Vibration, inflammation
Operations	
Experimental, technical	Cutting, breeding
Mental	Calculation, reasoning

A rather different set of facets may be used in the social sciences. For example, a classification for community development (19) first of all divides its terms into 10 fields relating to the individual, the family, the community, communication, arts and recreations, education, organization, economics, politics, and international. Within each field there are two basic facets: activities and personalities. The education field lists the following coded terms:

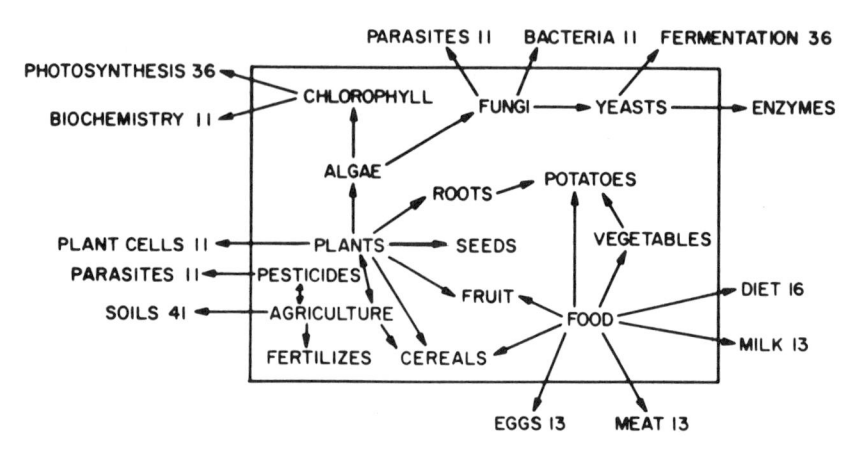

FIGURE 4. *Example of graphic display of groups of related indexing words.*

Activities
- Ha — Education, general
- Hab — School organization
- Ham — Teaching methods
- Hat — Curriculum
- He — Type of education
- Hed — Vocational training
- Heg — Technical education
- Hem — Physical education

Personalities
- Hib — Educands
- Hid — Education in the home
- Hif — Infants
- Hig — Primary
- Hij — Postprimary
- Hil — Secondary
- Hir — Exceptional children
- Hit — College, university
- Hiv — Specialists
- Hiw — Adults
- Hix — Communities

Terms within and among fields are combined to represent topics, thus "Teaching Methods for Exceptional Children" is represented by Hir Ham, "Technical University Education" by Hit Heg, and "Vocational Training in Home Economics" by Cag Hed (where Cag comes from a "family activities" facet).

One other variant of the systematic list has recently been developed: graphic displays of groups of related indexing words (20) (see Figure 4).

Construction of Terminologies

If a standard list of terms is to be constructed, the first point to be settled is its scope. A special list is usually compiled to meet the needs of a particular group of

Analysis of Information

users, and its boundary often does not coincide neatly with a traditional academic discipline. This may be illustrated by a special selection from the UDC compiled for metallurgy. It includes terms from the following sections of UDC:

33	Economics
51	Mathematics
53	Physics
54	Chemistry
62	Engineering, including
620.1	Testing, defects and protection of materials
621	Mechanical engineering
621.3	Electrical engineering
621.7	Workshop practice
622	Mining
66	Chemical technology
669	Metallurgy

It is clear that the scope of a standard list must be decided only after a close study of the interests of potential users of the system to be based on it. The obtaining of information about present interests is in itself not easy. It is still less easy to predict future interests; yet if the terminology is to be viable, the attempt must be made. Current interests can be identified by putting questions to users and by examining a representative range of material that directly expresses their interests, for example, their own publications, queries that they have put to information systems, and documents that they have stated to be relevant to their work. The future can perhaps be guessed by asking them for their own predicted interests 5 or 10 years ahead.

Once the scope of an information system is decided, the next step is to collect terms used. The material examined in deciding scope will lay the basis for this.

The survey can be extended by examining comprehensive texts in the fields of interest, as well as existing word lists (glossaries, subject-heading lists, thesauruses, classifications) in these and overlapping fields. The result of this work is a collection of terms that are candidates for inclusion in the standard list.

Candidate terms are then evaluated as to their estimated usefulness in the information system (21). Among the factors to be looked at are (1) any information on their frequency of occurrence in the field, (2) their preciseness and acceptability to users, and (3) their relations to other terms. Extremes of use frequency, high or low, may be a sign that a term is of little information value: either it is used so often that it will not act selectively in information search, or it is used so rarely that it will not be worth providing an index entry for it.

Relationships between terms are most readily displayed by structuring the list into classified form—particularly in the form of a faceted classification. This will reveal terms of overlapping meaning. For example, both "countryside" and "rural" may have been used for the same concept, or "balls" and "spheres," or "positioning" and "alignment." One of each pair may be chosen as a standard term. Again, classification will form groups of terms of narrower and broader meaning. In some cases the narrower term may be eliminated from the standard list as not sufficiently distinct or important, e.g.,

NT	replaced by	BT
Charring		Burning
Burnishing		Polishing
Fiberboard		Pressboard

In other cases both terms of a pair may be kept, with a cross reference between them:

NT	BT
Motorways	Roads
Monoxides	Oxides
Mirrors	Reflectors
Dazzle	Glare

Classification may reveal a cluster of overlapping terms that need more precise definition of usage. For example, in an engineering list, the words "deformation," "deflection," and "distortion" were amplified as follows:

Deformation (plastic)
Deflection (elastic deformation)
Distortion (unwanted plastic deformation)

A careful comparison of each candidate term with its class neighbors will thus help to standardize the list and reveal relations between terms. It is necessary during this work to decide whether the standard list is to be highly detailed—including a term for every distinct concept encountered in its subject field—or whether it is to consist only of general "descriptors," each representing a range of narrower and related terms. Many standard lists are lengthy and detailed, containing several thousand terms or even several tens of thousands. Other lists, although still covering a wide field, contain less than 1000 standard terms. The technical thesaurus of a chemical manufacturer lists 700 standard terms, each of which is used to replace, on average, 7 others. For example, "Mixing" is used to index concepts such as agitators (and subtypes such as paddle agitators), blending, homogenizing, and stirring, and "Drying" replaces concepts such as driers (and subtypes), dehydration, desiccants, and water removal. Professional opinion is divided as to the relative merits of detailed and limited lists.

After a standard list, showing relations between terms, has been compiled, the form in which it is to be displayed must be chosen. The alternatives have already been described: an alphabetic word list or thesaurus, a systematic list, or some combination of the two. The last gives the greatest ease of access to both indexer and searcher.

Coded Terminologies

An optional stage in subject analysis is to translate standard index terms into a code. Many systems do not include this step, but use natural language words as index entries. Nevertheless, there are situations in which coding is useful or even essential. Codes may be used for several purposes:

Analysis of Information

1. To maintain the filing sequence of a word list and index entries based on it
2. To decrease the amount of space needed to record terms
3. To indicate the physical location of a term on an index record, for example, its punching position on a card
4. To express relations between terms and between index entries

The number and letter codes attached to systematic word lists, already illustrated, may serve all these purposes. For example, the UDC code 669.183.2, for "Open-hearth processes" in metallurgy, (1) fixes the index entry at a certain position in a file; (2) provides a short filing number that may be inscribed on the spine of a book; (3) may be used for punch-card coding; and (4) by shortening, leads to adjacent related broader terms such as 669.183, "Reverberatory processes," and by lengthening, to adjacent related narrower terms such as 669.183.211.2, "Hearths."

The most complex code yet developed for index terms is the semantic code constructed at Western Reserve University (22). A paper on the theme "The Possibility of Changing the Brittleness of Cermet Materials by Modifying Their Microstructure" would be encoded as KOV. CERM. 2X. METL. 001, KWV. KAP. PAPR. 010, KAL. CIRS. MYTL. RANG. 13X. 001. There are three key indexing terms:

Cermet: CERM. 2X. METL. 001
Brittleness: PAPR. 010
Microstructure: CIRS. MYTL. RANG. 13X. 01

These are connected by role indicators showing relations between them: KOV means that a "property is given for" Cermet, the "property given" being KWV Brittleness; KAL means that there is an "influencing property" Microstructure, the "property influenced" being KAP Brittleness. Each key indexing term is encoded by combining "semantic factors" which together make up its meaning. Thus Microstructure is an aspect of Crystals (CIRS), characteristic of Metals (MYTL), and a species of Arrangement (RANG). This code allows very complex relations between index entries to be expressed. This entry can be retrieved whether we search for its specific code or for many more general subjects such as the following:

Microstructure of cermets: CERM. 2X. METL. 001, CIRS. MYTL. RANG. 13X. 001
Brittleness of metallic materials: METL, PAPR. 010
Crystal arrangement: CIRS. RANG. 13X

Codes for indexed subjects may also include codes for objects. Engineering product terms may be encoded for all the reasons given above. For example, a certain type of steel bar may be coded 78.65.16.120, specifying the form of the product, its material, and its dimensions:

Form, 78: bars
Material, 65: carbon tool steel
Subgroup, 16: SAE type WI, 1.2% carbon
Dimensions, 120: round, 3-inch diameter

Many such systematic codes are employed in industry.

One group of objects for which many codes have been developed is that of "chemical substances" (23). Chemical compounds can have special so-called "trivial" names, such as "aspirin." There is also a highly developed, fairly standardized systematic nomenclature for them, based on the structure of each substance. Each compound is represented by a set of parts (elements, radicals, functions, substituents) and relations between them. In standard nomenclatures, certain component parts are chosen for indexing and used as root names, prefixes, and suffixes. For example, in the name "3-acetamido-2-amino-5-methyl benzaldehyde" we have the following:

> Root name: benz
> Functional suffix: aldehyde
> Functional prefixes: acetamido, amino, methyl
> Relational signs: 3,2,5

The traditional method of coding in chemistry is to use elements as standard component parts, and to construct molecular formulas as coded index entries, for example, $C_{12}H_{18}O_2N_2Br_2As_2$. Indexes based on such formulas are much used. But many codes have also been developed using groups of atoms as functional component parts, analogous to the components of standard nomenclature.

Problems of Analysis

The last section has completed our look at the individual operations of analysis. From each document, characteristics of origin are first selected: a set of bibliographic elements is chosen, standardized with the aid of a cataloging code, and some elements are chosen as access points for the information search. Next, the subject information content of the document is analyzed: relevant subjects are identified and may be coded and their expression may be standardized with the aid of a standard list.

Practical cataloging and indexing uses a variety of aids. For subject analysis, the most important are the standard terminologies discussed previously, instruction manuals, and structured forms. In a sample of 50 technical information centers, 90% used a standard word list of some kind (24). Instruction manuals were used by 75%, and may contain indexing rules, mandatory indexing requirements, policy on depth of indexing desired, and so forth. Structured indexing forms were used by 38% of the sample. All these aids were believed to improve indexer accuracy and consistency.

Nevertheless, any examination of the practice of analysis within libraries and information services will reveal wide variations in what elements are selected to describe documents and how they are standardized. There is little in the way of clear principles to guide practice, and such principles as have been advocated by some are strongly disputed by others.

Thinking first of subject analysis, among the problems encountered is the degree of "exhaustivity." How detailed should subject indexing be? How many index terms per document? As explained in earlier sections, the trend is to increased exhaustivity. A sample of about 30 modern information systems shows the following distribution:

Terms per document	Number of systems
1–4	1
5	4
6–9	9
14–19	3
20–30	7
Over 30	6

We can measure the exhaustivity by the degree of condensation from original text. For example, the *McGraw-Hill Encyclopedia of Science and Technology* contains nearly 10 million words. It could be indexed in a library catalog under the two words "science" and "technology." The ratio of text to subject description would then be 5 million to 1. A more detailed information system might index each of the 7000 articles by a single word. The ratio of text to description would then be about 1400 to 1. In the index to the encyclopedia, there are eight two-word index entries per page of text; since each page averages 1000 words, the ratio of text words to index words is 60 to 1. What stage along this range of ratios —from 5 million down to 60—is the most effective in a particular set of circumstances? There is as yet little evidence to indicate the depth to which analysis should be taken.

A second problem of subject analysis concerns the degree of standardization of terminology. There are those who advocate and practice the selection of words for indexing just as they occur in each successive text examined. Other analysts develop and consistently use a strictly controlled word list. Once again, evidence as to the relative values of these policies is inconclusive. Coupled with this problem is the further one of deciding—if terminology is to be controlled—at what point in the information system it should be applied. This article has described its application during information analysis, but some systems use uncontrolled text words in analysis and introduce terminological variations during search. The standard word list is then used to indicate to the searcher what alternative text words may have been used in analysis.

Let us now look beyond the individual act of analysis and consider its place in the information system as a whole. Within this system, analysis of the same document is repeated over and over again by different agencies: publishers, libraries, indexing services, bibliographers, and so forth. There is a vast amount of duplicated, or at least overlapping, effort. Despite the existence of standard rules and lists, this duplication of work gives rise to endless variation between systems. Insofar as descriptive cataloging is concerned, it has been said that one can inspect catalog cards from 10 major U.S. libraries, all representing the same book, all based on the same cataloging rules, yet each begins with a different entry word (*25*). Of 938 subject headings used by nine industrial relations libraries, 57% were unique to one library and 23% showed significant alternative forms (*25*). Are such duplication and variation useful and necessary?

It has long been agreed that for descriptive cataloging uniformity is more valuable than the minor variations that may serve special local needs. In the United States the Library of Congress has taken the lead in promoting centralized and uniform cataloging. There is less agreement that uniformity is either desirable or achievable in subject analysis. Comparisons of different thesauruses (*25*) and of different coded vocabularies (*10*) have shown what a low degree of compatibility there is between standard word lists compiled by different agencies. There are those who argue that this is inevitable: A terminology must reflect the interests of its special user group, and each group will impose its own variant standard. Once again, we do not know whether the benefits to be gained from this individuality of approach are worth the effort engaged.

Analysis, it has been said, is the basic problem as well as the costliest bottleneck of information retrieval. There is a continuing need to develop principles that should guide the practice of analysis and standards that should aid cooperation, convertibility, and compatibility among information systems.

REFERENCES

1. A. Kent, *Textbook on Mechanized Information Retrieval,* 2nd ed., Wiley (Interscience), New York, 1966.
2. R. Strout, "The Development of the Catalog and Cataloging Codes," *Lib. Quart.,* 26, no. 4, 254–275 (1956).
3. There are many good texts on cataloging; one of the most interesting reports on its problems is that of S. Lubetsky, *Cataloging Rules and Principles,* Processing Department, Library of Congress, 1953. A standard modern textbook is L. J. Jolley, *Principles of Cataloguing,* Philosophical Library, New York, 1961.
4. *Coden for Periodical Titles,* American Society for Testing Materials, Philadelphia, 1963, and supplement 1, 1964.
5. *Directions for Abstractors and Section Editors,* Chemical Abstracts Service, Columbus, Ohio, 1952.
6. M. E. Stevens, *Automatic Indexing: A State-of-the-Art Report,* National Bureau of Standards, Washington, D.C., 1965.
7. C. A. Cutter, *Rules for a Dictionary Catalog,* 4th ed., U.S. Government Printing Office, Washington, D.C., 1904.
8. J. B. Kaiser, *Systematic Indexing,* Pitman, London, 1911.
9. E. J. Coates, *Subject Catalogues: Headings and Structure,* Library Association, London, 1960.
10. B. C. Vickery, *On Retrieval System Theory,* 2nd ed., Butterworth, London, 1965.
11. J. Pettee, *Subject Headings: History and Theory of the Alphabetical Subject Approach to Books,* Wilson, New York, 1947.
12. V. Earnshaw and A. Gautreaux, *Aviation Subject Headings and Classification Guide,* Special Libraries Association, New York, 1966.
13. *Thesaurus of Engineering Terms,* Engineers Joint Council, New York, 1964.
14. W. C. Berwick Sayers, *Manual of Classification for Librarians and Bibliographers,* 3rd ed., Grafton, London, 1955.
15. *Dewey Decimal Classification and Relative Index,* 17th ed., Forest Press, New York, 1965.
16. J. Mills, *The Universal Decimal Classification,* Graduate School of Library Service, Rutgers, The State University, New Brunswick, N.J., 1964.
17. R. S. Parkhi, *Decimal Classification and Colon Classification in Perspective,* Asia Publishing House, New York, 1964.

18. B. C. Vickery, *Faceted Classification Schemes,* Graduate School of Library Service, Rutgers, The State University, New Brunswick, N.J., 1966.
19. D. J. Foskett, *Classification and Indexing in the Social Sciences,* Butterworth, London, 1963.
20. *Euratom Thesaurus,* European Atomic Energy Community, Brussels, 1964.
21. D. J. Campbell, "Making Your Own Indexing System in Science and Technology," *Aslib Proc.,* **15**, no. 10, 282–303 (1963).
22. B. C. Vickery, "The Structure of Semantic Coding," *Amer. Doc.,* **10**, 234–241 (1959).
23. There are useful articles on chemical coding by L. E. Kuentzel and D. E. H. Frear, in *Punched Cards,* 2nd ed. (R. S. Casey et al., eds.), Reinhold, New York, 1958.
24. A. L. Korotkin et al., "Indexing Aids, Procedures and Devices," Rome Air Development Center Report RADC-TR-64-582, 1965; available from C.F.S.T.I. as AD 616342.
25. M. M. Henderson et al., *Cooperation, Convertibility and Compatibility Among Information Systems,* National Bureau of Standards, Washington, D.C., 1966.

DESCRIPTIVE CATALOGING

3
Descriptive Cataloging

Jay E. Daily / University of Pittsburgh, Pittsburgh, Pennsylvania

Unlike subject cataloging, which locates information in the resources of the library or information center, descriptive cataloging is used to identify a particular information source. Hence the underlying assumption of all descriptive cataloging is that someone already knows some identifying feature of the work. A further assumption is needed when all these identifications are combined in a single file. We assume that the most significant identifying features are reasonable points of access to the particular work sought. Only very recently has the work of descriptive cataloging led to another use which is purely statistical in nature. A computerized catalog is needed to answer such questions as, "How many books by a given publisher were obtained for a given year of publication?" Here the question is a part of a type to which studies of resources generally are closely allied. If it is understood that the file of descriptive cataloging information must provide points of access which enable research in several directions, then it is possible to discuss the topic not only from the standpoint of history and tradition, but as the evolution of a theory. Language data processing, having reached a stage of development where speculation can be tested experimentally, requires that modern descriptive cataloging be viewed not as the culmination of a long historical development but as the current solution to problems of identification utilizing the technology available.

Even as late as 1904, when the 4th edition of Cutter's *Rules for a Dictionary Catalog* were published posthumously, the concept of technology was largely limited to handwritten or possibly typewritten information, reproducible, if at all, only in a printed book catalog. Though printed cards available from the Library of Congress after 1901 produced the unit-card method of descriptive cataloging, the significantly different postulates, which account for points of access in a printed book catalog

---

From Daily, Jay E. *Descriptive Cataloging*. ENCYCLOPEDIA OF LIBRARY AND INFORMATION SCIENCE. Vol. 7. Edited by Allen Kent and Harold Lancour. Assistant Editor, William Z. Nasri. New York, Marcel Dekker, Inc., c1972. pp. 17-31.

and in a unit-card catalog, have only very recently come to light. Until reprography reached a point where locally produced cards could be fitted into a unit-card system, there was no need to distinguish between unit entry and main entry. Research now in progress tends to support the hypothesis that in a unit-card system title entry is most readily and efficiently utilized at all the steps in the system from order file to shelf list. In a computerized catalog, title entry is the searchable element required to identify a work from the point of first entry until complete entry is recorded. Indeed, in a main entry system, title entry can serve quite as well as author entry for the complete bibliographic description of a work (*1*).

The Bodleian Catalog of 1624, the rules produced by Panizzi for the British Museum Catalogue, and Cutter's rules all assume that author entry is the most efficient point of access to a file of bibliographic descriptions. This is true if the search is most usually made on the basis of author, if the work has a clearly defined author, and if the file of authors does not include any significant amount of ambiguity. In a manual file, sequentiality of information is important as well. That is, the names of authors must be arranged in some systematic fashion so that random access into the system is both immediate and precise. The Roman, Greek, and Cyrillic alphabets are ideal for this purpose; special rules are required for the Spanish, Swedish, and German alphabets; there are considerable problems with the Arabic and Hebrew alphabets; and the sequentiality is practically lost for syllabaries, such as Japanese and Amharic. The sequentiality is artificial and a great problem with Chinese. But in the intellectual climate of the eighteenth century, Latin and Greek were considered the linguistic height of man's endeavor, and these languages were accepted as the standard against which other languages were judged and to which they were made to conform. In any case, there were only books, broadsides, and manuscripts to consider and of these, only books were of such importance that bibliographic description was needed. Later in the century, with the development of serial publications, new problems arose, but the rules for main entry systems were not changed then, nor much later, because the printed book catalog needs only one place for full bibliographic description, and this can be identified in such a way that other points of access need not cite any more than is necessary to lead the searcher to the full description. Often the main entries were numbered, and title, additional authorship, and other points of access could refer back to this single entry. It was rather natural to think of author as main entry because scholarship relied on the principle of authority as the source of substantiation for any doctrine. Aristotle could settle almost any argument in favor of the contender who found the most oracular passage in an appropriate segment of the philosopher's opera.

As knowledge changed, the needs of researchers changed. By the early twentieth century it was not so much a matter of who said it as what was said. Learning consisted of an ability to cite the places where information could be found, and the author tended to represent a subject as well as explicate it. Hence the names which are utilized as words: Kantian, Hegelian, Darwinism, Marxism, and so forth. For the learned man, a knowledge of the principal authors in his field was amplified to include those who wrote at the periphery of a corpus of information. However, information could be stored in many different forms, and of these the book that had served as a standard source came to represent the ideal around which bibliographic description was organized as the terminology of cataloging shows.

Descriptive Cataloging

Early in this century, the Library of Congress adopted a rule that each frame of a motion picture film had to be printed on paper before the work could be copyrighted. When film was subject to fairly rapid deterioration, this rule was probably very wise. At the present, though, no such rule exists. The description of such photographic collections need differ in no great way from the description of random photographs copied and bound together as a book. However, motion picture films meant to be run through a projector require fuller and different description. There is no concept of authorship to guide the cataloger, so that the problem of entry is resolved only by adopting the title as the main entry. The length of the film, the running time at standard speed, and whether it is in color and has sound are all vital parts of the description.

Similarly the development of phonorecordings from cylinders, to discs, to wire, to magnetic tape, and in the future possibly to electronically activated crystals, has produced a need for description that includes not only the form of the recording but also an indication of what was recorded and by whom. An example is the recording of Debussy playing his own compositions for the piano in a process that allowed transfer from one form of phonorecording to another. *Clair de Lune* by Debussy is ambiguous in this context until we include who has performed the work. The technique of recording is an essential part of the description if a collection is meant to be used fully. The performer is sometimes more the identifying feature of a work than the original composer, as is the case with jazz musicians, many of whom are quite incapable of playing the same work twice in precisely the same way. All improvisation is unique and requires the performer as the principal point of identification and possibly the date as a further point of identification.

These methods of communication as information sources in the twentieth century were devolped concomitantly with rapid means of duplication, through photo-offset and other processes, so that, in effect, everybody could be his own publisher. The characteristic of the nineteenth century scholar, a lifetime devoted to a single work, gave way to the characteristic of twentieth century scholarship, a subject to which several different researchers devote their effort for a relatively short period of time. The change was from the subject equated with the author to the subject-shared or multiple authorship.

Cutter's most significant contribution to descriptive cataloging was the development of corporate entry as a point of access, to replace the nondescript entry "anonymous." This entry has the effect of grouping together all works where title is the most important point of description. Corporate bodies represent shared authorship in one fashion, and the Anglo-American Code has various rules which attempt to discern responsibility for the intellectual content of a work. This is, at best, a metaphysical problem adding nothing whatever to the bibliographic description.

Certain entries, such as uniform title and form headings for laws, constitutions, and other legal acts, are refinements of a title entry and do not really represent authorship in any degree. Anonymous classics. such as *The Arabian Nights,* only partly account for the problems of title entry where several different editions of the same work are published under different titles. A similarity may readily be seen between titles and subject headings especially as titles have become subject headings, not as uniform titles but, *faute de mieux,* topical headings for a new subject.

The development of the Anglo-American Code has generally followed rather than prescribed actual practice. The attempt to render into something like statute law all the possible bibliographic variations was shown to be the principal fault of the 1941 Preliminary Second Edition of the American Library Association Cataloging Rules of 1908. Osborn (2) established what can well bear his name as a principle of descriptive cataloging: No code of rules can predict all possible variation and prescribe methods of treating each as it may occur (3). We must rely on the judgment of the descriptive cataloger in order to produce a code of rules that will facilitate the work of the catalog department.

At the present, depending on what we wish to include, about 85% of descriptive cataloging in a general library is the work of technical assistants trained to follow specific rules and to call for help when the rules do not seem to apply. If we accept training as the characteristic background of technical assistants and education necessary for rendering judgment based on previous experience, personal and vicarious, as the characteristic of professional personnel, then much of the work of descriptive cataloging can be reduced to a fairly simple technique of transcribing what is found on the title page, recto and verso, and discovered elsewhere in the work at hand if needed. Training for such work is neither lengthy nor difficult. The failure of the original "Cataloging-in-Source-Project" (4) resulted from confusion over what must be included in a word to produce uniformity of cataloging and what may be omitted from a printed statement because the book at hand and a code of rules will produce uniform results. One of the chief complaints was that the card reproduced on the verso of the title page had the wrong collation. But the pagination was readily available within the book itself and the complaint is more a case of querulousness than reasoned criticism. As can be seen from the summary above, we can discuss descriptive cataloging at present under three headings: (1) What represents adequate description of an information source under which we can subsume such topics as brief-listing and cooperative cataloging; (2) what constitutes points of access and how they may be determined; and (3) what constitutes an effective method of organizing descriptive cataloging in a library or information center.

A librarian who manages a picture collection has no need for descriptive cataloging. It is sufficient to provide subject access to the collection and let the equivalent of author be treated as if it were a subject. This comparison is vital to an understanding of what descriptive cataloging achieves. It is well known that many other collections do not require an item-by-item description, whether an archival collection of letters and memoranda or a collection of technical reports, the authorship of which is quite inconsequential. The first decision to be made is whether descriptive cataloging is needed at all. Information retrieval systems have sometimes omitted and sometimes included bibliographic description, but a decision to omit any attempt at description is valid if no individual item will ever be needed. The decision need not be final nor need it cover all parts of a collection so long as access by subject is possible. It is always possible in a computerized catalog to add to the points of access and to make some identifying feature, such as a random number, serve in lieu of identification derived from the work itself.

From zero description we need proceed by degrees to the fullest possible description. As we extend the description of an item in the collection, we are guided by the type of information source and the need to identify it for a researcher. The fullest

Descriptive Cataloging

possible description is needed for an incunable or other rare work which may be as much an artifact as it is a book.

In the case of sixteenth, seventeenth, and some eighteenth century books, where hand-set printing resulted in a different copy for each title, the description that omits these marks of rarity is inadequate. Similarly for nineteenth and twentieth century books, each copy of which is identical (or so nearly so as to make no difference) with all the other copies produced in a given edition, there is no need to describe the book beyond that description that fits any copy of the edition. If the edition is not important and will never be important, as is the case with books in a public library system devoted to popular reading, then little more is needed than a description of the title as it might be found in any edition.

Each of the elements of the book that contribute to adequate description can be identified utilizing the standard terminology of catalogers through the ages.

(1) Title is the most important identifying feature of the book and may not be left out. This is especially true in the computerized catalog where title is the principal identifying feature.

(2) Subtitle, i.e., a portion of the entire name of the book which is considered by the author or publisher to be secondary to the principal name of the book, is primarily useful in identifying editions beginning with the first. At the time a book is cataloged, it is safest to assume that sometime in the future another edition will be published.

(3) Alternate title, i.e., another name for the book shown by the publisher to be equally as good as the name first listed, has a different significance altogether from subtitle. An alternate title may become better known than the original title. Since this is a possibility of the future, and the descriptive cataloger cannot predict that this will be impossible, an alternate title is as important as title in identifying the book regardless of edition. That an alternate title may be left out, expanded, or altered in another fashion in later editions is insignificant if change of edition is not important in the work. An alternate title can be identified with, and limited to, those titles included after a semicolon and the word "or" in the complete title of the book.

(4) Of equal importance with the title and alternate title is the author statement. This should be included in full if one or two authors are listed, but it may be shortened by any of the methods recommended in various cataloging codes if three or possibly four or more authors are included. Author statement is meant to include both editor and compiler as if they were authors, if the work has no author.

(5) Edition may be identified either as a number or some identifying feature of a particular work. Such identifying features include illustrator, translator, and editor, if the book has another type of authorship as well. Obviously if the work exists only because of an editor's work, then the editor is equivalent to the author. However, an editor of a particular edition deserves notice if the edition will be important in the system using the descriptive cataloging. Both illustrator and translator must be listed with the first edition of the book if a different edition will ever be important. In distinguishing between editions, marks of identification where numbers have been omitted are of capital importance.

(6) Imprint is a feature of identification necessary to distinguish editions, but most likely unnecessary to distinguish between different works. In the system that does not require identification of editions, publisher may be added on the basis of conflict; i.e., supposing a library already has a title identical with a different book, then imprint would be cited. This is a case that will rarely arise for mod-

ern books, considering the copyright laws now in effect in the United States and elsewhere in the world. Imprint is a vital part of edition and cannot be omitted in those systems where the edition of a work will ever be important. However, there is considerable question whether place as a part of imprint needs to be included. It should be understood that place is added on the basis that conflict may arise. However, there is no law which prevents two publishers of virtually the same name from maintaining offices in the same city, as occurred with Franklin Books Program and Burt Franklin, both of which are located in New York City and from time to time get each other's mail. It may be assumed that adding place in all cases is questionable even for the most complete bibliographic description, where place of publisher or date of publication may be discovered, if needed, more readily and more exactly in various guides to the publishing industry in a given country. Where place becomes important, as may happen with books from underdeveloped areas of the world, then it may be included after the name of the publisher, even though present rules insist that the only proper order of imprint is place, publisher, and date.

(7) Date of publication is not more significant than date of copyright. Some libraries utilizing fullest description have omitted publication date altogether, and quite successfully rely only on the copyright date. The Anglo-American Cataloging Rules and earlier rules of bibliographic description contain rubrics for citing dates and editions, including copyright, where it differed from date of publication. The date of a particular edition is far more significant than the date of a certain printing. If confusion exists over the distinction between printing and edition, the copyright date becomes a satisfactory method of determining whether a given title is an additional printing or is another edition. For a library which has no need of description beyond the identifying features of title and author, there remains a usefulness of including the copyright date of the edition at hand for scientific and technical works where the user may be mislead and seek a book that in the end will be too out of date for his purposes. Date then comes to be something more than bibliographic description and relates to the subject content of the work. Hence the necessity for including at least the copyright date in even the shortest method of cataloging.

(8) Collation has heretofore included either the number of pages or the number of volumes or both in the case of a work continuously numbered through more than one volume. This represents the pagination of the work or the volume count, either of which is quite important to a person utilizing a catalog even with the briefest description. Here again something like subject content is being indicated, although in an offhand manner, by the expanse of the work. Obviously a four-volume biography of George Washington will not suit the casual reader for whom brevity is important. Even less will lack of pagination serve students assigned a certain topic who will want to know how to get the burden of the matter in the fewest pages possible.

(9) Another part of collation is the statement regarding the presence of illustrative material, including maps, portraits, diagrams, facsimiles, and colored plates. The Library of Congress has ordinarily included music scores as if they were illustrative material. Maps folded out and some other description have been included as necessary for efficient function of the library because of the possibility of rebinding or as notice to the circulation librarian that the book has been damaged by a borrower. When the cataloging is being kept to the minimum to identify a given title it is generally efficient to include only the word illustrated for anything beyond one type of illustration and to include the name of that type of illustrative material if it is unique in the book. For instance, it would seem enough to make note of maps, if only maps are included, but not to use both illustrated and maps, if both are included.

Descriptive Cataloging

(10) The final part of the collation proper is the size of the book, and many libraries, even those where the cataloging by edition is of summary importance, will omit the size of the book unless there is something unusual for the reader to notice, such as an oversized book or an undersized book that is easily lost on the shelf. Standards for omission of size are very readily established so that only those books that do not fit the standard size may be noted on the catalog card.

(11) Series not included as a part of the collation represents another element crucial to the identification of a particular edition, but of much less importance when only the title will be sought as a point of identification. Books included in series, especially reprints, will satisfy few scholars in a research library, and yet be perfectly acceptable to casual readers in another kind of library. However, series statement has another importance in the cataloging process, especially to those librarians whose duty it is to determine whether the library already has a copy of the title or not. Often series is the uniquely identifying feature of the same book that has been published under two different titles. Different editions of a book may have different titles and, if so, all the editions should be brought together under a uniform title as if a series, even though the series itself has changed for the different editions. In view of this it can be stated that where cataloging by edition is important, then including a series statement is necessary, although the series may not be a point of access. It is equally important that series be omitted unless it is identified in some fashion with edition.

(12) Notes on catalog cards under present theory are best left to the few that constitute acceptable further description for the library; i.e., descriptive notes should be made only if essential. The general rule of the Library of Congress and hence the Anglo-American Cataloging Rules is to make notes on rather a generous basis when time is available for this purpose. However, it is surely wasteful to make notes for one set of books and not for another even though the validity of the notes has not changed. Contents notes, unlike descriptive notes, should be made whenever the book may be analyzed, but ought to be omitted if no analysis is done. At present contents notes frequently serve the purpose of including on a card what is being postponed or forfeited altogether, i.e., the preparation of adequate analytic entries. Contents notes are especially important if search will be made for each item within a book, and especially if the library has a portion of the book in another copy which represents an identical title separately bound. It seems unfortunate to rule on the basis of analytics by any means other than the usefulness of these entries in a catalog for the purpose of identifying the particular works in a library.

These elements represent adequate description based on a preliminary rule either to catalog each new edition of a work or to make entries only for different titles of a work. The latter process has been variously termed, but the idea is best understood under the rubric "brief-listing," a means of cataloging entirely suitable provided all members of the system are in complete agreement that no more is needed. Brief-listing represents an ideal form of cataloging which can effectively save money by providing adequate access to the titles in a system, but it seems far better to omit unnecessary forms of description rather than analytics where they will represent a considerable saving of time whether brief-listing or full-cataloging is done. Many library systems have chosen to include either place of publication or size and omit analytics on the basis that too much time is required for the latter.

Cooperative cataloging then can be seen as an agreement on standardized rules of adequate description depending entirely on whether the book is to be identified by edition or only by title. Forms of cooperation that cannot settle this point usually end in dissatisfaction and frustration. Even in a brief-listing system, all knowledge of different editions is not lost. The increasing coverage provided by the Library of Congress of its holdings in the printed reproduction of catalog cards gives adequate description of different editions for most works, and in any case, research into the nature of different editions should be conducted in a research library where sufficient bibliographic description abounds. Cooperative cataloging in the past, as seen in the Cataloging-in-Source project and in the shared cataloging projects, has often resulted in general frustration not only because of a confusion over adequate description but also because of confusion over the point at which technology may replace the decision of a cataloger. In general, rules have been made that no one will object to too much, and the fail-safe method of cooperation is to provide description beyond the state of adequacy into the conditions of abundance. The catalog of a library that might very well do with much less description of the works on its shelves is a kind of embarrassment of riches. Several different authors, beginning with Susan Grey Akers, have sought to discover what students require of a catalog, and in every case they have been rather dismayed that so much of the bibliographic description is of little meaning or importance to otherwise intelligent students. The results of the findings generally cast doubt on either the intelligence or previous instruction of students who do not make use of such parts of the description as are judged crucial by the surveyor.

Having gone this far in a description of books, we can develop rules for the description of other materials based on the concept of what is needed for identification and how this can be recorded. Obviously, if the information source lacks an element of description no effort should be made to include it. For instance, it is unwise to set up author equivalence for information sources where authorship is of no significance whatever. There is no justification except tradition for regarding all information sources as being like books. Rather, we should conclude that books represent a kind of bench mark of bibliographic description from which other information sources will vary.

Further, the benefit of subject analysis should not be lost by attempting to make bibliographic description serve that purpose. A case in point is the cataloging of music scores and phonorecordings. A title entry for a music score which is in effect a subject heading, such as string quartet, or symphony, or sonata, should not be made to serve also as the title of the work. An example may be seen in Beethoven's quartets, where a conventional title has been given to some of the works, such as the Rasoumovsky quartets. If title unit entry is employed for either music scores or phonorecordings, then the title as found on the music score must serve whether it says String Quartet no. 1 or String Quartet nos. 1 through 6, or The Rasoumovsky String Quartets, or String Quartet (Rasoumovsky One) no. 7. The purpose of title unit entry is to serve as the model of what will be included under each different entry. In this concept, the various entries, rather than the bibliographic description of a given score, serve as the points of access and the organizational features of the catalog. This method will permit the inclusion of entries for phonorecordings as well as music scores.

Music scores when they were made from engraved plates usually included a plate mark which was of great importance in identifying the particular form of the particu-

Descriptive Cataloging

lar revision or arrangement of a given piece of music. Such plate marks are no longer included with music produced by photo-reproduction. Here again the cataloger must decide how the music scores will be used and what the purpose of keeping them is. There is no need to make the music scores conform to the cataloging of books even though a collection of music scores may be similar to a collection of poetry, from single sheets to anthologies.

There is even less reason for making phonorecordings conform to the standards of books from which they must necessarily vary. The problem of phonorecordings is readily solved if a collection of single works by composers of serious music is the only thing to be cataloged. Whenever phonorecordings of jazz, or recordings of interesting or important performances, are included in the collection, then adequate description must include the performer even though this is never a question when books are being cataloged. The problem of analysis is equally important with phonorecordings because of the size of the disc which may include several different compositions by various composers and at times by various performers. Obviously each element of bibliographic description adds a dimension to the catalog. Phonorecordings of jazz performances must take into account not only the date of the recording and the method of transcription, but also the date of a performance.

The advantage of including nonbook, nonprint material as a part of the rules in the Anglo-American Cataloging Rules has practically been lost because of the dogma that such information sources must be made to conform to the rules established for books. The single unifying feature not only of books but also of serial publications, pamphlets, and off-prints, is the title. This is true also of nonprint materials such as phonorecordings, motion picture films, filmstrips, and films, or slides, and phonorecording combinations. In each of these cases authorship cannot readily be determined; for motion picture films the equivalence of authorship must be organized, more or less on an unsatisfactory basis, for adequate description to be possible. It is much better to devise separate rules of bibliographic description utilizing unit title entry as the method and providing for certain characteristics of motion picture films which apply to no other information source. A collection of motion picture film as photoplays, i.e., works of the imagination in motion picture form, must include not only the title of the film but also the director, the producer, and the main characters as well as the author of the photoplay and the author of the original work from which the photoplay was taken. Even video-tape or electronic recordings on magnetic tape can follow the same rules of description. A collection of documentary films will necessarily omit some elements of the description included as performers. If an equivalent to the author of books is sought in photoplays, it must be the director, who is principally responsible for the final product. Modern interest in motion picture films tends to center around the director's work, so that books of criticism and appreciation are being written about directors of motion pictures as if they were, in fact, authors, not the agent by whose effort an author's work comes to be exhibited.

In any case, the organization of points of access to a large motion picture collection must take into account the different reasons for which the motion picture film is sought. In a collection made up solely of documentary films, where the subject content is the only meaningful element, then the title of the film, the producer, the date of production, and the running time, with a conventional note for either color or black and white, and for sound as a part of the motion picture or in a separate recording, are sufficient to satisfy the needs of users of the collection. But it would be hoped that a collection for a research library would include photoplays of all periods, and these must be analyzed in the manner described above if their usefulness is not to be severely limited.

Libraries are frequently faced with the responsibility for organizing a collection of clippings, i.e., pieces taken from printed sources, and for other quite ephemeral material. In an era where reproduction in more permanent form is not only instantly available but relatively inexpensive, then the durability of the original information source is a secondary consideration if it is to be kept in mind at all. Clippings like slides may be organized solely by subject. It is conceivable that a series of clippings from a newspaper might illustrate the work of a given author, and if so then the clipping has the same significance as a group of poems by a given author or a group of paintings by a given artist. What is advocated here is methods of description that are adequate, not only for the present, but for any foreseeable future. This adequacy must be based on the nature of the collection, its permanence, and the permanence of each item in it, and the reason for which the collection was assembled in the first place.

Archival material, especially that of the modern era, is frequently filled with highly repetitive pieces, such as form letters sent out by businesses, if not by individual authors. The value of an archival collection is not so much in its uniqueness as in the fact that no more basic source of documentation can be utilized as an information source. Included in the general area of archival material are manuscripts dating from the period after the development of the modern publishing industry. The handling of these collections is most efficient when adequate description of the materials is included in a book catalog. This method is especially useful when the collection is of considerable permanence to which additions, when made, are few in number and at infrequent intervals. The book catalog may be prepared as a guide to a special collection of archival materials that provides a user not only with description but also information on the hours for use of the collection and any special regulations of which he should be aware. Such a guide may be cataloged as a book in the general collection with full subject analysis adding to its usefulness.

Adequate description may be defined as that description which provides all points of access needed to a given work. In the sense that bibliographic description includes all the likely clues to identification the user may have, then it is reasonable to make each clue a point of access. In practice, however, some points of access can be reached only with other works. This is especially true where a compilation of separate bibliographic entities is contained within a single volume. In this case analytics or some form of bibliographic analysis is necessary. In other cases, access is so rarely sought or if sought would result in so great a search that a portion of the bibliographic description may be omitted as a point of access. This is true for those works in which the number of the edition has no meaning except as it relates to the title and author of the work. This is equally true for publisher and for the collation. Hence adequate description is only in part governed by the necessity of points of access. Valid points of access include not only the title and the author statement but also the alternate title and editor, translator or illustrator if these names are significant in identifying the edition of the work. A further important point of access is the series statement for all but publisher's series used as a promotional device.

Descriptive Cataloging

What might be termed secondary points of access would be numbered edition and date along with publisher and, if included, place of publication. Collation is a secondary point of access but only insofar as pagination is concerned. If edition is identified by the illustrator, then that portion of the collation which includes illustrations will not be necessary as a point of access, perhaps not even as a secondary point of access. Descriptive notes are secondary points of access while contents notes are primary points of access. Contents notes should not be included in the bibliographic description if no analytics are to be made. The best subject description of a work may be found either in the table of contents or in the index or both, and the reader should be directed to the book itself for the purpose of assisting him to determine finally whether this is the work he wishes to consult. Points of access in a computerized system may include permuted titles and permuted authorship statements. Permuted titles with a program that suppresses words of purely syntactical importance, such as prepositions and conjunctions, can assist in solving problems when the user has only a sketchy notion of the title. Equally joint authorship may be established on the basis of rule which will make authors included in the computerized entry equally searchable under any name. This applies equally to bibliographic analytics made for those works that are in effect a one-volume container for many bibliographic entities. In the past the number of points of access has been severely limited because of the essential linearity of the printed bibliographic description in a book catalog or on a catalog card. When this linearity is no longer a constraint, methods can be found for making portions of the title as searchable as the main entry. Main entry systems of cataloging, especially those that exclude all other entries as in the National Union Catalog, will ordinarily provide only 50% retrieval for titles that are likely to be entered under a corporate author, as a conference, or under a personal name entry as editor. This fact has made these catalogs much less useful than they would be if the entire catalog were established in computerized form. The experimentation done for the various MARC projects of the Library of Congress has sufficiently established that searchable elements should be identified by some code while secondary points of access should be identified by a subsystem code which relates the secondary point of access to the searchable element.

These points of access in a computerized system are also useful in statistical studies which may be devised with a relatively simple programming relying on the code of searchability to establish the data sought. Analytics in cataloging serials are such that each issue of a periodical may be included in a computerized catalog as if this periodical were a separate, i.e., each volume cataloged as a monograph. However, in most cases it will be found that serials should be given brief listing, i.e., omitting the concept of edition altogether. Most of the union lists of serials produced with automated equipment have in effect followed established rules of bibliographic description for brief listing as opposed to the rules for bibliographic description of monographs in the system requiring identification of each edition. Points of access also determine the primary question with certain forms of material including maps, pictures, and other visual or graphic print materials.

If no part of the bibliographic description will ever be sought as an identifying feature, then no bibliographic description is necessary for a given information source. In the case of maps, which are to be used only for the subject content of the graphic displays, it is quite futile to include as points of access such inconsequential matters as cartographer and engraver. Rare maps, however, that are not to be used as actual guides to a territory may be cataloged as if they were manuscripts. Maps used solely for subject content, like all other graphic material the collection of which is meant for informational content not dependent upon the producer of the material, need no bibliographic description. Scale, projection, area covered, and other elements of description are more nearly subject analysis than identifying features of a given map.

The points of access when arranged in random fashion represent the easiest means of utilizing a clue in the user's mind to obtain the material he wants without elaborate investigation, but this can only be achieved by an on-line real-time computerized catalog. Various substitutions and economies are possible so that the real-time use of the catalog is reduced. Most important of these measures is the preparation of bibliographies based on a common need and answered by an arrangement of descriptions according to the most useful point of access sought. In a research library, for instance, all of the works in a collection of rare materials may be printed in a book catalog and this be made the primary point of access, even though it is at one time removed from the material itself. University and college libraries, similarly, now brief-list books on reserve for student's use as required or suggested by professors of various courses. Swank was probably 20 years ahead of his time in recommending that far more use be made of bibliographies for students than was common at his time. Even at the present time, when automated systems of cataloging are at least technologically and theoretically possible, very little attention has been given to the possibilities such methods would bring to light. Foremost among these is a reordering of priorities not only in the acceptability of materials, but also in the preparation of materials for cataloging.

As indicated above, some 85% of all book material cataloged by a library can be handled by technical assistants who are trained in the use of a relatively simple set of rules. Only the choice of main entry is a professional judgment. All the rest is derived from the work at hand following certain standard rules of description. It is possible, then, to arrange the processing of library materials in a kind of assembly line. The first stage in preparing the final entry in a computerized system is the ordering phase. The request for the material is first searched in the library's catalog, or in the Union Catalog of the system, and if it is established that the work is not on hand, then an order is placed for the work. At this point all bibliographic information found in the searching process can be included as a temporary entry meant to be revised when the actual copy is received.

For gift books and exchange books which are in effect obtained without prior searching, the entry begins with the receipt of the book. As soon as the book is received, in either case, bibliographic description can be made in the form shown in Figure 1. Usually the line of procedure would go from the assistant who receives the books and distributes them to various other less experienced assistants who will make the initial bibliographic description and pass the work on to a reviser. The reviser may or may not be a professional whose purpose is to see that all the rules of description have been followed correctly. From this point the bibliographic description goes to an input clerk who translates the material on the bibliographic sheet into machine readable language for the computer. Subject analysis, not an issue under this heading, may best be accomplished after the bibliographic description is com-

Bibliographic Description

(1) Identifying number

Body of the Entry

(2) Title

    Subtitle

(3) Alternate

(4) Author Statement

(5) Edition number

(6) Edition Statement

(7) Editor

(8) Illustrator, Translator

Imprint (9) Place

(10) Publisher

(11) Date, Copyright date

Collation, 12 Pages; Volumes

(13) Illustration

(14) Size

(15) Series Statement

Notes (16) Descriptive notes

(17) Contents notes

TRACING

FIGURE 1.

plete. If this is done, the need for a professional reviser is obviated. One of the professional tasks can be final review of the description as it appears in the catalog. The subject analysis once accomplished can be added to the entry whenever advisable. Until that time the work may be available for circulation by utilizing a random code or other device in lieu of a call number. The final preparation of the book may occur sometime after its value has been proven with circulation. The book prepared for the shelf represents the last stage of processing.

This concept removes the necessity for extensive cooperative cataloging, except for the remaining 15% of those works received by a general or research library that requires more sophisticated or special descriptive cataloging. The idea that it is unnecessary to catalog a book more than once still holds true, but as a practical measure it appears to be more economical to input information from the moment a request for a book is received until the actual book is at hand. Significant time waste in the cataloging process can be traced to the acquisitions department and the cataloging department each having unique functions and acquiring information which is never shared. Equally, time waste occurs because of matching problems where descriptive cataloging information is received independently of the book itself. The Cataloging-in-Source experiment came to grief because no clear distinction was made between those portions of the entry that required professional judgment and what was simply to be copied from the book at hand. Obviously if all the exogenous description, i.e., main entry and subject analysis, were included in the work from some central authority, as is now done in the Soviet Union and elsewhere, then descriptive cataloging becomes purely and clearly a sub- or nonprofessional task.

An extensive trial of this method resulted from the author's experience at the University of Mandalay from 1959 to 1962. The university had a library for all its students, departmental libraries for some of the students, and separate libraries for the Faculty of Medicine and the Faculty of Agriculture. The project established and funded by the Ford Foundation was to bring all the libraries into one unified system with a catalog for all the holdings in all the different libraries. In developing a method for the cataloging of the 30,000 titles in the main collection and the 10,000 additional titles in the other collections, the director of the library, U Htun Aung, and the author had to remember that none of the clerical or technical workers had ever been in a library or seen one in operation, let alone having any library experience. The solution was to break down each operation to its simplest component and train the clerks to do that task only. Later, as the clerk became more experienced, he was taught other components of the cataloging operation. A kind of assembly line was created so that the descriptive cataloging decisions were made by technicians (actually those graduates of the university who would go abroad for a professional degree) and their decisions were converted into card format by the typists. Each card had to be typed because of the lack of any equipment for creating unit cards, and the main entry system devised was such that any technician with some training could select a main entry with a reasonable expectation of arriving at the same decision that the Anglo-American Cataloging Rules dictated.

Despite the considerable distress which these methods caused the advisory committee of American Library Association, which acted as a backstopping agency and furnished professional advice, the experiment at least showed that other methods of descriptive analysis were as effective and much more economical than those which tradition dictated. As the computerized cataloging system becomes widespread, the opportunity to rethink previously developed rules is too good to be missed. Certainly there is little excuse for making the computer confirm what experience ought to have taught so far. The traditions of descriptive analysis have grown almost by accident from the bibliographer's solutions to problems of scholarship in previous times. The freedom from purely sequential information arranged with linear rigidity will help solve the problems of scholarship in an age of expanding information.

NATURAL LANGUAGE TEXT PROCESSING

4
Content Analysis

Carol E. Hicks / Cleveland State University, Cleveland, Ohio

James E. Rush / James E. Rush Associates, Powell, Ohio

Suzanne M. Strong / The Ohio College Library Center, Columbus, Ohio

> "Is there any other point to which you would wish to draw my attention?" Gregory asked.
> "To the curious incident of the dog in the nighttime," Holmes replied.
> "The dog did nothing in the nighttime," the inspector retorted.
> "That," said Sherlock Holmes, "that was the curious incident" [1].

Introduction

The ability to draw correct conclusions from apparently trivial or unrelated facts or incidents is a characteristic which mankind prizes highly. Although obscured in the wealth of detail which research in content analysis has generated, it is probably still true that the underlying motivation for content analytical studies is the desire to improve one's ability to infer correct conclusions from the wealth of data presented to him. It is precisely this inferential capability embodied in the fictional character Sherlock Holmes which provides the stories written by Conan Doyle the lasting interest and intrigue which so many people have enjoyed.

Content analysis is a field of endeavor devoted to the development of new tools and techniques through whose use one may improve his deductive abilities. The computer has lent considerable impetus to work in content analysis, and it is the use of computers in this area which draws our primary interest. To be sure, the person who reviews a book, abstracts a technical article, or interprets a diplomatic communique is performing content analysis, however ill-defined the procedures employed may be. While these activities are of general interest in

---

From Hicks, Carol E., James E. Rush and Suzanne M. Strong. *Content Analysis.* ENCYCLOPEDIA OF COMPUTER SCIENCE AND TECHNOLOGY. Vol. 6. Edited by Jack Belzer, Albert G. Holzman and Allen Kent. New York, Marcel Dekker, Inc., c1977. pp. 74-129.

content analysis, our attention will be focused more specifically upon techniques employing digital computers as aids in drawing inferences from textual data.

In this article we describe a variety of methods which have been employed in computer-based analysis of the content of English texts. We begin by considering some basic terminological definitions, then proceed to discuss content analysis studies in detail. Examples are employed throughout to illustrate the various methods, and important references are cited as appropriate. A more comprehensive listing of references may be found in the *Annual Review of Information Science and Technology*, Volumes 1–10 [2].

Basic Definitions

Content analysis may be defined as follows:

> Content analysis is a procedure for identifying those attributes of a message which have the greatest likelihood of leading to an accurate inference of the intention of the message source.

The disadvantage of this definition is that it employs a number of terms which are themselves undefined and whose definitions must thus also be given. In the first place, a message is that commodity transmitted in the communication process. Messages, as the following paragraph suggests, are essentially quantities of energy moved from a source to a receiver.

Communication may be defined as a system for sending and receiving observable signals (messages). The qualification "observable" is used to emphasize the fact that different organisms (or machines) can observe different kinds and degrees of signal. Most animals, for instance, can observe visual, olfactory, auditory, tactile, and gustatory signals, although in varying degrees depending upon the specific animal. Machines, on the other hand, are more likely to observe electrical or magnetic signals.

For communication to take place there must exist at least two entities (animals, machines, etc.) which are physically situated so as to be able to produce outputs (messages) observable by one another and to actually produce such outputs. Communication can be viewed in terms of the model depicted in Fig. 1 which is based upon the Shannon model of communication [3] modified to accommodate reciprocal signaling between the entities. In other words, communication is a system, for without reciprocity no communication can be said to have occurred.

An ensemble of messages forms a language. Thus language is defined within the context of communication, and amounts to the set of signals observable by source and receiver. Language must therefore be a shared ensemble of messages, but no other restrictions need be placed upon it.

Many different languages are known. Languages may be differentiated through examination of the characteristics of the individual elements or messages of which they are composed. These characteristics may relate to the manner of production of the message or to the manner in which it is received.

Content Analysis

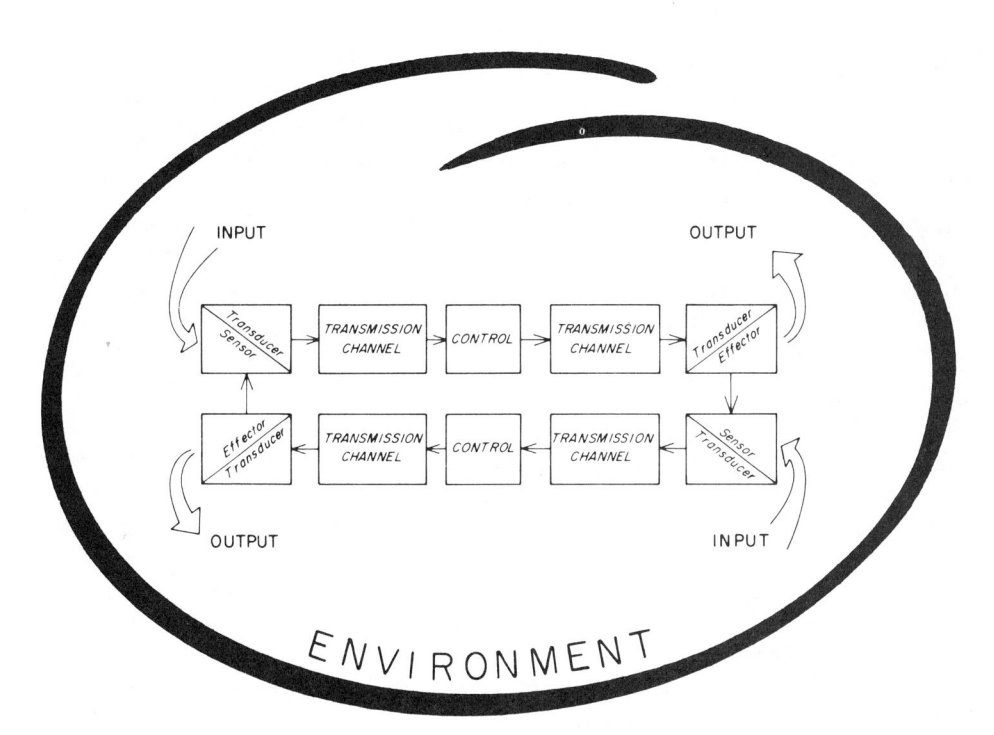

Fig. 1. A model of communication which emphasizes reciprocal signaling between source and receiver.

For instance, the gestures and movements that a person makes with his body are referred to as "body language" [4]. This language is used to communicate feelings of nervousness, attitudes of respect or fear, positions of weakness or power [5], and so on.

These examples of language are fairly obvious and the distinction between them is fairly easily made. However, language inferences are generally much more subtle and may be thought of as culturally oriented. A culture is a communication system, and since communication involves language, it is necessary for the components of a communication system to employ a common language if there is to be a reasonable expectation of effective communication.

We see, therefore, that language differentiation is a relatively complex and perhaps hazardous process because languages can be differentiated not only on the basis of elemental or structural characteristics, but on the basis of geography, on the basis of profession, on the basis of ethnic origin, or on religious grounds as well. As a consequence, it is necessary to be careful in content analysis to define the language with which one is dealing.

What we are concerned with in content analysis, therefore, is the study of language or, more properly, tracts of language utterences which we have called messages or which may be called texts, journals, articles, and so on, with the purpose of inferring the intention of the source of the message. In particular we are interested in developing computer aids to manual content analysis or in developing fully automated content analysis systems.

AREAS OF APPLICATION OF CONTENT ANALYSIS

In its broadest sense, content analysis has almost universal applicability. We shall restrict ourselves to its current manifestations in language processing. Other aspects of content analysis (even though not so categorized) are treated elsewhere in this *Encyclopedia*. We shall first mention several areas of application of content analysis as a means of introducing the reader to the ways in which content analysis can be used. Discussion of these applications will conveniently lead into specific techniques of content analysis.

Social Sciences

Automated content analysis has proved a useful, although not yet widely used, tool in the social sciences. A variety of techniques has been employed to provide the scientist with data from which inferences about the intention of the message source may be made. Suppose, for example, a political scientist is studying a reporter's articles dealing with a presidential candidate. Can the scientist make supportable statements about the reporter's bias with respect to the candidate? The scientist might attempt to answer this question by employing a group of people to read the article and to state their opinions about the attitude of the reporter. But such opinions or inferences are, like those of the scientist himself, intuitive and subjective in nature. Most people will find it difficult to state precisely why they feel that the attitude of the reporter is biased in one direction or another. What is called for, therefore, is a more objective method of handling content.

Content analysis can be performed objectively by categorizing words or groups of words used to describe the candidate. For example, was the candidate described as stodgy or as down-to-earth? Were his ideas described as creative or radical? In each pair of descriptors (words), one descriptor is inferred to have a positive connotation while the other is considered to have a negative connotation. If words can be so classified, then the totality of these words used in reporting the candidate's actions can serve as a measure of the bias of the report. If a preponderance of words in the report are of the negative sort, the report can be said to be unfavorable to the candidate.

Such an approach as this has, in fact, been employed [6] to infer the bias of news reports dealing with the presidential campaign of 1968 as broadcast by the three major television broadcasting companies in the United States.

This approach is not flawless. There may be disagreements about a particular positive or negative connotation. Or the connotation of a word may depend upon a particular usage or a particular context. For instance, in the following short paragraph from a *National Geographic* article dealing with the Russian-U.S. joint space venture, it seems to us that there is at least a noticeable difference in the manner of reference to the rockets of the respective countries.

> Shrugging free of its shackles, a Vostok rocket lifts Soyuz skyward at the U.S.S.R.'s vast Baykonur Cosmodrome in remote Kazakhstan. In a thunderous echo $7\frac{1}{2}$ hours later, a Saturn rocket hurled Apollo aloft from

Kennedy Space Center, Florida, beginning the 44 hours of complex maneuvers that would culminate in the linking [7].

Nevertheless, if categories are clearly formulated, such an approach to content analysis can be useful, and a small amount of error is usually tolerable. The advantage of this rather simplistic approach to content analysis is that inferences may be based upon a set of objective criteria rather than upon intuition. If there is disagreement about the conclusions drawn from the analysis, one may state more precisely why he disagrees [8].

Political Science

Studies similar to those described above have been performed by political scientists in attempting to assess the attitude of a given country toward the United States. By examining political correspondence, statements in state-controlled news media, and so on, it may be possible to determine whether a country's attitude is aggressive or passive, hostile or friendly toward the United States. Such analyses are typically performed by classifying words in a manner similar to that described in the preceding paragraph, and then observing the occurrence of these words in the correspondence or diplomatic communiques under examination [9, 10].

Psychology

Psychologists frequently use automated content analysis procedures to aid in the determination of the attitudes of their subjects. For example, the dialog between the psychologist and his subject will be tape recorded to be subsequently transcribed for analysis. The transcription of the subject's speech usually includes not only the basic texts but also the length of the pauses between statements and such other utterances as "um," "er," and "ah." Words, pauses, and syntactic structures are then interpreted as indicators of fear, anxiety, aggressiveness, or peace [11, 12].

A well-known attitudinal measure used by psychologists is Osgood's Semantic Differential [13, 14]. This measure requires that subjects rate specific qualities of some entity according to some scale terminated by strong opposites. Osgood's Semantic Differential is a reasonably reliable measure of strongly polarized attitudes. That is, distinction between positive and negative, strong and weak, active and passive, and other conceptually diametric pairs are rather easily distinguished using the Semantic Differential. See, for example, the work of Patton [15].

Anthropology

It is fairly well accepted that folklore and myth can convey a good deal of information about the deep-seated moral characteristics and social values of a particular culture of which the folklore or myth are a part [16]. Thus one aim of content analysis in anthropological studies is to establish the attitudinal relationship between a culture's folklore and its currently observable characteristics. For instance, it is of interest to determine what the members of a culture believe concerning honor, morality, and religion, or what values they place upon various artifacts or natural phenomena [17, 18].

Linguistics

Linguists employ content analysis procedures for a variety of purposes, including authorship attribution studies, interpretation of allegory, language translations, abstracting, and indexing. In fact, one might say that content analysis is concerned with the identification, isolation, and interpretation of metaphore. A well-known application of content analysis is in the work of Mosteller and Wallace, whose main purpose was to test Bayes' theorem in a textual discrimination problem, namely determination of the authorship of certain of the *Federalist Papers* [19]. A comparative analysis of certain of the *Papers* with confirmed authorship showed that Madison and Hamilton employed certain prepositions (to, from, by) with significantly different frequencies, and this fact enabled Mosteller and Wallace to establish authorship of other of the *Federalist Papers* with a high degree of confidence.

Stylistics is another area of study which has received considerable attention [20, 21]. Comparison of the styles of different authors, determination of basic characteristics of style, and the perception of theme are among the important aspects of stylistic analysis.

Information Storage and Retrieval

Although not usually mentioned in conjunction with discussions of content analysis, information storage and retrieval is basically concerned with ascertaining the content of documents (e.g., books, articles, case law). The creation of abstracts and indexes and the searching of machine-readable files of text data are content analytical processes. In preparing an abstract, it is necessary to identify and isolate the principal message of the author to form the basis of the abstract. Indexing similarly demands the selection of words and phrases that are significant of content. Extensive discussions of both abstracting and indexing may be found in Refs. 22 and 23; brief discussions of document retrieval, classification, question-answering, and inference systems are included in this article.

Music

Formal content analytical procedures have found their uses in music, principally in thematic analysis studies. Such studies have been used both in attempts to identify the recurrence of a theme in two or more of a composer's works, or to identify a theme common to the works of two or more composers. Such studies have also been carried out in an attempt to attribute a work of unknown authorship to some particular composer [24, 25].

Robotics

Once a science-fiction concept, robotics is now a more prosaic area for scientific research. In addition to problems of locomotion and control [26], robotics is concerned with the way in which commands are interpreted by a robot to carry out the task(s) expressed in the command [27, 28]. For example, the request

> Bring me a glass of water.

requires that the robot to which it is addressed correctly interpret "bring," "me," "a glass of water" in addition to knowing where to get a glass and some water, and where "me" is located. This example merely suggests the complexity of the problem and is but an illustration of the general notion of automated language processing.

Additional areas of application of content analysis may be imagined, many of which deal with languages other than the typical printed or spoken languages. Pattern recognition [29, 30] is a good example of such application areas. These are treated elsewhere in this Encyclopedia, usually under the name of the application.

TECHNIQUES OF CONTENT ANALYSIS

In preceding paragraphs we have mentioned a variety of applications of content analysis as a way of indicating its scope and as a means of suggesting the range of data to which content analysis may be applied. We turn now to the techniques of content analysis.

Content analysis procedures have frequently used manually derived categories of words which are thought to be distinctive of some particular idea or attitude. The value of the result of such content analysis studies depends upon the appropriateness of these categories to the particular application. If categories are not well-chosen and well-formulated, the value of the analysis may be low. Several more-refined techniques have been developed which may be employed in content analysis and which may yield results with greater validity. We discuss several of these techniques in the remainder of this article. For convenience of presentation, these techniques are categorized as pertaining to elemental analysis (e.g., identification of words, word groups, word frequencies) or to structural analysis (i.e., identification of elements and of the relations between them). The use of these terms will become clearer as the techniques are further defined. Applications illustrative of these analysis techniques conclude each section.

Techniques of Elemental Analysis

Techniques employed in a determination of the content of a tract of text by analysis of the elementary components of that text we call *elemental analysis techniques*. Such techniques include word frequencies and relative frequencies, use of thesauri, concordances, stemming, stoplists, and part-of-speech determinations.

Stoplists

The most frequently occurring words in most any text are those generally classified as function words. This class of words includes the prepositions, conjunctions, articles, and similar words that serve a syntactic function in the text but which do not serve directly to express content. We may also include other frequently occurring words which are deemed meaningless. It is possible to eliminate these words from consideration in a text through the use of a table of these words. This table, often called a "stoplist," need not be larger than perhaps a few hundred words (see Fig. 2 for example). Each word in the text is then compared with this stoplist and if it matches an entry in the stoplist, it may be ignored in subsequent processing (e.g., frequency counts). This simple technique makes it possible to eliminate function words from consideration and to concentrate attention on words with a higher probability of content expression.

One must, however, be careful not to exceed the bounds of reason in stoplist development. It is difficult to identify words which are meaningless in every context. The word "of" used as a preposition may well be a poor indicator of content, but when used as a noun, it becomes quite important.

Stemming

The correct identification of word frequencies may be confounded by the appearance of morphologically distinct but conceptually related words. For instance, the word "compute" may take many derivational forms such as computer, computing, computed, computes, computation, computerized, and computer-aided. Since all of these words are conceptually related, it would be desirable that they all be accounted for in the frequency of occurrence of the basic root concept. To do so requires the application of what is frequently

A	HOUSE
AMERICAN	INDIA
AN	INTERNATIONAL
BUREAU	NATIONAL
CALIFORNIA	NEW YORK
COMMITTEE	OF
CONFERENCE	ON
CONGRESS	SENATE
COUNCIL	SYMPOSIUM
DEPARTMENT	THE
DEPT.	U.N.
GT. BRIT.	U.S.

Fig. 2. A brief stoplist (from Ref. 31).

Content Analysis

referred to as a stemming procedure. In general, a stemming procedure is designed to reduce words to a common root, which may then be used in the word-frequency counts. Stemming algorithms have been developed which recognize and eliminate common inflectional suffixes and prefixes [32, 33]. A typical stemming algorithm embodies an iterative procedure for identification and elimination of inflectional affixes (see, for example, Fig. 3). These affixes may be subdivided according to whether they appear preceding the root word or following the root word.

A somewhat more arbitrary approach to the grouping of etymologically related words involves straightforward word truncation [34]. While this technique has been most often used in query formulation in retrieval systems, it can be used with equal success in refining word-frequency counts or in grouping etymologically similar words.

Vocabulary Control

> Yonder stands Barazinbar, the Redhorn, cruel Caradhras; and beyond him are Silvertine and Cloudyhead: Celebdil the White, and Fanuidhol the Grey, that we call Zirakzigil and Bundushathur [35].

In order to avoid boring repetiveness in a text, the author will often resort to the use of synonyms or analogs. While this technique may be beneficial to human readers, it is quite devastating to automated content analysis, particularly that involving the recognition of words representing a particular concept. In the case of frequency of occurrence techniques, for example, its use means that either the frequency counts will be unrelated to the frequency of occurrence of

worth	cis	al
ally	fer	an
ance	fic	at
ceae	ful	ch
diol	gen	ct
less	ide	ed
lide	ile	en
lite	ine	er
ment	ing	ic
metr	ion	id
ness	ism	ly
xide	ite	a
age	ity	c
ale	mic	i
ant	nol	o
ase	sis	x
bil	str	y
ble	vit	z

Fig. 3. Sample suffix list for use in stemming.

the concept or else interpretation based upon the frequencies obtained will be potentially at variance with the fact. In order to overcome such difficulties, it is necessary to utilize a dictionary of synonyms as part of the content analysis procedure. In order to cope with analogs as well, the dictionary is frequently expanded to a thesaurus so that various other relationships between words in addition to synonymy can be established. But even with the use of a thesaurus, some synonyms must be established dynamically. For instance, in a chemical article it is frequently the case that the author, who wishes to avoid repetition of a long chemical name, will employ shorter words or symbols to represent the compound in question. This might be thought of as dynamically established synonymy. In any event, the basic thesaurus must be augmented by such equivalences established within the text being analyzed. This is by no means a simple matter. It has formed the basis for a great deal of linguistic research and no generally useful solution of the problem has so far been found.

The authority list developed at the Chemical Abstracts Service for use in production of the index to *Polymer Science and Technology* (POST) is a good example of vocabulary control employing elemental analysis techniques [36]. A variety of relationships is employed (see Table 1); these relationships control the entries appearing in the POST index relative to the words or phrases which were present in the abstract or article being indexed. A few examples illustrating the results of application of the POST authority list are given in Table 2.

An extension of thesaurus techniques to provide an interface between a user and the vocabularies of two or more data bases has recently been described [37]. The interface amounts to a function which maps the user's terminology into that of the data base and is intended to obviate the user having to learn several different vocabularies.

TABLE 1
Definition of Relations Used in the Authority List for POST

Relation symbol	Definition of relation
US	Replace the main term (MT) with the subordinate term (ST)
US*	Cross refer MT to ST
UF	Approve MT
UF*	Cross refer from ST to MT
SN	Scope note—the intension of MT
BT	MT generic to ST (no action)
BT*	Cross refer from ST to MT (upward reference)
NT	MT species of ST (no action)
NT*	Cross refer from ST to MT (downward reference)
RT	MT related to ST (no action)
RT*	Cross refer from ST to MT (see also reference)
MU	Multiple entry. Generate added index entries
TC	Make index entry at MT and ST and connect with "see also" reference.
NC	Make index entry at MT and ST and connect with "see also" reference.
XX	Cross refer from ST to ST related to MT by US*

Content Analysis

TABLE 2
Examples Illustrating the Effect of the Relations Defined in Table 1

MT from text	Rel	ST	Result
occurrence	US	occurrence	
theory of indexing	US*	indexing theory	theory of indexing *see* indexing theory
eigenvalue	UF*	proper value	proper value *see* eigenvalue
copolymers	SN	excludes blends	copolymers (excludes blends)
nylons	BT*	polyamides	polyamides *see* nylons
Orlons	RT*	acrylans	acrylans *see also* Orlons

Concordances and Collations

Concordances are essentially word indexes which list and give the specific location of each occurrence of a word within the source document. Concordances may also display the immediate context in which a word appears. Concordances enable scholars to make inferences about the use of words by a specific author or to compare word usage by two authors as an aid in detecting similarities of style [38]. For instance, study of a concordance of the words of St. Thomas Aquinas indicated that he used the word "virtus" to mean "strength" or "driving force" rather than "self-control" [39]. The use of concordances to fill in missing words in a document has also been explored [40].

Collation of a text and its variant (e.g., a manuscript and the published edition) involves the identification of changes or variations between them. Moore [41] is attempting to formalize this aid to scholarly research and to develop efficient algorithms for producing collations.

Word Frequency Techniques

The frequency of occurrence of words in a text has often been used as a measure of the content of the text [42]. The hypothesis underlying this measure is that the more frequently a word occurs in a text the more likely is the text to be about the concept which the word represents. For example, if the word "computer" occurs frequently in a text, this may indicate that the article is about "computers." The measure is too simplistic to be employed in serious content analytical studies. Nevertheless, as we shall see, various refinements of the basic hypothesis stated above have led to useful word frequency techniques.

Because accurate frequency counts depend upon correct identification of synonyms or morphologically similar words, some of the techniques described above (stemming, vocabulary control) may be usefully employed as precursors to frequency analysis.

An excellent example of word frequency analysis is afforded by the work of Kucera and Francis on present-day American English [43].

Relative Frequency Techniques

In addition to the use of stoplists, stemming, and so on, the basic frequency criteria can themselves be refined. Instead of dealing with the simple frequency of occurrence of words in a text, one may consider the frequency of occurrence of a word in a text in contrast with its frequency of occurrence in a large body of text. To effect this comparison, a core of text which is considered to be representative in some sense must first be defined and each word's frequency of occurrence in that core must be determined. (The frequency of occurrence of a word in this core of text may be thought of as its frequency of occurrence in general usage.) Now the frequency of occurrence of a word in a specific text may be compared with the word's frequency of occurrence in general usage. For example, suppose a word occurs with a frequency of 20 in 1000 words of a given text, whereas its frequency of occurrence in the general corpus is 10 in 10000 words of text. Such a word would usually be considered a significant indicator of content in the specific text because its frequency of occurrence is 20 times that found in general text.

Several alternative theories of word significance have been propounded [44]. One theory states that the greater is the occurrence frequency of a word in a document the more indicative is the word of the document's content. Occurrence frequency is defined as

$$\frac{F_{w_i}}{\sum_{\forall i} F_{w_i}}$$

where F_{w_i} is the frequency of occurrence of the ith word, w_i, in the document ($1 \leq i$).

Relative frequency has also been determined using difference, ratio, and conditional probability measures. The frequency difference measure states that a word in a document (D) is significant of content if

$$\left(\frac{F_{w_i}}{\sum_{\forall i} F_{w_i}}\right)_D - \left(\frac{F_{w_i}}{\sum_{\forall i} F_{w_i}}\right)_C > 0$$

[where the subtrahend is the occurrence frequency of word i in a general corpus (C) of text]. The frequency ratio measure

$$\frac{\left(\dfrac{F_{w_i}}{\sum_{\forall i} F_{w_i}}\right)_D}{\left(\dfrac{F_{w_i}}{\sum_{\forall i} F_{w_i}}\right)_C} > \alpha$$

accords significance to a word when the ratio of its occurrence frequency in a document to that in a general corpus exceeds some prescribed threshold, α.

The conditional probability frequency is the probability that a given word type will not appear more frequently in a random sample than in a particular document. This can be calculated by using the hypergeometric distribution, the Poisson standard deviate, or the standard deviate [45].

The use of relative frequency of occurrence as a measure of content is usually more successful than the simple frequency-of-occurrence measure. The major difficulty in employing the relative frequency technique is that of establishing a word's frequency in a sample corpus. One other problem associated with the relative frequency technique is that occasioned by the constant change which language undergoes. This means that the frequency of occurrence of a word in general usage would need to be recalculated from time to time in order to keep pace with language changes.

Although the elemental analysis techniques discussed thus far are of considerable interest and have been used extensively, they are of very limited value in content analysis when contrasted with human analytical abilities. Hence a great deal of effort has been expended in the search for more suitable analytical methods. We shall conclude this discussion of elemental analysis by examining a number of techniques of considerably greater complexity and erudition. These techniques are all based upon a view of a text as a collection of words or word-aggregates, such as phrases, sentences, or clauses.[1]

At the word level, the role or function of each word is of interest. In traditional terms we may consider the analysis of text into word-classes to be equivalent to part-of-speech analysis. However, automated analyses usually gives significantly different results because the application of the results usually demands it.

Defining Grammatical Classes

The words which comprise the vocabulary of a language are traditionally classified into eight parts of speech or grammatical classes. Dionysios Thrax is credited with first proposing eight parts of speech: noun, verb, participle, article, pronoun, preposition, adverb, and conjunction [46]. The interjection is often added to this list. For English, Priestly classified words into the above eight parts of speech in 1761 [47]. Some parts of speech are given definitions based upon their *lexical meaning*. For instance, a noun is defined as the name of a person, place, or thing. On the other hand, an adjective is defined as a word which modifies a noun. Such a definition is based upon *function*.

Gleason [48] has suggested an alternative method of defining grammatical classes. Three criteria are used as a definitional basis. the first criterion consists of a model for each of the four classes: noun, verb, adjective, and pronoun. Each model consists of possible inflectional endings which signal membership in the appropriate class. the second criterion lists words whose membership in one of the four classes is signaled by a change in word form rather than by the addition of inflectional endings (e.g., mouse and mice). The third criterion is the

---

[1] These word-aggregates might be thought of as analogous to functional groups or molecular fragments in chemical terms.

syntax of the sentence in which a word occurs. This criterion, Gleason feels, is a less sure basis for word class identification than the first two.

Fries, in contrast with Gleason, has defined the parts of speech in terms of a basic structural frame or pattern [49]. Each position within a structural frame is occupied by a particular word class. Any word which can fit into a given position in the frame belongs to the corresponding word class. For illustration, consider the sample frame sentences:

1. The concert was good (always).
2. The clerk remembered the tax (suddenly).
3. The team went there.

A word which can replace either "concert," "clerk," "tax," or "team" belongs to *Class 1*. Words which can replace "was," "remembered," or "went" are members of *Class 2*. Any word which can replace "good" is placed in *Class 3*, and words which can replace "always," "suddenly," or "there" are placed in *Class 4*.

In addition to the four classes defined above, Fries defined a fifth class of words (*Class 5*) whose elements serve as structural markers within a sentence. These are frequently referred to as *function words*. The members of this class are most readily defined ostensively since there appear to be so few of them (Fries identified just 154). Some of the groups within this class are the auxiliary verbs, conjunctions, prepositions, relative pronouns, and determiners.

There are significant differences between the first four classes and *Class 5*. For the first four classes, lexical meanings are easily separable from structural meanings. For function words (*Class 5*) no clear distinction can be made, perhaps because such words may have no lexical meanings. Furthermore, whereas the first four classes are open ended, *Class 5* appears to be a closed class.

Fries found that function words accounted for almost a third of the total number of word occurrences in text. And in a more recent analysis of more than 1,000,000 words of text, Kucera and Francis have found that these words account for nearly 46% of the total number of words in the text studied [43].

Finally, it is easy to show that in order to understand certain structural signals within English text, *Class 5* words must be known as items. For instance, the two sentences

> The boys and the leaders were invited.
> The boys of the leaders were invited.

are indistinguishable on the basis of class assignment. In fact, the only way in which a structural distinction may be made between the two sentences is to know the words *and* and *of* as items.

The importance of the role which function words play in grammatical class assignment will be seen in the brief discussions to follow of several automated procedures for assignment of words of a text to their respective grammatical classes. In addition, the use of function words to resolve ambiguity in syntactic analysis has been described by Klein and Simmons [50], and Beckmann has shown that function words in English serve the purpose of an error-detecting code [51].

Procedures for Grammatical Class Assignment

Several procedures for assigning words of a text to their respective grammatical classes are described in the following paragraphs as a means of illustrating the variety of approaches which has been taken to solution of this problem.

The Economic Parser. A program called the Economic Parser, which assigns words to grammatical classes, identifies phrase types, and marks clause boundaries, was developed by Clark and Wall [52]. The program first performs a dictionary look-up. The dictionary consists of about 1000 entries. The entries include function words, inflectional endings, and a list of words which are exceptions to regular inflection (i.e., "thing" is not a verb even though it ends in "ing"). Words which are not found in the dictionary are assigned an ambiguous noun/verb category. In a second pass, phrase boundaries are tentatively identified. In the third pass clause boundaries are identified and clauses are tested for well-formedness. If a clause does not contain a verb, noun phrases are examined in a left-to-right manner and the first word which has been assigned to the noun/verb class is identified as a verb. The algorithm was applied to abstracts of technical material and is reported to attain 91% accuracy in the identification of grammatical classes.

The Computational Grammar Coder. Klein and Simmons have implemented a Computational Grammar Coder (CGC) which assigns words in English text to the appropriate grammatical class [50]. The CGC is the initial phase of a syntactic analyzer which is part of a question-answering system. The CGC contains two types of dictionaries: (1) a function-word dictionary containing about 400 words, and (2) two dictionaries containing those nouns, verbs, and adjectives which are exceptions in various suffix texts. These dictionaries contained about 1500 words.

The algorithm of the CGC begins by putting each word through a series of independent tests. These tests include a function word test, a capitalization test, a numeral test, and a series of suffix tests. Each test may result in the assignment of a set of codes to the word. If a particular test yields no information about a word, the system assumes that the classes noun, adjective, and verb are possible. A final set of codes is obtained by taking the intersection of the set of codes assigned in each test.

After each word in a sentence has been identified in this manner, the context-frame test is made. This test sequentially processes strings of ambiguously coded words which are bounded by uniquely coded words. Every possible combination of codes of an ambiguously coded string is checked against a context-triad-frame table which contains permissible combinations of codes in such strings.

In tests using scientific text, the CGC correctly assigned approximately 90% of the words.

The WISSYN System. The WISSYN system, designed to make grammatical class assignments to words in English text, was developed by Stolz, Tannenbaum, and Carstensen [53]. WISSYN contains dictionaries which are similar to those used in the CGC. The function-word dictionary contains about 300 words. If a word in a sentence is not found in the dictionary of function words, it is checked against a dictionary of suffixes and exceptions.

A third phase attempts to resolve the ambiguity of certain function words. For example the word "that" may be used in the following ways:

>that dog jumped
>the dog that jumped

In this phase, a set of frames similar to those implemented by Klein and Simmons is used to resolve residual ambiguity.

A final phase of WISSYN uses the statistical frequencies of structural patterns of English sentences to assign grammatical classes. The operation of this phase can be easily understood by considering an illustration. Given a sentence whose elements have been identified as:

$$T \ D \ N \ X_1 \ P \ D \ N \ P \ X_2 \ X_3 \ T$$

where T is a terminal marker, D is a determiner, N is a noun, P is a pronoun, and X_i is the *i*th unidentified word ($i \geq 1$). When an unidentified word is encountered, the probabilities of the three longest strings consisting of four or fewer words surrounding the unidentified word are considered. Thus the probability of X_1 being a noun, verb, adjective, or adverb would be calculated using the statistics of Table 3. The element X_1 would be designated as a verb, since this was the most probable case.

In a test of literary, scientific, and newspaper articles, an accuracy as high as 93% was attained.

MYRA. A grammatical class assignment procedure first reported by Marvin, Rush, and Young [54] and subsequently refined by Young [55, 56], called MYRA, is built on the premise that function words together with a set of rules (exemplified below) constitute necessary and sufficient conditions for the unambiguous determination of the grammatical classes of all words present in an English sentence. The principal classes to be determined are NAME and PRIMARY RELATION; SECONDARY RELATIONS are "known" *a priori* through use of a

TABLE 3
Conditional Probabilities

Predictor	Noun	Verb	Adjective	Adverb
D N X_1 P D	.046	.819	.013	.122
X_1 P D N P	.438	.359	.068	.135
N X_1 P D N	.017	.591	.078	.314
Joint product	.00034	.17377	.00007	.00517

Content Analysis

dictionary.[2] The rules constitute a set of context sensitive productions written by means of a simple notation. A simple example will serve to illustrate the rules. The rule:

$$\ldots \text{THR XXX} \ldots \Rightarrow \ldots \text{THR VRB} \ldots$$

means that if the function word subclass THR is immediately followed by an unclassified word (XXX) in a sentence, then the unclassified word is assigned to the class VRB.

MYRA accepts English text as input in a continuous string without any prior formatting or marking. (This fact has two implications. First, MYRA does not "know" that the input is English text, but the text will be processed as though it were. Second, MYRA must break the string up into individual words.)

MYRA operates on the input text in three stages.

In the first stage, the individual words, exclusive of punctuation, are looked up in the dictionary. If a match occurs, the code for the dictionary element is entered into a vector which corresponds with the sequence of words between elements of EOS. For instance, the input string

> The mouse ate the cheese.

would have already been partitioned as

> The/mouse/ate/the/cheese/.

The vector resulting at the end of stage one will be

> DTR XXX XXX DTR XXX EOS

In the second stage, MYRA applies the first 101 rules. Application is signalled by the presence in the vector of an element of FUNCTION WORD or of some other element(s) already classified, so that only rules which can reasonably be expected to produce classifications are applied. In the example, a rule for DTR can first be applied. Its application yields

> DTR ADJ NON DTR XXX EOS

Moving to the right in the vector, we see that a second rule for DTR is called for. Its application yields

> DTR ADJ NON DTR NON EOS

At the end of stage two, the vector may or may not be complete. It is completed and verified in stage three.

In stage three MYRA first classifies any previously unclassified WORDS. Finally, the vector is checked to see if a PRIMARY RELATION is present. If no PRIMARY RELATION is present, then elements of the vector are reclassified so that a PRIMARY RELATION is included. The analysis is thus completed and the results are output. In the example, at the end of stage two the vector contained no PRIMARY RELATION. Application of a final rule yields:

> DTR NON VRB DTR NON EOS

---

[2] Two alternative dictionaries were employed, one containing 217 entries and the other 431 entries.

MYRA was tested on some 6000 words of text and was reported to achieve an accuracy of 91% using the limited dictionary and 94% using the extended dictionary [56].

Knowledge of the classes to which words belong is essential to any subsequent syntactic analysis of text. In addition to the procedures described above, grammatical class assignments have also been made manually and embodied in dictionaries for use in automated syntactic analysis procedures.

Procedures for Syntactic Analysis

In the preceding section we described techniques for grammatical class assignment. These techniques may be used in isolation for content analysis, but they are principally used as the basis for syntactic analysis.

Syntactic analysis, which involves the identification and characterization of aggregates of words, is intermediate between elemental analysis and structural analysis.[3] Syntactic analysis procedures of many kinds have been developed, based upon a variety of theories. Several of the more important syntactic analysis procedures are described in the following paragraphs. We include syntactic analysis among elemental analysis techniques because the results they yield do not expose the conceptual structure of text but extend the basis for content determinations provided by word-analysis procedures.

The Multiple-Path Syntactic Analyzer. A well-known program for syntactic analysis is the Multiple-Path Syntactic Analyzer developed by Oettinger and Kuno [57]. This system is based on a context-free grammar of 3400 rules and a top-to-bottom (top-down) analytical procedure employing a pushdown store. The dictionary used by this procedure gives a highly refined division of syntactic classes. For example, "are" belongs to three syntactic classes: one when used as an intransitive verb, one when used as a finite copula, and one when used as an auxiliary to another verb. Each possible analysis of the sentence is explored in a left-to-right manner and verified or invalidated by the context-free grammar. The production of multiple analyses is useful for research purposes, but it is a decided disadvantage in practical application. Processing time is not directly dependent upon the length of a sentence but depends primarily on the number of possible surface structures which the sentence can generate.

Syntactic Analysis for Transformational Grammar. Zwicky [58] has included syntactic analysis in an attempt to implement a transformational grammar for sentences. The first phase of the program is a phrase-structure grammar which handles a subset (32 of a possible 134 rules have been implemented) of English. The initial step in Zwicky's procedure consists of a dictionary look-up of each word in a sentence. The dictionary contains all possible syntactic classes for a word, along with attributes such as tense, transitivity, and number. This lexical entry also represents an entry in terms of more abstract elements, for example, "none" is defined as "neg any." After all possible syntactic classes for a word

---

[3] It may be thought of as being analogous to functional-group analysis in chemistry.

Content Analysis

in a sentence have been retrieved, all possible analyses of a sentence are examined. The sentence

Can the airplane fly?

has 15 possible surface structures. In the next step a context-free grammar is applied to each of these analyses, and some structures are eliminated. Transformational rules are applied next in an effort to eliminate the spurious surface structures. No discussion of the lexicon or of the rules used in either the context-free grammar or the transformational grammar is given. Although the process has been only partially implemented, Zwicky concludes that highly efficient routines are needed to obtain the correct surface structures.

Syntactic Analysis Based on a Regular Grammar. Thorne, Bratley, and Dewar have written a syntactic analyzer as part of a system which assigns the deep structure and surface structure to English sentences [59]. In this syntactic analyzer, five types of sentences, six types of clauses, and several other syntactic categories including gerund subjects, active verbs, modifiers, and indirect objects are identified.

The analyzer employs a dictionary of fewer than 200 words. It contains function words (referred to as closed-class words), verbs, suffixes, and exceptions to these suffixes. The analyzer is based upon a form of transformational grammar [60]. The operation of the system is as follows. First, all of the function words in a sentence are identified. Based on these function words and on the information provided by the grammar as it relates to the sentence, a set of predictions is made. These predictions are tested, and based upon the results of these tests, new predictions are made for successive parts of the sentence. All of the possible predictions are tested, and every prediction which holds produces a distinct analysis for the sentence. See Fig. 4 for example.

In some sentences none of the predictions which are made are satisfied. This happens when the sentence is improperly constructed or because the grammar is not complete. In this case a program produces a message indicating that the analyzer has failed for this sentence.

The Economic Parser. The syntactic analyzer developed by Clark and Wall [52] and mentioned earlier in conjunction with grammatical class assignment, demonstrates that a relatively simple analysis may yield substantial syntactic information. Clark and Wall developed a limited phrase-structure parser for use in mechanized indexing. They adopted a "computational" dictionary similar to the one developed by Klein and Simmons. The grammar they employ identifies only phrases and clauses, and no attempt is made to mark relations between phrases. The difference between a "complete" phrase structure and the Clark and Wall model is illustrated in Fig. 5.

The Clark-Wall algorithm is a set of procedures for assigning an allowable syntactic structure to an input string. The first pass incorporates a dictionary look-up and phrase boundary placement. Pass two establishes clause boundaries and tests well-formedness. Clark and Wall report an average accuracy of 91%. Though encouraged with these results, Clark and Wall are careful to emphasize

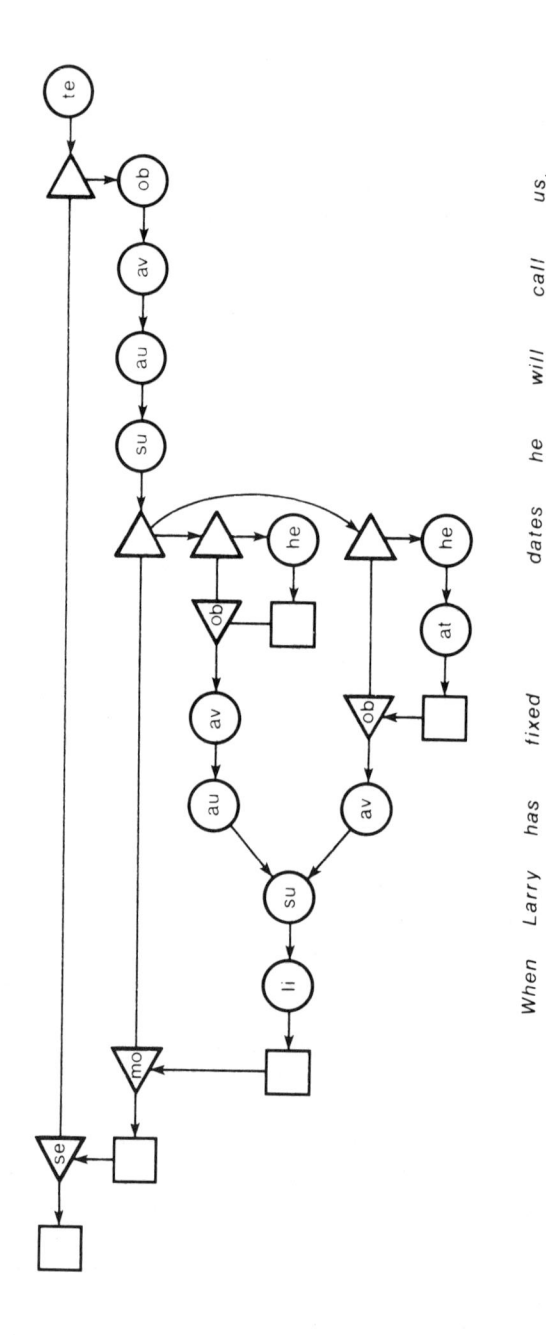

Fig. 4. A two-path analysis structure produced by the Thorne, Bratley, and Dewar procedure.

When Larry has fixed dates he will call us.

Content Analysis 77

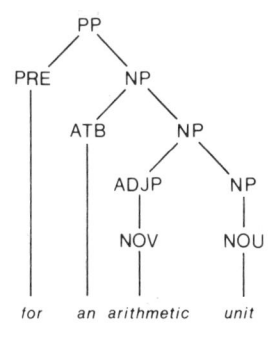

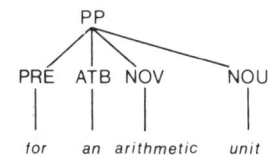

Fig. 5. Tree structure representations of a complete phrase-structure analysis (top), and a Clark-Wall modified phrase-structure analysis (bottom).

that the parser is of a limited nature and is "scored" solely on correct identification of phrases.

A Limited Program for Syntactic Analysis. Resnikoff and Dolby have written a program for grammatical class assignment which consists of fewer than 100 COMIT instructions [61]. This program utilizes a dictionary of 200 function words and 200 affixes. At the time their paper was published, Resnikoff and Dolby intended to expand the dictionary to about 1000 words. In preliminary tests on texts which include parts of *Ulysses* by James Joyce and a *New York Times* editorial, the results were reported as being "evidently high."

PROSE. Another theory of grammar is employed by Vigor, Urquhart, and Wilkinson in the parsing algorithm for their Parsing Recognizer Outputting Sentences in English (PROSE) [62]. Their analysis is based upon a dependency grammar analogous to the one described by Hays [63]. Figure 6 contrasts a phrase structure (such as used by Clark and Wall or Thorne, Bratley, and Dewar) with a dependency analysis.

A phrase structure postulates a hierarchy of phrases and subphrases comprising the nodes of a tree. In a dependency grammar, the words of the text are the internal nodes of the tree. Vigor, Urquhart, and Wilkinson have identified two measures of dependencies which they call binding and determinacy. Binding is a function of physical position. Determinacy is a function of possible contexts. The two values for binding are *bound* or *loose*; the two values for determinacy are *determinate* or *recursive*. The relationship of an article and its noun is bound determinate. The relationship of a conjunction to the words it relates is loose recursive.

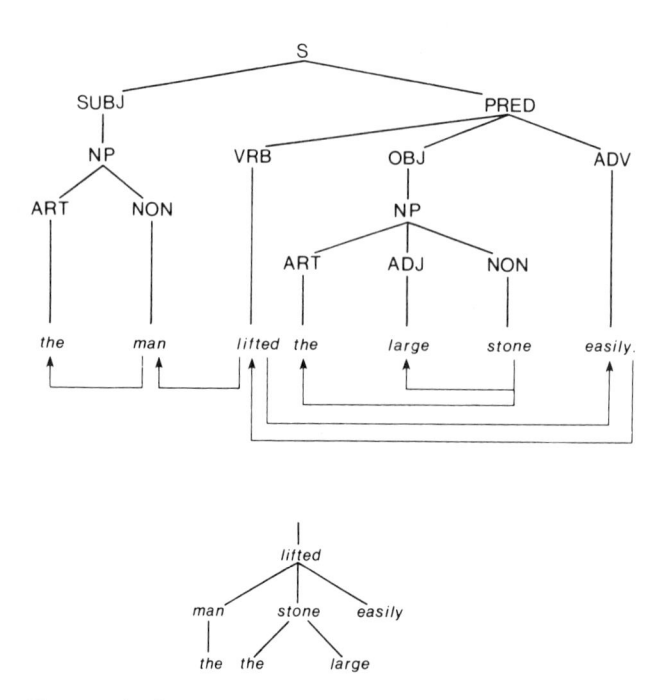

Fig. 6. A phrase-structured tree with word-dependency relationships marked (top), and a dependency-analysis tree of the type employed in the PROSE project (bottom).

Vigor, Urquhart, and Wilkinson describe the parsing process as setting up a dependency tree by "plugging in plugs." For example, "the" has a "plug" which can only be satisfied by a noun "outlet." "Sits" has a required "plug" for a singular noun or pronoun and an optional "plug" for a positional preposition.

Syntactic Analysis Based on String Analysis. In a project headed by Sager a string analysis grammar [64] is the basis of a syntactic analysis program. In this analysis a sentence is viewed as a set of elementary strings (clauses). Modifiers and prepositional phrases are defined as adjuncts. Thus the sentence

> Cars without brakes cause accidents.

is described by the elementary string N tV N (i.e., noun, tensed verb, noun) and an adjunction class P N (preposition, noun). Rules are developed for the analysis of relative clauses and of clauses joined by coordinate conjunctions. In the first step of the program, the possible syntactic classes of each word in the sentence are retrieved from a dictionary. The assignments made during this step are:

> Cars without brakes cause accidents.
>   N   P   N/tV   N/tV/V   N

In the next phase of the program, the syntactic categories are examined in a left-to-right manner while the grammar rules for elementary strings and adjuncts are matched to the possible analyses of the sentence. If a grammar rule fails to match up correctly with the sentence, the program backs up to the initial word of an adjunct or string and attempts to apply a different rule. Sager estimates that an adequate grammar for English could be accomplished with about 150 rules plus another 150 restrictions. These restrictions analyze elements of the elementary string and check for such things as subject-verb agreement and well-formedness.

Syntactic Analysis Based on Transition Network Grammars. Woods has developed a grammar described in terms of an augmented transition network [65]. A recursive transition network is a directed graph with labeled states and arcs. The labels on the arcs may be state names or terminal symbols. An arc labeled with a state name produces the following action: the state at the end of the arc is stored in a pushdown stack and control passes to the state indicated by the arc label. Control is passed back to the saved state by popping the stack. This network is augmented by adding to each arc of the transition network an arbitrary condition which must be satisfied in order for the arc to be followed and a set of structure-building actions to be executed if the arc is followed. The algorithm accepts as input words of a sentence along with the grammatical class of each word of the sentence. The algorithm produces a labeled bracketing of the phrases of the sentence; an identification of the subject, object, and verb; and an assignment of the sentence type (e.g., interrogative or declarative). The transition network model requires about the same processing time as predicative analyzers [66].

Syntactic Analysis in the Simulation of Natural Language Processes. Winograd has recently published a system designed to explore how humans process language [28]. The system includes procedures for both syntactic and semantic analysis. The syntactic analysis procedures are based on a systemic theory of grammar [67, 68]. Although the theories of this grammar have not been stated in a unified way, the emphasis of this grammar is on the "informational units" [69] of a language. Winograd interprets these "informational units" as amounting to clauses and phrases.

In his procedures for syntactic analysis, Winograd has defined 18 word classes, four group types (noun, verb, adjective, and preposition) and two clause types. The 18 word classes are a finer division of the traditional word classes. The two types of clauses are denoted as major and secondary. Associated with each of these units is a set of attributes. Every unit belonging to a word class, group, or clause is assigned a subset of these attributes. For example, a verb (e.g., "began") may have the attributes "past," "infinitive"; a preposition group (e.g., "in the kitchen") may have the attribute "locational object"; and a clause may have attributes such as "transitive," "passive," and "causality."

The components of the syntactic analysis process are a dictionary, a context-free grammar, and a pushdown list (PDL). The dictionary contains the vocabulary of the language along with each entry's syntactic class and attributes. The program which implements the context-free grammar contains several functions which give the grammar context-sensitive aspects. As an example, one function checks for agreement between subject and predicate. A bottom-up parser is used to apply the context-free grammar.

Syntactic Analysis Based on the Notion of Naming in Language. Young [56] has offered an approach to syntactic analysis based upon the notion that language is a system of things and relations between them, and that its vocabulary consists of *names of things* and *names of relations*. A "thing" is defined as any directly or indirectly observable entity, and a relation is defined as any observable change of state (behavior) of a thing with respect to time. For example, "driving a nail with a hammer" involves two sensible objects, "nail" and "hammer," which are related by "driving." Young refers to things simply as NAMES and to relations between things as RELATIONS.

Many researchers have, in one way or another, treated languages as relational systems. Rothstein has proposed the use of binary relations in representing strings of language [70]. In a model of verbal understanding, Simmons [71] has defined primitive elements of his model to be *concepts* and *relations*; these primitives are essentially equivalent to Young's *thing* and *relation*, and as will be seen subsequently, the views of Montgomery [72], Fillmore [73], Chafe [74], and others are also compatible with this relational view of language.

The Naming Process in Language.

> "The name of the song is called '*Haddocks' Eyes*'." "Oh, that's the name of the song, is it?" Alice said, trying to feel interested. "No, you don't understand," the Knight said, looking a little vexed. "That's what the name is *called*. The name really is '*The Aged Aged Man.*' " Then I ought to have said 'That's what the *song* is called'?" Alice corrected herself. "No, you oughtn't: that's quite another thing! The *song* is called '*Ways and Means*': but that's only what it's *called*, you know!" "Well, what *is* the song, then?" said Alice, who was by this time completely bewildered. "I was coming to that," the Knight said. "The song really *is* '*A-sitting On a Gate*': and the tune's my own invention" [75].

In Young's conception, NAMES and RELATIONS denote basic elements of a language, but it will usually be found that simple NAMES (single words) may be combined for naming many things or behaviors so that it is unnecessary to assign a unique name to every thing or behavior. In other words, the basic vocabulary of a language will be found usually to be rather quickly extended to practical limits, and that additional linguistic devices are required to continue to name things and behaviors in a practical way. For instance, there are many horses in the world and it would be cumbersome at best to have to assign a unique word as a NAME to each and every one, even though the language might provide the capability of doing so. Instead, languages provide for the modification of basic NAMES by permitting several NAMES to be related to one another in special ways. For example, the relation between "brown" and "horse" in the NAME "brown horse" is established, in English, by the juxtaposition of the words, while explicit relational words are often used as in "house of wax," where "of" serves this purpose.

By providing appropriately for combining single NAMES to form more complex ones, a language becomes more powerful without the burden of a huge vocabulary.

Content Analysis 81

This view of naming forms the basis for a type of phrase-structure syntactic analysis which emphasizes the centrality of RELATIONS. The decomposition of a sentence as a hierarchy of name-relation-name triples is shown in Fig. 7. An extensive treatment of this analysis procedure is given in [56]. Pepinsky has more recently discussed and amplified the name-relation-name concept [76].

CALAS. A rather comprehensive system of programs to aid in the analysis of text, called CALAS, has been developed [77, 78]. CALAS is an outgrowth of the earlier work of Young and her colleagues [54–56].

CALAS operates in three stages. In the first stage individual words are identified and are assigned to their respective grammatical classes. A feedback mechanism is provided so that assignment errors may be corrected, although an accuracy of about 95% is usually obtained without human editing.

In the second stage, words of a sentence are grouped into phrases. Again, a feedback mechanism provides for correction of analysis errors.

The third stage of CALAS marks clause boundaries and makes case role [73] assignments (case grammar is discussed later).

CALAS provides a great deal of information which humans can use to more objectively draw inferences about the content of text.

Application of Elemental Analysis Techniques

The elemental analysis techniques described in the preceding paragraphs have received application in a variety of processes. Among these are document retrieval, document classification, question answering, indexing, and abstracting. The first three of these areas of application are discussed in the following sections.

Document Retrieval

In document retrieval, elemental analysis techniques are frequently employed to determine the content of the documents of a collection and to construct a query which is to be processed against the document collection in order to identify documents to be retrieved therefrom.

The information storage and retrieval process, of which document retrieval is a part, is illustrated in Fig. 8. Documents are selected for acquisition and are

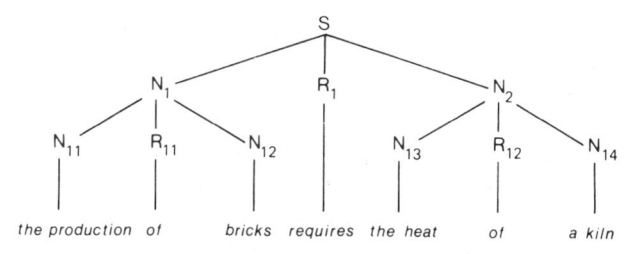

Fig. 7. Name-relation-name decomposition of an English sentence.

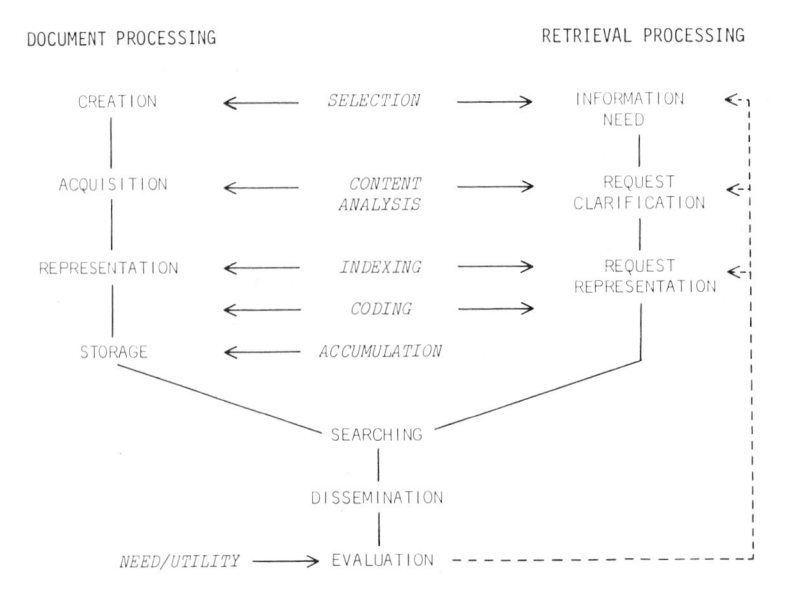

Fig. 8. The information storage and retrieval process.

represented in a form appropriate for the retrieval process. When a user has an information need, he formulates a question, or query, represented in a form acceptable to the system, and the document collection is searched to find the documents which satisfy the query specification [79].

The documents of the collection are rarely stored in their entirety in machine-readable form. A document is usually represented by its title, the authors, and the source (i.e., the journal citation or the publisher and place). This representation is occasionally augmented by the use of manually selected terms which improve the descriptive power of the document representation. Sometimes an abstract of the document is also used to augment the basic document representation. The document representation is usually further processed to produce an index consisting of words or terms derived from the document representation through application of one or more elemental analysis techniques. The semiautomated technique employed by Chemical Abstracts Service for the production of the index to *Polymer Science and Technology* (POST) illustrates such applications (see section entitled Vocabulary Control).

Once such an index has been created it serves as the basis for subsequent retrieval of documents from the collection. A search for desired documents presupposes that a user can identify with some precision the essential elements which characterize the desired documents and which set them apart from the remainder of a document collection. The user must characterize desired documents using terms which are consonant with those employed in the index. The user's document characterization takes the form of a query which is often constructed as a tabular representation as illustrated in Fig. 9. Inspection of Fig. 9 shows that in addition to the terms chosen for document description, the relationship between the terms expressed through the use of Boolean logical

Content Analysis

Query description: (word description)
Term relationship: $(A + B + C) \cdot (D + \bar{E}) \cdot (F + G + H)$
Threshold weight: 10

Entry	Logic	Term	Weight
01	OR	A	1
01	OR	B	1
01	OR	C	2
02	OR	D	3
02	NOT	E	2
03	OR	F	3
03	OR	G	4
03	OR	H	4

Fig. 9. Tabular representation of a query (from Ref. 80).

operators and the relative value of the terms expressed through the use of weights have also been employed. Further details concerning these refinements of the basic term description can be found in [81]. If a document is to be retrieved according to the specifications shown in Fig. 9, its set of index descriptors must include at least one term from within each entry group (i.e., from within each of the parenthesized terms in the Boolean expression shown in the term relationship). Weighting places further constraints on retrieval, requiring not only that the proper set of terms be identified, but also that the total sum of term weights equal or exceed the query threshold weight specification.

Additional refinements on the document retrieval process described above include the use of stemming or truncation, and the use of a thesaurus to control the term vocabulary employed in the query. These techniques may be applied manually or through computer programs.

Classification

Rather than indexing a collection of documents by use of words representative of document content, one may instead process the document collection to produce well-defined subsets or classes which are conceptually closely related. These classes may be formed either through a derivative process or through an assignment process.

In derivative classification, the document collection is analyzed and those documents most similar to each other in terms of text characteristics are declared members of the same class. In assignment classification, *a priori* classes are established whose members must satisfy some prescribed criteria. Documents are subsequently analyzed for these criteria.

A good example of derivative classification is the automatic hierarchy generation procedure described by Abraham [82]. It is necessary first to construct a term-document or term-property matrix. The matrix may be of simple binary form where the presence of a term T_i in a document is represented by a 1 in the kth cell of document vector v^i, otherwise $v_k{}^i = 0$. A weighting function, based perhaps on a frequency measure, may instead be used to give a broader range of values within the matrix.

The terms of the matrix are usually prescribed through a vocabulary-control device or through use of frequency techniques. From the term-document (property) matrix, a term-term similarity (correlation) matrix must be constructed. This matrix, which shows the similarity between terms T_i and T_j, may be formed in a variety of ways. For the purpose of hierarchy construction, an asymmetrical measure of similarity is needed because we are interested in generic/specific relationships. Salton [83] gives the measure

$$C_{ij} = \frac{\sum_k \min(v_k^i, v_k^j)}{\sum_k v_k^i}$$

where C_{ij} is the similarity (correlation) between terms T_i and T_j. If $T_i = T_j$, $C_{ij} = 1$. If T_i and T_j do not bear any similarity to each other, $C_{ij} = 0$. Of course, a threshold criterion K may be applied to C to arbitrarily differentiate between similar and dissimilar terms. A hierarchy may now be formed by means of the following algorithm [82]:

1. If $C_{ij} < K$ and $C_{ji} < K$, then T_i and T_j are dissimilar.
2. If $C_{ij} > K$ and $C_{ji} > K$, then $T_i \cong T_j$.
3. If $C_{ij} < K$ and $C_{ji} > K$, then $T_i \to T_j$ in the hierarchy.
4. If $C_{ij} > K$ and $C_{ji} < K$ then $T_i \leftarrow T_j$ in the hierarchy.

In contrast with manually derived hierarchical classification schemes, the hierarchy produced by this method is entirely arbitrary and may not, in fact, be a simple tree (a term may be related to more than one parent term). However, the method has the advantage of being fully automatic, and one can envision a number of refinements which may make the hierarchy more nearly acceptable.

Classification by assignment is a familiar manual process, but its automation has also been achieved with some degree of success. Fried *et al.* [84] proposed an automated technique of assignment classification based on the concept of sequential analysis [85], which has recently been implemented by White *et al.* [86]. The technique requires that a document be assigned to one of k previously established categories, $C_1, \ldots, C_k$. This, in turn, means that the k categories must be established by some means. White *et al.* employed both semiautomated and fully automated procedures for initial category generation and definition.

Content Analysis

Category definition is extremely important since the definitions serve as discriminators during the assignment of a document to a category. The usual method of category (class) definition is through the use of keywords. As we have already pointed out, words significant of content may be selected in many different ways.

Assume that n keywords are selected to define a category, $w_1, \ldots, w_n$. Next assume that some weight is computed for each word w_1 for each category in which it occurs. Let w_1' be a random variable whose value is the weight assigned to keyword w_1; generally, let w_i' be a random variable whose value is the weight assigned to keyword w_i. Given a document belonging to category C_j, the probability $P(w_1 \mid C_j)$ that the document will contain w_1 can be estimated by analysis of a sample document collection. More generally, the probability $P_n(w_1', \ldots, w_n' \mid C_j)$ that a *sequence* of keywords $w_1, \ldots, w_n$ will be found in a document belonging to C_j can be estimated. Once keyword selection and probability estimation have been completed for the k categories, documents may be assigned to these categories as follows.

The document is scanned (read) until a keyword (or a sequence of keywords) is found, then one of $k + 2$ decisions must be made: the document is assigned to one of the k categories, the document is considered unclassifiable, or more keywords must be read. At the extreme the entire document would have to be read, but the decision rule (see below) employed is designed to minimize this condition.

The decision rule should be one which permits a document to be assigned to a category as early as possible to avoid unnecessary processing. Each decision will be made with some prescribed limit of error α. That is, the decision rule must function so that the probability that a document is misclassified will be less than or equal to α. Hence the probability that a document will be correctly classified is $1 - \alpha$. The decision rule suggested by Fried *et al.* follows from a lemma on sequential analysis [86] and has the form

$$\frac{P_n^*(w_1', \ldots, w_n' \mid C_j)}{P_n(w_1', \ldots, w_n' \mid C_j)} \geq \frac{1}{\alpha}$$

where $P_n^*(w_1', \ldots, w_n' \mid C_j)$ is a probability distribution over the sequences $w_1, \ldots, w_n$ ($1 < n \leq N$) of keywords defining a category C_j for each j and each fixed n. For each j, $P_n^*(w_1', \ldots, w_1' \mid C_j)$ can be taken as an arbitrary but fixed discrete distribution over N^n points. (Several choices for P_n^* are possible, but the choice should result in minimum sample sizes.) $P_n(w_1', \ldots, w_n' \mid C_j)$ is the probability that a document which belongs to category C_j will be observed to contain the sequence of keywords $w_1, \ldots, w_n$. Several alternative methods of estimating $P_n(w_1', \ldots, w_n' \mid C_j)$ have been employed in the studies reported by White *et al.* [86].

The deicision rule is applied iteratively to a document until it is classified or until it is deemed unclassifiable. Figure 10 illustrates the successful assignment of a document to category C_{j_0} after n_0 steps.

Document classification employing the above procedures is also somewhat arbitrary, but the results are usually more nearly in accord with manual assignments than are the results of derivative classification procedures.

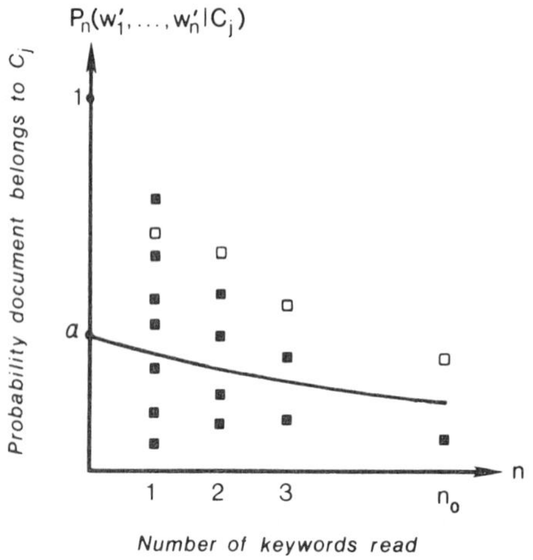
$P_n(w'_1, \ldots, w'_n | C_j)$
Probability document belongs to C_j
1
a
n
1
2
3
n_0
Number of keywords read

Fig. 10. Assignment classification based on sequential analysis.

Question Answering and Inference Systems

Another important area of application of elemental analysis techniques is that of question answering or inference making. We will briefly describe two of the many examples of these applications. The reader is referred to Borko [87], Simon and Siklóssy [88], and to the references therein for more detail.

General Operation of a Question Answering System. The question answering procedure can be conceptually divided into four phases: syntactic analysis, semantic analysis, data retrieval, and data processing, as illustrated schematically in Fig. 11.

The first phase consists of transforming the input sentence into a structure which explicitly represents the grammatical relationships among the words of the sentence. Using this information, the second (semantic analysis) component constructs a representation of the semantic content or meaning of the sentence. When actually implemented, the distinction between these two phases is seldom precise and their interaction is taken into account by the feedback loop shown in Fig. 11.

The third phase is that involving retrieval of relevant data from the data base. Any necessary processing of data is done by the fourth, or data processor, phase. Since data retrieval and deduction are closely linked, the relationship between the "Data Retriever" and the "Data Processor" phases could be compared to that between the "Parser" and the "Interpreter" phases of the system. The output of the "Interpreter" initiates and controls the operations of data retrieval and deduction.

The schematic of Fig. 11 contains a fifth block, called "Answer syntax computer." It may be observed that answer computation takes place in parallel with the four main phases of the question-answerer. The purpose of this block is to put together a syntactically and semantically acceptable natural language string as the answer, or response, to the query. Whatever the processes involved

Content Analysis

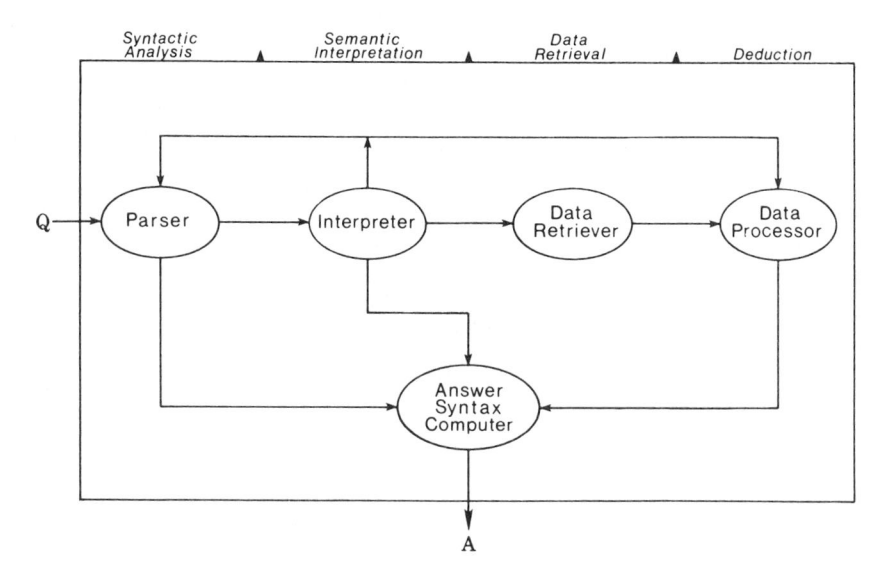

Fig. 11. The phases of a question answering system.

within the system may be, it is the output of this block which constitutes a meaningful response to the user and which controls interaction between user and system.

ELIZA. ELIZA is a program which makes certain kinds of natural language conversation between man and computer possible [89]. An example dialog is as follows:

> Men are all alike
> IN WHAT WAY?
> They're always bugging us about something or other
> CAN YOU THINK OF A SPECIFIC EXAMPLE?
> Well, my boyfriend made me come here
> YOUR BOYFRIEND MADE YOU COME HERE?
> He says I'm depressed much of the time
> I AM SORRY TO HEAR YOU ARE DEPRESSED.
> ⋮

The basic operation of ELIZA is as follows. Text is read and inspected for the presence of a keyword. If a keyword is found, the sentence is transformed according to a rule associated with the keyword; if no keyword is found, a context-free remark is put out or, under certain conditions, an earlier transformation is retrieved. A prepared script provides transformations for ELIZA. The script is a high level program whose statements are not necessarily sequential—the flow of control among command statements in the script is guided by the keywords of the input. Since ELIZA is actually not a question-answerer, no data base is used. Transformational rules and keyword dictionaries form the "brain" of the program. It is relevant to note that a system with such elementary semantic routines has shown promising capabilities in application to a number of computer-aided instruction (CAI) problems and to computer simulation of counseling behavior [90].

GRANIS. Coles has described a computer program designed to make inferences about both pictures and natural language [91]. The program, called GRANIS (GRAphical NAtural INference system), accepts a restricted subset of English together with elementary line drawings (input directly via a graphic display console).

GRANIS is made up of three major components: syntactic, semantic, and pragmatic. The syntactic component consists of clusters of productions for the recognition and translation of well-formed English sentences within the universe of discourse (organic chemistry, plane geometry, electrical circuits).

The semantic component consists of productions which cause the source string (text) to be translated into an expression in a predicate calculus. These expressions amount to interpretations of the input sentences.

A dictionary contains the terminal vocabulary of the source language which is partitioned into referent terminals (nouns, verbs, etc.) and function terminals (conjunctions, prepositions, etc.). The meaning of each lexical item in the set of referent terminals is also provided by the dictionary. The dictionary consists of a collection of Boolean procedures for evaluating predicates corresponding to the referent terminals.

The user of GRANIS draws a picture on a graphics device and then enters sentences (statements) about the picture. GRANIS will indicate whether the sentence is true or false for the given picture.

Other Applications

The use of elemental analysis techniques in automatic abstracting has been fully described elsewhere in this Encyclopedia [22]. More recently, Mathis and Young [92] have described the use of content analysis techniques in procedures for improving the quality of computer-produced abstracts, and Mathis [93] has employed similar techniques in abstract evaluation. Indexing applications have been described by Landry and Rush [23], and uses of elemental analysis techniques in psychology have been described by Pepinsky [76], Patton [15], and Fisher [94]. The reader should consult these sources, as well as the multitude of references cited therein, for details of many applications.

Structural Analysis

> All the innumerable substances which occur on earth—shoes, ships, sealing-wax, cabbages, kings, carpenters, walruses, oysters, everything we can think of—can be analysed into their constituent atoms, either in this or in other ways. It might be thought that a quite incredible number of different kinds of atoms would emerge from the rich variety of substances we find on earth. Actually the number is quite small. The same atoms turn

up again and again, and the great variety of substances we find on earth results, not from any great variety of atoms entering into their composition, but from the great variety of ways in which a few types of atoms can be combined... [95].

In structural analysis of messages or texts we are interested not just in the component parts (elements) of the message, but also in the relationships between the elements and how these relationships are used to signify content both on the part of the message source and on the part of the message receiver. In other words, structural analysis involves the transformation of texts into structural representations which facilitate the drawing of inferences from the text about the intension of the text source. It must be admitted that the study of structural analysis is not well developed and that many of the techniques and theories to be described are yet in their formative stages. Nevertheless, the work which has been done promises exciting results in the foreseeable future, so that we are moved to suggest applications which have not yet been developed. Consultation of the references cited will enable the reader to form his own conclusions.

Form and Content

The content of a message is inextricably linked with its form. Thus, in spite of earlier views, it is now generally accepted that message form is significant in content analysis, but this idea has been long in coming [96]. Viewing messages as linear strings of words seems to have been accepted for as long as language has been studied; this view reached its zenith with the work of Chomsky and his adherents on the notions of deep and surface structures and transformational grammars [60, 97–100]. The hypothesis that the content (meaning) of a message lies "beneath" the text we see (or hear) is a plausible one, but the further hypothesis that the underlying (deep) structures are fewer in number than the corresponding surface structures is not tenable. For instance, the two sentences

> The hiker was attacked by a bear

and

> A bear attacked the hiker

convey essentially the same idea, but do not in all particulars have the same content. There are many subtle aspects of language which the Chomskian view cannot explain. Nevertheless, Chomsky deserves credit for initiating a great resurgence of interest and progress in linguistics and content analysis.

The fact that messages are usually represented as linear strings of sounds or visual signals has, we believe, obscured the real structure (form) of messages and has, until recently, led researchers in the wrong direction.

Structural Prototypes

Among the earliest reports of work on the structural approach to content analysis were those by Bernier and Heumann and by Libbey.

Vocabulary Control. Bernier and Heumann [101] postulated a "vocabulary ball" consisting of related semantemes. The core of the ball represented the most abstract concept in a document collection. Succeeding layers are composed of terms which are of increasing specificity and of increasing numbers. In general, the structure can be viewed as a collection of ordered relationships among semantemes. A "first-order" relationship is defined as any link between semantemes on adjacent layers, while a "second-order" relationship is defined as any link between semantemes in the same layer. Bernier and Heumann claimed that these relationships constitute a comprehensive classification and that any term could be defined by use of all of its first-order relationships.

Libbey [102] described a somewhat similar approach to term definitions. Each term in a vocabulary is defined by the set of terms from the vocabulary with which the chosen term is most closely related. These strings of terms, called definitors, were designed to improve document retrieval by providing for conceptual linkage between vocabulary elements. The definitor also permits computation of a "pseudometric distance" between queries and documents. Libbey also suggested that the introduction of new terms to a vocabulary and alteration of the bias of descriptor indexes could be facilitated by use of definitors.

Association Maps. Sometime later, Doyle [103] proposed the association map, somewhat like a cardiovascular system where the arteries correspond to relationships involving many documents, arterioles fewer, and so forth. Doyle maintained that flexibility in the "capillary" regions was vital and suggested that these regions could be mechanically determined. He thought that the gross organization, however, should be manually determined and fixed. Statistical correlation graphs, called document proxies, were employed to position a document onto the map and to retrieve documents from it. Doyle contended that graphs are easily evaluated at a glance, that differences among documents may be made conspicuous, and that graphs are subject to dynamic control.

Dependency Theory. Following the work of Doyle, and independently of it, Hays [63] introduced his dependency theory of language analysis, which was aimed at producing a graph showing directly the interdependencies among words of a sentence, in contrast with a phrase structure in which word dependencies are only implicit. Dependency grammars have been employed in several subsequent studies, some of which are described later in this article.

Semantic Networks. Quillian has suggested a view of meaning involving what he called "semantic networks" [104]. Such networks combine the ideas embodied in the definitional notions of Bernier and Heumann and of Libbey with the network concept described by Doyle, but they also allow for predication or modification of a concept within the structure. All factual information is encoded either as a "unit" or a "property." A unit represents some thing, idea, or event, and a property represents any sort of predication. Each unit must contain a link to its superset, and may contain links to properties. Each property must contain links to an attribute and a value and may contain links to other properties. The attribute-value pair may represent the traditional category-value pair (for example, color-white) or any verb-object or preposition-object pair. Figure 12 may help to explain the model.

Content Analysis

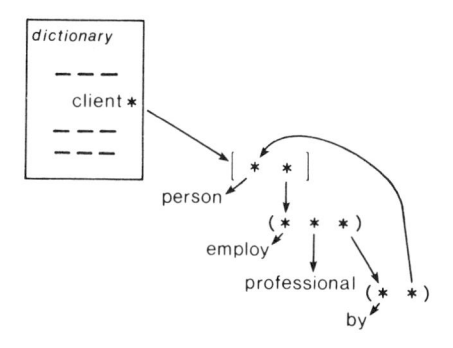

Fig. 12. A representation of Quillian's "semantic network" organization for "client" as a "person who employs a professional."

The unit (in brackets) represents the concept "client." It links to its superset "person" and its property whose attribute is "employ" and value is "professional." This property links to another whose attribute is "by" and whose value is "client." Quillian employed this memory model in his Teachable Language Comprehender (TLC). In theory, the TLC can be taught to alter its memory structure with "teacher guidance." Initially, however, it was "spoon-fed" a semantic structure.

Quillian's work, though primarily a semantic model, makes use of certain syntactic relationships (such as predicate-object) within the structural framework. This extension over the name hierarchy proposed by Bernier and by Doyle is an important step toward complete structural representations of texts or messages.

TOSAR. A somewhat different approach to structural organization is exhibited in Fugmann's Topological Method for the Representation of Synthetic and Analytical Relations of Concepts [105]. TOSAR is an attempt to expedite literature searches by a predictable indexing scheme. Unlike Bernier, Doyle, and Quillian, Fugmann makes no attempt to structure the document collection. Rather, each document or query is represented as an independent network. Organization is not a concept hierarchy, but rather a type of time line or event sequence. For each document or query, a graph is drawn manually. The graph is then coded and stored (or mechanically matched) with the graphs which represent the document collection.

The relations displayed by the graph are chemical in nature, but Fugmann asserts that "a method of representing relations between concepts precisely and clearly smooths the road to a consistent analytical treatment even of concepts that are not concerned with structural chemistry" [106].

Each process that is carried out is represented by a series of levels. The concepts before the process are arranged on one level and the concepts after the process are displayed at one point on a lower level. For example, the graph in Fig. 13 represents the process described by the sentence: Oligomerization of propylene with the aid of Al(Alkyl)$_3$ to obtain hexene, and separation and

Propylene   Al(alkyl)$_3$ Oligomerization

Hexene, Propylene

Fractional distillation

Propylene   Al(alkyl)$_3$ Oligomerization

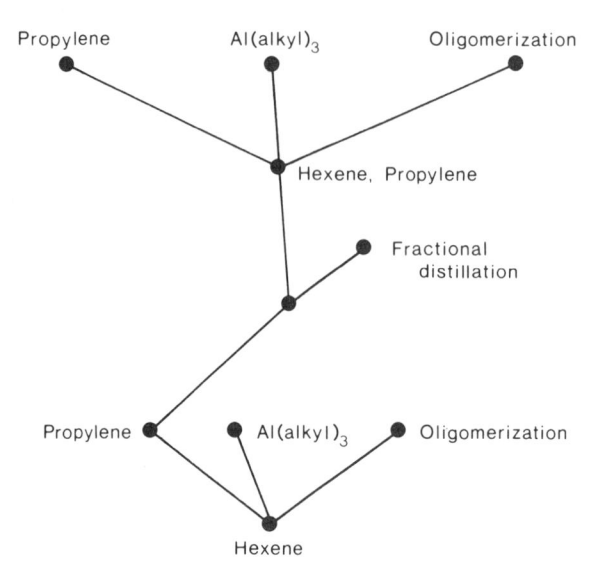

Hexene

Fig. 13. A TOSAR graph for a polymerization process.

purification of the excess propylene by fractional distillation and recycling of the propylene is reported.

Conceptual Dependency Parser. Shank and Tesler have described a method of structural representation based on the sentence [107]. Their Conceptual Dependency Parser operates on one word of an input sentence at a time, checking potential links to other words in the sentence with its knowledge of the world and past experience. A linked network is displayed upon the completion of each sentence. A typical network is shown in Fig. 14. The parser employs a five-step process to construct the network: A dictionary look-up, application of realization rules, an idiom check, rewrite procedures, and a semantics check. The dictionary consists of a list of "senses" each composed of a "conceptual category" (such as actor, action, location, etc.) and an "interpretation" (such as: fly—an insect). Guesses as to which sense applies are stacked for testing against the realization rules and conceptual semantics. The rules define how the word might be connected to previous and future words in the sentence to form the structure. These rules prohibit such constructions as the now famous "ideas sleep" [108] on the basis that such a connection has never been made (in the parser's experience). The semantics check is employed to choose between two feasible interpretations. For example, the parser would attempt to construct

John saw Texas flying to California.

in the same way it handled

John saw the birds flying to California.

until the semantic check disallowed the construction

Texas ⇔ fly

Content Analysis

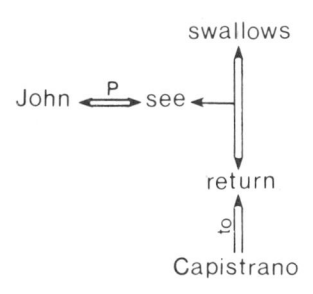

```
                swallows
                   ↑
   John ⇌ᴾ see ←——|
                   ↓
                return
                 ↑
                ⁻ᵗᵒ
                Capistrano
```

Fig. 14. A network produced by Shank and Tesler's "Conceptual Dependency Parser."

Although Shank and Tesler have stressed that the parser is a conceptual rather than a syntactic model, the categories they propose align closely (in English) with the traditional grammar classes and with case grammar roles.

Graphic Representations for Automatic Indexing of Text. In 1969, Rush described a method of representing text in structured form [109] which he developed as an outgrowth of work on the use of links and roles [110] to define term/term relationships. An example of Rush's structural representations is shown in Fig. 15. The structures were produced manually and were intended for machine encoding and processing in a manner analogous to that used to process chemical structures [111].

Young refined the relationships which Rush had used and suggested that the structures could be derived entirely by computer program.

Graphic Structures for Russian Sentences. Plath has described a procedure for constructing diagrams of sentences in Russian [112]. A program embodying the procedure and based upon a projective grammar is used as a means of presenting the output of a predictive syntactic analyzer. The program has also been used to analyze and classify sentences according to their structural properties. An example of Plath's structures is shown in Fig. 16.

Graphic Structures for French Sentences. A program designed to produce structural representations of sentences in French has been implemented by Tesnieré [113], who treats the verb as the central relator of the sentence. The verb appears at the apex of the graph; subject and object substructures appear to the left and right, respectively, and below the verb (see Fig. 17 for illustration).

Case Grammar

> Polonius: What do you read, my lord?
> Hamlet: Words, words, words.
> Polonius: What is the matter, my lord?
> Hamlet: Between who?
> Polonius: I mean the matter that you read, my lord [114].

The Woodward-Hoffman rules, which predict
 A   B   C   D
a disrotatory mode of opening, are obeyed.
 E   F   G   H

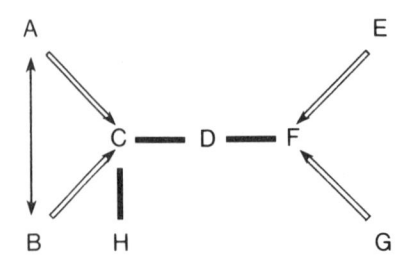

Fig. 15. Example of the graphical representations described by Rush.

Before proceeding further with our discussion of structural analysis, we must digress briefly to consider the notions of case grammar. In contrast with older views of case, which dealt with the role of pronominal forms (e.g., I–me and He–him) and, in some languages, also nominal forms, in the sense usually of subject or object, Fillmore has extended the notion of case in English to cover all nouns (and pronouns) in any syntactic situation.

Fillmore first described his theory of case grammar in 1968 [73]. He defined the sentence to be a modality plus a proposition. The modality constituent embodies the whole sentence and includes such elements as negation, time, and mood. The propositional constituent is a set of noun-verb relationships, called cases. The cases are called agentive, instrument, dative, factitive, locative, and objective, depending upon the role of the noun in the relationship. It is the noun which, in the Fillmore analysis, determines the case. Verbs are classified according to the cases which accept them.

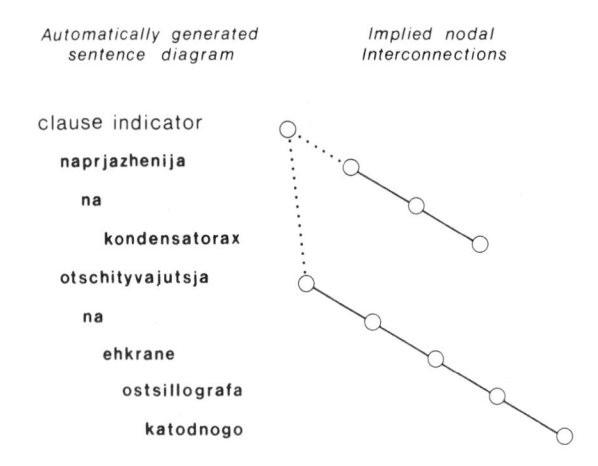

Automatically generated sentence diagram   *Implied nodal Interconnections*

clause indicator

naprjazhenija

na

kondensatorax

otschityvajutsja

na

ehkrane

ostsillografa

katodnogo

Fig. 16. A structural representation of a Russian sentence produced by Plath's procedure.

Content Analysis

A similar model of semantic structure has been proposed by Chafe [74]. A sentence in his analysis consists of one "predicative element" and optionally a set of "nominal elements." Chafe takes the position that "it is the verb which dictates the presence and character of the noun" and not the noun which controls the verb. Chafe then defines four "selectional units": state, process, action, and ambient. Verbs are classified according to these units, and it is these units which "select" the relationship of the noun to the verb. These relationships are the propositional cases Fillmore proposed. Chafe labels them experiencer, agent, benefactive, patient, instrument, locative, and so forth.

Another version of a case grammar was published by Anderson [115]. The labels he adopts for the case roles are different from those of Fillmore and Chafe, but his analysis is similar to theirs. Like Chafe he stresses the centrality of the verb. Anderson's work is important because he has suggested certain syntactic tests for distinguishing between cases.

Young and her colleagues have developed computer programs which implement a case grammar analysis [56, 77] This implementation recognizes the "essential cases" of agent, experiencer, beneficiary, and object and the "peripheral cases" of locative, time, manner, comitative, cause, and purpose. The analysis is a three-phase process. Phase 1 identifies the verb class by dictionary look-up or default. Essential cases are assigned based on the verb class case frame or secondary relators. Phase 2 assigns the time case based on dictionary recognition, and phase 3 assigns the remaining peripheral cases based on prepositions and other syntactic and lexical cues.

The basic verb types usually identified in case grammar analysis are defined in Table 4, after Cook [116]. The case roles assumed by nouns or noun phrases are given in Table 5, after Young [56]. The following examples serve to illustrate the assignment of case roles:

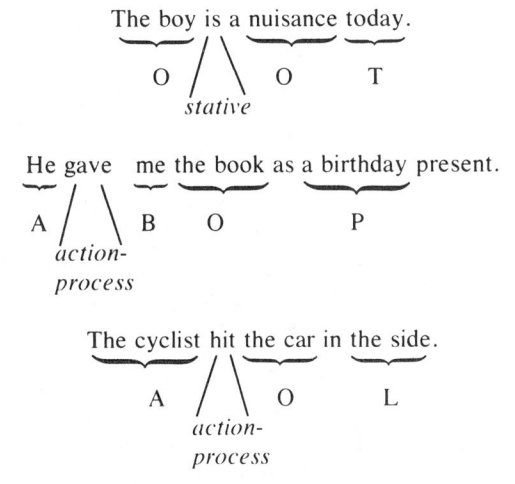

$$\underbrace{\text{The boy}}_{O} \overset{\text{is}}{\underset{stative}{\diagup\diagdown}} \underbrace{\text{a nuisance}}_{O} \underbrace{\text{today}}_{T}.$$

$$\underbrace{\text{He}}_{A} \overset{\text{gave}}{\underset{action-process}{\diagup\diagdown}} \underbrace{\text{me}}_{B} \underbrace{\text{the book}}_{O} \underbrace{\text{as a birthday present}}_{P}.$$

$$\underbrace{\text{The cyclist}}_{A} \overset{\text{hit}}{\underset{action-process}{\diagup\diagdown}} \underbrace{\text{the car}}_{O} \underbrace{\text{in the side}}_{L}.$$

Salton [117], Winograd [28], and Halliday [67] have also suggested or used methods of analysis which are essentially case grammar systems, and Montgomery [72] has suggested that Fillmore's case grammar provides a "linguistically-based formalism" for representing content in terms of relationships, although she suggests a lexical rather than computational approach.

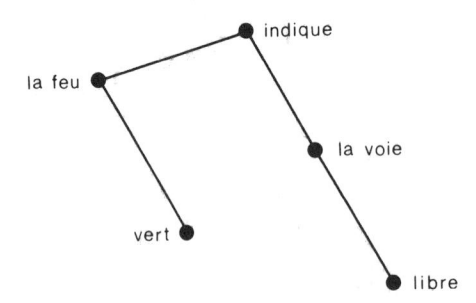

Fig. 17. A structure produced by the program described by Tesniéré.

TABLE 4
Verb Types and the Case Frames They Govern

Basic verb type	Case frames dictated by each verb type			
	Simple	Compound		
State	[O]	[E, O]	[B, O]	[O, L]
Process	[O]	[E, O]	[B, O]	[O, L]
Action	[A]	[A, E]	[A, B]	[A, L]
Action-process	[A, O]	[A, E, O]	[A, B, O]	[A, O, L]

TABLE 5
Definition of Essential and Peripheral Case Roles

Case role	Symbol	No.	Definition of case role
Agent	A	1	The source of the action specified by the primary phrase[a]
Experiencer	E	3	The one who experiences the feeling, sensation, etc., specified by the primary phrase
Beneficiary	B	4	The possessor (in its broadest sense) of some thing, whether the possession be temporary or permanent, positive or negative
Objective	O	2	The receiver of the action specified by the primary phrase
Locative	L	5	The place where the action specified by the primary phrase occurs
Time	T	6	The time when the action specified by the primary phrase occurs
Manner	M	7	The way in which the action specified by the primary phrase is performed
Comitative	C	8	The accompaniment case, a subject accompanying the source of the action specified by the primary phrase
Cause	Cs	9	The case giving the reason for the action specified by the primary phrase
Purpose	P	10	The case giving the purpose of the action specified by the primary phrase

[a] Primary phrase may be thought of as a verb phrase.

Content Analysis

The importance of case as described above is that it may well serve to provide the clues needed to identify the concepts contained in a message or text. We have already mentioned that structural analysis involves not only linguistic elements but the relationships between these elements as well. Certain of these relationships may be ascertained through syntactic analysis, but the more important relationships which are susceptible of identification through application of analytical procedures are those defined in the theory of case grammar. It is the answers to questions such as *who, why, where, how, when, what,* and *what for* that case grammar analysis provides, and it is precisely these answers that content analysis has heretofore been unable to deduce. This point may be made clearer by examination of two recent approaches to structural representations of text.

Derivation of Structures from Text

Structural Representation of English Sentences. Young has proposed a graphic representation of English sentences which builds upon her work in syntactic and case grammar analysis [56]. Each sentence is processed as a set of clauses, and a subgraph is produced for each clause. The nodes of the graph include verbs and nouns (adverbs and adjectives are treated as part of the verb or noun node). The arcs or edges of the graph represent what Young calls secondary relations (prepositions, conjunctions, etc.). Both nodes and edges are labeled, and verb nodes are assigned special symbols (see Table 6). The edge labels are case roles, as given in Table 4. A few examples, presented as Fig. 18, should suffice to illustrate the approach.

Young claims that such representations are susceptible of production by computer program and that they preserve and explicate the NAMES and RELA-

TABLE 6
Symbols Used by Young to Represent Case Grammar Classes of Primary Relations

Primary relation type (case)	Dominant	Participial	Infinitival
Stative	—•○•—	—•●•—	—•◐•—
Agentive	—■□→	—■■→	—■▨→
Experiencer	—▲△→	—▲▲→	—▲▨→
Beneficiary	←◇◇—	←◆◆—	←◈▨—
Reflexive	←●⬡—	←●⬢—	←●▨—

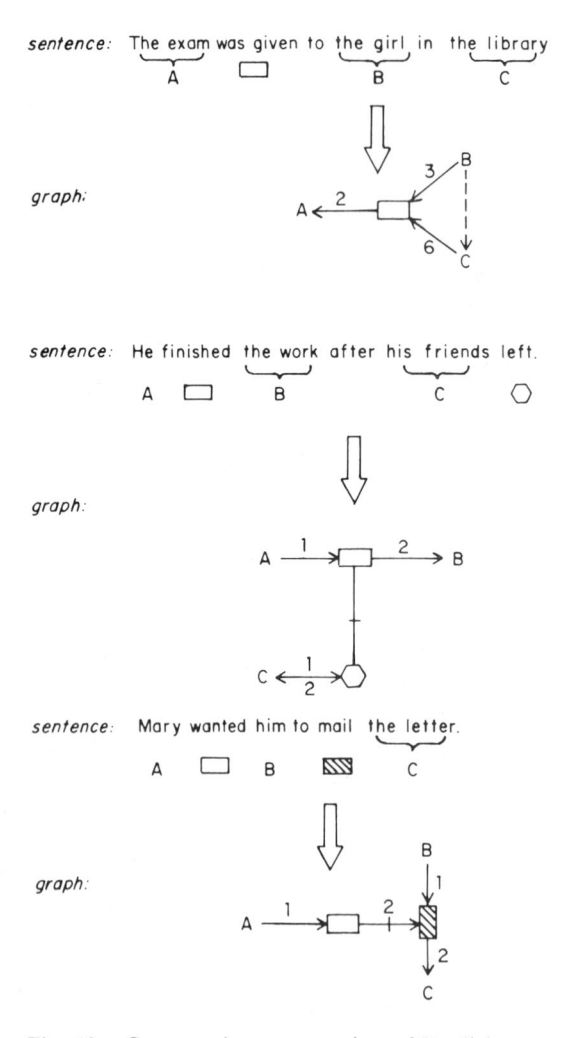

Fig. 18. Structural representation of English sentences by Young.

TIONS in a sentence in such a way that index entries of various types may be derived from them in addition to more complex aggregates analogous to structure-based retrieval in chemistry [118, 119].

AGNES. The most comprehensive procedure for generation of structural representations of English text so far reported is that described by Strong [120, 121]. She called the procedure an Algorithm for Graphic Notation of English Sentences (AGNES). Each sentence in English is represented by a network comprised of nodes and edges. A sentence is viewed as being composed of one or more clauses, each consisting of a predicate and, optionally, a subject, one or more objects, and/or modifiers. Each of these clause components is, when present in a sentence, represented in the network as a node. Relationships

Content Analysis

TABLE 7
Directionality of Edges in AGNES Graphs in Relation to Verb Type and Case Frame

	Edge type				
Verb type and case frame	Subject-predicate	Predicate-object	Modifier	Conjunctive	Phrase
Unspecified	/	\	↑	. . . .	↓ prep
Stative [O]	/				
Stative [O, O]	/	:\			
Action [A]	↗				
Process [O]	↙				
Action-process [A, O]	↗	↘			
Experiencer [E]	↙				
Stative [E, O]	↙	\			
Action [A, E]	↗	↘			
Process [E, O]	↙	↘			
Action-process [A, E, O]	↗	↘	⇕		
Stative [B, O]	↙	\			
Action [A, B]	↗	↘			
Process [B, O]	↙	↘			
Action-process [A, B, O]	↗	↘	⇓		

between nodes are represented as edges of the network. An edge may be labeled with a relational word. Several types of edge are employed; these are defined in Table 7. The basic network is augmented by directionality of the edges which specifies the major case frames extant in the network (see Table 7). Examples of AGNES graphs are given in Fig. 19.

An important extension of the basic AGNES procedures involves explication of intersentence relationships. Strong developed a set of rules which determine how sentences are to be linked. For example, the antecedent of a personal pronoun is linked to the pronoun by a double-dashed edge. Two or more occurrences of the same word in separate sentences will also be linked by a double-dashed edge. The individual sentence graphs of Fig. 19 are shown in Fig. 20 with intersentence relations identified. Although the figures show two-dimensional structures, Strong indicates that at least three dimensions are required for proper graphic representation [120].

Application of Structural Analysis

This proposal was met with great applause, until an Old Mouse arose and said, "This is all very fine, but who among us is so brave? Who will bell the Cat?" The mice looked at one another in silence and nobody volunteered.

It is easier to suggest a plan than to carry it out [122].

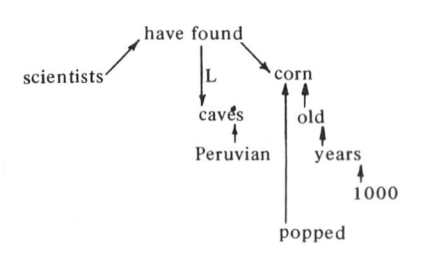

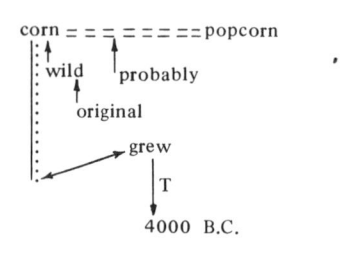

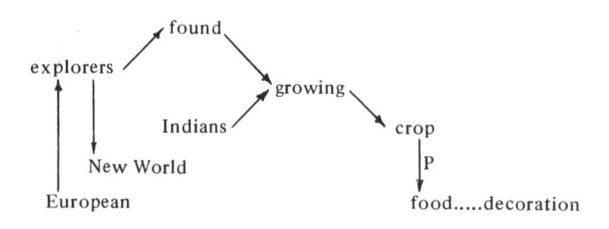

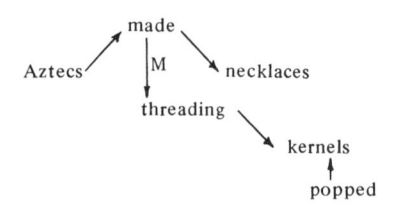

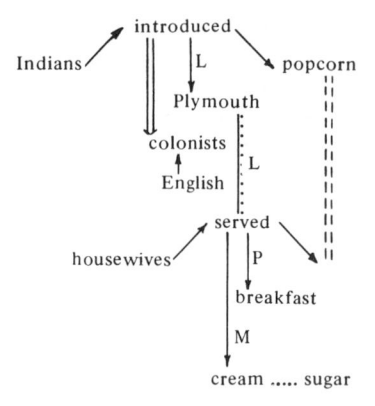

Fig. 19. Example of graphs of sentences produced by AGNES.

Content Analysis

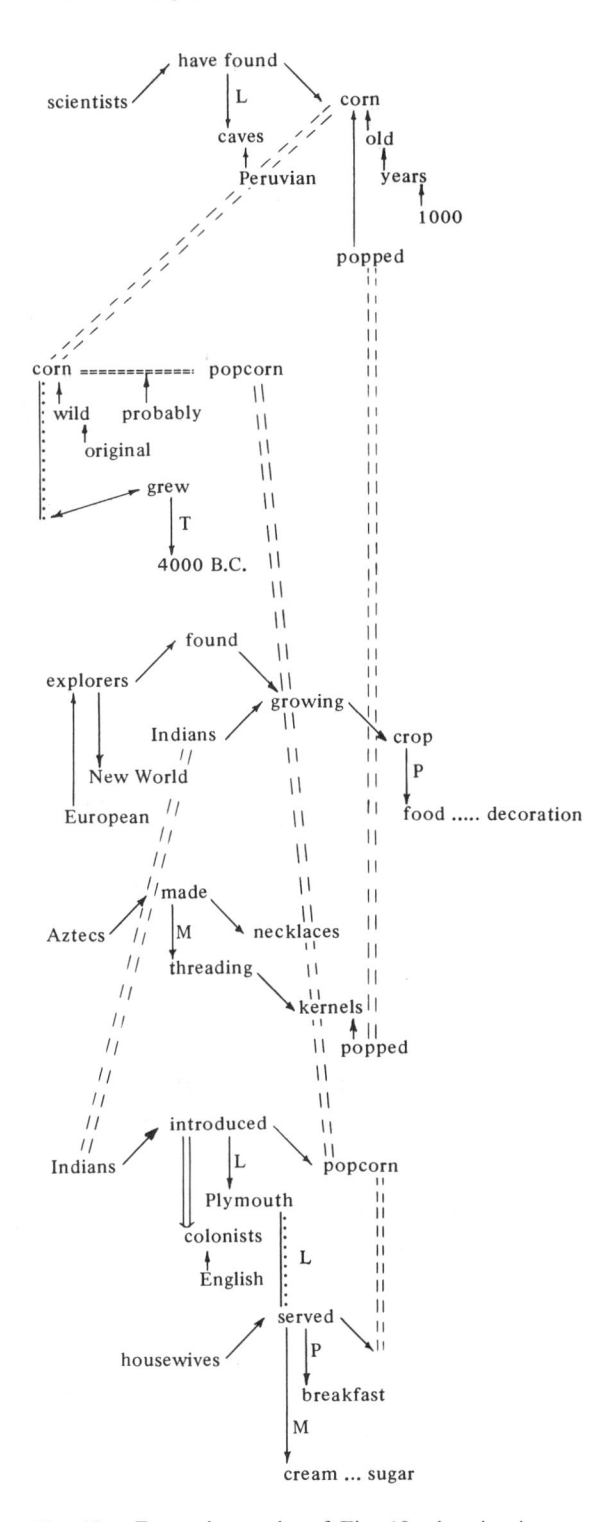

Fig. 20. Example graphs of Fig. 19, showing intersentence relations.

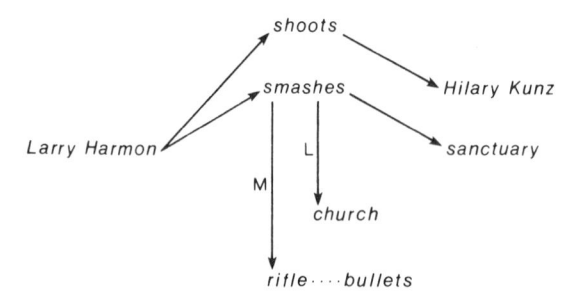

```
              shoots
             ↗
     ↗smashes────→ Hilary Kunz
                ↘
Larry Harmon ↗   │   ↘ sanctuary
             M│  │L
              │  ↓
              │ church
              ↓
           rifle····bullets
```

Fig. 21. Index display suggested by Strong.

While structural analysis is yet in its formative stages of development, and while many of the proposed techniques of structural analysis have not been reduced to computer programs, it is not unreasonable to suggest one or two applications.

The work of Fugmann and his colleagues on TOSAR [105, 123] has already led to computerized storage and retrieval processes even though the structures are produced manually. The basis for these retrieval techniques is the theory that concepts as expressed in words of a language are properly represented as nonlinear structures and that both the contents of texts and the contents of queries thus represented may be compared node by node and edge by edge to determine correspondence. This approach to retrieval at once overcomes a fundamental weakness of all existing retrieval systems: the inability to specify and/or identify relationships contained in the text or query. The situation is quite analogous to that of structural chemistry, wherein the search for specific structural complexes (structures or substructures) is made vastly simpler and more precise if the relations (bonds) between atoms (elements) as well as the atoms are available for retrieval.

Strong has suggested several applications related to machine indexing [120]. Among these are an index, similar to a Predicasts miniabstract [124], utilizing case roles. A second index proposed by Strong is a graphical one utilizing reduced portions of full structures which are dynamically produced for video display. The display is produced by selecting from the larger graph (with intersentence relations) those nodes with the highest degree (largest number of connections to other nodes) together with the relations directly linking these nodes. Augmentation of the basic graphical index display could then be produced on demand of the user to denote time, place, etc. A sample index display is shown in Fig. 21.

Other applications suggest themselves. We shall leave it to the reader to imagine some of them.

CONCLUSION

In the world of words, imagination is one of the forces of nature [125].

In this article we have attempted to survey the area of study loosely termed content analysis, and we have tried to organize many diverse studies according

Content Analysis

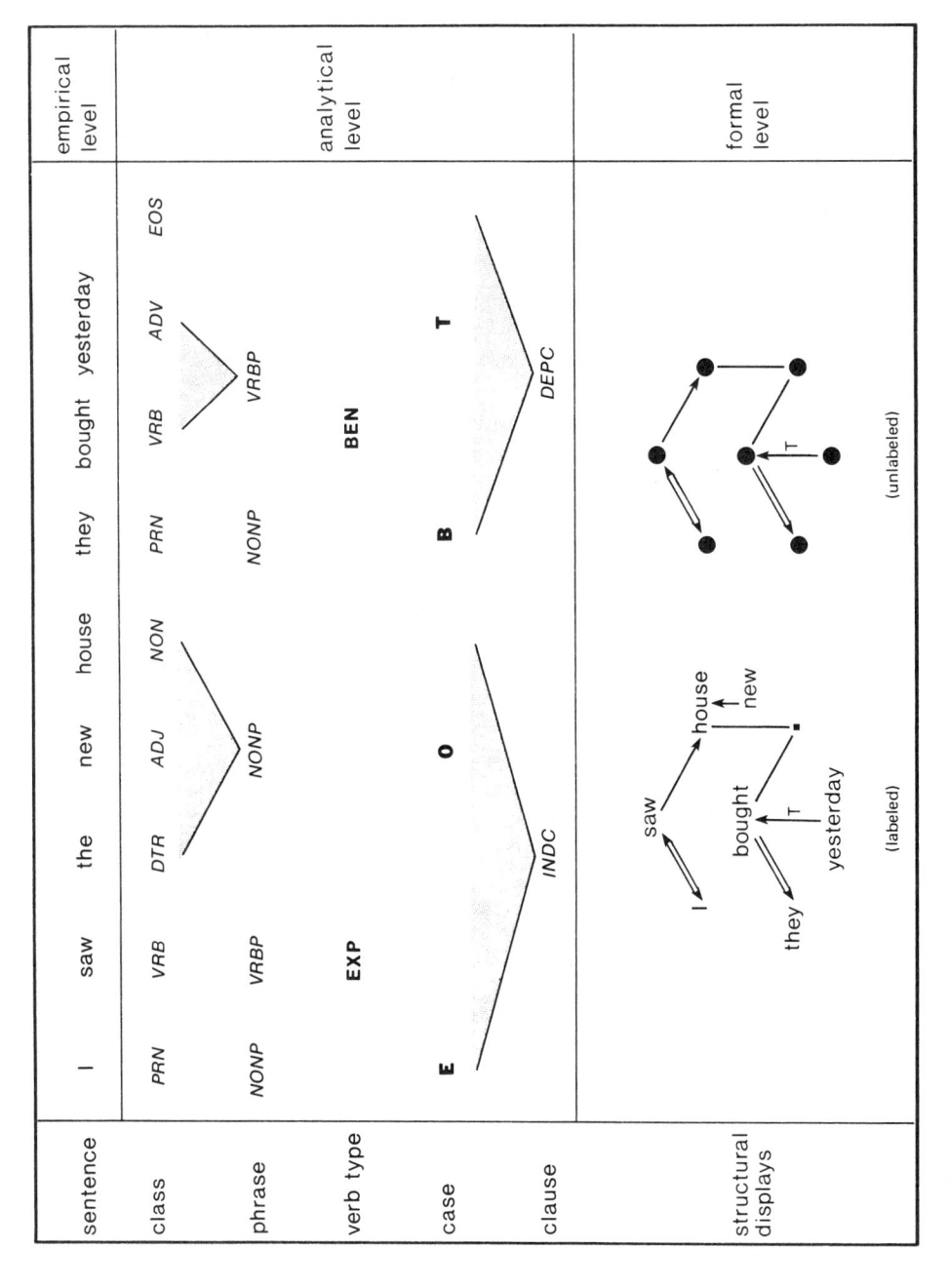

Fig. 22. Pepinsky's schemapiric representation of text.

to whether they concerned elemental or structural analysis. This organization is based upon a chemical metaphor which we believe to be of considerable importance in content analysis because there has been a serious inability to speak in precise terms about the variety of studies described in the literature and to do so in a way which makes evident their basic similarities. Pepinsky, in his "A Metalanguage of Text" [76], emphasizes the need for both analytical and formal levels of analysis in the study of and talk about language or text. His schemapiric representation of text, illustrated in Fig. 22, is a succinct and substantial way of concluding this article.

ACKNOWLEDGMENTS

The authors wish to thank Harold Pepinsky for the many hours of exciting discussion of many of the topics covered in this article. Thanks are also due Mrs. Corinne Garvey without whose help this article could not have been produced.

REFERENCES

1. A. C. Doyle, Silver blaze, in W. S. Barring-Gould, *The Annotated Sherlock Holmes*, Vol. 2, Potter, New York, 1967, p. 277.
2. C. A. Cuadra (ed.), *Annual Review of Information Science and Technology*, Wiley, New York (Vols. 1–2), 1966–1967; Encyclopedia Britannica, Chicago (Vols. 3–7), 1968–1972; American Society for Information Science, Washington, D.C. (Vols. 8–10), 1973–1975.
3. C. E. Shannon and W. Weaver, *The Mathematical Theory of Communication*, University of Illinois Press, Urbana, Illinois, 1949, p. 7.
4. J. Fast, *Body Language*, Pocket Books, New York, 1970.
5. M. Korda, *Power! How to Get It, How to Use It*, Random House, New York, 1975.
6. E. Efron, *The News Twisters*, Nash, Los Angeles, California, 1971.
7. T. Y. Canby, Handclasp in space, *National Geographic* **149**(2), 184 (1976).
8. P. J. Stone, D. C. Dumphy, M. S. Smith, and D. M. Ogilvie, *The General Inquirer: A Computer Approach to Content Analysis*, M.I.T. Press, Cambridge, Massachusetts, 1966.
9. S. J. Thorson, *Models, Theories, and Political Theory*, Polimetrics Laboratory, The Ohio State University, Columbus, Ohio, 1972.
10. A Bruschi, *Principles and Technique of a Political Metalanguage*, Research Committee 7: Committee on Conceptual and Terminological Analysis (COCTA), presented at the International Political Science Association Meeting, Montreal, 1973.
11. H. Garfinkel and H. Sacks, On formal structures of practical actions, in *Theoretical Sociology: Perspectives and Developments* (J. C. McKinney and E. A. Tiryakian, eds.), Appleton-Century-Crofts, New York, 1970, pp. 337–366.
12. L. C. Hawes, Interpersonal communication: The enactment of routines, in *Exploration in Speech Communication* (J. J. Makay, ed.), Merrill, Columbus, Ohio, 1973, pp. 71–90.
13. C. E. Osgood, G. J. Suci, and P. H. Tannenbaum, *The Measurement of Meaning*, University of Illinois Press, Urbana, Illinois, 1957.

14. J. G. Snider and C. E. Osgood (eds.), *Semantic Differential Techniques*, Aldine, Chicago, 1969.
15. M. J. Patton and A. Fuhriman, *Research on Psychological Counseling Using a Computer-Assisted Metalanguage*, paper presented before the Annual Convention of the American Psychological Association, Chicago, September, 1975.
16. D. Richardson, *Peace Child*, Regal, Glendale, California, 1974.
17. B. N. Colby, G. A. Collier, and S. K. Postal, Comparison of themes in folktales by the General Inquirer system, *J. Am. Folklore* **76**(302), 318–323 (1963).
18. B. N. Colby, Culture grammars, *Science* **187**(4180), 913–919 (1975).
19. E. Mosteller and D. L. Wallace, Inference in an authorship problem, *J. Am. Stat. Assoc.* **58**(302), 275–309 (1963).
20. W. A. Cook, S.J., Stylistics: Measuring style complexity, in *Georgetown University Working Papers on Languages and Linguistics No. 11*, Georgetown University Press, Washington, D.C., 1975.
21. S. Y. Sedelow, *Automated Analysis of Language Style and Structure*, Research Report ONR NR348-005, University of North Carolina, Chapel Hill, North Carolina, September 1970.
22. B. A. Mathis and J. E. Rush, Abstracting, in *Encyclopedia of Computer Science and Technology*, Vol. 1 (J. Belzer, A. G. Holzman, and A. Kent, eds.), Dekker, New York, 1975, pp. 102–142.
23. B. C. Landry and J. E. Rush, Automatic indexing: Progress and prospects, in *Encyclopedia of Computer Science and Technology*, Vol. 2 (J. Belzer, A. G. Holzman, and A. Kent, eds.), Dekker, New York, 1975, pp. 403–447.
24. T. Winograd, Linguistics and the computer analysis of tonal harmony, *J. Music Theory* **12**(1), 2–49 (1968).
25. H. B. Lincoln, Use of the computer in music research: A short report on accomplishments, limitations and future needs, *Computers and the Humanities* **8**(5–6), 285–289 (1974).
26. J. F. Young, *Robotics*, Butterworths, London, 1973.
27. C. Hewitt, PLANNER: A language for proving theorems in robots, in *Proceedings of the International Joint Conferences on Artificial Intelligence*, Mitre Corp., Bedford, Massachusetts, 1969, pp. 295–301.
28. T. Winograd, Understanding natural language, *Cognitive Psychol.* **3**(1), 1–191 (1972).
29. K. S. Fu, *Sequential Methods in Pattern Recognition and Machine Learning*, Academic, New York, 1968.
30. M. S. Watanabe (ed.), *Frontiers of Pattern Recognition*, Academic, New York, 1972.
31. J. D. Smith and J. E. Rush, The relationship between author names and author entries in a large on-line union catalog as retrieved using truncated keys, accepted for publication in the *Journal of the American Society for Information Science*, June 1976.
32. D. S. Colombo, *Automatic Retrieval Systems and Associated Retrieval Languages*, Computer and Information Science Research Center, OSU-CISRC-TR-69-17, The Ohio State University, Columbus, Ohio, 1969.
33. W. S. Stalcup and A. E. Petrarca, Automatic vocabulary control and its evaluation in computer-produced indexes, in *Proceedings of the American Society for Information Science National Convention*, Boston, 1975.
34. D. S. Colombo and J. E. Rush, Use of word fragments in computer-based retrieval systems, *J. Chem. Doc.* **9**(1), 47–50 (1969).
35. J. R. R. Tolkien, *The Lord of the Rings*, Part 1. *The Fellowship of the Ring*, Ballantine, New York, 1965, p. 370.

36. J. E. Rush, *Work at CAS on Search Guides and Thesauri,* presented at the Chemical Abstracts Service Open Forum, Miami Beach, Florida, April 12, 1967.
37. R. T. Niehoff, Development of an integrated energy vocabulary and the possibilities for on-line subject switching, *J. Am. Soc. Inf. Sci.* **27**(1), 3–17, (1976).
38. S. Y. Sedelow and W. A. Sedelow, Jr., Stylistic analysis, in *Automated Language Processing* (H. Borko, ed.), Wiley, New York, 1967, p. 182.
39. R. Busa, S.J., An inventory of fifteen million words, in *Proceedings of the IBM Literary Data Processing Conference,* September 1964, pp. 171–199.
40. P. Tasman, *Indexing the Dead Sea Scrolls by Electronic Literary Data Processing Methods,* IBM Brochure, November 1958.
41. D. J. Moore, Practical algorithms for computer collation of long natural texts for scholarly use, in *Abstracts of Research,* Computer and Information Sciences Research Center, The Ohio State University, Columbus, Ohio, 1975, p. 22.
42. H. Borko, Indexing and classification, in *Automated Language Processing* (H. Borko, ed.), Wiley, New York, 1967, pp. 99–125.
43. H. Kucera and W. N. Francis, *Computational Analysis of Present-Day American English,* Brown University, Providence, Rhode Island, 1967.
44. J. M. Carroll and R. Roeloffs, Computer selection of keywords using word-frequency analysis, *Am. Doc.* **20**(3), 227–233 (1969).
45. J. W. Sammon, Jr., *Some Mathematics of Information Storage and Retrieval,* Rome Air Development Center, Air Force Systems Command, Griffiss Air Force Base, New York, Technical Report No. RADC-TR-68-178, June 1968.
46. L. Bloomfield, *Language,* Holt, Rinehart and Winston, New York, 1933, p. 5.
47. J. Priestly, *Rudiments of English Grammar,* London, 1761, cited in C. C. Fries, *The Structure of English,* Harcourt, Brace and World, New York, 1952.
48. H. A. Gleason, *An Introduction to Descriptive Linguistics,* Holt, Rinehart and Winston, New York, 1961.
49. C. C. Fries, *The Structure of English,* Harcourt, Brace and World, New York, 1952, p. 74.
50. S. Klein and R. Simmons, A computational approach to grammatical coding of English words, *J. Assoc. Comput. Mach.* **10**(3), 334–347 (1963).
51. P. Beckmann, *The Structure of Language: A New Approach,* Golem, Boulder, Colorado, 1972.
52. D. C. Clark and R. E. Wall, An economical program for limited parsing of English, *AFIPS Conference Proceedings,* Vol. 27 (Part 1), 1965, pp. 307–316.
53. W. Stolz, P. Tannenbaum, and P. Carstensen, A stochastic approach to the grammatical coding of English, *Commun. ACM* **8** (6), 399–405 (1965).
54. S. Marvin, J. Rush, and C. Young, *Grammatical Class Assignment Based on Function Words,* Seventh Annual National Colloquium on Information Retrieval, Philadelphia, Pennsylvania, May 1970.
55. C. Young, Grammatical Assignment Based on Function Words, M.S. Thesis, The Ohio State University, 1970.
56. C. Young, *Design and Implementation of Language Analysis Procedures with Application to Automatic Indexing,* Computer and Information Science Research Center, OSU-CISRC-TR-73-2, The Ohio State University, Columbus, Ohio, 1973.
57. A. Oettinger and S. Kuno, Multiple-path syntactic analyzer, in *Proceedings of the International Federation of Information Processing Congress,* North Holland, Amsterdam, 1962, pp. 306–312.
58. A. M. Zwicky, J. Friedman, B. C. Hall, and D. E. Walker, The MITRE syntactic analysis procedure for transformational grammars, *Proceedings of the Fall Joint Computer Conference* Vol. 27(1), 1965, pp. 317–326.

59. J. Thorne, P. Bratley, and H. Dewar, The syntactic analysis of English by machine, in *Machine Intelligence,* Vol. 3 (D. Michie, ed.), American Elsevier, New York, 1968, pp. 281–310.
60. D. T. Langendoen, *The Study of Syntax,* Holt, Rinehart and Winston, New York, 1969.
61. H. L. Resnikoff and J. L. Dolby, Automatic determination of the parts of speech of English words, *Proc. Inst. Electr. and Electron. Eng.* **15**(7), 1029 (1963).
62. D. B. Vigor, D. Urquhart, and A. Wilkinson, PROSE—Parsing recognizer outputting sentences in English, in *Machine Intelligence,* Vol. 4 (B. Meltzer and D. Michie, ed.), American Elsevier, New York, 1969, pp. 271–284.
63. D. G. Hays, Dependency theory: A formalism and some observations, *Language* **40**(4), 511–525 (1964).
64. N. Sager, Syntactic analysis of natural language, *Adv. Comput.* **8,** 153–188 (1967).
65. W. A. Woods, Transition network grammars for natural language analysis, *Commun. ACM* **13**(10), 591–606 (1970).
66. R. K. Lindsay, Inferential memory as the basis of machines which understand natural language, in *Computers and Thought* (E. A. Feigenbaum and J. Feldman eds.), McGraw-Hill, New York, 1963, pp. 217–233.
67. M. A. K. Halliday, Notes on transitivity and theme in English; Part 1, *J. Linguistics* **3**(1), 37–81 (1967).
68. M. A. K. Halliday, Functional diversity in language as seen from a consideration of modality and mood in English, *Found. Language* **6,** 322–361 (1970).
69. M. A. K. Halliday, Notes on transitivity and theme in English, Part 2, *J. Linguistics* **4**(2), 179–215 (1968).
70. J. Rothstein, Relational languages, in *Report to the National Science Foundation, Office of Science Information Service,* Computer and Information Science Research Center, The Ohio State University, Columbus, Ohio, 1970, pp. 5.44–5.46.
71. R. Simmons, J. Burger, and R. Schwarcz, A computational model of verbal understanding, *Proceedings of the Fall Joint Computer Conference,* Vol. 33(1), 1968, pp. 411–456.
72. C. A. Montgomery, Linguistics and information science, *J. Am. Soc. Inf. Sci.* **23**(3), 195–218 (1972).
73. C. J. Fillmore, The case for case, in *Universals in Linguistic Theory* (E. Bach and R. Harms, eds.), Holt, Rinehart and Winston, New York, 1968, pp. 1–88.
74. W. L. Chafe, *Meaning and the Structure of Language,* University of Chicago Press, Chicago, Illinois, 1970.
75. L. Carroll, Through the looking-glass, and what Alice found there, from *Alice's Adventures in Wonderland and Through the Looking Glass,* Airmont, New York, 1965, p. 228.
76. H. B. Pepinsky, A metalanguage of text, in *Language and Logic in Personality and Society* (H. Fisher and R. Diaz-Guerrero, eds.), Academic, New York, in preparation.
77. J. E. Rush, H. B. Pepinsky, N. M. Meara, S. M. Strong, J. A. Valley, and C. E. Young, *A Computer-Assisted Language Analysis System,* Computer and Information Science Research Center, OSU-CISRC-TR-74-1, The Ohio State University, Columbus, Ohio, 1974.
78. M. D. Owdom, *Outline of a Computer-Assisted Language Analysis System (CALAS),* Instruction and Research Computer Center, The Ohio State University, Columbus, Ohio, October 1975.
79. K. L. Montgomery, *Document Retrieval Systems: Factors Affecting Search Time,* Dekker, New York, 1975.

80. P. M. Russo, Cellular Networks and Algorithms for Parallel Processing of Non-Numeric Data Encountered in Information Storage and Retrieval, Ph.D. Dissertation, The Ohio State University, 1975.
81. C. H. Davis and J. E. Rush, *Information Storage and Retrieval in Chemistry*, Greenwood, Westport, Connecticut, 1974, Chap. 5.
82. C. T. Abraham, Techniques for thesaurus organization and evaluation, in *Some Problems in Information Science* (M. Kochen, ed.), Scarecrow, New York, 1965, pp. 131–150.
83. G. Salton (ed.), *The SMART Retrieval System: Experiments in Automatic Document Processing*, Prentice-Hall, Englewood Cliffs, New Jersey, 1971, p. 140.
84. J. B. Fried, B. C. Landry, D. M. Liston, Jr., B. P. Price, R. C. Van Buskirk, and D. M. Wachsberger, *Index Simulation Feasibility and Automatic Document Classification*, Computer and Information Science Research Center, OSU-CISRC-TR-68-4, The Ohio State University, Columbus, Ohio, 1968, pp. 11–19.
85. A. Wald, *Sequential Analysis*, Wiley, New York, 1947, Chap. 10.
86. L. J. White, J. D. Smith, G. Kar, D. E. Westbrook, B. J. Brinkman, and R. A. Fisher, *A Sequential Method for Automatic Document Classification*, Computer and Information Science Research Center, OSU-CISRC-TR-75-5, The Ohio State University, Columbus, Ohio, 1975.
87. H. Borko (ed.), *Automated Language Processing*, Wiley, New York, 1967.
88. H. A. Simon and L. Siklóssy (eds.), *Representation and Meaning: Experiments with Information Processing Systems*, Prentice-Hall, Englewood Cliffs, New Jersey, 1972.
89. J. Weizenbaum, ELIZA—A computer program for the study of natural language communication between man and machine, *Commun. ACM* **9**(1), 36–45 (1966).
90. R. F. Simmons, Natural language question-answering systems: 1969, *Commun. ACM* **13**(1), 15–30 (1970).
91. L. S. Coles, Syntax directed interpretation of natural language, in *Representation and Meaning: Experiments with Information Processing Systems* (H. A. Simon and L. Siklóssy, eds.), Prentice-Hall, Englewood Cliffs, New Jersey, 1972, pp. 211–287.
92. B. A. Mathis, J. E. Rush, and C. E. Young, Improvement of automatic abstracts by the use of structural analysis, *J. Am. Soc. Inf. Sci.* **24**(2), 101–109 (1973).
93. B. A. Mathis, *Techniques for the Evaluation and Improvement of Computer-Produced Abstracts*, Computer and Information Science Research Center, OSU-CISRC-TR-72-15, The Ohio State University, Columbus, Ohio, 1972.
94. H. Fisher, An analysis of repression from the point of view of language and logic, *Interam. J. Psychol.* **5**(3–4), 167–181 (1971).
95. J. Jeans, *The Universe Around Us*, 4th ed., The University Press, Cambridge, England, 1945, p. 7.
96. M. Minsky, Form and content in computer science, *J. Assoc. Comput. Mach.* **17**(2), 197–215 (1970).
97. N. Chomsky, *Syntactic Structures*, Moulton, 's-Gravenhage, 1957.
98. N. Chomsky, *Aspects of the Theory of Syntax*, M.I.T. Press, Cambridge, Massachusetts, 1965.
99. R. A. Jacobs and P. S. Rosenbaum, *English Transformational Grammar*, Blaisdell, Waltham, Massachusetts, 1968.
100. E. H. Lenneberg, *Biological Foundations of Language*, Wiley, New York, 1967.
101. C. L. Bernier and K. F. Heumann, Correlative indexes III: Semantic relations among semantemem—The technical thesaurus, *Am. Doc.* **8**(1), 211–220 (1957).
102. M. A. Libbey, The use of second order descriptors for document retrieval, *Am. Doc.* **18**(1), 10–20 (1967).

103. L. B. Doyle, Semantic roadmaps for literature searches, *J. Assoc. Comput. Mach.* **8**(4), 553–578 (1961).
104. M. R. Quillian, The teachable language comprehender: A simulation program and theory of language, *Commun. ACM* **12**(8), 459–476 (1969).
105. R. Fugmann, H. Nickelsen, I. Nickelsen, and J. Winters, TOSAR—A topological method for the representation of synthetic and analytical relations of concepts, *Angew. Chem., Int. Ed. Engl.* **9**(8), 589–595 (1970).
106. Ref. 105, p. 593.
107. R. C. Shank and L. Tesler, *A Conceptual Dependency Parser for Natural Language*, International Conference on Computational Linguistics, Stockholm, Sweden, Preprint No. 2 (1969).
108. V. Mehta, Onward and upward with the arts (linguistics), *New Yorker*, pp. 44–87, May 8, 1971.
109. J. E. Rush, *A New Approach to Indexing*, presented before the Student Chapter of the A.S.I.S., Case-Western Reserve University, Cleveland, Ohio, January 1969.
110. B. A. Montague, Patent indexing by concept coordination using links and roles, *Am. Doc.* **13**(1), 104–111 (1962).
111. H. L. Morgan, The generation of a unique machine description for chemical structures—A technique developed at Chemical Abstracts Service, *J. Chem. Doc.* **5**(2), 107–113 (1965).
112. W. Plath, Automatic sentence diagramming, in *Proceedings of the 1961 International Conference on Machine Translation and Applied Language Analysis*, H.M.S.O., London, 1962, pp. 176–208.
113. L. Tesnieré, *Elements de Syntax Structural*, Klenchsuck, Paris, quoted by R. Pages, Relational aspects of conceptualization in message analysis, in J. M. Perreault (ed.), Proceedings of the international symposium on relational factors in classification, *Inf. Storage Retr.* **3**(4), 177–410 (1967).
114. W. Shakespeare, Hamlet, in *William Shakespeare* (A. S. Downer, ed.), Holt, Rinehart and Winston, New York, 1965, p. 208.
115. J. Anderson, *The Grammar of Case: Towards a Localistic Theory*, Cambridge University Press, Cambridge, England, 1971.
116. W. A. Cook, S. J., A case grammar matrix, in *Georgetown University Working Papers on Languages and Linguistics, No. 6*, Georgetown University Press, Washington, D.C., 1972, pp. 15–48.
117. G. Salton, Manipulation of trees in information retrieval, *Commun. ACM* **5**(2), 105–114 (1962).
118. M. F. Lynch, J. M. Harrison, W. G. Town, and J. E. Ash, *Computer Handling of Chemical Structure Information*, MacDonald, London, 1971.
119. W. T. Wipke, S. R. Heller, R. J. Feldmann, and E. Hyde, *Computer Representation and Manipulation of Chemical Information*, Wiley, New York, 1974.
120. S. M. Strong, *An Algorithm for Generating Structural Surrogates of English Text*, Computer and Information Science Research Center, OSU-CISRC-TR-73-3, The Ohio State University, Columbus, Ohio, 1973.
121. S. M. Strong, An algorithm for generating structural surrogates of English text, *J. Am. Soc. Inf. Sci.* **25**(1), 10–22 (1974).
122. Aesop's Fables, Belling the cat, in *The Family Treasury of Children's Stories Book II* (P. R. Evans, ed.), Doubleday, Garden City, New York, 1956, p. 6.
123. I. Nickelsen and H. Nickelsen, Mathematische analyse des TOSAR-verfahrens, *Inf. Storage Retr.* **9**(2), 95–119 (1973).
124. R. E. Maizell, J. F. Smith, and T. E. R. Singer, *Abstracting Scientific and Technical Literature*, Wiley-Interscience, New York, 1971, p. 74.
125. W. Stevens, *Opus Posthumous: Poems, Plays, Prose* (S. F. Morse, ed.), Knopf, New York, 1957, p. 170.

5
Machine Translation

Winfred Lehmann / University of Texas, Austin, Texas

AIM AND REQUIREMENTS

Aim

Machine translation (MT) has the aim of translating material from one human language into another by computer. It is designed primarily for the scientific and technical materials produced in great quantities by our advanced society, and in large part rapidly superseded. Since these lose much of their value unless translated virtually at once, MT seems an ideal means of making them more generally accessible, especially if it can be carried out reliably and cheaply.

Its most influential early proponent was Warren Weaver, secretary of the Rockefeller Foundation. In 1946, shortly after the computer had been developed, Weaver proposed that it be used for translation, arguing that languages are codes and could thus be translated by a machine designed for the management of symbols. Formulating his views in a paper labeled "Translation," he sent this on July 15, 1949, to several hundred colleagues. The paper led to the first serious work on MT, to conferences, and publications [18, 19, 26].

One of the most prominent early scholars in the field was the late Yehoshua Bar-Hillel who organized a conference at M.I.T. in 1952 and published a paper on the state of research [1]. He subsequently guided the direction of research by successive articles and papers [2, 3]. Work was inaugurated in other countries as well, notably England, France, Germany, and the USSR. Comprehensive surveys of this work were provided by Delavenay [9] and by Josselson [13].

Support for research was stimulated by a demonstration in 1954 arranged by Leon Dostert and Paul Garvin of Georgetown University in conjunction with Peter Sheridan of IBM. Subsequently various centers of research, notably Georgetown, Harvard (Anthony Oettinger), and M.I.T. (Victor Yngve), received grants and con-

---

From Lehmann, Winfred. *Machine Translation.* ENCYCLOPEDIA OF COMPUTER SCIENCE AND TECHNOLOGY. Vol. 10. Edited by Jack Belzer, Albert Holzman and Allen Kent, New York, Marcel Dekker, Inc., c1978. pp. 151-164.

Machine Translation

tracts to implement MT. By 1964 these had amounted to 20 million dollars, yet no system had been devised which produced translation without considerable postediting [6].

Sponsors of research then asked the National Academy of Sciences to set up a committee to review the situation. The report of the Automatic Language Processing Committee (ALPAC) under the chairmanship of John R. Pierce, issued in 1966, was highly critical of MT. It did not recommend further support for MT, but rather for computational linguistics in general and for mechanical aids to human translators. This report had a severe impact. Research was greatly reduced, so that progress virtually ceased. Some curtailed projects were maintained, especially where there was particular awareness that rapid translation of large quantities of material is essential, as in the Common Market and in countries with emphasis on bilingualism, like Canada. Of late, this realization has been strengthening, so that once again there are prospects for research support, as noted below.

Linguistic Requirements

A primary reason for the disillusionment with MT and the slow progress in MT research is the immense complexity of language and the inadequacy of the grammars and dictionaries available for even the most extensively studied languages.

A language is an open-ended system which can yield an infinite number of sentences. When people learn their native language, they master this system in such a way that they can produce and recognize sentences which have never been produced before. They also can distinguish between grammatical and ungrammatical sentences. No grammar, however, has been produced which encompasses this capability. The grammars which are available for learning a second language contain rules which permit speakers to recognize the similarities and differences between the target language and their own. But details are often mastered by individual observations rather than from carefully formulated rules. Second language learning, like first language learning, is then in part intuitive.

To carry out MT of any variety, extensive grammars with precise rules[1] must be produced. Precise rules are necessary because of the ambiguity in languages, and because one-to-one lexical correspondence between languages is rare; moreover, languages differ considerably in their surface structures.

A brief example may illustrate the ambiguity of natural language. In one context the statement He declined may mean "He refused"; in another it may mean "His health worsened." Words typically have multiple meanings, such as table in its concrete and figurative uses, and in its meaning "chart." Humans disambiguate by noting cotext or context of an utterance. Simulating this capacity on a computer involves considerable ingenuity and study.

Cotextual and contextual information must also be included in MT dictionaries because words can rarely be translated with single equivalents, especially common words. Thus English know must be translated with German kennen if its object is a person, with wissen if a fact, and with koennen if a skill. Rules can indeed be provided to assure such translations, but they involve considerable computer storage. Neither the early computer technology nor the computer programs were adequate to provide huge storage with rapid access.

---

[1] "Rule" in the sense of determination of normal usage—i.e., a "regularity" rather than a "regulation."

Other problems, as in the syntactic and semantic analysis of the languages concerned, had not been adequately identified, so that much linguistic research as well as improved computer technology was required before a partial MT system could be developed. Such problems may be illustrated by examining briefly the expression of definiteness in selected languages. In English this is conveyed largely by use of the definite article. Russian, on the other hand, one of the languages in greatest demand for MT, contains no articles; definiteness is expressed by other devices which are not described in available grammars. Before acceptable MT from Russian to English is possible, the Russian devices for indicating definiteness must be described.

Another language of concern for MT, Chinese, also lacks articles. Definiteness may be indicated in Chinese by placing a noun before the verb; thus the Chinese sequence: <u>man dog see</u> (to use English lexical equivalents) would correspond to English <u>The man sees the dog</u>, while <u>man see dog</u> would correspond to English <u>The man sees a dog</u>. Before MT research, grammars did not attempt to describe such details. English speakers who learned Russian and Chinese mastered them by practice based on observation and on trial and error.

Similarly, no adequate rules for use of the definite article in English had been provided. One rule was that nouns used a second time in an account require the definite article, as in fairy tales: <u>Once upon a time there was a beautiful princess. The princess</u> . . . . Yet this rule is not specific enough to program a computer to handle sequences like the following, which requires a definite article in the first use of a noun: <u>She was reciting Hiawatha. The poem excited her students.</u>

This example of the problems involved in achieving accurate translations of definite articles may illustrate that MT could not be instituted simply by programming the grammars that were available before the advent of computers. Rather, translations must be based on determination of deeper structures arrived at through syntactic and semantic analysis. This requirement, as noted below, led to the development of transformational grammars which deal with underlying as well as surface structure in their linguistic descriptions.

Linguistic descriptions involve dictionaries as well as grammars. Languages have traditionally been described in two processes: production of grammars, which deal with the arrangement and classes of elements, and production of dictionaries, or lexicons, which define those elements. Just as grammars of the past are inadequate, so are the dictionaries.

Large, so-called unabridged dictionaries contain approximately half a million words. Even in this large stock, many technical terms are omitted—the technical terms in one science alone, chemistry, far exceed a half million. Often, too, the definitions in available dictionaries are insufficiently precise to meet the requirements of MT. For example, a large German dictionary defines <u>beugen</u> as "bend, bow down" and the like, but does not indicate its widespread meaning in technical use: "diffract." Moreover, MT systems must include capabilities for dealing with new technical terms since MT is directed at translating journals, monographs, and other avenues of information while this is fresh and of vital concern. Dictionaries as well as grammars must therefore be amplified, and continuous lexical research must be maintained to account for new words as scientific disciplines develop. Even so, no MT system attempts to account for the entire language. Accommodation of technical and scientific lexica is the primary demand. In any event, the linguistic requirements for MT are formidable.

Computational Requirements

Computer requirements, both hardware and software, are similarly demanding. Early computers were particularly designed for purposes such as numerical analysis; MT, on the other hand, is carried out by data processing techniques. Early MT research therefore had to deal with steps necessary for adapting computational processes to data manipulation. Initially consideration was given to the development of special-purpose computers. Some were actually built, notably the Mark II used by the Foreign Technology Division (FTD) of the U.S. Air Force Base at Dayton, Ohio, at the time of the ALPAC report. Yet research in MT makes up such a comparatively small proportion of computer applications that the undertaking was soon abandoned and available general-purpose computers were used.

Likewise, the early computer languages such as FORTRAN were developed for the purpose of numerical manipulation. MT projects had the possibility of modifying these or of working directly with machine language. Either option required massive programming activity. This led to the development of the first computer language achieved for data-processing, COMIT, designed by Yngve. Currently, projects make use of the subsequently developed systems such as SNOBOL and LISP.

Whatever the choice of computer and programs, the storage requirements for even a carefully selected lexicon and the accompanying grammar vastly exceeded the storage capabilities available in computer. (Even today a dictionary as small as the Merriam-Webster Collegiate taxes the storage of the typical large computer facility characteristic of a university.) For an MT system to function at all, the lexicon had to be stored on tapes; access time was slow, as was translation.

The vision of MT proposed by Weaver thus required a huge amount of preparatory research before even simple MT systems could be tested. This research fell to two fields, one of which—computer sciences—was nonexistent in 1947, and the other—linguistics—was so new that there was only one small linguistics department in the universities of the United States. It is scarcely surprising that development was slow.

THE DESIGN OF MT SYSTEMS

MT is a problem in applied linguistics. To achieve the aim of automatic translation by computer, an algorithmic system for language analysis, including specialized grammars, lexicons, and programs, must be designed and implemented.

Linguistic Strategies in the Designing of an MT System

Traditional linguistics dealt with language as though it consisted of several strata. The recurrent patterns were treated in the grammar; the less frequent in the lexicon. The elements listed in dictionaries are generally words, but some are idioms. Thus expressions like go without saying are listed in the lexicon on the grounds that this is an idiom, but not sequences like go without saying goodbye. By appropriate entries for idioms one can distinguish between them and nonidiomatic patterns, such as go without one's overcoat. Each word of the latter type of sequence is listed separately in a dictionary, and the relationship between them is described in the grammar. Current linguistics also recognizes a distinction between the grammar and the lexicon, although the terminology is not always the same as that of earlier linguistics.

MT systems are designed to manage language by means of these two components. The lexicon is listed in stores; the grammar is handled by means of algorithms. In implementing these activities, various practical problems arise.

One must decide, for example, whether to analyze compounds, e.g., light-ray, and list each element separately, or to include the compound in the lexicon. The decision may vary, depending on the languages involved and on computer capabilities. German, for example, is notorious for its lengthy compounds, especially in technical writing: fire insurance company is one word in German: Feuerversicherungsgesellschaft. Moreover, such compounds may be created freely, like English nominal phrases. Accordingly, it seemed necessary in early MT projects to develop procedures for automatically analyzing compounds into their constituents rather than to list all possible compounds as separate entries. The decision was influenced by restrictions on storage capacity and access time to the data. Today, with the relatively recent development of huge storage capacities, a different decision might be warranted. Yet, however such problems are handled, the lexical difficulties are far smaller than are the grammatical.

One of the long-studied problems of grammars is the treatment of synonymous sentences. The formerly popular Advanced English Grammar of Kittredge and Farley [15] recognizes the equivalence of sentences like the following (p. 135): It was a pleasure to see him and To see him was a pleasure. Another example showing a similar equivalence relationship is: It is easy to understand you; compare You are easy to understand. Relating such semantically equivalent sentences (the relationships have been referred to as transformational) has occupied much of the attention of recent linguistics. Besides studying specific patterns like those with easy, linguists have explored the extent of all such relationships in languages, especially in English.

Another pattern which has received extensive attention is the passive. This also had been studied by traditional grammarians, who generally treated it as did Kittredge and Farley (p. 110):

> Any sentence of which the predicate is a transitive verb followed by an object, may be changed from the active to the passive without affecting the sense.
>
> ACTIVE   Richard shot the bear.
> PASSIVE The bear was shot by Richard.

In recent grammars the passive has been considered a transform of the active, yet there have been no analyses which are generally accepted by all transformationalists, for some passive-type constructions are not simple transforms of actives, e.g., They were taken by surprise.

Whatever the terms used, or the specific rules, a grammar is clearly much simpler if such related constructions can be considered equivalent, and the simpler or more natural variant can be treated as more fundamental. An MT grammar with such an approach would obviously be more economical than one which set out to analyze each sentence into a subject and a predicate, regardless of its relationships with other sentences.

Such a transformational approach may be applied by analyzing surface structures of sentences and determining the simpler varieties, e.g., Richard shot the bear. This is the procedure pursued by Zellig Harris who originated transformational grammar.

The approach can also be applied by assuming an underlying "simple variety" comparable to a concept which then is variously expressed and modified to become the actual surface sentence. This is the transformational approach pursued by Harris's student, Noam Chomsky. In the 1960s this approach aroused tremendous enthusiasm among young linguists and among nonlinguists such as psychologists [10], for it seemed that the underlying patterns posited for the surface structures permitted insights into the functioning of the mind. Yet today, many of the more active syntacticians are returning to research which agrees with the approach of Harris, combining it with simultaneous "semantic" analysis, in procedures inspired by the logician Richard Montague. (See Partee [22], for example.)

Linguists concerned with MT also tried the two approaches, but much of the publication on which they attempted to draw was directed at providing support for transformational generative theory rather than at describing languages more precisely. Accordingly, much research carried out in transformational generative grammar, some of it funded by MT projects, had little pertinence for MT.

The transformational approach, however, brought attention to formal structures into linguistics. These are clearly well-suited for computer manipulation of language. Moreover, they can be examined for their adequacy by procedures known as grammar testers; these analyze the rules proposed in a grammar, whether it is designed for MT or for theoretical purposes. Computational techniques thus came to be a powerful research tool for linguists [12].

Grammars designed for MT must devise procedures for relating surface structures with units of meaning. For this purpose "deep" structures are posited and related to the surface structures. Grammars must be produced for these various levels. The use of these grammars may be illustrated by reference to problems resulting from the presence of discontinuous elements in language, such as took . . . down in She took the unusual words down. After their identification in a surface grammar they are brought together in a further grammar, so that the verb and the particle can be treated as a unit. In such a grammar of the deep structure they are regarded as a semantic unit, equivalent to "note." An MT system in this way analyzes sentences of a source language with a surface grammar and various additional grammars to identify the underlying structures. These are then transposed into the target language using a comparable set of grammars for that language.

The grammars of an MT system are thus designed in accordance with the understanding of language achieved in linguistics. The rules they incorporate are highly precise and inclusive. In the same way, the dictionaries start from traditional dictionaries but proceed to more specific analyses of use and meaning, indicating these through subscripted features accompanying the lexical entries. Other components of an MT system, such as the recognition procedures, are determined at least in part by computer capabilities.

Computational Strategies: Search and Parsing

Search Procedures

However the linguistic analysis is produced, arrangements must also be made to recognize accurately the words of the initial input string and to relate them to other words in the sentence, that is, to simulate reading. The computerized process is known as search. A search may be done in various ways, one by identifying each word from left to right and matching it with an entry in the lexicon. After identification, parsing is produced. This procedure leads to complexities, especially in lengthy sentences, but also in a simple sentence like: <u>She took the unusual words down</u>. Here the analysis of <u>took</u> is determined in part by the last word. Procedures must then be included to move backwards as well as to read from left to right.

An alternate procedure, devised by Paul Garvin, focuses on the words of a sentence in accordance with their grammatical significance rather than by their linear order of occurrence. This procedure, called the fulcrum approach, first identifies the major syntactic elements, like the subject and its verb, and only later their modifiers. These, such as the adjective <u>unusual</u> in the example above, are then processed in their relation to the central structure.

At present the "reading" of input texts is readily accomplished as a result of extensive work in the early MT research.

Parsing Procedures

In designing an MT system, the rules for parsing sentences can be incorporated in the computer algorithm, or the algorithm and the grammar can be kept separate. By the first kind of design, the system would consist of two components: a lexicon and a translating algorithm. Such a system is known as bipartite. By the second, the system would be tripartite, consisting of a lexicon, a grammar, and a table of computational rules which could be used with any grammar of any language.

The initial MT systems, notably those developed at Georgetown University, were bipartite. These systems have been extensively used in production by the U.S. Air Force Foreign Technology Division (FTD), the AEC Oak Ridge National Laboratory, and the Scientific Information Processing Center of EURATOM, and commercially by LATSEC, Inc.

As late as 1971 Garvin argued in favor of a bipartite system, on the grounds that "the fundamental problem in the automatic recognition of grammatical structure of text is the correct sequencing of the application of the rules of the grammar which are supposed to effect the recognition. In this author's opinion, such a sequencing of the application of different grammatical rules can be effected only by making the rules of the grammar an organic part of the algorithm" [11, p. 109].

Yet bipartite systems have been criticized because they grow to be cumbersome. Such a grammar can indeed be readily programmed, but when it must be updated the added rules result in a minor program supplementing the original program. In time the translating algorithm of a bipartite system may come to be a patchwork which is very difficult to improve further.

In a tripartite system, on the other hand, the grammars may be extensively revised, with no need to modify the computational rules. Moreover, the same set of computational rules can be used for many languages, while in a bipartite system a new translating algorithm is necessary for each additional language. The tripartite design then would seem vastly superior. These differing approaches to parsing may illustrate that the design of a system is determined by strategies which are inherent in the new application of linguistics made possible by the development of computers.

Besides drawing on linguistics and computer sciences, MT also incorporates findings of rhetoric and stylistics. Sequences longer than sentences, often referred to as cotext in the domain of rhetoric, must be taken into consideration when translating.

One example was cited above: use of the definite article in English. Moreover, certain characteristics of language long studied in stylistics are especially prevalent among specific groups of language users or language used for specific purposes. Thus technical writing makes use of different patterns of expression from those of materials designed for a general audience. Technical German, for example, contains frequent preposed participial modifiers of nouns, which correspond to relative clauses; rarely found in the everyday form of the language, these modifiers constitute a special problem for any translation of scientific and technical German.

Support for this conclusion has been provided, especially in the computer-aided work of the New York University Linguistic String Project [24]. Concentrating on pharmaceutical texts, this has determined that technical writing makes use of special syntactic patterns as well as special vocabulary. "Intellectual verbs, like find, hypothesize, discover, which characteristically take human subjects" are found at the bottom of an analysis tree and "concrete words referring to objects in the science at the top," as in the example: "Carvalho and Leo found that the Ca^{++} uptake of skeletal SR involves the exchange of Ca^{++} with other cations in SR." Sager's analysis not only distinguishes the "words referring to the objects and relations in the science proper from statements the human investigator makes about those objects and relations" but also determines "definite classes, like quantity operators and causality operators" in characteristic positions [24, pp. 37-39]. Mechanical parsing has in this way led to the determination of characteristic semantic and syntactic patterning in scientific writing. Such results illustrate contributions of MT and related procedures to a deeper understanding of language. They also support the conclusion that MT is a distinct activity, requiring procedures that are best determined by drawing on a number of disciplines in relation to one another [16].

Summary of Strategies of Design

For more detailed information, interested readers might wish to refer to the specialized reports which are issued periodically by active research groups. Only a selection will be reviewed here, to illustrate the current situation and requirements for further improvements.

Any system must take the complex structure of language into consideration. Accordingly it must deal not only with the lexical elements, but also with syntax in its surface and deeper levels. In the brief history of MT there has been a progression from systems which basically translated word-for-word, to those which included attention to surface syntactic rules, and finally to those which deal also with deeper syntactic and semantic levels of language. These three progressively more sophisticated types of systems are referred to as first, second, and third generation systems. Current research groups generally aim at third generation systems [6, 17, 28].

THE CURRENT SITUATION

In view of its independent status, the field has suffered from not receiving steady support. Researchers, whether drawn from linguistics or computer sciences, may well develop competence in MT. But computational possibilities change so rapidly that continued experience is helpful for original research. Virtually all support for such research has been governmental, as is generally true for developing fields—and this has been interrupted, in Europe and the USSR as well as the United States, in great part as a result of the ALPAC report which led to virtually complete cessation of funding. Research groups were gradually disbanded, so that currently these are limited to relatively small projects, of which those at Grenoble, Saarbrücken, and Montreal will be noted briefly here. As evidence of the decline of research after the publication of the report, it may be noted that the March 18, 1977 issue of Science devoted to electronics does not even mention MT.

On the other hand, The Commission of European Communities recently arranged the Third European Congress on Information Systems and Networks, with the theme: Overcoming the Language Barrier [8]. The proceedings of this meeting contain reports on some of the ongoing research projects.

The Centre d'Études de la Traduction Automatique (CETA) at Grenoble, under the direction of Bernard Vauquois, has the longest record of continuous research [4, 25]. Moreover, its system has been tested with the largest quantity of texts. CETA draws on various linguistic theories, making use of dependency as well as transformational and phrase structure analysis. It deals with translation in three stages: analysis of the source language; interlingual mapping; and synthesis of the target language sentences, making use of a "language pivot." A parser has been developed for labeled tree structures in which the nodes of the tree include the morphosyntactic and semantic/logical data necessary for transfer to the target language. The primary aim of the project is translation from Russian to French, although grammars have been studied and tested for other languages as well, such as Japanese and English.

The Saarbrücken Automatic Translation System (SUSY) is being developed to carry out translation from Russian to German, with some work also being done on other languages such as French and English. Considerable attention is being given to automatic identification of lemmata (words reduced to their basic forms) in German texts. This is done by means of a mechanized lexicon containing 100,000 entries [20]. The grammars under development classify elements not simply by their syntactic use, but also by their function; thus pareil "similar" is treated as a "deictor" or article word rather than an adjective [27]. SUSY thus illustrates how MT may develop dictionaries and grammars designed specifically for the automatic analysis of languages rather than the work of traditional or contemporary linguistics.

MT research in Canada is prompted by the government's policy of biculturalism. In keeping with it the Canadian State Department's Translation Bureau "has undertaken to develop a second-generation system for machine translation of technical manuals" [7]. The system, being developed under a contract with the TAUM project of the University of Montreal, is to be put into operation in November 1978. Time requirements necessitate the immediate development of a system rather than further research, and hence the restriction to a second-generation level, involving only lexical and morphosyntactic analysis, on which English-French transfer will be based. Confidence in useful results is derived from the success of the METEO system "which is used for the translation of weather forecasts intended for the general public" [7].

In the United States, research at Austin and Berkeley is being done to incorporate advances in computational activity into systems devised earlier. The aim is production of a third-generation system. There is hope of close cooperation among these various research groups and also of utilization of previous accomplishments.

EVALUATION OF MT

As noted above, work on MT has been severely criticized. Taking no consideration of the obsolete system in use at the time, the ALPAC report concluded that translations performed by translators supported by the government were cheaper and better than those produced by FTD [23, p. 28]. It cannot be denied that the new field of MT attracted some inadequate workers, nor that the translations produced with TDS's Mark II required considerable postediting and accordingly were expensive. Computational costs have, however, been reduced as systems have been improved, while the costs of human translators are constantly rising. It is also acknowledged that there have been considerable advances in MT research [14, pp. 225-226]. Whether these advances could have been made without waste is a question that may be viewed in the larger context of all technological developments. The history of MT research might be compared with that of research to meet future energy needs; all the funds used for MT would scarcely maintain some energy projects for a fraction of a year. But as Kay states [14, p. 219], after the ALPAC report "any application . . . for financial support for a project involving language and computers . . . could expect a swift and categorical refusal." Human frailty seems to involve error and waste in any technological advance, whether it concerns transportation, energy, or communication.

MT gains its appeal and support from the problems arising from the huge amount of publication currently produced, and from the short-lived usefulness of that publication. Technological and scientific materials are made available in vast quantities, whether in English, Chinese, French, German, Italian, Japanese, Russian, Spanish, or other languages, and much of it is soon out of date. (Some scholars assert half-seriously that any scientific article is out of date by the time it is printed.) A scientific article written in a foreign language may then be of little use if it is not translated at once.

Moreover, bilingual countries like Canada mandate by law the translation of huge quantities of government documents virtually overnight. There are also projects such as the one currently under way in Canada for the translation of technical manuals associated with the employment of the Aurora missile [7]. And the European Common Market countries arrange translation of many materials from any of the official languages—English, Danish, Dutch, French, German, Italian— into any other, making a total of 30 combinations. These requirements gain urgency as educational systems have greatly reduced the study of foreign languages, even in Europe where the tradition of foreign language teaching was strong.

Yet the adverse criticisms have discouraged investigators as well as suppliers of funding. Linguists who consider themselves devoted to theory give MT little attention. In the 50 year index to Language, the journal of the Linguistic Society of America, there is only one reference to MT (Vol. 32, 1956) and this is a review of a collection of essays. Although MT does not enjoy a favorable evaluation today, its future will no doubt be determined by social needs, which when sufficiently pressing will change funding and attitudes.

Future research will be greatly assisted by the remarkable improvements in computer hardware and software. These will also affect the method of output. The huge data stores required for manipulation of human language are no longer such a problem for the computers of today, when rapidly accessible disk storage facilities are available. But systems will have to be carefully designed for economical storage of these data, with rapid access in spite of their bulk. Moreover, computer languages like LISP have now been designed for handling large data bases, so that programmers no longer have to modify the technically suited computer languages. Further, input and output facilities have been greatly improved. While scanning devices have not been developed as rapidly as was promised, language material is now widely available on magnetic tape; it can be transmitted to the computer in more flexible ways than through the cumbersome keypunch machine. Moreover, output can be quickly displayed on CRT terminals, diminishing the need for printout. These advances in computer technology will no doubt lead to MT which is displayed on a

CRT, with the possibility of simultaneous running display of the original. Users will then have the option of rapidly scanning a desired text in much the same way they would scan texts available in their native languages, and the cumbersome process of printing huge amounts of text of uncertain value can be dispensed with.

On the other hand the linguistic contributions to MT have made fewer advances than has the computational area. The necessary large, precisely defined lexical stores were not being assembled in the absence of funding. Nor were the necessary syntactic and morphological analyses being produced. To be sure, great attention is being given by linguists to syntactic study; but much of this focuses on specific problems in English which have come to be focal points in constructing theories. For example, though the relative clause and its relation to its antecedent has been examined copiously, the aim of the studies is to test theory rather than to provide improved understanding of the construction, which previous grammarians understood and described thoroughly. But for MT, complete grammars are equally required for both source and target languages. Hence it is necessary to continue research in compilation of large linguistic data bases. The development of the requisite systems is accordingly a long-range undertaking.

IMPLICATIONS AND SPIN-OFFS OF MT RESEARCH

As mentioned earlier, when MT research was undertaken languages were not precisely described nor were their lexical elements defined in detail. Language learning is so intuitive a process that even punctilious scholars failed to note all the properties of lexical items or grammatical constructions until computers produced the nonsensical output which incomplete descriptions of language yield. While computational linguistics on its own might have led to the detection of inadequacies, and then to improved grammars and dictionaries, work toward MT has made clear the accuracy and thoroughness required for the analysis and description of language.

Besides MT, computerized analysis is involved in automatic indexing, in data retrieval, and in fact retrieval. Indexing has been carried out from time immemorial, especially for texts of highest prestige in our society. Thus the Bible and the Homeric poems have been provided with indices and concordances which in the past might involve the life effort of one or even several scholars. Today such tools are produced readily by computer programs which are routinely used in MT research. Indexing, however, has remained at the lexical or first-generation level. The widely used KWIC (keyword-in-context) indexing has indeed developed skillful techniques. But these techniques yield only that information which can be derived from identification of word-forms. When indexing systems incorporate the parsers developed for mechanical translation, their usefulness will be greatly enhanced.

Research in MT will make contributions to other facilities as well, such as question-answering systems, and will profit from insights in such research. These systems are now used with relatively homogeneous data bases as in airline ticketing, in banking, and in accessing medical data. When combined with large lexical stores such as the syntactic and semantic algorithms developed in MT research, they may be extended to provide access to a wide variety of information.

The syntactic and morphological analysis carried out in second-generation MT research will permit the construction of data processing systems. When semantic analysis is added, systems can be devised which process facts. Queries then will not be restricted in their scope to the individual items included in data stores, but they will encompass related "facts," regardless of their linguistic expression.

Projection of such computerized capabilities has led to proposals in artificial intelligence whose essential aim is to simulate the activities of the human brain. This involves not only the retrieval of facts and data but also the understanding of a situation. Such understanding requires concern for the setting in which a linguistic utterance is produced as well as the analysis of that utterance. In aiming at such achievement, artificial intelligence research has led to the proposal of restricted settings, known by various names, among them "scenarios," which are important in determining the meanings of utterances. For example, speakers of English will interpret differently the following utterance depending on their knowledge of the actors involved in a given setting of the scenario: She ought to be here by now. If the referent of she is in some way under the authority of the speaker, the utterance will be interpreted: "There is an obligation which normally would require her to be here at this time." If the referent is someone not under such authority, the utterance will be interpreted: "She generally would have arrived by this time. (Some difficulty must have interfered with her expected behavior.)" The computational study of language has in this way led to fuller recognition of the complexities involved in human communication, which extends to the study of perception as well as of language.

When such complexities are revealed they are by no means studied only by computational linguists or specialists in MT. Miller and Johnson-Laird have produced an intriguing study relating perceptual knowledge about the world to language use [21]. This has led to their proposal of a procedural approach to semantics, and to the study of memory systems. In their introduction, Miller and Johnson-Laird state that "the wide range of theoretical possibilities that modern computers suggest provides much of our present motivation to search for psychological, linguistic, anthropological, or other substantive boundary conditions on hypotheses about lexical memory" [21, p. 6].

The manipulation of language by computer which began in the effort to achieve machine translation has accordingly disclosed many problems and opened many areas of research. As our knowledge of language and its use is increased, these will be illuminated, though possibly not before the accomplishment of improved mechanical translation. MT of technical materials is one of the simplest linguistic applications involving computers. Its progressive advances will provide data which will then be available for more complex research areas and applications, such as the study of perception, of memory, and of storage of information in the brain. MT thus has numerous implications for other areas of research, as well as its central purpose, the rapid and automatic translations of texts.

ACKNOWLEDGMENTS

I am grateful to Helen-Jo Hewitt, Zbigniew L. Pankowicz, and Solveig M. V. Pflueger for assistance in preparing this article.

REFERENCES

1. Bar-Hillel, Y., The present state of research on mechanical translation, Am. Doc. 2, 229-237 (1951). (Reprinted in Ref. 2.)
2. Bar-Hillel, Y., Language and Information, Addison-Wesley, Reading, Massachusetts, 1964.
3. Bar-Hillel, Y., Some reflections on the present outlook for high-quality machine translation, pp. 73-76 in Vol. I of Ref. 17.

4. Boitet, Ch., Un essai de réponse a quelques questions théoriques et practiques liées à la traduction automatique. Définition d'un système prototype. Thèse d'Etat, Grenoble, 1976.
5. Booth, A. D. (ed.), Machine Translation, North-Holland, Amsterdam; Wiley, New York; 1967.
6. Bruderer, H., Handbuch der maschinellen und maschinenunterstützten Sprachübersetzung, Fink, Munich, 1977.
7. Chandioux, J., Creation of a second-generation system for machine translation of technical manuals, pp. 613-621 in Ref. 8.
8. Commission of the European Communities, Overcoming the Language Barrier (Third European Congress on Information Systems and Networks, Luxembourg, May 3-6, 1977), Vol. 1, Verlag Dokumentation, Munich, 1977.
9. Delavenay, E., La Machine à Traduire (Que Sais-Je No. 834), Presses Universitaires de France, Paris, 1959.
10. Fodor, J. A., J. G. Bever, and M. F. Garrett, The Psychology of Language: An Introduction to Psycholinguistics and Generative Grammar, McGraw-Hill, New York, 1974.
11. Garvin, P. L., Operational problems of machine translation: A position paper, pp. 95-118 in Vol. I of Ref. 17.
12. Hays, D. G., Introduction to Computational Linguistics, Elsevier, New York, 1967.
13. Josselson, H. H., MT in the sixties: A linguist's view, Adv. Comput. 11, 1-58 (1971).
14. Kay, M., Automatic translation of natural languages, in Language as a Human Problem (E. Haugen and M. Bloomfield, eds.), Norton, New York, 1974, pp. 219-232.
15. Kittredge, G. L., and F. E. Farley, An Advanced English Grammar, Ginn, Boston, 1913.
16. Lehmann, W. P., Towards experimentation with language, Found. Language 1, 237-248 (1965).
17. Lehmann, W. P., and R. A. Stachowitz, Feasibility Study on Fully Automatic High Quality Translation, Vols. I and II (RADC-TR-71-295), Rome Air Development Center, Griffiss Air Force Base, Rome, New York, 1971.
18. Locke, W. N., Machine translation, in Encyclopedia of Library and Information Science, Vol. 16 (A. Kent, H. Lancour, and J. E. Daily, eds.), Dekker, New York, 1975, pp. 414-444.
19. Locke, W. N., and A. D. Booth (eds.), Machine Translation of Languages, Wiley, New York, 1955.
20. Maas, H. D., The Saarbrücken automatic translation system (SUSY), pp. 585-592 in Ref. 8.
21. Miller, G., and P. N. Johnson-Laird, Language and Perception, Harvard University Press, Cambridge, Massachusetts, 1976.
22. Partee, B. H. (ed.), Montague Grammar, Academic, New York, 1976.
23. Pierce, J. R. (chairman), et al., Language and Machines: Computers in Translation and Linguistics (A Report of the Automatic Language Processing Advisory Committee (ALPAC), Publication No. 1416, National Academy of Sciences-National Research Council, Washington, D.C., 1966.
24. Sager, N., Evaluation of Automated Natural Language Processing in the Further Development of Science Information Retrieval (String Program Reports No. 10), NYU Linguistic String Project, New York, 1976.

25. Vauquois, B., La traduction automatique à Grenoble, Dunod, Paris, 1975.
26. Weaver, W., Translation, pp. 15-23 in Ref. 19.
27. Weissenborn, J., The role and form of analysis in machine translation: The automatic analysis of French at Saarbrücken, pp. 593-611 in Ref. 8.
28. Yngve, V. H., Syntax and the problem of multiple meaning, pp. 210-213 in Ref. 19.

6

Machine Translation

William N. Locke* / Massachusetts Institute of Technology, Cambridge, Massachusetts

Machine translation, or automatic translation as it is sometimes called, is used here in the sense of translation from one natural language to another by computer. After some general considerations about translation, the challenges it offers, and the computer as a tool, the evolution of machine translation from the first conception to the present will be traced in three phases, ending with a discussion of a number of operating systems and a brief survey of current research.

Translation

Machine translation (MT) can be justified only if it is better, faster, or cheaper than human translation (HT); so comparisons between the two are in order, not only because economics will determine which wins out but more importantly because a better understanding of each can come from study and research into the other. HT may not be the best model for MT but it is the only one we have, so linguists and computer experts started from there. Up to now most of the work has been directed toward the translation of scientific and technical texts where the stylistic complications are less, speed is at a premium, and above all, there is more money.

Considering HT, let us ask two questions whose answers may seem surprising. First, what are the qualities that make a good translator of scientific and technical material? Experts generally agree that they are, in order of importance; (1) knowledge of the technical field of the text; (2) native command of the language to be translated into; and (3) knowledge of the language to be translated from. Intuitively, one would expect the order to be exactly the reverse.

From Locke, William N. *Machine Translation*. ENCYCLOPEDIA OF LIBRARY AND INFORMATION SCIENCE. Vol. 16. Edited by Allen Kent, Harold Lancour and Jay E. Daily. Assistant Editor, William Z. Nasri. New York, Marcel Dekker, Inc., c1975. pp. 414-444.
*Deceased

Second, how does a translator work? The commonly accepted model, that he takes the words and grammar of Language A and replaces them with words and grammar of Language B, is simply wrong. No translator works that way. What he really does is to read or listen to the text in Language A to get the idea—and it is here that a knowledge of the technical field is essential—then he expresses the same meaning in Language B. Meaning is the substance of communication. Words and grammar are arbitrary conventions which have evolved over the years and differ from one language to another.

MEANING

Meaning (semantics) involves the sum total of all human experience, including its interpretation. For an individual it is the experiential environment shared with people of the same culture—what has been called "the encyclopedia in your head." Each word in our language carries an aura of associations which we have to sense in order to interpret it: word + associations = meaning. There are never two completely synonymous words in the same language—all their associations would have to be identical. Likewise, no word is an exact translation of any word in another language. That is why a translator can work only with ideas, i.e., meanings. He is able to equate words plus associations with meanings in two languages. His translation process is: word in Language A + associations = meaning = word in Language B + associations.

We tend to think of reading or hearing as linear phenomena, the one in space, the other in time, but the process of understanding is far from linear. The first few words we see or hear tell us in general what meaning to expect. We are constantly racing ahead in our minds, predicting what the author is going to say, checking to see that our prediction was right, trying one or more other interpretations if we were wrong. It is a curious fact that we are able to use this error correction device simultaneously on several levels. In a conversation we predict successive sounds, words, phrases, and sentences; filling in gaps caused by noise, strange accent, or careless speech until they make sense. Likewise in written text we correct misprints without even seeing them and fix up missing words or transposed lines as best we can, always on the basis of what "makes sense." Making sense; that is, having a meaning that fits the total context, is the ultimate criterion.

Simmons shows the implications for the computers of the 1960s:

> Evidence from psycholinguistic studies indicates that humans can select a particular sentence interpretation only on the basis of probabilistic cues that result from linguistic and environmental contexts. No computer system yet planned is capable of dealing with this level of subtlety (*1*).

In other words, we humans hear what we expect to hear; we see what we expect to see. But we are always alert for any cue that indicates that our expectation was wrong. In that case, we take a second look at the text or play the spoken words back in our auditory memory and try a new interpretation that will make better sense.

But perhaps a computer does not have to understand the meaning of the text it is called upon to translate. After all, the "consumer" of the translation is a human with a brain. Maybe the computer can just translate words—a sort of automatic bilingual dictionary, giving several meanings if necessary, from which the human can choose. That is the way MT started, but the automatic dictionary is a poor crutch. It reminds one of the way foreign languages are frequently taught to humans—you give the student the translations of a few words and some grammar rules and he tries to work out the meaning of simple sentences. Then he tries to compose some. He is working from words to meaning and it is a frustrating process, slow and full of mistakes. This is not at all the way he learned his own language. According to Macnamara,

> ... infants learn their mother tongue by first determining, independent of language, the meaning which a speaker intends to convey to them and then working out the relationship between the meaning and the expression they heard. In other words, the infant uses meaning as a clue to language, rather than language as a clue to meaning (2).

Unfortunately, what Simmons wrote in 1966 is still true. Computers cannot predict meaning. This puts MT at a disadvantage with respect to each of the three requirements for a good human translator. With respect to the first, knowledge of the field, up to now no one has been able to build into a computer knowledge of a technical field such as a human specialist would have. As to command of human languages, native and foreign, involving as it does not only vocabulary and grammar but a whole encyclopedia of past experience of the individual and the race, this, too, is in the speculative future for computers.

Before going on, the matter of getting an input to a computer should be mentioned. From a written text it is a relatively easy matter of keyboarding or of optical recognition, but what of speech? To use the human analogy again, a baby hears and imitates the sounds its mother makes. It learns to map speech sounds into words and sentences with the aid of meaning. Macnamara says ". . . the main thrust in language learning comes from the child's need to understand and to express himself" (2).

Once again the computer has to work with less information than the human has. In normal speech there are no individual sounds or groups of sounds corresponding to letters or syllables or written words in any absolute sense. There are no pauses corresponding to the spaces between written letters or words.

Moreover, humans are able to interpret physically different combinations of sounds pronounced by different people with different voice quality and different accents as one and the same word. We do it, once again, by relying on the broad experiential context as well as the other words in the sentence. From this we predict the probable meaning, and decide what the individual words are.

Someone has likened the normal flow of speech to an omelette which you have to unscramble to find the individual words. Human beings do it effortlessly and unconsciously, but to get an input from speech to a computer requires a translation process analogous to that from one written language to another.

Though the terminology of some proponents of MT seems to imply that they are processing the spoken language, the fact is that no one has been able to get an input from speech to a computer. As Otten says,

Machine Translation

> The optimism expressed in the mid and late fifties that speech recognition is primarily a matter of developing faster and more powerful computers has been replaced by the realization that we know too little about speech even to specify the computer one would like to have, much less to speak of programming it (3).

Under the circumstance, research has concentrated on translating the written language, and that has provided a sufficient number of challenges; for instance, the resolution of ambiguity.

AMBIGUITY

When the meaning of a word or group of words is unclear, or when they have multiple meanings, they are said to be ambiguous. Rhodes (4) demonstrates the inevitability of ambiguity as follows: The human brain can engender 10^{100} concepts, far more than the 10^{80} elementary particles in the universe. An outside estimate for the number of words an individual might know is 10^6 or 10^7. So we cannot hope to coin a word for every new concept but are doomed to a situation where almost every word must bear several connotations.

Ambiguity, like its antonym, redundancy, is not only unavoidable, it plays a constructive role in communication. It allows one to remain vague when being precise would be wrong or harmful. Nevertheless, it may stand in the way of knowing exactly what the author meant. Redundancy helps resolve ambiguity. It makes assurance doubly sure. It is essential to get a message through in the presence of noise. In HT and in MT every available cue to the meaning must be used. The goal is to make the translation contain exactly the same amount of ambiguity and redundancy as the original. Otherwise *traduttore–traditore,* as the Italians say, translator–traitor.

Ambiguity can exist on the word, the syntactical, or the meaning level. Word ambiguity occurs mainly in isolated words. In Webster's Second Edition (5), "head" has fifty-one different meanings, thirty-six as a noun, eleven as a verb, and four as an adjective. Most word ambiguity disappears as soon as the word is in context.

Syntactical ambiguity occurs when two or more interpretations of the sentence structure are possible. An example is "Time flies." The ambiguity may not be immediately evident, but add a second sentence, "You cannot." Now the meaning of the first is changed but both are still ambiguous, as is shown by adding a third sentence, "Their flight is too swift." In any communication situation, syntactical ambiguity, like word ambiguity, is usually resolved by context. The speaker or writer usually makes sure that his meaning is clear. He should know his audience and be specific enough in his references to inform but not to insult them.

Semantic ambiguity is illustrated by the following:

> I called you Friday.
> I will call you Friday.

From the tense of the verb in the first sentence we know the day of the call was the previous Friday; from the tense in the second, the following Friday; but in order to know the date of either "Friday" we would have to know when the sentence was spoken or written. This is a first semantic ambiguity. There is a second. Perhaps the speaker is Robinson Crusoe. Now a whole new range of possible interpretations for both sentences comes to mind. Once again context, the total context, can resolve ambiguity.

Semantic ambiguity is compounded in translation. The area of meaning of a word in one language does not correspond exactly to the area of meaning of any one word in the other. Some Eskimo dialects have a number of words for "snow" depending on its quality. In English should we translate them all simply as "snow" or should we "annotate" each occurrence by adding an adjective like "grainy, flaky, mixed with water?" Obviously a lot has to be known about Eskimo as well as English usage to handle "snow."

If there are ambiguities, the translator tries to judge whether they are a function of differences in the two languages and cultures, in which case he tries to find the best way to resolve them in his translation, or whether they are purposeful on the part of the author, in which case he tries to find the right wording to retain them.

COMPUTERS AND PROGRAMMING

The "machines" of machine translation are a combination of hardware, which includes input and output devices plus one or more central processing units and memories, and software, which includes all the instructions to the computer. As to the hardware, its development has carried it far beyond the ken of the average educated individual. Computers were originally designed to compute, i.e., to work with numbers. In order to handle text processing, new I/O devices, new logic, and larger, faster memories were necessary.* These have been introduced in such variety that hardware is no longer a problem; almost everything needed for MT can be had "off the shelf." Fortunately the users of this advanced technology need not understand the detail of its design or operation.

Programming is a different matter. We have not yet reached the point where there are standard programs which will run translations and linguistic research problems but we have come a long way since the beginning of MT. In Winter 1957–1958, Yngve (6) at M.I.T. designed a programming language, which he called COMIT, for the use of linguists working on MT. This language was described by Sammet in 1972 as "The first realistic string handling and pattern matching language; most of its features appear (although with different syntax) in any other language attempting to do string manipulation." The influence of COMIT can be seen in most of the languages used for automated language processing, particularly SNOBOL, EOL, L^6, and PL/1. Advances in programming have to some extent kept pace with advances in hardware, but Sammet can still conclude, "We have not solved the problem of how to bridge the gap between what the person wants to say about solving his problem and the physical circuits in the machine"(7).

These few comments on computers and programming will serve primarily to indicate the importance of the subject. For further information, see the appropriate

*It is understood that language is processed in a computer in coded patterns of electric impulses, not in its original form.

entries. We shall now go back to the beginning of MT and trace the three phases of its evolution from 1946 to the present.

Phase I: 1946–1952

The earliest known suggestion that a machine could be made to translate languages was a patent application filed in Moscow in 1933 by Smirnov-Troyanski. He claimed a method of simultaneous translation into several languages but unfortunately his scheme was visionary. Digital computers such as he would have needed to carry it out were not available for another 10 years during World War II. In 1946 Warren Weaver, secretary of the Rockefeller Foundation, and A. Donald Booth, director of the Birkbeck College Computation Laboratory in London, tentatively discussed the possible application of computers to the translation of languages. Weaver brought up the idea, developed 3 years later in a memorandum, "Translation" (8), that different languages are just different codes, the meaning of which could be discovered by breaking them with a computer as had been done during the war. Booth stressed the more immediately feasible goal of storing a bilingual dictionary in the computer memory and translating scientific articles word for word.

In the next few years Booth with others, notably Kathleen H. V. Britten at the Institute for Advanced Study in Princeton and Richard H. Richens of the Commonwealth Bureau of Plant Breeding and Genetics, Cambridge, England, did some experimenting. Booth and Richens worked out a simple word for word translation program in 1947. The deficiencies of this approach will be clear to anyone who has tried to puzzle out the meaning of a text in a language he does not know by looking up the words in a dictionary. Still, it was a start.

In 1948 Richens suggested an improvement. An ordinary dictionary, he reasoned, contains only the basic forms of words, the nominative singular of nouns, the infinitive of verbs; yet the case and number of noun forms and the person and number of verb forms are essential to real comprehension. But all the possible forms of every word far exceeded the memory capacity of the computers of the time. Therefore, he proposed that two bilingual dictionaries be put in the computer, a stem dictionary and an endings dictionary. The computer would take each successive word in the Language A text and look it up. If there was no match with any stem, it would "strip off" a letter at a time from the end until there was. Then it would store the corresponding B stem. Next it would look up the "stripped off" letters in the endings dictionary and finally combine the appropriate B endings with the B stem to give the correct translation.

On July 15, 1949 Weaver sent his "Translation" to some 200 of his acquaintances. To most it was the first suggestion they had ever heard that a computer might be used to translate languages. Because of its initial and enduring importance as a prediction and a program, it will be summarized here at some length:

The multiplicity of languages impedes cultural exchange and international understanding, he said, but electronic computers may be able to contribute to the solution of the worldwide translation problem. The fact that computers can break codes leads one to suppose that there are certain invariant properties which are, "to some statistically useful degree, common to all languages."

Weaver then quotes from a 1947 letter of his own to Norbert Wiener, the mathematician:

> Recognizing fully, even though necessarily vaguely, the semantic difficulties because of multiple meanings, etc., I have wondered if it were unthinkable to design a computer which would translate. Even if it would translate only scientific material (where the semantic difficulties are very notably less), and even if it did produce an inelegant (but intelligible) result, it would seem to me worth while.
>
> Also knowing nothing official about, but having guessed and inferred considerably about, powerful new mechanized methods in cryptography—methods which I believe succeed even when one does not know what language has been coded—one naturally wonders if the problem of translation could conceivably be treated as a problem in cryptography. When I look at an article in Russian, I say: "This is really written in English, but, it has been coded in some strange symbols. I will now proceed to decode."

Wiener in reply eptiomized the semantic problem:

> I frankly am afraid the boundaries of words in different languages are too vague and the emotional and international connotations are too extensive to make any quasimechanical translation scheme very hopeful.

Booth and Richens, says Weaver, were not concerned at the time with multiple meaning, word order, idiom, etc., but only with the problem of mechanizing a stem dictionary. A mechanized dictionary cannot hope to be useful for literary translation

> in which style is important and in which problems of idiom, multiple meanings, etc. are frequent. . . . Large volumes of technical material might be usefully, even if not at all elegantly handled this way. . . . In mathematics . . . one can very nearly say that each word . . . has one and only one meaning.

The problems of multiple meaning of general terms such as "fast" meaning "rapid" or "motionless," he suggests, can perhaps be decided by consulting a certain number of adjacent words, i.e., the context.

We must go so deeply into the structure of languages as to come down to the level where they exhibit common traits:

> For widely varying languages, the basic logical structures have important common features. . . . Think, by analogy, of individuals living in a series of tall closed towers, all erected over a common foundation. When they try to communicate with one another, they shout back and forth, each from his own closed tower. It is difficult to make the sound penetrate even the nearest towers, and communication proceeds very poorly indeed. But, when an individual goes down his tower, he finds himself in a great open basement, common to all the towers. Here he establishes easy and useful communication with the persons who have also descended from their towers.
>
> Thus may it be true that the way to translate from Chinese to Arabic, or from Russian to Portuguese, is not to attempt the direct route, shouting from tower to tower. Perhaps the way is to descend, from each language, down to the common base of human communication—the real but as yet undiscovered, universal language—and then re-emerge by whatever particular route is convenient.

Statistical semantic studies should be undertaken as a basis for the cryptographic approach, Weaver felt:

> "Perfect" translation is almost surely unattainable. Processes, which at stated confidence levels will produce a translation which contains only X percent of "error" are almost surely attainable.

This memorandum triggered widespread response varying from one man who scoffed, "Rubbish," to the enthusiasm of Vannevar Bush, president of the Carnegie Institution of Washington, "I think the job could be done in a way that would be extraordinarily fascinating." Theoretical research was started by Yehoshua Bar-Hillel at the Research Laboratory of Electronics of the Massachusetts Institute of Technology. Erwin Reifler, a German-born associate professor of Chinese at the University of Washington started work on the translation of German and Chinese into English; William E. Bull, professor of Spanish at the University of California at Los Angeles began studying Spanish to English possibilities; Victor A. Oswald, Jr., professor of German, and Stuart L. Fletcher, Jr., a teaching assistant, also at UCLA, worked on German to English. But Russian to English MT, which was to become the major concern in the United States because of the importance of its scientific and technical literature and because few Americans could read it, did not get under way for a few more years.

The prolific Reifler in 1950 started a mimeographed series of memoranda "Studies in Mechanical Translation, MT," which he sent to all those he knew to be interested in MT. He was the first to suggest human intervention in the computerized translation process: a "pre-editor" would remove ambiguities by tagging words in the input text to indicate which of the many dictionary meanings was appropriate and a "post-editor" would polish up the style before final typing. Later he and others would suggest that authors should "write for MT" using a simplified and unambiguous vocabulary and syntax easily translatable by computers. Both the "pre-editor" and "writing for MT" were soon dropped as impractical. Editing the output of MT before publication was and is accepted today as desirable, just as it is for HT.

Bar-Hillel at M.I.T. became in 1951 the first full-time worker in the field. He soon wrote a paper describing the current state of MT research (9). The first published paper also appeared in 1951. This was by Oswald and Fletcher (10). Convinced that German word order must be rearranged for an adequate translation to English, the authors proposed tentative ways of doing it.

The initial phase of MT started by Booth and Weaver may be said to have ended with a conference at M.I.T. in the spring of 1952, financed by the Rockefeller Foundation and organized by Bar-Hillel, who invited all those known to be active in MT. The plan was to "contribute materially to progress in the field by bringing language and computer experts together in the same room, thus giving them a chance to learn each other's language as well as the power and limitations of each other's techniques." A start was made in learning to communicate, but the strongest impression was the disappointment of each group at the inability of the other to solve problems that looked simple. The computers of the day had not the capacity to cope with whole dictionaries, grammars, and large blocks of text, nor were there suitable programming languages for processing text. Nor was the linguists' theoretical and practical understanding of translation adequate to write the programs. Nevertheless, the direction that research should take was clear. Word frequency and translation studies for individual languages and for separate scientific fields would lay the groundwork for automatic dictionaries once sufficiently large memories became available, but since this seemed to be years away and since there was a clear trade-off between memory size and logical operations, more analysis of syntax was to be started immediately as a basis for more extensive logical operations.

The conference also saw the beginning of a continuing debate between the proponents of individual translation programs for pairs of languages and those in favor of an unambiguous, logical, intermediate language (sometimes also called a pivot, information, logical, or interlanguage) into which a text of the "source" language would first be translated and from which it could then be retranslated into any "target" language. Later it was to be pointed out that such an intermediate language would also be useful, if not essential, for information retrieval.

Phase II: 1952–1966

The M.I.T. conference had its intended effect of stimulating further activity in MT. In September 1952 the first discussion of MT was held at the Seventh International Congress of Linguists in London with forty present. The rate of publication picked up. Through 1952 there had been only one published paper, that by Oswald and Fletcher; in 1953 there were nine; in 1954, eight more; and for the next 10 or 15 years a gradually increasing number each year.

In March 1954 there appeared the first issue of a journal, *MT (Mechanical Translation),* edited and published by William N. Locke and Victor H. Yngve at M.I.T. with National Science Foundation support. In the same year the Ph.D. thesis of Anthony Oettinger (*11*) was accepted at Harvard University, the first of uncounted numbers of masters and doctors theses at many universities over the succeeding years. Oettinger described experiments in which a computer operating as an automatic Russian dictionary produced rough translations of technical texts which could be used effectively by specialists in the subject matter.

In 1954 also, MT "went public." Leon Dostert and Paul Garvin of Georgetown University worked with Peter Sheridan of IBM to prepare a public demonstration. A number of Russian sentences with a vocabulary of 250 words and their English equivalents were stored in an IBM 701 computer. Six rules of syntax were programmed to convert the Russian to English grammar. The result made headlines. The demonstration was a *tour de force* like a later one at the New York World's Fair in 1964. Neither could be generalized into operational MT. As Shreider wrote

> The first experiments in mechanical translation were started early in the fifties using very short texts; moreover, the translating algorithms were specially tailored just to these short texts, and it was for these reasons that demonstration effect was attained.... This illusion was due not only to the seemingly convincing demonstrations of machine translation capabilities referred to above, for the fiction of these demonstrations (supported by inordinately glib-tongued journalists) was not difficult to unmask. Nor had these demonstrations any significant impact in the

scientific community. Much more serious is another illusion which was supported by many investigators. This is the illusion that the problem at hand was of an engineering nature, that machine translation had already been resolved in principle, and that to be implemented in practice, only considerable organizational efforts were required (12).

The first book, *Machine Translation of Languages* by Locke and Booth (13), appeared in 1955. In the same year experiments on the BESM computer at the Institute of Precision Mechanics and Computation of the USSR Academy of Sciences indicated that "machine translation had a good probability of success." Two years later a Russian translation of *Machine Translation of Languages* was published in Moscow and the Russian effort, which was eventually to outdistance that in the United States, was under way.

In October 1956 the second MT conference was held at M.I.T., this time with NSF support. Some thirty papers from the United States, Canada, and the United Kingdom were presented, and Panov sent a paper from the USSR Academy of Sciences where the early Russian work was concentrated. He published *Avtomaticheskij Perevod (Automatic Translation)* in 1956 and at about the same time *Voprosy Iazykoznaniia (Problems of Linguistics)* started a regular section on MT. Work spread rapidly in the United States, England, and the USSR, and research was started in France, Italy, and Scandinavia. From then on conferences, reports, published papers, and books multiplied. Only a few can be mentioned.

In 1958 the first All Union Conference on MT in Moscow brought forth seventy-one papers (14); the Institute for Precision Mechanics and Computational Technology of the Academy of Sciences, Moscow, started publication of a *Trudi, Machinii Perevod (Machine Translation)*; and Booth, Brandwood, and Cleave (15) published *Mechanical Resolution of Linguistic Problems*. In France, Emile Delavenay published *La Machine à Traduire* in 1959 (16), and in the same year a Conference on Mathematical Linguistics in Leningrad dealt largely with MT.

In the United States an excellent, though occasionally caustic survey of the first years of MT "The Present Status of Automatic Translation of Languages," was published by Bar-Hillel in 1960 (17). Table 1 is a summary of his statistics. There was also some work in France, Germany, Poland, Hungary, Czechoslovakia, Switzerland, India, and a few more countries.

TABLE 1

STATUS OF MT, 1960

MT groups	Individuals	Annual expenditures ($)
14, US	~150	~1,500,000
3, England	~26	?
10, USSR	~300	~1,500,000
1, Milan	?	?
1, Jerusalem	4	4,000
29	~480	~3,004,000

Also in 1960 came the first move toward the creation of a professional society for MT in the United States. An Ad Hoc Committee on Professional Problems in Machine Translation and Related Areas was set up, and this in turn recommended the formation of an Association for Machine Translation and Computational Linguistics (AMTCL). The association was founded in 1962 and in 1964 started publication of a newsletter, the *Finite String* (a reference to the strings of characters that make up languages). President David G. Hays in the first issue wrote, "The title of our association is a claim that this field of knowledge [computational linguistics], necessary for MT, is broader in application; in effect, we claim the disciplinary integrity of knowledge underlying all linguistic applications of digital computers." He thus gave a foretaste of the evolution MT was to undergo in the next few years, broadening, fusing with automatic language processing, and to a large extent losing its identity in the field of computational linguistics.

As the money being expended on MT grew into annual millions, the sponsoring agencies in the United States decided that regular meetings of the research groups would result in better communication and faster progress. A National Symposium on Machine Translation in 1960 was followed by a number of conferences sponsored by Wayne State University, each devoted to a theme: dictionary design and grammar in 1960, grammar codes for Russian–English dictionary entries in 1961, syntactic analysis in 1962, and semantic analysis in 1965.

The First International Conference on Machine Translation of Languages and Applied Language Analysis was held in 1961 at the National Physical Laboratory at Teddington, England. Other international conferences have continued to be held at frequent intervals in various countries; for example, the Second International Conference on Automatic Language Processing held in 1967 at Grenoble and the 1969 International Congress on Computational Linguistics in Stockholm.

As MT research continued and became more widespread, two trends could be seen; the first was on the theoretical level, a realization that an understanding of human expression requires an understanding of thought; semantics (meaning) could no longer be left to philosophers; too many ambiguities could be resolved only on this level. The second trend, linked with the first, was organizational, the growth of research by teams including people from outside linguistics and computer science, anthropologists, philosophers, psychologists, physiologists, communications specialists, mathematicians, and systems engineers, each bringing the insights of his own background.

The 1960s in the United States and in the USSR were stimulating times for all science, and MT was accepted as a fledgling science. English was the language of the largest number of scientific publications; Russian was second. Reading each other's publications was of the highest priority. In the United States and in the United Kingdom few could read Russian and many translations were published, whereas in the USSR a knowledge of English was widespread and important books and journals were as likely to be reprinted in the original as to be translated.

In spite of a scarcity of competent translators for scientific and technical fields, NSF was able by 1965 to support the production of cover to cover translations of thirty-nine Russian journals. The Joint Publications Research Services (JPRS) had been set up in 1957 to service government agencies with translations,* and though the quality of translation and reproduction was poor and the service slow, a real need was met in many fields, including one called Foreign Developments in Machine Translation and Information Processing.

At the same time there was a rapid growth of commercial translating services and of commercially published translations of Russian books and journals. There were inevitable complaints at paying $40 for a translated book whose Russian original cost $2, or $150 to $350 for a subscription to a translated journal, but quality translation has always been expensive. It takes time, too. It was not unusual for a translated book to come out 2 or 3 years after the original, because the publishing process cannot start until the translation is done and edited. For journals a time lag of a few months was considered excellent. A year was not uncommon. The impetus given MT by these prices and these delays was considerable, though the growing availability of important books and articles in translated form eventually became a counterargument and one cause of a disillusionment with MT which set in in the middle 1960s in the United States.

Twenty million dollars had been poured into MT projects in the United States and abroad, but the goal of good, cheap, fast translations kept receding. At first any "intelligible" translation from a computer was an achievement, but for most people "intelligibility" is not enough. "Naturalness" has always been the goal of HT—a translation so good that people will not know it has been translated—but it is a goal rarely achieved and for MT it is usually conceded to be a remote possibility. In the middle 1960s, then, MT could produce intelligible but awkward translations of selected scientific and technical passages. To be acceptable for most purposes they had to be edited for clarity and style as HT is, and they often took longer and cost more than HT because for MT more editing was required.

Some time in 1963 or 1964 the sponsoring agencies led by NSF decided that the $20 million they had invested in MT had bought little in the way of practical results and that the end was not in sight. Leland Haworth, director of NSF, requested the National Academy of Sciences to set up a committee to advise NSF, the Department of Defense, and the Central Intelligence Agency on research and development in the general field of mechanical translation of foreign languages. The committee, under the chairmanship of John R. Pierce, a communications engineer from the Bell Telephone Laboratories, was called the Automatic Language Processing Advisory Committee (ALPAC) and it started work early in 1964. Members were John B. Carrol, an educational statistician; Charles F. Hockett, a linguist who resigned late in 1964 and was replaced by Eric P. Hamp, another linguist; David G. Hays, a linguist-philosopher; Anthony G. Oettinger, an applied mathematician; and Alan Perlis, a computer expert. The executive secretary was A. Hood Roberts, a linguist. ALPAC's charge was to study the strongly held but conflicting opinions about the promise of machine translation and recommend what were the most fruitful steps

*As of 1973, JPRS had in stock more than 50,000 translations of reports published since 1963 in Communist or Socialist countries, about half in scientific or technical fields. These are available to the public through the Clearinghouse for Federal Scientific and Technical Information and the U.S. Government Printing Office.

that should be taken. The committee interviewed seventeen witnesses, commissioned a number of studies, and in 1966 issued a report (*18*) which was to be as important in its own way for MT as Weaver's "Translation" had been. The committee concluded that MT was slower, less accurate, and twice as expensive as HT. Neither of the committee's two recommendations directly pertained to MT. They were: (1) continued and expanded support for computational linguistics, and (2) support for improvements in HT, including machine aids to translators such as automatic dictionaries. The general feeling throughout the world was one of incredulity. How could a committee of obviously capable people arrive at the conclusion that "there is little justification for massive support of MT?" The answer to this question has never been really clear.

First there were the exaggerated claims of success put out in advertising by computer companies. These were a two-edged sword. If they were believed, the need for support from government agencies was over. If they were not believed, then perhaps there was no future for MT and further support was a waste of money. Then, too, there was the swing toward more fundamental research in MT. Simmons notes, "However, most of these projects, notably those at M.I.T. and Harvard, had by that time redirected their efforts into more basic studies of the structure of languages and they considered MT only a distantly conceivable goal." (*19*)

The committee apparently decided that MT was a lost cause and that it should recommend support of the more general area of computational linguistics along with practical improvements in HT in order to keep government money flowing into linguistics research—this in spite of the gathering wave of antiscience feeling in government, which was to reduce radically the support of basic research by the Department of Defense, shift the emphasis of the NSF from basic to applied science, and eventually to see the abolition of top scientific advisory posts. Herbert A. Simon says, plaintively,

> To lay claims to the resources of his society, a scientist must produce what the society wants. And what it wants is a little knowledge and a lot of relevance. . . . We who have a thirst for knowledge can be thankful that basic knowledge usually does prove relevant to social needs. That's why we're tolerated and sometimes nurtured (*20*).

The ALPAC Report was widely condemned as narrow, biased, and shortsighted. The most thoroughgoing commentary according to Harry Josselson was that by Zbiginew L. Pankowicz of Griffiss Air Force Base, Rome, New York, the only man in a United States sponsoring agency who stood firm in the face of the panic flight from MT that followed the report. Pankowicz criticized the committee for

> (1) inferior analytical work resulting in factual inaccuracies; (2) a hostile and vindictive attitude toward machine translation; (3) the use of obsolete and invalid facts and figures as a basis for condemnation of machine translation; (4) distortion of quality, speed and cost estimates in favor of human translation; (5) concealment of data reflecting credit on machine translation (*suppressio veri suggestio falsi*), and (6) willful omission of dissenting statements on machine translation, presented to the Committee by some experts in this field (*21*).

The reaction in the USSR was equally negative. Kulagina, Mel'chuk, and Rozentsveig wrote:

We wish to declare decisively that this view has no real support: it is founded upon a failure to understand the problem in principle and confusion of its theoretical, scientific and practical aspects. The fact that machine translation has been ineffectual in practice to the present should, in our opinion, lead to an increase rather than a decrease in efforts in this area, especially in exploratory and experimental work. It is clear that no practical result can precede fundamental development of the problem, although the possibility is not excluded that useful practical results may be the product of early stages of research (22).

Josselson quotes a selection from *Nauchno-Tekhnicheskaja Informatsija (Scientific and Technical Information)*,

Those ideas which have originated and are originating in connection with MT are a contribution not only to the development of an MT system (a problem which is probably not acute in the United States) but also advance the resolution of one of the most important problems of the 20th Century—the problem of symbiosis of man and machines (21).

Phase III: 1966 to Present

After the enthusiasm of the first phase of MT work and the disappointments of the second, the third shows a spectrum of interests ranging from the practical to the theoretical with an experimental component in between. In the United States after the ALPAC Report a few organizations continued to provide gradually declining support for work on MT: Bunker-Ramo, IBM, and the Rand Corporation, for example. Government support disappeared except for the Air Force which continued to provide money for both operational and research MT.

Symbolic of the changed attitude toward MT in the United States is the reaction of the Association for Machine Translation and Computational Linguistics. In 1965 it had taken over sponsorship of the journal *MT (Mechanical Translation)* and had added *and Computational Linguistics* to the name. In 1968 AMTCL removed the MT from its name and became the Association for Computational Linguistics. Two years later it discontinued the journal.

Abroad the ALPAC Report caused a number of countries to re-evaluate their MT research but for the most part they continued it. Josselson (21) was able to list in 1970 the following research groups which had started work since 1960: The Centre d'Etudes pour la Traduction Automatique founded in 1962 at Grenoble; the Projet de Traduction Automatique of the University of Montreal; the Groupe de Linguistique Automatique, Brussels; Karlova University, Prague; The Computing Centre of the Hungarian Academy of Sciences; the Deutsche Academie der Wissenschaften, West Berlin; four groups in Japan; the Universidad Nacional Autónoma de México; the University of Nancy; the University of Debrecen, Hungary; the University of Saskatchewan; The Research Institute for Mathematical Machines, Prague; the University of Warsaw; the Institut Za Eksperimentalnu Fonetiku, Yugoslavia; and the Académie de la République Populaire Roumaine. In those 10 years reports of official research in MT had been issued by some seventy groups in fifteen countries: United States, USSR, Great Britain, France, Germany, Japan, Italy, Belgium, Canada, Mexico, Czechoslovakia, Yugoslavia, Rumania, Hungary, and Poland. These figures do not include research in computational linguistics or hardware. In 1970 a new journal *T. A. Informations* (23) was founded in France by the

Association pour le Développement de la Traduction Automatique et de la Linguistique Appliquée (ATALA).

OPERATING SYSTEMS

It is not generally known that there are a number of MT systems in operation: three in the United States, one in Italy, and one in Russia at last count. These will be discussed in the order in which they started operation.

"Georgetown" System

The "Georgetown" system takes its name from the fact that it was developed by the late Leon Dostert at Georgetown University with NSF and CIA support. It was installed in 1963–1964 at two locations, one at the AEC Oak Ridge National Laboratory at Oak Ridge, Tennessee and the other at the EURATOM Scientific Information Processing Center at Ispra, Italy. In both places the system is said to be still essentially the same as it was when it was installed except for some dictionary additions and a switch to upper and lower case. It is designed to translate Russian scientific and technical material into English. The following description of its operation is from Kay (24):

> the Georgetown system . . . incorporated neither the notion of a grammatical rule nor the notion of a syntactic structure. . . . If a word to be translated could, in the abstract, be either an adjective or a noun, the process examined the word's context to determine in which capacity it functioned in the given sentence. The grammatical classifications that were thus appended to the words in a text could be used later to determine which of a list of possible English alternatives would serve to translate the word and to help decide on the eventual order of the words in the second language.

At Oak Ridge translations are made on demand for government scientists and engineers. The EURATOM installation provides translations for its own people and for a growing number of outsiders through the European Translations Center in Delft, Holland, the Centre National de Documentation Scientifique et Technique in Brussels, and the Maschinenfabrik Augusbrug-Nurnberg in Germany. EURATOM had produced some 67,500 pages of translations in 7½ years and Oak Ridge some 51,000 in 6 years, prior to a study by Bozena H. Dostert (25) of the University of Texas Linguistics Research Center, wife of Leon Dostert. She attempted to find out what the customers of the Georgetown system thought of the product. The reasons given by those interrogated for using MT are that it is "quicker and cheaper" than HT, though it is difficult to know on what this judgment is based since, except in an emergency, MT translations are batched at both installations and run when the computers are free, and cost figures are unavailable, with the users themselves paying nothing. The output is "raw" (i.e., unedited) and users have to refer back to the original Russian text for formulas, diagrams, and illustrations. Nevertheless, 92.4% of the respondents judged the quality to be "acceptable" or "good." They said it took twice as long to read an MT text as the original English whereas HT took only 32% longer. Familiarity with subject matter was considered the primary factor in understanding MT texts, 93% of which were said to be "informative,"

81.5% "complete," and 71.1% "readable." As to misinformation, 82.4% "never had that experience." "MT 'style' can readily be gotten used to," they said, and 96.1% "have recommended or would recommend MT to their colleagues." In short, Mrs. Dostert concludes, the Georgetown 1964 system is an "acceptable substitute" for HT.

Moscow Patent Office

Since 1964 the Central Research Institute for Patent Information in Moscow has developed and operated a specialized and quite sophisticated MT system for translating the weekly Official Gazette of the U.S. Patent Bureau into Russian (26). The operation was originally programmed on a URAL-4 computer but may have been reprogrammed since. It is described by Josselson:

> An algorithm based on segment analysis provides for the delineation of operational units of text (syntagmas) such as noun groups and verbal combinations. The translation is carried out with the aid of a compiled dictionary of specified patterns of syntactic constructions (27).

The program of the Moscow Patent Office has approximately 20,000 instructions. Its sixteen subroutines can be divided into four groups for different phases of the operation:

1. Text preparation: arrange words, search for words in the dictionary, analyze unknown words (i.e., not found in the dictionary), process idioms, select homographs, segment text into phrases.
2. Syntactic analysis of segments: locate pronominal antecedents, work out case information (morphological), analyze predicative units of text, analyze noun word combinations.
3. Synthesis of Russian text: synthesize Russian text, print out translation.
4. Auxiliary programs: master program, write information on magnetic tape, transfer information from tape to drum storage, print out intermediate program results.

FTD

From 1964 to 1970 the Foreign Technology Division (FTD) of the Air Force operated what was called the Mark II Translator. The "photoscopic store" memory, Russian–English dictionary, and minimal grammar were developed by IBM. Kay describes the operation of the system:

> During the life of the system, a vast Russian–English dictionary of stems, prefixes, and suffixes was amassed and new disks were made periodically to incorporate the new information. The logical capabilities of the machine, however, were rudimentary. Each stem and affix on the disk was accompanied by a pair of codes indicating classes of stems and affixes that could occur before and after it. Thus, when a Russian word was sought in the dictionary, various alternative classes might be found, and the one chosen would be determined by the choice made for the item immediately preceding it (28).

The machine output was edited and printed complete with illustrations, which accounted for 70% of the high costs and most of the time consumed.

It was Mark II output which the ALPAC Committee compared with JPRS translations and found it no faster, no better, and higher in cost.

SYSTRAN

In 1970 FTD replaced Mark II with the more efficient SYSTRAN, which had been developed by Peter Toma of LATSEC, Inc., La Jolla, California. Since 1967 the Rome Air Development Center has supported various improvements in SYSTRAN. Editing and recomposition provide an output more attractive and more convenient than that of the Georgetown systems but at perhaps three times the cost.

The SYSTRAN system was evaluated in 1972 by Leavitt, De Haven and Giese (*29*). Their aim was primarily cost analysis and control, but the postediting and recomposition functions were studied in detail since they contribute 37 and 38%, respectively, to the total cost. Currently available technology for aiding the editor and for machine composition, said the authors, would reduce these figures and speed up the process.

In addition to Russian–English translation, SYSTRAN offers English–Russian, German–English, Chinese–English, and French–English. Examples of the output of a pilot French–English system (*30*) will give some idea of the quality of the machine output prior to editing:

French aeronautical text	SYSTRAN output
Il faudra en premier lieu, par des essais, déterminer le gouvernail le plus éfficace. On jouera sur le profil, sur le turbulateur, éventuellement on essayera une dérive évidée (comme W. Hauenstein). Le gouvernail le plus éfficace possible sera évidemment utilisé en atmosphère agitée, lorsqu'il est dangereux de s'attarder trop longtemps près de la pente. Au contraire, en air calme on emploiera un gouvernail moins éfficace pour mieux louvoyer.	It will be necessary first, by tests, to determine the elevator the most effective. One will play on the profile, on the Turbo-Jet, eventually one will try an hollowed leeway (as W. Hauenstein). The elevator the most effective possible will be evidently used in perturbed atmosphere, when it is dangerous to linger too long near the slope. On the contrary, in calm air one will will use an elevator less effective for better to manoeuver.

Logos

A third operating MT system in the United States is the Logos III System, also developed with the support of the Rome Air Development Center and commercially available. It operates on an IBM 370/145 with virtual storage and runs under the CMS (Cambridge Monitor System). It is said to be "language independent"; that is, the software will handle any language in the data base. English–Vietnamese and English–Russian are said to be operational, with other data bases in preparation.

One application of an earlier Logos system was technical English to Vietnamese MT for military training manuals. Input was by optical scanner. Translation was sentence-by-sentence; mistakes were corrected by an editor and were entered into the computer via an editing language developed by Logos. COM microfilm was produced off-line for proofreading and correcting. Formating instructions were entered in the system and transmitted to photocomposing equipment for the final composition of the translated text. Technically, this was a giant step toward the future.

According to the Logos Corporation, the MT text needed to be edited 25% of the time and changes broke down as follows: syntactical, 9.5%; lexical 10.7%; stylistic 1.5%; errors in data base, 2.5%; words not found, 0.8%. The cost was 8 to 10¢ a word, about what most human translators charge. Their report closed with a comment that goes to the heart of the translation problem:

> ... there are good reasons for questioning whether, with even the best of systems, the mission can be successfully accomplished. These reasons have to do with the vast differences in the technological levels of the English language and people and the Vietnamese language and people; it will take more than a computer to bridge the difference (31).

Two names stand out in the development of operating MT systems in the United States. The first is that of Leon Dostert, originally a skeptic, then a convert to MT, who directed the Georgetown University effort and inspired many of his students to become leaders in the field. The other name is that of Zbigniew L. Pankowicz at the Rome Air Development Center of the U.S. Air Force. Special tribute should be paid to this administrator of courage and vision. It is he who made possible the development of Mark II, SYSTRAN, and Logos, and it is he who has persevered in the support of the group at the University of Texas, the leader today in experimental MT research in the United States.

RESEARCH

Two opinions on research strategy will serve to introduce the work of several projects and individuals. First, Alexander Ljudskanov:

> By giving due consideration to the particular characteristics of the translation process and its study, as well as to the differentiation of the aims of mathematical linguistics from the theory of MT and of the fields of competence and performance from each other, research in this field would be channeled in a direction both more realistic for our time and more closely in accord with the facts.

He goes on to say with reference to books and articles on MT,

> they have confused the problem by comparing machine translation with the long-practiced human translation, by equating the problems of translating scientific materials with those involved in translating literary materials, and by using the same evaluation criteria for the results (32).

A second opinion is that of Paul Garvin who distinguishes three approaches:

> The "brute-force" approach is based on the assumption that, given a sufficiently large memory, machine translation can be accomplished without a complex algo-

rithm—either with a very large dictionary containing not only words but also phrases, or with a large dictionary and an equally large table of grammar rules. ... Both versions of the "brute-force" approach have yielded translations on a fairly large scale, but of questionable quality.

As opposed to this,

The "perfectionist" approach . . . is based on the assumption that without a complete theoretical knowledge of the source and target languages (based on a theoretical knowledge of language in general), as well as a perfect understanding of the process of translation both preferably in the form of mathematical models, the task cannot even be begun (33).

The "heuristic" or engineering approach which Garvin espouses falls between the two extremes. It is "translation oriented" and "probabilistic." The algorithm is

a linguistic pattern recognition algorithm which, instead of matching portions of sentences against rules stored in a table, directs searches at the different portions of the sentence in order to identify its grammatical and lexical pattern. Thus, the essential characteristic of the algorithm is the sequencing of the searches, and in each search subroutine, only as much grammatical and lexical information is used as is appropriate to the particular search (34).

Four substantial research projects will now be described, then the work of a number of smaller ones and individuals.

LRC

The first project will be considered in some detail. It is at the Linguistics Research Center (LRC) of the University of Texas at Austin and is directed by Winfred P. Lehmann with Rolf A. Stachowitz as research director. Fully automatic high quality German–English and English–German translation with no, or at least minimal, human editorial assistance is the goal, though the programs are language independent and can be applied to other pairs of languages. The translation process consists of "recognition" (analysis) of the elements of the "source" language text and "production" (synthesis) of the "target" language text. Meaning is to be transferred from one language to another through the substitution of linguistic and semantic units. Meaning can also be simplified or paraphrased as in automated indexing or abstracting by using the same languages for input and output.

The key to the LRC approach is expressed as folllows:

We may posit the existence of a universal base [of language structures] . . . the surface structures of any language can be related to such a universal base. Since the universal base in turn can be used for deriving the surface structures of any language, the universal base can serve as the intermediate language between any source language and any target language (35).

We are reminded here of Weaver's analogy of towers with a common substructure.

Large German and English dictionary data bases have been prepared in which codes for syntactic and semantic selection criteria are assigned to each entry. In addition, recognition grammars have been written at various levels of abstraction:

a "natural languages" grammar which, by a context-free parsing program, can derive from each natural language sentence one or more "standard strings" that bring together those words that logically belong together; a standard string grammar, also context-free, which identifies acceptable strings; and a "normal form" syntactic-semantic grammar which gives deep structures. The reverse of the recognition process, called "production" by LRC, starts with normal form deep structures identical with those of the recognition phase and derives one or more standard strings in the output language; the standard string grammar selects acceptable output strings and supplies corresponding natural language strings; finally the natural language grammar selects the appropriate constructions to make up a sentence and plugs in the lexical items with the correct endings (see Figure 1).

German verb–noun combinations illustrate the necessity of taking semantic relations into consideration in the transformation of surface structure to underlying structures. Thus a phrase like *Abstand nehmen (von)* corresponds to the English "to refrain, desist (from), give up."

Er nahm von diesem Plan Abstand. He gave up this plan.

To bring together discontinuous elements, such as *nahm Abstand,* the surface strings must be rearranged by deriving tentative standard strings from surface strings as:

Er nahm Abstand von diesem Plan.

An idea of the number and complexity of the rules which the LRC uses to resolve syntactical ambiguity may be had from the fact that seven steps are required to determine whether "page" in "the page slept" refers to a person or a piece of paper. The amount of new research is very substantial; for example, the classification of verbs and their complements into twenty-nine patterns used in *The Advanced Learner's Dictionary of Current English* by Hornby, Gatenby, and Wakefield was found after several years of experimentation to be incomplete, so a new classification was developed. The same had to be done for adjectives and for adverbs (35).

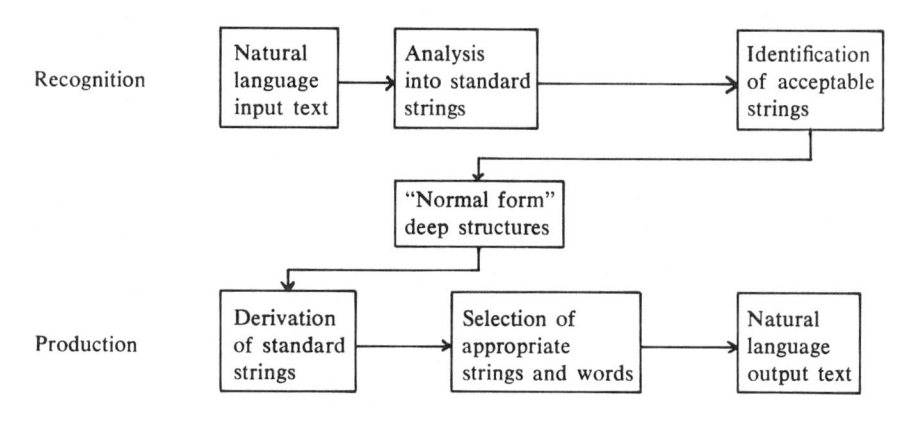

FIGURE 1. *Block Diagram of LRC System.*

A most important survey of the state of the MT art was published in a report by LRC in December 1971 (*36*). This report stresses the fact that Bar-Hillel, one of the first proponents of MT, who in the 1960s changed his mind and took the position that fully automatic high quality translation was an illusory goal because of the "semantic barrier," has once again become somewhat more optimistic. He writes,

> It is therefore, for instance, not inconceivable that a translation program with an unsatisfactory output for a certain user under given conditions might turn out to be more satisfactory if the conditions are changed, for instance, if the user is allowed to ask back certain questions and the computer is programmed to answer these questions upon request . . . [the human user] is the first and final judge, and it is he who will have to tell whether he is ready to trade quality for speed, and to what degree (*37*).

This is a challenge which the authors of the report are happy to accept. Rapid advances in computer hardware and software have removed the technological barriers to MT (except in the case of Chinese, Japanese, and similar languages), leaving only linguistic obstacles arising from incomplete analysis of linguistic performance at all levels. They conclude,

> Current linguistic theory is inadequate for machine translation . . . semantic representations derived from syntactic structures in the source language must be associated with syntactic structures in target language . . . comprehensive grammars do not yet exist for any languages . . . research in discourse analysis should be increased. . . . Machine translation can be designed with varying degrees of adequacy . . . (*38*).

LRC, like many other MT research projects, makes use of transformational grammar to go from surface structure (natural language syntax) to "deep structure" (logical syntax). A "tree diagram" is widely used to represent transformations. Kay gives an example,

> the sentence [S1], "Claims that John had passed the examination surprised the professor." The subject of this sentence is "Claims that John had passed the examination," which contains the second sentence [S2], "John had passed the examination," which has its own subject, "John." The relationships of these various parts to one another can be conveniently represented in a tree diagram. (See Figure 2.)

It will be noted that linguists' tree diagrams represent roots rather than branches because they start with surface phenomena and work down to the underlying logical relations. In actual translation operations on random sentences, a number of different surface structures (e.g., "John inherited the estate" or "the estate was inherited by John") may be represented by a single deep structure. This causes no difficulty at the analysis stage, but during synthesis the computer has to decide which of the possible surface structures shall be used. It depends partly on stylistic considerations. The situation may be even more complicated. Any syntactic ambiguity means more than one possible deep structure for the surface structure. Then both analysis and synthesis become a multiple choice guessing game. As said earlier, humans are adept at this game, eliminating such ambiguities with the

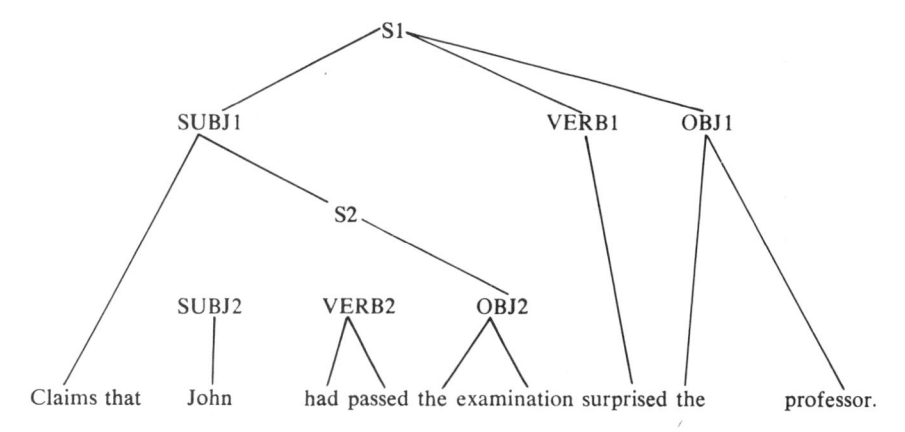

FIGURE 2. *(Reprinted from Ref. 24, p. 220, by permission of the American Academy of Arts and Sciences.)*

help of context. To understand this process well enough to program a computer to do it is the challenge that faces LRC and everyone who wants to perfect MT.

Berkeley

A second ongoing MT research program in the United States is the Chinese–English project at the University of California, Berkeley, also supported by the Rome Air Development Center. It is described as "a practical combination of the theoretical and the pragmatic approaches to machine translation" (*39*). Further, "although the system is designed to be capable of translating standard modern written Chinese in general, it is at present intentionally biased in its data bases toward the translation of scientific texts in the fields of nuclear physics and biochemistry" (*40*).

It will be immediately recognized that the characters of Chinese and Japanese present special input difficulties. In the first place each character, of which there are several thousand in everyday use, has to be coded for input. Optical recognition would be the answer, but until it is perfected, skilled human interposition will be necessary. Second and no less important, individual characters represent syllables; there is no indication whatever of word boundaries. To identify the words, a series of characters has to be compared with the dictionary until a matching series is found. The longest possible match is used. In a more sophisticated routine a two way lookup operation matches first from left to right then right to left. If both find the same word, fine; if different words are found, they have to be carried along into later stages of the processing in the hope that syntactic or semantic information can resolve the ambiguity. Chinese verbs have no tense endings, nouns no sign for the plural. Context may provide the necessary information, if not it may be impossible to compose a correct English sentence.

The present status of the Berkeley project is described as follows:

> The cumulative efforts of the past several years have resulted in the materialization of a large dictionary, a complex grammar [or hierarchy of grammars], a sizeable

corpus of machine-readable Chinese text and a sophisticated programming system.... Chinese sentences constitute the source language input. This is submitted to the parser and analyzed into structural trees. Interlingual processes then apply to these structures to map them into the appropriate equivalent English structure. These structures are then used for synthesis into the target English output by applying the necessary surface structure rules (*41*).

Postediting is necessary at present, but the eventual goal is "Chinese translations that could be used by casual readers directly and happily" (*42*).

G.E.T.A.

The Groupe d'Etudes pour la Traduction Automatique (G.E.T.A.) in Grenoble was founded in 1962 under the name Centre d'Etudes pour la Traduction Automatique and is directed by Bernard Vauquois. G.E.T.A. It is developing computerized methods for translating written texts from Russian into French with a small-scale effort also in German and Japanese. Poetry and other purely literary texts are excluded. A report on work up to 1970 (*43*) states the philosophy: Word for word translations are worthless even if the word order is rearranged; attempts to perfect the output by analyzing the syntax of sentences of Language L and synthesizing corresponding sentences in Language L' have still not given high quality translation; the problem of automatic translation is the transformation of written text into meaning and the reverse transformation.

Like Nikolai D. Andreev in Leningrad and Sidney M. Lamb at Yale University, G.E.T.A. has proceeded on the assumption that a semantic interlanguage, a "pivot language," would have to be developed to formalize meaning "so that any text of any language could be formulated in it and then an equivalent text in any other language created from it" (*44*). By 1970 a series of models for the automatic translation process had been developed and parts of them had been programmed. The analysis of Russian into Pivot Language I and the generation of French had been debugged, expanded, and checked on more than 400,000 words of Russian text. "Intermediate results" could be shown as follows:

Analysis of Language L:
   (a) segmentation of words into stems and endings (morphological analysis)
   (b) 1) segmentation of sentences into phrases
       2) resolution of syntactical ambiguities
   (c) semantic analysis in Pivot Language II
Synthesis of Language L':
   (d) Construction of new sentence patterns (syntactical synthesis)
   (e) Construction of words from stems and endings (morphological synthesis)

Pivot Language II has a more precise expression of basic concepts such as "time" or "determinacy" in invariant form and syntax such that deep structures can be generated from surface structures and vice versa. In reality the pivot languages are families of languages having a syntax closely allied to French but with vocabularies from the different "source" languages. The analysis stage of translation decomposes the sentences into elementary statements and shows the semantic relations between these statements. The final phase is called transfer rather than generation because little more than the substitution of lexical items is involved.

G.E.T.A. has chosen to treat only one sentence at a time, which limits the difficulties but means that words whose antecedent is outside the sentence, pronouns for example, cannot be handled. It should be added, however, that a few workers elsewhere have tackled "proforms" with some success.

After 1970 G.E.T.A. went through the trauma that every MT research project eventually goes through when an obsolete but reliable computer is replaced by a new, larger, faster but less reliable one. They took advantage of the disruption to create a new software system for handling the strings and tree structures in different linguistic models. They are making a careful study of the kinds of ambiguity in their large body of Russian text in order to devise ways of resolving them. Again and always, ambiguity is the key.

TAUM

The Project for Automatic Translation of the University of Montreal (TAUM), directed by Richard I. Kittredge, has as its goal the analysis of all grammatical features of all words in the text, plus a certain number of semantic ones: for nouns, whether they are animate, concrete, or abstract; for verbs, the kinds of subject and objects they can take and their possible constructions. These help resolve ambiguity at the word and syntactical levels. Kittredge writes,

> The purpose of the syntactic parsing . . . is to provide in a single tree structure the most important elementary sentences of which the input sentence was (transformationally) composed. . . . The ultimate aim is to represent each sentence (text) in predicate argument form where an argument is either a noun phrase or a sentence. In addition to the lexical items which are then hierarchically arranged, there are category symbols attached to constituents and their sub-parts, and features to represent syntactic and semantic sub-classes (*45*).

Jules Dansereau explains the two step operation,

> "Transfer" includes the decomposition of the English structure, the dictionary and the recomposition of French structure . . . "generation" receives the trees as reconstructed by "transfer"; its job is to decompose them in order to arrive at a syntactically well formed French string, giving all the necessary information to the morphological rules (*46*).

There is great diversity in the work of the smaller projects and individual researchers. Brian Harris at the University of Ottawa; Margaret Masterman and her group at the Cambridge Language Research Center, Cambridge, England; and Richard L. Bisbey and Martin Kay at the Rand Corporation Linguistics Research Project, Santa Monica, California, subordinate the machine to the human in Machine Aided Translation (MAT). Yngve's "partial translation" (*47*) (only stems of words translated) reappears in the "pidgin translation" of Harris (*48*) (stems and endings translated) and in Masterman's (*49*) "pidgin" word for word MT system. Loh Shiu-Chang (*50*) proposes for Chinese to English to resurrect Reifler's "preeditor." Bisbey and Kay (*51*) would use not only a "pre-editor," who needs to know only the source language and "disambiguates" the input by identifying the correct syntactic analysis whenever more than one is furnished by the computer, but also a "posteditor," who needs to know only the target language and polishes up the style.

Masterman is also known for her work on "translating semantic meaning" by means of a hierarchically arranged bilingual thesaurus (52,53). Her work prefigures much of the later work on structural semantics by Silvio Ceccato (54) in Italy, Tunco Tamati and Tosihiko Kurihara (55) in Japan, and especially the imaginative work of I. A. Mel'chuk and A. K. Zholkvosky (56) in the USSR. Gardin comments on the latter:

> What these two linguists have achieved, indeed, is not only an original method of automatic translation, in which syntax and semantics are cleverly blended; the metalanguage which plays such an important part in this method can also be regarded as an information language, to the extent that it purports to carry basic meaning contents variously expressed in natural language forms (57).

Semantics theories continue to be many and varied as set forth by Bobrow, Fraser, and Quillan:

> We will not recount here the multifarious disagreements involved in all this, much less take sides. However, we would like to propose one sort of "dimension," along which it seems many of the semantic theories may be located. Essentially, this dimension is the degree of complexity of the material that is assumed to constitute semantic information. For a performance model, this information is what would have to be stored in the memory of the device that produced and/or comprehended language. A position lying near the "complexity" end of this dimension would assume semantic information consists of complex configurations, forming overall a network of nodes, interrelated to one another by different kinds of links. A position closer to the middle of this continuum might assume that semantic information is structured into trees, but still trees using several different kinds of labeled linkages. Further along on this continuum one might find a theory that assumed a tree structure for semantic information but now one that used a single kind of linkage between nodes of the tree. Finally, a position near the "simplicity" end of our continuum might assume that semantic information consists simply of unordered aggregates of semantic features. Semantic theories of today seem to be spread all along this continuum (58).

Some of the most promising recent contributions are in the field of artificial intelligence, one of whose goals may be defined as the invention of a Turing machine which can carry on such an "intelligent" conversation that a person on the other end of the telephone will not know that he is talking to a machine rather than a human.

A recent book, which includes a useful summary of the work of a number of others, is that of Wilks, who writes,

> My approach, on the other hand, takes meaningful language as the basic material for analysis and explanation. It does not assign any theoretical status to a class of "grammatical sequences" over and above their being what some particular grammar produces, or admits, as well formed. *One aim of the present work, therefore, is to construct a theory that enables us to detect semantic forms directly, and not via a strong and conventional syntax analysis* (59).

He goes on,

> It is no more a priori foolish to classify semantic forms than to classify logical or syntactic ones. In fact they are related enterprises. In syntactic classification one examines the behavior of a word within a coarse framework of structures, and assigns it to large substitution classes. In semantic classification the framework mesh is finer and the substitution classes correspondingly smaller. I think it could be shown that there are syntactic analogues to basic semantic message forms . . . *(60)*.

Wilks quotes John McCarthy,

> . . . Mathematical linguists are making a serious mistake in their concentration on syntax and, even more specially, on the grammar of natural languages. It is even more important to develop a mathematical understanding and a formalization of the kinds of information conveyed in natural language *(61)*.

A large number of researchers in the Soviet Union are at work on linguistic semantic models, at the Institute of Linguistics, the Institute of the Russian Language, the Institute for Applied Mathematics, and the All Union Institute of Scientific and Technical Information (VINITI) of the Academy of Sciences, at the Moscow State Pedagogical Institute of Foreign Languages, not to mention groups in Leningrad, in other provincial cities, and in the other Soviet Socialist Republics. The trend seems to be toward what Rozentsveig *(62)* calls an "explanatory-combinatorial dictionary," which combines explicit descriptions of the ways, both semantic and syntactic, in which each word can combine with others; i.e., a dictionary that adds the functions of a thesaurus and a grammar, as the best dictionaries always have to a limited extent. Wilks affirms that the traditional distinction between syntax and semantics (and he might have added lexicography) is unnecessary in practice. His "templates" combine all three. He explains,

> I am not suggesting, though, that the manipulations to be described here are merely "dictionary based," if that is to be taken to mean having no theoretical presuppositions. There are in fact three important linguistic presuppositions on which the following analysis is based: namely, the use of templates for analysis, and stereotypes for generation . . . in addition the principle . . . that by building up the densest, or most connected, representation that it can for a piece of language, the system of analysis will be getting the word senses and much of the grammar right *(63)*.

None of the above-mentioned researchers limit their interests to MT. Most are simultaneously making contributions to the broader field (called automated language processing by information scientists and computational linguistics by linguists) which includes information retrieval, fact retrieval, question answering systems, automatic indexing, and abstracting (extracting). Sparck Jones and Kay *(64)* rightly regret that mutual understanding and interaction of information science and linguistics have up to now been slight. Each needs the insights of the other. Semantics, meaning, lies at the heart of the difficulties in all these areas. On that point nearly everyone agrees, but there the agreement ends. There are nearly as many theories about how to use meaning in automated language processing as there are individuals thinking about it. This is a healthy situation. The challenge is worthwhile because it goes deep into the nature of the human intellectual process. If we learn enough to do MT, we shall have contributed something even more important to the understanding of how the mind works.

Conclusion

In its 25 year history, machine translation became an internationally recognized field of research, then lost its identity in the larger field of computational linguistics to which it gave birth—except for operational MT which continues to be substantial in quantity but poor in quality.

The remaining barriers to improved quality lie in our incomplete understanding of the linguistic and psychological mechanisms of translation. Research is going forward with substantial assistance from specialists in other disciplines. Not only may any paper in linguistics or information processing be pertinent, but also papers in such disparate fields as logic, mathematical modeling, topology, the psychology and neurophysiology of perception and cognition, computer programming, and artificial intelligence.

Computers themselves have progressed to the point where they are efficient tools for MT with their direct input output hardware; large, fast, random access memories; and, equally important, procedural- and problem-oriented languages which facilitate efficient representation and manipulation of text. Computers can now be programmed to analyze written, but not yet spoken, text on the morphological and syntactical levels, and perhaps eventually to assign probabilities in order to predict meaning and resolve ambiguities as humans do.

Perhaps MT is now entering a third and final phase. Following a first phase of enthusiasm coupled with ignorance of the extent of the difficulties came a second of discouragement and loss of financial support. Now we see a new optimism that the deeper intellectual problems may be soluble.

REFERENCES

(An asterisk indicates a key item)

1. R. F. Simmons, "Automated Language Processing," *Ann. Rev. Inform. Sci. Technol.,* **1,** 163 (1966).
2. J. Macnamara, "Nurseries, Streets and Classrooms: Some Comparisons and Deductions," *Mod. Language J.,* **57**(5-6), 250-251 (September-October 1973).
3. K. W. Otten, "Machine Recognition of Speech," *Advan. Comput.,* **11,** 162-163 (1971).
4. I. Rhodes, "Glossary Storage in MT," in *Machine Translation* (A. D. Booth, ed.), North Holland, Amsterdam; Wiley, New York, 1967, p. 433.
5. *Webster's New International Dictionary of the English Language,* 2nd ed., unabridged, Merriam, Springfield, Massachusetts, 1952, pp. 1147-1148.
6. V. H. Yngve, *Computer Programming with COMIT II,* M.I.T. Press, Cambridge, Massachusetts, 1972, p. XIII.
7. J. E. Sammet, "Programming Languages: History and Future," *Commun. ACM,* **15,** 601-610 (1972).

*8. W. Weaver, "Translation," in *Machine Translation of Languages* (W. N. Locke and A. D. Booth, eds.), Technology Press of M.I.T., Wiley, New York, 1955.
9. Y. Bar-Hillel, "The Present State of Research on Mechanical Translation," *Amer. Doc.,* 2(4), 229–237 (1951) [not published until 1953].
10. V. A. Oswald, Jr., and S. L. Fletcher, Jr., "Proposals for the Mechanical Resolution of German Syntax Patterns," *Mod. Language Forum,* 36(3–4), 1–24 (1951).
11. A. Oettinger, "A Study for the Design of an Automatic Dictionary," Ph.D. Thesis, Harvard University, 1954.
12. Y. A. Shreider, "Automatic Translation: Illusions and Reality," Introductory Report presented at the SMEA Symposium, "Mash-perevod-67," Budapest, October 1967, p. 3.
*13. W. N. Locke and A. D. Booth (eds.), *Machine Translation of Languages,* The Technology Press of M.I.T., Wiley, New York; Chapman and Hall, London, 1955.
14. "Tezisi Konferencii po Mashinomu Perevodu," Ministerstvo Vyshego Obrazoudnija, Moscow, 1968.
15. A. D. Booth, L. Brandwood, and J. P. Cleave, *Mechanical Resolution of Linguistic Problems,* Butterworths, London, 1958.
16. E. Delavenay, *La Machine à Traduire,* Que Sais-Je (No. 834), Presses Universitaires de France, Paris, 1959.
*17. Y. Bar-Hillel, "The Present Status of Automatic Translation of Languages," *Advan. Comput.,* 1, 91–163 (1960).
*18. Automatic Language Processing Advisory Committee, *Language and Machines—Computers in Translation and Linguistics* (Publication No. 1416), National Academy of Sciences–National Research Council, Washington, D.C., 1966.
19. Ref. *1,* p. 151.
20. H. A. Simon, Editorial, *Science,* p. 613 (August 17, 1973).
*21. H. H. Josselson, "MT in the Sixties: A Linguist's View," *Advan. Comput.,* 11, 1–58 (1971).
22. O. S. Kulagina, I. A. Mel'chuk, and V. Yu. Rozentsveig, "More on the Problem of Realizing MT (Machine Translation)," *Avtomatizatsiia Perevoda Textov, NTI,* 2(No. II), 28–32 (1969).
23. *T. A. Informations—Revue Internationale du Traitement Automatique du Language,* 1, (1970), publié par A.T.A.L.A. (Association pour le développement de la Traduction Automatique et de la Linguistique Appliquée avec le concours des Editions Klincksieck, Paris).
*24. M. Kay, "Automatic Translation of Natural Languages," *Daedalus* (Summer 1973); issued as *Proc. Amer. Acad. Arts Sci.,* 102(3), 219 (1973).
25. B. H. Dostert, "Users Evaluation of Machine Translation, Georgetown MT System, 1963–1973," *Final Tech. Rept.,* RADC-TR-73-239, Rome Air Development Center, Griffiss Air Force Base, Rome, New York, August 1973.
26. L. G. Kravec, A. L. Vasilevskij, and A. M. Dubickaja, "Eksperimental'naja sistema avtomaticheskogo perevoda publikacij iz Amerikanskogo pattentnogo ezhenedel'nika 'Official Gazette,'" *Nauch.-Tekh. Inform.* 2(1), 35–40 (1967).
27. Ref. *21,* pp. 43–44.
28. Ref. *24,* p. 218.
29. A. W. Leavitt, R. C. De Haven, and G. W. Giese, *Final Tech. Rept.,* RADC-TR-72-293, Synectics Corporation, Rome Air Development Center, Griffiss Air Force Base, Rome, New York, 1972.
30. "SYSTRAN: The Operational Machine Translation System," LATSEC, Inc., La Jolla, California, undated, pp. 31–36.
31. "Optimization of Logos I System (Phase II)," *Final Tech. Rept.,* RADC-TR-71-142, Logos Development Corporation, Rome Air Development Center, Griffiss Air Force Base, Rome, New York, July 1971, p. VI-1.
32. A. Ljudskanov, "Is the Generally Accepted Strategy of Machine-Translation Research Optimal?," *MT,* 11(1–2), (March and June 1968).
33. P. L. Garvin, *On Machine Translation,* Mouton, The Hague, 1973, p. 10.
34. P. L. Garvin, "Heuristics in MT," *Lingua,* 21, 162–184 (1968).
35. W. P. Lehmann and R. A. Stachowitz, "Development of German–English Machine Trans-

lation System," *Tech. Repts.,* RADC-TR-72-47-74, and 73-260, Rome Air Development Center, Griffiss Air Force Base, Rome, New York, March 1972, April 1972, and August 1973.
*36. W. P. Lehmann and R. A. Stachowitz, "Feasibility Study on Fully Automatic High Quality Translation," *Final Tech. Rept.,* RADC-TR-71-295, 2 vols., Rome Air Development Center, Griffiss Air Force Base, Rome, New York, December 1971, Vol. 1, p. 19.
37. Y. Bar-Hillel, "Some Reflections on the Present Outlook for High-Quality Machine Translation," in Ref. *36,* Vol. 1, p. 76.
38. Ref. *36,* Vol. 1, pp. 44-47.
39. "A Description of the Berkeley Chinese-English Machine Translation System," Machine Translation Group, Project on Linguistic Analysis, University of California, Berkeley, June 30, 1972, mimeographed, p. 1.
40. Ref. *39,* pp. 29-30.
41. W. S. Y. Wang, S. W. Chan, and B. K. T'sou, "Chinese Linguistics and the Computer," *Linguistics,* **118,** 100 (December 15, 1973).
42. Ref. *39,* p. 33.
43. "Rapport d'activité du Centre d'Etudes pour la Traduction Automatique jusqu'en 1970," Centre National de la Recherche Scientifique, Section 28, Paris, France, mimeographed.
44. Ref. *43,* pp. 1-2.
45. R. Kittredge, "An English Analysis Grammar," in *TAUM 73,* Projet de Traduction Automatique de l'Université de Montréal, August 1973, p. 26.
46. J. Dansereau, "La Génération du Français," in Ref. *45.* Original French, "Le 'transfert' comprend la décomposition de la structure anglaise, le dictionnaire et la recomposition de la structure française," p. 41; "La 'generation' reçoit les arbres tels que reconstruits par le transfert. Elle a pour tâche de les décomposer pour arriver à une chaîne française, syntaxiquement bien formée, en donnant aux règles morphologiques toute l'information nécessaire," p. 46: Translation by W. N. Locke.
47. V. H. Yngve, "Syntax and the Problem of Multiple Meaning," in Ref. *13,* pp. 210-213.
48. T. R. Hoffman and B. Harris, "Pidgin Translation," University of Montreal, prepublication draft, 1969.
49. M. Masterman, "Mechanical Pidgin Translation," in *Machine Translation* (A. D. Booth, ed.), North Holland, Amsterdam; Wiley, New York, 1967, pp. 195-227.
50. L. Shiu-Chang, "Translation of Chinese Scientific Texts into English by Computer," Computing Center, Chinese University of Hong Kong, August 1972, mimeographed.
51. R. Bisbey and M. Kay, "The Mind Translation System," Rand Corporation, Santa Monica, California, undated, P-4786.
52. M. Masterman, "Essays on and in Machine Translation," Cambridge Language Research Unit, Cambridge, England, 1960, mimeographed.
53. M. Masterman, "Semantic Message Detection for Machine Translation Using an Interlingua," in *Proceedings of the First International Conference on Machine Translation, Teddington, Middlesex, 1961,* HMSO, London, 1961.
54. S. Ceccato, "Correlational Analysis and Mechanical Translation" in *Machine Translation* (A. D. Booth, ed.), North Holland, Amsterdam; Wiley, New York, 1967, pp. 77-135.
55. T. Tamati and T. Kurihara, "A Semantic Approach to the Automatic Analysis of Japanese and English," Kyusyu University, Fukuoka, Japan, March 1968.
56. I. A. Mel'chuk and A. K. Zholkovsky, "Toward a Functioning 'Meaning-Text' Model of Language," *Linguistics,* **57,** 10-47 (1970).
57. J. C. Gardin, "Comments on the Working Paper: *Linguistic Problems of Scientific Information,*" ICSU-UNESCO Joint Project on the Communication of Scientific Information, Moscow, 1968, mimeographed, p. 13.
58. D. G. Bobrow, J. B. Fraser, and M. R. Quillan, "Automated Language Processing," *Ann. Rev. Inform. Sci. Technol.,* **2,** 166 (1967). Reprinted by permission of John Wiley & Sons, Inc.
*59. Y. A. Wilks, *Grammar, Meaning, and the Machine Analysis of Language,* Routledge & Kegan Paul, London, 1972, p. 94.

60. Ref. *59,* p. 100.
61. J. McCarthy, "A Basis for a Mathematical Theory of Computation," in *Computer Programming and Formal Systems* (P. Braffort and D. Hirschberg, eds.), North Holland, Amsterdam, 1963, p. 69.
*62. V. Yu. Rozentsveig, "Models in Soviet Linguistics," *Soc. Sci., Dept. Soc. Sci., Presidium USSR Acad. Sci.,* **3,** 82–94 (1971).
63. Y. A. Wilks, "An Artificial Intelligence Approach to Machine Translation, in *Computer Models of Thought and Language* (R. C. Shank and K. M. Colby, eds.), Freeman, San Francisco, 1973, pp. 117–118.
64. K. Sparck Jones and M. Kay, *Linguistics and Information Science* (FID Publication no. 492), Academic, New York, 1973.

7
Natural Language Analysis and Processing

Naomi Sager / New York University, New York, New York

Because of the complexity of language material in its given form, the initial, and major, problem is to reduce the successive sentences of a discourse (i.e., a text or conversation) to a simpler regular form in which the meaning elements necessary for useful processing can be located by straightforward procedures. This process is generally thought of as consisting of a syntactic component and a semantic component. In some kinds of applications it is followed by a so-called pragmatic component related to the specific task to be performed. The syntactic component segments the sentence into subunits which are grammatically connected, and identifies the grammatical role of words within the subunits. The semantic component furnishes a representation of the sentence which aims to capture the underlying relations of words, which are essential in conveying the information in the discourse.

OBJECTIVES OF NATURAL LANGUAGE PROCESSING

The general objective of work in this field is to develop procedures which make it possible to process the informational content of texts and conversation. An implicit goal is to learn more about language structure and use. Since the procedures are for the most part analytical (start with the text, produce the analysis) and must be both precise and penetrating, there is promise that the ways of organizing the linguistic facts and carrying out the analysis will reflect, at least in part, the inherent organization of data in language and the means by which sentences are processed by the human mind.

Applicational goals include the use of these procedures to make information which is recorded in natural language more readily accessible to users. Where the documents are stored in computer readable form, it would be desirable to have

From Sager, Naomi. *Natural Language Analysis and Processing.* ENCYCLOPEDIA OF COMPUTER SCIENCE AND TECHNOLOGY. Vol. 11. Edited by Jack Belzer, Albert G. Holzman and Allen Kent. New York, Marcel Dekker, Inc., c1978. pp. 152-167.

computer programs that could extract and assemble the relevant information from the computer store by processing the natural language documents. This goal becomes more prominent as natural language data bases become increasingly available.

A major goal is to develop systems for man-machine communication in natural language. Such a "front end" would be useful in information retrieval, to enable users of computer search systems to state their requests in natural language. Question-answering systems are one type of development in this direction. In these systems questions in natural language which apply to a given structured data base (table or the equivalent) are interpreted and an answer is returned. There would also be applications of natural language "front ends" in automatic programming, where it would be desirable to have a system which can interpret instructions given in natural language (or in a language very like a natural language) and can interpret declarative statements giving information required for programming tasks.

Applications of automatic language analysis in the language domain itself include mechanical translation, one of the earliest goals, and the use of the computer in language and literary research, such as in the testing of grammars and in style analysis. Use of natural language processing in computer-aided-instruction (CAI) and specifically in language teaching is also a possibility.

NATURAL LANGUAGE VS FORMAL LANGUAGES

There are reasons why natural language can be processed by computer programs. Overtly, it is composed of linearly arranged discrete elements which, like the symbols of mathematics and various codes, occur only in particular combinations. For this reason, a properly formulated grammar, which specifies the rules of formation for well-formed sequences of the language, can be used in a procedure to recognize the syntactic structure of sentences. Such a procedure produces a structural description of a sentence (or more than one if the sentence is ambiguous) which shows how the sentence was composed of elements specified by the grammar, combined according to the rules of sentence formation. In this respect natural language resembles its near-neighbors, the formal languages of mathematics, logic, and programming, for which recognition procedures have been devised. But there are significant differences between natural languages and formal languages which have made the computer analysis of natural language a special area of research. Some of the unique features of natural language from a computational point of view are the following.

Differing Acceptabilities

While the symbols in syntactic formulas for natural language represent word classes (e.g., N noun, TV tensed verb) analogous to the variables of mathematics, not every combination of members of the classes in a formula makes an equally acceptable instantiation, as though the formula $(a + b)^2 = a^2 + 2ab + b^2$ were to be more true for some numbers than for others. Thus, "Fire spreads" is a well-formed assertion of the N TV type whereas "Fire requires" is not. No matter how refined the word classes represented by formula symbols are made (e.g., making transitive verbs and intransitive verbs major classes), some differences in the acceptability of particular words in particular syntactic relations remains.

Grammatical Subclasses

As a result of the above property of natural language, a grammar contains constraints which refer to subclasses of the major classes. Words must be assigned attributes that indicate subclass memberships, and analysis procedures must be equipped with the ability to access the lexical entries for words and to eliminate readings in which words are assigned syntactic roles incompatible with their subclass memberships. Otherwise, nonwell-formed input strings will be accepted (e.g., "Fire requires") and wrong analyses of correct sentences will be obtained (e.g., "Fire requires oxygen being present," analyzed like "Prices rise everything being equal").

Selection

In some cases the unacceptability of particular word combinations is grammatical in character (sharp yes-no) as in the example "Fire requires," where a transitive verb is in the position of an intransitive verb. Another example of a grammatical constraint involving subclasses is number agreement: "John walks," but not: "John walk." However, a characteristic of natural language is that over and above what can be captured in grammatical constraints, the acceptability of word combinations in grammatically well-formed sequences is graded and dependent on the universe of discourse. Thus "John walks to school" is normal and "John breathes to school" marginal, while "John floats to school" might be acceptable if John's school is on a waterway and someone gives his boat a strong schoolward push in the morning. For a given word w, the set of words which w commonly co-occurs with in a given syntactic relation is called (following the linguist Bloomfield) the selection of w in that relation; e.g., if w is a verb, then it has a selection of subject nouns, and if transitive a selection of object nouns.

The selection of a word is closely related to its meaning. If two words in the same grammatical class have identical selections, they are exact synonyms, and conversely, if they have few linguistic environments in common, their meanings are very different. Selection is difficult to state precisely for the words of a whole language and differs markedly from field to field (consider the varied uses of the word "field" itself). However, in particular areas of discourse, especially those where the vocabulary is limited and usage is regular (e.g., science subfields), selectional classes can be defined precisely and selectional rules have virtually the force of grammatical constraints. E.g., in cell biology: "Ions enter the cell," but not: "The cell enters ions."

MAJOR GRAMMATICAL THEORIES

Certain major schemata, or theories, of grammatical structure in linguistics have also been used in computational efforts to treat language on a broad scale.

Immediate Constituent Analysis (ICA) was initially formulated by Leonard Bloomfield [1]. It describes the structure of a sentence as a sequence of certain kinds of segments (e.g., noun phrase + verb phrase), each of which is characterized as being composed in turn of certain segment sequences, down to the words or morphemes of the language. This type of grammar is readily expressed as a set of context-free productions, i.e., as rules of the form A → B, where A is a symbol from a given alphabet of symbols, and B is also such a symbol or sequence of symbols. This formalism is well suited for specifying the gross structure of sentences (whether in terms of ICA or of other grammatical formulations) but does not provide a means for treating such essential features of natural language as grammatical subclass constraints and selection, noted above. ICA was used in a context-free formulation in an early system developed by the RAND Corp. The system employed a fast bottom-up parsing algorithm, but because of the limits of context-free grammar was unable to overcome the problem of multiple analyses.

String analysis is a grammatical formulation that was developed (by Harris in 1959) specifically for language computation. It differs from ICA primarily in that it isolates in any given sentence an elementary sentence, called the center string, on which the rest of the sentence is built. Further additions to the center string are elementary word strings of given types, called adjunct strings, which adjoin to the left or right of particular elements in other strings in the sentence. When one compares a string analysis with an immediate constituent analysis of a sentence, one sees that the successive words of an elementary string are the centers of endocentric constructions (constructions of the type X containing an X in them) in the constituent analysis. E.g., "A small dog barks loudly" has the immediate constituents Noun phrase = "a small dog" and Verb phrase = "barks loudly," both of which are endocentric. The centers of these constructions are, respectively, "dog" and "barks," which together constitute the center string of the sentence under string analysis.

String analysis is used in the system developed by the Linguistic String Project at New York University (NYU). The utility of string analysis for computation lies in the fact that there are simple rules for combining elementary strings to form sentences, and that grammatical and selectional constraints apply to words within one elementary string or in contiguous strings related by adjunction. This means that the grammatical and selectional constraints that are needed to obtain the correct analysis can be applied locally, without extensive searches of the parse tree. For example, number agreement and other constraints can be tested by the same procedure in elementary sentences ("A dog barks") and in more complicated sentences ("A small dog which confronts a large dog barks loudly") because the relevant words are contiguous in the elementary string. This is true regardless of how many words intervene between the relevant words in the given sentence. It is also found that the component elementary strings in a given sentence S bear a close relation to the elementary sentences that are the components of S under transformational analysis.

Transformational analysis was introduced into linguistics (by Harris in 1952) as an outgrowth of work on discourse structure. In that work it was clear that many sentences and sentence parts, while differing in grammatical form, were similar in content and, in fact, contained the same vocabulary items except for certain grammatical words or affixes, e.g., "which," "by," "-ing." When two or more such forms satisfied certain conditions, they were called transforms of each other. The forms were understood to be sequences of variables of the type N noun, V verb, etc. (called variables because their values are different words in different sentences) and grammatical words or affixes, called constants of the transformation. A classic example is the active-passive transformation:

$$N_1 \; t \; V \; N_2 \longleftrightarrow N_2 \; t \; be \; V\text{-en} \; by \; N_1$$

Here N_1, t (tense), V, and N_2 are the variables and "be," "-en" (past participle marker), and "by" are the grammatical constants. For example, if N_1 has the value

"Withering," t the value "-ed" (past), V the value "use," and N_2 the value "digitalis," we have the transformational relation between two sentences:

Withering used digitalis in 1784 ⟷ Digitalis was used by Withering in 1784

Note that the information content is the same in both forms though a shift in emphasis or other stylistic change may be introduced by the transformation.

Transformations become the basis for a grammar when it is seen that all (or virtually all) the word-string components of a sentence—say, under string analysis—are derivable by known transformations from independent sentences. Thus, from "Withering used digitalis in 1784," we might have in addition to the above: "digitalis, which was used by Withering in 1784," "the use of digitalis by Withering in 1784," "Withering's 1784 use of digitalis," etc. A sentence, then, under transformational analysis, is decomposed into elementary source sentences plus transformations operating on the elementary sentences or on already transformed sentences. Some transformations, such as the active-passive, and the replacing of a particular noun by a pronoun, are purely paraphrastic; that is, they add no information and are only a rearrangement of parts or a change in the shape of words. Others add a fixed increment of meaning to the operand sentence, the same addition of meaning to all operand sentences (for example, "seems" in "The heart seems to respond," "The child seems to understand," etc.).

A question-answering system (REQUEST) that includes transformational analysis has been developed at IBM. The NYU Linguistic String Project system includes transformational decomposition of text sentences, operating on the string parse outputs. The relevance of transformational analysis is that while being a grammatical procedure, it nevertheless yields a uniform representation of the information in sentences. If, for example, two sentences contain the same information presented in different styles, or if they overlap in their information content, then the information which they carry in common will appear in the transformational analysis of the sentences as identical component elementary sentences with the same incremental transformations; they will differ only in the paraphrastic transformations in the decomposition. This means, in principle, that sentences can be compared in a standard fashion for sameness or overlap in content.

<u>Transformational generative grammar</u> was introduced by Chomsky [2, 3] as a system for generating sentences. The system combined elements of immediate constituent analysis (in the form of phrase structure rules) with transformations. The grammar contains a small set of phrase structure productions, with the root symbol S for sentence (e.g., S → NP VP, NP → Det N, VP → verb), and a mechanism for realizing terminal symbols as words. These are used to generate the "deep structure" of the sentence. Transformational rules operate on the deep structure tree and on successive trees produced by the operation of transformations until a final "surface structure" tree is obtained. This structure is then interpreted by means of phonological, semantic, and logical rules.

This formulation of grammar has been used in several computational systems, chiefly at the MITRE Corp. and IBM. However, reversing the generative process in order to analyze sentences requires a number of extra steps that are necessitated by the fact that the grammar is oriented toward generation rather than analysis. First a set of surface structure trees must be obtained for the sentence. This requires a parsing, or covering, grammar which is different from the transformational grammar. The set of surface·structure trees which are obtained should contain the one which would be generated for the given sentence by the transformational grammar. The procedure must determine which sequence of transformations operated to produce the surface structure and what was the deep structure tree that was generated using the phrase structure rules. One source of difficulty is that too many surface structure trees may be generated, requiring that many different sequences of reverse transformations be tried. Another problem is that at each point where a reverse transformation is to be applied, a number of reverse transformations might qualify, thereby increasing the number of paths that have to be checked. In practice, special measures to increase efficiency are required or the process takes too long. Also, because of the multiple sources of error, each analysis which is obtained must be verified by a forward generation process.

For dependency grammar, see the article under that heading in Volume 7.

BRIEF HISTORY OF LANGUAGE COMPUTATION

Early research projects in natural language processing, in the period dating from the late 1950s through the mid-1960s, for the most part had large applicational goals and were optimistic about rapid progress. Many projects were directed toward mechanical translation (MT), and some projects were concerned with processing texts for information retrieval. In virtually all the major efforts, the goal was to be able to treat the language as a whole, not a particular subset relating to a specific subject matter or application. One might mention from this period the earliest translation program (Russian to English) of Ida Rhodes at the Bureau of Standards in 1959, based on Predictive Analysis, a method which was later extended and adapted to English by Oettinger and Kuno in the system known as the Harvard Predictive Analyzer. The earliest English syntactic analysis program was developed at the University of Pennsylvania in 1958-1959 in a system which combined ICA with string analysis. This program was used to provide the language analysis in the first question answering system (Baseball 1961). String analysis was extended and implemented for practical applications of text analysis at New York University from 1965 onward, and was used in a program for analyzing narrative surgical reports at Roswell Park Memorial Institute in Buffalo. A major effort in language analysis for information retrieval in French was the SYNTOL Project (cf. references in Sparck Jones and Kay [4]). In the 1960s several large projects were based on the transformational generative grammar, principally those of the MITRE Corp. and IBM. The early systems were mainly documented in report series, of which the major ones are listed in the Resources section at the end of this article.

The initial hopes of rapid progress toward large-scale applications received serious setbacks when the language problem proved to be more complex and unwieldy than had been realized at first. Many MT projects had relied primarily on dictionary look-up and were faced with problems due to the syntactic complexity of text sentences and the differences in grammatical requirements in language pairs, as well as the lexical problems of translation. The MT field fell under serious criticism when the large expenditure of research funds failed to yield commensurate results (1966 Report of the Automated Language Processing Advisory Committee of the National Academy of Science, Language and Machines—Computers in Translation and Linguistics). Also, in the area of single-language text analysis, although there was progress, the magnitude of the linguistic data which had to be organized and the problem of ambiguities in the analysis turned out to be major stumbling blocks, requiring the development of special tools.

The result of these developments was that in the late 1960s and in the 1970s, much of natural language processing research concerned itself with what could be accomplished using sophisticated software on narrowly delineated language areas.

Question-answering systems flowered, since here the scope of the problem was limited syntactically to question forms and semantically to the exact categories of the given data base, which was usually a numerical table or the equivalent. Some systems reached practical operational status (e.g., Bolt Beranek and Newman's system for lunar rock data retrieval, and IBM's REQUEST system operating on business statistics). Systems which combined syntactic, semantic, and task-oriented procedures were referred to as integrated systems, and included experiments in robotics with natural language instructions. Of the early projects, the Linguistic String Project has continued the development of a large grammar with a broad capability for text analysis.

Renewed interest in natural language processing on the part of information scientists and others arose in the 1970s with the advent of machine-readable natural language data bases, interactive on-line systems (that can take over some of the burden of analysis in man-machine dialog), and the steady advance on all fronts in the computer field, providing lower costs, increased availability of components, and more sophisticated software. Medicine, education, business, and government all appeared to have one eye cocked toward natural language processing should it indeed prove possible to communicate with machines in natural language and to access computer-stored written information by means of computer programs.

REQUISITES FOR COMPUTER ANALYSIS OF LANGUAGE

Part of the reason why progress in natural language processing was slower than anticipated was the fact that the requisite linguistic and computational tools were not available and had to be developed.

Enriched Formalisms

As was noted above, natural language differs from formal languages in important respects. Before successful language computations could be performed, enriched formalisms and their associated recognition procedures had to be developed. One approach has been to specify the grammar on two levels. Context-free productions, or the equivalent, are used to define parse tree structures, and procedures which operate on the generated parse trees are the means for expressing grammatical and semantic restrictions and transformations. This approach has proved suitable in several forms, e.g., using string analysis and transformations as the framework, and using augmented transition network (ATN) grammars.

Computer Grammars

The possibility of incorporating into a computer program the large number of linguistic facts needed for correct analysis of sentences depends on having an appropriate linguistic theory and a sufficiently rich formalism. But this is not enough. The actual grammar has to be written, and if semantic interpretation is to be done, the lexical coding and the procedures for this stage of processing also have to be written. The writing of a computer grammar of a natural language is a big undertaking. One could imagine, as many early investigators did—hence their optimism—that existing grammars of languages would provide the necessary rules and that the problem would simply be one of coding the rules for use in procedures.

But that has proven not to be the case. A conventional grammar, such as Jespersen's monumental seven-volume work on English, while rich in detail, is not organized or formulated in such a way that the observations can easily be assimilated into a formal framework. On the other hand, much of the grammatical work that has been done in a formal framework, chiefly in transformational generative grammar, has not led to an integrated grammar of the whole language, and does not deal with the issues faced in recognition. Computational linguists have therefore had to write their own grammars, or parts of grammars, covering the range of language material their systems are intended to handle.

The positive side of this is that some linguistic phenomena have been formulated in greater detail than ever before. The negative side is that in most cases a "grammar" which is specified for a particular subset of a language is not readily extendible to cover the whole language, or a significant portion thereof. The reason is that the treatment of one phenomenon affects how others can be treated, so that a global view of the grammar is needed from the start or the system becomes unwieldy on expansion, with conflicts and redundancies in the analysis. Thus the field has seen very many small coverage systems which are extendible in principle but which are short-lived in practice because of this problem.

Treatment of Ambiguity

In addition to the fact that a suitable grammar has to be written, the computational linguist faces the problem that a syntactic analyzer "sees" possible readings of the sentence that a person is unaware of. Partly, this points to the need for selectional or semantic constraints. However, in addition to these, some weighting as to which are the more likely grammatical configurations appears to be necessary. For example, in the following instance of syntactic ambiguity, all three readings obtained by a parsing program were semantically possible, but the grammatical analysis on the first parse was the more likely of the three. The program obtained the following three analyses for the sentence "We have studied membrane potentials recorded with intracellular microelectrodes." The first was the intended reading, in which "have studied" is a verbal unit occurring with "membrane potentials recorded with intracellular microelectrodes" as its noun phrase object. In this noun phrase, "recorded . . ." is a passive adjunct of "potentials." However, the program also found two other possible uses of "have" in this sentence, each of which meshed with another source of ambiguity so as to produce an additional reading. In one, the main verb is "have" ("We have potentials") and "studied" is a passive modifier of "potentials," paraphrastic to "We have potentials which were studied." The other spurious reading contains the same analysis of "studied potentials" as a noun group, but this time as the embedded subject of "recorded" under the verb "have": "We have potentials recorded," paraphrastic to "We have arranged that potentials be recorded." The ambiguity in this sentence illustrates a new kind of problem to be studied: what are the more likely combinations of grammatical forms.

In addition to those syntactic ambiguities which involve different segmentations of the sentence, illustrated above, alternative readings arise due to the reassignment of a given segment to be a modifier of a different element in the sentence, e.g., "He wrote a book on cooking in the Chinese style." Eliminating the unintended readings in these cases usually depends on selectional constraints for the type of discourse or on regularities observable in the context. Ambiguity resolution often requires constraints on several levels and is not usually attainable without restricting the system to a particular subject domain.

Treatment of Implicit Elements

In addition to treating the words that are present in a discourse, a natural language processor has to deal with some words that are present in "zeroed" form, that is, are not physically present but are reconstructible from the context, e.g., "left" after "she" in "He left and she too." Also, some words refer to other words or stretches of the discourse, e.g., personal pronouns and phrases like "this process," "the foregoing." To complete the analysis and to perform content-oriented tasks, the zeroed words must be supplied and the antecedents of referentials identified. In addition, on the discourse level, one might have to supply entire implicit sentences (sentences assumed by the reader in order to read the text as a coherent discourse). These and related matters are discussed in the literature in papers on conjunctions, reference resolution, discourse structure, and inference systems.

Approaches to Meaning

There is no single path, valid for the language as a whole, from the syntactic analysis of sentences to their meaning. The syntactic analysis clearly provides some information (e.g., what is the subject and what is the object of the action expressed by a verb in an assertion), but to arrive at an exact and useful characterization of the contents of sentences, special processing using specialized lexicons is required. One approach is to derive the relevant categories for the words in an area of discourse by examining detailed co-occurrence patterns (selection) of words in subject-verb-object and similar relations in samples of the textual material. Another approach has been to provide the relevant categories from general knowledge, based on the view held by various investigators that semantic categories are largely independent of syntactic relations in the texts and can be stated a priori for the language as a whole, or significant portions of it. The purely semantic approach has yet to be demonstrated on a broad enough range of subject matters so that its merits can be evaluated.

STAGES OF PROCESSING

Although systems differ as to how they distribute the burden of analysis between the syntactic component and the semantic component, both types of processing are present in some form, and can be presented here as operating serially. It should be noted that both components require a lexicon in which words are given classifications needed for processing, and that this represents a considerable share of the cost and effort of setting up a workable system.

Parsing

When a sentence is read into the computer for processing, the first step is to look up the words in the lexicon and associate with each successive word of the input string its major classifications and subclassifications. (In some applications not every word need be coded prior to processing.) For example, the major classes associated with each word of the following sentence from a medical record are

Patient was admitted to hospital for meningitis.
N/ADJ TV TV/VEN P   N   P   N.

In addition, grammatical subclass information such as the following might be noted: "Patient" as a noun is singular, and so are the nouns "hospital" and "meningitis" and the verb "was." Also, for semantic processing it might be noted that in the medical sublanguage from which the words are drawn, "patient" is in a distinguished class (PATIENT), "admit" is a medical action verb (V-MD), "hospital" is a medical institution word (INST), and "meningitis" is a diagnosis word (DIAG). The set of subclasses for a particular sublanguage can be obtained by the analysis of word co-occurrence patterns in samples of the textual material.

The determination of syntactic structure is accomplished by a parsing algorithm that draws upon the grammar and the lexical attributes of the sentence words. The object of parsing is to produce a structural representation of the sentence, such as the one shown in Fig. 1, for the sentence: "Significant past history—Patient was found to have sickle cell disease during first admission to Bellevue for H. Influenzae Meningitis," a typical sentence from a hospital discharge summary. (The dropping of the definite article is typical of the telegraphic style of reports and records.) In the parse tree of Fig. 1, sibling nodes are connected by a horizontal line and the parent node is attached to the left-most daughter node only; branches end in terminal nodes (e.g., N, TV) or literals (e.g., "to") associated with sentence words (shown just below the terminal symbol or literal) or in NULL (not shown). The paragraph heading ("Significant Past History") is not parsed.

Parsing strategies differ. Figure 1 was obtained using a top-down algorithm in conjunction with a grammar that had two components, a set of context-free productions for generating parse tree structures of the linguistic string type, and a set of procedures, called restrictions, associated with particular elements in the productions, for checking the well-formedness of word-subclass combinations (e.g., number agreement, selection). Briefly, the top-down parser generates a parse tree from the context-free productions and attempts to match each successive terminal node of the tree with a word class assignment of the current sentence word, stepping from left-to-right through the sentence. If a terminal node X matches the X category of the current sentence word, a pointer is created from X in the parse tree to X in the lexical entry for that word. Thus, in Fig. 1, when the terminal node N under SUBJECT matched the N category of "patient," the subclassifications of "patient" in the lexicon (e.g., SINGULAR became attributes of the N in the parse tree.

The parser is also equipped with a restriction interpreter, tree climbing operators, logical operators, and attribute-testing operators. These enable it to test the parse tree, including the attributes (subclasses) that have been attached to terminal nodes. Thus, after the SUBJECT and VERB subtrees have been completed, the parser can apply an agreement restriction by making the following test: Starting at the node VERB, descend to the node TV and test for the attribute SINGULAR/PLURAL; store the result. Now start again from VERB, go to the sibling SUBJECT; descend to the noun; test for SINGULAR/PLURAL; compare this with the stored attribute and register success if the items match. (This is a much simplified version of the real restriction.) If all the restrictions associated with a node succeed, the parsing continues; if not, the subtree is rejected and the parser "backs up" to try other grammar options for building the tree.

For a description of alternative parsing algorithms, a survey such as Grishman 1975 in the Courant Report Series (cf. Resources section below) can be consulted.

Grammatical Regularization

The parse tree gives valuable information about the sentence but it has several limitations as a structural representation for information processing. Language

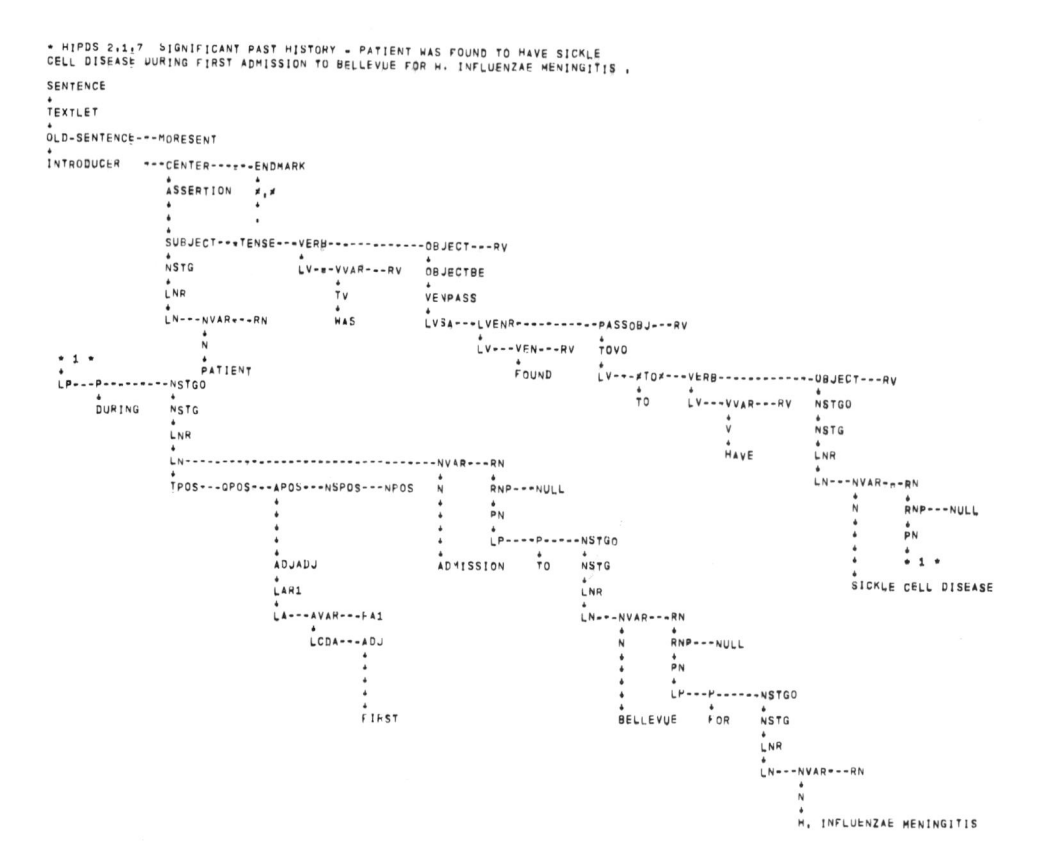

```
* HIPDS 2.1.7  SIGNIFICANT PAST HISTORY = PATIENT WAS FOUND TO HAVE SICKLE
CELL DISEASE DURING FIRST ADMISSION TO BELLEVUE FOR H. INFLUENZAE MENINGITIS .
SENTENCE
    •
 TEXTLET
    •
OLD-SENTENCE---MORESENT
    •
INTRODUCER   *---CENTER---*---ENDMARK
             ASSERTION   #,#
                •
                •
                •
             SUBJECT--*-TENSE---VERB------------OBJECT---RV
             NSTG         LV-*-VVAR---RV   OBJECTBE
             LNR          TV               VENPASS
             LN---NVAR---RN   WAS          LVSA---LVENR--------PASSOBJ---RV
             N                             LV---VEN---RV     TOVO
 * 1 *       PATIENT                       FOUND       LV-*-*TO*---VERB------------OBJECT---RV
 LP---P-------NSTGO                                    TO     LV---VVAR---RV    NSTGO
   DURING    NSTG                                             V                 LNR
             LNR                                              HAVE              LN---NVAR-*-RN
             LN-------------------------NVAR---RN                               N     RNP---NULL
             TPOS---QPOS---APOS---NSPOS---NPOS   N   RNP---NULL                       PN
                •                                    PN                               * 1 *
                •                                    LP---P-----NSTGO          SICKLE CELL DISEASE
             ADJADJ                ADMISSION  TO   NSTG
             LAR1                                  LNR
             LA---AVAR---FA1                       LN-*-NVAR--*-RN
             LCDA---ADJ                            N     RNP---NULL
                                                         PN
                                                         LP---P------NSTGO
             FIRST                                 BELLEVUE  FOR   NSTG
                                                                   LNR
                                                                   LN---NVAR---RN
                                                                   N
                                                                   H. INFLUENZAE MENINGITIS
```

FIG. 1. Parse tree (Figs. 1-3 are outputs of the NYU Linguistic String Project System.) Node names—terminal symbols: N noun, P preposition, ADJ adjective, TV tensed verb, VEN past participle.

Types of nonterminal symbols: For X = a terminal symbol: LX left adjuncts of X; RX right adjuncts of X; LXR a sequence of LX + X + RX or of LX + XVAR + RX; XVAR local variants of X; XPOS position of X-occurrence among ordered adjuncts.

Other node names: SA sentence adjunct; NSTG noun string; NSTGT noun string of time; NSTGO noun string in object; PN prepositional phrase; ADJADJ repeating adjectives; LCDA left adjuncts of compound adjective; OBJECTBE object of be; VENPASS passive string; LVSA left adjuncts of verb in participial SA string; PASSOBJ object in passive string.

Output conventions: A prepositional phrase PN which has several possible positions of adjunction is assigned in the parse tree to the nearest PN slot (here BELLEVUE FOR MENINGITIS rather than ADMISSION FOR MENINGITIS). The later stages of processing correct the assignment on the basis of word co-occurrence classes.

has too many different grammatical structures to deal with, and some of the different structures contain the same information. Adding a stage of transformational analysis eliminates grammatical paraphrases; it results in fewer forms and leads to a canonical representation of information. For example, two sentences which contain, respectively, "Ca^{++} exchanges with other cations in SR" and "the exchange of Ca^{++} with other cations in SR," carry the same information over these stretches, and it would be a definite gain to have only one representation for it. Furthermore, it is hoped that the structural representation of the sentence after transformational analysis will be closer to a representation of its contents than either the original word string or, in most cases, the syntactic parse.

An example of a transformational decomposition obtained by applying (reverse) transformations to the output of a string parsing program is shown in Fig. 2 for the same sentence as in Fig. 1. Figure 2 shows the computer output for a transformational decomposition obtained by applying reverse transformations to the parse tree output shown in Fig. 1. In this form of output the sentence is decomposed into elementary ASSERTION structures in which the VERB (or adjective or preposition— also labeled VERB) precedes the SUBJECT and OBJECT node as in Polish notation. The transformations used to obtain each ASSERTION appear as T-nodes above the ASSERTION. Thus the main ASSERTION was obtained from the original parse tree structure for "Patient was found to have sickle cell disease" by the application of the PAST tense transformation and the PASSIVE transformation. The PAST tense transformation recognized "was" as a past tense verb and replaced it by a tenseless form of "be" (later itself replaced). The PASSIVE transformation in effect turned "Patient be (past) found to have sickle cell disease" into "( ) find (past) patient to have sickle cell disease," where ( ) represents an unstated subject. Under the OBJECT node of this ASSERTION the T-NTOVO transformation converted the object structure (called NTOVO) covering "patient to have sickle cell disease" into a tenseless ASSERTION "Patient have sickle cell disease." With regard to T-SA-PN in this analysis, the time expression "during first admission . . .," which modifies the main assertion, is transformed into an assertion which has the main assertion as its subject, the transformational paraphrase being: "Patient was found to have sickle cell disease, and this (act of finding) was during the first admission . . ." (see legend of Fig. 2 regarding HOST). An example of the nominalization transformation T-VN-ACT in Fig. 2 is the expansion of "admission to Bellevue for . . . meningitis" to "( ) admit ( ) to Bellevue for . . . meningitis," where again ( ) represents unstated arguments. A difficult part of the nominalization transformation is identifying the arguments of the verb which usually appear as prepositional phrases among other prepositional modifiers.

Complete transformational decomposition is important for calculating word co-occurrence similarities, since then we wish to have every occurrence of the same root word in a form where it can be counted with the others. In other applications it is possible to regularize the representation without actually carrying out every reverse transformation. For example, "admission" can be recognized as related to "admit" via subclassification rather than decomposition (as in Fig. 3) if the purpose is to develop an underlying semantic representation for the particular material rather than to reduce the sentences to a very general informational representation.

Semantic Representation

Most applications require a representation of sentences that is quite specific to the subject matter of the language material to be treated. At the same time the

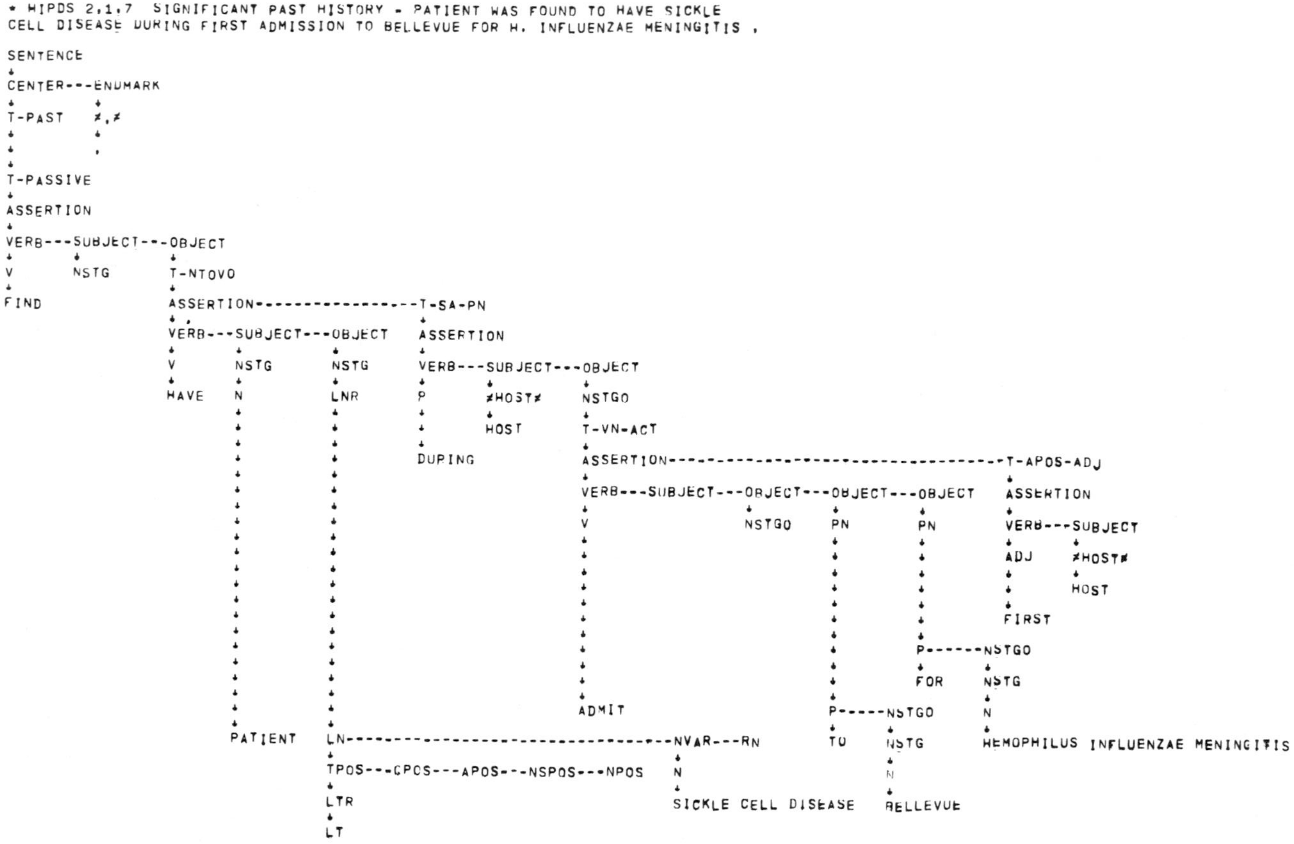

FIG. 2. Transformational decomposition. The subtree under a transformational node (labeled T-x) is the result of applying the reverse transformation named by T-x to the appropriate parse tree structure. If the subtree under such a node contains a node N_1 which is a copy of a node N_2 in the structure to which T-x is connected, then the value of N_1 is a node HOST which contains a pointer to N_2. In the figure the HOST nodes each contain a pointer to the second ASSERTION above HOST in the tree.

Natural Language Analysis and Processing

```
* HIPDS 2.1.7  SIGNIFICANT PAST HISTORY - PATIENT WAS FOUND TO HAVE SICKLE
CELL DISEASE DURING FIRST ADMISSION TO BELLEVUE FOR H. INFLUENZAE MENINGITIS .

FORMAT ---CONNECTIVE ---FORMAT
 +           +             +
DATA         CONN          DATA
 +           +             +
 +           REL-CLAUSE    TREATMT --------------------------TR-ST-CONN---PT-STATUS
 +           +             +                                  +
 +           +             INST------------------------VER3-MD    FOR    FINDING
 +           +             +                            +      +         +
 +           +             BELLEVUE---LEFT-ADJUNCT    V-MD              QUAL
 +           +             +           +              +                 +
 +           +             +           +              +                 DIAG
 +           +             +           +              +                 +
 +           +             +           +              +                 H.INFLUENZAE MENINGITIS
 +           +             +           +              +
 +           EXPAND-REFPT  TO                     ADMISSION---LEFT-ADJUNCT
 +           +                                                  +
 +           QUAL                                                FIRST
 +           +
 +           ADMISSION
 +
PATIENT ---TREATMT ---PT-STATUS
 +         +             +
 PT        VERB-MD       VERB-PT ---FINDING
 +         +             +          +
 +         +             V-PT       QUAL
 +         +             +          +
 +         +             HAVE       DIAG-----------------TIME
 +         +             +          +                     +
 PATIENT   V-MD---TIME              SICKLE CELL DISEASE  EVENT-TIME
           +     +                                        +
           FIND  V-TENSE                                 TPREP2---REF-PT
                 +                                        +        +
                 PAST---PASSIVE                          DURING   ADMISSION
```

FIG. 3. Information structure.

method of obtaining that representation must be general enough so that it covers paraphrastic variations and is not so special to the subject matter that a new system has to be built for each application. A sufficiently rich syntactic component which includes the reduction of grammatical paraphrases, such as was illustrated above, can with few adjustments provide the gross structure of sentences in any language material. This leaves the well-defined task of determining the more detailed relations of the words within these structures. It is found that in a given subject area the patterns of word co-occurrence in these structures correlate with the different kinds of information being transmitted. For example, in medical reporting, verbs that characteristically take as their subject such nouns as "hospital," "doctor," "clinic," and some other words, conveniently labeled the "medical institution class," generally have the semantic character of "actions taken in treating a patient." This is hardly surprising. However, the fact that this type of correlation between distribution and meaning occurs widely means that the classes needed for information processing and other applications can be derived from a study of co-occurrence patterns in samples of the language material.

In addition to determining semantic word classes, word co-occurrence patterns that are characteristic of a given subject matter can be systematized into formats for the information that is carried by the discourses in that subject area. A program can then map regularized parse outputs into the format. An example of such a structure for the medical reports sentence that has been carried through the stages of computer processing here is shown in Fig. 3. Each format unit for this material contains a TREATMENT part and a PATIENT STATUS part, though both are not present in every sentence. (Only format headings that subsume sentence words are printed.) References to the patient are brought out to the left; otherwise the order of entries follows normalized syntactic order. In Fig. 3 the first format unit has the medical action "find" and the patient status "have sickle cell disease," each with its own associated time. The second format unit has the medical action verb "admit" (in its untransformed state "admission") under TREATMENT and a connective ("for") between TREATMENT and PATIENT STATUS. In this case the admission was for the diagnosis "meningitis" (under FINDING under PATIENT STATUS). The connective between the two format units in Fig. 3 is the expansion of the time reference point "admission" of the first unit.

Figure 3 illustrates one kind of semantic structuring; other types are referenced in the Resources section. Here, node labels correspond to the types of entities and relations that are important in the subject area and are present in a regular way in the discourse. The syntactic relations of words in the sentence (after removing the effect of paraphrastic transformations) provide the skeletal structure of the format. In subject areas where such information formats can be defined, a system equipped with the three stages of processing—parsing, regularizing, and formatting—can map the sentences of documents into the formats. This provides a structured data base containing the same information as the documents. From this data base, programs can answer questions automatically and generate statistical summaries, such as (for the data base of the sample sentence): How many patients with symptom X also had symptom Y within time period Z ? And so forth. It can be seen that while computers cannot "understand" natural language, they can be programmed to utilize the structural regularities of the language—both the syntactic regularities of the language as a whole and the usage regularities of specialized areas—so as to analyze the sentences of a discourse and arrange its informational content in relevant ways.

REFERENCES

1. L. Bloomfield, Language, Holt, Rinehart and Winston, New York, 1933.
2. N. Chomsky, Syntactic Structures, Mouton, The Hague, 1957.
3. N. Chomsky, Aspects of the Theory of Syntax, M.I.T. Press, Cambridge, Massachusetts, 1965.
4. K. Sparck Jones and M. Kay, Linguistics and Information Science, Academic, New York, 1973.

8
Automatic Analysis

Mary Elizabeth Stevens* / National Bureau of Standards, Gaithersburg, Maryland

Recognition and Detection

How is automatic analysis carried out by machine? First, we may consider machine capabilities for the sensing of prespecified patterns of physically encoded selection criteria. If, for example, there are machine-usable circulation records, then a periodic machine check can produce a list of all borrowers with overdue books. This compilation is possible by virtue of machine capabilities for counting, sorting, tabulating, and comparing, especially in the sense of determining whether the recorded due date, e.g., "5-15-67," is greater or less in numeric value than today's date, e.g., "5-19-67." If, for example, the record for a given item is indeed 5-15-67 and today's date is equal to or greater than this, this item and all others similarly equaling or exceeding the recorded numeric value for "today's date" will be selectively sorted out so that overdue notices may be sent to the specific clients involved.

Another early form of automatic analysis was that of selection of certain items or records on the basis of mask matching. Suppose, for example, we used a simple code for documents stored in the form of blacking out the individual letters comprising the last name of each author:

From Stevens, Mary Elizabeth. *Automatic Analysis.* ENCYCLOPEDIA OF LIBRARY AND INFORMATION SCIENCE. Vol. 2. Edited by Allen Kent and Harold Lancour. Assistant Editor, William Z. Nasri, New York, Marcel Dekker, Inc., c1969. pp. 147–154; 158–159.
*Presently retired

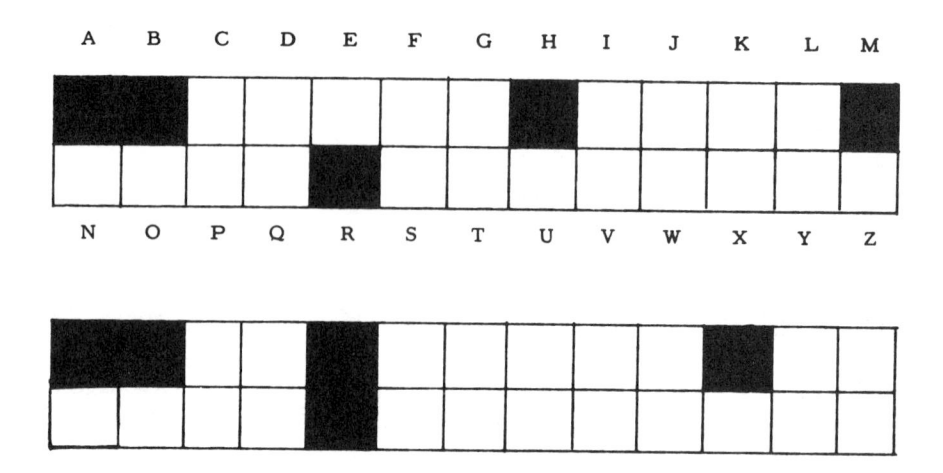

Then a photographic negative image of the code for "Baker":

would, when compared with or superimposed on those shown above, select only the second, as by the extinction of light that is beamed against the superimposed records to a photosensitive cell (on much the same principle that some automatically controlled doors open when one approaches). Now suppose that these codes are physically recorded on or adjacent to a facsimile or micro-image copy of the documents to which they refer and that the code selection is automatically accompanied by retrieval or printout from the record of the indicated document on microform. This is the principle of the Bush Microfilm Rapid Selector as proposed in the 1930s and of the later Minicard system.

A closely similar technique was used in some of the earliest approaches to automatic analysis as applied to optical character recognition problems. In the mask or template-matching technique, as shown in the accompanying illustration (Figure 1) of some common recognition techniques (line a), we will find, for example, that an input character A will leave large patches of nonconforming black or white when scanned against the corresponding mask for the character B.

In other techniques, such as shown on line d, the input character is sliced, in effect, into a number of successive vertical portions and in each portion the relative amount of ink is determined (either by the amount of blackness in the area scanned or, in the case of bank checks, by its relative magnetization).

In still another type of technique, the entire input character area is looked at as though through a superimposed rectangular grid and the relative blackness or whiteness to be seen in each cell or box is checked. For example, a stylized A might appear as shown in line c of the illustration to a particular automatic analysis device designed for character recognition with stylized fonts such as that adopted as a standard character set by the United States of America Standards Institute.

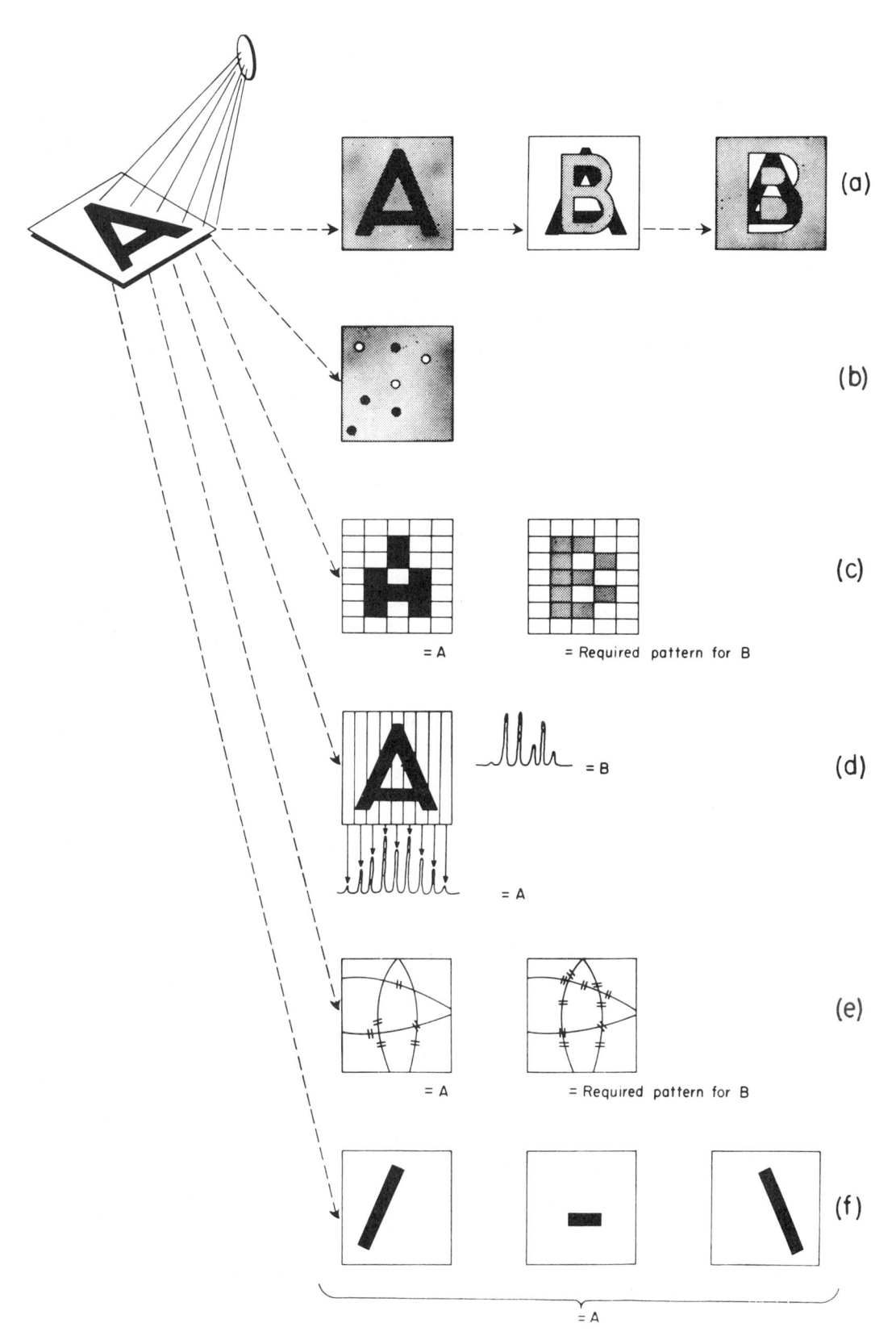

FIGURE 1. *Some common recognition techniques.*

Then there are techniques that involve what might be termed discriminating or "criterial crossings" detection (e.g., that character strokes cross or do not cross superimposed lines, as in line e of the illustration, or that they do or do not occur in certain arbitrary areas of an input image field). Such techniques, in particular, have been investigated in experiments on the recognition of constrained handprinted characters.

In still other character recognition techniques, the black-white boundary of the input image of an unknown character or symbol or photographic image of one or more objects can be traced, and the machine can keep track of the number, direction, and magnitude of changes in direction of the tracing device. The final formula can then be compared with prestored formulas that are typical for A's, B's, and other characters. Such a technique may also be applied in automatic analysis of aerial photographs where the machine is looking for parallel straight lines that are close together to detect streets or for other combinations that may indicate particular configurations typical of various airport runway patterns.

Thus beyond the questions of automatic character recognition are problems of other types of pattern recognition including those of speech, stenotype records, photographic and microphotographic records, patterns in sonic wave measurements or seismological events, and the like. At another level, pattern recognition problems are involved in format differentiations, such as automatic discrimination between text and graphic material on a printed page so that appropriate layout information may be preserved for later reconstruction.

Where the input pattern to be subjected to the techniques of automatic analysis is nearly identical to previously observed exemplars of its pattern class, the problem is relatively easy to solve with a variety of currently demonstrable techniques. Hence, the problems of pattern identification (whether of handwritten signatures, fingerprint impressions, or spoken passwords) may be complex but they are typically less so than those of pattern recognition in the case of many ambiguous identification clues and of pattern detection generally. Specific problems of automatic pattern recognition are exemplified by those of detecting the presence and determining the identity of signals that are embedded in noise.

In terms of the detection of patterns in the presence of noise, the technology of automatic analysis is directed first to the extraction of criterial or salient features or properties in the general input-image area. That is, the machine may be directed to look for a leading left or right black stroke when scanning successive "slices" of an imprinted character. This is one of the reasons, for example, for the slightly odd appearance of the numeral 1 in many bank-check account or credit card number imprintings.

Thus there are character and pattern recognition techniques which look for significant or "criterial" features. This might be done, for example, as in line f of Figure 1, by moving over the input-image area masks for a diagonal sloping upward to the right, a short horizontal bar, and a leftward sloping diagonal and noting whether or not coincidence occurs for all three. Similarly we might look for a white area entirely enclosed by black in the upper part of the input-image area and another in the lower part and so recognize either a B or the numeral 8.

Such techniques of analysis may also be extended to whole printed or written words. That is, in the case of block-printed words, such as the written-out form of the 10 digits, we may find that the numerals 9 and 4 each have six consecutive instances of some vertical black, but that one and not the other has, first, no horizontal at the top where the other has; next, both have some horizontal at the top; and so on, with differentiating features occurring on "some horizontal, bottom" for the third and fourth letters.

Because of both contextual and significant feature considerations, among other factors, whole-word recognition schemes may have certain advantages over character-by-character optical recognition systems. Examples have been provided in long-range investigations of possibilities for machine recognition of cursive handwriting and in certain more application-oriented experiments such as those directed toward postal address identifications.

Still further extensions of such techniques could be used to extract automatically keywords that match a presupplied list, stored in the machine, from a text that is being automatically scanned, then, to count the number of such extractions, and to use the results of these operations perhaps to prepare a concordance, perhaps to compile a keyword index, or perhaps to route a new document to a client who has expressed interest in all documents that discuss supersonic jet fighters.

Quite similar or analogous techniques are applied in the case of automatic speech recognition, including, for example, the use of frequency bank filters to extract from speech frequency spectra certain discriminating features. Thus the frequency spectra for fricatives, sibilants, and vowels in human speech exhibit noticeable differences when converted, for example, into a two-dimensional graphic plot or into discriminatory codings suitable for machine processing. Voice and speech recognition may eventually be applicable in libraries not only for vocal inquiries but also for applications such as the "Bibliofoon" at Delft University Library.

If these differences are distinct enough, we may build a recognition matrix such that if any member of the class "s" or "sh" or "ts" or "z" occurs, followed by "e" or "i," then by "b" or "v," again by "e" or "i," or a null signal, and finally by "n" or "m," then the output of the automatic analysis procedure as applied to English will be the decision that the spoken numeral 7 has occurred. In a practical example the German 7 which may be variously pronounced as "sieben," "zieben," "siben," "ziebn," "siebm," and so forth, can also be successfully identified by such a technique.

In general, however, the state-of-the-art in automatic analysis as applied to voice recognition up to 1967 lags behind that of automatic character recognition. Speech recognition vocabularies (that is, the number of distinct words that can be recognized by machine) are very limited and specialized; differences as between male and female speakers of the same words present continuing problems; and there remain substantial differences of opinion as to what the discriminating features of utterances of a given phoneme or word really are.

There are, however, two closely related aspects of voice recognition applications of automatic analysis techniques. The first is that of speech synthesis, whereby techniques that automatically reproduce the sound frequencies and timings of a given word or of a sequence of words may be used for data or message transmission and may contribute to more economical usage of transmission or communication links, networks, and media.

The second area of applicability is that of automatic speaker identification and the recognition of a specific individual's voice. Here it can be shown experimentally that "voice prints" are probably as unique to individuals as are their fingerprints and that machine techniques of detection and analysis can in many cases distinguish between the same words and word sequences as spoken by a given person and as spoken by professional imitators, where the human ear alone might easily be confused. Such automatic analysis possibilities are of particular importance when considered in terms of guarding against unauthorized access to shared data banks and programs and to mechanized search systems of various types.

A final example of pattern recognition problems to which the available techniques of automatic analysis may be applied is that of various image or information *enhancement* operations such as increasing and improving the black-white contrast of pictorial data inputs, especially at edges or boundaries, or of reducing the synonymity occurring in input text by referring variant expressions to a common, preferred term.

Suppose, for example, that an unknown, jagged-edge character has been looked at by a bank of photocells which each detect the amount of black it sees in its own area, with results as shown in part below:

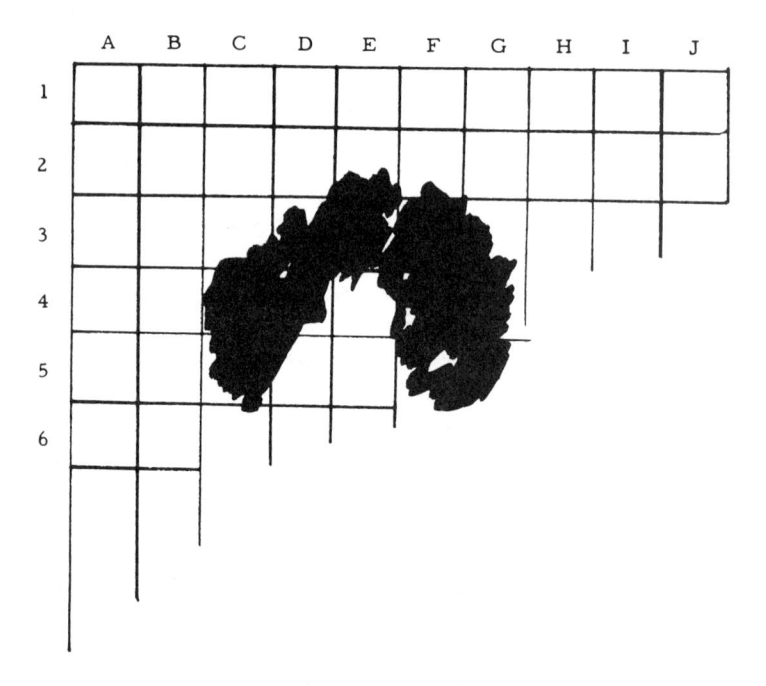

We notice first that square E2 has as much as or more black in it than square E4. However, looking at E2, we find that there is more white than black in the *majority* of its neighboring squares (D2, D1, E1, F1, and F2), whereas E4 has neighboring black squares (D3, E3, F3, D4, F4, and F5). Thus a rule can be given to the automatic analysis procedure: Wherever, for a given square x, the majority of its immediate orthogonal neighbors are black, count square x as black, and, conversely, if most of the neighbors are white, treat x as white. Such techniques reduce the amount of spurious information (the ragged character edge or superimposed dirt such as flyspecks on the paper), they sharpen and smooth the line of the character edges, and they fill in holes or gaps which result from irregular typing or printing.

The importance of this type of automatic analytic capability can be seen from Figure 2, which is a photographic enlargement of actual typewritten characters. Another important feature in this connection is the ability of some machine techniques to check for context clues. Thus, if after image enhancement operations it is still impractical to decide between a possible lower-case "o" with breaks in its right-hand curve and a possible "c" with considerable fill-in on the right, then if the ambiguous character is preceded by a distinct "c" and is followed by "w," then it is obviously "o," and if preceded by "a" and followed by "t," it is, at least in English, a "c."

The equivalent information enhancement operations for the processing of textually recorded information also involve reducing redundant information and other operations. For example, they may include both lexical and syntactic normalizations (such as transformations from the passive to the active voice and substitutions of preferred terms for various synonyms), resolutions of problems of homography, and applications of rules involving considerations of context. Such operations may be performed either entirely automatically or manually with the aid of various mechanized procedures.

In general, the techniques of automatic analysis as applied to problems of character and pattern recognition are of interest with respect to the current state-of-the-art in the information and library sciences for two major reasons. First, these techniques offer means to sense, transcribe, or rerecord information whether it occurs as data values or as textual statements. For example, the information may have been originally inscribed in a prepared format for mark-sensing, visually encoded as by means of a dot or bar code or handprinted, drawn, typed, or printed as alphanumeric characters and other graphic symbols. Second, insofar as these techniques incorporate adaptive, self-organizing, or self-classifying features, they provide significant areas for the further development and application of advanced research principles of these sciences.

FIGURE 2.

Analysis of Documentary Data

We are now at the point where it can be seen that automatic analysis operations in the area of character and pattern recognition provide one possible method of preparing documentary and textual material for machine processing and therefore for other types of automatic analysis. Unfortunately, as of mid-1967, automatic character readers capable of recognizing a wide variety of characters such as may be found on a printed page or even on a library catalog card were not yet generally available.

Major difficulties encountered with various techniques for character recognition, moreover, are that in realistically large character sets in a variety of fonts, or of sets of symbols and symbol configurations, the differences that distinguish one character from another may be small and difficult to detect, such as the small tail that distinguishes "Q" from "O," that many real characters are "noisy" in the sense of mutilation or of spurious additions such as superimposed dirt or smudging or smearing of ink, and that it is difficult to establish adequately discriminating reference patterns for large numbers of characters including different alphabets and many mathematical and other special symbols. In addition, there are many noncharacter clues to the meanings of messages conveyed by a typical page or by the physical format and layout of a catalog card.

There are two major alternatives to the use of character recognition techniques for the input of documentary materials to a mechanized system. The one which holds considerable future promise is the use of the punched paper or magnetic tapes that are used to control typesetting equipment or that provide a reusable record of information typed on a tape-producing typewriter. Such tapes contain the texts already encoded in machine-usable form. As more and more printing is done by automatic techniques, this alternative will be available for input to machine processing of new documentary materials, but it obviously cannot be applied to catalogs, indexes, abstract journals, documents, books, and libraries already in existence.

Therefore, the prevalent method today is the other alternative, that of the use of a manual keyboard device to transcribe previously written, typed, or printed information onto punched cards, punched paper tape, or magnetic tape. Here, the depression of the key for the character "A," for example, results in the encoding of the appropriate pattern for that character in a particular machine language such as that of the position of one or more holes punched out in a given column of a punched card.

Given, then, that we have information such as names of authors, titles, subject headings assigned, other bibliographic citation data, and perhaps the full text in machine-readable form, we may next ask how machine operations similar to those developed for character and pattern recognition might be applied to the automatic analysis of documentary identification data, including subject-content indicators, and to the text itself.

Automatic Syntactic Analysis and Machine Translation

An obvious extension of the syntactic code dictionary and thesaurus approach is to supply for each word an indication of the possible syntactic roles in which it may serve. Thus we may take a sentence, defined as the string of characters and spaces that occurs between a period followed by two spaces and another period followed by two spaces, and look up each substring of characters both following and preceding a single space. Suppose, to illustrate better the automaticity of the procedure, that the sentence is in a hypothetical "foreign" language, such as the following: "Rohm eh rasén tunai rohenen eh larineh démocaréeh tih lah hian marian." We find from the dictionary stored in the machine that the following syntactic role possibilities occur:

Rohm: preposition
Eh: definite article
Rasén: adjective, plural, subjective or objective case
Tunai: noun, singular or plural, subjective or objective
Rohenen: nominal adjective indicating possession
Larineh: noun, singular, subjective
Démocaréeh: verb, intransitive, past tense, third person singular, active voice
Tih: preposition
Lah: quantifying adjective
Hian: pronoun, possessive, third person singular
Marian: noun, plural, subjective or objective, or noun, singular, objective

With this information it is then possible to apply various rules of parsing or grammar recognition. For example, we will expect to find in every well-formed sentence a subject and a predicate. For subject we will seek to find a noun, noun phrase, or pronoun in the subjective case. Our candidates are "tunai," "larineh," and "marian.'" Next, we need a predicate indicated by a verb or verb phrase which must agree in number with our subject. The only verb is "démocaréeh," which our lookup says is singular; therefore our subject is "larineh," and it is preceded by the definite article. Therefore, the "larineh" did something that does not require a direct object.

Actually the other information available could equally well have helped us to eliminate "tunai" and "marian" as possible subjects. Thus our machine rules would tell us that prepositions govern nouns or noun phrases in the objective case, and so on, so that, without knowing the meaning of the words themselves, we can come up with an analysis such as the following: The "larineh" did something in, with, of, for, through, from (etc.) the (adjective) things of somethings (or someones) in, with, of, for, by, or from (etc.) some, any, all, none (etc.) of his, her, or its, something or somethings, with only the word "marian" retaining homographic ambiguity.

If lexical meanings are now supplied, we might come up with the following: "The general came down from the distant mountains of the kings with all his arms (or army?)." In the succceeding sentence we might find that "they were glad to rest" and so decide on "army" as the proper meaning for our still-ambiguous word.

The above example thus also illustrates some of the potential promise and some of the difficulties of automatic analysis techniques as applied to machine translation from one natural language to another. Actually the sample sentence is a quite simple and straightforward one, whereas in many cases the presently available techniques both of automatic syntactic analysis and of machine translation typically result in many different possible analyses and interpretations of the same input sentence.

As of mid-1967, then, the state of the art in automatic syntactic analysis and in machine translation must be viewed somewhat pessimistically for the near future at least. The difficulties range from the practical, such as the present high costs of input of texts (typically about a penny per word) or of computing the multiple analyses often required for a single sentence, through the requirements of constructing adequate dictionaries with effective syntactic coding, to the theoretical problems of language and meaning.

For the case of automatic translation between languages, generally, we face the problem of polysemia (the problem of multiple meanings available in the target language for a symbol sequence in the source language), as well as problems of possible homography in both languages (multiple meanings attached to a symbol sequence in a given language for that language). Again, combinational problems may compound (sic) the issue, as in the case of "compound number" or "complex fraction" in translating from Russian to English.

Other areas of linguistic data processing to which techniques of automatic analysis have been experimentally applied include those of sentence normalizations, such as those involved in the transformational analysis investigated by Harris and others, and in automatic paraphrasing, especially minimum paraphrasing. This might mean, for example, conversions from passive to active voice, stripping away adjectives or adverbs, isolating action verbs, and the like.

INDEXING

9

Coordinate Indexing

Susan Artandi* / Rutgers University, Brunswick, New Jersey

Coordination in its most general sense means the combination of two or more terms to create a subject class that will differ from the classes represented by the terms individually or in some other combination. For example, when the terms *University, Libraries,* and *Administration* are coordinated in the proper order the new class that is created at their intersection is *University library administration.*

The coordination described in the above example corresponds to the Boolean connective AND, and it has been extensively used in the construction of index languages for precoordinate document retrieval systems in which index terms are frequently generated through the coordination of two or more terms to describe specific subjects. These precoordinated terms also serve as search terms in the form in which they were assigned by the indexer without further manipulation.

In postcoordinate systems coordination takes place at the time of searching. This means that in indexing complex subjects are broken down into simpler concepts and in searching complex subjects are defined through coordination. This introduces flexibility to the system because of the large number of combinations of terms that is theoretically possible.

To use the previous example, in a precoordinate system *University library administration* would serve as both the index term and the search term. In a postcoordinate system the universe of documents would be searched to determine which documents have all three terms, *University, Library,* and *Administration,* assigned to them.

Coordination viewed as an index language device falls into the category of precision devices. Precision devices are intended to decrease the probability that non-relevant documents will be retrieved. By increasing the specificity of the term (nar-

---

From Artandi, Susan. *Coordinate Indexing.* ENCYCLOPEDIA OF LIBRARY AND INFORMATION SCIENCE. Vol. 5. Edited by Allen Kent and Harold Lancour. Assistant Editor, William Z. Nasri. New York, Marcel Dekker, Inc., c1971. pp. 679-682.
*Presently retired

rowing the scope of the class), coordination will increase the ability of the system to filter out nonrelevant documents. This, however, is accomplished at the expense of filtering out some relevant materials at the same time (*1*).

Historically, the introduction of coordinate indexing has been closely associated with Mortimer Taube, although there were others who used this approach to indexing before him—Batten in England and Cordonnier in France. When the method was first applied by Taube in 1953 to organize a group of ASTIA (Armed Forces Technical Information Agency) documents, he used a small vocabulary of single-word terms called *uniterms* in the system. Uniterms were taken from the text of the documents and no attempt was made at any kind of vocabulary control (*2*).

Today's coordinate indexing systems gradually evolved from this early concept. They are no longer based exclusively on single-word terms and terms made up of two or more words are freely used. These may be regarded as precoordinate terms that are postcoordinated at the time of searching. Free vocabularies were gradually replaced by controlled vocabularies, codified in thesauri, displaying the structure of the index language. Index languages used in coordinate indexing systems frequently include complex relationships among terms which make sophisticated searching possible.

Sophisticated searching methods also became possible through the advent of computer based systems. Whereas manual and "peek-a-boo" coordinate indexing systems are largely limited to the use of the logical connective AND, primarily because of limitations inherent in the methods of implementation, computerized systems allow the use of the Boolean connectives AND, OR, and NOT in the formulation of logical expressions to describe the class of documents to be searched for. For example, if one class of documents is about indexing (Class A) and another class of documents is about chemical journals (Class B), then a logical AND (A.B) will specify a search for all documents in the system that have both A and B assigned to them—documents dealing with the indexing of chemical journals. A logical NOT (A.$\bar{B}$) will specify those documents that have A assigned to them but not B also—documents dealing with indexing with the exception of those that deal with the indexing of chemical journals. A logical OR (inclusive) (A + B) will specify those documents to which A or B or both have been assigned—documents dealing with indexing or with chemical journals, or with the indexing of chemical journals. The Venn diagrams in Figure 1 illustrate the above; in the three diagrams the shaded areas represent A.B, A.$\bar{B}$, and A + B, respectively (*3*).

As coordinate indexing systems became more widely known and used, some of the limitations inherent in postcoordination became evident.

The assumed advantage of the almost unlimited possibility for the combination of terms proved in many cases to be disadvantageous. To prevent unwanted coordinations, *links* were introduced; and to indicate the function of a particular term in the indexing description, *roles* were assigned. For example, if a single document deals with the extrusion of polyethylene and the molding of polypropylene, then a link between *Polyethylene* and *Extrusion* and a link between *Molding* and *Polypropylene* would prevent false coordinations between *Extrusion* and *Polypropylene*, and *Molding* and *Polyethylene*, respectively. As a result of the link the document would not become a false drop in response to queries on the extrusion of polypropylene or the molding of polyethylene.

Coordinate Indexing 183

Automatic indexing (of) chemical journals A
B A.B logical AND
Shaded area indicates the class of documents which have both A and B assigned to them.

Automatic indexing except automatic indexing of chemical journals A
B A.B̄ logical NOT
Shaded area indicates the class of documents which have A assigned to them but not B also.

Automatic indexing, chemical journals, and automatic indexing of chemical journals A
B A+B logical OR
Shaded area indicates the class of documents which have A or B (or both A and B) assigned to them.

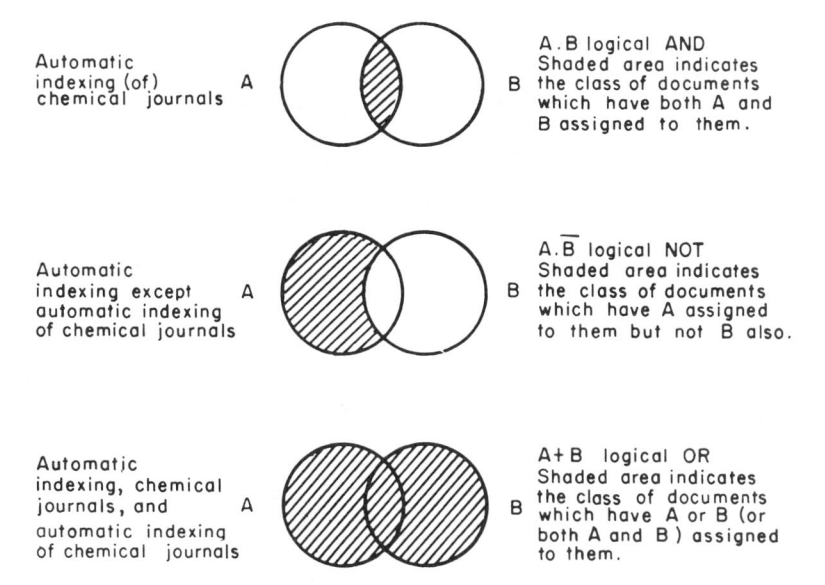

FIGURE 1. (*From Susan Artandi,* An Introduction to Computers in Information Science, *Scarecrow Press, Metuchen, N.J., 1968.*)

However, links, though they can eliminate noise, may prevent some potentially useful coordinations. This can be illustrated with Taube's classical example of a document on the subject of "lead coatings for copper pipes." To avoid the possible false coordination between *Lead* and *Pipes* links can be introduced between *Lead* and *Coatings,* and *Copper* and *Pipes,* respectively. However, though this will prevent the possibility of false coordination, it will also prevent the potentially useful coordination between *Coatings* and *Pipes* to answer a query about "coatings for pipes" (*4*).

Roles are intended to improve the precision of search results by explicitly stating the relationship existing between document classes. They add an element of syntax by specifying the function of a term in the index description or in the query. In essence this means that a given term, through the addition of various role indicators, is broken down into several more specific terms. The principal way in which this method differs from the straightforward use of more specific terms is that the relationships described through role indicators are usually standardized within a given system.

The Engineers' Joint Council System, for example, includes an elaborate system of roles. In that system a document on the molding of plastic housing, for example, would be indexed with the following terms and roles: *Molding* (Role 8), *Plastics* (Role 1), and *Housing* (Role 2)—Role 8 to indicate principal subject of discussion, Role 1 to indicate raw material, and Role 2 to indicate product (*5*).

Many coordinate indexing systems operate without roles and links. Generally speaking, the trend in coordinate indexing seems to be away from the use of roles and links because of problems related to their consistent application and because of the additional cost involved in their use.

In view of the fact that the use of roles and links can increase indexing costs substantially, their use in terms of economic efficiency can only be justified if the added costs involved in their use are compensated for by savings resulting from improved quality of output.

However, the use of roles does not necessarily improve retrieval significantly. A recent study of the MEDLARS system showed that less than 10% of the false coordinations could have been prevented through the use of role indicators. There is also some indication that the usefulness of roles will vary with the subject field, the complexity of the queries, and the size of the file. The more precise and unambiguous the language of the field, the more complex the queries, the larger the file, the more successful roles are likely to be.

It is likely that the specificity of the index language that can be achieved through the use of role indicators can also be accomplished by increasing the specificity of the index terms in other ways. Subheadings, for example, can act as roles and links simultaneously. It was found that increased specificity in the MEDLARS vocabulary could prevent most of the precision failures occurring in the system that could be corrected by role indicators. For example, the coordination of the terms TOXINS and FISH, in a search for toxins produced by fish, retrieved a number of nonrelevant documents dealing with bacterial toxins affecting fish. Although this kind of false coordination could be prevented by role indicators (fish as a producer, fish as a target), it could also be prevented by the use of the more specific terms ANIMAL TOXINS and BACTERIAL TOXINS (6).

Postcoordinate systems can be implemented in a number of ways, ranging from a manual card file to a computer file. The particular file organization used in these systems depends to a large extent on the method of implementation. Coordinate indexing systems in their manual or optical coincidence form are usually based on an inverted file in which each record corresponds to a term. Computerized systems in recent years have been operating largely with direct files on magnetic tape in which each record corresponds to a document. A number of large computerized systems use the combination of a direct and an inverted file. The inverted file is used to reduce the domain of interest and the serial file, corresponding to the reduced domain, is used for the detailed search on the query (7,8). Increase in the size of systems and advances in computer technology will no doubt significantly affect methods of file organization for coordinate indexing systems in the future.

REFERENCES

1. Cyrill Cleverdon, "The Cranfield Test on Index Language Devices," *Aslib Proc.*, 19, 173–194 (June 1967).
2. Susan Artandi and Theodore C. Hines, "Roles and Links, or Forward to Cutter," *Amer. Doc.*, 14, 74–77 (January 1963).
3. Susan Artandi, *An Introduction to Computers in Information Science*, Scarecrow Press, Metuchen, New Jersey, 1968, pp. 34–35.
4. Mortimer Taube, "Notes on the Use of Roles and Links in Coordinate Indexing," *Amer. Doc.*, 12, 98–100 (April 1961).
5. John C. Costello, *Coordinate Indexing*, Vol. VII of *Rutgers Series on Systems for the Intellectual Organization of Information* (S. Artandi, ed.), Grad. School of Lib. Serv., Rutgers, the State University, New Brunswick, New Jersey, 1966.
6. F. W. Lancaster, "On the Need for Role Indicators in Postcoordinate Retrieval Systems," *Amer. Doc.*, 19, 42–46 (January 1968).
7. *The Combined File Search System*, IBM Corp., Hawthorne, New York, 1966.
8. I. A. Warheit, "File Organization of Library Records," *J. Lib. Automation*, 2, 20–30 (March 1969).

10

Subject Indexes

Charles L. Bernier* / State University of New York at Buffalo, Buffalo, New York

Subject indexes are the most popular and most used of all kinds of indexes. Subject indexes of abstract journals, for example, wear out before other kinds of indexes and have to be rebound. This popularity is well deserved; people want to learn about what others are doing and what they have researched, studied, and reported. People are interested in subjects that are drawn, debated, sculpted, painted, photographed, researched, studied, reported, thought, considered, planned, completed, discussed, sketched, hypothesized, theorized, created, invented, analyzed, debunked, criticized, praised, advocated, promised, developed, explained, concluded, expounded, taught, and so on. Subject indexes guide searchers to all kinds of subjects.

Differentiation from Concept, Topic, and Word Indexes

Subject indexes are different from, and can be contrasted with, indexes to concepts, topics, and words. Authors, debaters, painters, photographers, researchers, sculptors, and others have subjects on which they are working and reporting. Authors et al. (that is, authors, debaters, researchers, etc.) also have many concepts about which they think and report. Authors often organize their writings on subjects into topics; also, they use many words in their writings.

Indexes to concepts that authors et al. have and report (concept indexes as contrasted with subject indexes) include subjects, but they also include much more than subjects. Concept indexes are bulky; entries to the subjects in them are greatly diluted. For example, a researcher reporting on research on the

---

From Bernier, Charles L. *Subject Indexes.* ENCYCLOPEDIA OF LIBRARY AND INFORMATION SCIENCE. Vol. 29. Edited by Allen Kent, Harold Lancour and Jay E. Daily. Assistant Editor, William Z. Nasri. New York, Marcel Dekker, Inc., c1980. pp. 191-204.
*Presently retired

loss of volumes of encyclopedias from libraries may have many hypotheses as to how the volumes are taken, who has taken them, why they were taken, how to regain the volumes, how to prevent future loss, and the use of statistics in this kind of research. Some or all of these concepts may be reported in the work being indexed. The subject actually studied may be the correlation between course assignments and the disappearance of encyclopedia volumes. All of these concepts might be indexed for a concept index; only the subject studied and reported would be indexed in a subject index.

Many presentations are organized into topics. Topics guide readers, and especially those who return to the work to read parts of it again. Topic indexes guide searchers to chapter headings and subheadings; they also guide users to topics such as historical introduction, purpose of the work, research protocol, survey instrument, experimental precautions, conduct of the research, results obtained, analysis of the results, conclusions from the work, and the summary (perhaps followed by appendixes, tables, etc.). Usually the topics into which a work is divided are not the subject(s) on which the author reports, because these topics are related mainly to the method of presentation of the work rather than to the work itself.

It has been found to be very easy for indexers to drift into indexing concepts and words rather than subjects—when they are making subject indexes. For example, this drift may occur when a new word comes into the language to express an interesting apparatus, concept, material, process, etc. An example of this drift into concept and word indexing, and away from subject indexing, occurred when *chromatography* (the process and the word) was introduced into chemistry and thence into the chemical literature. Chromatography was such an effective and elegant method for the separation of substances formerly separated only with great difficulty, that it intensely interested chemists and became a popular subject for study, especially by analytical chemists. At first, all studies on chromatographic separations involved new subjects. Certainly the substances studied at first had never before been separated chromatographically. The techniques of chromatography itself were developed. New kinds of chromatography were invented and perfected. Chemists studied and reported on chromatographs and on their ancillary equipment. The excellence and popularity of chromatography as a separation technique resulted in thousands of papers, reports, and books on chromatography. Then—with time, and as effective chromatographic procedures and apparatus were developed for many important classes of substances that needed to be separated—chromatography became a standard technique of chemical analysis. The interest of chemists and the subjects studied by them gradually shifted elsewhere. Of course, the word *chromatography* continued to be used in the reports of these subsequent studies, although nothing new about chromatography was reported. The subject of most of these studies was no longer chromatography. Although chromatography was not a subject studied and reported in most of these later papers, it was a concept considered and expressed by chemists who were working on other subjects and who used chromatographic separations in their work. Subject indexers mistakenly indexed nearly all of these works under the subject heading **Chromatography.** As the

Subject Indexes

number of studies on the subject of chromatography gradually decreased, indexers continued to index the *concept* (chromatography), and to index the *word* (chromatography). The number of articles and of index entries on the *subject* of chromatography gradually decreased as the field became "mined out." However, the number of entries under the subject heading **Chromatography** continued to increase in subject indexes. This indexing of the concept and of the word was noted by users of indexes, who looked up entries under the heading **Chromatography,** only to find material on the techniques and apparatus that they already knew. These users correctly objected that chromatography was no longer being exclusively subject indexed. They correctly objected to looking up entries only to find that textbook chromatographic techniques were described in a work that concerned other chemical subjects. This concept indexing and word indexing of chromatography was brought to the attention of the indexers, and they reverted to subject indexing only. These indexers were astonished to see how easily and gradually they had been led down the garden path by the concept of chromatography and also by the word *chromatography*, to make subject index entries under **Chromatography,** the subject heading. Subject indexers are expected to detect and to resist the indexing of concepts and words that do not lead to subjects reported by authors.

The Process of Subject Indexing

In the process of subject indexing, subject indexers first identify subjects reported in the work to be indexed. If the subject is that of a photograph, the subject may not be expressed immediately in words in the mind of the indexer. The second step is to embody the subject in words—to paraphrase the subject. "Still life of purple dahlias in blue Chinese vase on mahogany table before red velvet drapes" might be a subject paraphrase. Another paraphrase could be "Crime suggestibility by mass media." Yet another might be "Techniques of great comedians." Subject paraphrases are as complete as necessary, terse, and independent of other contexts. That is, they do not omit significant parts of the subject studied; they are not redundant; and they have no pronouns, so that they do not depend on other material for their meaning. Also, they have no verbs, adverbs, or articles; these parts of speech are unnecessary and are omitted to make the index entries derived from the subject paraphrases more easily developed, more easily used, and more terse. For the professional indexer, the subject paraphrase is not written, but "coined" and carried in memory during the indexing. One subject paraphrase is coined for each subject reported by the author of the work being indexed. The specificity of the subject paraphrase is made great enough to enable the index entries (or index entry) derived from it to be distinguished from all other subject index entries from other works that appear under the same subject headings in the index.

SUBJECT INDEX ENTRIES

Next, subject indexers create the subject index entries from the paraphrases. Each entry consists of the subject heading, a modification (modifying phrase, subheading), and a reference (locator), in that order. (The word *locator* is a neologism that was coined to avoid possible confusion between *reference* and *cross-reference*.) Examples of subject index entries are:

    Niagara Falls, mist clouds from, shapes of, 1234
    Carpets, cleaning (commercial) of, 4321
    Crime, suggestibility by mass media, 3214
    Suggestibility, of crime by mass media, 3214
    Mass media, crime suggestibility by, 3214
    Dahlias, still life of purple, in blue Chinese vase on mahogany table before red velvet drapes, 2314

SUBJECT HEADING DERIVATION

The subject headings are derived from the subject paraphrases. It has been found to be relatively easy to select the best words of a subject paraphrase to serve as guides to the paraphrase. However, it has been found difficult to define and to describe this process of selecting the best words. Indexers can do it without being able to say how they do it. Also, people who are not indexers can do it with astonishing reliability—and also without being able to tell how they do it. As an experiment, try to select the *one* "best" word (not term or phrase) in each of the following paraphrases, to guide a searcher to that paraphrase:

    Review on swords
    Review on sword scabbards
    Review on sword manufacture
    Writing the critical review
    Laboratory synthesis of hydroxyurea
    Tuberculosis therapy prior to 1900
    Biography of Rev. Dr. Martin Luther King, Jr.

Of course, a subject paraphrase usually requires more than one subject index entry; also, a given document may require several subject paraphrases.

TERM TRANSLATION

Once words or terms that are useful as guides to the subject paraphrase have been selected by the subject indexer, the next step is to alter the few terms that need translation into standard index headings. Subject index headings are standardized to eliminate scattering of like entries—the bane of all poor indexes (*1*). Nearly always, the words of the subject paraphrase will be identical with the subject heading words; this means that translation is usually unnecessary. Of course, the words in the subject paraphrase are nearly always identical with the words of the author of the work being indexed. Hence, most subject headings will be identical (or nearly identical) with the words used by the authors. This identity avoids distortion of the authors' meanings and places entries in the subject index where authors and others will most likely look first.

Much of the standardization of index headings involves the singular and the plural forms of the words used. Plural subject index headings are generally:

1. Classes of things, e.g., **Animals, Apples, Automobiles,** and **Ketones**
2. Multiple parts of the body, e.g., **Eyes, Fingernails, Kidneys,** and **Toes**

Singular headings are generally:

1. Unique, specific things, e.g., **Vega** and **Acetone** (however, specific animals are usually given plural headings, e.g., **Cats, Dogs, Horses,** and **Zebras;** and specific apples are plural-term entries, e.g., **Winesap apples, Delicious apples,** and **McIntosh apples)**
2. Singular parts of the body, e.g., **Skin, Liver, Nose,** and **Stomach**

Whichever sounds best, singular or plural, is often used.

Another kind of standardization of subject headings concerns organic-chemical nomenclature, nomenclatures of microorganisms, codes for agency names and report numbers, and the like. The use of standard nomenclatures is often described in the introduction to the index.

Standardization might also involve the conversion of adjectives and gerunds into nouns. For example, *oscillatory* might be converted into **Oscillation,** and *abbreviating* into **Abbreviation.** Obsolete terminology is translated, with care, into current terminology. Examples are:

Accumulators into **Storage batteries**
Roentgen rays into **X-rays**
Wireless telephony into **Radio**
Pianoforte into **Piano**

This kind of translation requires great care so as not to distort the author's meaning. For example, in the field of mental health, the equivalence of terms such as insanity, mental illness, derangement, and unbalanced person is for the author—and generally not for the indexer—to decide. Translation of terms of the subject paraphrase into subject index headings is the exception rather than the rule, unless nomenclatures are involved.

MODIFICATIONS

Once a subject heading term has been selected from the subject paraphrase and translated (if necessary) into a standard subject heading, the next step is for the subject indexer to coin a modification or to select a subheading. Modifications (modifying phrases) modify the subject heading much as adjectives modify a noun. Modifications make the index entry (consisting of subject heading, modification, and reference) much more specific than it would be without them. In effect, modifications tailor the entry to fit the subject reported. Modifications are coined to be as specific as necessary to differentiate among all entries having the same heading in the index.

Ideally, the modification should be specific enough to differentiate among all potential entries under the heading. Such great specificity would enable the searcher to decide definitely for or against looking up the entry. Actually, such great specificity (even if it could be attained) is unnecessary and impractical. This degree of specificity would involve prediction of what subjects are going to be studied, even in the distant future; such accuracy of prediction is impossible.

In actual indexing, the subject indexer may adopt a policy of using a little overspecificity of modifications because it is much easier to delete overspecificity later, during the editing of the index and during the compilation of a cumulative index, than it is to add the required specificity later. When the modification has more than seven or eight words in it, the indexer starts to wonder about overspecificity. Subheadings are a kind of modification that are used in place of coined modifications. Subheadings are selected from a list of standard subheadings. Modifications are coined ad hoc by the indexer to fit (as precisely as is desired and necessary) the subject studied. Standard subheadings are used to make indexing in computers and computer search easier. Examples of modifications are given in the index entries shown in previous sections. Indexers create and note many highly specific rules for writing modifications for a given index. Some general rules for writing modifications are:

1. Avoid redundancy and repetition.
2. Use, if possible, the words of the subject paraphase.
3. Start the modification with an action word that refers to the heading; e.g., **Paper,** preservation by ammonium carbonate, 1234.
4. If the heading is an action (process) word, start the modification with the thing acted upon; e.g., **Preservation,** of paper by ammonium carbonate, 1234.
5. Use all prepositions necessary; e.g., **Salt,** purification of, 3421; and not **Salt,** purification, 3421 (the latter is ambiguous).
6. Omit articles, pronouns, adverbs, and verbs.
7. Alphabetize parallel substantives in modifications unless there is some logical order: e.g., **Dyeing,** with anthraquinone, azo, and phenanthrene dyes, 4321; and, as an example of logical order, **Lead ores,** crushing, grinding, screening, ball-milling, flotation, and drying of, 2341.
8. Favor having the heading read into the start of the modification. Second-best is reading into the end of the modification, and third-best is reading into the middle of the modification—usually after a comma.
9. Use, as the starting word in the modification, the standard nomenclature term used as a heading in the index, rather than the term selected from the subject paraphrase.

These few rules are not complete; hundreds of additional, more specific, rules are used by subject indexers for specific headings.

REFERENCES

Once the heading and modification part of the entry has been created, the reference (locator) is added to complete the entry and to guide the searcher from the entry to the work indexed. If the heading and modification have been dictated, it may be most efficient for the transcriber to add the reference separately, without its being dictated.

The reference may be a column or page number, or the reference could be the number of an abstract or a patent. Abstracts may be located by their serial number as reference. Some reference numbers may contain codes; for example, codes for the names of the agencies producing reports (that is, a report number is used as the reference example; for example, "AD 346 292") Thus, the complete subject index entry consists of three elements: subject heading, modification (e.g., a coined modifying phrase or a subheading), and reference (or locator).

CHECKING

As the subject index entries are made, all of them are checked by another indexer, who is usually more experienced than is the first indexer. This complete check is necessary to reduce the number of errors to an acceptable level. Even experienced indexers regularly have about 20% of their entries changed by the checker. About 15% of these changes are of a minor nature, such as reworded modifications, correction of misspellings, removal of mistakes in punctuation and format, deletion of entries to concepts and words, and deletion of overspecificity of modifications. Only about 5% of the entries involve serious errors, such as omissions, misunderstandings, wrong interpretations, and incorrect references.

After the index cards are alphabetized, they are edited to eliminate unnecessary headings, indicate double indentions, combine identical entries, separate blocks of references, correct errors, detect omissions, etc.

The product of all of this effort is a subject index—the finest tool for finding subjects reported by authors. Indexes in book form use modifications. Indexes in computers for correlative search have no modifications as yet; instead, subject headings are correlated with other terms to make searches more complete and more specific (2). Correlative subject indexes (e.g., manipulative, coordinate, and computerized indexes) make use of terms selected from subject paraphrases. Some of these terms would not be used as subject headings or be translated into subject headings because they would become headings that were too broad and heterogeneous; that is, heterogeneous headings have too many varieties of unrelated entries under them. Examples of terms that probably would be too broad and heterogeneous for most indexes are *manufacture, formation, preparation,* and *synthesis.* However, all of these broad terms can be correlated during search by means of Boolean logic (*and, or, not*). It should be noted here that distinctions among subject, concept, topic, and word indexes hold whether the indexes are computerized or in book form.

Use of Subject Indexes

The efficient use of subject indexes requires education, training, and skill on the part of the searcher. This statement holds whether the indexes are published as books or stored in computers. As can be surmised from the previous discussion, subject indexes are not very useful in searching for concepts, topics, and words of authors simply because subject indexers do not index concepts, topics, and words; subject indexes were not designed for this purpose.

There are indexes to concepts, topics, and words (concordances) that should be used for search in these areas. As has been pointed out, subject indexers may drift into indexing concepts, topics, and words; however, this drift is by accident and not by design.

In finding subjects reported by authors, the searcher turns to the subject index(es) with paraphrases of questions about subjects of interest. From these paraphrased questions, the searcher selects terms (words and phrases) that seem to be the best guides to the paraphrased questions. Translation of terms first selected by the searcher into the subject headings actually used in the index is aided by quality indexes through their syndetic systems. Syndetic systems include introductions to the index as well as cross-references, interfiled notes, and inverted subject headings. If the index lacks cross-references and nomenclature guidance, the searcher is left to his own resources so far as finding the suitable subject headings is concerned. Knowledge of the field, technical thesauri, dictionaries, and encyclopedias are of great help in finding the appropriate subject headings for search. Usually, finding all of the appropriate headings is an iterative process in which the searcher approaches the index with the terms first found; discovers works on the topic of interest; reads these works; refines the term list after this experience; again consults dictionaries, thesauri, etc.; and then again returns to the index with the expanded search vocabulary and increased knowledge of the field. Often preliminary reading of a few works in the field is helpful in expanding the search vocabulary as well as in increasing the precise understanding of what is sought and read.

MANUAL INDEXES

In the use of manual indexes (in book or card form), the searcher simply looks up each of the search terms, one at a time. Then the searcher reads, scans, or skims *all* of the modifications under each of the search terms. If the modifications are categorized, the searcher may find it possible to skip whole categories—usually after some experimentation. If standard subheadings are used, some of these can be skipped after experience shows that it is safe to do so. The reason that all uncategorized modifications must be read is because it has been found to be impossible to predict the starting words that control the alphabetical positions of the modifications that lead to relevant references. Language is so delightfully flexible that the same thing can be said in many ways and with many different words. Another reason that it is impossible to predict starting words is that several different items may be included in the same modification, and the existence and the order of these items in the modification cannot be predicted.

COMPUTER SEARCH

In the use of computerized subject indexes, the searcher finds relevant terms in the same way that he does for book indexes. Nearly always, a thesaurus or standard list of subject headings is provided as an aid. *Medical Subject*

Headings (MeSH; Ref. *3*) is an example of an excellent thesaurus. Since there are no modifications in the computerized system, the searcher uses the correlation of two or more terms by the Boolean *and,* in place of reading modifications; this limits the search to those works indexed by *all* of the terms used in the search. In this kind of search, the number of references retrieved is usually smaller than in a search by the use of one term alone (a deck search); however, this reduction in the number of references retrieved is not a goal but an incident in the search. It is irrational to reduce the number of works discovered without also knowing if the references so rejected contain relevant material. It has been pointed out elsewhere that the use of too many terms correlated by Boolean *and* can result in rejection of all references and can also result in invisible loss (*4*). Correlation by Boolean *or* is used to expand the search to include related material. In this case also, the objective is not to increase the number of references found, but to increase recall (the percentage of relevant references retrieved from the collection). Correlation by Boolean *not* is used to reject completely irrelevant material. The use of Boolean *not* may reduce the number of references retrieved; however, again this is not an objective, but an incident in the use of Boolean *not*. The use of the Boolean *not* can inadvertently exclude relevant material; that is, cause invisible loss. For example, it might be thought that excluding either **Male** or **Female** would separate the collection of desired references into two mutually exclusive groups. A little reflection will show that this is not so because there may be a set of documents in the collection that will be indexed by both **Male** and **Female.** This set will be excluded by the use of Boolean *not* **Male** and also by the use of the Boolean *not* **Female.**

The absence of modifications in computerized search systems has necessitated the use of weights, links, and roles in order to improve the relevance of material selected to the question asked. The article "Correlative Indexes" in this encyclopedia has the details (*2*). Despite all of these ramifications of computerized search systems, subjects will be retrieved only if subject indexing was done.

Alphabetic and Categorized Subject Indexes

Nearly all subject indexes have the entry headings and the modifications arranged alphabetically. The reason for the use of alphabetical order is because it is so widely known. However, it is not necessary to use alphabetical order; headings and modifications (especially subheadings) can be put into classified or categorized order. Classification systems and categorization are used to bring related entries and modifications together. Alphabetization tends to scatter related material; for example, **Lactose, Maltose,** and **Sucrose,** widely separated alphabetically, can all be categorized under **Disaccharides.** Likewise, **Fructose, Galactose,** and **Glucose** can all be categorized under **Monosaccharides.** Both **Disaccharides** and **Monosaccharides** can be categorized under **Sugars. Sugars** can be categorized under **Carbohydrates,** and so on.

The principal objection to classification systems and to categorization is that they are not obvious to the searcher and must be learned, or an alphabetical index to the classification system must be consulted. If one must first consult an index to the classification system, then why not use an alphabetical arrangement of the entries in the first place and save the extra step of consulting an alphabetical index to the classification system? This objection has generally been powerful enough to ensure the use of alphabetical order for subject indexes. As an alternative to the use of a classification system, the index can easily carry as an appendix a technical thesaurus designed for the subject area. This seems to be the best way to handle the problem of alphabetical versus classified arrangement. The semantic relations shown in the technical thesaurus are nearly always permanently valid, and they guide the searcher to all related material (5).

The use of alphabetical order in the subject index permits new terms to come into use, as they will, and to be accepted smoothly into the alphabet without disrupting a classification scheme. The thesaurus lexicographer can then categorize the new terms in the next edition of the thesaurus or on correction sheets to guide users to the newly related material. Even without a thesaurus, the alphabetical index can, through internal cross-references, guide searchers to semantically related material as well as a thesaurus does. Perhaps the ideal index is one in which the entries are alphabetical with a comprehensive internal syndetic system consisting of cross-references, interfiled notes, inverted headings, and a complete introduction to the index. In addition, for the ideal system, there would be a comprehensive thesaurus that would show all of the permanent relations among the terms in the language—often at a glance for a specific subject area. Such an indexing system would place a minimum load on the searcher; and the load on the searcher is an inverse measure of the quality of an index (1).

Whether the order of the entries is alphabetical, categorized, or classified, the index is still a subject index if it guides searchers to subjects reported by authors.

Collective and Cumulative Subject Indexes

Searching through one alphabet (i.e., index) for entries under a set of search terms may be considered necessary by the searcher; however, finding the same set of search terms and reading all modifications in 12 alphabets (indexes) for the annual set of issues of a monthly publication or searching in the 10 annual indexes of a decade of volumes is apt to be tedious and irritating. Such effort may appear to be unnecessary to the searcher, who may reason that cumulative indexes should have been provided. This reasoning by the searcher has led to the authorization and creation of cumulative indexes. Collective indexes, in which the individual indexes are bound side-by-side as separate alphabets, provide a slight (very slight) improvement over having the indexes in the separate issues or volumes. Cumulative indexes, in which the individual alphabets are merged and edited into one index, are clearly superior to collective indexes in saving the time of searchers. Editing of the cumulative indexes has been found to improve them considerably, mainly because of the changes that have occurred during the period for which they were cumulated; the earlier indexes are (or can be) brought up to the quality of, and reorganized by, the cross-references of the later indexes. It should be noted that collective and cumulative indexes are still subject indexes if they guide searchers to subjects reported by authors and if the component indexes are to subjects.

Quality of Subject Indexes

Some searchers may be astonished to learn that subject indexes, as well as diamonds, come in different qualities (*1*). The most general measure of quality is the lightness of load that the index places on the user; the heavier the load, the poorer the quality of the index. Causes of an increased work load include:

1. *Omission of valid subject entries:* Omissions can cause loss of guidance to relevant information, for which loss the searcher may be held responsible. The searcher could lose his job for missing critical or vital material, or he could do a lot of unnecessary work because he might repeat something already in the literature. Omissions may be invisible—which makes them sinister. Detected or suspected omissions cause the user to turn to other indexes—which is an additional load. In high quality indexes, 100% of the entries of which have been carefully checked, the percentage of omissions is probably well under 1%; in concordances (word indexes) to titles of articles (and in which there has been no editing), as many as 66% of the subject entries may be missing (*6*).
2. *Scattering of related entries:* Scattering among headings necessitates discovery of the scattered headings and looking under each. Scattering among synonyms is especially time wasting and irritating; the indexer should have eliminated this kind of scattering. Guidance to entries that cannot be assembled should be provided by the syndetic system of the index, mainly by cross-references from synonyms. Nomenclature information in the introduction can save hours of searching. Scattering among modifications under headings is reduced by the editing of the index cards before publication of the index.
3. *Incorrect references:* Errors in references may cause failure to locate the material. Also, they may cause the index user to take time trying to find the correct reference. The number of incorrect references should be less than 0.1%. Simple clerical checks of the index cards can reduce this kind of error to any desired level. The cards are checked before alphabetization; all cards made from the same page, column, galley, etc., have the same number on them. Variant numbers are very easy to find in this kind of check, provided that the checker is alert.
4. *Errors of all sorts in entries:* Errors that are noticed become puzzles for searchers that waste their time and are irritating.
5. *Entries not leading to subjects reported by authors:* Such entries waste the time of searchers and give a bad impression of the index. Every entry should lead to material that the searcher doesn't know or to material that he wishes to recall. Entries may not lead to subjects because of concept, topic, and word indexing.
6. *Nonspecific modifications:* These are not specific enough to enable the searcher to say, "Yes, I want to look up the entry" or "No, I don't want to look up the entry"; rather than saying, "Maybe I want to look up the

entry." "Maybe's" waste time of searchers because they all have to be looked up in order to avoid missing relevant material.
7. *Long modifications:* Modifications that are too specific take extra reading time. This, actually, is a very minor source of load.
8. *External cross-references:* Cross-references that are not interfiled with the index entries must be remembered and searched outside of the index, perhaps in a thesaurus or word list. This constitutes an added load.
9. *Inconsistencies:* Inconsistencies in headings, modifications, format, and spelling become puzzles to the user, who must waste time trying to solve the puzzles.
10. Failure to supply cumulative indexes.

Quality of indexes is ensured by the proper education and training of indexers, by checking procedures (often 100% checking), by editing of the index entries, by proofchecking and proofreading, by feedback from the users, and, most important, by design and support of indexes that are of high quality. There are high quality indexes; we know all of the quality factors of indexes, and we know that quality can be designed, maintained, and improved. Users should be sophisticated enough to expect high quality and to demand it when quality is inadequate.

Teaching Subject Indexing

One of the first things to be learned is the distinction between subject indexes and indexes to concepts, topics, and words (concordances). Then, selection of subject(s) for paraphrasing is considered and taught, often by having students select material for indexing from the literature of indexing or library and information science. Paraphrasing of the subjects selected is interesting and fun. Next comes the selection of all terms suitable to guide the searcher to the subject paraphrase. Translation (when necessary) of the selected terms into subject headings is learned next. Students may try to translate all of the terms selected, not realizing that the best subject headings are the terms of the author. Modifications are coined next, or subheadings are selected from a list of them. Finally, the use of cross-references and of other syndetic devices is learned. Programmed instructions have been written for these steps as a preliminary guide to learning them.

In general, actual practice in subject indexing is the best way of learning it. The decisions made during subject indexing teach the process. If the instructor makes the decisions, the result is unsatisfactory. Practice in subject indexing can be in subject fields of interest to the student. Examples of such fields are library science, information science, teaching, education, learning, history, and the other sciences. Courses that include subject indexing are offered in library schools. Professional societies can help beginning indexers; two such societies are the American Society of Indexers and the Society of Indexers (Great Britain).

REFERENCES

1. C. L. Bernier, "Correlative Indexes: X. Subject-Index Qualities," *J. Chem. Documentation*, **4**, 104–107 (1964).
2. C. L. Bernier, "Correlative Indexes," in *Encyclopedia of Library and Information Science* (A. Kent and H. Lancour, eds.), Dekker, New York, 1971, Vol. 6, pp. 189–205.

3. *Medical Subject Headings (MeSH),* Department of Health, Education, and Welfare, Public Health Service, National Library of Medicine; available from Superintendent of Documents, U.S. GPO, Washington, D.C. 20401. (A new edition appears each year.)
4. C. L. Bernier, "Correlative Indexes: V. The Blank Sort," *Amer. Documentation,* **9,** 32–41 (1958).
5. C. L. Bernier and K. F. Heumann, "Correlative Indexes: III. Semantic Relations among Semantemes—The Technical Thesaurus," *Amer. Documentation,* **8,** 211–220 (1957).
6. C. L. Bernier, "The Indexing Problem," *J. Chem. Documentation,* **1**(3), 25–27 (1961).

11

Automatic Indexing: Progress and Prospects

Bertrand C. Landry / Martin Marietta Corporation, Denver, Colorado

James E. Rush / James E. Rush Associates, Powell, Ohio

An index is an array of symbols, systematically arranged, together with a reference from each symbol to the physical location of the item symbolized.

Taube [1]

Automatic indexing is the use of machines to extract or assign index terms without human intervention once programs or procedural rules have been established.

Stevens [2]

The problem of automatic analysis reverts to the problem of automatic *translation*, where the target language is no longer a natural language but an artificial one, constructed for the expression of the document content.

Gardin [3]

THE NATURE AND DEFINITION OF INDEXING

Introduction

To R. L. Collison [4], "The trouble with indexing is that even today we are still at the elementary stage of learning how to do it. We do not know enough about its technique . . ." and we certainly do not know enough about its theory. Indexing and its associated paraphernalia constitute a strange process. Consequently, the researcher and reviewer are confronted by an interesting situation: on the one hand, examples of the product of indexing—the index—are plentiful and ubiquitous; on the other hand, attempts to formalize either the process of indexing or the relationship between its exemplars are virtually nonexistent. Unfortunately, this lack of order in (or, should

From Landry, Bertrand C. and James E. Rush. *Automatic Indexing: progress and prospects.* ENCYCLOPEDIA OF COMPUTER SCIENCE AND TECHNOLOGY. Vol. 2. Edited by Jack Belzer, Albert G. Holzman and Allen Kent. New York, Marcel Dekker, Inc., c1975. pp. 403-447.

we say, lack of a science of) the fields of indexing and indexing theory is reflected in the diversity of studies in automatic indexing.

It is not the goal of this article to present an exhaustive coverage of the field of automatic indexing. Rather, attention is directed to an analysis and critique of present-day approaches and a discussion of some possible future directions in automatic indexing. Should further in-depth information be required, the reader is referred to the following comprehensive state-of-the-art reports: Edmundson and Wyllys [5], Artandi [6], Stevens [2, 7], and the System Development Corporation [8]. Additionally, the *Annual Review of Information Science and Technology* [9] contains considerable discussion related to advances in automatic indexing.

Plan of the Article

After a brief consideration of the various levels of mechanized or automatic indexing, we shall consider the role of the *index* and of the *indexing system* in the process of information storage and retrieval. Following a formal definition of indexing, we shall discuss and present examples of current techniques of automatic indexing with respect to the operations of document input, document analysis, index entry creation, and index compilation. Finally, we shall consider why the achievement of truly automatic indexing is dependent on advances from current research in document representation.

Indexing: From Manual to Automatic

The history of indexing is a history of manual indexing. Developments in manual indexing have followed an unbroken line from the literary expansion that took place during the Hellenistic period of ancient Greece to the present-day development of specialized information centers. Despite its lengthy history, indexing remains much of an art. It is only within the last decade that this artful practice has been placed under the scrutiny of the scientific method. We believe that advancements in the formalization of indexing will come from the extension of indexing theory [10–13] and further in-depth studies of the composition and growth patterns of actual large indexing systems.

Unfortunately or fortunately, depending on whether one is an historian or a reviewer, automatic indexing does not have a lengthy history. Actually, development of techniques of automatic indexing have, by and large, followed developments in computer processing technology. In the way of a milestone, the shift from number-oriented to character-oriented processing (in both hardware and software developments) gave impetus to research in the automatic indexing of textual data. However, as the following opinions by Artandi [14] and Carroll [15] suggest, the general level of success of automatic indexing techniques is open to criticism:

> Computer-aided indexing methods are mainly concerned with the computer manipulation of the product of manual indexing. Automatic indexing and extracting methods are still largely limited to the definition of content through text characteristics [14].

> In most classification or indexing procedures, some intelligent being still must read every document acquired and make some rational judgment regarding its content. The ultimate goal of automatic indexing is to make these steps unnecessary [15].

Even to the not-so-casual observer, there seems to be some confusion as to the goals of automatic indexing: should attempts be made to automate the operations of the human indexer? Or, should attempts be directed toward the automation of some representational scheme? Or, rather, should automatic indexing research be directed toward a combination of these two approaches? We shall return to this problem in the section entitled Toward Automatic Indexing.

The term automatic indexing is really a misnomer. The concept "automatic" is usually associated with the concept algorithmic.[1] An algorithm, as a logical, well-defined sequence of instructions or operations, could be implemented by either a human or by a machine. For example, the algorithm depicted in Fig. 1 could be applied to documents by either a human indexer or a computer if the document were in suitable machine-readable form. Consequently, for the purpose of the discussion in this article, we shall restrict our attention to *computer-based* indexing.

At this point one may wonder what are the possible implementations of computer-based indexing? Figure 2 presents a hierarchy of the possible uses of computer-based indexing involving either manual or mechanized (via computer-applied algorithms) index-entry selection. In terms of the sophistication of the computer algorithms, the hierarchy spans the range from simple machine compilation of *manually* selected entries to the machine compilation of *mechanically* assigned entries (see Stevens [7]). In mechanical entry selection, index terms are either *extracted* from the text of the document or *assigned* (from a master list) based upon the identification of keywords in the text of the document. In the case of extraction, the index terms either are unaltered text words (*free vocabulary*) or are created as the result of *prescribed* rules of usage (examples include synonyms, use of generic or related terms, removal of plural endings). When entry selection is effected by means of assignment rules, the index terms, by definition, are the result of the application of a *controlled vocabulary*. In computer-based indexing systems, an index entry may be formed using either multiple terms or a single term. In the case of a multiple-term entry (used as a conjunction of several concepts), we describe the vocabulary of the index as being *precoordinate*; in the case of the uniterm entry, we describe the vocabulary of the index as being *postcoordinate* (i.e., the creation of a multiterm concept is done through the intersection of index entries at the time of the search of the index).

With this brief overview of the various possible implementations of computer-based indexing techniques, we direct our attention to some pertinent history. Table 1 presents some of the important developmental work that has contributed to the current state-of-the-art of computer-based indexing. Many of these research efforts are discussed in the section entitled Examples of Computer-Based Indexing. We have chosen, for ease of presentation, to make the distinction between computer-based indexing of textual data and of nontextual data. By this partition we draw a distinction between textual document processing and, for instance, chemical formula/structure processing. In each case the object is to create index entries that in some manner serve to represent the original document.[2] Furthermore, within each category of document processing we have found it convenient to make a distinction between index entries

---

[1] Loosely, an algorithm is a procedure that terminates in some finite time [16].

[2] We consider both aggregates of words and chemical formula/structures to be examples of documents [12].

Automatic Indexing

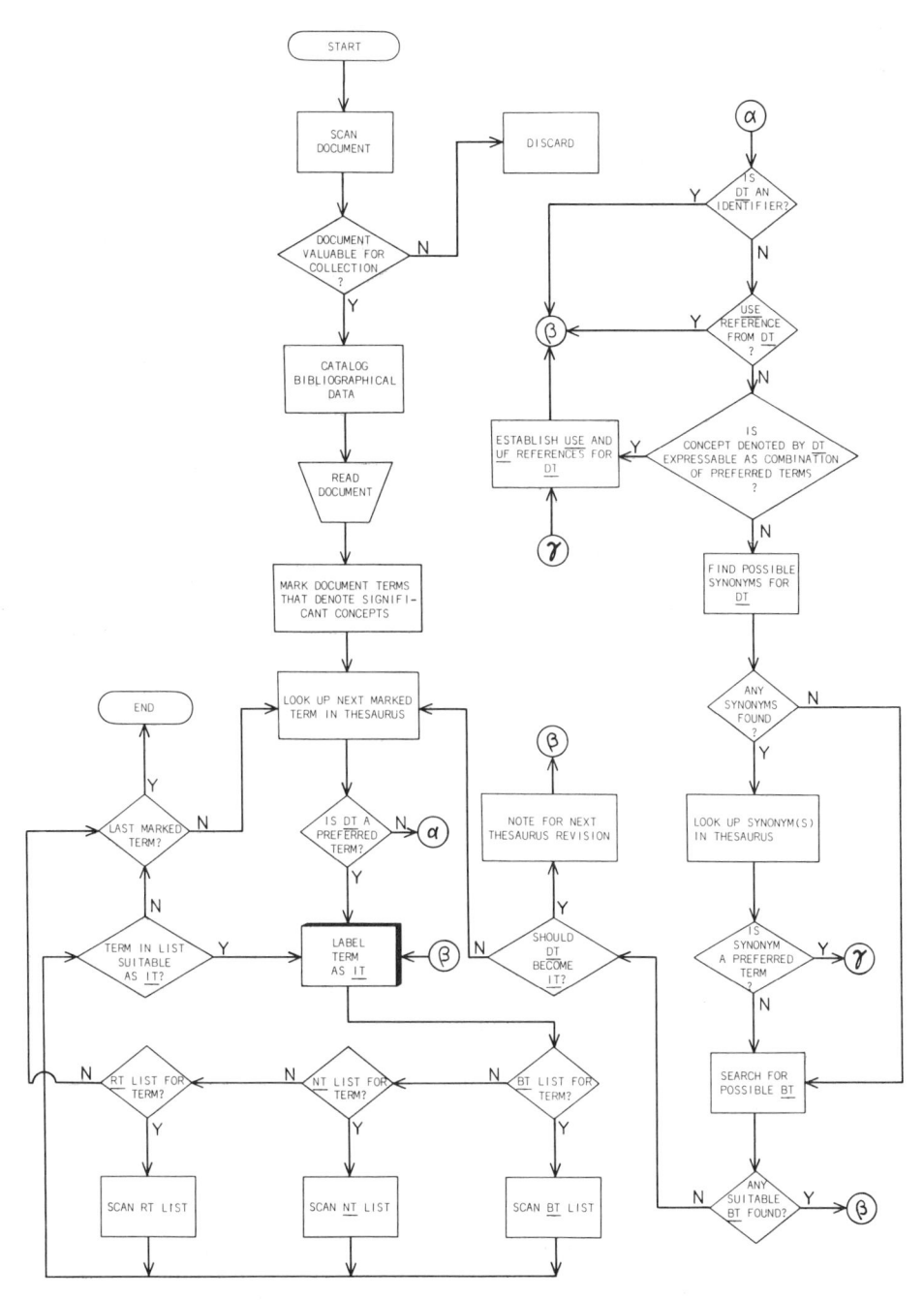

Fig. 1. A flow chart for indexing with a thesaurus.

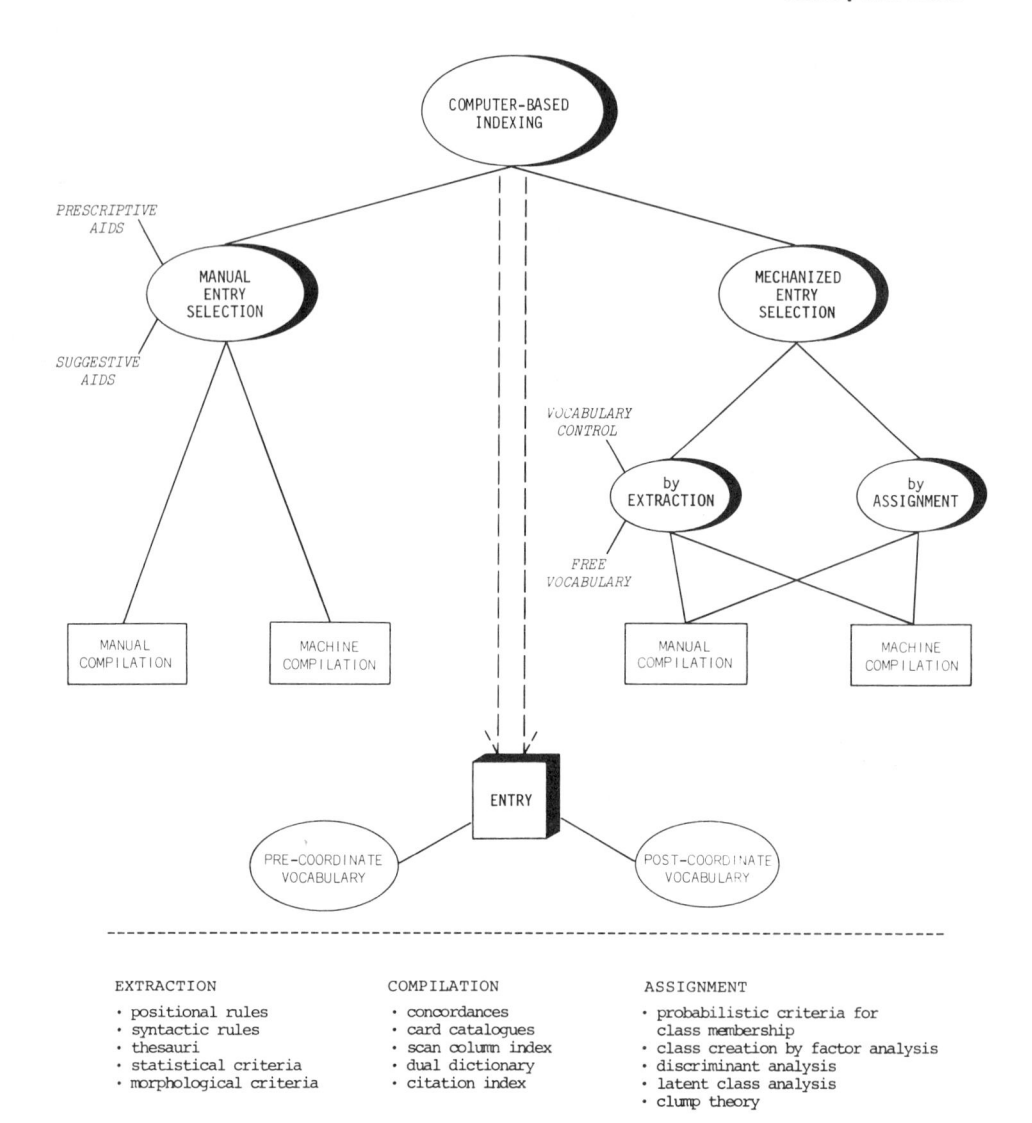

Fig. 2. Hierarchy of the uses of computer-based indexing with examples of the operations of extraction, compilation, and assignment.

EXTRACTION
- positional rules
- syntactic rules
- thesauri
- statistical criteria
- morphological criteria

COMPILATION
- concordances
- card catalogues
- scan column index
- dual dictionary
- citation index

ASSIGNMENT
- probabilistic criteria for class membership
- class creation by factor analysis
- discriminant analysis
- latent class analysis
- clump theory

that are independent of the context of the original document and those entries that preserve some degree of the context of the original document. Hence

Noncontextual index entries:

KWOC: Key Word Out of Context—uniterm or precoordinated terms.

Contextual index entries:

KWIC: Key Word In Context—a keyword within a display of some portion of its contextual environment in the source document.

RELATIONAL: A keyword with a display of some portion of its contextual/relational environment in the source text.

TABLE 1

Landmarks in Computer-Based Indexing[a]

	Text			Nontext		
		Contextual			Contextual	
Procedure	KWOC	KWIC	Relational	KWOC	KWIC	Relational
Manual	Classification schemes	Latin squares	Roget's Thesaurus			
			Dictionaries			
	Concordances		Concordances			
Computer-based	Luhn 1957	Luhn 1959	Bernier (thesaurus) 1957	Fugmann GREMAS 1963	ISI Rotaform 1963	Mooers 1951
	Baxendale 1958	Many variations	Doyle (semantic maps) 1962	CAS screen generation 1965	ISI Wiswesser 1968	Meyer 1962
	Maron 1961	,,	Gardin (SYNTOL) 1964		Petrarca et al. 1971	Gluck, Rasmussen 1963
	Edmundson, Wyllys 1961	,,	Hays 1964			Morgan 1965
	Salton 1969	,,	Quillian 1968			
	Borko 1970	Petrarca, Lay 1969	Shank, Tessler 1969			
			Fugmann 1970			
			Rush 1972			

[a] This table is not exhaustive; no judgmental value should be associated with exclusion.

It is interesting that the conceptual operations associated with textual relational indexing are the reverse of those associated with nontextual relational indexing. In textual relational indexing one starts with a linear string (sentence) of data elements and the object is to create a structure that represents or identifies the relations between the elements in the linear string; in nontextual relational indexing the goal is to derive index entries from a linearization of complex (relational) structures. The problem of the linearization of chemical structures has been essentially solved (see Morgan [18] and Davis and Rush [19]); however, the identification of textual relations is, in contrast, in its infancy. We will return to the problem of document representation in the section entitled Toward Automatic Indexing.

Before considering specific examples of computer-based indexing techniques, we shall attempt to be a little more precise about the nature and role of indexing in the process of information transfer.

Communication, IS&R, and Indexing

We shall present, without extensive introduction or motivation, some basic definitions which are germane to the analysis of computer-based indexing techniques:

Data element: A data element is the smallest entity which can be recognized as a discrete element of that class of entities named by a specific attribute for a given unit of measure with a given precision of measurement.

Document: A document is a well-ordered set of data elements.

Indexing process: The indexing process is characterized by the operations of identification (recognition) and representation of data elements and relations.

Indexing system: An indexing system is a system for the application of the indexing process to the document space. The output from the indexing system is the index.

Document space: A document space is an ordered set of documents.

Index: An index is the image of composite order-preserving mappings performed on the document space.

Index entry: An index entry is an expression such that the following data element (d) relation (REL) holds: d_j REL d_k, where for each j $\exists$ $\{k\}$ s.t. d_j REL d_k $\forall j,k$. $\{k\}$ are the partitions of the document, d_j is the jth data element of the document.

As depicted in Fig. 3(a), an indexing system serves as the intermediary between a set of data sources and a set of data users (receivers). The problem becomes one of

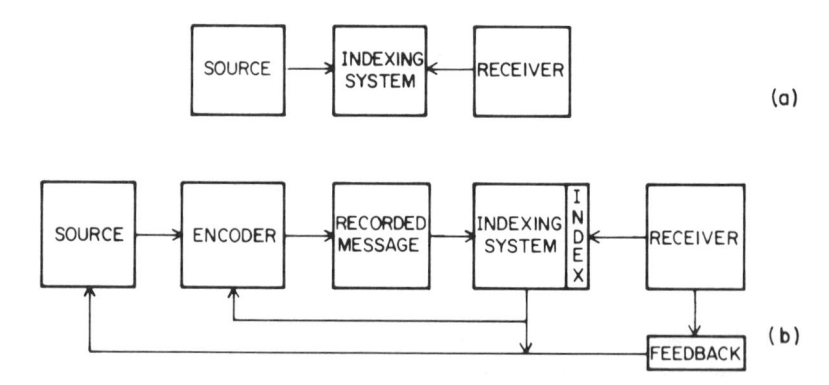

Fig. 3. (a) The position of the indexing system in data transfer. (b) The indexing system and feedback operations.

Automatic Indexing

representing messages that come from a number of unrelated sources. We assume that each message (document) is an ordered collection of data elements and relations between data elements. It should be obvious that message representation must be effected so as to guarantee the maximum degree of overlap between the experience set that *is* the representation and the experience sets of the classes of potential receivers. In this way the meaning of the document is preserved.

The indexing system provides the transformations and the interface experience set required for effective communication between the source(s) and the receiver. As a result of the operation of the indexing system, a receiver is able to *discover* the existence of a source; this permits the existence of the feedback loop depicted in Fig. 3(b). Feedback between a receiver and a source is often a prerequisite for effective communication. The crucial point is that not only is the index the product, but it is all that remains of the original document space. Accordingly, we assume that the original documents are not directly available to the receiver; hence the index is the receiver's only point of access to the document collection. Under such constraints it should be clear that accurate retrieval depends on the exactness of the operation of the indexing system.

Let us now consider the function of the indexing system from a more abstract level. Information storage and retrieval (IS&R) systems can be described in the terminology of Marschak [20] as the combination of two *purposive processing chains*. These two chains are depicted in Fig. 4. We have chosen to call them *document processing* and *retrieval processing*. Both processes, which are greatly simplified in this figure, actually involve multilevel and multistep operations designed to expedite the transfer of data.

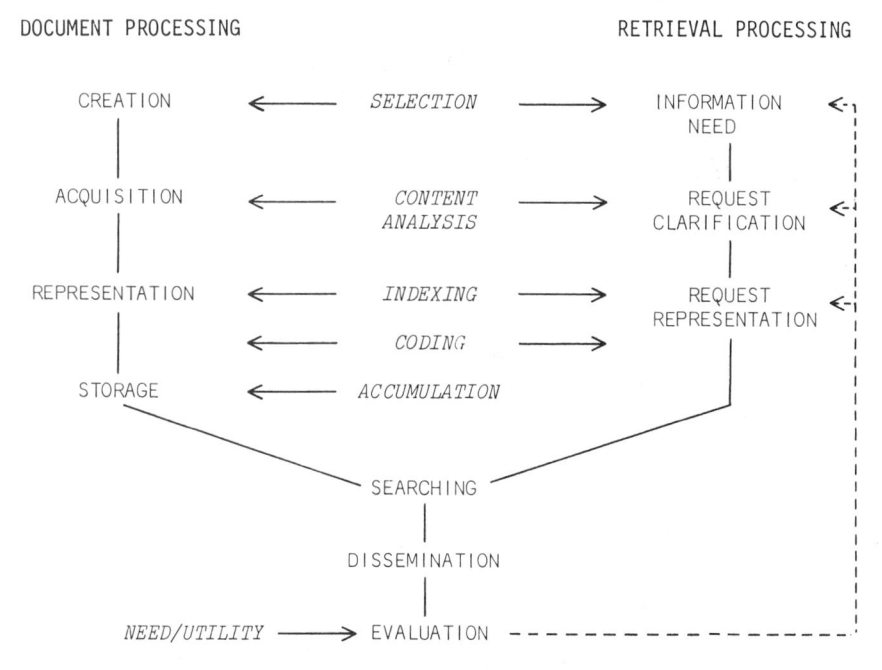

Fig. 4. The index as the interface between IS&R processes of document processing and retrieval processing.

The document processing chain shows the flow from document creation to document acquisition (by the IS&R system), representation, and storage. The first three stages are paralleled by the retrieval processing chain in the conception (realization) of the information need, the clarification of the request, and the representation (coding) of the request. Both chains share, through the representation stage, the operations of selection, content analysis, indexing, and coding. Document storage involves, in addition, the process of accumulation. The two processing chains merge at the searching operation where retrieved data (potentially, information) are disseminated for evaluation. The dotted lines in the figure indicate the possibility of repeated cycling through the retrieval process. The indexing system operates on the document space (and the document representation) produced by the first stages of the document processing chain. Thus the index is the *document* which the retrieval processing chain uses for the search operation. To reiterate, *accurate retrieval depends on the exactness of the operation of the indexing system.*

It should be clear, at this point, that there exists a problem in delineating the precise scope of a general computer-based indexing system. The actual itemization of the components/operations that fall within the box labeled "indexing system" depends on the specific implementation, i.e., the number of manual inputs and operations, the scope of the operating system being used, the set of utility programs that are available, etc. Accordingly, we have selected the operations of *input,*[3] *identification, representation, entry creation,* and *output* as being germane to a description of a particular computer-based indexing system.

Input relates to those operations required to obtain data in computer-manipulatable form. Thus input includes keyboarding, optical scanning, magnetic-character reading, and the whole range of analog signals (e.g., voice) which may be operated on by a computer program.

Once data have been obtained in machine-readable form, they must be partitioned according to a set of well-defined *identification* procedures. Among these are identification of document boundaries, titles, bibliographic data, and various other elements which are of interest within a particular indexing system.

The process of identification is followed by that of *representation*, a process involving essentially symbol/symbol transformations. For instance, a word may replace a word, a phrase a paragraph, a molecular formula a structure, and a name a picture.

Entry creation is the process of constructing an index entry from data element representations. This process involves, in particular, formatting operations such as inversion, articulation, and keyword extraction.

Finally, the set of entries created at the previous step is ordered in some way, redundancies are eliminated, final formatting operations are performed, and the resultant document is made available to a class of users in some way. This process we call *output*.

While these five classes of procedures are not cleanly separated in most indexing systems, we consider them to be the basic processes in indexing and will use them as the basis for subsequent discussion.

---

[3] We believe that a distinction should be made between input as a *product* (e.g., a magnetic tape resulting from a previous document processing operation) and input as a *source* (e.g., the text of this article).

EXAMPLES OF COMPUTER-BASED INDEXING

An Overview

Figure 5 presents a matrix of the possible levels of automation associated with the five classes of computer-based indexing procedures mentioned above. It should be recognized that although an indexing system may be described as computer based, in actuality only a minority of its procedures may be performed automatically, while the remaining procedures are accomplished either manually or by means of some semi-automatic process (i.e., with limited manual intervention). As an example of this range of degrees of automation, the procedure of document input (depending on whether the document is viewed as a source or as a product) could involve either manual keypunching, optical character recognition (with some manual editing), or direct processing from a previously prepared magnetic tape.

As has been implied in the section entitled The Nature and Definition of Indexing, the processes of data element identification and document representation are the crucial steps for successful computer-based indexing and subsequent document retrieval. Consider the following title (a document resulting from *identification*):

> Effect of a selective beta-adrenergic blocker in preventing falls in arterial oxygen tension following isoprenaline in asthmatic subjects.

If, for the sake of exposition, we postulate the existence of a computer-based indexing system that incorporates role indicators (R), generic-specific relations, formula lists, and a word guide or controlled vocabulary as *analysis documents*, then the following system *representation* might be obtained:

> R_{19} of a selective beta-adrenergic receptor (beta receptor) blocking drug (drug) in R_6 R_3 in arterial (cardiovascular system) oxygenation tension (airway resistance) R_{30} isoprenaline ($C_{14}H_{22}N_2O_3$) in asthmatic subjects.

It is conceivable that this indexing system would automatically generate (among others)

PROCEDURES	OPERATION		
	MANUAL	SEMI-AUTOMATIC	AUTOMATIC
INPUT			
IDENTIFICATION			
REPRESENTATION			
ENTRY CREATION			
OUTPUT			

Fig. 5. Matrix of the level of automation associated with the computer-based indexing procedures.

the following entries from the system representation of the document (*entry creation*):

> beta-blocking drug
> beta receptor
> airway resistance
> $C_{14}H_{22}N_2O_3$
> beta-adrenergic blocker,
>   effect of, in preventing falls following isoprenaline in asthmatic subjects

Virtually all computer-based indexing systems automate the index-output process. We wish to stress that although output procedures are sometimes very complex, there is a considerable difference in computational sophistication between algorithms that are designed to format index entries and algorithms that are designed to create the system's representation of the document space. However, one should not minimize the importance of the format of the "index display" as the vehicle for a receiver's rapid assimilation and comprehension of index data.

Specific Examples of Computer-Based Indexing Systems

With the foregoing as background, we turn to a discussion of specific examples of computer-based indexing systems. Table 2 presents a summary of some general, specific, and experimental computer-based indexing systems. The column labeled "type" is derived from the partition depicted in Table 1 and the subsequent columns are a compression of the matrix of Fig. 5. These representative indexes are described and characterized in the sections entitled General Indexes, Specialized Indexes, and Experimental Indexes.

General Indexes

KWIC Indexes. The *Biological Abstracts* subject index called B.A.S.I.C. (Biological Abstracts Subjects in Context) (Fig. 6) exemplifies the KWIC index, the only type of index that is widely produced by automated means. The purpose of the KWIC index is to permit the user to locate documents of potential interest to him by first locating a keyword within an alphabetical listing and then, by checking the contextual settings in which the keyword occurs, to enable him to narrow his choices to those that he judges correspond to his interests. Many variants of the KWIC index have been produced, but all are based upon the notion of the cyclic Latin square, known for centuries [40]. A typical KWIC index entry may be characterized as follows:

C	K	C'	A

where C and C' represent segments of the context in which the keyword, K, occurred in the document (either C or C' might be empty, but not both) and A is a pointer (address) to the location of the keyword (and its context) within the document.

In the example of Fig. 6, the keyword occurs near the middle of the entry and the address is an abstract number. Shading is introduced to facilitate visual location of the keyword.

TABLE 2

Examples of Computer-Based Indexes[a]

Name	Ref.	Type	Input	Identification	Representation	Entry creation	Output
General indexes							
B.A.S.I.C.	21	KWIC	M	A	A	A	A
Biosystematic index	22	KWOC/REL	M	M	A	A	A
Chemical Industry Notes	23	KWOC	M	S	A	A	A
Project MEDICO	24	KWOC/REL	M	A	S	A	A
Double KWIC	25	KWIC/REL	M	S	A	A	A
Articulated	26	KWOC/REL	M	S	A	A	A
Citation	27	KWOC	M	M	S	A	A
Multiterm	28	KWOC/REL	M	A	A	A	A
Specialized indexes							
HAIC	29	KWIC	A	A	A	A	A
Chemical Substructure index	30	KWOC/REL	M	A	A	A	A
GREMAS (chemical reactions)	31	REL	M	M	M	A	A
KLIC	32	KWIC	A	A	A	A	A
DuPont CS[4]	33	REL	M	A	A	A	A
CAS Patent Concordance	34	KWOC	A	A	A	A	A
Experimental indexes							
SYNTOL	35, 36	KWOC/REL	M	A	A	A	A
On-line indexing (Doyle)	37	REL	M	S	—	—	—
On-line indexing (Thompson)	38	REL	M	S	A	S	A
Book indexing (Borko)	39	KWOC	M	S	A	S	A

[a] A = automatic, M = manual, REL = relational, and S = semiautomatic.

```
EEN BACTERIA EXPOSED TO    MONOCHROMATIC LIGHT OF DIFFERENT WAV    22030
EELY MOVING EYE GRATING    MONOCHROMATOR /SPECTRAL SENSITIVITY     46414
S-SP ISOCHRYSIS-GALBANA    MONOCHRYSIS-LUTHERI DIURON NEBURON M    22258
A CLADOSPORIUM FUSARIUM    MONOCILLIUM CONIOTHYRIUM-OLIVACEUM S    16322
F CONDUCTING BUNDLES OF    MONOCOT AND DICOT PLANT LEAVES SORGH    10630
IA AMSINCKIA-HISPIDIA-D    MONOCOT DICOT LIST/ ADDITIONS TO THE    58993
ND IN 24 PARGANAS INDIA    MONOCOTS DICOTS/ A BOTANICAL EXPLORA    23827
RAMS BINOMIALS PRIORITY    MONOCOTS DICOTS/ A RECONSIDERATION O    17950
CT OF MURSHIDABAD INDIA    MONOCOTS DICOTS/ A SKETCH FLORA OF C    23825
SIDES OF LEAVES IN SOME    MONOCOTYLEDONOUS AND DICOTYLEDONOUS     16829
ICHOTOMOUS BRANCHING OF    MONOCOTYLEDONOUS TREES ASCLEPIAS-D H    44067
   MALAD-MADH AREA PART 1    MONOCOTYLEDONS HABITAT FLOWERING FRU    58986
  TAXONOMIC NOTES ON SOME    MONOCOTYLEDONS OF ALASKA AND NORTHER    35699
 AL NOTES ON NEW OR RARE    MONOCOTYLEDONS OF THE FRENCH ANTILLE    35701
   FRENCH ANTILLES MARINE    MONOCOTYLEDONS 39TH CONTRIBUTION HAL    35701
```

Fig. 6. Illustration of the B.A.S.I.C. index (author's reproduction).

Input of the data to be processed by the KWIC indexing procedure is typically manual (automatic if a prior processing step yields the appropriate input as a by-product), but the remaining processes of identification, representation, entry creation, and output are usually automatic.

KWOC Indexes. There are a multitude of examples of the KWOC index of which that to *Chemical Industry Notes*, illustrated in Fig. 7, is typical. A simple noun phrase, consisting of a noun modified (optionally) by one or more adjectives, serves as the keyword. A KWOC index entry may be characterized as

$$\boxed{K \mid A}$$

where K is a keyword and A is a set of addresses.

In the example of Fig. 7, input is manual, identification is partly manual (flags introduced into the input), and the remaining processes are automatic. The addresses are abstract numbers.

Textbooks are often indexed by the KWOC technique, although in the vast majority of cases the entire index is produced manually. Hybrid indexes combining some KWOC entries and some KWOC/relational entries are also commonly used with textbooks. Again, the indexes are manually produced.

A rather unique example of the KWOC index is afforded by the Science Citation Index (SCI) [27, 41], illustrated in Fig. 8. An entry in this index is characterized as

$$\boxed{K_p \mid I_s}$$

where K_p is a primary keyword of the form

$$\boxed{N \mid S}$$

where N is an author name and S is a specifier amounting to a bibliographic citation, and I_s is a set of secondary index entries of the form

$$\boxed{K_s \mid A}_1$$
$$\boxed{K_s \mid A}_2$$
$$\vdots$$
$$\boxed{K_s \mid A}_n$$

where K_s is a secondary keyword (an author name), and A is a bibliographic citation amplified by a code indicative of document type.

The significance of an SCI entry is that the document represented by K_p (and authored by element N of K_p) has been cited by one or more of I_{s_i} ($1 \leq i \leq n$, $n =$ total number of citings of K_p). The interpretation is that since one knows what the document represented by K_p is *about*, one can reasonably assume that the document(s) represented by the I_{s_i} are also at least in part *about* the same thing. The SCI is the only index which permits a user to trace data both forward and backward in time.

KWOC/Relational Indexes. In this category we include those indexes whose entries are KWOC in nature but which are modified by a relational element of some kind.

```
ANCHOR CHEMICAL CO. ltd.          K216, F235, E462
ANGUS                             D308
ANTHRAQUINONE                     A259
ANTHRAQUINONE-BASED DYES          A259
ANTI-FOAMS, SILICONE              E530
ANTIOXIDANTS                      D270, F284
ANTIOZONANT AFD                   E531
ANTIOZONANTS                      D270
APPLIED SYNTHETICS CORP.          E436
AQUITAINE CHEMICALS INC.          D292, K203
AQUITAINE-ORGANICO          D291, D292, K203
```

Fig. 7. Illustration of the Chemical Industry Notes index (author's reproduction).

Typical relational elements are those called *role indicators* [42]. For instance, a keyword that has a *set* of referents may be modified by some means so that the combination has a single referent. The keyword ASH might be modified as follows.

ASH (the plant)
ASH (wood)
ASH (residue of combustion)
ASH (process)

To be sure, the increase in specificity is not perfect (e.g., many kinds of trees called "ash" exist). Nevertheless, the purpose of the KWOC/REL index is to provide a degree of specificity that the keyword alone does not provide.

In the example of Fig. 9 [43], input is manual, but the processes of identification, representation, entry creation, and output are automatic. Examination of Fig. 9 reveals a series of partial index entries (no address has been appended to the keyword/ relation string), the first element of which represents a keyword and successive elements of which represent relations. For instance, 57432 is a keyword (a number standing for a specific chemical compound). This keyword is found (by computer) in a dictionary in which certain other elements are contained that (1) bear specific relationships to the keyword or (2) specify certain relationships into which the keyword may enter (determined by the context of the keyword in the document). A normalized frequency is also computed for each keyword, and its value is appended to the keyword as a

```
CORNELIUS RJ------*58*P AUSTR I MIN METALL  65   185
        BJORLING G     J CHEM UAR       66    9   187
CORNELIUS WO------*33*Z FISCH-------------  31   535
        PANDIAN TJ     MARINE BIOL      67    1    60
CORNELIUSSEN R----*   *IN PRESS-------------=
        PETERLIN A     J POLY SC A2     67    5   957
        --------------  -PRIVATE COMMUNICATIO=
        MEINEL G       J POL SCI B    L 67    5   613
CORNELL CM--------*50*SURGERY-------------   28   735
        SALVINI E      MIN RAD FIS      67   12    70
CORNELL D---------*60*CHEM ENGNG PROG-----   56    68
        REISS LP       IND ENG PDD      67    6   486
        SEMMELBA.R     CHEM ENG SC      67   22  1237
```

Fig. 8. Illustration of the Science Citation index (author's reproduction).

```
BUCHANAN DS
AN APPROACH TO MANAGEMENT OF STATUS EPILEPTICUS.
SOUTHWEST MED 47,187-9, JUL 66

NO. OF WORDS = 1760
(2) BARBITURATES

57432 (2) AMOBARBITAL, 5-ETHYL-5-ISOAMYLBARBITURIC ACID, BARBITURATES,
    AMYTAL

50066 (3) 5-ETHYL-5-PHENYLBARBITURIC ACID, PHENOBARBITAL, BARBITURATES

(2) ANTICONVULSANTS

57410 (3) DIPHENYLHYDANTOIN, 5,5-DIPHENYL-2,4-IMIDAZOLIDINEDIONE,
    HYDANTOINS


AMYTAL/ THERAPY (1)
AMOBARBITAL/ THERAPY (1)
PHENOBARBITAL/ ADMINISTRATION (1), EFFECT (1), THERAPY (2)
ANTICONVULSANTS/ EPILEPSY (1), THERAPY (1)
DIPHENYLHYDANTOIN/ DOSAGE (2)
BARBITURATES/ ACTIVITY (1)
```

Fig. 9. Illustration of a KWOC/REL index (after Ref. 43).

measure of the keyword's importance in the document. Thus 57432 has "importance" 2, is called AMOBARBITAL (synonym), 5-ETHYL-5-ISOAMYLBARBITURIC ACID (synonym), is a member of the class BARBITURATES, and has the trade name AMYTAL. In addition, AMYTAL is seen to be modified by the term THERAPY and the combination AMYTAL/THERAPY has weight 1. The entire set of index entries, together with the bibliographic data, constitute something of a telegraphic abstract [44].

A second example of the KWOC/REL type of index is afforded by the articulated index. Classic examples of manually produced articulated indexes include the *Subject Index to Chemical Abstracts* and the *Subject Index to Nuclear Science Abstracts*. Lynch has studied articulated indexes with the aim of automating their production [45]. Full automation has not been achieved, but an articulated index has been produced by Lynch *et al.* by semiautomatic means (see Fig. 10) [46]. The principal problems to be resolved before articulated indexes may be produced entirely automatically are (1) the construction of normal-form strings and (2) the selection of keywords.

A normal-form string consists of noun phrases separated by articulation points (usually function words, such as prepositions and conjunctions), viz.,

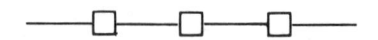

———□———□———□———

where ——— represents a noun phrase and □ represents an articulation point. Each noun phrase is a candidate keyword (heading, in Lynch's terminology). Articulated

Automatic Indexing

```
        ABSTRACTS
            OF CURRENT PUBLICATIONS, SMRE(2)
            EXCHANGE OF PUBLICATIONS + BIBLIOGRAPHIES +,
                ON MINE SAFTEY RESEARCH, GRICE C.S.W.(19)
        ACCIDENTS
            ANALYSIS OF DATA ON, MAGUIRE B.A.(2)
                IN HAULAGE AND TRANSPORT FOR 1960, MAGUIRE B.A.(7)
            CALCULUS TO STUDY OF, IN MINES, APPLICATION
                OF PROBABILITY, WYNN A.H.A.(3)
            CONTROL OF, CHARTS + SUMMARIES FOR, DAWES J.G.(17)
            CONTROL CHARTS, WIDGINTON D.W.(1)
            DUE TO HAULAGE, CAUSES OF, NORTH OF ENGLAND INSTITUTE
                OF MINING AND MECHANICAL ENGINEERS(7)
```

Fig. 10. Illustration of Safety in Mines index (author's reproduction).

index entries may be characterized by an algorithm of the following kind [47] (assume n noun phrases in the normal-form string):

Assume a normal-form string

$$K_1 \square K_2 \square K_3 \ldots \square K_n$$

Generate from this string n *canonical notations*, each of the form

$$K_i \mathrel{\text{———}} K_1 \square K_2 \ldots \square K_{i-1}\square, \square K_{i+1} \ldots \square K_n \qquad (1 \leq i \leq n)$$

where K_i is the ith noun phrase as subject heading (keyword) and the string following the dash is a *canonical modifier*. Call the portion of the canonical modifier to the left of the comma the *initial part* and that portion to the right of the comma the *final part*. Apply the following procedure to each canonical notation, in turn, to obtain all articulated index entries for a normal-form string of n components ($n - 1$ articulation points).

1. If there is no initial part of the canonical modifier, the index entry is complete.
2. For each incomplete index entry, form complete entries as follows.
    a. Beginning with the last component of the initial part, generate i subheadings (secondary keywords) and canonical submodifiers by extracting the last, the last two, ..., the last $i - 1$, and last i components.
    b. If the initial part exists, extract the first, and only the first, component of the final part as a subheading.
3. Continue application of 1 and 2 until all entries are complete.

Various alternatives may be introduced, but the above algorithm suffices for illustration.

The segments of an articulated index entry may be thought of as answers to questions such as WHERE, WHY, WHAT, HOW, WHEN, and WHOSE, with respect to one of the noun phrases as keyword. For instance, the articulated index entry

Sulfur isotopes,
    in pyrite from Black Forest, 00000

contains two segments both of which answer WHERE with respect to "sulfur isotopes." But in the entry

        Pyrite,
           sulfur isotopes in, from Black Forest, 00000

the segments answer the questions WHAT and WHERE with respect to "pyrite." When the KWOC/REL index is viewed in this way, it can be seen that the *Predicasts Abstracts* of Fig. 11 exhibit the properties of a KWOC/REL index just as does the articulated index, but in a more highly organized form.

    A final example of the KWOC/REL index is illustrated in Fig. 12. This index, the multiterm index developed by Skolnik [28], consists of index entries of the form

$$\boxed{M \mid A}$$

where M is a multiterm of the form B/C/D/... and A is an address. The sequence of elements B, C, D, ... in the multiterm is established as *generic* to *specific* or, where such a succession of relations is not possible, by *chronology* or by some prescribed order, as for chemical reactions, where the order is

    product/reactant(s)/process/conditions/catalyst, solvent, etc./equipment/use of product/
    property of product

Each element of the multiterm may also have one or more role indicators appended to it.

KWIC/Relational Indexes. The Double-KWIC (D-KWIC) index provides a level of relational capability not easily realized through use of the standard KWIC index [25]. The relational aspects of the D-KWIC index are purely syntactic. From the illustration of Fig. 13, it can be seen that an index entry such as

        File management
           evaluation of * software packages ... the 215

provides a useful syntactic relationship between "file management" and "evaluation" from which one may infer the existence of some conceptual relationship.

    The D-KWIC index is produced by procedures that, except for input which is usually manual, are fully automatic. The input strings (titles, etc.) are first KWICed in the usual fashion, then the keyword is isolated and is replaced by an asterisk (to mark the location of the keyword in the original string; see Fig. 13). The remainder of the string is again KWICed, but only selected strings are subordinated to the keyword previously isolated. In this way, a better organization of "secondary keywords" is obtained than is possible using the standard KWIC procedure.

    A D-KWIC index entry may be characterized as

$$\boxed{K_p \mid K_s \mid C \mid A}$$

where K_p and K_s are primary and secondary keywords, respectively, C is context, and A is an address. Control over the specific values of K_p and K_s may be obtained by use

Automatic Indexing

SIC NO.	PRODUCT A	EVENT	PRODUCT B	YEARS B S L	QUANTITIES B S L	UNIT OF MEASURE	JOURNAL	SOURCE DATE	PAGE
28153 205	Phenol	used in	plastic materials	65 80	.6± 1.2±	bil lbs	Chem Week	11/23/68	10
28153 206	Phenol, synthetic	capacity by	producer	69 71 72	1550.d 2375.d 2576.d	mil lbs	#OPD Rep	3/ 3/69	29
28153 206	Phenol, synthetic	consumption		71	1020.	mil lbs	OPD Rep	4/21/69	30
28153 206	Phenol, cumene-based	consump of	cumene as % of phenol	66 69 75	48. 70. 75.	% of total	O&G Jour	3/ 3/69	92

Fig. 11. Illustration of the Predicasts abstracts (author's reproduction).

```
REACTANT -R / PROCESS / CATALYST / USE / PROPERTY / PRODUCT -PQ /
PROCESS / CATALYST / USE / PROPERTY / PRODUCT -PQ / REACTANT -R /
CATALYST / USE / PROPERTY / PRODUCT -PQ / REACTANT -R / PROCESS /
USE / PROPERTY / PRODUCT -PQ / REACTANT -R / PROCESS / CATALYST /
PROPERTY / PRODUCT -PQ / REACTANT -R / PROCESS / CATALYST / USE /
```

Fig. 12. Illustration of the Multiterm index (author's reproduction).

of word control lists (stop lists or thesauri), frequency criteria, and procedures for the standardization of inflectional suffixes [25, 47, 48].

Specialized Indexes

The distinction we make between general indexes (discussed in the previous section entitled General Indexes) and specialized indexes is based upon the nature and scope of the subject matter indexed rather than on index type. Thus we consider a subject index for chemistry or physics to be a general index, but a molecular formula index or a star catalog to be specialized indexes. There are many specialized indexes, a few of which are discussed below. The examples have been chosen to illustrate a range of specialties. The selections have been arbitrary and they are by no means exhaustive.

KWIC Indexes. The *Hetero Atom in Context* (*HAIC*) index, illustrated in Fig. 14, is a good example of a specialized application of the KWIC indexing technique to a set of data whose elements have a well-defined structure, namely molecular formulas. In this index the truncation or "wrap-around" of the input string common in general KWIC indexes is avoided because the index entry is made to be self-addressing. That

```
FILE ACTIVITY
   INFLUENCE OF *, FILE SIZE, AND PROBABILITY OF SUCCESSFUL
      RETRIEVAL ON EFFICIENCY OF FILE STRUCTURES  .............. 175
FILE MANAGEMENT
   EVALUATION OF * SOFTWARE PACKAGES  ........................THE  215
   PACKAGES  .......................THE EVALUATION OF * SOFTWARE  215
   SESSION SUMMARY  ......................................* SYSTEMS:  525
   SOFTWARE PACKAGES  ....................THE EVALUATION OF *  215
   SUMMARY  ...........................................* SYSTEMS: SESSION  525
   SYSTEMS: SESSION SUMMARY  .......................................*  525
FILE ORGANIZATION
   CONTROLLED *   ..................................................USER  245
   CONTROLLED * AND SEARCH STRATEGIES  ........................USER  183
   SEARCH STRATEGIES  ......................USER CONTROLLED * AND  183
   STRATEGIES  .......................USER CONTROLLED * AND SEARCH  183
   USER CONTROLLED *   ............................................. 245
   USER CONTROLLED * AND SEARCH STRATEGIES  ....................... 183
FILE PROCESSOR
   THE HUMAN-READABLE/MACHINE-READABLE (HRMR) MASS MEMORY AS THE *
      FOR A NETWORK OF DOCUMENTATION/ANALYSIS CENTERS  .......... 339
```

Fig. 13. Illustration of the Double-KWIC index (author's reproduction).

Automatic Indexing 217

$$\begin{aligned}
&\text{Mn}_2 \text{ Ni } \text{O}_4\\
&(\text{C}_2\text{H}_8\text{N}_4 \text{ Ni } \text{O}_4)_x\\
&(\text{C}_3\text{H}_{10}\text{N}_4 \text{ Ni } \text{O}_4)_x\\
&(\text{C}_4\text{H}_{12}\text{N}_4 \text{ Ni } \text{O}_4)_x\\
&(\text{C}_6\text{H}_2\text{N}_2 \text{ Ni } \text{O}_4)_x\\
&(\text{C}_8\text{H}_{12}\text{N}_4 \text{ Ni } \text{O}_4)_x\\
&(\text{C}_{10}\text{H}_{16}\text{N}_4 \text{ Ni } \text{O}_4)_x\\
&(\text{C}_{12}\text{H}_8\text{N}_2 \text{ Ni } \text{O}_4)_x\\
&(\text{C}_{14}\text{H}_{24}\text{N}_4 \text{ Ni } \text{O}_4)_x\\
&(\text{C}_{18}\text{H}_{16}\text{N}_4 \text{ Ni } \text{O}_4)_x\\
&(\text{C}_{18}\text{H}_{20}\text{As}_2 \text{ Ni } \text{O}_4)_x\\
&(\text{C}_{22}\text{H}_{18}\text{N}_4 \text{ Ni } \text{O}_4)_x\\
&(\text{C}_{22}\text{H}_{24}\text{N}_4 \text{ Ni } \text{O}_4)_x\\
&((\text{C}_{24}\text{H}_{22}\text{N}_4 \text{ Ni } \text{O}_4)_x\\
&(\text{C}_{38}\text{H}_{28}\text{As}_2 \text{ Ni } \text{O}_4)_x\\
&(\text{C}_{42}\text{H}_{36}\text{As}_2 \text{ Ni } \text{O}_4)_x\\
&\text{C}_{12}\text{H}_8 \text{ Ni } \text{O}_4 \cdot \text{C}_2\text{H}_8\text{N}_2 \cdot 2\text{H}\\
&\text{C}_{26}\text{H}_{20}\text{N}_{10} \text{ Ni } \text{O}_4 \cdot 2\text{C}_5\text{H}_5\text{N}\\
&\text{C}_{12}\text{H}_{28}\text{N}_8 \text{ Ni } \text{O}_4 \cdot 2\text{Cl}\\
&\text{C}_{27}\text{H}_{27}\text{N}_6 \text{ Ni } \text{O}_4 \cdot \text{ClO}_4\\
&\text{C}_{29}\text{H}_{31}\text{N}_6 \text{ Ni } \text{O}_4 \cdot \text{ClO}_4
\end{aligned}$$

Fig. 14. Illustration of the HAIC index (author's reproduction).

is, it serves as a pointer into the *Formula Index to Chemical Abstracts*. The relationship between a HAIC index entry and a CA abstract is illustrated below.

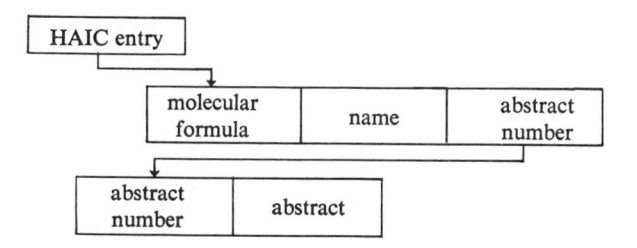

```
HAIC entry
   ↓
   ┌──────────┬──────┬──────────┐
   │molecular │ name │ abstract │
   │ formula  │      │  number  │
   └──────────┴──────┴──────────┘
        ↓
   ┌──────────┬──────────┐
   │ abstract │ abstract │
   │  number  │          │
   └──────────┴──────────┘
```

The HAIC index also differs from general KWIC indexes in that several levels of sorting are applied to each set of entries having a particular keyword. For instance, it can be seen from Fig. 14 that within the group of formulas with **Ni** as the keyword, the formulas are secondarily ordered by the portion of the context to the left of the keyword. This makes it possible to locate not only formulas having a particular element (e.g., **Ni**) but those having, in addition, say, the grouping $\mathbf{O_4P_2S_4}$.

Input for the HAIC is obtained in machine-readable form as the by-product of other operations, hence all processes necessary to its production are automated. (The HAIC index was discontinued in 1971.)

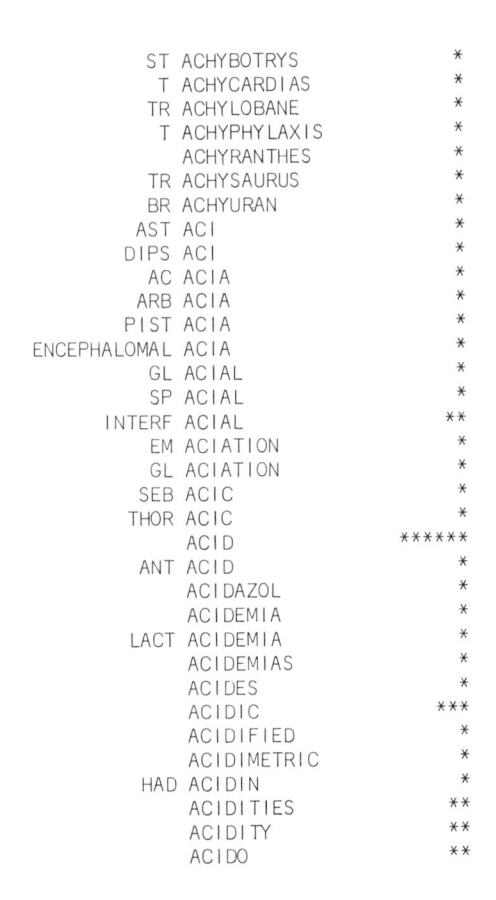

```
           ST ACHYBOTRYS         *
            T ACHYCARDIAS        *
           TR ACHYLOBANE         *
            T ACHYPHYLAXIS       *
              ACHYRANTHES        *
           TR ACHYSAURUS         *
           BR ACHYURAN           *
          AST ACI                *
         DIPS ACI                *
           AC ACIA               *
          ARB ACIA               *
         PIST ACIA               *
ENCEPHALOMAL ACIA                *
           GL ACIAL              *
           SP ACIAL              *
        INTERF ACIAL             **
           EM ACIATION           *
           GL ACIATION           *
          SEB ACIC               *
         THOR ACIC               *
              ACID               ******
          ANT ACID               *
              ACIDAZOL           *
              ACIDEMIA           *
         LACT ACIDEMIA           *
              ACIDEMIAS          *
              ACIDES             *
              ACIDIC             ***
              ACIDIFIED          *
              ACIDIMETRIC        *
          HAD ACIDIN             *
              ACIDITIES          **
              ACIDITY            **
              ACIDO              **
```

Fig. 15. Illustration of the KLIC index (author's reproduction).

A second special application of the KWIC indexing technique is exemplified by the Key Letter In Context (KLIC) index [32] illustrated in Fig. 15. Here words are processed to provide the user a means of determining those words that contain a particular sequence of letters in common. In the illustration of Fig. 15, it is easy to see that 14 words contain the letter sequence ACID. The asterisks to the right in each entry provide frequency-of-occurrence data for the word indexed (* = low frequency, ***** = high frequency). The KLIC index serves simultaneously as the index and as the set of data indexed. Its use in automated retrieval systems has been discussed elsewhere [32, 49].

The production of the KLIC index, like the HAIC, is entirely automatic, although in both instances input could be manual.

KWOC Indexes. The *Patent Concordance* [34], prepared by the Chemical Abstracts Service, is illustrative of a specialized KWOC index (see Fig. 16). The index entries take the form

$$\boxed{K \mid A_1 \mid A_2}$$

PATENT NUMBER	CORRESPONDING PATENT		CA REF. NUMBER
156474	BRIT	1177240	72, 12416Q
	GER	1643961	
156630	GER	1902078	
156810	BRIT	1212613	72, 79085Z
	FR	1603226	
	US	3542779	
156951	GER	1814293	
157057	GER	1920222	
157087	GER	1918042	
157288	BRIT	1243646	73, 18869G
	US	3607104	
157467	GER	1900711	
157475	GER	1931090	
157593	GER	1810836	

Israeli

21179	NETH	6504911
24062	BRIT	1108848
24642	BRIT	1073039
24981	DAN	112814
25131	BRIT	1120152
25260	NETH	6608865
26022	S AFR	67 03320
26256	FR	AD92917

Fig. 16. Illustration of the Patent Concordance (author's reproduction).

where K is a keyword consisting of the *name* of the country in which the patent was issued and the *number* assigned by that country to the patent (e.g., Israeli 25131). In other words, K is a noun phrase consisting precisely of ADJECTIVE-NOUN. A_1 and A_2 are two addresses, the first of which points to the corresponding patent issued in another country and the second points to a CA abstract (the second may be empty). If A_2 is empty, the entry acts like a HAIC entry in that A_1 addresses another location in the *Patent Concordance*. This index enables the user to locate all patents issued that correspond to a given patent.

KWOC/Relational Indexes. The *Biosystematic Index to Biological Abstracts* [21] is both a KWOC index and a relational index because the keyword is accompanied by a series of elements related to it either taxonomically or subjectively. As illustrated in Fig. 17, a *Biosystematic Index* entry takes the form

$$\boxed{K \mid TC_1 \mid TC_2 \mid \ldots \mid TC_n \mid SH \mid A}$$

where K is a keyword, a major taxonomic category name such as Spermatophyta; TC_i ($i \geq 0$) are the names of the taxonomic categories hierarchically subordinate to the keyword (e.g., angiospermae → monocotyledonae → agavaceae); SH is a set of subject headings (as abbreviations) associated with the abstract containing mention of the organism, and A is the address (abstract number). Referring to Fig. 17, one finds, for example, the entry

SPERMATOPHYTA
ANGIOSPERMAE
MONOCOT   ARACEAE   PL MORPH   10582

which indicates that Abstract 10582 has been associated with the subject heading PLANT MORPHOLOGY and an organism of the arum family,[4] the implication being that if one is interested in the morphology of *Araceae*, one should examine Abstract 10582.

The input and the identification steps in the production of the *Biosystematic Index* are manual. The remaining procedures are effected automatically.

A second example of a specialized KWOC/REL index is afforded by the Chemical Substructure Index (CSI) produced by the Institute for Scientific Information [30] and illustrated in Fig. 18. The data element processed to produce a CSI entry is a Wiswesser linear notation [50] for a chemical entity. Given a canonical form of such a notation, certain structural features, expressed explicitly within the notation, are selected to serve as keywords, the remainder of the notation being appended to the keyword to specify the relation of the substructure represented by the keyword to the chemical structure represented by the entire notation. An additional KWOC-like feature of the CSI entry is the portion referred to as QUIKSCAN, an alphabetical sequence of the Wiswesser symbols that cause CSI entries to be produced. The form of the CSI entry is

| K | R | Q | A |

where K is the keyword, R is the relational framework in which the keyword is found, Q is the QUIKSCAN feature, and A is the address (abstract number plus compound number within the abstract). The CSI makes possible a degree of manual generic searching that an alphabetically ordered list of Wiswesser linear notations cannot possibly afford. Of course, since the notation in its original form occurs as a CSI entry, specific searches may also be carried out.

Relational Indexes. In this category we include those indexes whose organization is based upon the relational aspects of the data indexed. Most of the examples in this category are unsuited to direct use by people. Rather they serve as the basis for automatic retrieval based upon a person's interests. Two examples from the many available are discussed.

The DuPont Company's Chemical Structural Storage and Search System (CS[4]) [33] consists in part of a relational index whose entries have the form

| R | A |

---

[4] A familiar example of which is the jack-in-the-pulpit (Indian turnip).

Automatic Indexing

SPERMATOPHYTA					
			MONOCOT	AGAVACEAE	ECOL PLANT	6452
			MONOCOT	ALISMATACEAE	ECOL PLANT	7204
			MONOCOT	AMARYLLIDA	FD MICR FERM	7215
			MONOCOT	AMARYLLIDA	FLOR DISTRIA	7701
	AVES STST	6681	MONOCOT	ARACEAE	ENT BIO CONT	6435
	COLEOP SYST	8448	MONOCOT	ARACEAE	PL GROW SUB	7271
	DIPTERA SYST	8495	MONOCOT	ARACEAE	PL MORPH	10582
	ECOL ANIMAL	7109	MONOCOT	BROMELIACEAE	PL RESP FERM	8987
	ECOL ANIMAL	7125	MONOCOT	CYPERACEAE	FD MALT BREW	10650
	ECOL ANIMAL	7144	MONOCOT	CYPERACEAE	ECOL GEN	7750
	ECOL PLANT	7147	MONOCOT	CYPERACEAE	FLOR DISTRIB	7150
	FORESTRY	7200	MONOCOT	CYPERACEAE	HOMOP SYST	6641
	FORESTRY	7772	MONOCOT	GRAMINEAE	PL GROWTH	8509
	PALEOBIOLOGY	7778	MONOCOT	GRAMINEAE	AN PROD FEED	5570
	PL DIS FUNG	9782	MONOCOT	GRAMINEAE	AN PROD FEED	5929
	PL DIS OTHER	10408	MONOCOT	GRAMINEAE	AN PROD FEED	5936
	SOIL FERTIL	10447	MONOCOT	GRAMINEAE	AN PROD FEED	5938
	SOIL MICRO	11199	MONOCOT	GRAMINEAE	AN PROD FEED	5941
	SOIL MORPHOL	11184	MONOCOT	GRAMINEAE	AN PROD FEED	5942
	WILDLIFE TER	11223	MONOCOT	GRAMINEAE	AN PROD FEED	5943
ANGIOSPERMAE	BOT GEN SYST	7259	MONOCOT	GRAMINEAE	AN PROD FEED	5944
ANGIOSPERMAE	BOT GEN SYST	6451	MONOCOT	GRAMINEAE	AN PROD FEED	5945
ANGIOSPERMAE	CHLAMYDOSPERM	6452	MONOCOT	GRAMINEAE	AN PROD FEED	5946
ANGIOSPERMAE	CONIFEROPSIDA	NEOPLM THERA	9500	MONOCOT	GRAMINEAE	ASCHEL EXPT	8382
ANGIOSPERMAE	CONIFEROPSIDA	ARACHNI SYST	8409	MONOCOT	GRAMINEAE	BAC GEN SYST	5976
ANGIOSPERMAE	CONIFEROPSIDA	AVES SYST	6678	MONOCOT	GRAMINEAE	BAC GEN SYST	5977
	BEHAV ANIMAL	5985	MONOCOT	GRAMINEAE	BAC PHYSL	10318

Fig. 17. Illustration of the Biosystematic index (author's reproduction).

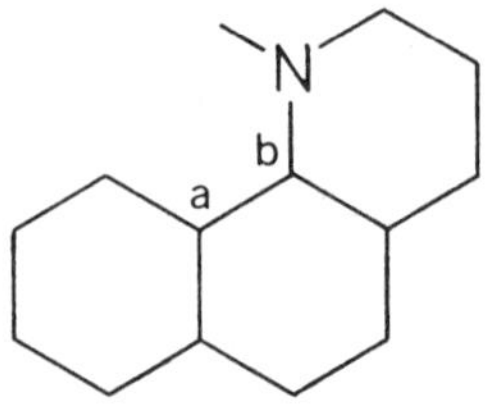

WLN	QUIKSCAN	ABSTR	CPD

TB666 CN

...MV&T&J	MNTV	175602-	1
...NV BUTT&J D	NTUV	"	25
...NV BUTT&J DIR	NRTUV	"	27
...NV&T&J D	NTV	"	2
...NV&T&J DIR	NRTV	"	5
...NV&T&J DIVR	NRTV	"	7
...NV&T&J D2	NTV	"	3
...NV&T&J D2- AT5NTJ	NTV	"	11
...NV&T&J D2- AT6N DNTJ D	NTV	"	15
...NV&T&J D2- AT6N DOTJ	NOTV	"	9
...NV&T&J D2- AT6NTJ	NTV	"	13
...NV&T&J D2G	GNTV	"	4
...NV&T&J D2N1&1	NTV	"	14
...NV&T&J D2R	NRTV	"	6
...NV&T&J D2UU1	NTUV	"	8
...NV&T&J D2Y	NTVY	"	12
...NV&T&J D3N1&1	NTV	"	10

TB666_

...COVJ FQ	OQTV	175494-	33
...COVJ FQ E1- AT6NTJ	NOQTV	"	28
...COVJ FQ E1M- BT5N CSJ ER	MNOQRSTV	"	16
...COVJ FQ E1M- BT5N CSJ ER D	MNOQRSTV	"	17

Fig. 18. Illustration of the Chemical Substructure index (author's reproduction).

where R is a relational network and A an address.[5] The relational network is a chemical structural formula represented as a canonical-form string (Fig. 19), the production of which has been fully described elsewhere [18, 44]. This relational index, which serves for the location of those structures which possess some element(s) in a specified relational framework, is clearly unsuited to direct manual use. Hoffman has described its use within the CS[4] [33].

---

[5] In the literature this component of the entry has been called a "registry number" [51] or an "identification number" [52]. We recognize that the problems inherent in attempts to automate addressing are nontrivial, but we cannot treat them here. See Ref. 52 for more detail.

Automatic Indexing

CANONICAL FORM

Atom	Code	Bond 1 Type	Bond 1 No.	Bond 2 Type	Bond 2 No.	Bond 3 Type	Bond 3 No.
1	C	2	14	1	6	1	9
2	C	2	15	1	7	1	10
3	C	1	4	1	9	1	10
4	C	2	5	1	3		
5	C	2	4	1	8		
6	C	1	1	1	11		
7	C	1	2	1	12		
8	C	1	5	1	13		
9	O	1	1	1	3		
10	O	1	2	1	3		
11	C	1	6				
12	C	1	7				
13	C	1	8				
14	O	2	1				
15	O	2	2				

COMPACT LIST

Atom	Code	Attached Atom	Bond Type*
1	C	2	–
2	C	5	1
3	O	6	1
4	O	–	2
5	C	–	1
6	C	7	1
7	C	9	1
8	O	10	1
9	C	11	2
10	C	12	1
11	C	14	1
12	C	15	1
13	O	–	2
14	C	–	1
15	C	–	1

* Of the bond joining the atom with this row number to the lowest numbered atom attached thereto.

Fig. 19. Illustration of the CS[4] index (author's reproduction).

Input to the CS[4]'s relational index is effected manually. All other processes are automatic.

The second relational index that we shall describe is one concerned with chemical reactions. The index, which we shall call the Chemical Reactions Index (CRI), was developed as part of a general information storage and retrieval system by Fugmann and his colleagues at Farbwerke Hoechst [31].[6] In this index a sequence of chemical reactions, such as that depicted in Fig. 20, is transformed into an index entry by representing those parts of the chemical species involved in the reaction that undergo change, together with the chronology of change [53]. Structural features are represented in the GREMAS notation. Finally, an index entry is completed by affixing an address to the reaction representation.

The form of the CRI entry is

$$\boxed{R \mid A}$$

where R is a set of relational strings $R_1 \ldots R_n$ and A is an address. A relational string, R_i, has the form

---

[6] This index does not exist entirely as an isolate. Rather, it, with other indexes, forms the central data base of the IDC [54].

| M | SC | PC | N |

where M is a sequence marker (e.g., @DR marks the start of an R), SC is the code for the starting reactive center, PC is the code for this center in the product, and N is the number of the affected center in the entire structure (N may also indicate a class of reactions). If SC or PC would otherwise be empty, the code ZZZ is used. When a set of relational strings, R, would contain essentially redundant elements, these may be eliminated (see Fig. 20), otherwise, as many strings R_i as are necessary to describe all changes that have occurred in the reaction are included in R.

This relational index is generally intended for computer-based searching, although its manual use is feasible (especially if transformed into a KWOC/REL or KWIC/REL index).

Input, identification, and representation are manual, although studies leading to the automation of these steps are underway [54]. The remaining processes are automated.

Although each CRI entry pertains to a one-step reaction, multistep reactions can be traced by observing whether two or more CRI entries form a linked list, all elements of which have the same address. For the example of Fig. 20, this idea can be depicted as follows:

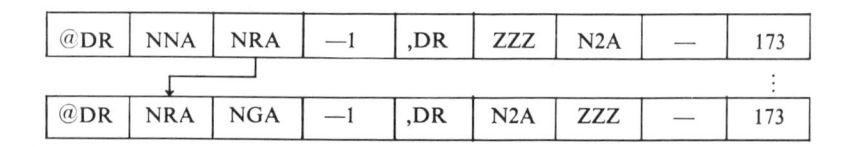

| @DR | NNA | NRA | —1 | ,DR | ZZZ | N2A | — | 173 |

| @DR | NRA | NGA | —1 | ,DR | N2A | ZZZ | — | 173 |

```
@DR  NNA  NRA  --1           @DR  NRA  NGA  --1
,DR  ZZZ  N2A  ---           ,DR  N2A  ZZZ  ---
/DR  NNA  NRA  --2           /DR  NRA  NGA  --2
,DR  ZZZ  N2A  ---           ,DR  N2A  ZZZ  ---
```

This representation may be simplified to:

```
@DR  NNA  NRA  --1           @DR  NRA  NGA  --1
,DR  ZZZ  N2A  ---           ,DR  N2A  ZZZ  ---
```

Fig. 20. Illustration of the GREMAS "Chemical Reactions Index" (author's reproduction).

Experimental Indexes

In this section we shall briefly consider some examples of indexes and indexing methods that we characterize as "experimental." It should be obvious that a considerable research effort has also preceded the development of each of the indexes described in the sections entitled General Indexes and Specialized Indexes; however, we are unable, within the scope of this article, to describe all of these important research efforts. We have chosen the following examples of indexing research because they either provide a basis for some present-day computer-based indexes or else they serve as an introduction to some of the representational research described in the section entitled Toward Automatic Indexing.

Indexing Based on the SYNTOL Model. The SYNTOL model of language [35] was designed to provide a nonambiguous representation for all natural language propositions. In addition, the representations were designed to be amenable to subsequent computer manipulation. Following DeSaussure, language was viewed as the composition of two reference axes: the syntagmatic and the paradigmatic. Syntagmatic relations described the linear order of the discourse (descriptors and the relations that tie them together) and paradigmatic relations consisted of an *a priori* designation of the underlying thought represented by the discourse (i.e., semantic classes).

The computer-based implementation of the SYNTOL model (see Bely *et al.* [36]), which produces a KWOC/RELATIONAL index, utilizes a lexicon and a dictionary that, together, comprise some 25,000 entries (the paradigms) and a set of routines that perform a syntactic analysis on the input text. Three types of relations are identified: type 1, *coordination* (formal relations, e.g., equality); type 2, *associative* (association of subject to action); and type 3, *consecutive* (presence of one element that affects another). Figure 21 illustrates an input text, an intermediary analysis, and the final document representation. The output from the intermediary analysis lists the text words, their grammatical classes, their morphological codes, and the extracted keywords and relations. The final representation lists the syntagms that have been identified, the unrelated uniterms, and those syntagms that have been rejected by the processing. The format of the entry is

$$A \mid K_1 \mid R \mid K_2$$

where A is the document number, K_1 and K_2 are keywords (K_2 may be absent), and R is one of the previously defined relations.

Keyword Structures. Doyle [37] has demonstrated that a text can be reduced to a "semantic roadmap," a two-dimensional network of terms and relations which it is argued would, ultimately, make information retrieval more effective. Doyle opines:

> The association map is a gigantic, automatically derived thesaurus. Confronted by such a map, the searcher has a much better "Association network" than the one existing in his mind, because it corresponds to words actually found in the library and, therefore, words which are best suited to retrieve information from that library [55].

```
                    RESUME 58-12-01417
(
RECHERCH           NX  FP                      EXPERIMENTAL
EXPERIMENTA        AF  FP
SUR                PU  O
LA                 RC  FS   DL  FS
PREVENTION         NX  FS                              N32
DES                PO  P
CRISE              NX  FF                      CRISE
PAR                PR  O
LA                 RC  FS   DL  FS
PROCAINE           NX  FS                      PROCAINE
INTRAVEINEU        AF  FS                      INTRAVEINEUX
)

            58-12-01417

            LISTE DES SYNTAGMES

                PROCAINE        /3/   CRISE
                PROCAINE        /3/   EPILEP
                PROCAINE        /2/   PROTECTION
                PROTECTION      /2/   EPILEP
                DIRECT          /2/   CORTEX
                ELECTROCHOC     /2/   CORTEX
                ELECTROCHOC     /2/   STIMULATION
                STIMULATION     /2/   ETRE
                XYLOCAINE       /3/

            LISTE DES ISOLATS

                EXPERIMENTAL
                INTRAVEINEUX
                SUJET

            SYNTAGMES REJETES PAR R.N.

                PROCAINE              INTRAVEINEUX
                ELECTROCHOC           ETRE
                SUJET                 PROCAINE
```

Fig. 21. Illustration of SYNTOL input text, intermediary analysis, and final document representation (author's reproduction).

As depicted in Fig. 22, the "relations" among terms are actually statistical weights which represent *associations* between terms. The associations are represented as normalized frequencies of cooccurrence of pairs of words and are generated utilizing the Pearson correlation coefficient. Operationally, the association map could be implemented as a relational index to the various associations between words in a document. Implicit in Doyle's approach is the assumption that frequency of cooccurrence is a valid relation for an indication of the content of a document.[7]

---

[7] For completeness, we wish to point out that there is a considerable body of literature dedicated to statistical and probabilistic methods of index term selection. The early Luhn study [58] that postulated a relationship between word frequency and its "importance" in a document has fostered studies on various forms of statistical association, clump theory, factor analysis, and probabilistic indexing (to mention but a few). The interested reader should consult Stevens [2] for a review of these approaches. Probably the most sensible application of these techniques can be found in Salton's SMART stystem [59].

Automatic Indexing

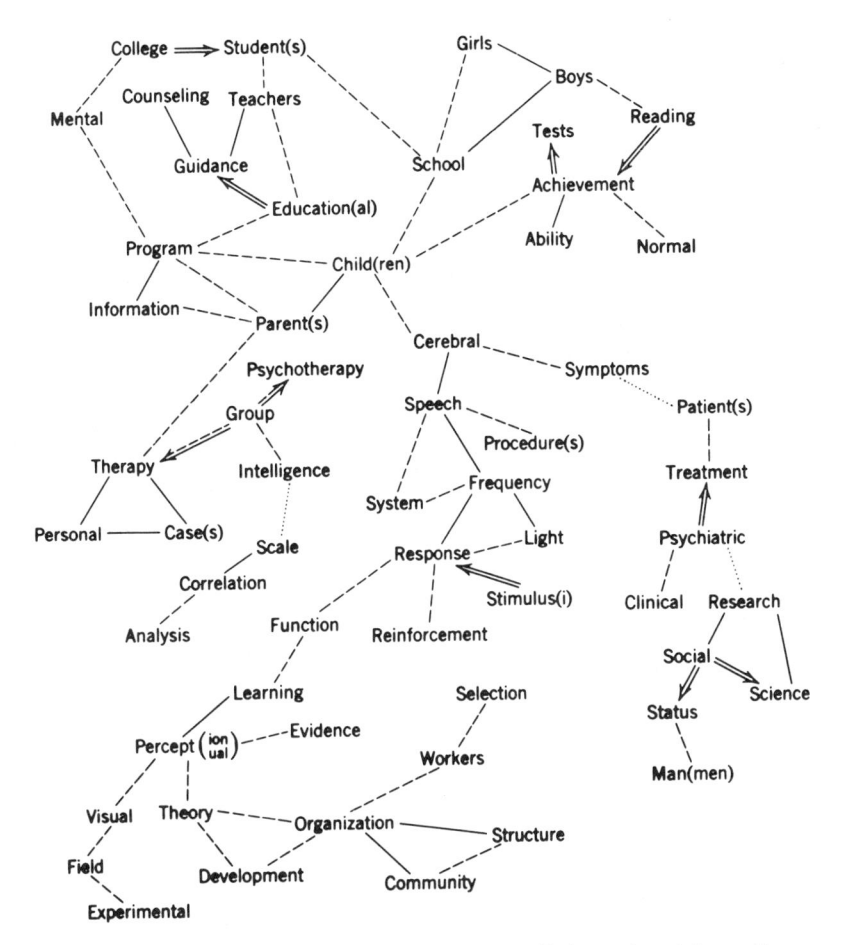

Fig. 22. Illustration of a "semantic roadmap" (reproduced from H. Borko, *Automated Language Processing*, Wiley, New York, 1968, by permission of the publisher).

Thompson [38], at the Stanford Biotechnology Laboratory, has recently developed an on-line retrieval system that utilizes an index term display that is conceptually related to the "roadmap" developed by Doyle. Thompson describes his system as a "classification index" that displays the system's hierarchical classification structure to the searcher. Thus, utilizing an interactive CRT, the user is able to "merely point at alternatives which seem most appropriate to him" while remaining within the constraints of the indexing system. Figure 23 depicts a CRT display where the searcher has narrowed his search term to "hepatitis" and "bacteriophage" and "vascular diseases." The result of this search is a list of matching documents.

Other "on-line indexing" systems include the *Negotiated Search Facility* developed by Bennett [56] and the *Browser* system developed by Williams [57].

Computer-Based Book Indexing Techniques. What is possibly the oldest form of index, the back-of-the-book index, still is derived essentially through manual processes.

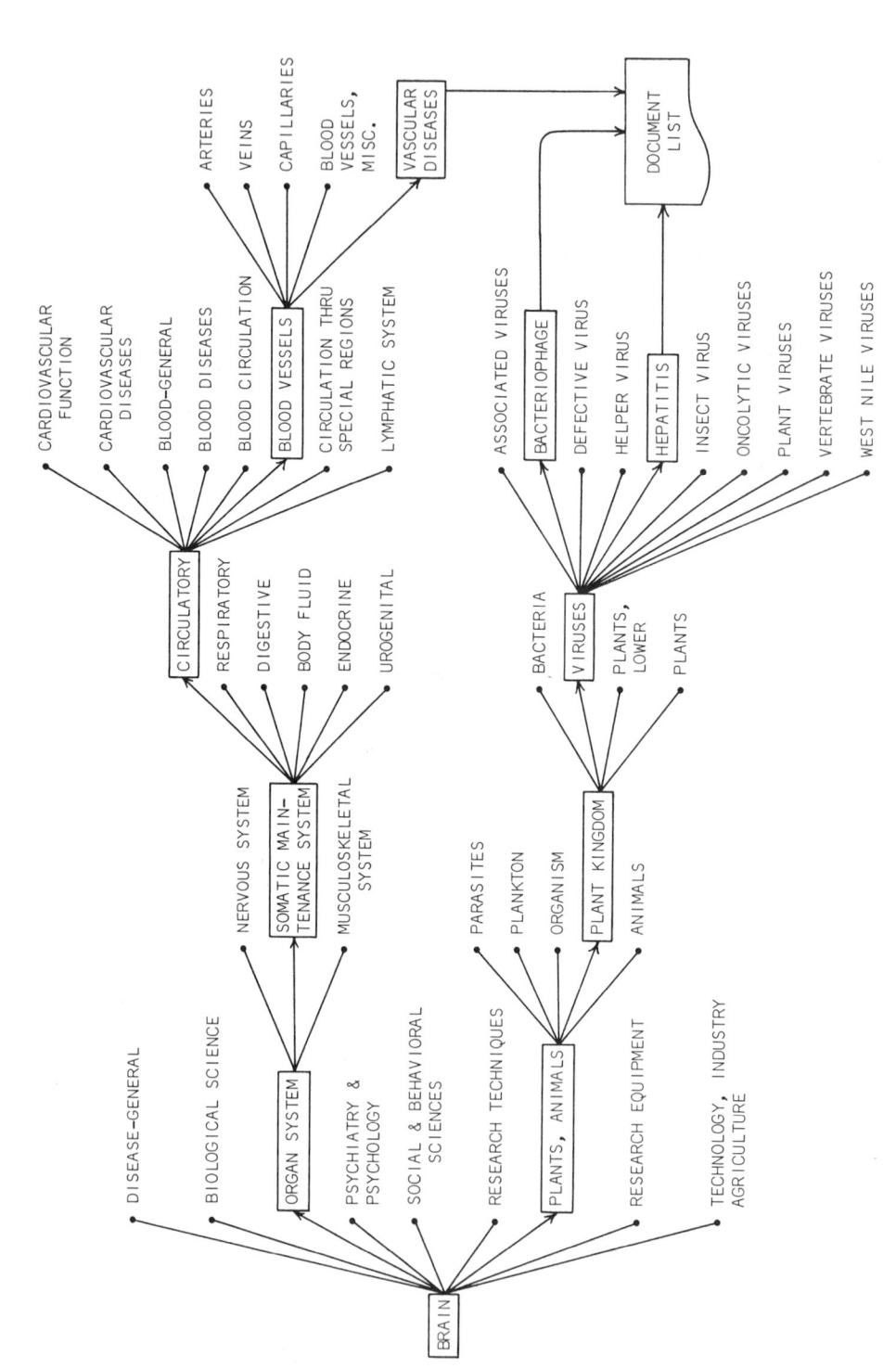

Fig. 23. Illustration of Thompson's classification index. Reprinted with permission from the *Journal of the American Society for Information Science*.

Automatic Indexing

As we have shown, certain specific forms of documents (with some restriction as to content or to length) lend themselves to application of computer-based indexing; however, the automation of the steps of representation and index creation for books remains essentially unsolved. We are forced to admit that, despite the apparent sophistication of computer-based indexing techniques, the field remains in its infancy.

A notable advance toward automatic book indexing has been reported by Borko [39] who has developed the SAINT (Semi-Automatic Index for Natural Language) system for the computer-assisted indexing of books. This system uses the power of the computer to process rapidly the input text, to count, sort, eliminate duplication, and finally *suggest* lists of two-word terms which are then manually edited by an experienced indexer. The operations performed by this computer-based indexing systems include:

Reading of text (including page and paragraph numbers)
Elimination of function words
Counting occurrences of words
Sorting words alphabetically and by frequency
Printing of word lists (manual editing)
Combining of synonyms and words having the same root form
Listing of word pairs (manual editing)
Compilation of cross references
Printing of the index (manual editing)

Figure 24 depicts a typical final output from the SAINT system. The general form of the entries is as follows:

$$K_1 \quad page_{i_1}, para_{j_1} \quad \ldots \quad page_{i_n}, para_{j_n}$$

or

$$K_1 \quad \begin{array}{l} See \\ See\ also \end{array} \quad K_2$$

where K_1 and K_2 are words and the synonym and related term references (*See* and *See also*) for a given K_1 point to the document partitions ($page_i$, $paragraph_j$) occupied by K_2.

```
AUTOMATA
                    14  5      14  6      15  3      31  1      34  5      37  3      61  1
                    61  2      62  2      62  3      67  1     241  2     287  1     330  5
                   366  1     367  1
AUTOMATED ANALYSIS                        SEE ALSO AUTOMATIC ANALYSIS
AUTOMATED ANALYSIS
                     1  2       6  4       7  4      99  3     120  2     120  4     204  1
                   211  1     248  1     250  1     288  1     316  4
AUTOMATED BILINGUAL DICTIONARY
                   294  3     294  4     294  5     316  4
AUTOMATED CLASSIFICATION                  SEE ALSO CLASSIFICATION AUTOMATIC
AUTOMATED CLASSIFICATION                  SEE ALSO DOCUMENT CLASSIFICATION
AUTOMATED CLASSIFICATION                  SEE      CLASSIFICATION AUTOMATED
AUTOMATED CONTEXT ANALYSIS
                     6  4     120  2     211  1     288  1
```

Fig. 24. Illustration of the SAINT system index (author's reproduction).

Summary

In the foregoing discussion we have attempted to provide an overview of the principal types of indexes currently in use. The illustrative examples, although varied, represent no more than a small sampling of those available in every subject area. We have certainly slighted the fields of music, art, literature, law, medicine, and many others. But we believe we have dealt fairly with the general concepts and expect that the reader may be able to extend his knowledge of indexes and indexing beyond that gained from the discussion. A few bibliographical clues are provided following the list of references at the end of this article.

TOWARD AUTOMATIC INDEXING

Every word that a native speaker of a language uses in his natural language has a definite and useful function. Contrary to some erroneous popular notions, natural languages are highly economical and efficient systems. In most cases no word in a properly formulated sentence is redundant or dispensable. Thus . . . artificial English like systems which permit the deletion of words in sentences often lose information or create misinterpretations.
Moyne [60]

By definition, the function of a metalanguage in semantic analysis is to singularize or to differentiate—the two notions are interchangeable—the documents of a corpus by the interplay of complex correspondances between natural language formulations and equivalent expressions in a metalanguage.
Gardin [61]

. . . an index node points to each relational statement. Other pointers (arguments of particular predicates) point to the index nodes of the relational statements they represent.
Montgomery [62]

General Directions

We have repeatedly stressed that the accuracy and the utility of an index are directly related to the completeness and the accuracy of the indexing system's representation of the document space. It is through this representation that a user can be alerted to, and can be placed in contact with, a source's message. Although many of the example indexes presented in the section entitled Examples of Computer-Based Indexing show considerable sophistication and a reasonable level of automation, it can be argued that they fail to provide both a complete and a *flexible* representation of the original document. We have further argued that the direction of current research in computer-based text processing (and indexing) is toward a "structural" representation of the source document. However, a distinction should be made between structures which are *physically derived* from a linear string of words and those structures which are *intellectually imposed* on a linear string. Both interpretations of structure are pertinent to the development of enhanced document representations.

Automatic Indexing

Consider the following example from Lewis Carroll's *Through the Looking Glass*:

> '*Twas* brillig, *and the* slithy toves
> *Did* gyre *and* gimble *in the* wabe:
> *All* mimsy *were the* borogoves,
> *And the* mome raths outgrabe.

Thanks to an abundance of function words, this "nonsense" passage exhibits considerable structural information—i.e., we can derive syntactical, positional, and relational information concerning the unidentified words in this passage without recourse to knowledge of words like "brillig." Thus, with a theory of the logical structure of function words (see Fries [63]), we can physically derive structural information about utterances of our language. However, a single structural analysis may admit a multitude of interpretations. If we say "ship sails today" do we mean "the ship sails today"? or "ship the sails today"? or even "shipped sails today"? Our thesis can be clearly stated: each symbol has a set of referents in someone's world; the logical structure of an utterance provides the means and the locants for the selection of a specific (person-specific) set of referents.

Research in document representation should not be interpreted as being purely syntactical in nature; rather, the identification of syntactical features is a prerequisite for the identification of higher order relations between data elements. As depicted in Fig. 25, research in document representation must be complemented by further basic research concerning how humans communicate (see Montgomery [62], Pepinsky [64]) in order to model satisfactorily how an index user presents his own "unique reality." We believe the goal of automatic document representation is to provide a scheme that permits the facile integration and interpretation of a user's *experience space*. In this way, the indexing system, rather than being rigid, provides a flexible interface that is adaptive to a user's intellectual structure (i.e., the relations that the user perceives among the classes of data contained in the document store).

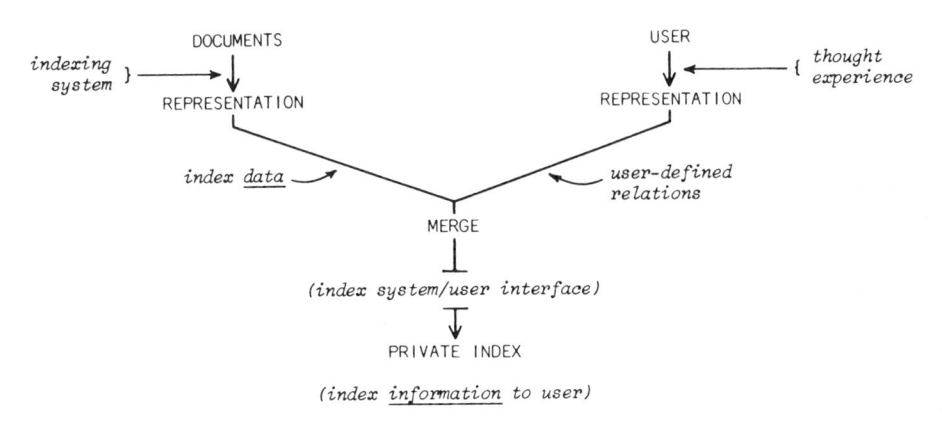

Fig. 25. Dynamic system representation amenable to user intellectual imposition of "meaning."

In the remainder of this section, several research efforts are described and certain experimental indexes are presented which should suggest to the reader the directions that the study of automatic indexing is tending.

Examples of Research Efforts in Document Representation

TOSAR

Fugmann [65] has recently described the TOSAR—topological method for the representation of synthetic and analytical relations of concepts—system for the manual generation of graphical displays of concepts and relations. This system was developed to characterize chemical reactions, but the approach also appears to be valid for the representation of data contained in natural language utterances. For example, a string like "the processing of oxidized polypropylene" is represented by the graph

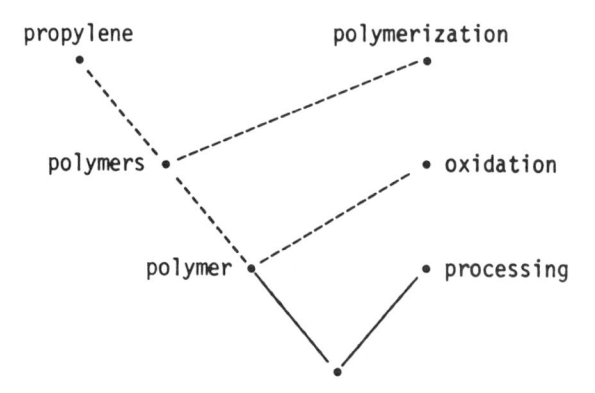

(where dashed lines indicate inferences drawn from the text). In this scheme, labeled nodes represent substances or processes. Each level of the graph (unlabeled nodes) represents a particular stage of a complex chemical process (e.g., combination, separation, and action of a catalyst). While this representation process is manually implemented at present, a detailed discussion of an algorithm for the computer manipulation of these structures may be found in Nickelsen and Nickelsen [66].

It should be obvious that once such graphs are prepared, they can be used for "substructure" searches or for "full-structure" searches, i.e., for "polypropylene processing" or "the processing of oxidized polypropylene." Figures 26a and 26b depict a more elaborate TOSAR graph. For additional details on the philosophy and implementation of this novel approach, the reader is directed to Refs. 65-67.

GRAIT

Drawing on the Dependency Grammar introduced by Hays [68], the Conceptual Dependency Parser of Shank and Tesler [69], and the Quillian [70] concept/relation

Automatic Indexing

In the oligomerization of olefins, such as propylene, to obtain unsaturated oligomers, *e.g.* hexenes and nonenes, the activity of the catalyst steadily decreases as a result of the catalyst being loaded with the oligomers formed. A reusable catalyst is regenerated from the oligomerization mixture as follows.

Propylene and the oligomerization products are distilled off from the catalyst in a fractionation column A under pressure. In a second column B in series with the first, propylene is separated from the oligomer mixture, which consists mainly of hexene and nonene, by fractional distillation. The propylene is partly returned to the oligomerization reactor, while the remainder is introduced into the lower part of the column A to free the catalyst collecting there from the last traces of oligomer. This operation is carried out at a temperature below the decomposition range of the catalyst and below the boiling point of the contaminating oligomers.

The purified trialkylaluminum catalyst is continuously removed from the base of the column A and returned to the oligomerization reactor. The hexene fraction formed can be used for the production of isoprene by cracking.

Fig. 26a. Patent abstract.

network model of human memory, Rush *et al.* [71–75] have developed a series of research algorithms generically labeled GRAIT (Graphic Representations for Automatic Indexing of Text), designed to transform English text into a metalanguage suitable for a variety of automatic indexing processes. Among these algorithms are procedures for automatic syntax analysis, clause identification, and role analysis by means of case grammar.[8]

Basic to the GRAIT processing is the definition of *sentence* as an ordered triple, $N_i R N_j$ where N_i, N_j are names and R is a relation. Briefly, a *name* is a language string assigned to an object or construct and a *relation* is (1) a language string assigned to a behavior imputed to an object or construct, or (2) a language string which has only a linguistic function. Thus names are associated with nouns and noun phrases, and relations are associated with predicates and selected function words (see Young [73]).

In one experimental implementation of this categorization, a graph is formed for each input sentence in the following way. Construct a chain of names and primary relations. The names will consist of simple names or of the right-most word of a composite name. The relations in complex names are used to determine how the components of a complex name are to be joined to the main chain. Secondary relations are represented in the graph by directed edges (arcs) whose type and direction depend upon the specific secondary relation. Furthermore, pronouns and relative pronouns are replaced by their referents whenever these exist. The results of this procedure are illustrated in Fig. 27. An interesting variation of this basic procedure is depicted in

---

[8] For an extensive review of case grammar, see Refs. 76 and 77.

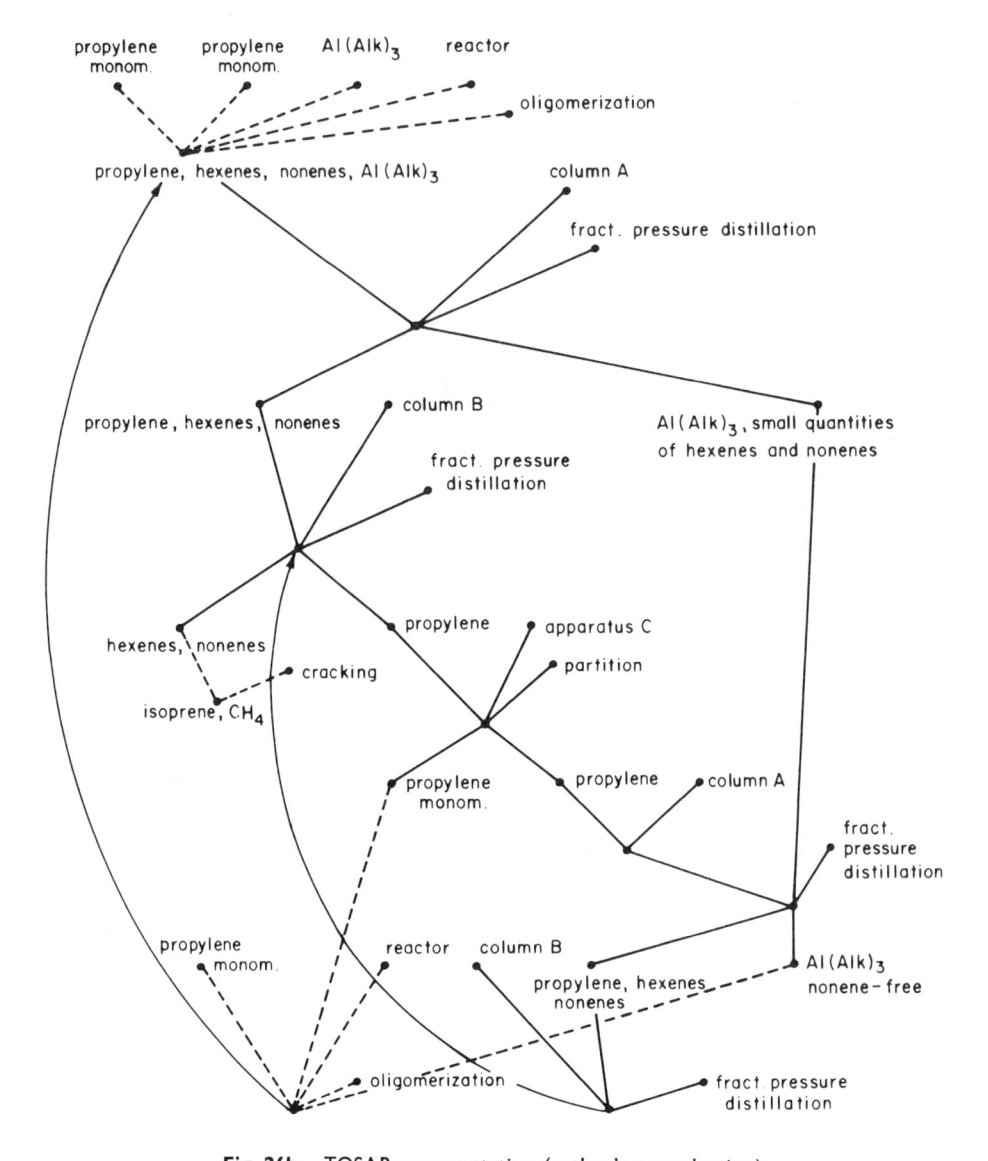

Fig. 26b. TOSAR representation (author's reproduction).

Fig. 28. This representation, developed by Young [73], shows the names in the basic name–relation–name triple.

It should be pointed out that these structures, exhibited as graphical structures, are the result of computer manipulation of input data; hence only a linearization of the structures is stored in the memory of the computer system.

Finally, we consider the representation scheme (an extension of GRAIT) in the early stages of development by Strong [74]. The network displayed in Fig. 29 is based on a syntactic analysis and is constructed as follows. The verb (the primary element of each clause) is connected to its subjects and objects with diagonal edges. Vertical

Automatic Indexing

SENTENCE: The routine microscopic blood inspection that is a universal feature of present medical practice is generally depended on as one of the mose useful indicators of the state of a person's health.

STRUCTURAL REPRESENTATION:

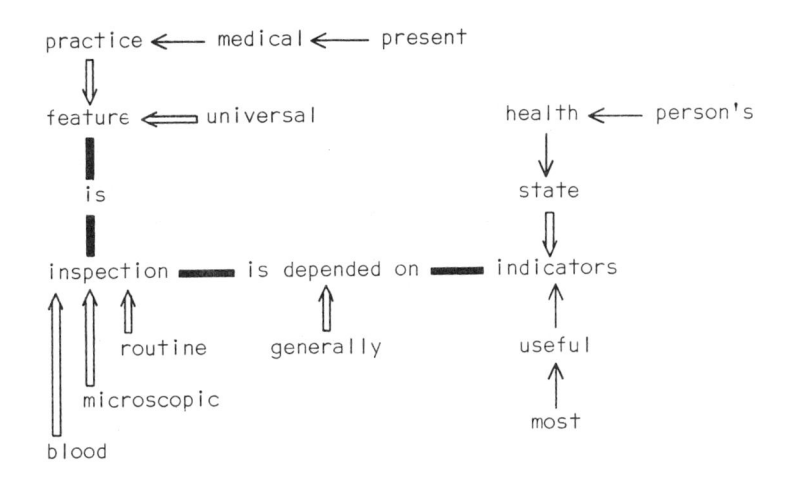

```
practice ⇐── medical ⇐── present
   ⇓
feature ⇐══ universal              health ⇐── person's
   ▮                                 ↓
   is                               state
   ▮                                 ⇓
inspection ▬▬ is depended on ▬▬ indicators
  ⇑ ⇑              ⇑               ↑
  ‖ ‖  routine   generally        useful
  ‖ ‖                              ↑
  ‖ microscopic                   most
  ‖
blood
```

Fig. 27. Graphical representation developed by Rush et al. [75].

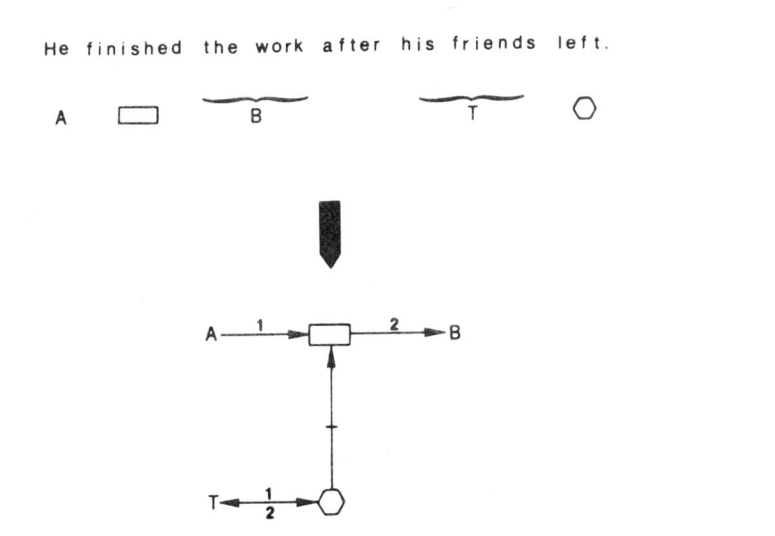

He finished the work after his friends left.

A ▯   B ︵   T ︵   ⬡

A ──1──▶ ▭ ──2──▶ B

T ◀──½── ⬡

Fig. 28. A case grammar structural analysis and representation (after Young [73]).

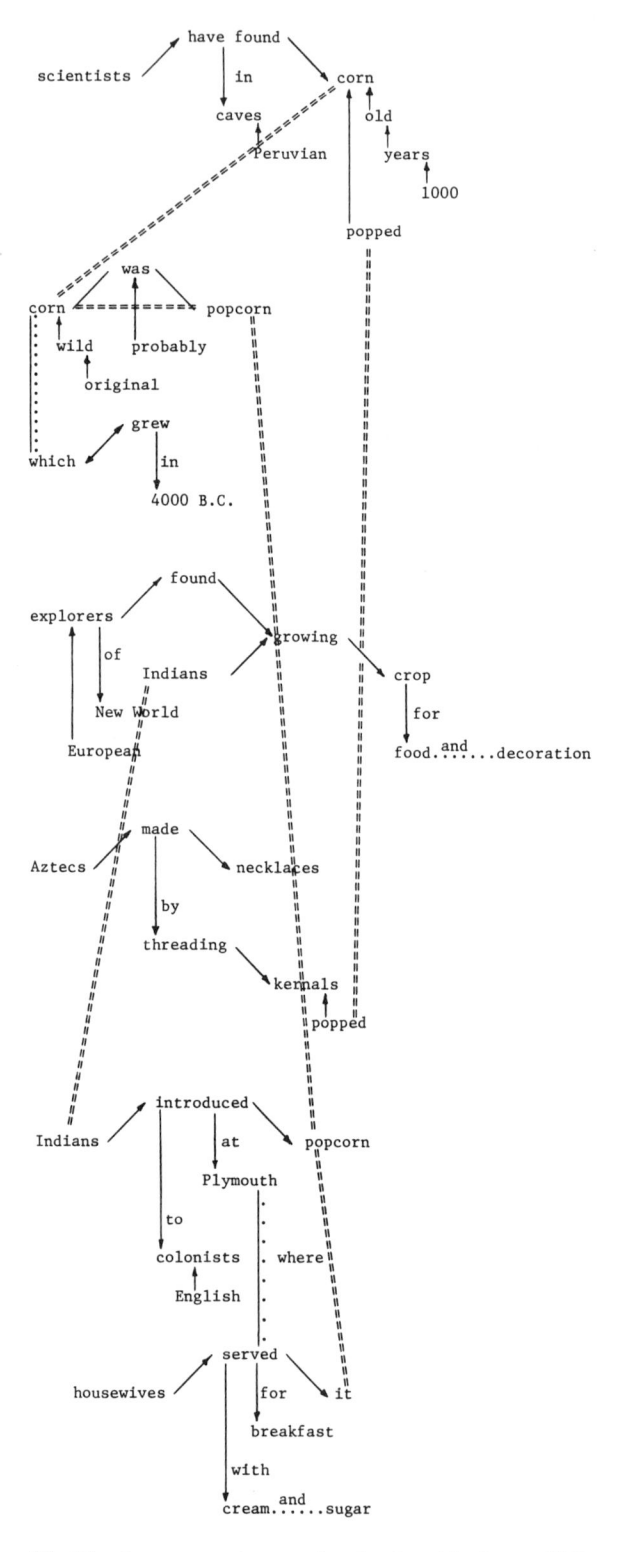

Fig. 29. Sentence representation developed by Strong [74].

edges denote modification and dotted edges denote conjunction. Dashed edges depict implied and intersentence relationships. Major case grammar roles are identified by the type of verb-noun edge, and minor case roles may be used to label the modifier edges. It is believed that the resultant network constitutes an improved representation of text for natural language processing.

CONCLUSION

The purpose of an index is to provide the user direct access to items of data in a collection which would otherwise be accessible only by sequential means. The problem of indexing is that of providing, *a priori*, direct access to data items that meet the unknown demands of unidentified users. The degree to which an index satisfies the demands of a user (or a collection of users) is in direct relation to its fidelity as a representation of the original data collection in which the user is interested. Thus, as we have said, accurate retrieval depends on the exactness of the operation of the indexing system. Any process which renders an item of data inaccessible is an undesirable element of an indexing system.

The question is: Can an index be devised that will make all items of data in a collection directly accessible to all users all the time? The answer to this question is not known. But we can identify certain characteristics which such an index should exhibit:

1. The index, as the retrieval interface, must be dynamic rather than static.
2. The index must represent both *data elements* and the *relations* (explicit and implicit) among them.
3. The index must represent the original collection of data with high fidelity.

If such an index is to be realized, as we believe it can, then research effort needs to be directed toward those steps in the indexing process that we have called *identification* and *representation*. The work of Fugmann and his colleagues in Germany and of Rush and his associates in the United States appears to be converging to a solution of the representation problem, but no important results have yet been obtained toward the solution of the identification problem. Yet the development of data description languages [78], the work of Strong [74], and various developments in computational linguistics [62], pattern recognition [79], and artificial intelligence [80] suggest that the identification problem is solvable.

Computer-based indexing is in its infancy. A great deal of interesting and challenging work remains to be done to bring computer-based indexing to maturity.

REFERENCES

1. M. Taube, *Studies in Coordinate Indexing*, Documentation Incorporated, Bethesda, Md., 1956.
2. M. E. Stevens, *Automatic Indexing: A State-of-the-Art Report*, National Bureau of Standards Monograph No. 91, March 30, 1965, p. 3.
3. J. C. Gardin, Semantic analysis procedures in the sciences of man, *Soc. Sci. Inf.* **8**(1), 24 (1969).
4. R. L. Collison, *Indexes and Indexing*, deGraff, New York, 1959, p. 20.
5. H. P. Edmundson, and R. E. Wyllys, Automatic abstracting and indexing—Survey and recommendations, *Commun. ACM* **4**(5), 226–234 (1961).

6. S. Artandi, A selective bibliography survey of automatic indexing methods, *Spec. Lib.* **54**(10), (1963).
7. M. E. Stevens, *Progress and Prospects in Mechanized Indexing*, working paper presented for the Symposium on Mechanized Abstracting and Indexing, Moscow, September 28–October 10, 1966.
8. System Development Corporation, *A System Study of Abstracting and Indexing in the U.S.*, 1966, PB-174-249.
9. C. A. Cuadra (ed.), *Annual Review of Information Science and Technology*, Wiley, New York (Vols. 1–2); Encyclopaedia Britannica, Chicago (Vols. 3–7), 1966–1972; American Society for Information Sciences (Vols. 8–10), 1973–1975.
10. L. B. Heilprin, *Mathematical Model of Indexing*, Documentation Inc., Bethesda, Md., 1957, AD-136-477.
11. B. C. Landry and J. E. Rush, Toward a theory of indexing, *Proc. Amer. Soc. Inf. Sci.* **5**, 59–64 (1968).
12. B. C. Landry and J. E. Rush, Toward a theory of indexing—II, *J. Amer. Soc. Inf. Sci.* **21**(5), 358–367 (1970).
13. B. C. Landry, *A Theory of Indexing: Indexing Theory as a Model for Information Storage and Retrieval*, Computer and Information Science Research Center Technical Report No. TR-71-13, The Ohio State University, 1971.
14. S. Artandi, Document description and representation, in *Annual Review of Information Science and Technology*, Vol. 5 (C. A. Cuadra, ed.), Encyclopaedia Britannica, Chicago, 1970, p. 161.
15. J. M. Carroll and R. Roeloffs, Computer selection of keywords using word-frequency analysis, *Amer. Doc.* **20**(3), 227 (1969).
16. B. C. Landry, B. A. Mathis, N. M. Meara, J. E. Rush, and C. E. Young, Definition of some basic terms in computer and information science, *J. Amer. Soc. Inf. Sci.* **24**(5), 328–342 (1973).
17. H. Wellisch, A flow chart for indexing with a thesaurus, *J. Amer. Soc. Inf. Sci.* **23**(3), 185–194 (1972).
18. H. L. Morgan, The generation of a unique machine description for chemical structures—A technique developed at Chemical Abstracts Service, *J. Chem. Doc.* **5**, 107–113 (1965).
19. C. H. Davis and J. E. Rush, *Information Retrieval and Documentation in Chemistry*, Greenwood, Westport, Conn., 1974, Chaps. 8 and 9.
20. J. Marschak, Economics of information systems, *J. Amer. Stat. Assoc.* **66**(333), 195 (1971).
21. *The Subject Index to Biological Abstracts*, BioSciences Information Service of Biological Abstracts, Philadelphia.
22. *The Biosystematic Index to Biological Abstracts*, BioSciences Information Service of Biological Abstracts, Philadelphia.
23. *CIN Index*, Chemical Abstracts Service, American Chemical Society, Columbus, Ohio.
24. S. Artandi, Computer indexing of medical articles—Project MEDICO, *J. Doc.* **25**(3), 214–223 (1969).
25. A. E. Petrarca and W. M. Lay, The double-KWIC coordinate index, *J. Chem. Doc.*, **9**(4), 256–261 (1969).
26. J. Armitage and M. Lynch, Computer generation of articulated subject indexes, *Proc. Amer. Soc. Inf. Sci.* **6**, 253–257 (1969).
27. E. Garfield, Science Citation Index—A new dimension in indexing, *Science* **144**, 649–654 (1964).
28. H. Skolnik, The multi-term index: A new concept in IS&R, *J. Chem. Doc.* **10**(2), 81–84 (1970).
29. *HAIC Index*, Chemical Abstracts Service, American Chemical Society, Columbus, Ohio.
30. C. E. Granito and M. D. Rosenberg, Chemical Substructure Index (CSI)—A new research tool, *J. Chem. Doc.* **11**(4), 251–256 (1971).
31. R. Fugmann, W. Braun, and W. Vaupel, GREMAS—ein Weg zur Klassifikation und Dokumentation in der organischen Chemie, *Nachr. Dok.* **14**(4), 177–190 (1963).
32. A. K. Kent, The Chemical Society Research Unit in information dissemination and retrieval, *Sven. Kem. Tidskr.* **80**(2), (1968).
33. W. S. Hoffmann, An integrated chemical structure storage and search system operating at DuPont, *J. Chem. Doc.* **8**(1), 3–13 (1968).
34. *Patent Concordance*, Chemical Abstracts Service, American Chemical Society, Columbus, Ohio.
35. R. C. Cross, J. C. Gardin, and F. Levy, *L'automatisation des Recherches Documentaires, Un Model Generale: le SYNTOL*, Gauthier-Villars, Paris, 1964.

36. N. Bely, A. Borillo, N. Siot-Decauville, and J. Virbel, *Procédures d'analyse Semantique Appliquées et la documentation Scientifique*, Gauthier-Villars, Paris, 1970.
37. L. B. Doyle, Indexing and abstracting by association, *Amer. Doc.* **13**, 378–390 (1962).
38. D. A. Thompson, Interface design for an interactive information retrieval system: A literature survey and a research system description, *J. Amer. Soc. Inf. Sci.* **22**(6), 361–373 (1971).
39. H. Borko, Experiments in book indexing by computer, *Inf. Storage Retr.* **6**(1), 5–16 (1970).
40. J. R. Sharp, *Some Fundamentals of Information Retrieval*, London-House and Maxwell, New York, 1965, p. 94.
41. E. Garfield, Citation indexing for studying science, *Nature* **227**, 669–671 (1970).
42. B. A. Montague, Patent indexing by concept coordination using links and roles, *Amer. Doc.* **13**(1), 104–111 (1962).
43. S. Artandi, *Automatic Indexing of Drug Information, Project MEDICO—Final Report*, Graduate School of Library Science, Rutgers, The State University, New Brunswick, N.J., 1970, PB-190-807.
44. C. H. Davis and J. E. Rush, *Information Retrieval and Documentation in Chemistry*, Greenwood, Westport, Conn., 1974, Chap. 4.
45. J. Armitage and M. Lynch, *Articulation in the Generation of Subject Indexes by Computer*, presented at the 153rd National Meeting of the ACS Chemical Literature Division, Miami Beach, Florida, April 1967.
46. J. Armitage et al., Experimental use of a programme for computer aided subject index production, *Inf. Storage Retr.* **6**(1), 79–87 (1970).
47. W. M. Lay, The Double-KWIC Coordinate Indexing Technique: Theory, Design, and Implementation, Ph.D. Thesis, Department of Computer and Information Science, The Ohio State University, 1973.
48. A. E. Petrarca and W. M. Lay, The double-KWIC coordinate index II: Use of an automatically generated authority list to eliminate scattering caused by some singular and plural main index terms, *Proc. Amer. Soc. Inf. Sci.* **6**, 227–282 (1969).
49. D. C. Colombo and J. E. Rush, Use of word fragments in computer based retrieval systems, *J. Chem. Doc.* **9**(1), 47–50 (1969).
50. E. G. Smith, *The Wiswesser Line-Formula Chemical Notation*, McGraw-Hill, New York, 1968.
51. F. A. Tate, Handling chemical compounds in information systems, in *Annual Review of Information Science and Technology*, Vol. 2 (C. A. Cuadra, ed.), Wiley, New York, 1967, pp. 285–309.
52. M. J. Ebersole, A General Method for Automatic Generation of Data Record Descriptors, M.S. Thesis, The Ohio State University, 1971.
53. R. Fugmann and W. Bitterlich, Reaktionen Dokumentation mit dem GREMAS System, *Chem. Ztg.* **96**(6), 323–329 (1972).
54. E. Meyer, The IDC System for chemical documentation, *J. Chem. Doc.* **9**(2), 109–113 (1969).
55. Ref. 37, p. 383.
56. J. L. Bennett, On-line access to information: NSF as an aid to the indexer/cataloger, *Amer. Doc.* **20**(3), 213–220 (1969).
57. J. H. Williams, Browser: An automatic indexing on-line text retrieval system, AD-693-143, 1969.
58. H. P. Luhn, The automatic creation of literature abstracts, *IBM J. Res. Develop.* **2**(4), 159–165 (1958).
59. G. Salton, *Automatic Information Organization and Retrieval*, McGraw-Hill, New York, 1968.
60. J. A. Moyne, Information retrieval and natural language, *Proc. Amer. Soc. Inf. Sci.* **6**, 259–263 (1969).
61. Ref. 3, p. 34.
62. C. A. Montgomery, Linguistics and information science, *J. Amer. Soc. Inf. Sci.* **23**(3), 195–219 (1972).
63. C. Fries, *The Structure of English*, Harcourt, Brace & World, New York, 1952.
64. H. B. Pepinsky (ed.), *People and Information*, Pergamon, Elmsford, N.Y., 1970.
65. R. Fugmann et al., TOSAR—A topological method for the representation of synthetic and analytical relations of concepts, *Angew. Chem. Int. Ed. Engl.* **9**(8), 589–595 (1970).
66. I. Nickelsen and H. Nickelsen, Mathematische Analyse des TOSAR-Verfahrens, *Inf. Storage Retr.* **9**, 95–119 (1973).
67. R. Fugmann, The theoretical foundation of the IDC system: Six postulates for information retrieval, *ASLIB Proc.* (February 1972).

68. D. G. Hays, Dependency theory: A formalism and some observations, *Language* **40**(4), 511–525 (1964).
69. R. C. Shank and L. Tesler, *A Conceptual Dependency Parser for Natural Language*, Preprint #2 from the International Conference on Computational Linguistics, Sweden, 1969.
70. M. R. Quillian, Semantic memory, in *Semantic Information Processing* (M. Minsky, ed.), MIT Press, Cambridge, Mass., 1968.
71. J. E. Rush, *A New Approach to Indexing*, presented before the Student Chapter of the A.S.I.S., Case-Western Reserve University, Cleveland, Ohio, January 1969.
72. *The Ohio State University, Computer and Information Science Research Center*, Report to the National Science Foundation, August 1972, p. 2.1.
73. C. E. Young, Development of Language Analysis Procedures with Application to Automatic Indexing, Ph.D. Thesis, The Ohio State University, 1973.
74. S. M. Strong, An Algorithm for Generating Structural Surrogates of English Text, M.S. Thesis, The Ohio State University, 1973.
75. J. E. Rush, H. B. Pepinsky, B. C. Landry, N. M. Meara, S. M. Strong, J. A. Valley, and C. E. Young, *A Computer Assisted Language Analysis System*, The Ohio State University, Computer and Information Science Research Center, 1973.
76. W. A. Cook, S.J., *Introduction to Tagmemic Analysis*, Holt, Rinehart & Winston, New York, 1969.
77. C. J. Fillmore, The case for case, in *Universals in Linguistic Theory* (E. Bach and R. Harms, eds.), Holt, Rinehart & Winston, New York, 1968, pp. 1–88.
78. Anon., *June 1973 Report of the CODASYL Data Base Task Group*, available from the Association for Computing Machinery, New York, 1973.
79. M. S. Watanabe (ed.), *Frontiers of Pattern Recognition*, Academic, New York, 1972.
80. M. A. Arbib, *The Metaphorical Brain*, Wiley-Interscience, New York, 1972.

12

Automatic Analysis

Mary Elizabeth Stevens[*] / National Bureau of Standards, Gaithersburg, Maryland

Considering next, then, techniques for the automatic extraction of keywords from text as directly analogous to those of detection and extraction of features in character patterns, we may now ask what procedures of automatic analysis can be applied in the machine derivation of documentary or information alerting and search tools. The first and most obvious example is that of machine preparation of KWIC or permuted title indexes.

For any word (or name or symbol sequence) encoded and recorded in machine-usable form, automatic data-processing systems and general purpose machines can compare the input symbol or sequence of symbols with prestored possible equivalents and determine whether or not, and when, a match occurs. Next, the machine procedures can copy that sequence of encoded symbols for which a match does occur into its file of records or into what is, in effect, a worksheet area.

Typically for KWIC indexes this capability is used to eliminate from further consideration words that are presumed to be insignificant for indexing purposes by running all the words of a title against a prepared "stop" or "purge" list which thus serves as an exclusion dictionary for all words that match. Then the machine capabilities include that of shifting the positions of individual symbols or of groups of symbols either to the left or to the right in a given sequence of groups of symbols.

Furthermore, the machine can count. This may mean, for example, that the number of individual character symbols (including those for "blank" or "space") that are being assembled and have been transferred one by one into an area for eventual printout are tallied and when the count for the tally reaches the maximum allowed length for a desired printout line, a new "line" will be started.

From Stevens, Mary Elizabeth. *Automatic Analysis.* ENCYCLOPEDIA OF LIBRARY AND INFORMATION SCIENCE. Vol. 2. Edited by Allen Kent and Harold Lancour. Assistant Editor, William Z. Nasri. New York, Marcel Dekker, Inc., c1969. pp. 154–157; 164–166.
[*]Presently retired

Consider, for example, the title "The Encyclopedia of the Information and Library Sciences." First, the word "the" will be eliminated from further processing consideration by reference to the stop list or exclusion dictionary, although it will be retained for later printout of the permuted or rotated title. Thus by eliminating the "little" words, index entries will be generated for "Encyclopedia," "Information," "Library," and "Sciences." Each of these entry or access words will be sorted alphabetically with other words from other titles and the permuted titles will be printed out in this sorted order, typically as follows:

```
                            ENACTMENT OF LAWS. THE
    ATION AND LIBR          ENCYCLOPEDIA OF THE INFORM
    OF    STATISTICAL       ENGINEERING. THE HANDBOOK
    GINEERING.   THE        HANDBOOK OF STATISTICAL EN
    CYCLOPEDIA    OF        INFORMATION AND LIBRARY EN
                            LAWS.  THE   ENACTMENT  OF
    ENCYCLOPEDIA O          L I B R A R Y  SCIENCES. THE
    LOPEDIA OF INF          SCIENCES.  T H E   E N C Y C
    ERING. THE  HA          STATISTICAL     E N G I N E
```

When produced by computer with high-speed printer output of the sorted and assembled index listings, arbitrary line length and upper-case limitations such as exemplified above are quite common. In addition, other disadvantages can be and have been cited against KWIC or KWOC indexes, such as the scattering of actually synonymous entries throughout the index and the confounding of index entry words with significantly different meanings in the same long blocks of entries under the same keywords. Nevertheless, a major advantage of timeliness has been achieved by these techniques, and many users have been emphatically enthusiastic.

An improved typographic quality of output of such machine-produced permuted title keyword indexes, which can be achieved by the use of augmented chain printers to produce both upper and lower case, by the use of overprinting to highlight the index access keyword, and especially by the use of computer-controlled typesetting techniques with a full range of case, font, boldness, and size of characters, will undoubtedly increase the popularity of this type of index in the near future.

A similar timeliness of index production and use is promised by more advanced techniques of automatic analysis that have been at least experimentally demonstrated for other types of "derivative" indexing (i.e., relying on the author's own words alone), for modified derivative indexing (i.e., augmenting the author's own words either by manual or mechanized means), and for automatic assignment indexing (i.e., where the words in the author's text act as clues to appropriate subject headings, subject classification codes, or indexing terms which may or may not coincide with any of the words or phrases used by the author himself). That is, similar advantages may be promised, provided that present problems such as text input cost can be solved.

The original proposals of the late H. P. Luhn for autoencoding of documentary materials have of course been most dramatically realized in the form of the KWIC indexes for titles alone. Yet, in fact, they were as much directed toward the automatic generation of condensed representations serving the current-awareness-alerting function of conventional abstracts as to the extraction of indexing entries for subsequent retrospective search.

In this technique as originally proposed, the machine counts the number of times each different word appears in the text of an abstract or full document. When the counts have been completed, the words can be ranked in the order of frequency of occurrence. Then, those words which have occurred most frequently are disregarded. These are typically the "little" words (articles, conjunctions, prepositions, pronouns) and words that are likely to be common to many texts. Next, the words that occur very infrequently are also disregarded on the grounds that if they occur very seldom they are unlikely to be good indicators of the subject content of the text.

Those words that remain for consideration can now be used for either indexing or "autoabstracting" purposes. That is, a small number of sentences, in which words having a significant frequency of occurrence in the text as a whole appear together, can be extracted and printed out. Text words can be extracted as index entries either on the basis of their frequencies of occurrence as such or because of their occurrence in the sentences that have been extracted.

A number of variations on the basic word frequency approach have been proposed by Luhn and other investigators. These variations include considerations of relative word frequencies with respect to a given subject area or to a given collection, giving special attention to nouns and nominal phrases occurring in prepositional constructions, and considerations of word pairs and longer n-tuples of words. Various means may be employed to combine different forms of the same root word, such as singulars and plurals, and this modification is of considerable importance in applying the autoencoding technique to texts written in highly inflected languages.

This type of automatic analysis has certain obvious advantages, most notably in the use of the author's own words in the preparation of condensed representations of his text. On the other hand, time-consuming and costly processes of preparing the text in machine-readable form are involved, and also the sentences selected from text are usually presented separately and out of context with each other and sometimes with the main intent of the text itself. In addition, the indexing that results is strictly "derivative" (or word rather than concept indexing) with all the disadvantages of scattering of synonyms, failures to resolve problems of homographic ambiguity, and other problems stemming from a particular author's use of terminology and language.

Automatic Indexing and Classification

Word-word and word-term associations may also be applied in automatic indexing procedures based on "teaching samples" (or "training sequences") of items that are exemplars of presumably effective *manual* assignments of certain desired terms, descriptors, or subject headings to items in a given collection. We may, for example, choose 100 or more items that have presumably been adequately indexed for our own subsequent search and retrieval purposes. Suppose, next, that we provide machine-readable records of the titles, abstracts, and listings of the terms, descriptors, headings, or classification codes previously assigned to these items. We may then, by the primitive machine operations of counting, sorting, comparing, and extracting, as conditions of identity and nonidentity (or greater or less in "numeric" value) are recognized, proceed first to eliminate presumably nonsignificant words (for indexing purposes at least) and then to establish a master vocabulary of the remaining words together with statistical data as to their relative frequencies of co-occurrence with descriptors previously assigned to items in which these words appear.

Suppose, for example, that the following titles occurred for sample items to which one or more of the descriptors "Adaptive Systems," "Automatic Pattern Recognition," "Boolean Functions," "Computer Applications," and "Electrical Networks" had previously been assigned:

"Electrical Network Performance and Computer Simulation"
"Boolean Minimization in Electrical Network Synthesis"
"Network Analysis as Applied to Electronic Circuit Design"
"Network Analysis in Terms of Boolean Functions"
"Recognition of Sloppy, Handwritten Characters"
"Pattern Recognition Techniques as Applied to Bank Management Operations"
"Adaptive and Self-Organizing Systems in Pattern Recognition"
"An Aided Adaptive Character Recognition System for Computer Translation of Languages"
"Simulation of Character Recognition by Computer"
"Adaptive System Recognizes Patterns"

The texts of these titles are now processed against a previously prepared stop list to eliminate the little words and words that are expected to appear very frequently, such as "applied," "system(s)," and "technique(s)."

Next, for each of the remaining words, tallies are made of their co-occurrences, if any, with each of the five descriptors, resulting in a table such as Table 1. We notice that singular and plural forms of the same word have been combined and that some nonsignificant words ("aided" and "sloppy") have been retained because they had not been anticipated when the stoplist was prepared.

Let us now suppose that a new item has been received. Its title ("Pattern Recognition with an Adaptive Network"*) and its abstract ("This paper presents the results of several experiments with a class of adaptive networks, in which recognition of hand-printed characters selected from the English alphabet reached the 94% success level in 40 trials per character. The object of the experiments and analysis was to develop efficient reinforcement procedures for such adaptive systems. A major result was the development of a new, symmetric reward function.") are prepared in machine-usable form either by keypunching or by use of a tape-producing typewriter.

This material is then read into the computer where each word is looked up in the vocabulary table and, for each word found there, a tally is made for the frequency of its prior co-occurrences with each descriptor with which it has co-

---

* This is an actual case (a paper by L. G. Roberts) used in machine-indexing experiments conducted by Stevens and Urban.

Automatic Analysis

TABLE 1

	D_1, adaptive systems	D_2, automatic pattern recognition	D_3, Boolean functions	D_4, computer applications	D_5, electrical networks
Adaptive	111	111		1	
Aided	1	1		1	
Analysis			1		11
Bank		1			
Boolean			11		11
Character(s)	1	111		111	
Circuit(s)					1
Computer(s)	1	11		111	1
Design					1
Electrical			1	1	11
Electronic					1
Function(s)			1		1
Handwritten		1		1	
Language(s)	1	1		1	
Management		1			
Minimization			1		1
Network(s)			11	1	1111
Pattern(s)	11	111			
Performance				1	1
Recognition	11	~~JHT~~		111	
Recognizes	1	1			
Self-organizing	1	1			
Sloppy		1		1	
Synthesis			1		1
Translation	1	1		1	

occurred. In somewhat oversimplified terms, since there would really be many more sample items, many more vocabulary words, and more descriptors than we have shown, the results might be as given in Table 2.

Finally, the machine assigns the three highest scoring descriptors to the new item, namely, "Automatic Pattern Recognition," "Adaptive Systems," and "Com-

TABLE 2

	D_1	D_2	D_3	D_4	D_5
Pattern	11	111			
Recognition	1111	~~JHT~~ 1111		~~JHT~~ 1	
Adaptive	~~JHT~~ 1111	~~JHT~~ 1111		111	
Network			1111	11	~~JHT~~ 111
Character(s)	11	~~JHT~~ 1		~~JHT~~ 1	
Analysis			1		111
Function			1		1
Total	17	27	6	17	12

puter Applications," all of which are appropriate since the work reported in the real paper was based on computer simulations. In the actual case, moreover, this item had previously been indexed twice by human indexers using descriptors similar or identical to those shown. The two indexers agreed with each other in the descriptor assignments to precisely the extent that they each agreed with the machine's assignments; neither of the human indexers assigned a descriptor indicative of the adaptive feature, and one of them erroneously assigned the descriptor "Electrical Networks."

This example has been pursued at some length because it is easier to simplify for illustrative purposes than some of the more sophisticated techniques that have been investigated and yet it is representative of the results that can be obtained in a variety of automatic indexing or classification techniques. For example, clue words and their descriptor associations may be developed on the basis of computing the conditional probabilities that if word "i" occurs, then category (or descriptor) "j" is likely to be appropriate, or on the basis of mathematical and related techniques such as factor analysis, latent class analysis, discriminant function analysis, and "clumping" or "clustering" techniques. These have been applied to the grouping of psychological test data with personality traits or aptitudes, to separations and groupings of archeological artifacts, to medical symptoms associated with various diseases, and to experiments in automatic indexing or classification of documentary items.

In the latter case the "properties" measured may be the relative frequencies of co-occurrence of words in texts, of words with descriptors or subject headings, of descriptors with other descriptors, and of documents with other documents on various bases such as being cited together by one or more documents or having one or more cited references in common. Thus an important area of application of automatic analysis operations is again the development of statistical association factors.

TERMINOLOGY CONTROL

13

Authority Files

Jay E. Daily / University of Pittsburgh, Pittsburgh, Pennsylvania

A separate listing of entries and the authority on which they are based is commonly called an authority file; these files may, for example, simply record decisions which are based on a single authority, in which case the listing of the authority may not be given, in the interest of simplification. All decisions, however, which may later be questioned and the basis on which they were made must be recorded in some fashion if consistency of entry is to be maintained. As will be shown below, often the file itself is the authority, especially when the entries are derived from an authoritative source in the form of preprinted cards, photoreproductions of entries, or printouts of magnetic tape prepared in advance by the authority. Such files are commonly maintained for names, subjects, and series. In addition, large libraries very often maintain a general information file of its serials, especially periodicals, which lacks a common name in the literature and is locally called anything from Serials Information File to O.G. File (for *Omnium Gatherum* File).

Name-Authority Files

Those libraries which adhere to the literary units principle, which would bring together all the works by an author, must rely on some authority for the establishment of the entry of the name. If, however, the library bases its entries on a no-conflict rule and the appearance of the name in the work at hand, authority files are unnecessary. While Panizzi is usually cited as the source of rules of entry, and his rules do not provide for research that would bring all of an author's work together, the literary principle was established early, and early courses of cataloging

---

From *Authority Files*. ENCYCLOPEDIA OF LIBRARY AND INFORMATION SCIENCE. Vol. 2. Edited by Allen Kent and Harold Lancour. Assistant Editor, William Z. Nasri. New York, Marcel Dekker, Inc., c1969. pp. 132–138.

included work on authority files as a necessary adjunct of cataloging (1). The 1941 ALA rules included authority files and rules for establishing them (2), and Tauber has provided a description and example of coding techniques (3). But the literature is scant on the subject and for the most part inapplicable. Official catalogs may be considered an authority file as well as the catalog itself, especially when the entries are obtained from an authoritative source. With the sale of Library of Congress cards, the practice of making authority files decreased, because authority and style of entry were established at the moment the cards were obtained, and any further work would have been fruitless. Very few libraries would challenge the authority of the Library of Congress in its entry (Figure 1).

The publication of the 1967 Anglo-American Rules and the decision of the Library of Congress to employ a policy of superimposition raises the question of name-authority files once more. Superimposition of the 1967 rules will be utilized to reduce recataloging, because wherever an entry has been established, it will not be changed to fit the rules, but the 1967 rules will be used for the establishment of new entries. The Library of Congress will base its decisions on its own catalogs, not on a consensus of practice elsewhere; hence what is new to the Library of Congress may be an established entry elsewhere and vice versa. If the literary units principle is the governing philosophy of a given catalog, there seems to be no convenient way to deal with the change of rules and the decisions of the Library of Congress except by establishing name-authority files, particularly when variations from the Library of Congress practice are required. A decision on the need for authority files ought to be a decision on the character of the catalog itself rather than a consideration of the cost alone.

The literary units principle as it appears in the works of Seymour Lubetzky (4) states that all the works of an author should be brought together in the catalog under one form of his name, including works to which he has contributed as joint author, or joint editor, and in analytical entries. To follow this rule strictly would require a name-authority file, even when Library of Congress cards are purchased for the catalog. The card itself can be considered the authority for anything the

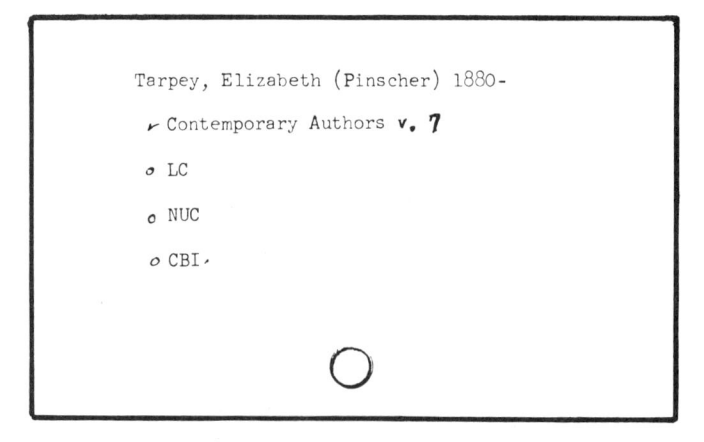

FIGURE 1. *Example of a card from a name-authority file.*

Library of Congress has cataloged but a name must be established correctly when it is first used if the principal authority has not done so. When authorship was rare enough so that persons who wrote books were also persons about whom books (or at least entries in reference works) were written, the search for name and date was not so long or difficult as it is now. With the expansion of literacy and the increase of authorship, especially in countries which scarcely had a written literature before World War I, the task becomes far more difficult and impossible in a significant number of cases. Even the Library of Congress has dropped the strict application of the literary units principle insofar as it applies to the unique work of a single author, preferring to establish entry only when a significant body of literature is obtained or when a conflict with a name as given in the catalog is discovered. Because the time for a search of authorities has been changed, the expression no-conflict is accurate. Authority cards are made only when needed to resolve a problem of entry.

This practice has given rise to a special kind of name-authority file in libraries which use Library of Congress cards. An entry is made when an author appears only in an added entry and is maintained until the author's name is given as main entry. The Library of Congress provides a complete entry for added entries so that when the name is established, even as an added entry, all further entries must be in conformity. Customarily the added entry card is withdrawn from the file when it appears as main entry, hence there is close connection between this practice and the provision of information obtained when a search of the catalog was conducted prior to the purchase of the item. Libraries which do original cataloging of works must make their entries conform to Library of Congress practice if the printed cards are to be utilized.

There are many problems, not all of them easily resolved, with the entry of personal names; the difficulties increase when the names of corporate bodies are included in the literary units principle. There would be good reason for not attempting to provide the history of the organization in changes of names as they appear in the references in the catalog. It would be sufficient to adopt a rule that an organization is considered defunct when its name changes and the new name under the rule is applied to a new institution. Lacking such a rule, it is necessary to maintain a corporate entry name-authority file. In addition, the old problem of society or institution and entry by place or entry by name is complicated by the 1967 rules which would eradicate the distinctions and adopt, in effect, what was previously a rule and an exception. If Library of Congress cards are used, the general rule of entry under the name when it is distinctive and under the place when it is not will compete with the previous attempts at divining whether a given organization was a society or an institution. The latter were entered under place, but an exception to the rule provided for institutions with a proper name and further exceptions provided, in the 1949 rules, for entry by place when the proper name was, in fact, quite commonplace, in such names as Carnegie Library or St. Mary's Hospital. There can be little argument that a rule which requires an exception to an exception is hardly better than no rule at all.

The question remains whether the literary units principle is not more suitable to a formal bibliography than to a library catalog. The no-conflict rule establishes a precedent for entry under the name as found in a book, but few are willing to accept Panizzi's rules which would provide that the work to be cataloged is the source of all bibliographic detail, even though this rule is likely to have been used in other, but certainly not all, bibliographies. Exacting studies on the history of the entry of names by the Library of Congress and the work of various authors (5) show that if the literary units principle is to be followed, as it must somewhere, then the problems of names are just becoming known. We must conclude that cultural and linguistic studies are necessary to establish methods of entry for names of every description. An example is the problem of names of nobility, a point of contention between British and American practice in the ALA rules since 1908, for the British usage requires entry by the family name and the American usage would enter under the descriptive place name associated with the title. The problem of names becomes especially difficult when there are no surnames, as in medieval European names, Arabic authors who wrote before recent changes in custom, and present-day Burmese authors.

Unfortunately we cannot look to automated equipment to resolve the puzzle. This is a problem of what we will do at the outset and decisions based on such sketchy evidence are a purely human task. Authority files assume a choice of authority and these notably differ when the questions are at all problematic, so that much study is needed to provide some central bibliographic authority with a known basis for resolving difficulties in a consistent fashion, and this leads to an open field for the study of names of every description. Once names have been established, a central repository of authority can be developed such that an inquiry into a form of a name as found in a work may be corrected with the standard entry to be utilized in all major bibliographic works, for with authority comes standardization, its only purpose for being. As literacy expands throughout the world, the need for a personal name authority becomes all the greater, especially as convincing precedent is found in the standardization of geographic names (6).

Subject-Authority Files

A similar problem but one which is even less of moment in library literature is the question of what subject-authority files to maintain and how to maintain them. It has been the practice of many libraries to accept a standard list and employ this for all modifications of the list as they appear in the subject catalog (interfiled with other entries in a dictionary catalog and hence a subject portion of a catalog). Equally useful is a card file of all subjects used in a catalog, amended as changes occur. Unfortunately both methods have several problems inherent in the arrangement and utilization of the authority file. The book is likely to be reprinted and every purely local heading not in the standard list must be copied from the old edition into the new. The card file requires much typing in its upkeep and must be consulted by each cataloger as a heading is employed unless the public catalog is considered the authority except for local headings, those not found in the standard list. Studies are suggested to determine which is better (3) but it appears that neither is very good.

In any case the standardization of subject headings, something close to half, will be composed following the rules of main entry, so that whatever has been said of names as bibliographic description applies just as well to names as subjects, so that many libraries regard the public catalog as the subject-authority file and make the addition of see references when a new subject is added.

While the addition of see references may be made routinely, no such action is possible if see-also references are included in the public catalog. It is necessary to break the routine so that all suggested see-also references can be traced if blind references are to be avoided. The utilization of the subject-heading list as a source of see-also references, there being no assurance for the user that a reference listed in the book will also be in the public catalog, is the only method of avoiding both the complications of using the catalog as a subject-authority file for see-also references or the construction and maintenance of a separate subject-authority file in card form, with its attendant complications. Very little has been written on the management of subject headings in a library, although there is some consideration of subject headings on a purely theoretical basis. It appears, though, that practices vary widely and no library is in a position to say whether the maintenance of a subject-authority file in either form does much more for the user than routinely follow the practices of the body which issues the cards. With the whole question of a tool which is worth the cost of subject cataloging in abeyance, pending further use studies, subject-authority files are considered a necessity but may be simply those headings used in the public catalog with the printed list as the further authority.

A more profitable study would seem to be the use of automated equipment to provide a current list in alphabetic and classified order of all the subjects utilized and their form. Such a procedure exists for some kinds of indexing, especially where natural language is rationalized into consistent form and arrangement according to subject area, as in a thesaurus. Automated equipment provides an answer to both objections; it can be as current as the library is willing to pay for and printed in sufficient copies so that every cataloger has one. The only easy part of automating library procedures is speculation on the possibilities and their rewards. A systematic study is needed to determine whether the computer offers the average library a way out of its dilemma in the maintenance of a subject approach to the collection.

Series-Authority Files

If a library uses Library of Congress cards or does original cataloging, a file showing the treatment of a series, either omitted or as an added entry, is generally maintained because of the vague rules which prevail in this area. Series-added entries are made when the work is, in fact, a set rather than a series, but is treated as separate works and cataloged separately volume by volume when the series might reasonably be considered a set and cataloged under one heading and classified together, that is, when the series constitutes a subject entity where a choice is made whether to classify together or to treat on a more specific basis. Commonly works which are given as a part of a series, but are in fact a series only insofar as the publisher is concerned and then principally as a means of selling titles and controlling the issuance of publications, are not entered with series-added entries in the catalog. Neither are works which appear to be periodicals but are, in fact, separate treatises on remotely related subjects and are called a bulletin series for purposes of gaining the postal privileges accorded periodical publications. It is not a mistake for a library to include a series of one item, so that some files are unnecessary if they are maintained because a series entry may be added when other items in the series are obtained. However, the decision not to make series-added entries for items of a certain kind or to do so cannot be more than an individual judgment and hence must be recorded. Series-authority files are also used to maintain consistency of entry, especially when the publisher changes the name of the series but continues the numbering or alters some part of the series titling without, in fact, creating a new series.

The series-authority file is, in fact, a decision file and this leads to the reason for maintaining any kind of authority file, especially those which are used to show the routing and treatment of periodicals. Where subjective judgments are made about individual items which do not form a readily identified class of materials, then a file showing the decision, its basis, its date, and any modification is a method of saving time and avoiding error.

Librarians have learned, even if they have not seen fit to explain, that some authority files are time-saving devices, especially those which cannot be replaced by other files. The serials information file sometimes records occasions when material received as a periodical is in fact a set, issued in fascicles, but can readily be accounted for as if it were a periodical; equally the serials information files will direct booksellers' catalogs to the proper persons and provide for immediate discard of some classes of material which the library receives but does not want. Where the method of entry into the serials records may be problematic, the serials information file will record other possible entries and direct the clerk handling the mail to the correct entry.

Conclusion

It is too easy to say that authority files are a memento of the past and should not be maintained at all, because the principle in their favor is one that must affect every library which employs clerical and professional personnel, and even one-man libraries will find use for an authority file which records a decision. What is a valid field of research is whether a central-authority file for author's names, locally computer-produced subject-heading authority files, and card files for decisions regarding series and periodicals are not the minimum files required which provide the maximum usefulness. There seems every good reason to hypothesize these as the authority files likely to be maintained regardless of changes in bibliographic method and centralization of technical services.

REFERENCES

1. J. D. Fellows, *Cataloging Rules, with Explanations and Illustrations,* H. W. Wilson, New York, 1926.

2. American Library Association, *Cataloging Rules: Author and Title Entries,* 2nd ed., ALA, Chicago, 1949.
3. M. F. Tauber, *Technical Services in Libraries,* Columbia Univ. Press, New York, 1954.
4. S. Lubetsky, "The Cataloging of Publications of Corporate Authors: a Rejoinder," *Lib. Quart.,* 21, No. 1, I (1951).
5. A. M. Abdul Huq, *Treatment of Bengali Muslim Personal Names in American and British Catalogs,* unpublished seminar paper, Univ. of Pittsburgh, Graduate School of Library and Information Sciences, 1967.
6. *United States Board on Geographical Names, Decision List,* U.S. Department of the Interior, 1940.

14

Subject Headings

Jay E. Daily / University of Pittsburgh, Pittsburgh, Pennsylvania

Crestadoro is usually given credit for establishing that the cataloger should provide a standardized guide to the subject content of a book by giving it a heading that would be appropriate and recognizable by the public (*1*). An author could call his nonfiction work anything, but the librarian would supply a word that enabled the user of the catalog to search for books whose authors and titles were unknown to him. Charles A. Cutter, in the four editions of his *Rules for a Dictionary Catalog*, codified the procedure and made some suggestions for the form that headings should take, each edition elaborating this element of his rules (*2*). At that point in the 19th and early 20th centuries, the cataloger was supposed to supply the headings from a list he prepared himself. This put a great burden on anyone who constructed the descriptive cataloging from a combination of rules and observations, and it added a creative element that was beyond the capabilities of some catalogers. The answer to the dilemma was a list of subject headings, supplied by the American Library Association and made up of the headings used in the largest libraries (*3*). The final edition of this list was published in 1911, a few years after the first edition of the Library of Congress list. With the development of a card distribution system that included headings constructed by the Library of Congress, most libraries preferred to use the LC list to create a kind of automatic conformity. This has continued to the present. The list of subject headings used most often in a general library is the latest edition of *Subject Headings Used in the Dictionary Catalogs of the Library of Congress* (*4*). Even in that list, a great many headings are not included, in the expectation that the librarian will be able to supply them as need arises. These are especially the

---

From Daily, Jay E. *Subject Headings.* ENCYCLOPEDIA OF LIBRARY AND INFORMATION SCIENCE. Vol. 29. Edited by Allen Kent and Harold Lancour. Assistant Editor, William Z. Nasri. New York, Marcel Dekker, Inc., c1969. pp. 178-191.

Subject Headings

names of individuals, of corporations, of specific buildings, ships, etc. The list is meant to supply topical headings in the interests of uniformity in libraries.

If a list of subject headings is at the same time a list of formalized titles of books—a handy definition that seems to serve better than any other—then topical headings are the very ones where there might be the most variation. The Library of Congress developed a syndetic structure, following the prescriptions of Cutter, that would seem to organize subject headings by categories through the use of *see also* lists. The concept was unassailable; a user could go through the list of books under one heading and find a list of related headings where he could look for more titles. The Library of Congress violated its own rules for inclusion of headings by providing *see* references from unused headings to those that were established. For purposes of keeping the records clear and avoiding blind references, *see also from* and *see from* lists were kept under the headings referred to by using *x* for *see from* and *xx* for *see also from*. While this was meant to provide an internal organization of the list, it provided a complexity that militated against dropping headings that were no longer used or changing those that lagged behind the public's use of a term—to such an extent that a list of subject headings is a museum of language.

The number of headings has consistently grown and there have been, overall, many fewer changes than were needed. When complaints arose after the publication of the fifth edition (that the new edition was simply a reprint of the fourth edition), Carlyle Frarey wrote a thesis showing conclusively that changes, all in the form of additions, had been made (5). The Library of Congress, while generally insensitive to criticism, began to publish additions and changes as they were made and was at some pains to describe the procedure by which these changes were made (6). Shortly after, David Judson Haykin published a book about the form of headings in the Library of Congress list (7). Haykin seemed to prescribe the form that new headings should take rather than explain the form of the headings already established in the list. Although a large number of examples which would contradict his statements were apparent to anyone familiar with the list, the book was used for many years in cataloging courses.

Daily's dissertation applied the techniques of grammatical analysis as established in linguistics in a study of the main headings of the list, with some passing attention to the subdivisions (8). In the manner of a linguist studying a language unknown to the world of scholarship, Daily established the morphology in order to determine those features that were "morphemic" in the list; and on this basis he then studied the use of these features, the syntax of the list. Finally, he created a kind of grammar of subject headings showing how uniformity could be achieved. His work, like most dissertations, attracted almost no attention, partly because the use of linguistic techniques in studying subject analysis was new (if not original) with Daily and partly because his rules seemed to require a complete reorganization of the list—when even a minor alteration was impossible or vastly expensive. Frarey dismissed the work as "arbitrary," apparently under the misconception that language ought to be something else (9).

A study of the semantics of the list was attempted by Lilley, who used only the headings that related to English literature as the basis of his conclusions

(*10*). Further studies of subject headings resulted from Daily's original work, all by students at the University of Pittsburgh. The basic principles were expanded and related to Arabic by Muhammed Aman (*11*). They were tested experimentally: in Farsi by Ebrami (*12*); in another list by Sinkankas, who used *Sears* in English (*13*); and by Koh, who used the Korean adaptation of *Sears* (*14*). At this writing, the topic seems a dead issue, despite the work done by Harris (*15*) and the complaints based on selected examples used by Chen (*16*).

The *Sears List* of subject headings was created in the 1920s by Minnie Earle Sears and has been kept up to date by a succession of editors—notably Bertha Frick, who worked with Sears in the creation of the original list. *Sears*, like the Library of Congress list, included suggested classification through the eighth edition (*17*). It was dropped from the ninth edition, ostensibly because school librarians, the principal users of the list, were employing the suggested classification numbers instead of the Abridged Dewey Decimal Classification as intended by the editor of the original list. Sears and Frick believed that a list had to be classified if problems of excessive synonymy were to be avoided. However, the list was not published in classified order until it appeared in this encyclopedia, the result of Sinkankas's devoted effort (*18*). The heart of Daily's work was his statement that the list should be classified and the problems of syndetic structure removed by this process. The reason for this was explained in Daily's preface to *Classified Library of Congress Subject Headings,* by Williams, Manheimer, and Daily (*19*). Although Sears and Frick believed firmly that classification was necessary in the formative stages of a subject heading list, Daily intended that the users would employ the classified guide instead of the *see also* structure, which Sinkankas had effectively shown simply did not organize headings in the same way (*20*). The possibility that a new subject heading list for a specific area of science and technology (e.g., atomic energy) would result in a kind of hidden classification was effectively disproved by Mellott (*21*).

The seventh edition of the Library of Congress list was criticized by Daily shortly after its appearance (*22*). One feature, however, was appreciated: the list was available in machine-readable form. Efforts to create a classified list from this tape went on for many years. The information on the tape was transferred to cards, but the cards could not be sorted out efficiently. A succession of students attempted to develop a program for utilizing the tapes, only to be defeated by the curious programming of the Library of Congress in preparing the tapes. They were never meant for such experimental work and existed only because the seventh edition had been printed from camera-ready copy prepared by a computer. James Williams succeeded where all others had failed, and *Classified Library of Congress Subject Headings,* in classed and in alphabetic order, was the result. A large number of headings were not given classifications, a point made in the critical review of the book by Atherton (*23*). Following the general belief of librarians that all the headings should be included, Atherton suggested that the headings on cards be sorted out with classification numbers from the entries on the MARC tapes and these supplied, so that all the headings would be classified. Another method would be simply to sit down and classify the headings, not so much an intellectual challenge as an inordinate clerical task. Early on in the experimentation, it was observed that the headings as found on the MARC tapes did not gibe very well with the list. A comparison of classification and headings was revealing only in the sense that either the list or the schedules had been used with remarkable license. A large number of topical headings not listed in the seventh edition nor in the *Additions and Changes* published by the Library of Congress made this procedure chancy at best and would have created, in effect, an entirely new list.

A further experiment comparing the LC subject headings and the Dewey classification was much more successful so far as similarity between subject headings and the Dewey schedules was concerned. The reason for this can be found in the fact that the classifiers for the Dewey number are the last to see the work and all the previous work is available to them. They are naturally free to disagree in any way they wish, but usually they accept the subject headings and are guided by them, to some degree, in the choice of Dewey number.

Eighth Edition of the Library of Congress List

Many changes were made in, and proposed with the publication of, the eighth edition of *Subject Headings Used in the Dictionary Catalogs of the Library of Congress*. These included the simplification of the title to *Library of Congress Subject Headings,* or possibly just *Subject Headings.* The name Quattlebaum is missing from the title page and also from the work itself. As editor of the list through the seventh edition, Quattlebaum achieved a remarkable degree of correctness. The latest list is so filled with error that a project to produce a classified guide has been stalled by the enormous clerical task of inputting hundreds of entries that are in some fashion incorrect, and by the question whether such license taken with the list would not also justify classifying those headings that so far do not have suggested Library of Congress classification numbers. The list is in two volumes, showing the great increase in headings over the one-volume seventh edition. Like the last edition, this one is also available in machine-readable form, but the programming was completely changed, evidently in an effort to make it more accessible to libraries. At the time the tapes were made available, it was announced that the list would be updated in machine-readable form as well so that a library could maintain a computerized authority file for subject headings. So far as is known at this writing, the computerized tapes are still not available.

Table 1 is a comparison of the fifth edition with the eighth edition. It shows, in general, the increase of headings in a period of nearly 30 years and the decrease of suggested classification numbers. In the fifth edition, 21,451 headings were counted as the maximum. There was a built-in statistical error of about 0.5%. In the eighth edition, there are at least 95,920 headings. The distinction between classed and unclassed headings is shown where clearly

TABLE 1
Comparison of Fifth and Eighth Editions of the Library of Congress List

Type of heading	Fifth Edition Classed	Fifth Edition Un-classed	Fifth Edition Total	%	Eighth Edition Classed	Eighth Edition Un-classed	Eighth Edition Total	%
One word	5,671	1,019	6,690	31.8	1,393	8,923	10,316	10.8
Gloss	809	463	1,272	6.0	6,391	4,263	10,654	11.2
Hyphenated	871	108	979	4.7	4,002	4,519	8,521	8.9
Two words	5,858	1,374	7,232	34.4	10,814	22,578	33,392	35.0
Three or more words	466	118	584	2.8	2,831	4,715	7,546	8.0
Function words	1,679	513	2,192	10.4	5,390	5,699	11,089	14.0
Inverted headings	—	—	1,434	6.8	—	—	9,026	9.5
Models	—	—	642	3.0	—	—	1,000	1.1
Series	—	—	24	0.1	—	—	1,376	1.4
Excluded and error			(412)					
Totals	15,354	3,595+	(18,949) 21,451		30,821	50,697+	(81,518) 95,920	
Percent	81.02 (of 18,949)	18.98	—	100.0	37.81 (of 81,518)	63.19	—	100.0

applicable, and the relationship is emphasized at the bottom of the table. Although the unclassed headings made up only some 20% of the list in the fifth edition, the unclassed headings are now the majority, about two-thirds of the eighth edition. This represents a further decrease from the seventh edition, and it leads one to suppose that the Library of Congress now believes that classification of headings is not desirable, for whatever reason. Along with a decrease in the percentage of one-word terms, there is a corresponding increase in all the other forms. By definition, this represents a growing complexity of the list, since one-word headings are less susceptible to grammatical and semantic variation. As the table shows, this illustrates the great increase in headings. However, the old favorites are still available: "Photography of the invisible" (2:1375)* and "One-leg resting position" (2:1291) with the *see* reference from "Standing on one foot." The correct heading is "Selters water" (2:1631) not "Seltzer water," which is a *see* reference. However, the list now includes as *see also from* references "Astronomical photography" and "Photography, Ballistic." The previous edition listed these as *see* references. The cataloger can select either "Tablets (Medicine)" (2:1791) or "Pills" (2:1389). There is a *see also from*

---

*Pagination is continuous in the two volumes. Examples are located by showing the volume first, then the page number. The column on the page has been omitted.

"Enteric-coated tablets" but "Pills" is an orphan, in the parlance adopted by Sinkankas in his paper on the syndetic structure of the Library of Congress list (*18*). An orphan is a heading without any reference whatever, not even a *see* reference. The significance is that these headings cannot be found unless the user and the cataloger happen to know the heading or chance upon it. The likelihood is that the heading "Pills" was used briefly and forgotten, while "Tablets (Medicine)" was amplified when the new heading "Enteric-coated tablets" was added (1:610). Interestingly enough, both "Pills" and "Tablets (Medicine)" are listed together because of similar suggested classification numbers in *Classified Library of Congress Subject Headings*.

The problems with the list can be seen further in the expansion of the front matter, which gives the user a much more complete explanation of the headings and of the kinds of headings omitted, those left to the cataloger to add. A very useful series of examples is given, showing not only the preferred form of heading but also the kind of cross-referencing that should be added. These are called "nonprint" headings, meaning that they are headings which are omitted from the list but exist in the dictionary catalog of the Library of Congress.

A further useful feature of the front matter is the effort at standardization of subdivisions. A count of the main headings in boldface type cannot establish the number of subject headings since they may be subdivided essentially—by form ("—— Bibliography," "—— Abstracts," etc.) or by place, though no longer with the haphazard distinction between direct and indirect subdivision—or topically. Daily's dissertation established that topical subdivisions vary according to the semantic area of the main heading, but these topical headings might vary considerably in the terminology of the subdivisions.

It is apparent that the Library of Congress contemplates a time when the subject heading list can be revised from a museum of language into a working tool for user and cataloger—granting that the computer reduces the clerical operations to a minimum. Recataloging for purposes of changing a heading seems to incur great expense for little gain. Bringing all the subdivisions used into conformity will greatly enhance the work. Although not mentioned in the front matter, the Library of Congress adopted the convention developed for *Classified Library of Congress Subject Headings:* A dash is added for each subdivision so that the first has one dash; the second, two; the third, three; and the fourth, four; for example, "United States – History – – Civil War – – – Personal Narratives – – – – Confederate side." This is very useful if the sequence of subdivisions must be followed from one column to the next and especially if the subdivisions continue on the next page.

As will be shown later, a classified list is very readily kept up to date. Such headings as "European War, 1914–1918" (1:631)—which cannot now be changed because of the huge bulk of cards bearing this heading—reflect the changing of terminology. The heading was established while World War I was in its early phases. Japan had not yet joined the Allies and there was no fighting in Asia or Africa. The present system of cross-referencing, even in a computerized file, imposes extreme burdens on the user and the cataloger, who must rely on the alphabet to find the heading needed even though the alphabet is in itself a distraction. The current definition of the Library of Congress catalog, according to some, is "A great bibliographic tool where information is lost in alphabetic order." This applies to the subject heading list as well, in part because of the form of headings.

Changes which are purely typographical in nature—such as the decision not to print "Hot water—Therapeutic Use" (1:848) in boldface type, thereby violating a rule for subdivision—are easily detected by the scope note "This heading is used only with subdivisions." All 47 examples found in the fifth edition have been corrected and the practice has been discontinued.

Changes in the form of headings cannot be made, except as already noted, and the practices established with the first subject heading lists are maintained. This is seen in the curious use of the word *the* in the headings "The West" (2:1980), "State, The" (2:1729), and "East" (1:551). The three headings are alphabetized alike, in the case of the first two as if no article were printed. The Library of Congress catalogers may avoid using these headings, but they are still part of the list. Similarly, forms used for a kind of morphological grouping within the alphabet remain, and they are equally used for dispersal of headings. These are primarily the gloss (a word in parentheses completing the heading) and the inverted heading (a term followed by another term, separated by a comma). Music headings are customarily grouped with terms in parentheses that establish the instruments to be considered; for example, "Trios" (2:1870), which is followed by nearly 10 columns of headings specifying every kind of trio from "Trios (Accordion, flute, violoncello)" (2:1870) to "Trios (Vina, percussion, violin)" (2:1873). This principle of use for the gloss differs from the many headings specifying "—— (Islamic law)," like "Real property (Islamic law)" (2:1525) and "Marriage (Islamic law)" (2:1102). Even though the latter heading is in a string specifying different kinds of laws, the usage differs from the string of headings beginning with "Trials (Adultery)" (2:1868) and ending with "Trials (Witchcraft)" (2:1869)—a total of 52 headings—because neither "Adultery" (1:17) nor "Witchcraft" (2:1994) are used commonly as words within parentheses.

Inverted headings are numerous and used capriciously. If there is any principle underlying the use, the cataloger, the user, and the researcher alike are challenged to find it. Several authors have asked why, for instance, there should be the heading "Photography, Ballistic" (2:1873) and yet another heading "Astronomical photography" (1:122). In each case there is a string of headings beginning with the entry word, 12 using "Astronomical ——" and 38 using "Photography ——." There are, for instance, 8 headings that begin "Submarine ——" (2:1759–1760) and 84 that begin "Military ——" (2:1155–1160). It is not enough to argue preponderance of headings in one form or another to account for "Photography, Submarine" and "Photography, Military." In the fifth edition, inverted headings were 6.8% of the total of 21,451 headings. Inverted headings are 9.5% of the 95,920 headings counted in the eighth edition. The percentage is increasing, so that this is obviously a preferred form of the subject headings. A user accustomed to the list will look under both forms of the heading, and if he is wise, under the inverted form first. A *see* reference is always made from an inverted heading.

Although the gloss serves a useful purpose when it truly explains the meaning of a heading—as in "American (Artificial language)" (1:61)—there is no argument for "Languages, Artificial" (2:1009), not even the handy reference to general practice by the Library of Congress. Morphological groupings reflect, possibly, catalogers' yearnings for order and symmetry, even in a language that can boast of it only in word order, and not always there. The fact that headings can be left in natural order is one of the reasons for providing a classified list of headings. The effort of classifying is certainly no greater than the time wasted in systematic mystification.

At times, the Library of Congress list verges on the ungrammatical, as in "Community plays, etc." (1:394). Most freshman English courses include the instruction not to use *etc.* for fewer than two items. The eighth edition includes 1,376 examples of a series, almost all of them rather more acceptable than the heading just noted. There are 24 examples in the fifth edition, although this comparison may be fouled by inclusion of other elements counted together in the eighth edition and separated in the fifth. A further difficulty in the Library of Congress list is the use of hyphens. Sears noted the distinction between hyphenation as she preferred it and that of the Library of Congress (*24*). The fifth edition included "Grape-fruit" (p. 479), which has become "Grapefruit" (1:785); however, "Egg-plant" (1:565) has been kept with the hyphen in place. Headings with several words sometimes include hyphens where they are scarcely expected, as in "Steam-boilers, Water-tube" (2:1734), and omitted where a hyphen would reduce ambiguity, as in "Red cotton bug" (2:1330). It is very difficult to guess what the practice of the Library of Congress will be, although headings used for works dealing with agriculture and technology, especially the technology of an earlier period, seem to include the greatest use of hyphens. However, even here one is likely to guess wrong. Although "Fruit-flies" (1:729) is the accepted form, the correct heading is "Horn-fly" (1:842). It seems, though, that for the newer headings the Library of Congress has adopted the rule that coordinating modifiers are hyphenated, as in "Computer-assisted instruction" (1:399).

Supposing that a student of cataloging learns not to question why a heading is in one form and why another in the same general semantic area is in a different form, he must still learn some of the idiosyncrasies of the list. Main headings may be subdivided indirectly and appear as topical subdivisions of place names. In general, this rule applies to institutions which are characteristic of nations or states and specifically located in or near cities, like "Cemeteries" (1:284). The student must learn not to use the subdivision "- - Biography" after the names of persons, confirmed by examples like Lincoln, Washington, Napoleon, Wagner, and St. Thomas Aquinas. The astute student will ask about Shakespeare and learn that if the subdivision is itself to be subdivided then it is included, so that the heading is "Shakespeare, William, 1564–1616 – Bibliography – – Youth" (2:1647). The student must also learn that headings with brackets—there are an even 1,000 in the eighth edition—are models and that other headings can be constructed utilizing the same form; for example, "Songs, American" (2:1701), even though only English and French are shown in the brackets. However, the list goes on to show "Songs, English" and "Songs, French" (2:1702) along with 21 other headings. Because of the example of "Songs, English (Middle English, 1100–1500)" the student may wonder just what the model is and why it is given. The student is wise not to ask why certain headings are subdivided by place directly—meaning that the local place name is given without showing the whole hierarchy of its location, as in "Sick leave" (8:1663)—while indirect subdivision requires that the hierarchy must be worked out, omitting country for the United States, Canada, and Great Britain. The correct subdivision, for instance, would be "Siderite – Wales – – Aberystwyth" (2:1662), supposing that anyone ever wrote on the topic and that the kind of iron ore is found in that part of Wales. The student must further learn that the notation "Direct" or "Indirect" may follow the main heading or it may follow a subdivision or it may follow both. If either of the words follows the subdivision, then the place name follows the topical subdivision. If not, the local subdivision is interposed between the main heading and the topical subdivision. Students in practica have regularly reported that subject headings are the most difficult part of the work they do under the supervision of the head cataloger.

It can be concluded from the table comparing the forms found in the fifth edition with those of the eighth edition that the problems of the subject heading list have grown along with the number of headings included. Along with this problem of form is the problem of organization. The *see also* structure is incomplete even at best. There are innumerable examples of the note which explains that the heading is also a subdivision and should be looked up under each heading that can include it; for instance, the note under "Caricatures and cartoons" (1:266). The subdivision appears under certain subjects, "*e.g.* Marriage – Caricatures and cartoons; Triple alliance – Caricatures and cartoons," and may also appear as "Humor, caricatures, etc. *under the names of wars, etc., e.g.* European War, 1914–1918 – Humor, caricatures, etc." Under the names of persons, the subdivision is "Cartoons, satire, etc." or "Portraits, caricatures, etc." This note, if followed, would make it impossible for the user to find out what was included in a library's collection of visual art that is humorous in nature; equally it would be impossible for the cataloger to put in the *see also* references required to provide this access.

The procedures required to keep a catalog current with editions of the list are so extensive, costly, and fraught with undetectable error that most libraries do not attempt to put *see also* references in the catalog. Because a library does not obtain all the books received by the Library of Congress, care must be taken to include only those headings in the *see also* structure which apply to books already cataloged. This, in turn, means that the references in the catalog must be constantly altered to be current with new items as they are cataloged. In view of the slapdash method of the *see also* references in any case, the list itself is generally pressed into service to supply the user with additional locations for the subjects he wants.

A further problem arises with authority files for subjects. Libraries which keep these in card form must assign a cataloger and a clerk to the task full time to avoid creating a bottleneck in the use of precataloged material. Some libraries let the catalog serve as the authority file. Others must keep records of changes made. Some catalogers simply cannot accept headings like "Photography of the invisible" or "Cookery (Frogs)" (1:436), and the decision to revise a heading makes an authority file essential, however difficult it may be to maintain if it includes the cross-references. The Library of Congress proposed authority files in machine-readable form, but these may be subject to the same imponderables that Manheimer found in the change from one subject authority list to another which included cross-referencing. At the same time, several apparently minor changes were made in the form of headings, which made the original file unusable (25). The Library of Congress list of subject headings is rather like a white elephant inherited from earlier generations and reflecting the changing standards and methods of librarianship since the latter part of the 19th century. It could be revised, but it is highly doubtful that it will be except on the piecemeal basis applied so far. The changes made since the cut-off date of the eighth edition have been no more numerous than those made previously. The method of revision is set forth in Daily's rules and has been tested repeatedly, first in the dissertation itself and then by dozens of students as part of the course work in Daily's Theory of Classification course at the University of Pittsburgh (26). These rules apply to subject headings for small as well as large collections, to special as well as general coverage, and (granting some alteration to fit the language) to headings in any language at all, as observed previously.

Revision of Subject Heading Lists

This section could as well be entitled "Preparation of Subject Heading Lists for Special Collections." However, in view of the proposed computerization of the subject heading list by the Library of Congress, the revision of the general list is considered. One of the greatest problems is avoided at the outset: the choice of a suitable classification method. The Library of Congress would have to reverse its trend and classify all the headings. Some headings have as many as eight classifications; and to give each heading a single location in the classified list, these would have to be reshaped to show the area intended within the heading. This is already done as part of the information provided with the subject headings. For instance, "Propaganda" (2:1460) would have to be expanded to account for its classification in "Diplomacy," "European war," "Lobbying," and "Public opinion," utilizing the rules of form that would give the following headings: *Propaganda : Diplomacy. JX 1674–5; *Propaganda : European war. D639.P6–7; *Propaganda : Lobbying – – United States, JK 1118; *Propaganda : Public opinion. HM263.

While this appears to be an enormous labor, it would also provide a uniform index to the classification schedules. As Immroth demonstrated, the indexes are of highly varied quality, and the often proposed and sometimes executed project of combining the existing indexes into one alphabet is no more useful than the present system because a term may vary in form in the schedule, the index, and the subject heading list (27). The Library of Congress classification and the subject headings were developed from actual books, so that the first rule, taking the heading from the literature, is not so difficult to follow. However, throughout the list there is evidence that some headings are cataloger's creations and would not be found in the literature. Other headings can be supplied. The method does not require *see* references in the classified list, as both the preferred heading and other possible headings are listed together; for instance, TR 705 Scientific application : Photography.

The principal changes of form would omit prepositions unless they are parts of standard, accepted terms where the whole term is equivalent to a word; for instance, "Freedom of information" (1:720). Many of the prepositional phrases used in the eighth, and even more in earlier editions, were simply nonce formations useful to the cataloger but a complete mystery to the user. The phrases that end "– – – in literature" and "– – – as a profession" have served as models for several strings of headings all using the preposition, sometimes with rather curious results, as in "Photography in boring" (2:1374). The revision would require the heading to be *Earth boring : Photography. The advantage of the colon in replacing prepositions is that it has no meaning at all, while prepositions have some scant residue of meaning even though, as syntactic markers, this is very hard to define.

A further principal change of form would eliminate all the inverted headings. These may serve a purpose in the index of a book, but except for names (where the most important element must be used first; importance being guided by a decision on which element is most varied in expression), inverted headings only reflect a desire to shape the list into some kind of symmetry, which is frankly impossible in English. In some languages this is not a problem; Esperanto, for instance, where a modifier can either precede or follow the head of the construction and where a rule to provide that it always follow does not violate the grammar of the language. The inverted headings in the Library of Congress list require special alphabetic rules and very careful cross-referencing, and they are completely unnecessary when a classified guide is provided, since the variation in entry word is desirable.

Finally, words in parentheses could be used, but only when the word is truly an explanation of the term or a variant spelling. The strings of headings that use parentheses as a means of grouping headings would have to be completely changed, so that "Trials (Adultery)" would become *Adultery trials and "Cookery (Apples)" would become *Apples : Cookery, if not some more practical term like *Apple cooking. The reason for these rules is that the classified guide brings together all the different headings which are dispersed in the subject heading list. Such curious headings as "Yeomen (F)" (2:2017) would have to be rephrased as *Yeomanettes or (depending on the number of books with this heading) be included with *World War, 1914–1918 in the classified guide under D639, with the general heading *Women's work : World War, 1914–1918.

One of the rules is already being followed in the eighth edition: vague historical terms have been replaced by precise dates so that periods of history and biography can be filed semantically from earliest date to latest.

As it now stands, the revision of the Library of Congress subject heading list would provide a means whereby the user of an automated catalog could have a given subject area displayed on a terminal screen and select from that the headings that would provide a display of books coming closest to meeting his needs. At present, there is no possibility of devising a program whereby the *see also* structure could provide the same amount of information. As Sinkankas stated, the structure leads a user out of the subject area rather than into it (*13*). Such orphans as "Carob" (1:266) would finally find a location in relation to other headings. One orphan is "Bleak (Fish)" (1:198), which has neither *see* reference nor *see also* reference nor suggested classification to locate it among all the others.

Subject headings have acquired so bad a reputation that developers of computerized indexes have called the natural-language subject access to their system "descriptors." Word magic, however, does not change the fact that the natural-language portions of all methods of subject analysis—from concordance to subject headings, and including the schedules and index of a classification system—are related. For many years it was believed that there was no relationship, or at best a complimentary relationship, between subject headings and classification systems. The work of classifying was done in one department at the Library of Congress and the adding of subject headings was the task of another department. The Cataloging and Classification Section of the American Library Association had two committees, one dealing with classification and the other with subject headings. The distinction has now been lost, if it ever really existed. A thesaurus for access to a compilation of data must use a kind of subject heading, the difference chiefly lying in the depth of indexing. Subject headings are meant to provide access to an entire book while index terms provide access to a few paragraphs. A self-contained index that will never grow may take liberties of form that become disastrous in a larger system.

Whether the Library of Congress will begin work on a major revision of its method of subject analysis or shift to another system, such as Precis, is unknown as of this writing. Precis, despite its attractiveness and possibly because of the strict control of grammatical forms, has yet to be proved. Intended as the beginning of a general classification (which so far has not materialized), Precis provides a method of access which has proved at least as successful as subject headings in its use by the British Library.

The initial steps toward a classified guide were taken with publication of Williams, Manheimer, and Daily's *Classified Library of Congress Subject Headings*. Further progress might be made along the same lines so that the present revision of the Library of Congress schedules could more completely reflect the subject heading list. However, the general tendency of the Library of Congress has been never to admit an error and to utilize whatever it wished in the literature without acknowledging its existence. This has been of enormous benefit to the researcher, who would have been much hampered in his studies if he had been tied to some general project involving the very data he was observing.

Subject headings will always be of greatest usefulness to the novice in a subject area. The expert tends to know the names of authors and the sources of continuing information in a subject area. The novice must have some place to begin, which is provided by the subject access to the material. It is only when the novice begins to study the means of subject access closely that he becomes aware of its deficiencies. Usually he will condemn his own lack of knowledge long before he realizes that his ignorance was shared and compounded by the makers of the subject heading list.

REFERENCES

1. Andrea Crestadoro, *The Art of Making Catalogues*, British Museum, London, 1856; University Microfilms, Ann Arbor, Mich., 1968.
2. Charles Ammi Cutter, *Rules for a Dictionary Catalog*, 4th ed., Government Printing Office, Washington, D.C., 1904, 173 pp.; and *Rules for a Printed Dictionary Catalog*, Government Printing Office, Washington, D.C., 1876, 89 pp.
3. *List of Subject Headings for Use in Dictionary Catalogs*, American Library Association, Chicago, 1911.
4. U.S. Library of Congress, Subject Cataloging Division, *Subject Headings Used in the Dictionary Catalogs of the Library of Congress*, Government Printing Office, Library Branch, Washington, D.C.: 1st ed., 1897; 2nd ed., 1919 (2 vols.); 3rd ed., 1928; 4th ed., 1943 (2 vols.); 5th ed., 1948; 6th ed., 1956; 7th ed., 1966; 8th ed., 1975 (2 vols.).
5. Carlyle James Frarey, *Subject Heading Revision by the Library of Congress, 1941–1950*, University of Rochester Press for the Association of College and Reference Libraries, Rochester, N.Y., 1954, 97 pp.
6. U.S. Library of Congress, Subject Cataloging Division, Processing Department, *Supplement to LC Subject Headings*, Library of Congress, Washington, D.C. (Supplements to each edition recording additions and changes are published as much as 2 years before the publication date—for the eighth edition, January 1974.)
7. David Judson Haykin, *Subject Headings, a Practical Guide*, Government Printing Office, Washington, D.C., 1951.
8. Jay Elwood Daily, *The Grammar of Subject Headings: A Formulation of Rules for Subject Headings Based on Syntactical and Morphological Analysis of the Library of Congress List*, Columbia University, New York, 1957.
9. Carlyle J. Frarey, "Subject Headings," in *Cataloging and Classification* (Maurice Falcolm Tauber, ed.), Graduate School of Library Service, Rutgers–The State University, New Brunswick, N.J., 1960.
10. Oliver Linton Lilley, *Terminology, Form, Specificity and the Syndetic Structure of Subject Headings for English Literature*, Columbia University, New York, 1958.
11. Muhammad Muhammad Aman, *Analysis of Terminology, Form and Structure of Subject Headings in Arabic Literature, and Formulation of Rules for Arabic Subject Headings*, University of Pittsburgh, Pittsburgh, 1968.
12. Hooshang Ebrami, *Catchword Indexing, Subject Headings and Chain Indexing: The Formulation of Rules for Subject Analysis in Farsi*, University of Pittsburgh, Pittsburgh, 1970.
13. George Sinkankas, *An Investigation and Comparison of Three Associative Systems in a General Subject Heading List*, University of Pittsburgh, Pittsburgh, 1974.
14. Gertrude Soonj Lee Koh, *The Semantic Problems of Translated Subject Headings Exemplified in the List of the Korean Subject Headings*, University of Pittsburgh, Pittsburgh, 1977.
15. Jessica Lee Harris, *Subject Headings: Factors Influencing Formation and Choice; with Special Reference to Library of Congress and H. W. Wilson Practice*, Columbia University, New York, 1969.

16. Lois Chen, " 'American Poetry' but 'Satire, American': The Direct and Inverted Forms of Subject Headings Containing National Adjectives," *Lib. Resources Tech. Serv.*, **17**, 330–339 (Summer 1973).
17. Minnie Earle Sears, ed., *List of Subject Headings for Small Libraries, Compiled from Lists Used in Nine Representative Small Libraries,* H. W. Wilson, New York: 1st ed., 1923; 2nd ed., 1926; 3rd ed., 1933; 4th ed., 1939 (edited by Isabel Stevenson Monro); 5th ed., 1944; *Sears List of Subject Headings,* H. W. Wilson, New York: 6th ed., 1950; 7th ed., 1954; 8th ed., 1959 (6th–8th eds. edited by Bertha Margaret Frick); *List of Subject Headings,* H. W. Wilson, New York: 9th ed., 1965; 10th ed., 1972; 11th ed., 1977 (9th–11th eds. edited by Barbara Marietta Wesby).
18. George M. Sinkankas, *A Study in the Syndetic Structure of the Library of Congress List of Subject Headings,* University of Pittsburgh, Graduate School of Library and Information Sciences, Pittsburgh, 1972.
19. James G. Williams, Martha L. Manheimer, and Jay E. Daily, *Classified Library of Congress Subject Headings,* Dekker, New York, 1972.
20. Sinkankas, Ref. *18,* pp. 59–60.
21. Constance May Mellot, *Analysis of an Alphabetical Special Subject Heading List to Determine Elements of Classification,* University of Pittsburgh, Pittsburgh, 1977.
22. Jay E. Daily, "Many Changes, No Alteration," *Lib. J.,* **92**, 3961–3963 (November 1, 1967).
23. Pauline Atherton, [Review of *Classified Library of Congress Subject Headings*], *Lib. J.,* **98**, 1895–1896 (June 1973).
24. *List of Subject Headings for Use in Dictionary Catalogs,* American Library Association, Chicago, 1911.
25. Martha Lose Manheimer, *The Applicability of the NASA Thesaurus to the File of Documents Indexed Prior to Its Publication,* University of Pittsburgh, Pittsburgh, 1969.
26. Daily, Ref. *8,* Appendix 3.
27. John Phillip Immroth, *Analysis of Vocabulary Control in Library of Congress Classification and Subject Headings,* Research Studies in Library Science, No. 3, Libraries Unlimited, Littleton, Colo., 1971, 172 pp.

15
Thesaurus

Douglas J. Foskett / University of London Library, London, England

The word *thesaurus* derives from Greek and Latin words which mean "a treasury," and it has been used for several centuries to mean a lexicon or treasury of words. An interesting and entertaining historical account has been given by Karen Sparck Jones, who traces the origins of "synonymy" in dictionaries and identifies the main difference from natural language: the thesaurus involves "vocabulary normalisation" (*1*). Modern usage may be said to date from 1852, when the first edition of the *Thesaurus of English Words and Phrases* was published by Peter Mark Roget. His subtitle reads: "classified and arranged so as to facilitate the expression of ideas and to assist in literary composition." The value and importance of *Roget* may be judged from the fact that new editions have appeared regularly right up to the present day. The addition of "and phrases" in the title has great significance, as anyone knows who has used *Roget* for literary composition; and it is also significant in a discussion of the role of the thesaurus in information storage and retrieval.

This role began in earnest in the early 1950s, particularly through the work of Hans Peter Luhn. Luhn himself was clear about the relation of his own use of the word to that of Roget, but the confused way in which the idea was applied by several others was pointed out in 1960 by B. C. Vickery, who showed that at least four different meanings were used in the literature of information science at that time. The most common interpretation was as an alphabetical list of single words, with related words listed under each, in various ways. Since then, attempts have been made to tidy up this situation, and the definition used here is that of the World Science Information System of UNESCO, known as UNISIST:

From Foskett, Douglas J. *Thesaurus.* ENCYCLOPEDIA OF LIBRARY AND INFORMATION SCIENCE. Vol. 30. Edited by Allen Kent, Harold Lancour, and Jay E. Daily. Assistant Editor, William Z. Nasri. New York, Marcel Dekker, Inc., c1980. pp. 416-462.

Thesaurus

A thesaurus may be defined either in terms of its function or its structure.

In terms of function, a thesaurus is a terminological control device used in translating from the natural language of documents, indexers or users into a more constrained "system language" (documentation language, information language).

In terms of structure, a thesaurus is a controlled and dynamic vocabulary of semantically and generically related terms which covers a specific domain of knowledge.

Roget's own thesaurus is very far from being a simple alphabetical list of words; the main structure is in fact the list of words and phrases set out in a series of categories defined in very general terms such as Existence, Quantity, Time, Space, Matter, Intellect, and Sentient and Moral Powers. Each of these categories has a number of subdivisions, each containing several words. Each word is identified by an arabic numeral, and below it are listed all the synonyms and other related words and phrases which concern the same concept. Under Space, for example, we find the subdivision "relative space," which includes the following entry:

183. **Situation** — *N.* situation, position, locality, locale, status, latitude and longitude; standpoint, post; aspect, attitude, posture, pose.

place, site, base, station, seat, venue, whereabout, environment, neighbourhood; bearings, &c. 278; spot &c. 182.

top- ge-ography; map &c. 554.

V. be-situated, -situate; lie; have its seat in.

Adj. situ-ate, -ated; local, topical, topographical &c. *n.*

Adv. in situ; here and there; here-, there-, where-abouts; in place, here, there.

As can be seen, each of the words and phrases listed under each term heading is assigned to a grammatical category: noun, verb, adjective, and adverb. Following the section that lists all the terms in categories there is a second list of all these terms in alphabetical order; under each term in this section there appears a list of related terms with different category numbers. The heading term also appears in those categories, according to its various shades of meaning:

position
circumstances 8
term 71
situation 183
proposition 514
assertion 535
situation
circumstances 8
place 183
location 184
business 625
out of a — 185

Thus *Roget's Thesaurus* is a classification scheme for terms with a relative alphabetical index. It can be seen at once that its value consists in being a structure for relating concepts to one another through their various meanings; this is what makes *Roget* familiar to all concerned with the quality of style in writing. As Roget put it in his own original introduction, he did not set out to provide a dictionary but a structure of concepts in which:

> ... the idea being given, to find the word or words by which that idea may be most fitly and aptly expressed. For this purpose, the words and phrases of the language are here classed, not according to their sound or their orthography, but strictly according to their signification.

The use of a thesaurus in modern information storage and retrieval systems has not been so much for the purpose of finding fit and apt means of expression as for controlling a vocabulary in the process of analysis of information. According to Mary Elizabeth Stevens, in her biographical note on Luhn, he was thinking about "families of notions" as early as 1951 (2). He certainly advanced this idea in his work at the Research Center of the I.B.M. Corporation, where he was looking for a simple way of using a computer to record a system of authorized words for use in subject indexing, with a regular structure of cross-references. His paper of 1957, "A Statistical Approach to Mechanised Literature Searching," is usually held to be the first published expression of this opinion, and in it he specifically states:

> The procedure to be described is similar to the one used by P M Roget for compiling his Thesaurus for English Words. . . . the third step is a preparation of a card index for all transcribed sentences. A concordance that can then be worked out with the aid of these cards will result in the grouping of words of similar or related meaning into "notional families." This is so similar to the work required for the creation of Roget's thesaurus that basic organization of his book may well serve as the skeleton for this process (3, p. 89a).

Most of the modern thesauri, on the other hand, began by making the alphabetical list the major element; in the early days, some had no listing in categories at all. But it was soon found that even in a computerized system some kind of classificatory structure was an advantage for both indexer and searcher, and consequently there have been introduced arrangements of terms in categories for most of the more recent thesauri. There is now an enormous literature on the subject, including several books; in English, there are works of an introductory nature by Jean Aitchison and Alan Gilchrist (4, 5), and a vast, encyclopedic survey by Dagobert Soergel (6). All of these can be strongly recommended. The journal *International Classification* has as its subtitle "Journal on Theory and Practice of Universal and Special Classification Systems and Thesauri," and a review of recent work has been made by F. W. Lancaster (7).

Even if the modern thesaurus does on occasion help an author to find an appropriate or felicitous word and therefore enhance his style, its primary object is to act as an indexing language for use in information storage and retrieval. Any such language must be based on the literature of the subject field which it sets out to cover; it must be able to accommodate all the terms found in that literature, and this will certainly include many words that are not germane to that field but belong to marginal fields. Although this causes trouble for indexers and searchers, it is nonetheless a reflection of the nature of knowledge itself, which is of course not neatly divided into self-contained and mutually exclusive compartments but is an intricate mesh of ideas which react with other ideas; each individual person has such an intricate network stored in his brain, derived from his unique set of experiences. It is for this reason that any index language must contain as many guides to related concepts as are necessary to cope with the many different "patterns of knowledge" that already exist in the heads of the indexers and searchers who use that index language. Such a scheme of words must be a growing organism, always subject to revision, and thus there must be some means for introducing new words and concepts at appropriate places. This particular need has always been advanced as the strongest argument in favor of the simple alphabetical list, on the grounds that any such new word can easily be inserted in its correct place in the alphabetical order. Against this must be set the fact that this applies only to a single-language system, whereas the growing need today is for multilingual thesauri which can be used in several different countries. In addition, unless an index has some form of structure, a user will have no means of knowing whether he has selected the correct term when making or consulting the index. Even with a structure, it is still somewhat cumbersome to pursue a train of references in alphabetical indexes. For example, the article "Nine Years' Toxicity Control in Insecticide Plants," from *Index Medicus* though not indexed under either "toxicity" or "toxicology," may still be traced from the cross-reference from "toxicology" to "poisons," despite the fact that the article is not indexed under "poisons" either; the explanation is that in this index "poisons" stands next to "poisoning" and it is here that the article is actually indexed. This is a cumbersome and chancy process, but there is a path to be found if the searcher thinks to look for it and takes the trouble to follow up the trail of cross-references.

Purpose of a Thesaurus

The major purposes of a thesaurus include the following:

1. To provide a map of a given field of knowledge, indicating how concepts or ideas about concepts are related to one another, which helps an indexer or a searcher to understand the structure of the field.
2. To provide a standard vocabulary for a given subject field which will ensure that indexers are consistent when they are making index entries to an information storage and retrieval system.
3. To provide a system of references between terms which will ensure that only one term from a set of synonyms is used for indexing one concept, and that indexers and searchers are told which of the set is the one chosen; and to provide guides to terms which are related to any index term in other ways, either by classification structure or otherwise in the literature.
4. To provide a guide for users of the system so that they choose the correct term for a subject search; this stresses the importance of cross-references. If an indexer uses more than one synonym in the same index—for example, "abroad," "foreign," and "overseas"—then documents are liable to be indexed haphazardly under all of these; a searcher who chooses one and finds documents indexed there will assume that he has found the correct term and will stop his search without knowing that there are other useful documents indexed under the other synonyms.
5. To locate new concepts in a scheme of relationships with existing concepts in a way which makes sense to users of the system.
6. To provide classified hierarchies so that a search can be broadened or narrowed systematically, if the first choice of search terms produces either too few or too many references to the material in the store.
7. A desirable purpose, but one which it would be premature to say is being achieved, is to provide a means by which the use of terms in a given subject field may be standardized.

In practice, the use of a controlled vocabulary to make subject indexes in libraries is by no means new. Lists of "subject headings," such as those of Minnie E. Sears and the Library of Congress, have been in popular use since the 19th century. E. J. Coates has made an analysis of some of them in his book *Subject Catalogues: Headings and Structure* (8), showing how imperfect is the relationship between the Library of Congress list and its own classification scheme. On the whole, such lists were designed as aids to indexing only—that is, with the compiler of an index in mind, rather than a searcher. Naturally, an indexer would take on the role of a searcher when consulting the subject catalog to ensure that a new book would be entered under the same headings as previous books on the same subject. It is surprising, therefore, that the modern development of the thesaurus, with much the same objectives, should originate from users rather than from librarians. Significant features were that it happened in the area of scientific and technical literature and in institutions having easy access to computers, with their ability to process large amounts of data in a very short time. Searches carried out in such circumstances demanded ready access to highly specific subjects with many facets. If we take the relatively simple article mentioned earlier, "Nine Years' Toxicity Control in Insecticide Plants," it will be clear that this might be approached from at least four different directions: toxicity (poisons, poisoning, health, hygiene), control (measurement, restriction), insecticide (insects, pests, infestation), and plants (factories, industry, production). Approaches beginning with any one of these words should lead the searcher to this particular article.

It will also be clear that using only one facet will bring the searcher a large number of documents from the collection, and that many of them will not be helpful. The search must be narrowed down by coordinate indexing. The order in which the words are arranged has considerable significance too, because a searcher will not be looking for documents which deal with, for example, the control of toxicity of insecticides in plants, a subject in the same general area of knowledge but not the same specific subject.

A thesaurus which acts efficiently as a controlled language for indexing and retrieval therefore has to provide specific terms, general terms to which the specific terms are related, and a secondary network of other terms which may from time to time be related in the subject literature. It is, in fact, an improved version of the "list of subject headings," and in at least one case, the Medical Subject Headings (MESH) used in the MEDLARS scheme of the National Library of Medicine, the present thesaurus has grown out of the original list and continues to use the same title.

It should be noted that not everyone agrees on the need for a controlled vocabulary in information storage and retrieval. At a symposium on "A Comprehensive On-line Computer System for Special Libraries" held at the Building Research Station in England in December 1974, H. H. Neville and his colleagues announced their intention of moving over to a "natural language system" (9)—mainly on the grounds that controlled-language systems are becoming ever more elaborate, need increasing amounts of staff time at input, and perform no better in retrieval. A middle road has some advocates: "free language entry," that is, a system with no restriction on the number of terms in use and with a minimal structure of references to cope with synonyms and similar close relationships. There seems to be little difference between this and the "list of subject headings" used in most libraries.

Yet the fact remains that more and more organizations are compiling thesauri and continue to find them useful, to the extent that several "guidelines" for construction have been published: Guidelines for monolingual and for multilingual thesauri have been produced by UNISIST (*10*), and the British Standards Institution has completed a draft specification. Most of the organizations which have published a thesaurus have included information on its structure and use, and two international centers for collecting thesauri have been set up, at Case Western Reserve University in the United States and at the Central Institute for Scientific, Technical, and Economic Information in Warsaw. Each of these centers now holds several hundred examples, and new ones are reported in every issue of the *FID/CR Newsletter* published by the Documentation Research and Training Center of the Indian Statistical Institute in Bangalore.

In this article, therefore, no attempt is made to give a complete list or even to cite all the major thesauri; a selection is provided, and anyone wanting to use a thesaurus for their own field will be well advised to consult one of the centers to find out whether any example already exists.

Format

A thesaurus usually has at least two major parts: (*a*) a list of words grouped systematically into sets or categories, now often called "facets," in each of which all the words have some intrinsic relation to each other (such as chemical elements, mammals, industrial occupations, and member states of the United Nations); and (*b*) an alphabetical list, which may take more than one form, of all the terms from all the categories, with a notation which refers each term to the category of which it is a member. C. van der Merwe, in his *Thesaurus of Sociological Research Terminology*, published by Rotterdam University, expresses this relation thus:

> This combination of a systematic classification scheme and a controlled index language determines the structure of the thesaurus. Although an alphabetical index of terms has been added as an extra aid, the thesaurus in a more narrow sense consists of terms that have been arranged in a logical order by subject rather than in an alphabetical order (*11*, p. 7).

The relative importance of these two parts varies greatly from one thesaurus to another, and in some cases the principles on which the categories are based are far from clear.

The *Thesaurus of Engineering and Scientific Terms* (TEST), one of the largest and best known, covers a very wide range of subjects, as its name implies (*12*). It was produced as a cooperative effort between the Engineers Joint Council and the Department of Defense of the United States, and its object is "to produce a comprehensive thesaurus of scientific and technical terms for use as a basic reference in information storage and retrieval systems and to provide a vocabulary groundwork by means of which the interchange of information might be enhanced" (*12*, p. 1). In addition to compiling a data bank of some 150,000 terms, an important early step was the formulation of rules and conventions; these were first published as the *Manual for Building a Technical Thesaurus* (ONR-55) by the Office of Naval Research and were later included as an appendix to the printed TEST. These are commonsense rules and have been followed to a greater or lesser degree by several other compilers; they are, however, somewhat less detailed than later examples such as the *UNISIST Guidelines*. The major part of TEST is the alphabetical list, which is actually called "Thesaurus of Terms," as distinct from the other sections: "Permuted Index," "Subject Category Index," and "Hierarchical Index." There is much duplication between these groups, especially the Thesaurus of Terms and the Permuted Index. Since the Thesaurus of Terms includes entries for "vocational guidance" and "vocational interests," for example, it is hard to see the necessity for entries of "vocational guidance" and "vocational interests" under "vocational" in the Permuted Index. The Subject Category Fields and Groups include those shown in Figure 1, and although these categories are identified by subject, they are in fact arranged in alphabetical order (with the exception of No. 10); the subgroups are likewise alphabetical, without regard for closely related subjects. Some subgroups appear more than once, but not consistently; for example:

05 09 Personnel selection, training, and evaluation
06 14 Personnel selection and maintenance (medical)

Such a subgroup could better be treated only once, in 05 09, or alternatively, in every category where personnel are involved. It could also be given the same subgroup number in each category.

A similar type of arrangement can be found in the thesaurus of the American Psychological Association (APA), which has three sections: "Relationship Section," "Rotated Alphabetical Terms Section," and "Postable Terms and Term Codes Section." Extracts from the three sections of the APA thesaurus are given in Figures 2, 3, and 4 (*13*). Duplication between the Relationship Section and the Rotated Alphabetical Terms Section is reduced by not including in the latter those terms which are not to be used for indexing documents—like "concept (self)," "conditioned reflex," and "conditioning (classical)," from all of which there are references to the term which is to be used. As in TEST, the normal sequence of terms is alphabetical. In the second edition of the APA thesaurus, some 180 terms have been deleted because an analysis showed that they had never been used as access points to the psychological literature in the cumulated machine-readable data base of *Psychological Abstracts* (PA). The new Rotated Alphabetical Terms Section includes terms having several words, listed in alphabetical sequence under each word in turn. The Postable Terms and Term Codes Section replaces the former alphabetical section and includes the numeric codes for each term from the PA data base.

If the compiler follows the principles of facet analysis, the place of each term should be easy to see, since the facets will be based on a logical approach to the subject field. Probably the best-known example of this is the *Thesaurofacet*, compiled by Jean Aitchison and her colleagues for the English Electric Company (*14*). This is certainly one of the most thoroughgoing and successful attempts to construct for a thesaurus a detailed and systematic analysis or classification of a very

Thesaurus

Subject Category Fields and Groups

01   Aeronautics
    *01 01
    01 02 Aeronautics
    01 03 Aircraft
    01 04 Aircraft flight instrumentation
    01 05 Air facilities

02   Agriculture
    02 01 Agricultural chemistry
    02 02 Agricultural economics
    02 03 Agricultural engineering
    02 04 Agronomy and horticulture
    02 05 Animal husbandry
    02 06 Forestry

03   Astronomy and astrophysics
    03 01 Astronomy
    03 02 Astrophysics
    03 03 Celestial mechanics

04   Atmospheric sciences
    04 01 Atmospheric physics
    04 02 Meteorology

05   Behavioral and social sciences
    05 01 Administration and management
    *05 02 Information sciences
    05 03 Economics
    05 04 History, law, and political science
    05 05 Human factors engineering
    05 06 Humanities
    05 07 Linguistics
    *05 08
    05 09 Personnel selection, training, and evaluation
    *05 10 Psychology
    05 11 Sociology

06   Biological and medical sciences
    06 01 Biochemistry
    06 02 Bioengineering
    06 03 Biology
    06 04 Bionics
    06 05 Clinical medicine
    06 06 Environmental biology
    06 07 Escape, rescue, and survival
    06 08 Food
    06 09 Hygiene and sanitation
    *06 10
    06 11 Life support
    *06 12 Medical equipment and supplies
    06 13 Microbiology
    06 14 Personnel selection and maintenance (medical)
    06 15 Pharmacology
    06 16 Physiology
    06 17 Protective equipment
    06 18 Radiobiology
    06 19 Stress physiology
    06 20 Toxicology
    06 21 Weapon effects

07   Chemistry
    07 01 Chemical engineering
    07 02 Inorganic chemistry
    07 03 Organic chemistry
    *07 04 Physical and general chemistry
    07 05 Radio and radiation chemistry

08   Earth sciences and oceanography
    08 01 Biological oceanography
    08 02 Cartography
    08 03 Dynamic oceanography
    08 04 Geochemistry
    08 05 Geodesy
    08 06 Geography
    08 07 Geology and mineralogy
    08 08 Hydrology and limnology
    08 09 Mining engineering
    08 10 Physical oceanography
    08 11 Seismology
    08 12 Snow, ice and permafrost
    08 13 Soil mechanics
    *08 14 Geomagnetism

09   Electronics and electrical engineering
    09 01 Components
    09 02 Computers
    09 03 Electronic and electrical engineering
    09 04 Information theory
    09 05 Subsystems
    09 06 Telemetry

*10   Nonpropulsive energy conversion
    10 01 Conversion techniques
    10 02 Power sources
    10 03 Energy storage

11   Materials
    11 01 Adhesives and seals
    11 02 Ceramics, refractories, and glasses
    11 03 Coatings, colorants, and finishes
    11 04 Composite materials
    11 05 Fibers and textiles
    *11 06 Metals
    11 07 Miscellaneous materials
    11 08 Oils, lubricants, and hydraulic fluids
    11 09 Plastics

FIGURE 1. *Extract from TEST.*
Reproduced by permission of the Engineers Joint Council.

RELATIONSHIP SECTION

Community

Community Welfare Services — (Continued)
    Welfare Services (Government)
  Related Business Organizations

Companies
  Use Business Organizations

Comparative Psychology
  Broader Psychology
    Sciences
    Social Sciences

Compatibility (Interpersonal)
  Use Interpersonal Compatibility

Compensation (Defense Mechanism)
  Broader Defense Mechanisms

Compensatory Education
  Broader Curriculum
    Education/
  Related Educational Programs

Competition
  Broader Social Behavior

Complex (Electra)
  Use Electra Complex

Complex (Oedipal)
  Use Oedipal Complex

Complexity (Cognitive)
  Use Cognitive Complexity

Complexity (Stimulus)
  Use Stimulus Complexity

Complexity (Task)
  Use Task Complexity

Compliance
  Broader Social Behavior

Comprehension
  Used for Understanding
  Narrower Listening Comprehension
    Number Comprehension
    Reading Comprehension
    Sentence Comprehension
  Related Meaning
    Meaningfulness

Comprehension Tests
  Related Measurement/

Compressed Speech
  Broader Speech Processing (Mechanical)
    Verbal Communication

Compulsions
  Narrower Compulsive Repetition
  Related Mental Disorders/

Compulsions — (Continued)
  Related Obsessions
    Obsessive Compulsive Neurosis
    Obsessive Compulsive Personality

Compulsive Neurosis
  Use Obsessive Compulsive Neurosis

Compulsive Repetition
  Used for Repetition (Compulsive)
  Broader Compulsions

Computer Applications
  Narrower Computer Assisted Diagnosis
    Computer Assisted Instruction
    Computer Simulation
  Related Computers

Computer Assisted Diagnosis
  Broader Computer Applications
    Diagnosis
  Related Medical Diagnosis
    Psychodiagnosis

Computer Assisted Instruction
  Used for Instruction (Computer Assisted)
  Broader Computer Applications
    Teaching
  Related Teaching Methods
    Individualized Instruction
    Programed Instruction
    Teaching Machines

Computer Programing Languages
  Used for FORTRAN
    Programing Languages (Computer)
  Related Computers
    Data Processing

Computer Programs
  Use Computer Software

Computer Simulation
  Broader Computer Applications
    Simulation
  Related Simulation Games

Computer Software
  Used for Computer Programs
    Programing (Computer)
  Related Computers
    Data Processing
    Systems/

Computers
  Broader Apparatus
  Narrower Analog Computers
    Digital Computers
  Related Automation

Computers — (Continued)
  Related Computer Applications
    Computer Programing Languages
    Computer Software
    Cybernetics
    Data Processing
    Systems/

Concentration Camps
  Used for Camps (Concentration)
  Related Correctional Institutions

Concept (Self)
  Use Self Concept

Concept Formation
  Used for Conceptualization
  Broader Cognitive Processes
  Related Concepts
    Conservation (Concept)
    Egocentrism

Concept Learning
  Narrower Nonreversal Shift Learning
    Reversal Shift Learning
  Related Concepts
    Learning/

Concepts
  Used for Information (Concepts)
  Related Concept Formation
    Concept Learning
    Information/

Conceptual Imagery
  Used for Imagery (Conceptual)
  Broader Imagery
  Related Imagination

Conceptualization
  Use Concept Formation

Concussion (Brain)
  Use Brain Concussion

Conditioned Emotional Responses
  Used for CER (Conditioning)
  Broader Classical Conditioning
    Conditioned Responses
    Conditioning
    Emotional Responses
    Operant Conditioning
    Responses

Conditioned Inhibition
  Use Conditioned Suppression

Conditioned Reflex
  Use Conditioned Responses

FIGURE 2. *Extract from the Relationship Section of the* Thesaurus of Psychological Index Terms. *Reproduced by permission of the American Psychological Association.*

ROTATED ALPHABETICAL TERMS SECTION

Obstetrical	**Complications**	Atmospheric	**Conditions**
Postsurgical	**Complications** (Physical)	Working	**Conditions**
	Comprehension	Bone	**Conduction** Audiometry
	Comprehension Tests		**Cones** (Eye)
Listening	**Comprehension**		**Confabulation**
Number	**Comprehension**		**Conference** Proceedings
Reading	**Comprehension**		**Confession** (Religion)
Sentence	**Comprehension**		**Confidence** Limits (Statistics)
	Compressed Speech		**Conflict**
	Compulsions	Marital	**Conflict**
	Compulsive Repetition	Role	**Conflicts**
Obsessive	**Compulsive** Neurosis		**Conformity** (Personality)
Obsessive	**Compulsive** Personality	Mental	**Confusion**
	Computer Applications		**Congenital** Disorders
	Computer Assisted Diagnosis	Drug Induced	**Congenital** Disorders
	Computer Assisted Instruction		**Congenitally** Handicapped
	Computer Programing Languages	Self	**Congruence**
	Computer Simulation		**Conjoint** Therapy
	Computer Software		**Connective** Tissue Cells
	Computers		**Connective** Tissues
Analog	**Computers**		**Connotations**
Digital	**Computers**		**Consanguineous** Marriage
	Concentration Camps		**Conscience**
	Concept Formation		**Conscious** (Personality Factors)
	Concept Learning		**Consciousness** Disturbances
Conservation	**(Concept)**		**Consciousness** Raising Groups
Self	**Concept**		**Consciousness** States
Temporal Spatial	**Concept** Scale		**Conservation** (Concept)
Tennessee Self	**Concept** Scale		**Conservation** (Ecological Behavior)
	Concepts		**Conservatism**
God	**Concepts**	Political	**Conservatism**
Mathematics	**(Concepts)**	Wilson Patterson	**Conservatism** Scale
	Conceptual Imagery		**Consistency** (Measurement)
Brain	**Concussion**		**Consonants**
	Conditioned Emotional Responses		**Constipation**
	Conditioned Responses	Test	**Construction**
	Conditioned Stimulus	Mental Health	**Consultation**
	Conditioned Suppression	Professional	**Consultation**
	Conditioning		**Consumer** Attitudes
Avoidance	**Conditioning**		**Consumer** Behavior
Classical	**Conditioning**		**Consumer** Protection
Escape	**Conditioning**		**Consumer** Psychology
Eyelid	**Conditioning**		**Consumer** Research
Operant	**Conditioning**		**Consumer** Surveys

FIGURE 3. *Extract from the Rotated Alphabetical Terms Section of the* Thesaurus of Psychological Index Terms. *Reproduced by permission of the American Psychological Association.*

large subject area, engineering—using the technique of facet analysis and deriving the whole of the alphabetical listing from the classification schedules. Figure 5 shows how the two parts of the *Thesaurofacet* complement each other and contrasts the amount of information given by this relationship with that provided by the type of entry found in more conventional systems.

Experience has proved, therefore, that in order to provide maximum efficiency and ease of use, a thesaurus should have at least two major parts, the systematic and the alphabetical, and in fact there are many thesauri which have more than two parts. The extra ones usually turn out to be variations on the two basic forms.

POSTABLE TERMS AND TERM CODES SECTION

09920	Cobalt	11040	Conceptual Imagery	12390	Creativity Measurement
09930	Cocaine	11070	Conditioned Emotional Responses	12400	Credibility
09940	Cochlea	11090	Conditioned Responses	12430	Crime
09950	Cochran Q Test	11100	Conditioned Stimulus	12440	Criminal Conviction
09960	Cockroaches	11110	Conditioned Suppression	12450	Criminal Law
09970	Codeine	11120	Conditioning	12460	Criminals
10000	Coeducation	11190	Cones (Eye)	12470	Criminology
10040	Cognition	11200	Confabulation	12490	Crises
10050	Cognitive Ability	11210	Conference Proceedings	12510	Crisis Intervention
10060	Cognitive Complexity	11220	Confession (Religion)	12520	Crisis Intervention Services
10070	Cognitive Contiguity	11230	Confidence Limits (Statistics)	12530	Critical Flicker Fusion Threshold
10080	Cognitive Development	11250	Conflict	12540	Criticism
10090	Cognitive Discrimination	11270	Conformity (Personality)	12570	Crocodilians
10100	Cognitive Dissonance	11290	Congenital Disorders	12590	Cross Cultural Differences
10110	Cognitive Generalization	11300	Congenitally Handicapped	12610 †	Crowding
10120	Cognitive Mediation	11310	Conjoint Therapy	12620	Cruelty
10130	Cognitive Processes	11320	Connective Tissue Cells	12630	Crustacea
10140	Cognitive Style	11330	Connective Tissues	12640	Crying
10150	Cohabitation	11340	Connotations	12650	Crying Cat Syndrome
10200	Cold Effects	11350	Consanguineous Marriage	12670	Cuba
10220	Colitis	11360	Conscience	12680	Cues
10230	Coll Ent Exam Bd Scholastic Apt Test	11370	Conscious (Personality Factors)	12690	Cultism
10250	Collective Behavior	11380	Consciousness Disturbances	12700	Cultural Assimilation
10260	College Academic Achievement	11387 †	Consciousness Raising Groups	12710	Cultural Deprivation
10290	College Dropouts	11390	Consciousness States	12730	Cultural Test Bias
10300	College Environment	11400	Conservation (Concept)	12750	Culture (Anthropological)
10320	College Students	11403 †	Conservation (Ecological Behavior)	12760	Culture Change
10330	College Teachers	11405	Conservatism	12770	Culture Fair Intelligence Test
10350	Colleges	11420	Consistency (Measurement)	12780	Culture Shock
10370	Colon Disorders	11430	Consonants	12790	Curare
10380	Color	11440	Constipation	12800	Curiosity
10390	Color Blindness	11470	Consumer Attitudes	12810	Curriculum
10400	Color Perception	11480	Consumer Behavior	12820	Curriculum Development
10410	Color Pyramid Test	11490	Consumer Protection	12830	Cursive Writing
10430	Colostomy	11500	Consumer Psychology	12840	Cushings Syndrome
10440	Columbia Mental Maturity Scale	11510	Consumer Research	12850	Cutaneous Sense
10450	Coma	11520	Consumer Surveys	12860	Cybernetics
10470	Commissioned Officers	11540	Contact Lenses	12875 †	Cyclic Adenosine Monophosphate
10480	Commitment (Psychiatric)	11548 †	Content Analysis	12880	Cycloheximide
10510	Communes	11550	Content Analysis (Test)	12890	Cyclothymic Personality
10540	Communication Skills	11560	Contextual Associations	12900	Cynicism
10550	Communication Systems	11580	Contingency Management	12910	Cysteine
10560	Communication Theory	11630	Contraceptive Devices	12920	Cytochrome Oxidase
10570	Communication/	11710	Conversation	12930	Cytology
10580	Communications Media	11730	Conversion Neurosis	12940	Cytoplasm
10590	Communism	11750	Convulsions	12950	Czechoslovakia
10600	Communities	11756 †	Cooperating Teachers		
10620	Community Attitudes	11760	Cooperation		
10627	Community College Students	11790	Coping Behavior	12970	Dance
10630 †	Community Colleges	11800	Copper	12980	Dance Therapy
10640	Community Facilities	11830	Cornea	12990	Dark Adaptation
10647	Community Mental Health	11860	Coronary Thromboses	13000	Darwinism
10650	Community Mental Health Centers	11900	Corpus Callosum	13020	Data Processing
10658 †	Community Mental Health Services	11910	Correctional Institutions	13040	Daughters
10660	Community Mental Health Training	11980	Cortical Evoked Potentials	13070	Day Care Centers
10670	Community Psychiatry	12000	Corticosteroids	13080	Daydreaming
10680	Community Psychology	12010	Corticosterone	13090	DDT (Insecticide)
10690	Community Services	12020	Corticotropin	13100	Deaf
10700	Community Welfare Services	12040	Cortisone	13110	Death and Dying
10720	Comparative Psychology	12045	Costs and Cost Analysis	13115 †	Death Anxiety
10740	Compensation (Defense Mechanism)	12070	Counseling Psychology	13120	Death Attitudes
10745	Compensatory Education	12080	Counseling/	13150	Death Rites
10750	Competition	12090	Counselor Attitudes	13160	Decarboxylases
10810	Compliance	12100	Counselor Characteristics	13166 †	Decentralization
10820	Comprehension	12120	Counselor Education	13170	Deception
10830	Comprehension Tests	12150	Counselor Role	13180	Decerebration
10840	Compressed Speech	12160	Counselor Trainees	13190	Decision Making
10850	Compulsions	12170	Counselors	13200	Decompression Effects
10890	Compulsive Repetition	12180	Counterconditioning	13210	Decortication (Brain)
10900	Computer Applications	12190	Countertransference	13230	Deer
10910	Computer Assisted Diagnosis	12195	Countries	13240	Defecation
10920	Computer Assisted Instruction	12210	Courage	13250	Defense Mechanisms
10930	Computer Programming Languages	12215 †	Course Evaluation	13260	Defensiveness
10950	Computer Simulation	12260	Cousins	13290	Dehydrogenases
10960	Computer Software	12300	Crabs	13297 †	Delay of Gratification
10970	Computers	12310	Crafts	13300	Delayed Auditory Feedback
10980	Concentration Camps	12330	Cranial Nerves	13310	Delayed Development
11000	Concept Formation	12340	Cranial Spinal Cord	13320	Delayed Feedback
11010	Concept Learning	12360	Crayfish	13340	Deletion (Chromosome)
11030	Concepts	12380	Creativity	13360	Delirium

† New term added in 1978

FIGURE 4. *Extract from the Postable Terms and Term Codes Section of the* Thesaurus of Psychological Index Terms. *Reproduced by permission of the American Psychological Association.*

THE COMPLEMENTARY PARTS OF THE THESAUROFACET

i) Thesaurus entry

Information not in classification schedules

	Television Camera Tubes	MCE *Class number*
UF	Camera tubes (television)	
	Emitrons	
	Iconoscopes	
	Image iconoscopes	
	Image orthicons	
	Orthicons	
	Pick up tubes (television)	
	Vidicons	
RT	Photomultipliers	
	Phototubes	
	Television cameras	
BT(A)	Television apparatus	

ii) Classification schedules

Information not in Thesaurus
Related terms (RT):
  (i) Image converter tubes
  (ii) Image intensifiers
  (iii) Storage tubes
  (iv) Television picture tubes
  (v) Television colour picture tubes
Narrower terms (NT):
  Television colour camera tubes
Broader terms (BT):
  (i) Cathode ray tubes
  (ii) Electron beam deflection tubes
  (iii) Electron tubes

M	*ELECTRONIC ENGINEERING*	
MA	**ELECTRON TUBES** (Cont'd) *BT*	
MBT	Electron beam deflection tubes *BT*	
MBV	Indicator tubes (tuning)	
MBW	Trochotrons	
MC	Cathode ray tubes *BT*	
MC2	*RT* { Image converter tubes	
MC4	Image intensifiers	
MC6	Storage tubes	
MCE	**Television camera tubes**	
MCI	Television colour camera tubes *NT*	
MCL	*RT* { Television picture tubes	
MCO	Television colour picture tubes	
MCQ	X ray tubes	

CONVENTIONAL THESAURUS ENTRY

In the Thesaurofacet underlined items are shown in the classification schedules and not in the thesaurus

	Television Camera Tubes
UF	Camera tubes (television)
	Emitrons
	Iconoscopes
	Image iconoscopes
	Image orthicons
	Orthicons
	Pick up tubes (television)
	Vidicons
RT	<u>Image converter tubes</u>
	<u>Image intensifiers</u>
	Photomultipliers
	Phototubes
	<u>Storage tubes</u>
	Television cameras
	<u>Television colour picture tubes</u>
	<u>Television picture tubes</u>
NT	<u>Television colour camera tubes</u>
BT	<u>Cathode ray tubes</u>
	<u>Electron beam deflection tubes</u>
	<u>Electron tubes</u>
	Television apparatus

FIGURE 5. *Extract from* Thesaurofacet.
Reproduced by permission of the English Electric Company.

Terms

The basic elements in a thesaurus are the individual words, terms, or phrases, and these are often called "descriptors" or "keywords." Some writers use these two as synonyms; others make distinctions of various types. The *UNISIST Guidelines* chooses "descriptor," which is a general term used in documentation systems. But there is an important psychological factor to be borne in mind, namely, standard usage, which clearly favors the use of the word "term." This will be evident when (before dealing with the form of the descriptors themselves) we consider two other pieces of thesaurus apparatus: (*a*) definitions and explanations and (*b*) the symbols of relationships. Both of these are usually found only in the alphabetical part, though they can also have value in the systematic part, and some compilers use them there as well.

Definitions and explanations have to be given wherever there is a need to state the precise meaning of a particular term in the particular context of any thesaurus. The term "elevation" has several different meanings in technology, and the terms "pavement" and "public school" have more or less opposite meanings in the United Kingdom and the United States. To ensure consistency in use, and in order not to mislead searchers, it is necessary to add a "scope note" (SN) immediately under the term, thus:

> Public School
> SN   In the United Kingdom, an independent foundation which does not receive funds from the state, and which is a member of the Headmasters Conference or the Girls' Public Day School Trust.
> In the United States, a school established and supported by the state system of education.

Dagobert Soergel gives good examples of such homographs (6):

> Seal 1 (*marine animal*)
> Seal 2 (*documents*)
> Drill 1 (*instruction*)
> Drill 2 (*agriculture*)
> Drill 3 (*fabric*)

Not every term needs a scope note, but their presence is of considerable help in using a thesaurus correctly and, indeed, in reaching a correct understanding of the field of knowledge concerned.

Relationships and the symbols used to express them have always been an integral part of lists of subject headings. They have been of two simple forms, nearly always called "see" and "see also" references. Their significance is plain from their names: a "see" reference is added to a term not used in the system, pointing to the term used instead, a synonym or near-synonym, a "see also" reference is added to a term which can be used, pointing to other terms at which additional useful information may also be indexed. The well-known *Sears List of Subject Headings*, now edited by Barbara Westby (*15*), has an additional refinement, using *x* and *xx* to show the reciprocal references from the "see" and "see also" references themselves:

Classical dictionaries
  x Dictionaries, Classical
  xx History, Ancient
History, Ancient
  See also **Archeology; Bible; Civilization, Ancient; Classical dictionaries; Geography, Ancient; Inscriptions; Numismatics**; also names of ancient races and peoples (e.g. **Hittites**; etc.); and names of countries of antiquity
  x Ancient history
  xx **World history**
History—Atlases. *See* **Atlases, Historical**
History, Biblical. *See* **Bible—History of Biblical events**
History—Chronology. *See* **Chronology, Historical**
History, Church. *See* **Church history**
History, Constitutional. *See* **Constitutional history**
History—Criticism. *See* **Historiography**
History—Dictionaries
  x Historical dictionaries

This simple solution has also been used by MESH, with X for "see" and XU for "see under"; it also has XR for "related" and XS for "specific" terms:

Armed Forces Personnel
    X Military Personnel
Kefir
    XU Milk

The symbols to express these relationships in thesauri have now become more or less standardized, as follows:

SN	Scope note
USE	Equivalent to "see" reference
UF	Use for, the reciprocal of USE
BT	Broader term, in a hierarchical array
NT	Narrower term, in a hierarchical array; the reciprocal of BT
RT	Related term, expressing any useful relationship other than BT/NT

There are many, usually minor, variations of these. The *Information Retrieval System Subject Authority List* of the American Petroleum Institute, which has gone through a number of revisions, now has "see" and "see also" references in addition to "use" and "used for." The *Thesaurofacet* has extra symbols to mean that a term may appear in more than one hierarchy according to context, and that the term may form part of a multiword term which is in common use and so must appear in the system as such:

BT	Broader term
BT(A)	Additional broader term
NT	Narrower term
NT(A)	Additional narrower term
RT	Related term
Synth	Synthesized
S	Constituent term in synthesized index term
UF	Use for
*	Cross-reference in classification schedules

As will now be clear, the word "term" is the one most commonly used to name a "descriptor" and to point to other "descriptors" in the system. None of the thesauri published so far use symbols based on "descriptor"; for example, BD, ND, RD. It would therefore seem sensible to standardize use of the word "term" for these individual basic elements of a thesaurus, and this word is henceforward used with this meaning in this article.

Forms of Terms

The *UNISIST Guidelines* identify two major types of term: (*a*) terms denoting concepts or concept combinations and (*b*) terms denoting individual entities. The latter terms are also called proper names (or identifiers). Proper names may be:

Project names
Nomenclatures
Identification numbers or symbols
Geographical or geopolitical names
Trademarks
Names of persons and organizations
Abbreviations and acronyms
Other proper names (e.g., programming systems)

Identifiers differ from concept terms in that they are specific to one, named entity and cannot usually be attached to another as an alternative. When they appear in the literature, they have to be used in the index, since they are more or less unique to their own entity (in much the same way that an author's name uniquely identifies his work). It is true that a search for information about, say, the State of Illinois may be helped by documents about the United States or the Middle West, but such part-whole relations are not a common feature among identifiers. One such example is the Geographical List in the *Thesaurus of Terms for Indexing the Literature of Mineral Processing and Metals Extraction*, published by Warren Springs Laboratory of the U.S. Department of Industry in 1974. Where it is necessary to include identifiers of such a common type, a compiler might better turn to an existing list rather than begin to invent his own, which is not likely to end up very different. An identifier naming a new form of entity, such as Hovercraft, must always be included, because this is the term which searchers will naturally expect to find in the index. This applies even where, as in the case of Hovercraft, it would be possible to synthesize a description from terms already in the thesaurus.

Most of the identifiers listed here have already been published in lists which are in fact easily available, and there should be little difficulty in attaching them to a thesaurus. It would be desirable for more use to be made of them, again in the interests of standardization and of its concomitant, compatibility between different systems.

In most thesauri, terms are single-word, plural nouns. Exceptions always have to be made where this use results in ambiguity, unfamiliarity, or nonsense. Nouns are chosen because they are the most concrete part of speech; a single-word adjective or adverb would not usually convey much specific meaning, while a verb concept, though it can be specific, is usually converted into the gerund form used as a noun: "cleaning," "reading," etc.

The choice between singular and plural forms is much more complex. Some words have two different connotations in the two forms: in law, "damage" is not the singular of "damages." The plural form is the more favored choice, on the grounds that most thesaurus terms represent classes of things and it therefore seems more like natural usage to prefer the plural: "automobiles," "children." On the other hand, the singular form often makes more sense when used to synthesize a compound; in the *London Education Classification/Thesaurus*, the singular is preferred for this reason. "Child" is used instead of "children" in order to be able to synthesize "child development," "child psychology," and similar commonly found compounds. Some guidelines are necessary, and the rules given for TEST, one of the largest thesauri, show the complexity of the issue (see Figure 6).

But many concepts cannot be adequately represented by single words, and compounds are of necessity included in most thesauri. Since a major objective of a thesaurus is to facilitate coordinate indexing, it seems logical to avoid compounds as entry terms, though it will be desirable to put in a "use" reference from any compound not used. This often occurs when a form of adjective-plus-noun is in common use as an inquiry term, but the inclusion of such forms would result in unhelpful bulking under the adjective, with hosts of such compounds enumerated. In the field of education, for example, the adjective "educational" is commonly found in compounds: "educational philosophy," "educational psychology," etc. In that context, the adjective is actually nonsignificant as an identifying term, yet the *ERIC Thesaurus* has nearly 100 such compounds listed at "educational," covering several pages. It is better to invert, using "philosophy of education" and "psychology of education," which are equally readily understood and used as inquiry terms. "Educational technology," on the other hand, has now become a term of art and cannot be replaced by "technology of education," which has a somewhat different meaning. TEST has very many compound terms: In addition to "boundaries" and "boundary layer," for example, it includes "boundary layer control," "boundary layer flow," "boundary layer separation," "boundary layer stability," and "boundary layer transition"—in spite of the fact that terms like "flow" and "stability" also have substantive entries of their own. The Introduction to the *ERIC Thesaurus*, commenting on the "multiword term problem," points out that this is one of the most difficult tasks facing anyone constructing an indexing scheme, and states that ERIC prefers to draw far more heavily on multiword terms on the grounds that these are more often used by educators than is necessary in the physical sciences. The author of this Introduction, Frederick Goodman, warns that this approach must be used with care:

> ... it might be dangerous to have the following four descriptors: GROUP TESTS, GROUP INTELLIGENCE TESTS, GROUP TESTING, and GROUP INTELLIGENCE TESTING. A searcher might search on one or two of those terms and assume that he had found all the relevant documents (*16*).

Some commonly used compound terms may be avoided by the expedient of coordinating two (or more) single-word terms which will be required in the thesaurus anyway. This gives greater flexibility and escapes the problem mentioned by Good-

TYPE OF TERM	USE SINGULAR FORM	USE PLURAL FORM
Material terms, such as: 　chemical compounds 　mixtures 　materials	When term is specific, as: 　urea 　cellophane 　beeswax	When term is generic, as: 　amines 　solvents 　plastics
Terms representing properties, conditions, characteristics	When term is specific, as: 　viscosity 　temperature 　purity 　opacity	When term is generic, as: 　physical properties 　process conditions
Terms representing equipment, devices, physical objects, and elementary particles	Do not use singular	Use plural, as: 　pulverizers 　regulators 　mesons 　teeth 　stars
Class of use terms	Do not use singular	Use plural, as: 　adhesives 　catalysts
Process terms	Use singular, as: 　constructing 　installing 　modulating	Do not use plural
Proper names (A proper name is defined as the name for a *single unique* item)	Use singular, as: 　Hookes Law 　Pluto	Do not use plural
Disciplines, fields, subject areas	Use singular according to common usage, as: 　chemistry 　hydraulics 　engineering	Do not use plural (Words such as "hydraulics" are actually singular)
Events or occurrences	Do not use singular	Use plural, as: 　ambushes 　explosions 　discharges

FIGURE 6. *Extract from TEST (Table 1. Guidelines to Singular-Plural Usage). Reproduced by permission of the Engineers Joint Council.*

man. E. J. Coates points out another interesting factor here (8): the terms "child psychology" and "animal psychology" are well known and used, and their inclusion would be justifiable. But no one would ever think of using "boy psychology" or "chimpanzee psychology," though both are logical subsets of the others and there is plenty of literature on each. Coates makes the point that in these cases, inversion or coordination will produce the perfectly acceptable compounds "psychology-plus-animals," and "psychology-plus-children." The *UNISIST Guidelines* go even further, giving as an example the single word "shipbuilding," which is to be separated into "ships" plus "building." The advantage of such a procedure is that it releases both terms for use in other combinations. Where this is done, the *UNISIST Guidelines* also suggest the addition of another symbol, UFC (use for combination), to the symbols of relationship in order to draw attention to the fact that a compound is involved; the TEST practice is to place a dagger (†) in front of a term to show that two or more terms have to be used in combination to identify the term not used:

    Bombs (Ordnance)   1902
    UF   † Smoke bombs

    Smoke bombs
    USE   Bombs (Ordnance)
    and   Smoke ammunition

Thesaurofacet recognizes the problem by providing a pair of symbols: *Synth* at a term which should be made by synthesis, with *S* as its reciprocal:

    Cold rolling   TH/TD 2

    Synth
           RT   Cold mills
    S   BT   Rolling
    S   BT(A) Cold working

There are many terms with "cold" which are syntheses, but there are also exceptions, such as "cold cathode tubes."

To deal with the question of which form to use, some authors have advocated the device of truncation, in which only the root part of a word is used, with several alternative endings. In many cases, this will cover noun, adjective, verb, and adverb forms—even, in some instances, more than one of each. Thus the root "machin-" would cover all the words beginning with those letters: "machine," "machined," "machining," "machinable," etc. The device can achieve particularly good results in a computerized system containing many compound or precoordinated terms, but it needs to be used with care; its apparent simplicity can easily result in the unlucky searcher receiving a pile of references which are irrelevant because the different suffixes add meanings from different contexts, such as "machination" and the "damage"/"damages" example in law.

Relationships

In addition to synonyms/near-synonyms, the other two types of relationship are those of hierarchy and association, or co-occurrence. These are usually symbolized by BT/NT and RT. Broader/narrower terms are reciprocals because they cannot exist without each other: To be a broader term necessarily implies at least one other term which is narrower. Related terms are also reciprocal in a different sense; one would expect that if Term *A* is RT to Term *B*, then Term *B* must be RT to Term *A*, but in practice this is not always expressed in the schedules, being catered for by other means such as classification.

The hierarchical BT/NT relationship is a classificatory one. A BT must be a class term with (usually) an array of NT listed beneath it. On the other hand, each NT will normally have only one BT listed beneath it, though exceptions to this can arise, partly because some terms can actually exist as members of more than one class, but also because the NT itself may be a compound, in which each element of the compound has an upward reference to its own BT:

    AC generators
        BT   AC machines
              Electric generators

Where the thesaurus includes a detailed systematic part based on a scheme of classification, the selection of BT/NT is simple, because these terms will already be set out there in a series of classified arrays; they will usually have indentations in the schedule to show which terms are subordinate to which. The more general the term, the more terms will be subordinate to it, but the division of a generic term into its various species will be shown in a series of steps:

    Mammals
        Primates
            Apes
                Gorillas

    Criminology
        Delinquents
            Juvenile Delinquents
                Hooligans

In such hierarchies, all the indented terms are subordinate, or NT, to the main heading, or class term, which is likewise BT to all of them. In practice, it expands the size of the thesaurus considerably to list all such NT under the main heading, and it is almost equally effective for search purposes to list only one step of any multistep hierarchy. Thus, from the example given, we could derive the following:

    Criminology
    NT   Delinquents

    Delinquents
    BT   Criminology
    NT   Juvenile Delinquents

    Hooligans
    BT   Juvenile Delinquents

    Juvenile Delinquents
    BT   Delinquents
    NT   Hooligans

Some thesauri, however, do refer to more than one level of a hierarchy. In the *SPINES Thesaurus* produced by UNESCO for the UNISIST Project, it was decided to do this, and the thesaurus refers to several levels of NT (*17*). Under R&D (an abbreviation for research and experimental development) we find:

```
5757    R&D
NT 1    EXPERIMENTAL DEVELOPMENT
NT 1    RESEARCH
  NT 2    APPLIED RESEARCH
    NT 3    PROCESS RESEARCH
    NT 3    PRODUCT RESEARCH
  NT 2    FUNDAMENTAL RESEARCH
```

The reciprocal entries include:

```
435     APPLIED RESEARCH
BT 1    RESEARCH
  BT 2    R&D
NT 1    PROCESS RESEARCH
NT 1    PRODUCT RESEARCH
```

An intermediate step is taken by the *INSPEC Thesaurus* produced by the Institution of Electrical Engineers in London, in the areas of physics, electronics, electrotechnology, and control (*18*). This specifies that BT means one level up and NT means one level down, but it introduces the relationship of TT (top term[s]) in a hierarchy to show the main class term of any specific term:

```
a.c. generators
UF      alternators
NT      asynchronous generators
        synchronous generators
BT      a.c. machines
        electric generators
TT      electric machines
```

TEST offers an economy of a slightly different kind. By prefixing a dash (—) symbol before a term, it indicates that the term has other NT shown only under the main entry:

```
Bomb fuzes
RT      Acoustic fuzes
—       Impact fuzes
        Nose fuzes
—       Time fuzes

Impact fuzes
RT      Base fuzes
—       Bomb fuzes
        Grenade fuzes
```

Another very effective means of economy in the alphabetical part may be gained where the systematic part consists of a correctly laid out scheme of classification, as in *Thesaurofacet* and in the *Thesaurus of Education Terms* by G. C. Barhydt and C. T. Schmidt (*19*). Both use a reference to the classified schedules instead of those BT/NT entries which are derived from the same hierarchy in the classification. In the Barhydt-Schmidt thesaurus, Facet 1 is "people," and Subfacet 1003 is "teaching staff," which includes the following:

        FACET 1
            SUB-FACET 1003
    ASSISTANT PROFESSOR
    ATHLETIC COACH
    LECTURER
    PROFESSOR
    SCHOOL TEACHER
    TEACHER

The related alphabetical array entries include the following (where * means a very general term which should only exceptionally be used):

    PROFESSOR
        RT 1003
    SCHOOL TEACHER
        USE TEACHER
    TEACHER
        SN *
        UF INSTRUCTOR
            SCHOOL TEACHER
        RT 1003

The notation 1003 thus refers the user to the faceted section, where that entry contains a number of other related terms: "exchange teacher," "relief teacher," "visiting teacher," and so on. Only occasionally does this particular thesaurus use BT and NT; the explanation lies in the fact that the terms in each subfacet are set out in alphabetical order, as shown in 1003, with no visible distinction between coordinate and subordinate terms (as would be shown in a regular classification schedule).

Most thesauri, however, do make a clear distinction. But whereas BT and NT are reasonably simple to identify, related terms present a much more complex issue, and no system has yet succeeded in defining precisely which terms should be enumerated as RT to any other term. One reason is that the RT relation may be designed to suit specific user groups, and so no actual generalized rule is possible. Using a properly designed classification schedule as a basis, one could say that, for a beginning, coordinate terms with the same generic term have a prima facie claim to be shown as RT to each other; they are related in at least one aspect, because they are members of the same class and are neither BT nor NT to each other:

    TRANSPORT INDUSTRY
        Water Transport
            Inland Water Transport
            Sea Transport
            Dock Work

Here, the last three terms can be listed as RT to each other, since a searcher looking at one term will be glad to be reminded of the other two. But compare this sequence:

    TRANSPORT INDUSTRY
        Air Transport
        Rail Transport
        Road Transport
        Water Transport

Thesaurus

Here, the last four terms are coordinates in relation to the generic term "transport industry," but the case for making them RT in the alphabetical part of a thesaurus is much less obvious.

The *UNISIST Guidelines* state that "the associative relation is usually employed to cover the other relations between concepts that are related but are neither consistently hierarchical nor equivalent (e.g. similarity, antonymity)" (*10*). The *Guidelines* then go on to list a number of types of relation that may be symbolized by the use of RT in the thesaurus:

- antonymity, i.e. a concept is the opposite of another concept: HARDNESS RT SOFTNESS
- co-ordination, i.e. concepts are derived from a superordinate concept by the same step of division: GENERIC RELATION RT PART-WHOLE RELATION
- generic relation, i.e. something is the predecessor of another thing: FATHER RT SON
- concurrent use of two concepts: EDUCATION RT TEACHING
- cause and effect: TEACHING RT LEARNING
- instrumental relation: WRITING RT PENCILS
- material relation, i.e. something is the material of which another thing is made: PAPER RT BOOKS
- similarity of different kinds (physical similarity, similarity of material, similarity of processes etc.): TEACHING RT TRAINING

These *Guidelines* admit, however, that even this list covers only some of the possible examples, and they add the necessary warning that any additional relations should be clearly defined and coded. Aitchison and Gilchrist suggest that "the part-whole relationship is the strongest non-hierarchical relationship, the other relationships being more tenuous and difficult to categorize" (*4*, p. 29). The types they offer are derived from the work of the British Classification Research Group, expounded by B. C. Vickery (*20*):

Species of same genus	B Scope displays RT C Scope displays (both being types of two-dimensional radar displays)
Thing	
Thing/part	Doors RT Knobs
Thing/property	Lasers RT Coherence
Thing/process	Roads RT Road engineering
Thing/thing as attribute	Arcs RT Arc furnaces
Thing/application	Adaptive filters RT Signal processing
Property	
Property/process	Charge (electric) RT Charge measurement
Property/property as attribute	Skew RT Skew girders
Process	
Process/thing (agent)	Temperature measurement RT Thermometers

Process/property	Detonation RT Detonation waves
Near synonym	Fretting RT Spalling

Where a strictly faceted classification scheme is used as the basis, it will often be found that certain terms in one facet have a very close relationship in practice with particular terms in another facet. This may well occur in fields like product engineering, where certain materials will be treated by specific tools and processes, such as "aluminum—extrusion—presses." This can be a valuable source of RT, and is in fact a combination of two of the relations itemized by Aitchison and Gilchrist. It is also one of the serious arguments in favor of using a faceted structure in the systematic part of a thesaurus, since it is a sure technique for itemizing such terms precisely in conceptual relations with each other, according to the logic and practice of the subject field in question.

The most extensive research in this area is probably that carried out at the Documentation Research and Training Center in Bangalore under the direction of A. Neelameghan; his paper, presented with several others at the 1975 DRTC Seminar, contains a detailed analysis of nonhierarchical associative relations and the computer generation of RT links. He identifies these links as "facet relation (FR), speciator relation (SpR), co-ordinate relation (CR), and phase relation (PR), according to Ranganathan's model for structuring of subject" (*21*).

Another method of reaching a similar result by means of computer processing has been examined by Karen Sparck Jones in her *Automatic Keyword Classification* (*22*). She has expounded the concept of "substitutible terms," that is, terms which are able to substitute for one another in a document or request: "A request containing *b* could be satisfied by a document containing *b* or *e* or *f* indifferently, on the assumption that documents which contained any of these words would be about the same thing" (*22*, p. 8). From this starting point, she went on to carry out computer analyses of texts, noting those words which appear concurrently with one another, and identified four distinct types of term associations. These she called strings, stars, cliques, and clumps, which are best illustrated graphically:

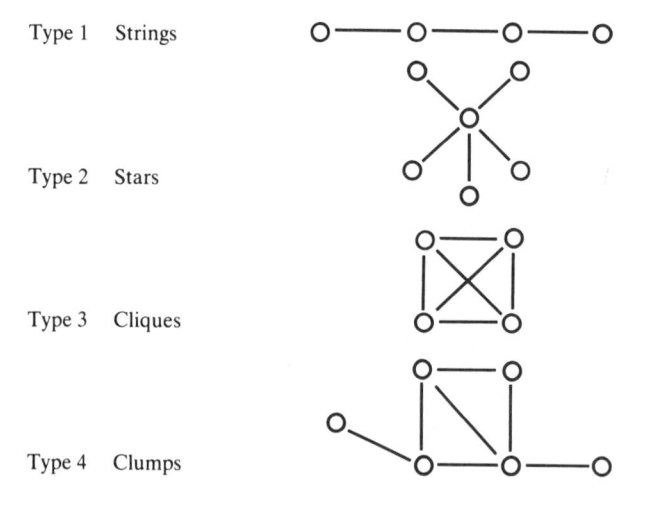

Type 1   Strings

Type 2   Stars

Type 3   Cliques

Type 4   Clumps

As she admits, this is a simplified view of these types, and other relationships could also develop in the strings and stars; but from the point of view of a thesaurus, such patterns could well be helpful in deciding which terms ought to be specified as RT in dealing with a particular subject literature, on the basis of co-occurrence in that literature. Furthermore, since this work was based on an actual set of documents, and tested on them, it has also served to underline the important fact that information retrieval systems have to cope with real literature, and that the literature in any subject directly reflects the way in which those working in that subject think about it.

Many research workers, particularly in the fields of language and comprehension, have shown that this type of associative relationship performs a most important function in the communication process. In brief, by ordering terms into more or less mutually exclusive categories, we come to understand the structure of subjects and are more easily able to learn about them. One of the clearest statements on this point was made by the eminent psychologist J. S. Bruner, reporting on a conference on education in science held at Woods Hole, Cape Cod, in September 1959: "Perhaps the most basic thing that can be said about human memory, after a century of intensive research, is that unless detail is placed into a structured pattern, it is rapidly forgotten" (*23*, p. 24).

The logical relation of genus/species has been of fundamental importance to our understanding of the world around us at least since the time of Aristotle, and all of the major schemes of bibliographical classification are based on it. But it is clearly not the only relationship that can exist, and furthermore, any entity may be a species of more than one class. Many psychologists have carried out tests on the role this relation plays in the development of the child's thinking powers, and they have shown that other relations come into the picture very early in life. For example, an orange is a species of citrus fruit and also of the class of round objects, and a child will demonstrate an understanding of the latter by bowling it along the floor. In the classic work *The Early Growth of Logic in the Child: Classification and Seriation*, J. Piaget and B. Inhelder show that multiplicative classifications develop in the child's mind as early as simple linear arrangements: that is, the ability to put things in groups as well as in straight lines (*24*).

In the simple generic hierarchy, each step of division is made by separating out those entities in a group which display one particular property, giving in principle two groups symbolized as *A* and *not-A*. This is not sufficient to express the multiple relationships between phenomena which exist in the real world and are described in the literature, and therefore any index language system which aims to reflect the literature has to be able to deal with more than the genus/species, or BT/NT, relation. R. A. Fairthorne once put it very succinctly when he wrote that "bibliographic classifications have no unique complement, and are therefore lattice systems, not Boolean Algebras" (*25*). In any subject field, a lattice of terms can easily enough be formed by dividing the terms, not into single hierarchies as in the Decimal Classification but into several categories of facets which are mutually exclusive. If we look at the literature of a subject, the topics written about soon reveal the appropriate facets. This approach is used in many thesauri; in the *Construction Industry Thesaurus* of the U.K. Department of the Environment, for example, the facets are Time, Place, Properties and Measures, Agents of Construction, Operations and Processes, Materials, Parts, and Construction Works (the end products, what Ranganathan would call the "Personality facet" of the subject) (26). In the alphabetical index, terms are referred by notation symbols to their place in the faceted schedules, as in *Thesaurofacet*.

To give a brief practical example—if we take the field of occupational safety and health, we find topics like these in the literature:

> Chromate dermatitis from chrome glue
> Dust sampling methods in the pottery industry
> Safety precautions for use with blind workers
> Statistics of accidents in the iron and steel industry
> Provision of spectacles for oxy-acetylene welding

From examination of these and other documents, we can easily deduce several facets, as shown in the *CIS Thesaurus* of the International Occupational Safety and Health Information Center at the International Labor Organization in Geneva (27):

1. Occupational hazards (chromates, dust)
2. Consequences of these hazards (dermatitis, accidents)
3. Techniques of investigation of hazards and consequences (sampling)
4. Protective and remedial measures (safety precautions, spectacles)
5. Places of occurrence (pottery industry, welding)
6. Groups of persons affected (blind workers)

It will be obvious that, with rare exceptions where a term has more than one significance, terms selected on this basis can logically belong to only one category.

This technique has several important values. It enables a thesaurus to be constructed in a highly systematic way, using only elementary terms in the vast majority of places; it gives a clear guideline for the enumeration of many RT; it can be used as a check on the completeness and consistency of the listings. A negative example will serve to underline these advantages. The *ERIC Thesaurus* has some 50 "Descriptor Groups" added to later editions, which are set out in alphabetical, not systematic, sequence with no apparent logical structure or connections. Many compound terms are listed, often even when their component single terms are also listed. Thus in "Group 010 Abilities," we find the term "readiness," and in "Group 440 Reading," we find the term "reading"; but in addition, in "Group 180 Education," we find the compound precoordinated as "reading readiness."

In "Group 010 Abilities," in fact, some 80% of the terms are actually compounds. Of these, 29 out of 60 are compounded with the term "skills"; these include "agricultural skills," "alphabetizing skills," and "locational skills (social studies)." The term "skill obsolescence" is also included in 010, but "skill development" accurs in "130 Development," and "skill analysis," in "150 Employment."

Separation of related terms occurs with and without cross-references. "Group 060 Behavior" has a reference "*see also* Psychology," but in "Group 420 Psychology" there are no "see also" references at all. Many inconsistencies occur between "Group 040 Attitudes and "Group 420 Psychology":

040	Attitudes	420	Psychology
	Parent Attitudes		Affection
	Persistence		Curiosity
	Resentment		Insecurity
	Self-esteem		Parent Influence
	Teacher Motivation		

"Group 040 Attitudes" also includes "family attitudes" and "mother attitudes" but not "father attitudes," and "social attitudes" and "scientific attitudes" but not "artistic attitudes."

Other inconsistencies occur in the placing of curriculum subjects:

110	Curriculum	140	Education
	Science Courses		Art Education
	Science Curriculum		Music Education
	Science Programs		Science Education
	Sciences	260	Humanities
	[but not Humanities	480	Social Sciences
	or Social Sciences]		

In Groups 260 and 480, the mixture of terms can only indicate a haphazard method of selection.

The introduction of Descriptor Groups constituted a great improvement for users of the *ERIC Thesaurus* compared with the first drafts, but once it had been decided to include a section for such groups, more attention might have been given to their nature and their relations with each other.

The conclusion is inescapable: A thesaurus benefits greatly in use, both for indexing and for searching, if the choice of terms and relations can clearly be seen to reflect the logical structure of a subject, instead of appearing to be a haphazard collection of terms which happen to turn up in the literature. This applies most strongly in those fields of knowledge—in the social sciences especially—where the terminology used by the experts themselves is not very precise.

Layout of the Thesaurus

The simplest way to lay out a thesaurus is to have one single list of terms in alphabetical order, with a minimum of references; such a product would certainly also be the least effective in practice. This reflects one of the great contradictions in the production of any bibliographical tool, and one that is very hard to resolve. It is this: How far can one reasonably go in refining the tool so that great effort may be required at the input stage, in the hope and expectation that many small individual efforts will be saved at the output stage? Clearly, the more complex the structure of a thesaurus, the more closely it will approach the complexity of the real world and the literature that describes the real world. It will give the indexer a refined and powerful technique, but one which will require a great deal of subtle thinking and skill if it is to be used to maximum advantage. For the searcher, on the other hand, it should present no difficulties because it will have foreseen and catered for all possible approaches, so that whatever search term may be chosen, it will lead unerringly to the relevant documents. In principle, one should always choose the best tool, because that will be the one to do the best job with the least effort. But economic considerations may make it necessary to choose a cheaper model, which will put more effort on the shoulders of the searcher.

One finds, in fact, a very wide variety of forms of presentation. The *London Education Classification (28)* has a highly structured faceted scheme as the basis, from which the alphabetical listing and its references have been made (see Fig. 7). The *EUDISED Multilingual Thesaurus (29)*, which took the London scheme as its starting point, also has a strongly faceted structure but arranges its terms in a somewhat different way, bringing the references into each facet and making much more use of alphabetical order of terms in facets. This is probably easier to produce by computer, but it does, of course, result in some nonlogical sequences, and it is different in different languages, as shown by comparing the English edition with the Spanish (see Figs. 8 and 9). The sequence of the subfacets themselves is unchanged, since this depends on the numerals (10100, etc.) and not on the alphabet, and thus much of the original classificatory relationship is preserved. Like many thesauri which are computer generated, the *EUDISED Thesaurus* also has an alphabetical index which resembles a keyword-in-context (KWIC) type and brings together all the compound terms that include the same single-word terms (see Fig. 10).

A very different type of layout, though based on the same principle of displaying related terms in the classified section, is used by C. van der Merwe in the *Thesaurus of Sociological Research Terminology* (see Fig. 11). The classified array, shown in the left-hand column headed "Category," follows the sequence indicated by the notational symbols D.331.3, D.331.31, D.331.32, etc. Other classes where related terms will be found are also indicated by notational symbols, and these are shown in the right-hand column headed "Related Terms": "paired selection (D.21)," "factorial design (C.132.22)," etc. The alphabetical index, by inverting headings in the classified section, brings together all those terms which relate to "sampling," can be located from "sampling," or are accidental to "sampling" with two or more random starts.

Linking by classified notation also occurs in the bilingual *CIS Thesaurus*, where RT are listed in the "faceted thesaurus" while the "alphabetical index" lists all those places in the facets where a particular term occurs in compound combinations (see Fig. 12).

In his excellent manual, D. Soergel discusses the question of layout in considerable detail in his Chapter D, and he is in no doubt as to the proper example to follow: "Notwithstanding the deviation in the arrangement of most other thesauri, notably TEST, Roget has found the most meaningful form, the one most appropri-

Facet 1   Educands
  Educands, general
  Pre-school child, Infant, under 5 years
  Schoolchild, pupil
    Child, pre-adolescent
    Adolescent, "Teenager"
  Student
  Youth outside of school and college
  Adult
  Exceptional Educand
    Genius, prodigy
    Gifted, brilliant, able
    Handicapped
      Physically handicapped
      Mentally handicapped
      Maladjusted, Emotionally disturbed
      Socially handicapped, Culturally deprived
Facet 2   Educational Institutions: Schools, Colleges, Universities
  Educational Institutions, and systems
  Home Education
  Nursery
  Primary, Elementary (5-11)
  Secondary (11-18)
    Stages
      Lower
      Middle
      Upper
    English types of school (or favoured country)
      Comprehensive
      Grammar
      "Public School"
  Post-Secondary Education
    University
    University of the Air
  Further Education
  Adult Education
  Continuing Education, Lifelong Education

FIGURE 7.   *Extract from* London Education Classification.
Reproduced by permission of the University of London Institute of Education Library and the authors.

ate to the intended use of a thesaurus" (6, p. 183). Soergel has improved on the original, however, in the "Roget-Soergel Model," which has these sections: (0) introduction to the thesaurus, (1) classified index (schedule), (2) main part in classified arrangement, and (3) alphabetical index. He gives as an example (6, pp. 185-191) the subject "electron tubes," worked out in full according to this model, and he contrasts its obvious clarity and simplicity with an extract from the TEST Subject Category Index, which he rightly characterizes as a "coarse hierarchy."

```
ADOLESCENT - ADOLESCENT - JUGENDLICHER
    UF: TEENAGER
    NT: BOY
        GIRL
    RT: ADOLESCENCE
        PUBERTY
        YOUTH

ADULT - ADULTE - ERWACHSENER
    BT: AGE GROUP
    NT: ELDERLY PERSON
        PARENTS
    RT: ADULT EDUCATION
        MATURITY

BOY - GARCON - JUNGE
    BT: ADOLESCENT
        MAN
    RT: BOYS' SCHOOL
        SEX

CHILD - ENFANT - KIND
    NT: ADOPTED CHILD
        BACKWARD CHILD
        CHILD OF DIVORCED PARENTS
        ILLEGITIMATE
        INFANT
        NEGLECTED CHILD
        ONLY CHILD
        PRE-SCHOOL CHILD
        PROBLEM CHILD
        WAIFS AND STRAYS
    RT: CHILD CARE
        CHILD DEVELOPMENT
        CHILD LABOUR
        CHILD PROTECTION
        CHILD PSYCHIATRY
        CHILD PSYCHOLOGY
        CHILD REARING
        CHILDHOOD
        CHILDREN'S BOOK
        FATHER-CHILD RELATION
        MOTHER-CHILD RELATION
        ORPHAN
        PAEDIATRICS
        PARENT-CHILD RELATION
        PRE-ADOLESCENCE
        PUPIL

ELDERLY PERSON - PERSONNE AGEE - ALTER MENSCH
    BT: ADULT
    NT: RETIRED PERSON
    RT: OLD AGE

GIRL - JEUNE FILLE - MAEDCHEN
    BT: ADOLESCENT
        WOMAN
    RT: GIRLS' SCHOOL
        SEX

INFANT - ENFANT DU PREMIER AGE - KLEINKIND
    BT: CHILD
    RT: CHILD REARING
        DAY-NURSERY
        INFANCY
        INFANT MORTALITY
        NURSERY RHYME

PRE-SCHOOL CHILD - ENFANT D'AGE PRE-SCOLAIRE -
VORSCHULKIND
    BT: CHILD
    RT: PRE-SCHOOL AGE

RETIRED PERSON - PERSONNE RETRAITEE - RUHESTAENDLER
    BT: ELDERLY PERSON
    RT: PENSION
        RETIREMENT

TEENAGER
    USE: ADOLESCENT
```

FIGURE 8. *Extract from the* EUDISED *Multilingual Thesaurus (English version). Reproduced by permission of the Council of Europe and Jean Viet.*

```
ADOLESCENTE - ADOLESCENT - ADOLESCENT
   NT:  MUCHACHA
        MUCHACHO
   RT:  ADOLESCENCIA
        JUVENTUD
        PUBERTAD

ADULTO - ADULT - ADULTE
   BT:  GRUPO DE EDAD
   NT:  PADRES
        PERSONA DE EDAD
   RT:  EDUCACION DE ADULTOS
        MADUREZ

JUBILADO - RETIRED PERSON - PERSONNE RETRAITEE
   UF:  RETIRADO
   BT:  PERSONA DE EDAD
   RT:  JUBILACION
        PENSION DE JUBILACION

MUCHACHA - GIRL - JEUNE FILLE
   BT:  ADOLESCENTE
        MUJER
   RT:  ESCUELA FEMENINA
        SEXO

MUCHACHO - BOY - GARCON
   BT:  ADOLESCENTE
        HOMBRE
   RT:  ESCUELA MASCULINA
        SEXO

NINO - CHILD - ENFANT
   NT:  HIJO DE PADRES DIVORCIADOS
        HIJO NATURAL
        HIJO UNICO
        NINO ABANDONADO
        NINO ADOPTADO
        NINO DE PRIMERA INFANCIA
        NINO DESATENDIDO
        NINO PROBLEMA
        NINO RETRASADO
        PARVULO
   RT:  ALUMNO
        AYUDA A LA INFANCIA
        DESARROLLO DEL NINO
        HUERFANO
        INFANCIA
        LIBROS PARA NINOS
        PEDIATRIA
        PREADOLESCENCIA
        PROTECCION A LA INFANCIA
        PSICOLOGIA DEL NINO
        PSIQUIATRIA INFANTIL
        PUERICULTURA
        RELACION MADRE-NINO
        RELACION PADRE-NINO
        RELACION PADRES-NINO
        TRABAJO DEL NINO

NINO DE PRIMERA INFANCIA - INFANT - ENFANT DU PREMIER
   AGE
   BT:  NINO
   RT:  CANCION DE CUNA
        GUARDERIA
        MORTALIDAD INFANTIL
        PRIMERA INFANCIA
        PUERICULTURA

PARVULO - PRE-SCHOOL CHILD - ENFANT D'AGE PRE-SCOLAIRE
   BT:  NINO
   RT:  EDAD PREESCOLAR

PERSONA DE EDAD - ELDERLY PERSON - PERSONNE AGEE
   BT:  ADULTO
   NT:  JUBILADO
   RT:  VEJEZ

RETIRADO
   USE: JUBILADO
```

FIGURE 9.   *Extract from the* EUDISED Multilingual Thesaurus (*Spanish edition*).

```
CHILD
    ABNORMAL CHILD      10310
        USE:  EXCEPTIONAL
    ADOPTED CHILD      10350
    BACKWARD CHILD     10340
    CHILD      10100
    CHILD CARE     25720
    CHILD DEVELOPMENT      17200
    CHILD EMPLOYMENT      25550
        USE:  YOUTH EMPLOYMENT
    CHILD LABOUR     25550
    CHILD OF DIVORCED PARENTS      10350
    CHILD PROTECTION      25720
    CHILD PSYCHIATRY      18651
    CHILD PSYCHOLOGY      17100
    CHILD REARING      11200
    CHILD-FATHER RELATION      17760
        USE:  FATHER-CHILD RELATION
    CHILD-MOTHER RELATION      17760
        USE:  MOTHER-CHILD RELATION
    CHILD-PARENT RELATION      17760
        USE:  PARENT-CHILD RELATION
    CHILD-SCHOOL RELATION      16320
        USE:  TEACHER-PUPIL RELATION
    FATHER-CHILD RELATION      17760
    MOTHER-CHILD RELATION      17760
    NEGLECTED CHILD      10350
    ONLY CHILD      18150
    PARENT-CHILD RELATION      17760
    PRE-SCHOOL CHILD      10100
    PROBLEM CHILD      10350
    RETARDED CHILD      10340
        USE:  BACKWARD CHILD
    SCHOOL CHILD      10210
        USE:  PUPIL
CHILDHOOD
    CHILDHOOD      18160
CHILDREN
    CHILDREN'S BOOK      14220
CHILE
    CHILE      30200
CHINA
    CHINA      30300
    CHINA MAINLAND      30300
        USE:  CHINA PR
    CHINA PR      30300
    CHINA R      30300
CHOICE
    CAREER CHOICE      16130
        USE:  OCCUPATIONAL CHOICE
    OCCUPATIONAL CHOICE      16130
    VOCATIONAL CHOICE      16130
        USE:  OCCUPATIONAL CHOICE
CHRISTIAN
    CHRISTIAN EDUCATION      12680
CHRISTIANITY
    CHRISTIANITY      26430
CHURCH
    CHURCH      26430
CINEMA
    CINEMA      14530
    CINEMA CLUB      14530
```

FIGURE 10. *Extract from the* EUDISED *Multilingual Thesaurus* Index. *Reproduced by permission of the Council of Europe and Jean Viet.*

Category	Descriptors	Unauthorized Terms	Related Terms
	Random start		
D.331.3 Stratified sampling	*Stratified sampling*	Stratified probability sampling Density sampling	Paired selection (D.21) Lattice sampling (D.22) Design effect (D.33) Stratified cluster sampling (D.331.4) Optimum stratification (H.216) Relational analysis (K.221)
	— *Balanced sample*		
	Poststratification	Stratification after selection	
D.331.31 Proportionate sampling	*Proportionate sampling*	Proportional stratified sampling Self-weighting sample Equal allocation	Representativeness (D.32) Systematic sampling (D.331.2)
D.331.32 Disproportionate sampling	*Disproportionate sampling*	Disproportional stratified random sampling Controlled sampling	Factorial design (C.132.22)
	— *Oversampling*		Sample size (D.321)

FIGURE 11. *Extract from* Thesaurus of Sociological Research Terminology. *Reproduced by permission of Rotterdam University Press.*

Graphic Display

Graphic, or two-dimensional, displays of sets of terms and their interrelationships—like lists of subject headings—are not exactly new to librarians. The idea, also like that of lists of subject headings, has been greatly developed and refined by some of the compilers and theoreticians of thesauri. The simplest and oldest form is the "family tree" type of structure, in which the various steps in the hierarchical subdivision of a class are shown; another familiar example is the management organization chart, which is also usually cast in this form. An example is:

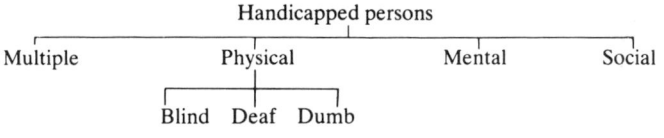

```
                    Handicapped persons
       ┌──────────────────┼──────────────┬─────────┐
    Multiple          Physical         Mental    Social
                   ┌──────┼──────┐
                 Blind  Deaf  Dumb
```

Such a list of connected terms is monohierarchical, in the sense that all the subdivisions stem from one main class, and from any one term there is only one chain of connections upward to that main class term. But a major use of graphic display in descriptions of thesauri has been precisely in order to illustrate the polyhierarchical nature of the relationships that the thesaurus can show—namely, that a concept represented by a term, whether single or compound, may often have a hierarchical

Fewo	**WOOD PRODUCTS - PRODUITS DU BOIS**
	RT: WOODWORKING INDUSTRY
Fewob	**BLOCKBOARD - PANNEAUX LATTES**
Fewod	**PLYWOOD - BOIS CROISE**
Fewof	**FIBREBOARD - PANNEAUX DE FIBRES**
Fewol	**WOOD WOOL - LAINE DE BOIS**
Fewon	**WOODPULP - PATE MECANIQUE**
	RT: CELLULOSE
	PULP AND PAPER INDUSTRY
Fewop	**PAPER - PAPIER**
	RT: PACKAGING MATERIALS
	PAPER AND PAPER PRODUCTS INDUSTRY
	WASTEPAPER
Fewoq	**CARDBOARD - CARTON**
	RT: PACKAGING MATERIALS
Fewor	**NATURAL RESINS - RESINES NATURELLES**
Feworc	**COLOPHONY - COLOPHANE**
Fewos	**TANNINS - TANINS**
	RT: TANNING
	TANNING AGENTS
	TANNING INDUSTRY
Fewot	**TURPENTINE - TEREBENTHINE**
Fewou	**CAMPHOR - CAMPHRE**
Fewov	**NATURAL RUBBER - CAOUTCHOUC NATUREL**
	RT: RUBBER INDUSTRY
	SYNTHETIC RUBBER
Fewova	**GUM ARABIC - GOMME ARABIQUE**
Fewove	**LATEX - LATEX**
Fewovi	**FOAMED RUBBER - CAOUTCHOUC-MOUSSE**
Fewox	**CHARCOAL - CHARBON DE BOIS**
Fewoxa	**ACTIVATED CARBON - CHARBON ACTIVE**
	RT: ACTIVATED CARBON PNEUMOCONIOSIS
	ADSORBENTS
	CARBON PRODUCTS
Fewoy	**WOOD TAR - GOUDRON DE BOIS**

(a)

LOG	
LOG HANDLING	
→ ROUND TIMBER HANDLING	Jdiko
LOG HAULAGE	Jso
LOG PONDS	
→ SAWMILLING INDUSTRY	Xeha
LOGGING	
FORESTRY AND LOGGING	Xap
LOGGING	Xapo
LOGGING EQUIPMENT	Jsy
LOGGING OPERATIONS	Js
PAPER	
PAPER	Fewop
PAPER AND CARDBOARD CONVERTING INDUSTRY	Xejo
PAPER AND PAPER PRODUCTS INDUSTRY	Xej
PAPER CONVERTING MACHINES (WEB-FED)	Hns
PAPER GUILLOTINES AND TRIMMERS	Hrapa
PAPER HANGING	Jql
PAPER MAKING MACHINES	Hnr
PAPER REAM HANDLING	Jdise
PAPER ROLL HANDLING	
→ REELED MATERIALS HANDLING	Jdir
PAPER SHREDDERS	Hryd
PULP AND PAPER INDUSTRY	Xeja
PAPERBOARD	
PAPERBOARD MILLS	
→ PULP AND PAPER INDUSTRY	Xeja
PAPERS	
FILTER PAPERS	Hufmo
TEST PAPERS	Qicup

(b)

FIGURE 12. *Extracts from the* CIS *Thesaurus: (a) from the "faceted thesaurus" and (b) from the "alphabetical index." Reproduced by permission of the International Occupational Safety and Health Information Center, Geneva.*

relationship with more than one main class term. A simple example appears in the *UNISIST Guidelines:*

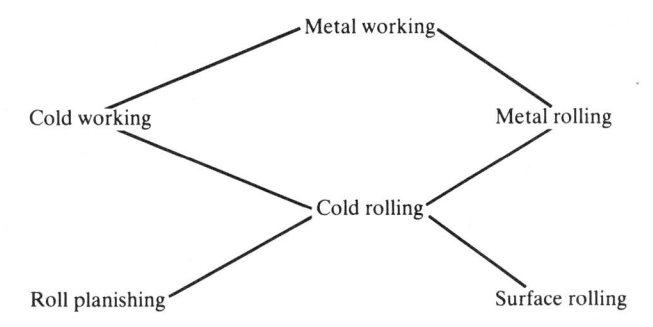

```
                    Metal working
    Cold working                    Metal rolling
                    Cold rolling
    Roll planishing                 Surface rolling
```

The extensive use of graphic display in this field, to the point that it has become an integral part of subsequent work on the thesaurus, probably began with that introduced into the Euratom Information and Documentation Center in Luxembourg. This was described in detail by its principal architect, L. N. Rolling, at the Second International Study Conference on Classification Research, organized at Elsinore, Denmark, in 1964 by the FID/CR Classification Research Committee of the International Federation for Documentation and the Danish Center for Documentation (*30*). Rolling gave a very complete account of the use of graphic displays, beginning with simple Venn or Euler Diagrams, and then enlarged on them in a number of different forms of graphic display, showing how they can demonstrate quite highly complicated networks. An arrowgraph is a stage more elaborate than the UNISIST example just given, and it is able to show reciprocal relations working in both directions between two terms (see Fig. 13). A more complex box-chart not only shows "neighbor" or contiguous relationships but can also include heirarchical relationships depending from the main term in each box (see Fig. 14).

Without going into the production of three-dimensional models, it is difficult to envisage a more thoroughgoing use of graphic display than the three-volume *SPINES Thesaurus* produced by UNESCO for the UNISIST Project (*17*). The whole of Volume 3 is devoted to "Terminological Graphic Displays," though the enthusiasm of the designers appears to have somewhat got the better of their bibliographical judgment, and the volume is of a very large and unwieldy format, about the size of an elephant folio. There are 34 of these displays showing, in two dimensions, all the terms in the thesaurus in their various contexts of meanings and relationships. Each right-hand page shows a term in a central box, with lines joining it to its related terms in the other boxes, or "polygons"; these links are mainly those to terms in the same hierarchy as the central term, but they also indicate synonymous terms not used. On the back of each page there are an explanatory note on how to use the displays, a list of all the RT which relate to the central term (or "Top Term") on the front of the page, and a complete display of all the relations between the complete set of the 34 graphic displays. Each display, of course, has a different term in its central box, so that any term may be looked at in the context of all its relations included in the thesaurus (see Figs. 15–17).

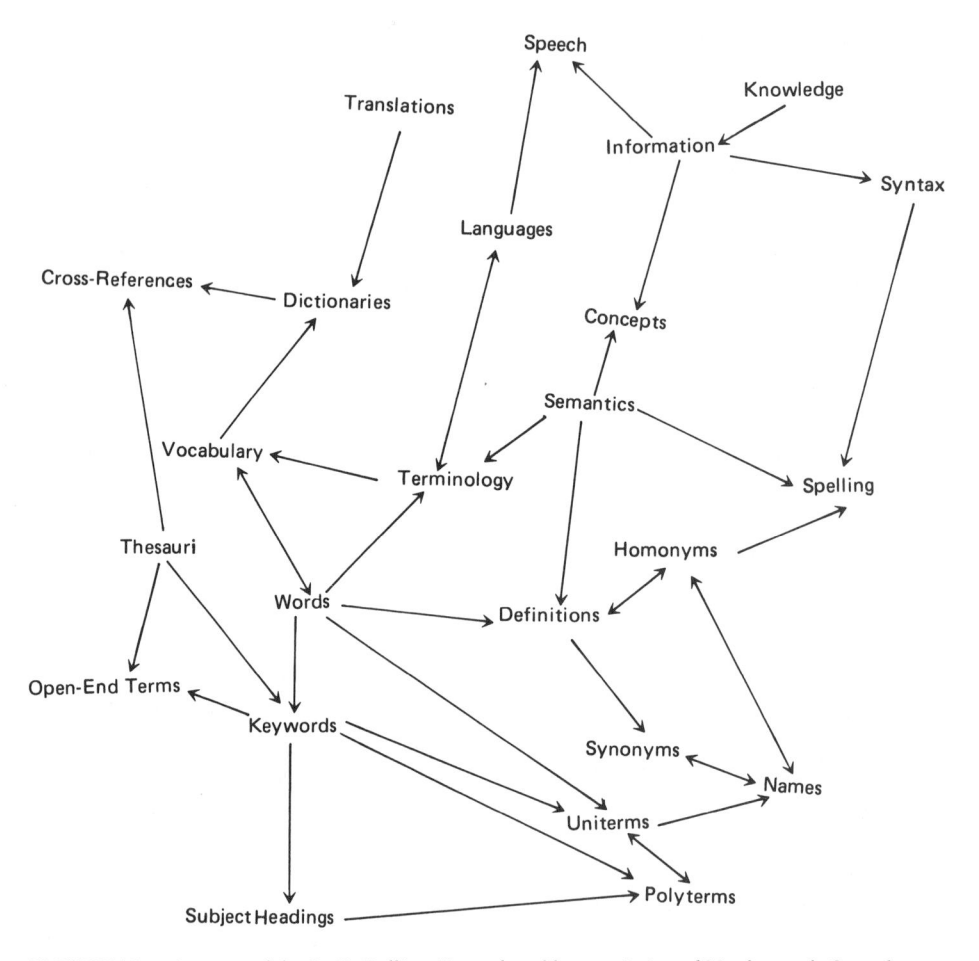

FIGURE 13. *Arrowgraph by L. N. Rolling. Reproduced by permission of Munksgaard, Copenhagen.*

Revision

An argument often leveled against schemes of classification as instruments for arranging and indexing documents is that, once published, they at once become fossilized and unable to cope with the ever-advancing dynamic continuum of knowledge—which is, of course, precisely what they set out to do. The thesaurus, it is claimed, does not suffer from this disability and is thus to be preferred as a superior tool. Such comments seem to indicate an unawareness of two factors: (*a*) the well-constructed thesaurus itself depends on a classificatory structure, whether this is acknowledged or not; and (*b*) keeping up to date, for any indexing language, simply means adding new words to an existing list, according to the format of that list. It makes little difference whether the list is in alphabetical or classified sequence, the new words have to be inserted in their appropriate place. At first blush, it appears easier to add to a simple alphabetical list, provided that all are ac-

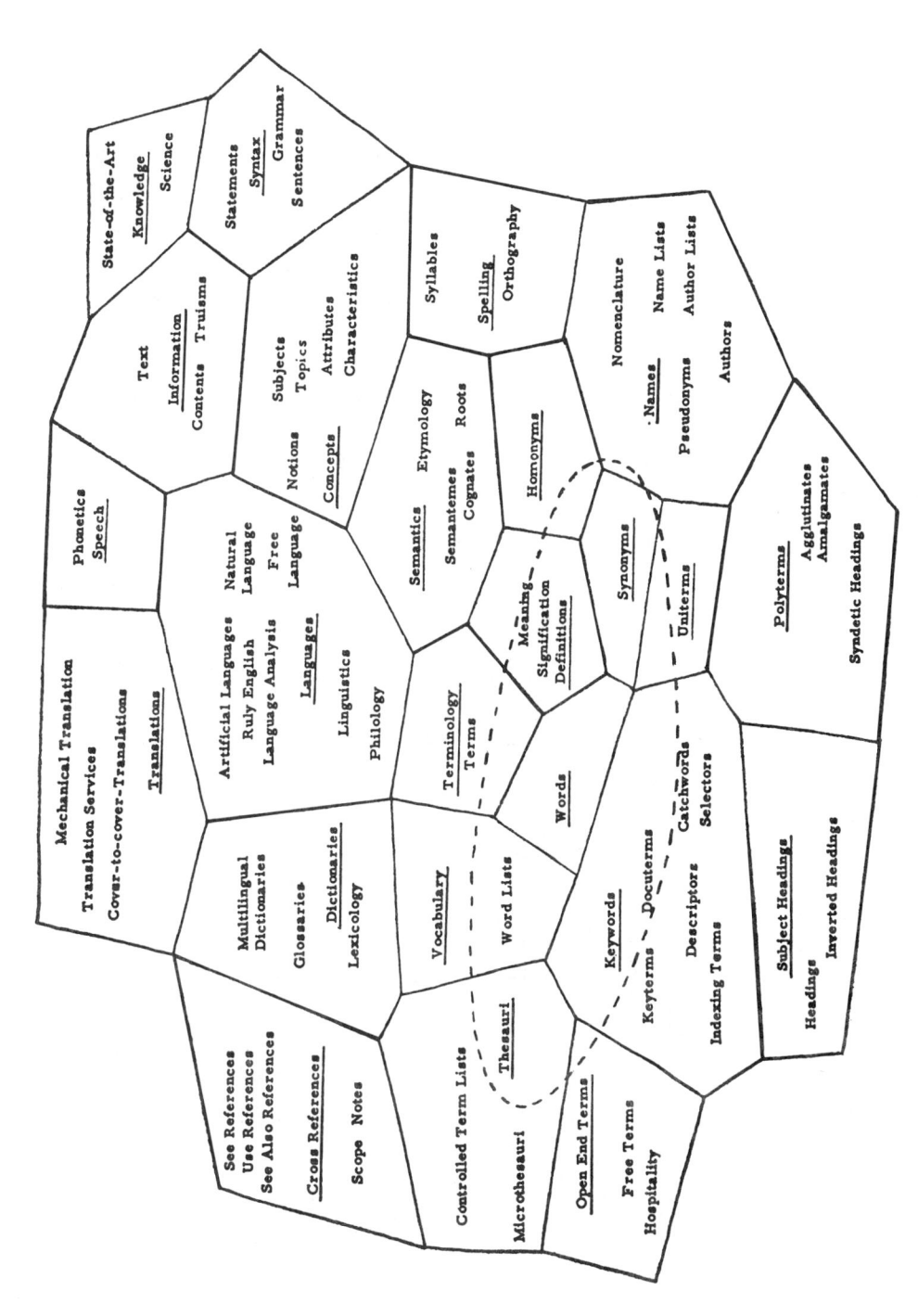

FIGURE 14. Box-chart by L. N. Rolling. Reproduced by permission of Munksgaard, Copenhagen.

FIGURE 15. *Extract from the* SPINES *Thesaurus. Reproduced by permission of UNESCO, Paris.*

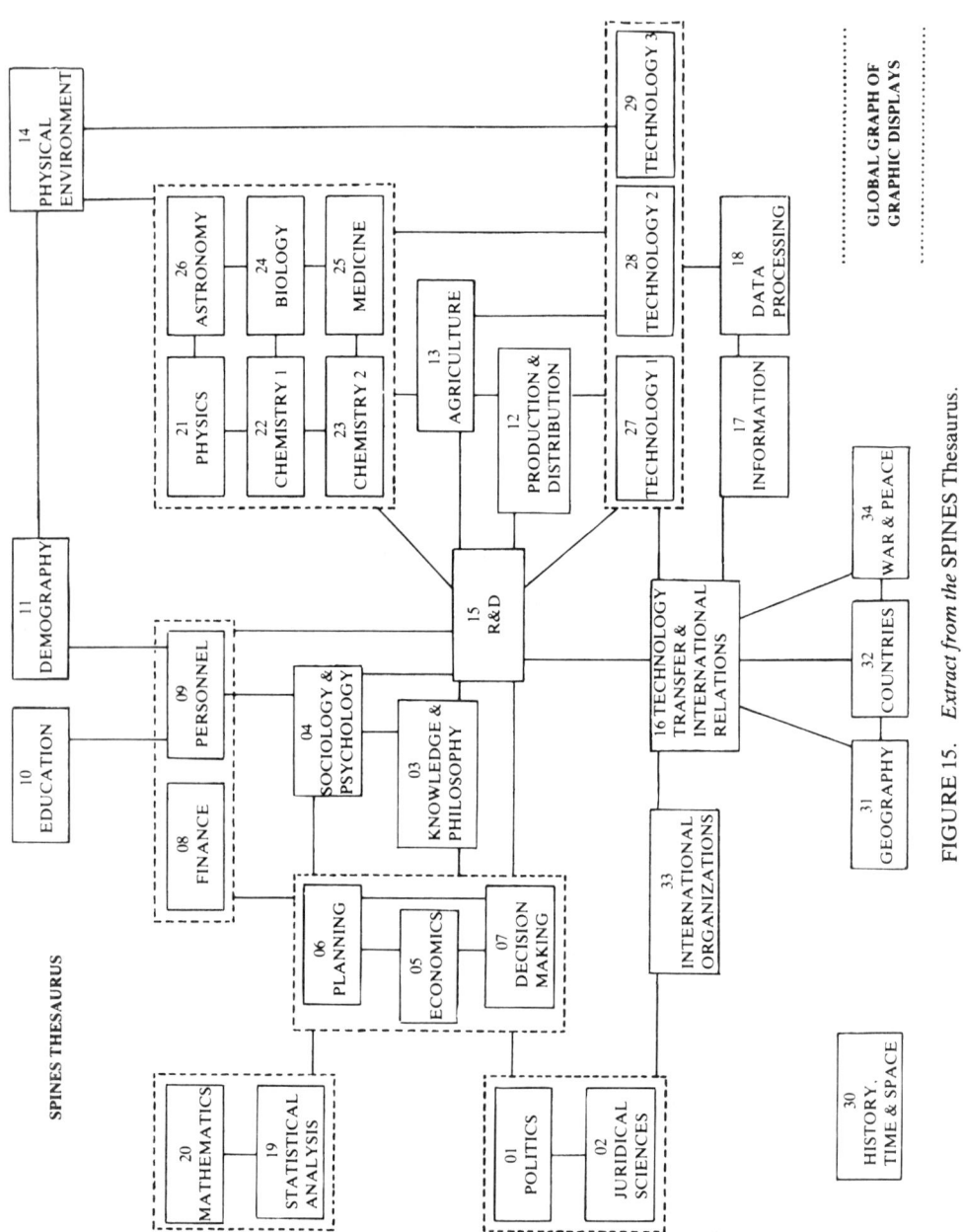

ASSOCIATIVE RELATIONS BETWEEN TOP DESCRIPTORS OF
GRAPHIC DISPLAY 18, AND EXTERNAL TOP DESCRIPTORS

18-01	DATA PROCESSING EQUIPMENT		18-02	DATA PROCESSING		18-03	COMPUTER SOFTWARE	
	ELECTRONIC TECHNOLOGY	27-11		INFORMATION SCIENCES	17-07		SYSTEMS	07-03
	OFFICE EQUIPMENT	29-17						

FIGURE 16. *Extract from the* SPINES *Thesaurus.*
Reproduced by permission of UNESCO.

tually agreed on the form of the word (which often differs even between the United Kingdom and the United States). But once the question of BT, NT, and RT arises, we are at once in the realm of classification, like it or not. Those who protest that new terms cannot be "fitted" into a classification scheme have overlooked the 19 editions of the Decimal Classification, the P-Notes of the Universal Decimal Classification, the new editions of Library of Congress Classification classes, and so on. As a matter of fact, they are also confusing classification with notation, which is another matter entirely.

A thorough and well-conceived scheme for the process of revision is essential for any indexing language. All that has to be decided is how to do it. This boils down to two main choices, with some variations: (*a*) new editions of the whole scheme, published as often as possible; and (*b*) piecemeal revision, adding new terms as they arise.

The first method has been the most favored and is used by the Engineers Joint Council for TEST and by the National Center for Educational Communication for the *ERIC Thesaurus*. It is much tidier, much more satisfactory for the compiler, who sees the product in a new and up-to-date dress; and it is more convenient for the user, who does not have to keep making amendments to his probably already battered copy. But it has some disadvantages. New editions are more costly to produce, and inevitable delays are involved because it only becomes worth publishing a whole new edition when enough amendments have been accumulated to provide an edition that is significantly new. It is also more expensive for the user, who will be buying a lot of material which he already has, in the form of everything that has not been amended. Preparation of new editions encourages the compiler to tamper with the existing text, not always effecting an improvement. As an example of how alterations which are unsatisfactory and inconsistent come about, largely through lack of a proper structure, we may consider the treatment by ERIC of the terms "ability," "creative ability," "creativity," and "intelligence," which varies considerably between the first and the subsequent editions, with no apparent reason for the changes and no improvement in the relational structure. Where a complete new edition is published, especially if this is within a relatively short time after the

DATA PROCESSING EQUIPMENT

calculators
— accounting machines
— calculating machines
— desk calculators

COMPUTERS
— business computers
— industrial computers
— scientific computers

minicomputers
microcomputers
general purpose computers
special purpose computers
analog computers
hybrid computers
digital computers
synchronous computers
asynchronous computers
first generation computers
— vacuum tube computers
second generation computers
— solid state computers
third generation computers
— solid logic computers
virtual machines
— virtual computing machines

COMPUTER PERIPHERAL EQUIPMENT
— computer auxiliary equipment

computer consoles
— computer control panels
— console typewriters (computer)
computer display devices*

COMPUTER TERMINALS

remote terminals
— teleprocessing devices

curve followers
data processing collators
key punches
plotters
— graph plotters
storage devices converters*
summary punches

film readers
— microfilm viewers
printers (data processing)

COMPUTER HARDWARE
— hardware (computers)
— computer systems

offline equipment
online equipment

CENTRAL PROCESSING UNITS
— central processors
— CPU

microprocessors

STORAGE DEVICES
— computer memories
— memory devices

storage capacity
random access
— direct access
serial access
computer registers
core storage
delays lines (computers)
magnetic cards
magnetic discs
magnetic drums
magnetic tapes
punched cards
— aperture cards
punched tapes
— paper tapes
thick film storage
thin film storage
input output devices*
— computer input devices
— computer output devices
computer circuits

character recognition devices
— magnetic ink character recog.
— mark detection
— mark sensing devices
— optical character recognition
punched card equipment*
— unit record equipment
punched tape equipment
— paper tape punches
— punched tape readers

FIGURE 17. *Extract from the* SPINES *Thesaurus.*
Reproduced by permission of UNESCO.

previous, an explanation of changes should be given. This is not only desirable from the user's point of view, but it also forces the compiler to think deeply about any proposed changes and their justification. Where this cannot be done, and where the previous edition is out of print and still in demand, it would seem preferable simply to issue a reprint.

Piecemeal revision means publishing additions and corrections as often as the occasion arises. The obvious advantage of this is that users can keep their copies continuously up to date with a minimum of labor for both compiler and user. It does require a certain firmness of purpose on the part of the user, however, and amendment slips are fragile things which can easily get lost. The most necessary feature of this type of revision procedure, therefore, is a vehicle of regular communication between compiler and users. Experience with the UDC P-Notes, each of which arises from a separate operation and is issued separately, shows that it can become a very laborious, even haphazard process.

But since a complete edition must itself, in the nature of things, be compiled piecemeal, there seems to be no reason why both revision methods should not be used in combination, especially if there is a regular means of communication to hand. ERIC, for example, publishes "New Thesaurus Terms" in its *Research in Education* and *Current Index to Journals in Education;* both of these are organized by means of its own thesaurus, and so a subscriber will need to possess a copy of the thesaurus if he is to make the best use of the two indexes to current documents. This not only provides regular and continuous communication between compiler and user, it can also mean that a user in straightened circumstances may not have to buy every new complete edition, so long as he faithfully adds all new terms to his own copy.

For both compiler and user, this combination of methods provides the best system. A thesaurus compiler who hopes and expects that his scheme will be widely used would be well advised to set up a regular revision service if he cannot make use of an already existing vehicle. This has a further advantage: If the users recognize that they have such a regular channel of communication, they may be encouraged to use it in the other direction and offer helpful suggestions for improvements based on actual practice in retrieval systems.

Machine Compilation

The development of computer technology has greatly assisted in the compilation and revision of thesauri, and most major organizations now use this technique, so that several programs are available. Much of the research in this area—like that of Karen Sparck Jones (*22*) and Gerard Salton (*31*)—has been based on the analysis of texts in order to work out the relations that occur between the semantic contents of words and phrases as they appear in actual documents. Although this contribution has considerable theoretical interest, probably the most important advantage of the use of computers is that the whole of a thesaurus is held in machine-readable form, available for immediate consultation in an on-line dialogue with a user, who then knows that he is accessing the thesaurus in its most up-to-date form. In his article "Vocabulary Control in Information Retrieval Systems" (*7*), F. W. Lancaster discusses several important functions that may be performed by storing a thesaurus in machine-readable form:

1. Checking for consistency and acceptability of terms
2. Maintaining statistics on the use of terms
3. Maintaining the "tracings" necessary to ensure that, if a term is deleted from the vocabulary or modified in some way, all the terms that are connected with this term (through some form of reference) are also appropriately modified
4. Maintaining records of term "history"
5. Automatic optimization of a searching strategy
6. Facilitating the conduct of generic searches
7. Automatic generation of cross-references for printed indexes

To these may also be added the facility for editing at the terminal whenever the need arises, so that the machine-stored thesaurus is always kept up to date in a quick, efficient, and relatively inexpensive way. If it can thus be made available for on-line access to users, they too can easily check to bring their own copies up to date without having to wait for a printed amendment.

Relations Between Thesauri

With so many organizations finding the need for a thesaurus, and so many thesauri being compiled, it seems surprising that more attention has not been given to the question of compatibility between the various schemes. In particular, one might expect this to apply to publishers of thesauri which cover the same or similar ground. That it has not happened so far is due to a variety of circumstances. First, only in recent years has there been any attempt to set up standard methods of construction. Second, many organizations seem to set about their task in total unawareness of either traditional subject heading lists or existing thesauri in their own or in related fields. Making a virtue out of such accidents, it is often claimed that one of the major attractions of a thesaurus is precisely that it can be tailor-made to suit the particular requirements of a particular organization—an attraction, it is said, which more than compensates for the costs of constructing a thesaurus in intellectual isolation.

The situation is changing, and the trend toward cooperation will doubtless continue—because there is a greater need, and because of the greater facility which has arrived in the wake of developments in the computer industry; and also, of course, because of growing awareness of the value of international cooperation in intellectual matters, in a world becoming ever more conscious of the value of cooperation in science and industry. The United Nations and its many specialized agencies, other international organizations such as Euratom, and the transnational corporations have all played a role in this development, and they are now being followed by international governmental organizations such as the European Communities Commission and the Council for Mutual Economic Assistance.

Where the method of construction is the same, it is a simple matter for one scheme to borrow parts of another. The *London Education Classification* thesaurus and the *Thesaurofacet* are both constructed by means of facet analysis, and so is the *London Classification for Business Studies* (LCBS), from which a new thesaurus is now being compiled. The LCBS has a facet for education which is an abridged version of some sections of the *London Education Classification;* the *Thesaurofacet* has a facet for management which is in its turn extracted from the LCBS.

A determined effort at this sort of economy has been started by the United Nations family of organizations, mainly through work in the social sciences by G. K. Thompson at the International Labor Organization (ILO). The result is the *Macrothesaurus* (*32*), described in a background paper by Thompson in 1974 (*33*). An "Interim Caretaker Group for the Macrothesaurus" was established at the ILO by the International Committee on Social Sciences Documentation, which has for many years stressed the need for coordination in the social sciences, where fields of study have large areas of overlap and the terminology is not nearly as precise as it is in the physical sciences. The initiative was taken in the late 1960s by the Organization for Economic Cooperation and Development (OECD), whose Development Center was active in the field of information storage and retrieval. This brought together the ILO, the Food and Agriculture Organization (FAO), the International Committee on Social Sciences Documentation, and the Deutsche Stiftung für Entwicklungsländer [German Foundation for International Development]. The "Aligned List of Descriptors" was first published for discussion in 1969. Many other organizations in the international field expressed interest; some had already compiled their own lists, and contributed them, so that the original Aligned List came to be much larger and more wide ranging. It is now "an authority list of terms on economic and social development, for use in the international context." It is titled *Macrothesaurus* because it was derived from several separate lists, and it endeavored to incorporate all of their terms in one single framework which would be acceptable to all of the original compilers. Each institution can take those parts of interest to itself, develop them more fully if necessary for its own purposes within the overall framework, and use the remainder to deal with the ever-present problem of "marginal fields."

The *Macrothesaurus* is divided into 19 facets, as follows:

- 01 International Cooperation. International Relations.
- 02 Economic Policy. Social Policy. Planning.
- 03 Economic Conditions. Economic Research. Economic System.
- 04 Institutional Framework.
- 05 Culture. Society.
- 06 Education. Training.
- 07 Agriculture.
- 08 Industry.
- 09 Commerce. Trade.
- 10 Transport.
- 11 Currency. Financing. International Monetary Relations.
- 12 Management. Productivity.
- 13 Labour.
- 14 Demography. Population.
- 15 Biology. Food. Health.
- 16 Environment. Natural Resources.
- 17 Atmospheric Science. Earth Sciences.
- 18 Science. Research. Methodology.
- 19 Information. Documentation.

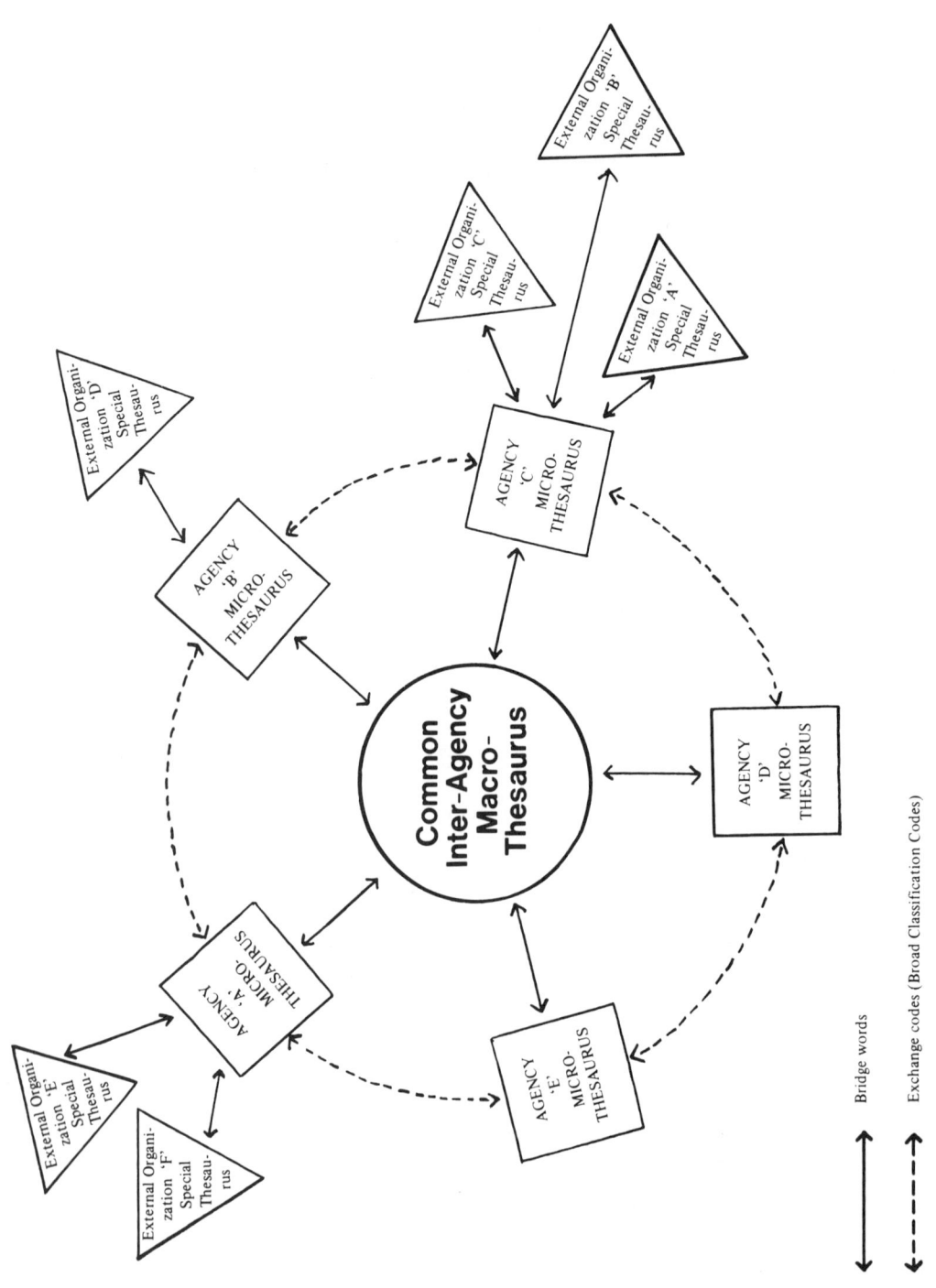

FIGURE 18. *Relations between thesauri.*

It is published by the OECD in English, French, German, and Spanish, and responsibility for its upkeep has been assumed by the United Nations family. Headquarters for the *Macrothesaurus* are based at the ILO, where G. K. Thompson has acquired much valuable experience in the use of computers for compiling and printing thesauri, and for their use in all aspects of information storage and retrieval. Already a number of improvements have been incorporated based on the suggestions of the cooperating bodies. Considerable reference was made, for example, to Jean Viet's *Thesaurus for Information Processing in Sociology* (34) for several sections, and in turn, Viet drew on "Section 06 Education" when he later compiled the *EUDISED Thesaurus*.

The kinds of relationship that may exist between such a "macrothesaurus" and the several "microthesauri" in its family are shown schematically in Figure 18.

In 1977 UNESCO published its own *Unesco Thesaurus*, which is subtitled "A Structured List of Descriptors for Indexing and Retrieving Literature in the Fields of Education, Science, Social Science, Culture and Communication." This was compiled by Jean Aitchison, and it follows to some extent the pattern which she established with the *Thesaurofacet*. It has been designed to be the working tool of the Computerized Documentation System (CDS) of UNESCO and will be used in indexing and retrieval of all documents and publications processed through the CDS. The terms from the *Unesco Thesaurus* are already being used to retrieve information from the data base established by the CDS, both for retrospective searches and in selective dissemination of information. It is in two volumes: Volume 1 contains the Introduction, the Classified Thesaurus, the Permuted Index, and the Hierarchical Display of Terms; Volume 2 contains the alphabetical part of the thesaurus. The *Unesco Thesaurus* was compiled originally by preparing an unstructured list of terms based on the *Macrothesaurus*, which was drafted in 1973/74 and circulated to many institutions, particularly in the UN family. As a result of this process, a new version was prepared, and the final version contains nearly 8,500 terms in all. There is a very good introduction, as one would expect from Jean Aitchison, and all aspects of the subjects are catered for. The *Unesco Thesaurus* also sets a fine example in the way in which considerable effort has been made to ensure compatibility with other thesauri and classification schemes such as the second edition of the *Bliss Bibliographical Classification*, the *London Education Classification*, and the *London Classification of Business Studies*.

The Thesaurus in Use

As this survey shows, the thesaurus can take several different forms, from the deceptively "simple" alphabetical list of terms to an intricate network of relationships like the *SPINES Thesaurus* and the *Thesaurofacet*. In every case, it will require an introductory section which explains how it can best be used. If this is not provided, the unlucky users will have to produce one for themselves; and this, paradoxically, is particularly true for the "simpler" types, because experience shows that they are the most difficult to use with consistency, especially where more than one person is involved in indexing. The reason for this becomes clear when we consider the purposes for which the thesaurus may be used. First, the purpose may be to index into one system subject information derived from several different sources which cannot be subjected to the constraints of the index system itself. Most of those sources are documents produced by individual authors who all base their writings on the thought patterns in their own minds, which are not necessarily the same pattern as that of the index system, even though all may be aiming at the same target: the accurate reflection of the real world and real phenomena. Second, the thesaurus may be used as an entry means for searching the file created by the index system, in order to find information for yet a third category of individual, an inquirer who may well be neither an author nor an indexer. This "matching" of terms cannot be done consistently if the thesaurus in use carries no rules of operation to guide the user to a correct selection of terms which will act as the bridge or intermediary between author and reader.

If the director of an information storage and retrieval system chooses to make use of a published thesaurus, he will naturally follow the rules set out by the original compiler; sometimes, unfortunately, these are not as full or precise as they should be, and compilers would do well to note that this is a fault which will certainly detract from the use and value of their systems. If, on the other hand, one chooses to compile one's own thesaurus (and the intellectual attraction of this is not to be underestimated), then a lesson may be learned from examples like TEST and the *Thesaurofacet*, which have well-written and detailed introductions giving both full explanations of how the thesaurus is constructed and all the information a user will require in order to use it efficiently. An introduction should therefore aim to cover all the sections that make up this article: the limits of the field or fields covered, the choice and form of terms, the network of relations, the form of presentation, and the use of special features like the graphical displays of the *SPINES Thesaurus*.

Conclusion

The thesaurus as a tool for librarians and information scientists represents the latest stage in a long line of works whose aims are to codify the language of discourse for the purposes of information storage and retrieval, and as a result, to improve the effectiveness of communication between people. Since language itself is constantly developing as the human race progresses, we cannot expect to find one perfect and absolute form, nor even one absolute set of rules and principles that will endure forever without change. Indeed, it will be to our advantage to recognize the need for constant revision of old forms and invention of new. What is important is that we should follow the advice we often give to others: Make use of the literature and so of the efforts and achievements of our predecessors. In this way, and only in this way, can each generation build on the foundations already laid by its forbears; and in this way too, we will learn more readily from our contemporaries. If we have the will to do this, then the thesaurus, being an instrument for effecting communication, can play a small but significant part in the improvement of understanding and harmony among the peoples of the world.

REFERENCES

1. Karen Sparck Jones, "Some Thesauric History," *Aslib Proc.*, **24**, 408–411 (July 1972).
2. Mary Elizabeth Stevens, H. P. Luhn: Information Scientist," in *H. P. Luhn* . . . , Ref. *3*, p. 26b.
3. Claire K. Schultz, ed., *H. P. Luhn: Pioneer in Information Science*, Spartan Books, New York, 1968, 320 pp.
4. Jean Aitchison and Alan Gilchrist, *Thesaurus Construction: A Practical Manual*, Aslib, London, 1972, 95 pp.
5. Alan Gilchrist, *The Thesaurus in Retrieval*, Aslib, London, 1971, 184 pp.
6. Dagobert Soergel, *Indexing Languages and Thesauri: Construction and Maintenance*, Melville Publishing Co., Los Angeles, Calif., 1974, 632 pp.
7. F. W. Lancaster, "Vocabulary Control in Information Retrieval Systems," in *Advances in Librarianship* (Melvin J. Voigt and Michael J. Harris, eds.), Academic Press, New York, 1977, Vol. 7, pp. 1–40.
8. E. J. Coates, *Subject Catalogues: Headings and Structure*, Library Association, London, 1960, 186 pp.
9. H. H. Neville, "Comprehensive On-line Computer System for Special Libraries, *Aslib Proc.*, **27**, 188–216 (May 1975).
10. UNESCO, *UNISIST Guidelines for the Establishment and Development of Monolingual Thesauri*, UNESCO, Paris, SC/WS/555, 1973, 37 pp.
11. C. van der Merwe, *Thesaurus of Sociological Research Terminology*, Rotterdam University Press, Netherlands, 1974, 471 pp.
12. Engineers Joint Council, *Thesaurus of Engineering and Scientific Terms*, EJC, New York, 1967, 890 pp.
13. American Psychological Association, *Thesaurus of Psychological Index Terms*, 2nd ed., APA, Washington, D.C., 1977, 282 pp.
14. Jean Aitchison et al., *Thesaurofacet: A Thesaurus and Faceted Classification for Engineering and Related Subjects*, English Electric Co., Whetstone, 1969, 491 pp.
15. Barbara Westby, ed., *Sears List of Subject Headings*, 9th ed., H. W. Wilson Co., New York, 1965, 641 pp.
16. Frederick Goodman, "Introduction," in *ERIC Thesaurus*, CCM Information Corp., New York, 1972, 330 pp.
17. UNESCO, *SPINES Thesaurus: A Controlled and Structured Vocabulary of Science and Technology for Policy-Making, Management and Development*, UNESCO, Paris, 1976, 3 vols.
18. B. J. Field, *INSPEC Thesaurus (a Thesaurus of Terms for Physics, Electrotechnology, Computers and Control)*, Institution of Electrical Engineers, London, 1973, 2 vols.
19. Gordon C. Barhydt and Charles T. Schmidt, *Information Retrieval Thesaurus of Education Terms*, Case Western Reserve University, Cleveland, 1968, 133 pp.
20. B. C. Vickery, *Classification and Indexing in Science*, 3rd ed., Butterworths, London, 1975, 228 pp.
21. A. Neelameghan, "Non-hierarchical Associative Relationships: Their Types and the Computer Generation of RT Links," in *Seminar on Thesaurus in Information Systems*, Bangalore, December 1–5, 1975, pp. A1–A8.
22. Karen Sparck Jones, *Automatic Keyword Classification for Information Retrieval*, Butterworths, London, 1971, 253 pp.
23. J. S. Bruner, *The Process of Education*, Vintage Books, New York, 1960, 97 pp.
24. Bärbel Inhelder and Jean Piaget, *The Early Growth of Logic in the Child: Classification and Seriation*, Routledge and Kegan Paul, London, 1964, 302 pp.
25. R. A. Fairthorne, "The Mathematics of Classification," *Proc. British Soc. International Bibliography*, **9**, 35–42 (October 1947).
26. M. J. Roberts et al., *Construction Industry Thesaurus*, Department of the Environment, London, 1972, 341 pp.
27. International Occupational Safety and Health Information Center, *CIS Thesaurus*, International Labor Organization, Geneva, 1976.
28. D. J. Foskett and Joy Foskett, *The London Education Classification: A Thesaurus/Classification of British Educational Terms*, 2nd ed., University of London Institute of Education Library, 1974, 165 pp.

29. Jean Viet, *EUDISED Multilingual Thesaurus*, Mouton, Paris, 1973, 391 pp.
30. Lol N. Rolling, "The Role of Graphic Display of Concept Relationships in Indexing and Retrieval Vocabularies," in *Classification Research: Proceedings of the Second International Study Conference* (Pauline Atherton, ed.), Munksgaard, Copenhagen, 1965, pp. 295–320.
31. Gerard Salton, *Experiments in Automatic Thesaurus Construction for Information Retrieval*, Cornell University, Ithaca, N.Y., 1971, 27 pp.
32. Organization for Economic Cooperation and Development, *Macrothesaurus: A Basic List of Economic and Social Development Terms*, OECD, Paris, 1972, 225 pp.
33. George K. Thompson, *Background Paper on the Macrothesaurus*, International Labor Organization, Geneva, 1974, 14 pp.
34. Jean Viet, *Thesaurus for Information Processing in Sociology*, Mouton, The Hague, 1971, 336 pp.

16
Subject Headings

Martha L. Manheimer / University of Pennsylvania, Pittsburgh, Pennsylvania

HOW SUBJECT HEADINGS APPEAR ON CATALOG CARDS

> SUBJECT CATALOGING
> Chan, Lois Mai.
>   Library of Congress subject headings : principles and applications / Lois Mai Chan. --
> Littleton, Colo. : Libraries Unlimited, 1978.
>   347 p. ; 24 cm. -- (Research studies in library science ; no. 15)
>   Bibliography: p. 333-339.
>   Includes index.
>   ISBN 0-87287-187-8
>   1. Subject cataloging. 2. Library of Congress. Subject cataloging Division. Library of Congress subject headings. I. Title. II. Series.

Library of Congress Subject Headings (LCSN)

Forms in which the headings may appear. The examples below may be found on p. 252 and 254 of the *Library of Congress subject headings*, 8th ed., 1975.

	Examples
Common nouns	Calves; Cambric

From Manheimer, Martha L. *Subject Headings.* CATALOGING AND CLASSIFICATION: A WORKBOOK. 2nd Ed. New York, Marcel Dekker, Inc., c1980. pp. 83-86.

Proper nouns	Calvinists; Calypso (Game); Cambrai, League of, 1508. There are very few proper nouns on the list. Proper names are added as needed by individual libraries, in the form used for the entry of the name.
Modified nouns	Campus parking; Canaanite literature
Phrases	Camps for the handicapped; Canada in art
Inverted headings	Cambrai, Treaty of, 1529
Glossed headings	Camps (Military); Camel (Fighter planes)

1. *Scope note.* A note defining the applicability of the heading. There is a scope note following the heading "Camps."
2. *Syndetic structure.* The relationships among the terms on the list implied by the cross-reference structure.
3. *See also (sa) references.* These are other legal headings that are related in some way to the heading under which they appear.
4. *See (x) references.* A direction under an illegal heading referring the user to the legal heading, i.e., the one used in the catalog, e.g.,

    Can-Am Road Race
    See Canadian-American Challenge Cup

    The "x" is the reciprocal, i.e.,

    Canadian-American Challenge Cup
    x Can-Am Road Race

5. *XX references.* This means that the main heading will appear under the xx reference (when it appears in the alphabetic array as a main heading) as a *sa* reference, e.g., see the relationship between "Camps for mentally handicapped children" and "Camps for the handicapped."
6. *Special subject subdivisions.* Under some headings special subdivisions appear that are of importance to that heading or are related only to that heading. They are preceded by one, two, three or four dashes. The number of dashes indicates the hierarchical level of the subheading.

    Canada--Description and travel
    Canada--Description and travel--Guide-books
    Canada--History--To 1763 (New France)--Juvenile literature

7. *Most commonly used subdivisions.* These are subheadings applicable to any main heading within specified limitations defined under the subheading. See p. xviii-lxxii in *LCSH*. One example is "Accidents" which can be used as a subheading with main headings in the list.

    Camps--Accidents

8. *Local subdivisions practice: Direct and Indirect.* The following information has been excerpted and, in part, paraphrased from *Cataloging Service,* Bulletin 118 and Bulletin 120.

    Direct and Indirect. These are parenthesized, italicized directions that immediately follow the heading or subheading. They indicate that a geographic location may be added to the main heading or subheading. A geographic location cannot be added unless *direct* or *indirect* appears following the heading or subheading. Both directions should now be interpreted as *indirect. Indirect* means that the larger geographical, i.e., political, jurisdiction is interposed between the heading and the specific place name.

> Camping--Pennsylvania--Elk County

When *direct* or *indirect* also or only follows the subheading, the place name is added following the subheading rather than the main heading.

> Camps--Safety regulations--Pennsylvania--Elk County

However, when the instruction *direct* or *indirect* follows only the main heading, the place name must follow the main heading,

> Camps--Pennsylvania--Elk County--Accreditation

because the instruction *direct* or *indirect* follows "Camps" and "Safety regulations" but does not follow "Accreditation."

Exceptions. For the following countries, the first-order political divisions are assigned directly:

Countries	*Divisions*
Canada	Provinces
Great Britain	Constituent countries
Soviet Union	Republics
United States	States

These divisions may be further subdivided by the names of countries, cities and other subordinate units.

> Music--Quebec (Province)--Quebec (City)
> Sports--England--London
> Nursing--Ukraine--Kiev (Province)
> Education--California--San Francisco

Assign as a direct subheading the name of any region which does not lie entirely within a country or first-order political subdivision of the four countries above.

> Europe   Rocky Mountains
> Great Lakes   Nile Valley
> Mexico, Gulf of

Assign directly the names of the following cities, Berlin, New York, Washington, D.C.

9. *Class references.* These are class numbers in the Library of Congress classification scheme which may represent an appropriate class for the book designated by the subject heading. They may follow either a main heading or a subheading and appear italicized within parentheses following the heading.

> Canada goose *(QL696.A5)*
> Camels *(QL737.U5; Animal industries, SF249)*

Class references are not part of the subject heading. They do not appear in the tracings. They are useful as a partial index to the classification scheme.

Other Directions

10. Under "Gilds" there is the following note:

> *sa particular gilds, e.g.* Dunfermline, Scot.
> Weavers' Incorporation; *and
> subdivision* Gilds *under names of
> cities, e.g.* Edinburgh--Gilds

The first part of this note means that specifically named gilds appear as subheadings under the names of cities. The second part of the note means that when used with the name of a city, the heading "Gilds" is used as a subheading under the name of the city.

> Gilds--France

but

> Paris, France--Gilds

11. *Reciprocal headings.* Under Canada--Foreign relations--United States, the reference

> *Note under* United States--Foreign relations--Canada, (France, Japan, etc.)

refers the user to the following instruction under United States,

> Duplicate entry is made under Canada, (France, Japan, etc.)--Foreign relations--United States.

These are reciprocal headings and entries must always be made under both countries involved.

12. *Exemplary headings.* The headings "Calvinists in Brazil, (etc.)" and "Cameo glass, English, (French, etc.)" are exemplary headings and indicate, in the first example, that the name of any country can be substituted for Brazil, and in the second example, the adjectival form of any national name.

13. *Biography.* Individual biography should be assigned the subject heading consisting of the name of the person in the form used for entry in the catalog. In addition, for most classes of persons, an additional heading, the one that would be used for collective biography for the class of persons to which the individual belongs, should be assigned in the following format.

> (Class of persons)--(Place)--Biography

For example:

> Librarians--Texas--Biography

CLASSIFYING

17

Abstract Classification

Jay E. Daily / University of Pittsburgh, Pittsburgh, Pennsylvania

A classification system which is based on the subject contents of books is called a "natural classification." Abstract classification systems can be devised without reference to the contents of books or other library materials. Abstract classifications fall into three basic classes: artificial classification, accidental classification, and the purely abstract. An artificial classification is based on some characteristic of books, independent of general subject matter. An accidental classification relies on those characteristics of the book which do not relate to subject content, such as size or color of binding, and is at times independent of the book itself, as in schemes based on accession numbers. Artificial classifications are often based on chronology, geographic location, form of material, author's nationality or name, and at times combinations of several of these. It can be seen that almost all regular classification schemes have artificial elements—and very likely accidental elements as well. Examples are the form divisions in the Dewey decimal system, the elements of the Library of Congress system with its characteristic provision for early works and tables for subdivisions by authors' names, and the provisions in many libraries for size of book.

Accidental classifications are generally employed in fixed-location schemes, and one of the simplest is a classification based on the receipt of the material. Each time an item is received, it is given a number, usually with a numbering machine, which shelves it in sequence by receipt and the accidents that occur as the numbers are stamped onto the item. Until recently, the Rangoon University Library used a classification scheme of this sort; because it is a closed-stack library, this classification is as useful as any other. Another accidental classification very similar to this is a fixed-location scheme which gives range number, stack number, and

---

From Daily, Jay E. *Abstract Classification.* ENCYCLOPEDIA OF LIBRARY AND INFORMATION SCIENCE. Vol. 1. Edited by Allen Kent and Harold Lancour. Assistant Editor, William Z. Nasri. New York, Marcel Dekker, Inc., c1968. pp. 12–16.

shelf number in some fashion. The Biblioteca Mayor of the University of Concepcion in Chile employs a fixed-location scheme that is modified so that broad subject areas are shelved in the same room. There is very little difference in this classification method and that employed by the New York Public Reference Library. Its classification scheme is unique and quite satisfactory, even though extremely simple. A number, usually composed of letters of the English alphabet, locates the material by stack level and range, where it is shelved in alphabetic order by author. Some broad, general subject analysis is done so that accidental classifications may partake of natural features.

Fixed-location schemes are employed for shelving books where some automation is used in obtaining the book for a patron. Various methods are used so that the patron by punching keys at the circulation desk can cause a light to flash on at the location of the particular volume. At the page post a light also flashes, showing that a book is sought. This greatly reduces the amount of clerical effort required to obtain the book and deliver it to the user.

All abstract classifications employ a simple notation, usually of a mixed type (letters and numbers). The notations can remain simple because all abstract classifications are closed systems, that is, do not provide for internal expansion either as infinite dense sets or as infinite discrete sets. Nevertheless, expansion is possible through the addition of whole blocks of unused numbers. An example of a notation for an accidental classification scheme would be as follows: the letters Z, W, X, and Y to represent book sizes from smaller than octavo to larger than quarto, numbers to indicate stack range, a letter to indicate the stack within the range, and another number to indicate the shelf on which the book is located. That is, W17G6 would indicate a book of about 22 centimeters shelved in range 17 on stack number 7 on the sixth shelf. This is a purely imaginary scheme for a purely imaginary library, and yet the entire classification could be worked out very precisely. This exemplifies the term "abstract classification."

Various explorations in the nature of classification have been conducted by Licklider (1), Vickery, and others. These are abstract in the purest sense of the word; they often rely on symbolic logic and linguistics to provide models for information storage organization. The relations between terms in natural language have been studied by Osgood et al. (2) and have been described as "semantic space" and "semantic differential." In a factor analysis of human scaling judgment relating statements to an attributive scale, Osgood and his coauthors found only a half-dozen factors which appear consistently, even in many different ethnic and linguistic contexts. So far as is known, all natural classification methods revert to the basic structure of languages, disclosing the classification function of statements in a natural language and the close relationship between the organization of natural classification schemes and the syntactical organization of statements.

Abstract classification schemes have been devised in advance of the examination of any material to be stored, and in a sense all natural classifications provide essentially for material not yet examined (or even written) if they are to serve for more than the material at hand.

The basic structures of classification schemes are as follows:

1. Hierarchical
2. Associative
3. Sequential
4. Attributive

It is a rare natural classification scheme which attempts to utilize only one of these features, or even attempts to omit one. Excepting attributive schemes, both artificial and accidental classifications can be so described and are distinct in relying on only one or two features of basic structure. For instance, fixed-location schemes are essentially hierarchical, as can be seen by comparing taxonomic hierarchies with a fixed-location scheme:

    I. Phylum   I. Library
        A. Family   A. Deck
           1. Genus   1. Range
              a. Species   a. Stack
                 (1). Race   (1). Shelf
                    (a). Individual   (a). Book

That not all statements of natural language fit into the scheme is obvious.

Associative schemes add distinctions such as size and thereby simplify the notation, especially where size becomes synonymous with deck or range. In natural classifications the coordinate indexing methods of Tauber (4) and his followers show the associative feature of natural classification very precisely, as does the Dewey decimal classification in its relative index. A term tends to take on the meaning ascribed to it by another term.

In a sequential classification all items having the same description are listed together; in an accidental classification books are simply numbered as received and shelved one by one. In the Dewey decimal classification the hierarchical organization breaks down completely into sequences such as the languages listed in 490–499, in which a vague attempt to list by families of language is only partly successful. In the Library of Congress classification many of the schedules are simple lists providing for organization by alphabetic codes which are essentially sequential, especially in the listings under specific subjects.

Attributive natural classification schemes, notably Ranganathan's Colon Classification and the Universal Decimal Classification, are matched in information storage organization with "role" descriptors automatically added at times to every term. In such schemes provision is made for both nonce relationships and specified, if not permanent, relationships. Attributive schemes are always related to natural classification and are the closest to the condensation principle of natural language whereby much can be said with few terms, the meaning of which depends on the role of the term in relation to other terms in the statement. Some writers seem to believe that all classification is purely hierarchical, but this is rarely the case. Rather it can be stated that, taken in the broadest sense, all natural classification relies on the attributive function of terms for syntactical organization. The work of Chomsky (3) in transformational analysis of grammar has made this apparent and has shown that questions about the subject content of books rely on a structure which states attributes of given terms in a given context.

The advantages of artificial and accidental classifications are readily apparent. Where no subject analysis of the book at hand is needed, processing tends to be extremely simple and standard bibliographies can be used in place of subject headings or other subject analyses. The shelving of the books is also very simple, especially in fixed-location schemes. Circulation procedures can be devised with great facility for fixed-location classifications, and there is good reason to argue that the lavish expenditure of funds for the subject classification of closed-stack libraries is largely a waste of money. Nevertheless, wherever the public is admitted to the stacks of a library, no abstract classification can provide for the users the advantages which are obvious with a natural classification. The experiments in purely abstract classifications may ultimately lead to a mathematical–linguistic model for the evaluation of classification schemes.

The enlargement of the library collection to include such materials as motion pictures, slides, phonograph recordings, and microtext has generally required that librarians devise abstract classifications which will locate the material by its form and in some useful sequence. Several different classification schemes have been proposed for phonograph recordings which would locate material not only by the type of recording, whether plastic disks or magnetic tapes, but also by the general type of information recorded, such as symphony music, opera, jazz, spoken word, and so forth. A proposal to put works of literature on phonograph recordings with the books was attempted in some public libraries and found to be very unsuitable. The phonograph recordings are now generally kept together in a separate *ad hoc* classification, which can be called abstract in the precise sense of the definition.

REFERENCES

1. J. C. R. Licklider, *Libraries of the Future,* M.I.T. Press, Cambridge, Mass., 1965, pp. 70–71.
2. C. E. Osgood, G. J. Suci, and P. Tannenbaum, *The Measurement of Meaning,* Univ. of Illinois Press, Urbana, 1957.
3. N. Chomsky, *Syntactic Structures,* Mouton, The Hague, 1957.
4. M. Tauber, *Technical Services in Libraries,* Columbia Univ. Press, New York, 1953.

18

Classification and Categorization

Jay E. Daily / University of Pittsburgh, Pittsburgh, Pennsylvania

This description of classification is meant to serve as a general introduction to some special research in classification and a summary of results so far. It is not meant as history nor as a summary of all research which has been done with varied results in various places. Usually such research has accepted as a basic assumption the idea that subject indexing differs from classification and has proceeded along very limited lines to whatever conclusions can be reached with this assumption. To accept this assumption is to deny the researcher the one system of methodology that makes research both objective and fruitful. One must assume that language, in its broadest sense, affects the subject indexing and that there is no distinct difference between classification, which is identified by its structure of notation, and the alphabetical list, however organized. "Subject indexing is a classification process" [1].

If, however, one accepts the idea that natural language has as one of its primary attributes a method of classification, then the classification process becomes clear and several tools available for research can be used freely. Without invading the interpretations of language current among philosophers, it is safe to dismiss all that theory dealing with language as a system of signals and as a means of expressing feelings. We are concerned only with the segment of natural language that is meant to convey the experiences of reality as messages. The definition is best left in its present sloppy form, and we need only go a little further and state that "reality" as here used refers to the portion of the environment that has weight and occupies space upon which operations may be performed and the results serve as the basis of communication. We are concerned with the expression of mood and feeling only as it serves for messages with a content greater than simple expression.

From Daily, Jay E. *Classification and Categorization.* ENCYCLOPEDIA OF LIBRARY AND INFORMATION SCIENCE. Vol. 5. Edited by Allen Kent and Harold Lancour. Assistant Editor, William Z. Nasri. New York, Marcel Dekker, Inc., c1971. pp. 43–66.

That natural language is classificatory can be identified readily in two different ways. The first, derived from onomastics, the study of names, leads us from such constructs as "John Smith, 901 East 19th Street, New York, New York, 10016," to "my friend 'Smith,' " to "John," to "the Smiths," and even to "all Smiths." It is of little importance that we are dealing with an imaginary person at an imaginary, indeed impossible, address, because we could devise a system that is as precise in structure as our example which identifies a certain person, and him only, and generalize from this individual at the level of absolute specificity through assumed contexts to the level of broadest generality. We can even trace this development in the transition from name into word. The second method is grammatical, grouping and identifying morphemes in order to trace the development of transformations from kernel, that is, absolute, statements to those that assume a context as segments of language to those that are so broadly general as to exist only for the purpose of making the transformation acceptable.

The briefest way to describe a particular person or place or thing is to name it. When the name is acceptable all further description is unnecessary except as we wish to teach another person the name. We cannot assume that an individual knows a name without identifying the particularity meant by another system. A recitation of names leads to a categorization of them which serves as the briefest possible description. For example, the list "gold, silver, lead, chlorine, oxygen, radium, sulfur, iron, sodium, calcium, etc." can be categorized as chemical elements. If we begin the statement "the chemical elements such as radium, sulfur, iron, gold" we further develop the categorization as a level that includes the particular names as well as the category. Regardless of how we symbolize these elements, the category and the names remain as indicators of particular substances which can be predicted to react in a given fashion, that is, upon which operations may be performed without regard to the individual except that he follow all the steps in the operation correctly.

Starting with names which identify a particular person, place, or thing, we can build transformations that are capable of changing the name to a generalization, and similarly, we can start with a generalization and build transformations that will lead us to identify a unique part of the experience of reality which everyone shares. These transformations are accomplished in natural language by various means inherent within the specific tongue, whether by variation of vowels between consonants in the Semitic languages, by postpositional syllables in the Mongolian and Japanese languages, by additional vowels or consonants in the Indo-European languages, or by arrangement of words in the Chinese languages, or by combinations of these in such *lingua franca* as English and Swahili.

Hence an analysis of morphology and of syntax can establish levels of specificity in the nominal structure of any language. We can go further and compare one linguistic system with another by comparing the methods of word-building and the system of transformations that regulate the employment of words in statements. In classification, we deal only with the nominal structure. We cannot be concerned with such philosophical problems as truth, validity, and usefulness. We have to assume that all statements are valid, that each represents an ordering of facts that amounts to truth, and that any statement is potentially useful if it is worthy of classification.

Classification and Categorization

Having accepted the techniques of general linguistics this far, we can go further and postulate that notational systems are artificial, or invented, systems for the translation or transliteration of natural language. The purpose of the notation is to identify a given nominal construct in such a way that the inherent system of the natural language is no longer a governing factor in the use of the name. Thus, when we categorize a list of names, as in the chemical elements, we can use a cipher which takes the letters of the names and substitutes for some or all of them other symbols. Just as easily we can utilize a code that will substitute one nominal construct for another, or we can utilize an artificial language that will enable us to rearrange names in some more useful system. In any case, we are dealing with a method of identification that is no longer governed by the necessary rules of a given natural language.

The Library of Congress system of classification and subject heading can be used to identify this procedure. J. P. Immroth has shown that titles of Shakespeare's works are at the first level of abstraction so that a specific play is meant by each title and the Library of Congress classification provides a means of identifying each play, even spurious and doubtful works, by utilizing the numbering system of two letters and four Arabic numerals. Elsewhere in the Library of Congress classification first-order abstractions are identified sometimes by one Cutter number, a typical cipher, or by two Cutter numbers (2). In research now being conducted, Immroth shows that there is no necessary relationship between the subject headings in the Library of Congress list and the classification, so that similarity of a term in the index, the schedules, and the subject heading list may be considered accidental, dependent only on the nature of English as the language used.

Subject heading theory, as it can be traced from Crestadoro through Cutter to Frarey, Lilley, Harris, and others, assumes that natural language can be made to serve the purpose of classification without the employment of notational devices. Such an assumption seems acceptable only because of the wide variety of transformations possible in English. A language such as French introduces different restraints and a very highly inflected language such as Russian imposes so many constraints that a natural language system of classification, as represented by subject headings, is impossible. Indeed, in English, it is only partially feasible. Natural language, which always begins as speech and hence may be described as a system of vocables, can convey in written form no messages so complete as those in spoken form, and even these are further amplified by the inclusion of nonverbal features of facial expression and gesture. McLuhan and many others have noted the increase in message content when television is the means of transmittal rather than radio.

Although many different methods of printing have been employed, marks of punctuation systematized, and rules of spacing on a page established, the written form of a natural language is only a part of the communication possible within the system of vocables, whether in written or spoken or unspoken form. A further assumption is that only the written form is necessary for classification purposes. However, such an assumption is rather easily disproved if it is restated as a hypothesis: the nominal structure employed for classification purposes is sufficient in only the written form. A heading like "Criminal statistics" is meaningful only if the proper intonation is employed to establish the transformation meant. If "criminal" is an adjective, then the intonation of the phrase in spoken form will differ from that intonation which establishes "criminal" as a substantive. We need the spoken form in order to work further transformations so that the imbedded kernel form may be transformed into such statements as "Statistics which are criminal" and "Statistics of those persons who are criminals." Even these transformations are wide of the mark that the subject heading is supposed to designate: "Statistics of crimes and those who commit them" (3).

Notation is necessary to free the nominal structure from the constraints of natural language. It establishes a context that shows the level of abstraction at which the term must be read. A notational device can widely separate the term "Criminal statistics" as a means of fraud from the term "Criminal statistics" as a description of methods of recording crimes and those who commit them. While the first possible meaning seems farfetched, it is nevertheless possible, and the second as the most familiar ought not to distract any reasonable person who would be looking for nothing else, in the present state of knowledge about crimes. It is this assumption of clarity that has made the possibility of a free use of natural language for indexing purposes seem a most useful method of simplifying and accelerating the process of classification. Furthermore, the fact that ambiguity increases only as the number of messages increase has led to the apparent support for the hypothesis that indexing systems may be independent of notational devices and yet function adequately for retrieval purposes. The hypothesis is valid to the extent that the number of messages is limited.

A further difficulty in the development of theory has been the confusion between notation and classification. This is readily seen when the notation constitutes an artificial language, as in the Dewey Decimal Classification. The notation apparently functions on its own and is purely hierarchical if we assume that the numbers from 000 to 999.999+ are all subdivisions of an unstated maximum number (1000). The natural language translation of the various possible terms in Dewey's notation, however, are not purely hierarchical. They constitute a series of hierarchies which the notation establishes as purely hierarchical, not the natural language. All language is arbitrary, in the sense that the user must turn to arbiters to establish differences of significance and employment of terms. The tendency of language to classify is readily established, but there is no single system of classification that can be equated to a given natural language except one derived from an analysis of its morphology and syntax. Even this may leave one with a broad system of categorization rather than the classification that limits levels of abstraction. While such a system may be employed usefully and readily, the number of messages that can be retrieved is strictly limited by the tendency of the language toward ambiguity and the means by which ambiguity is reduced.

The syntactical systems of natural language increase the context of a given term so that ambiguity may generally be stated as a function of redundancy. If the context is assumed and agreed upon, then ambiguity will not arise, but as we go further from an established context we must increase the number of terms which by themselves do nothing but amplify and categorize the level of abstraction meant by the given term. That classification systems are arbitrary is no surprise. The fact that arbitrary decisions may be used to reduce ambiguity by a means other than redundancy is noteworthy.

Classification and Categorization

It is often noted that even related natural languages cannot be translated exactly the one into the other. This difference arises from different contexts which sufficiently limit the ambiguity of the term. The contexts vary according to what has been called the deep structure of the term, using Chomsky's terminology, or what may be designated as the conceptual identification of the term. Early in Chomsky's development of transformational grammar, he discerned the possibility that the technique might lead to a method of objective analysis of semantic values (4). The fact that translation is precise for equal terms within those contexts which are the same indicates that what is translated is the context rather than the term. From this fact, we may work toward the possibility that the arrangement of terms in a classification that utilizes an artificial language will exhibit the deep structure of the term. If it were necessary to define concepts before we could classify terms, we would make a functional classification virtually impossible. We can suppose that a concept cannot adequately be stated in any term except that of the artificial language, so that the term used in natural language is considered a translation of the artificial language term, and as such, the natural language term is free of context except as a translation and is independent of the necessary contexts within the natural language to reduce the ambiguity of the term.

This leads to accepting the undefinability of concepts as axiomatic. Such a decision is less dangerous than may seem because philosophic systems have long accepted this, for instance Zen Buddhism, and the work of the Spanish mystics including San Juan de la Cruz and Santa Teresa de Jesus. The logical positivist system includes the basic idea from the Vienna Circle to the American group which formed around certain immigrant philosophers after World War II. The development of symbolic logic by Whitehead and Russell is based on the inadequacy of natural language to deal with the transformations necessary for logical statements without the confabulation that arises as a constraint of the language itself. Thus a given proposition in symbolic language may not have any exact equivalent in natural language (5). If concepts are definable only in the terms of the artificial language itself, then the translation may be made into any language and, granting the different contexts possible in different languages, we should expect to find that not all the terms of the artificial language are translatable in all languages. Preliminary research so far unpublished by E. Useriu and N. Deines confirm this so far as the Dewey Decimal Classification, in the former case, and the Universal Decimal Classification, in the latter case, are concerned. This is rather hard news for those who believe that an exact word for word translation of these classifications is possible, but in every case the area of context determined by the notation as a system of artificial language delimits the utilization of language and brings about translations of terms which are as unique as some that have been devised for translations of poetry. It is the failure of translation to bring the poetic form and force from one language to another that gave rise to the Italian proverb "Traduttore, traditore." Even here, the subtlety of natural language is exhibited. "Translator, traitor" lacks the provocative similarity of the vocables in Italian.

However this may defeat the efforts of the poet to recreate in his own language what has been effected in the verse in another language, it is a highly useful feature in the analysis of classification systems. Semantic analysis can proceed on the basis of three kinds of meaning: lexical, contextual, and conceptual. We can also postulate certain values which can be established by computational methods. So far four such values have been identified, although full testing and establishment of these values awaits further research: semantic weight, semantic limitation, semantic shift, and semantic lag. Finally we can arrive at a ranking of semantic content as orders of abstraction, borrowing liberally from the general semanticists (6). Absolute specificity, the identity of a nominal structure and a particular part of the physical environment, is the only portion that cannot be ranked except as the minimal unit of indexability. (With the ranking of orders of abstraction we discover a key to the indexability of certain terms.) Above this, the first order of abstraction is the category formed only of items of absolute specificity. Next is the category of those categories that include only items of absolute specificity. After this come high-order abstractions that can be summarized as categories of categories formed from nonspecific terms at any level.

Lexicography is the science of establishing lexical meaning for terms and is dependent upon the determination of word boundaries within contexts and the distinction between contexts which reduce ambiguity by different means and those which establish a different conceptual identification of a term. The result of lexicographical effort can be judged by the extent to which all the terms within a language have been identified and the contexts in which the terms are used with different conceptual meanings have been recorded. No lexicographical work is complete after it is made public because of the dynamic nature of language. This dynamism is seen first in the values we give to terms as they are used. Only by comparing these values can we establish a conceptual meaning.

Semantic weight is a function of the use of a term in different contexts. The greater the number of different contexts in which a term may appear, the less the semantic weight. It is as if some of the meaning is rubbed off whenever a term is used in a different context. The limit of conceptual meaning can only be the metaphors in which a nominal term may be used. The procedure for establishing semantic weight is that of the concordance: all the terms are identified in all of the contexts used. A raw total shows all the contexts, a refined total will identify contexts that are virtually the same and the degree of match may be established quite clearly by seeking similar nominal structures which appear with the contexts established. This method becomes more effective as it is used more widely so that a concordance of a particular author's work establishes the semantic weight of the term only within that work and for that author. As the number of authors and works increases, a very good "suppress" list for an indexing system may be devised so that words of purely syntactical function can either be omitted or can be utilized only as "prop words" which exist for the sole purpose of providing an acceptable arrangement of words. This characteristic is enough to defeat the noun rule which was last advocated seriously by M. Prevost (7). This concordance function is useful in establishing a classification system, because those terms that are used the least number of times in different contexts have sufficient semantic weight to make them indexable.

Semantic weight is a direct function of semantic limitation. The greater the number of terms needed to establish context, the less the semantic weight. Consequently, we can define semantic limitation and semantic weight as opposing functions of specificity. The adjective "runcible" appears to exist for the sole purpose of modifying "spoon." The semantic limitation is complete. We can, however, suggest

Classification and Categorization

a runcible afternoon and convey some slight poetic meanings. The verb "sit" has no synonyms in English, a further indication of semantic limitation and semantic weight. All the contexts in which the term is used will have the conceptual meaning of reclining on the haunches. "It sits well with me" is an example of metaphorical use of the term.

Further we can establish that the term of greatest semantic weight will tend to color the context in which it appears. This is seen most clearly in the use of taboo words and accounts for the growth of synonymous structures surrounding those terms of such intense emotional charge that their use is restricted by social proprieties and custom (8). Such semantic shift tends to reduce the semantic weight of those terms which are used even in a metaphorical sense, so that a term which is frequently used in a given context may come to represent the entire context. In Chinese, a character used in a classic tends to bear its connotation into every context in which it is used, so that each sentence of a classic acquires the force of an aphorism which any character may represent. The same tendency is seen in English. If a speaker refers to a "cherry picker," we expect to find a long arm reaching up.

Finally we can account for the constant development and change in language by postulating that the number of terms available is always less than the number of terms needed. This may be described as semantic lag. It is seen most clearly in the status of such languages as Korean, Burmese, and other tongues which reflect the intellectual stagnation during a period of colonial domination. In Korea, the Japanese prohibited the use of the native tongue of the Koreans and punished those who openly broke the rule. Korean became a language of the home, and all the technical development took place in Japanese. When World War II ended, the Korean language was instantly re-adopted as the official language of the country, but only recently has it acquired a terminology sufficient for the development of a technology within the country. However, even in English, perhaps the most developed of all the languages for the transfer of technical information, there is a measurable lag in the terminology available within a classification system. This is demonstrated by Appendix Two, which lists the 598 changes of terminology made for the ninth edition of the Sears list.

To exhibit just how these characteristics of language affect the analysis of an information retrieval system, the terms of the Sears Subject Heading list, 8th edition, the last to include a classification number, are included as Appendix One. They have been reorganized into a categorized list following the mathematical principles of the Dewey Decimal Classification and the numbers may be construed as similar to the abridged edition of the Dewey Decimal Classification.

In research now in progress, G. M. Sinkankas establishes three methods of syndesis in an alphabetic list: by morphology, that is, the use of grammatical structures, including punctuation, to attempt to bring like terms into alphabetic relationship with each other. This feature was adequately discerned in the Library of Congress list of subject headings, 5th edition, by the author (3). The accepted method is by a see-also structure, which Sinkankas investigated in two papers, so far unpublished, for a sample of headings derived from the Library of Congress list, 7th edition (9). Finally, there is the method of classification and categorization. It is only the latter which will concern us, as the nature of semantic analysis to establish contextual meaning is demonstrated below. We can dismiss conceptual meaning as beyond the level of our capability at present and not essential to the establishment of a classification, and equally we can establish that all the terms in the list are, in fact, also to be found in various lexicons of the English language. It is best to use a lexicon contemporary with the list itself, in view of the likelihood of semantic lag, and the one chosen for the first experiment is the *Oxford Universal Dictionary on Historical Principles, prepared by William Little* (rev. and ed. by C. T. Onions), Oxford at the Clarendon Press, c1955.

Lexical Meaning

Our first hypothesis may be stated as "All the subject headings in the classified list will be found in the O.U.D." Successive samples will establish that this is true except for a paradigmatic class which includes 027 Chicago—Libraries; 027.5 U.S. Library of Congress; 136.4 Africa—Native Races; 277.3 Ohio—Church History; 923 Nero, Emperor of Rome, 37–68; etc. However, we would find that the O.U.D. includes an entry for Jesus, p. 1063, col. 1, which is a partial match for 232 Jesus Christ. The entry is fully explained in the definition. There is also an entry for Mary, p. 1211, col. 3, which is similar, in that the term in the list is 232.93 Mary, Virgin. Further exploration would establish a series of transformations that would partially identify the distinction between 923 Nero, Emperor of Rome, 37–68, and 232 Jesus Christ. We would find that the paradigmatic class represented by headings not in O.U.D. are at the level of null abstraction with notable exceptions which we would have to explain by another method.

The larger paradigmatic class would consist of the very numerous one-word headings which are not capitalized in formal English prose. These represent an exact match in some cases, a partial match in others. Those headings in the list which consist of one or more words, especially those which include a mark of punctuation, would be only partial matches, in that one word would be listed but not necessarily the other word in the subject headings. A rather elegant and simple support of an amended hypothesis is possible, so that we can state that all of the terms have a lexical meaning.

This may seem trivial, especially when the list in question is based largely on words evident with great frequency in a wide variety of texts commonly found in the small library. The method is not so trivial when the list in question is a thesaurus for a very limited technological or scientific field. The establishment of lexical meaning may be crucial in distinguishing between semantic areas of terms which are alike in shape but differ in usage. Such terms, by definition, have very little semantic weight and are therefore usually not indexable. Just as semantic shift generally will create new lexical meanings from old ones, so words of little semantic weight may be employed in a highly specialized sense which is comprehensible only when sufficient context is added to establish the semantic limitation of the term. Assumed context will account for much of the polysemy which the raw term exemplifies. In the development of a thesaurus, lexical meaning is an ideal place to begin. The relationship to contextual meaning is obvious: lexical meaning is a choice of the most frequent contexts in which a given term may be found. Lexical meaning can be established by computational methods taking the contexts as they occur and analyzing the terms within these contexts, a procedure followed by Michael West in the development of his list of most frequent found words in a given corpus of literature (*10*).

Lexical meaning, however, is not equivalent to indexability, except that neologisms are likely to be unacceptable as index entries, and this operates to such an extent that even unusual morphs may be rejected by users of a given language as incomprehensible. There must be a standard method of syntax not only in the given contexts of a term, statistically determined, but also all morphemes employed must be acceptable within the grammatical structure of the language. A word in any natural language can only be understood within the syntactical and morphological limits of the tongue. In the Sears list one is instantly aware of inflectional mismatches with the O.U.D. These are most often plural forms of words, for instance, 335.4 Battles, where O.U.D. lists Battle, p. 154, col. 3. These are partial matches adequately accounted for by the inclusion of explanatory matter in the definition of the term: "3. (Without article or pl.): Fighting, war. . . ."

Contextual Meaning

The establishment of context may be lexical for common terms, especially in an alphabetical list, but it must be remembered that context is not only the sentences in which a given nominal structure may be found, but also context is established by any other word used with a given nominal form. Thus several languages create words by the accretion of previously accepted terms which are in themselves words. As in the example above, 335.4 Battles appears as the root form in such words as "battle-cry, battlefield, battleground, battle-piece, and battle-wise." Unfortunately English has not established rules for the use of the hyphen so that the above terms look as familiar when shown as "battlecry, battle-field, battle-ground, battlepiece, and battlewise." Further, the language permits open compounds, as indicated above, so that we might conjecture such spellings as "battlecry, battle-field, battle ground, battle-piece and battlewise." Editors will sometimes set up quite artificial rules for hyphenization and style manuals establish these as well, but the language is not capable of relating the hyphen to the pattern of intonation and stress which identifies a term as a single nominal structure. Even lexical sources may differ widely on a given term, and so far any effort to establish standardization has more or less been a failure. The most notable example is the hyphenization in the Library of Congress list of subject headings, as noted by M. E. Sears, when the Sears list was first proposed (*11*).

Copious examples of the establishment of context exist in Appendix One, but to return to the example previously cited, one finds this list: "335.4 Battles, Class Struggle, Communism, Communism and religion, Materialism, (and) Proletariat." If we look for the term 'Battles' in an area where we would expect it, for instance, 355 Military art and science, we do not find the term, even as a secondary term nor one following a mark of punctuation. We do find a variant term, 940.4 European War, 1914–1918—Battlefields. This would be a case of partial match. The context which establishes Battles as in the same semantic area as Class struggle and

Communism makes it necessary for us to assume that Battles here refers only to social warfare not to actual warfare. That this is a permissible context established by our lexical authority is soon shown. Battle in a figurative sense can mean struggle.

There is no implication that such a context is in any way impossible. Dealing with an arbitrary system, the analysis must avoid contamination of a classification by references to lexical authority beyond that established. What is shown in this example is the value of semantic shift. We can transform various words, using acceptable near synonyms contrasted with antonyms, and determine which term is effecting the coloration within the context. We can then hypothesize that this is the term of greatest semantic weight (Table 1).

As Table 1 plainly shows, the word "Battles" colors all the other terms in 335.4. Omitted, the subsequent terms are plainly an established context. If we take the other place in the classification where an exact match can be found, 904 Battles, and compare the context we find this list: 904 Battles, Courts and courtiers, Disasters. It is possible to interpose any of these terms in the list following 335.4. A recheck of the alphabetic list will establish that 335.4 Battles . . . is a simple clerical error. The Sears list, page 89, gives two suggested classifications: for Battles: 355.4, which we would expect, and 904, which seems as far-fetched as the erroneous inclusion of 'Battles' with Class Struggle, Communism, etc. The long way round to show a clerical error discovered by happy accident, demonstrates how the analysis of a classification can be accomplished without reference to another authority than the chosen lexical arbiter.

Throughout the list, legitimate groups which differ in no way from that shown in Table 1 can be found, for example, 394 Courts and courtiers, Dueling, Festivals, Festivals—U.S., Fairs, Gifts, Gladiators, Knights and knighthood, Rites and ceremonies, (and) Suicide. Here the semantic weight of "Suicide" colors the

TABLE 1
Transformations of Context

Battles, Class Strife, Communism, Communism and religion, Materialism, Proletariat.
Battles, Class Struggle, Marxism, Marxism and religion, Materialism, Proletariat.
Battles, Class Struggle, Communism, Communism and religion, Material universe, Proletariat.
Battles, Class Struggle, Communism, Communism and religion, Materialism, Working men.
Strife, Class Struggle, Communism, Communism and religion, Materialism, Proletariat.
Agreements, Class Struggle, Communism, Communism and religion, Materialism, Proletariat.
Battles, Class Peace, Communism, Communism and religion, Materialism, Proletariat.
Battles, Class Struggle, Capitalism, Capitalism and religion, Materialism, Proletariat.
Battles, Class Struggle, Communism, Communism and religion, Transcendentalism, Proletariat.
Battles, Class Struggle, Communism, Communism and religion, Materialism, Capitalists.
Agreements, Class Peace, Capitalism, Capitalism and religion, Transcendentalism, Capitalists.
Class Struggle, Communism, Communism and religion, Materialism, Proletariat.

Classification and Categorization

whole category. It occurs in another category: 179 Ambition, Animals—Treatment, Charity, Courage, Dueling, Honesty, Justice, Morale, Self-Control, Suffering, Suicide, (and) Toleration. Semantic shift, then, is a useful means of establishing contextual meaning within a given category.

Semantic limitation occurs throughout the list. In any given category the term is limited by the other terms in the same category. An example is seen in the heading "Gift" which will also be found in 336.1 and 360 as well as in 364. In the first category we find 336.1 Gifts, Monopolies, Public lands, (and) U.S.—Public lands. This occurs as a lower order of abstraction under 336 Income, the only heading listed. We can therefore extrapolate this implied morphology by using the colon to show that there is some hierarchical relationship implied by the classification, hence we are justified in the following transformations: 336 Income, 336.1 Gifts: Income, Monopolies: Income, Ohio—Public lands: Income, (and) U.S.—Public lands: Income. If we are to assume that 390 represents the higher order of abstraction for all the terms with those two numbers, then the category first cited becomes more limited in contextual meaning. 390 Manners and customs, hence the following category transformed as above for 336 Income:

> 394   Courts and courtiers: Manners and customs
> Dueling: Manners and customs
> Festivals: Manners and customs
> Festivals: U.S.—Manners and customs
> Fairs: Manners and customs
> Gifts: Manners and customs
> Gladiators: Manners and customs
> Knights and knighthood: Manners and customs
> Rites and ceremonies: Manners and customs
> Suicide: Manners and customs

The semantic limitation is then clear between 336.1 Gifts: Income and 394 Gifts: Manners and customs. However, we have picked an example where the hierarchical organization is acceptable and the semantic limitation seems reasonable. It breaks down completely if we attempt the same transformations with 360 Charity organization, Endowment, Gifts. We must transform each of the subsequent terms in categories 361, 362, 363, 364, 365, 366, 367, 368, and 369 as well. What G. M. Sinkankas discovered about the see-also structure of the Library of Congress subject headings can be compared here (9). The categorized list does not lead us out of the subject rather than through it, as his first paper clearly demonstrates is the effect of the see-also structure, but it does not put together terms where the semantic limitation is not justified by reference to a lexicon in existence. That is, choosing terms which seem most misused, we cannot assert that such transformations as 364 Crime and criminals: Gifts, or Crime and criminals: Endowments, or Crime and criminals: Charity organizations, are equivalent. Even less so are such terms as 365 Concentration camps, Convict labor, Education of prisoners, Escapes, Penal colonies, Prisons, (and) Punishment.

If semantic limitation is a function of semantic weight, then we can assert that semantic weight may be measured by the number of terms that are acceptable only in a metaphorical sense when limited as the context of the categorization requires. That is, such transformations are justified by the notation as Concentration camps:

Endowments, Convict labor: Gifts, and Education of prisoners: Charity organization. A table of transformations will show how we reach a metaphorical association of terms, especially if all the terms are transformed as above, including the terms subsumed under 364.1 Counterfeits and counterfeiting as a part of the category of 364 Crime and criminals, Crime and criminals—U.S., (and) Policewomen. The semantic shift which is apparent in this list makes the implication that policewomen are involved with crime and criminals and policemen are not. "Police," the heading given, is found in category 364.4 Law enforcement, Police, Public opinion.

It is important to note that any effort to match a hierarchy in natural language to that of an artificial language is usually very wide of the mark and generally unacceptable to the average user, leading to logical propositions which may be valid but would quickly be labeled untrue.

Even in the haphazard, largely accidentally classified list shown in Appendix One, there is a closer development of contextual meaning than provided by the even more haphazard association of terms by means of the see-also structure. A full analysis of the see-also structure of the Sears list is now in process, not so much for the purpose of showing the technique of semantic analysis as to show the nature of syndesis. While this research by G. M. Sinkankas is indicative, even at this early stage, a full report should provide an exact means of establishing semantic weight other than by the analysis of textual material. In any case, some examples can be shown here, always with the *caveat* that these are indicative, rather than conclusive.

To take as our example the word Gifts, p. 275, we have a see-also to Gift wrapping, p. 275, which leads to three more see-also references, Gifts, Packaging, (and) Paper work. The first is not an example of a circular reference, because these are see-also from references indicated by "xx." From Paper work we have a see-also reference to Gift wrapping. However, from Packaging we are led by see-also from references to Advertising and Retail trade. Under Advertising we find the following list of see-also references: Advertising cards, Commercial art, Electric signs, Mail-order business, Marketing, Packaging, Posters, Printing—Specimens, Propaganda, Public relations, Publicity, Radio advertising, Salesmen and salesmanship, Show windows, Sign painting, Signs and signboards, and see-also from references to Business, Propaganda, Public relations, Publicity, Retail trade, Salesmen and salesmanship. If we were to pursue this development of categories further we might find that all the headings in the list, except those which have no see-also references at all, are in some way related to Gifts. Obviously, this is a less useful method of categorization than the classified list shown. Until the hypothesis can be disproven, and so far all attempts have failed, we must accept the view that a classification, using a natural language, provides most control over contextual meaning. The really conclusive study will be based on that system which utilizes all three methods of syndesis.

To summarize, contextual meaning can be established by a review of all the contexts in which a given term occurs, and this meaning can be analyzed for certain values which indicate the nature of categorization to be provided: semantic weight which varies from terms of purely syntactical function, function words, to terms whose only purpose is to serve as the head of a construction of which the

Classification and Categorization 339

modifier is the distinguishing element, to abstractions which are abstract classes, or high order abstractions, having no references in the physical environment and in the communication of factual information to primary level indicators which are indentifiable with a part of the physical environment. The purpose of classification and categorization is to utilize a means whereby the contextual meaning of a term may be controlled in such a way that semantic lag will not grievously affect the reliability of the system for information handling. That classification can serve as a means of objective analysis of the semantic values of the nominal structures in a natural language may prove highly useful in areas allied to the library and information sciences. The attentive reader has probably already noted the close proximity of semantic shift to the methods of propagandistic description.

There are still three matters to be discussed under this heading. Studies in the characteristics of notation, studies of class logic as it relates to classification in the sense used here, and studies of indexability as a product of studies of semantic value.

Notation

As indicated above, notation may be divided into three separate areas: ciphers, codes, and artificial languages. Certain mathematical rules govern the use of each of these.

The first is the rule that all sequences, regardless of the symbol, constitute a workable series so long as they provide for endless addition of one to the number zero and each succeeding sum. All mathematics stems from a given number as unity and the possibility of an operation that will transform the number successively into different and measurable sums. Hence whether the alphabet, the Arabic numbers, or another system is used, the result is the same. However, when there is no inherent sequence in the symbols, they cannot be arranged in any way except by decree of an authority. The difference is that an inherent sequence already is accepted by the same convention which leads to contextual meaning.

The second is the rule of transfinite numbers. For some time it could neither be proven nor disproven that there were only two infinite sets: the infinite discrete set defined as a series to which another member of the series may be added, and the infinite dense set defined as a series such that between any two adjacent members of the series there is another member of the series and after the last member cited another may be added. These two sets are readily exemplified by the series of whole numbers, an infinite discrete set, and the series of decimal fractions, an infinite dense set. To show that one discrete set provides as many locations as another discrete set, it is necessary only to put them into a one-to-one relationship, hence anything that can be put in a one-to-one relationship with a discrete set is also a discrete set and governed by the same rules. That a dense set is larger than a discrete set is readily shown. In fact, there is the possibility of showing that an infinite dense set has more numbers between 1 and 2 than an infinite discrete set may have all together.

There are many other transfinite sets; how many depends on the means of serialization. In fact, we can postulate that there are as many transfinite sets, differing in extent of infinity, as there are mechanisms for increasing the density of the set. That is, compacted sets utilize more than one method of establishing density, and we can assume that there are infinite compacted sets as well which are still dense sets but are larger than the one exemplified by decimal fractions. The set that uses the letters of the English alphabet in place of a decimal point cannot be put into a one-to-one relationship with the set of decimal fractions. Obviously, there are an infinite number of possibilities when we create a rule of serialization which makes A equivalent to 0 and all the numbers through Z, omitting O, equivalent to 1 to 24 so that a numbering system to the base 25 is constructed. Then there are an infinite number of items in the series between 1.1 and 1.2, but fewer than the number possible between 1A1 and 1A2.

Finally, we can establish that the transfinite set represented by an association of terms provides for an infinity larger than any other. These are no longer dense sets and for want of a better term, we may call them infinite associative sets. The density is far greater than even the infinite compacted sets, as we can readily show by establishing that a one-to-one relationship is impossible if we compare the numbers from 1A1 to 1A2 with the associates possible from 1A1:1 to 1A1:2, where we have not ventured even to 1A2:1. As we increase the mechanisms of association we increase the range of infinity, so that the number of locations possible in a standard classification like the UDC (Universal Decimal Classification) can be established as far greater than those available in the DDC (Dewey Decimal Classification).

Customarily, notations were described as "pure" or "mixed" but these descriptions say very little. We may establish four kinds of notation: discrete sets, dense sets, compacted sets, and associative sets. Just what mechanism is utilized will help to establish the nature of the notation, which in turn helps to establish the hospitality of the notation and often its usefulness. A discrete set can use only one series. A dense set can use one inherent sequence but must provide for random inclusion and subinclusion by some notational means. A compacted set increases the range of inclusion, hence the hospitality. An associative set increases the hospitality still further and makes possible further random access beyond what is feasible in any of the other infinite sets. That this may be accomplished with both letters and numbers is of little moment. What is important is the predictability of hospitality based on the inherent sequence of the system utilized and on the rules governing its employment.

Ciphers

If a term in one inherent sequence is replaced according to rules of transliteration by a term in another sequence, the result is a cipher. This is widely used in crytography, but it is of summary importance in classification systems as well. The only means of providing a notational symbol for a term at the minimal level of abstraction is by means of a cipher or a code. In the Sears list, the inclusion of the numbers —973 for U.S. and —9771 for Ohio and —97731 do not represent ciphers, though this seems the case. Rather what has been done is to employ a code which can be established by reference to the Dewey Decimal Classification.

Classification and Categorization

A true cipher is seen in the frequent use of Cutter numbers, developed to its highest extent in the class PZ3, by the Library of Congress. This ciphering system has been widely used for the establishment of book numbers when the Dewey Decimal Classification is used so that books with the same classification number may be provided with a number which has a good chance of being unique. That it is not necessarily unique has been discovered by many libraries, so that the book numbering system becomes highly complicated, even though unnecessary, in most cases, for the shelving of books.

Ciphers serve the useful purpose of keeping the notation of a classification equivalent to the inherent notation of the alphabet. For instance, if it were desired to give each term in the Sears list categorized in Appendix One a locational symbol independent of the apparently hierarchical notation employed, a Cuttering system would rapidly accomplish this. Thus the category 546 Acids, . . . could be numbered as in Table 2.

TABLE 2
Cipher for Use in Categorization

546   /   /
.A2 Acids
.A4 Air
.A5 Alkalies
.A54 Alloys
.A58 Aluminum
.A582 Aluminum alloys
.B6 Brass
.C2 Carbon
.C4 Chemical elements
.C42 Chemistry, Inorganic
.C6 Copper
.D3 Deuterium
.G2 Gases
.G6 Gold
.H3 Helium
.H9 Hydrogen
.I6 Iron
.L3 Lead
.M3 Mercury
.M37 Metals
.N4 Nickel
.N46 Nitrates
.N466 Nitrogen
.O9 Ozone
.P5 Platinum
.P6 Potash
.R2 Radium
.S2 Salt
.S4 Silver
.S8 Sulphur/i.e. Sulphur/
.T4 Tin
.U6 Uranium
.Z4 Zinc

Such ciphers may be employed with proper names of any kind where no further classification is desirable or proper and the category formed is at a primary level of abstraction.

Codes

Codes may be employed in place of ciphers with greater freedom. Both ciphers and codes may be infinite dense sets by employing the simple rule of inherent sequence found in alphabetic structures. The inherent sequence of Arabic numbers is 1, 2, . . . 10, 11, 12, . . . 21, 22, 23, . . . 31, 32, 33, . . . 100, 101, 102, 103, . . . 110, 111, 112, 113, . . . 331, 332, 333. An alphabetic sequence which is automatically a dense set without any mark of density would be 1, 10, 11, 12, 100, 101, 102, 103, 110, 111, 112, 113, 2, 21, 22, 23, 3, 31, 32, 33, 331, 332, 333.

Codes may be generated from random numbers which permit a recategorization without reference to the natural language. These codes are particularly useful in testing for semantic values. Equally, such codes may be used for book numbers with a consistent measurement of risk of duplication. What is lost is the alphabetic arrangement within a category. If this is not desirable, and it rarely seems necessary, then random codes are an efficient way of providing unique numbers without the necessity of verifying that the number has not been used previously.

Codes may be infinite dense sets so that the code establishes a sequence which can be manipulated for other purposes, for instance in the assignment of accession numbers which will indicate the number of items received by simple subtraction, while it establishes an address for locating each item.

In an experiment conducted to ascertain the usefulness of a method of controlling books without professional intervention, a code was established after the books were arranged by binder's title on the shelves. This code can be maintained and adjusted so that it becomes virtually the equivalent of a cipher. The use of the decimal point is inconsequential so long as alphabetic rather than numerical arrangement is provided.

Artificial Languages

The inclusion of grammatical features that regulate the syntax and morphology of numbers to equate with implied meanings establishes the artificial language as the most useful notational system for natural classification, that is, classification based on the semantic evaluation of a given work, as in an analysis of its subject matter. Artificial languages can be profitably employed in abstract classification systems, but this is treated elsewhere in this Encyclopedia.

The artificial language employed in the Sears list cited in Appendix One may be analyzed *a posteriori* by the establishment of paradigmatic classes and by the use of transformations. However, the basis of an artificial language is the development of grammatical rules which govern the utilization and nature of the nota-

Classification and Categorization

tional devices. A study of these grammatical possibilities establishes four different kinds of grammatical systems, although there may be more so far undetermined.

Sequential grammars provide only that the set is used in precise sequence, one locational symbol following another in such a way that the individual parts of the symbol have no semantic value. Such sequential grammers would constitute a simple code, if there were no provision that numbers may be constructed from previously devised tables so that an *a posteriori* analysis would show certain sequences occurring with sufficient regularity to form a paradigmatic class. A purely sequential notation is a code, but where grammar is employed to provide semantic value for any given sequence, the notational system may be analyzed as an artificial language. Sequential grammars provide for much of the enumeration of the Library of Congress classification. As Immroth shows in his Guide (2), tables are used in Class B, Class H, and Class P with considerable regularity. In addition, the first two or three symbols used in the notation are alphabetic characters employed with some hierarchical significance. So far only Class K employs a three-letter notation, but the possibility exists elsewhere in the list. The only way to account for much of the Library of Congress classification is by establishing a sequential grammar where it applies.

Hierarchical grammars establish a syntax for the organization of symbols to equate to levels of abstraction in the arrangement of terms in the classification. The obvious example is the Dewey Decimal Classification and an example is provided in the categorized Sears list included as Appendix One. Here it can be shown that the numerical sequence is an infinite dense set such that all numbers provided are subdivisions of an unstated number (1000) equivalent to the world of knowledge. Each symbol is arranged in alphabetic sequence (the alphabet is 0, 1, 2, 3, 4, 5, 6, 7, 8, 9) with the morphological rule that only three numbers may be employed as whole divisions of the unstated maximum number. After three numbers, the decimal point indicates further subdivision. The hierarchy is established by rules governing the use of the zero. The highest levels of abstraction are shown by the use of two zeroes to locate the term at the far left of the sequence, so that 400 Language and languages establishes the hierarchy that follows. The schedules are arranged in such a way that the natural language term is meant to show hierarchical structures.

Within the classification itself, the zero is also employed as a means of nexus, or association, to provide for the inclusion of standard tables within the classification proper. This rule is necessary lest an adventitious term conflict with one for which a translation into natural language has been provided. With hierarchical classifications, such as the DDC and the UDC, devices for the prevention of ambiguity are important if the artificial language is to serve its purpose. A conflict may exist in the mind of the user of the classification if the hierarchical notation does not compare with his own levels of semantic abstraction; however, there is no logical system that can be made to apply both to natural language and to artificial languages. Rather logical systems are employed syntactically in artificial languages and are used as the notation of a classification for the purpose of avoiding implied hierarchies existing in a natural language.

Faceted notations provide that a given position of each term will establish the nature of its employment and that all classification utilizes the facets as implied context. Thus the Colon Classifications of Ranganathan establish five facets which always occur in the same order. The value of facets is that when a term does not require the facet it can be indicated by a blank stating that the facet exists but is not used. No hierarchy is implied by the facets, except as additional description leads to a hierarchical interpretation. That is, levels of abstraction may be established in different ways in different contexts, as indicated above. The faceted classification of Ranganathan, who first discerned its usefulness, provides that position one will always be "personality" and position two will always be "matter" and position three will always be "essence." That these terms are of widest possible semantic interpretation is inescapable as the classification is reviewed (*12*). The two remaining facets, "space" and "time," are actually of narrower semantic interpretation, referring to geographic and to temporal subdivisions. There is no implication that any of these facets are hierarchical, but rather that subdivisions can be hierarchical if desired. The class structure is rather one of association but with the number and kind of associations fixed. Such notational systems employ compacted dense sets.

A purely associative notational system removes the limitations of facets by providing that associations may occur in any fashion and need only be signaled by some device. These devices may be given an order in the rules, but the necessity for this order as a convenience has been established by Ranganathan. The relation of faceted classifications to fixed field and associative classifications to free field arrangement is obvious. The Universal Decimal System provides for associative development of any term through a system of signals. Unfortunately, at this writing a convention establishing the rank or even the semantic value of these signals is lacking. That the signals are functional implies they have only scant semantic weight, and the lack of conventional order results from the signals employed. They are largely marks of punctuation that have never been assigned an inherent order by convention. Such notational grammars as that employed by the UDC can be established in almost all the ways that natural language is analyzed, providing both a morphological and syntactical basis for the hypothesis that natural language is most readily adjusted to an associative classification. The notational system utilizes an infinite associative set with the result that hospitality is at its maximum.

The hospitality of finite discrete sets may be determined by counting the number of empty classes. In infinite discrete sets, the number of empty classes is still a method of determining the total possible random inclusions. The number of empty classes in infinite dense sets will determine the random inclusions that are not governed by the rules of structure, so that a hierarchical classification is infinitely expansive only if the grammar of the notation provides for random inclusions at all levels of the hierarchy.

There seems little point in discussing the hospitality of infinite compacted and infinite associative sets, because the limitation of hierarchies no longer applies and, in any case, the value of the transfinite number is apparently that of the kind of infinite set represented by a natural language. In any case, the development of a natural classification can follow the rules of morphology and syntax of a given natural language providing only those features most useful in the subject analysis of the material at hand. As a general rule, call it a canon rather than a hypothesis;

Classification and Categorization

it will be found that a minimum grammar is most efficient in determining the kind of notational system needed for a classification. The nominal structure of a language cannot account for all the possibilities of communication, it can only label them. Hence the notation enables the classifier to develop those arrangements that provide greatest semantic limitation, hence semantic weight, for the terms included. The existence of semantic lag makes the use of finite sets dangerous, and the general need for random inclusion makes the use of discrete sets equally dangerous. Thus notation can either dominate the classification or it can very liberally assist. The classifier must determine which notational system achieves maximum semantic limitation and obviates possibility ambiguities.

Class Logic and Library Classification

Efforts to explain the function of classification in terms of class logic have so far proven fruitless. It is quite apparent that the freedom of language has generally defeated all attempts at developing a class logic that will explain the organization of standard library classification. Rather, class logic has been used to develop search strategies in information retrieval systems. However, it is possible to design classification systems that will exhibit all the possibilities of modern class logic. Matrices have been developed that are especially useful in determining the nature and kind of associative systems and in establishing what kind of classification structure is needed in a given area of classification. Further, the transformations of class logic are especially applicable in determining the choice of terms.

For example, Table 2, showing category 546 Acids can be redesigned by constructing a matrix that will distribute the terms on the basis of statements relating each term to every other term, as Acids: Air, Alkalies, Alloys, etc. Here the colon indicates some kind of relationship, whether inclusion, exclusion, subinclusion, or subcontrariety. The colon does not indicate material equivalence. We immediately see that only one transformation is meaningful, Acids: Alkalies. We can then formulate statements and test for validity and truth. We find that the transformation: Acids, Nonacids and Alkalies: Nonalkalies, leads us to complementary classes so that we can reformulate the statement as "The classes of Alkalies and Acids are exhaustive and exclusive and therefore the class of nonacid nonalkalies is empty." When $A'B$ is equal to 0 we can formulate a relationship of subcontrariety, which we will symbolize as v, whence Acids v Alkalies. Obviously Salt: Alkalies and Salt: Acids will lead us to formulate another relationship between Salt: Acids, considering the chemical method of creating a salt by replacing the hydrogen ion with a metal. Since no acid is a salt, no alkali is a salt, we can formulate three exhaustive and exclusive classes, and simply list them sequentially.

546A	Acids
546B	Alkalies
546C	Salt

Similar logical operations will account for the addition of Gases and Metals to this list and the inclusion of gases and metals as subclasses of Chemical Elements. Further logical operations will establish that the statement of inclusion that transforms the simple relationship will lead us to an indication of diminished semantic weight for the term Gases. For we find that the following statements of inclusion are true and valid: Air—) Gases, Helium —) Gases, and yet Helium—) Chemical Elements, but Air cannot be included in the class Chemical Elements. Hence a hierarchy which began Chemical Elements and included Gases which included Air would be untrue. We must reformulate the term, providing that semantic limitation which will give us sufficient semantic weight to make the term classifiable in this fashion: Gases: Chemical Elements and Gases: *Chemical Mixtures. Rearranged, following the use of class logic, we may restate the sequence as follows utilizing an asterisk to show terms which do not yet exist in the list.

> 546.1 Chemical Elements
> 546.12 Gases
> 546.121 Helium
> 546.122 Hydrogen
> 546.1221 Deuterium
> 546.123 Nitrogen
> 546.124 *Oxygen
> 546.1241 Ozone
> 546.13 Metals
> 546.131 Aluminum
> 546.132 Copper
> 546.133 Gold
> 546.134 Iron
> 546.135 Lead
> 546.136 Mercury
> 546.137 Nickel
> 546.138 Silver
> 546.139 Tin

It can be seen at this point that the basing system of the Arabic numbers is too small. Further a problem of hierarchies results which class logic will clearly show. We can formulate such relationships as Aluminum: Alloys or as Aluminum Alloys, showing a logical product. We can also suppose Copper Alloys but this leads us to the term Brass, which we can formulate as Brass: Copper, Alloys: Copper, Brass—) Copper Alloys. Thus we could retain the hierarchical structure by altering the notation so that it will fit. A close perusal of Dewey's introduction to his classification will show that such alteration was considered legitimate. Hence, we might organize the list as:

> 546 Inorganic Chemistry
> 546.1 Chemical Elements
> 546.A Gases
> 546.1A1 Helium
> 546.1A2 Hydrogen
> 546.1A2D Deuterium
> 546.1A3 Nitrogen
> 546.1A4 /---------/
> 546.1A4Q Ozone
> 546.2 /---------/
> 546.2A Air
> 546.B Metals

Classification and Categorization 347

>   546.1B Aluminum
>   546.BA Aluminum Alloys
>   546.1C Copper
>   546.CB Brass
>   . . .
>   546.3 Acids
>   546.4 Alkalies
>   546.4PP Potash
>   etc.

The propositions and methods of class logic can be used to determine the extent of classification needed and its organization. The precise symbols used in stating the propositions are not really significant, though those of Blyth and Jacobson have been employed with considerable success (*13*).

It is this use of class logic which G. M. Sinkankas showed destroys the expectation that the see-also structure of subject heading lists can serve as a means of categorization. This is true only if the categories are not extended beyond first list of see-also references. When the see-also references are traced further into the structure of the list, the result is either a circular reference or a false syllogism. If we attempt a reformulation of our basic relationship, X:Y, we find that there is no logical possibility which will account for the presence of a given term in a given see-also category, and even less when categories of categories of see-also references are constructed. Thus the presence of "Public relations" as both a see-also reference and a see-also reference from Advertising exhibits a circular reference, and if we assume that "Packaging" is a part of the category "Advertising" and "Gift Wrapping" is a part of the category "Packaging," then we must assume that "Gift Wrapping" is also a part of the category "Advertising." The Sears list does not exhibit the false syllogism as well as the Library of Congress list where it is possible to show that "Pimps" is a part of a category which includes "Game Birds" and "Outdoor Cookery." Class logic enables us to establish contexts where they may seem vague or doubtful, and it is from a study of contextual meaning that we arrive at the key problem, indexability.

Indexability

All the research briefly reported on above, a large part of it, unfortunately, still unpublished, fails to disprove the hypothesis "Chain indexing procedures which are independent of pre-arranged notation or which develop notation that fits the index proposed provide for objective determination of terms to be indexed and govern the morphology and syntax of the nominal structure employed."

The reader is invited to use the terms in Appendix One to perform all the tests described above to assist in the disproof of the hypothesis stated above. If we cannot disprove the hypothesis, then we must live with it, even though it sentences the person preparing a thesaurus or information retrieval system to the lengthy tasks described above. That is, to formulate a thesaurus a concordance method of locating terms and contexts will establish terms at the level of abstraction needed. This categorization will provide that only terms of greatest semantic weight are indexable. Terms with insufficient semantic weight, that is, those used in several different contexts as established by formulations in class logic, are indexable only if limited. The techniques of semantic limitation acceptable in an indexing procedure must utilize minimum grammatical structures in such a way that the notational system employed may be adequately hospitable to provide for semantic lag. (It is possible to conceive of artificial languages with grammars so complex that they match the existing statements of natural language and hence provide no hospitality whatever.)

The test of the categories established is by looking for cases of semantic shift. These can be tested in several ways, by forming synonymous and antonymous categories, by the operations of class logic, and by investigation of the point at which contextual meaning becomes purely metaphorical. We can postulate that all the nominal structure of a language is interrelated, at least to the extent of a metaphor, but that only a whole metaphor, not a part of it, is indexable. Metaphoric contexts represent the ultimate extent of meaning, and the terms of greatest semantic weight will be found to create metaphorical structures when the context is altered from that already established.

Semantic lag includes alteration of contextual meaning as the natural language changes by usage. Such alteration becomes lexical when the most prevalent contexts are cited in an authority. Classification and categorization is far more often performed and can be studied much more deeply than has been apparent in the past. While there is no law that states that development of a chain index is a necessity for an information retrieval system, there is a kind of iron law of language that becomes operative as the system expands and is finally enough to crush the whole system. In dealing with indexing we are constrained by the natural language as the primary means of communicating messages with informational content. Even systems of bibliographic identification classify and categorize, often employing a notational system, usually a code, to establish the identity of a given description in a larger list. If it were not for semantic lag, the old Schlagwort system of the German bibliographers would provide an adequate method of classification. As it is, the method falls down when the alteration of contextual meaning leads to an alteration of the semantic weight of a term and demands further and further limitation if its significance is to be apparent.

Finally, utilizing the methods of comparative grammar, where equivalent systems are compared in use, we can establish the validity of the system by evaluating the degree of similarity. Very likely at some time in the future such procedures will be used to predict the reliability of search strategies in retrieving information which is relevant. Early efforts in this direction, especially that of M. Manheimer (14), enable us to utilize a method whereby the existing morphology and syntax of two systems can be compared, leading to what an ideal arrangement in a chain indexing procedure would establish.

Lacking a means of relating terms, except by inherent structures, requires the person wishing to retrieve information to have prior knowledge of which he may be ignorant if he intends to search by means of subject alone. Only the establishment of controlled contextual meaning in an array that leads to the prediction of inclusion and formulates exhaustive classes can provide information not only to the person who knows the subject area but to one who is just beginning to learn the extent of coverage and the terminology employed.

It is important to explain that this article is not meant to apply only to indexing in English. M. Aman has shown that the method is independent of language, since one of the primary uses of a classification is to provide for a polyglot dictionary (*15*). It is not surprising, therefore, that the Universal Decimal Classification is the most widely employed and most widely translated standard classification method. Present research leads to the supposition that an associative classification of adequate hospitality will provide the greatest and most facile means of classification. Further, that a faceted classification, where it is possible to employ it, provides greatest efficiency by establishing contexts that are always necessary. However, the hospitality of a faceted classification is always less than that of an associative classification.

REFERENCES

1. F. W. Lancaster, *Information Retrieval Systems: Characteristics, Testing and Evaluation,* Wiley, New York, 1968, p. 6.
2. J. P. Immroth, *Guide to the Library of Congress Classification,* Libraries Unlimited, Rochester, New York, 1968.
3. J. E. Daily, "The Grammar of Subject Headings, a Formulation of Rules, for Subject Headings Based on a Syntactical and Morphological Analysis of the Library of Congress List," Unpublished D.L.S. dissertation, School of Library Service, Columbia University, 1957.
4. N. Chomsky, *Syntactic Structures,* Mouton, The Hague, 1968.
5. S. Langer, *Introduction to Symbolic Logic,* 3rd ed., Dover Press, New York, 1964.
6. A. Korzybski, *Science and Sanity,* 10th ed., The International Non-Aristotelian Library Publishing Company, New York, 1957.
7. Marie Prevost, "An Approach to Theory and Method in General Subject Headings," *Lib. Quart.,* 16, 140–151 (1946).
8. J. E. Daily, "Don't Touch My Dirty Words," *Alternatives* (1969).
9. G. M. Sinkankas, *"Orphans . . . ,"* Unpublished Seminar Paper submitted in fulfillment the requirements of LS 351, Graduate School of Library and Information Sciences, University of Pittsburgh, 1968.
10. M. P. West, *A General Service List of English Words,* Longmans, London, 1960.
11. M. E. Sears, "The Hyphen—Subject Headings," *Wilson Bull.,* 2, 497–498 (1925/26).
12. S. R. Ranganathan, *Colon Classification,* Asis Publishing House, New York, 1963.
13. J. W. Blyth and J. H. Jacobson, *Class Logic, A Programmed Text,* Harcourt, Brace & World, New York, c1961, c1963.
14. Martha L. Manheimer, "A Methodology for the Evaluation of Thesaurus; Specifically the NASA Thesaurus," Unpublished Ph.D. dissertation, Graduate School of Library and Information Sciences, University of Pittsburgh, December, 1967.
15. Muhammed M. Aman, "Analysis of Terminology, Form and Structure of Subject Headings in Arabic Literature and Formulation of Rules for Arabic Subject Headings," Unpublished Ph.D. dissertation, Graduate School of Library and Information Sciences, University of Pittsburgh, February 1967.

19

Natural Classification

Jay E. Daily / University of Pittsburgh, Pittsburgh, Pennsylvania

Definition

A classification is called natural for the same reason that a language is called natural. It arises from the needs and methods of communication utilized in everyday life from time immemorial among all the peoples of the world. A natural language cannot be traced to its ultimate origin, although it would be possible to define human beings as those primates which use language. Although library classifications can be traced quite clearly, if not entirely accurately, at least back to classical sources (*1*), only those library classifications developed first by Melvil Dewey and then by those who followed in his path need concern us here.

Natural classification is closely linked with natural language and may be defined as a means by which the subject content of information sources is made accessible within established semantic contexts. Natural classification differs, first, from taxonomies and then from abstract classification. A taxonomy is a method of establishing classes of real things by establishing ranks of similarities and differences. An abstract classification utilizes nonlanguage characteristics of information sources for purposes of providing access to them. If accidental, then the classification is based upon features that may be added (such as accession number) or observed (such as color of binding of books, size of reports, etc.). If artificial, then the classification is based upon such characteristics as author's name, point of origin (issuing body), or other features that do not provide a reliable guide to the subject content.

Natural classification, however, is inextricably dependent upon natural language for its existence and may be a feature of language so far only imperfectly under-

---

From Daily, Jay E. *Natural Classification*. ENCYCLOPEDIA OF LIBRARY AND INFORMATION SCIENCE. Vol. 19. Edited by Allen Kent, Harold Lancour and Jay E. Daily. Assistant Editor, William Z. Nasri. New York, Marcel Dekker, Inc., c1976. pp. 186-206.

stood. Semantic context, the means by which language achieves its purpose in providing a tool of communication, accounts both for the paradigmatic classes of language and for the mechanisms by which subject content is grouped into semantic contexts in classification. Both language and classification, to be natural, arise without intervention as a tool of communication, the one for the expression of immediate needs, moods, preferences, opinions, ideas, and so on, and the other for providing a grouping of all the recorded communication. Grammatical categories which account for the existence of paradigmatic classes in natural languages explain as well many of the groupings of natural classification and the essential communicative process which is served by classification.

It is for this reason that the use of the word "logical" in the definition of a natural classification is perilous at best, and usually inaccurate. Just as natural language fails to convey logical concepts accurately, natural classification fails to exemplify them. When logical procedures are utilized in natural classification, its communicative value is greatly reduced. A grammar of classes, expressed in symbolic form, is both the primary method of construction and test of taxonomies, but even in the classification of taxonomies, natural language prevents the development of symbolic forms that can be utilized to develop a natural classification. This is due to the variation of subject content arising from the form of presentation—verse, prose, pictorial, fiction, nonfiction, native or foreign language, alphabetic or nonalphabetic, its position in an assumed chronology of such presentations; and its purpose—dictionary, encyclopedia, teacher's manual. Granted that the subject content is not the primary feature of the classification, it is at least the deep structure, as observed in natural language. It is not surprising, then, that all attempts to construct a symbolic logic that will account for the features of successful natural classifications have been failures.

Natural classification has served as a primary tool of communication in libraries and grew both in content and method as open-stack libraries became the rule rather than the exception. It should not be assumed that natural classification was adopted by the users of the libraries as their means of gaining access to library materials, but that it served to provide spatial regularity which library users rapidly come to rely upon. Reshelving a library, without changing the classification, will often bring complaints from users that "their books" have been discarded, when they have only been moved. It is quite sanguine to assume that the user will utilize the classification as anything other than the address at which he can locate material that interests him. Sometimes users will complain that a book has been misclassified, as sometimes it has been, and few users will not observe that an error has mixed the wrong sort of books with those that interest them. Nevertheless, the mechanics of classification remain mostly a mystery, and an uninteresting perplexity, to library users who customarily check a location to see if anything new has been added.

The study of classification has come to be named the theory of classification. Although at first glance this seems as much a misnomer as any other study labeled a theory when it is, in fact, an ongoing investigation, there is good reason to state that, in the scientific sense, considerable theory exists which explicates and provides a frame of reference for further studies, just as in linguistics and other areas of investigation. Obviously, the scientific sense is not that of physics or chemistry nor even of mathematics, but it is nevertheless a good way of knowing something and testing its reliability. Furthermore, certain rigid laws of efficiency have been stated that seem to explain many of the problems of classification. The theory of classification seeks to explain the purpose as well as the mechanics of natural classification, the constraints and possibilities inherent in arrangements of semantic context utilizing an organization independent of natural language.

In this sense, alphabetic order and random order can be considered features of classification worthy of study. But neither fulfills the essential requirement of a natural classification that semantic contexts be arranged without recourse to the method of any natural language. In providing groupings of semantic contexts, random order and alphabetic order may not be considered as methods of organization. The former is a contradiction and the latter an impossibility. No natural language provides for the consistent arrangement of semantic contexts in alphabetic or any other order. All attempts at twisting natural language into some kind of consistency have been resounding failures. While natural classification must employ natural language to be understandable and useful, its greatest utility is found in its freedom from natural language such that it can serve as an artificial language based upon consistency of arrangement of semantic contexts by creating its own set of indicators and controlling them with a unique grammar.

Just what information sources are classified is much less important than that a natural classification provide access to semantic contexts in such a way that the most significant feature of all communication is not obscured, all knowledge is related, and every information source occupies a specific location. Though the pathways to the location may be varied, the location remains. Direct classification of material arranges the material itself; indirect classification arranges the access points to the material. The most obvious advantage of natural classification is that it may be direct or indirect, and probably should be both to provide maximum access to information at minimum cost of energy.

The test of natural classification is, therefore, efficiency of access. It is the purpose of the theory of classification to explain how the maximum of access is achieved and what procedures represent an unprofitable expense of energy either for the classifier or the user, or both. The purpose of classification is seen in its arrangement of semantic contexts independent of natural language. Indexes, which are useful arrangements of topics and names, are valid only within a single work or, at best, within the works of a single author. Linguists now realize that each speaker of a language, in effect, uses a language uniquely and that the semantic boundaries of words and terms must broaden as many different speakers of a language employ terms. A classification is capable of setting its own semantic boundaries and establishing contexts that can accommodate the differences of language of many writers in many languages. Classification is, therefore, a means of achieving efficiency of retrieval of material, assuring complete recall and maximizing the relevance of information sources, depending on how well the classification is employed, supposing that it can be employed efficiently.

The early days of information retrieval studies assumed that classification was unnecessary, that speakers of a language could use the terms of an index to provide complete recall, without investigating how great an assumption this is. The indexer must accurately apply all those terms that the user is likely to utilize to gain access to the material. At times the indexing system simply fails to furnish the needed number of terms so that the indexer can at best provide only a superficial coverage of the information sources so far as the original author is concerned (2). This may assure efficient recall of material but only at the cost of relevance. At other times the index contains so many terms that the indexer is bound to forget many of them if they are left in alphabetic array. Attempts to provide interrelationships between terms, the *see also* structure, are notoriously unsuccessful. The *see also* structure, particularly in computerized systems, introduces rigidities of form so complete that the index is incapable of change. While terms may be added, none may be dropped, and minute changes of form make the system unusable (3). Even a haphazard classification system is better than the *see also* structure in showing the relationships between terms, whether direct or indirect indexing is employed. The several studies of subject headings seem to bear this out completely, especially the study of the last classified edition of the Sears subject heading list (4).

We may define a natural classification as a systematic arrangement of semantic contexts meant to provide maximum access to information sources at minimum expense of energy, independent of the constraints of natural language. To be complete, a natural classification must display the systematic arrangement which implies a notational representation of semantic contexts as well as the labels for these contexts in one or more natural languages. It is necessary as well to provide an index of these labels if they are capable of assuming an orderly array through some inherent feature. Alphabetic order is the most obvious, although the stroke-count radical system of Chinese characters, while very much more complicated, still represents an array utilizing inherent features of the labels employed. A natural classification is complete only if the schedule terms are indexed and the notation that provides for the systematic arrangement is included both in the schedules and the index. Schedule terms, the labels of semantic contexts in natural language, must not be altered in the index. Incomplete or erroneous indexing of the schedule terms is an obvious cause of inefficiency (5). In sum, a natural classification employs natural language to provide a display of semantic contexts in both a systematic arrangement and an arrangement utilizing inherent features of the natural language employed as labels of the contexts. A natural classification, then, needs schedules, notation, and index. Lacking any part, the classification is incomplete and inefficient. More than one natural language may be employed as labels, but all must be indexed if the classification is to achieve its purpose. One of the most amazing facts of library and information science is the length of time necessary to realize that subject heading lists and classification systems are intimately and necessarily related.

Semantic Contexts

Linguists long ago observed that several features of natural language were related to its use as a tool of communication. This general area, the study of the meaning and use of words to convey thought among people—semantics—has been remarkably incalcitrant to methods of systematic study. Nevertheless, homonyms—words that are the same shape but mean different things to different people—can be identified, and as the problems of morphology and syntax were resolved, a clearer idea of semantics as an area of objective study was gained (6).

A semantic context is the area of meaning in which a given term in a given language may be used. Not to belabor a simple word but highly complex idea, meaning is used to designate the communication value of a given term, that is, a word or words that can be employed by a native speaker with the intention of conveying his thoughts to another person or to any number of persons at any time. Natural classification does not attempt to arrange words or terms according to their meaning, but it can arrange semantic contexts to show the relationship between them. It is this independence of natural language that constitutes the primary value of, and need for, classification. Polyglot dictionaries and the thesaurus of a given language are arranged by semantic contexts, generally in a highly systematic fashion (7, 8).

Even alphabetically arranged dictionaries of a single language, or bilingual dictionaries, generally include a context for the terms in order to distinguish between the usage of certain terms. There are many jokes about the misuse of terms through inappropriate semantic context. (The diplomat, upon arriving in Washington with his wife, was asked by journalists if he had any children. "No," he explained, "My wife is unbearable. I mean inconceivable. I mean impregnable.") The correct term for this semantic context is "barren" or possibly "sterile." To find the appropriate term, the foreign diplomat may have consulted a bilingual dictionary which gave him a choice among five terms and unluckily he tried only the wrong ones.

One of the first assumptions a non-native speaker makes is that the language he is learning has the same semantic boundaries as the language he knows and that the semantic contexts are equally represented in both languages. Only a brief comparison of the Universal Decimal Classification makes it obvious that terms found in one language may not exist in another and that a single term in one language may include semantic contexts represented by several different terms in another language, each of which has its own area of correct usage. While every semantic context within a language has its own terminology ranging from the narrowest of meanings to the broadest of relationships among terms, these contexts do not precisely match any other language, either because the term has never been needed, hence never established by convention as appropriate, or because the grammar of the language does not admit of the possibility of a semantic context that exists in another language. Grammar introduces constraints through the mismatch of grammatical categories. While in Japanese and Korean the verb necessarily indicates the social position of the person to whom or about whom you are speaking, this cannot be conveyed precisely in European languages. Similarly, the grammatical category indicated by definite and indefinite articles in Western European languages is lacking in Japanese and Korean.

All this is not especially significant in classification systems, except to rule out an expectation that an exact translation is possible or desirable. At best, classification systems must be adapted from one language into another. An even more important conclusion is that the language used by one writer is generally not the language of another, even though both use a tongue learned as native speakers. This is especially true when the writers are reporting the results of research into the vast unknown, where even the terminology is new. The vocabulary of any language is less than is needed to express new ideas. As a science grows, its terminology solidifies and becomes generally adopted, but semantic differences are wide enough so that two authors dealing with the same phenomena have to define their terms before they can argue successfully about anything other than the meaning of their words.

This is the reason that indexes are generally unsuccessful except for a single work. As the number of works to be indexed increases, the semantic boundaries widen and the semantic contexts blur. The early studies of information retrieval often neglected this point, so that some of the early theorists were either busy proving the futility, or worse, of classification, based on a few documents—or were reinventing library classification, usually hierarchical, because of the surprising results that a study of many documents from many sources occasioned. Almost all the conclusions were drawn from a study of English, a remarkably intractable language grammatically, although furnished with an abundant and highly flexible vocabulary.

So far the arrangements of semantic contexts fit into three patterns: sequential, hierarchical, and what we may call associative or attributive. A faceted classification is actually an attributive system with fixed fields, distinguished from an associative classification with free fields. Library classification systems that are essentially natural classifications are rarely, if ever, purely one of the three possibilities. An admixture is expected both of different arrangements and even of such abstract features as author sequences and size of books. Perhaps significantly, the four best known classification systems each fit into one of the four types established. The Dewey Decimal Classification is meant to be essentially hierarchical; the Library of Congress Classification is largely sequential; the Universal Decimal Classification is associative, that is, attributive but with free fields; and Ranganathan's colon classification is faceted, that is, attributive but with fixed fields. Each is, in fact, a mixed classification utilizing one principle in a given subject area and another elsewhere, but the guiding purpose is most clearly seen in the different notations for each of these classifications.

These kinds of classification can easily be paralleled in the nominal structure of English with its easy utilization of modifiers. Nouns and adjectives can be employed as modifiers and even phrases, although verbs are usually employed only with morphological changes. Grammarians generally regard adverbs as adjectives when they modify nouns, so that Never-never Land makes never into an adjective. The repetition is employed for emphasis rather than as a device to create an adjective of an adverb. Sequences are seen in the repetition of the head of the construction in such series as big dogs, little dogs, pedigreed dogs, and mongrel dogs. A sequential classification is also seen when the semantic boundaries are assumed: puppies, whelps, lap dogs, hunting dogs, mongrels, curs, pariah dogs. When these terms are arranged into semantic contexts wholly contained within the semantic boundaries of another semantic context, a hierarchy is established. For instances, dogs of many sizes: big dogs, little dogs, from monstrous hunting dogs to miniature lap dogs; and dogs of every ancestry, pedigreed dogs, dogs of mixed breed, mongrels, curs, and pariah dogs. Because English has a fixed order for adjectives used in series with a single head of construction, a kind of faceted classification is seen in such phrases as "a small, brindled, short-haired dog." The order of adjectives is more flexible here than in such a phrase as "an expensive, small, black, Korean, lacquer box." The meaning of the adjectives changes if the order is not preserved. Since other adjectives and adjectival phrases may be added, positioned before and after the head of the construction, an associative grammar can be demonstrated.

Semantic contexts, however, are not controlled by the grammar of a natural language in a natural classification, so that the grouping of terms is independent of all save their accepted meaning. What is rigidly controlled by these possibilities of arrangement is the notation, even though the semantic contexts may seem to show another kind of arrangement. The sequential notation of the Library of Congress Classification is used willy-nilly, whether or not the particular part of the classification arranges semantic contexts into hierarchies or provides for associative features in the use of tables. Geographical tables are, of necessity, hierarchical but they constitute a feature of an associative classification. The trick in using the notation of the Library of Congress is to preserve its sequential arrangement regardless of the semantic contexts. Thus the tables in the H classification provide for different associative arrangements in different parts of the schedules, even though the semantic contexts are all geographical, all hierarchical, and the same for each of the columns that designate where the geographical subdivisions are to be used. The columns differ in the notation, providing more possibilities in one place and fewer in another. When completely elaborated, however, it is seen that each of the columns fits neatly into designated places in the H schedules. In other parts of the classification, even within the H schedule, the tables are not used. The geographical arrangement within a subject area is carefully designed to fit that subject area and no other.

Requirements that preserve the hierarchical notation in the Dewey Decimal Classification can be demonstrated by the use of zeroes, both before and after the decimal point, especially in the 18th edition, where the tables provide associative features in Volume 1 that can be used throughout the classification. However, the notation requires that the numbers supplied in the table occur in the places where the hierarchy of the notation will not be disturbed. Otherwise, severe ambiguity would result, with one number meaning two different things.

Ranganathan's great discovery of a faceted classification, a limited and fixed number of necessary associations, utilized a principle of Arabic numerals, actually invented in India, whereby the expression of a number is dependent upon the number of positions used for the digits. All faceted classifications having fixed fields must indicate an empty field. The Universal Decimal Classification with its signals of fields has no such requirement. There is reason though to align these signaled fields in a fixed sequence so that the search time can be reduced and the preparation of a classification number can follow rules which increase efficiency.

The designators of geographic subarrangement, chronology, language, and so on are each distinct, so that a number will have any of these facets only if needed. Ranganathan makes no provision for empty facets, though later designers of such schemes have found it useful to do so, generally by showing a blank field with a single indicator, such as a hyphen, in the appropriate position.

The significance of the rigidity of arrangement for the notation is that it provides a larger semantic context for any given one, however minute, and relates this to all the other semantic contexts, thereby establishing both a principle of growth and easily utilized location symbols. A rather frequent error is concealed in the studies of hierarchical systems that assume a necessary hierarchy of terms in a given language. The hierarchy, if it exists, is to be found in the semantic context of the term, and this is not fixed by the term itself but by semantic boundaries that the notation creates. That is, words cannot be grouped in absolute hierarchies. Aside from such features as homonymy, a word assumes the semantic context of its location within a natural classification. Mongrels are not subdivisions of dogs, but first of all a word that may indicate this distinction along with many others. This perplexity derives from a misunderstanding of the significance of terms within a natural classification. They are not absolutes but the best available translation of the artificial language and its terms as established by the notation. A taxonomy, which is meant to arrange observable actual things, usually establishes natural hierarchies, but a word is not the thing it indicates. A word remains a word and the thing it indicates remains a thing regardless of the word used as indicator. Hence we must treat semantic contexts as a feature of natural classification established by the guiding principles of the notation, so that the semantic boundaries of the contexts are clearly delineated by the notation. The more numerous the subdivisions of a semantic context, the more precise that context becomes (9).

Notation

The notation of a natural classification is an artificial language having its own rules of grammar and its own system of graphemes, the smallest units that are combined to create semantic contexts. Notations, to be efficient, must be at once economical of graphemes but hospitable to semantic contexts not yet discerned. Hospitality is achieved by creating empty classes, hence the notation of a natural classification must always be an infinite series. That these series differ in dimension is easily tested by comparing each unit of the series on a one-to-one basis, like counting on the fingers. If the series match, they are the same size. This leads to several conclusions that may be startling and in opposition to accepted fact. A whole is greater than any of its parts, but not necessarily if an infinite series is the whole. A sequential notation is a good example of this phenomenon. Infinite sequential series are formed by addition that reaches no ultimate number. Basically, the whole integers constitute a series formed by adding one to the sum of the previous number: $0 + 0 = 0, + 1 = 1, + 1 = 2, + 1 = 3, + 1 = 4, + 1 = 5$, etc. In library classification, the sequential notation may begin anywhere and, at least in theory, have no final number. This is most usually not the case, so that the

Library of Congress Classification, although sequential, is not infinite because the final number in any given combination of letters and numbers is 9999. Empty classes may be created either by systematic avoidance of certain numbers (0, 1, and 9) or by alternate use. Libraries of the 19th century often used accession numbers as classification numbers, so that the original accession books were shelf lists and the classification accidental, utilizing an infinite series. If the accession book had utilized only the even numbers, empty spaces would have been created so that other books could be interfiled using the odd numbers. The two series are of equal size, even though odd numbers constitute a part of the series of whole integers. The rigidity of infinite discrete sequences, whether even numbers or odd or both, has led to problems in the numbering of items in book catalogs. Any attempt to insert an item between two numbers is doomed to failure once those items have successive numbers. Empty classes cannot be created except by guessing where expansion can occur. The Library of Congress Classification system uses an infinite notation, but this is accomplished by means other than those provided by a discrete set of numbers, finite or infinite.

The alphabetic arrangement of materials utilizes an infinite dense set simply by constructing a rule of arrangement. Since the alphabet may be considered the notation of a basing system using 26 characters rather than 10, the Arabic numbers can be arranged alphabetically. In fact, arranging them numerically is a semantic filing system that comes to grief when anything but numbers is arranged. In alphabetic arrangement, the number 11 follows the number 1, therefore the numbers created beginning with 1 will be filed together, no matter the size. When a library classification begins 000 and ends with 999, it may be either sequential or hierarchical, depending on the filing rules. In the Dewey Decimal Classification, the numbers are arranged as an infinite dense set that provides for infinite division of each number in the series. The decimal point is more or less a convenience, but it is not an essential feature of the notational system. The numbers are arranged alphabetically, in effect, before as well as after the decimal point.

Empty classes are very easily created in this system, each new number after the decimal point creating 10 new subclasses. Early theorists considered this a distinct advantage and thought that "infinite expansibility" is a desirable feature of classification systems. Knowledge was assumed to expand rather than change. However, the classification system was meant to provide for the systematic arrangement of books on shelves, and since there is only finite space, infinite expansion may be more a liability than an advantage. The problems of the Dewey Decimal Classification arise from this fact. Knowledge, as it is reported in libraries, does not simply expand, it changes in several ways besides. The boundaries between subjects and disciplines blur, and those between disciplines as well, so that music becomes a consideration of biological experiments, something that was never considered in the period when Dewey constructed both his classification scheme and this theory of classification. Each subsequent edition has had to take into account the changes in knowledge as they appear in information sources, often with severe dislocations so far as the previous edition is concerned.

An infinite dense set may expand, creating empty classes readily, but it cannot change the primary system of arrangement. This rigidity requires alteration of

Natural Classification 359

semantic contexts that makes previous arrangements unusable or at least extremely inconvenient. Knowledge is now assumed to be not a fixed arrangement of subjects and disciplines but a regrouping of information sources to which new information is added. It is constantly changing, in the sense that disciplines are a convenience to be avoided when not needed.

To achieve a notation that provides for an infinity of change without disturbance of structure, a kind of infinite series is needed that is larger and not so rigid as the infinite dense and discrete sets. Until fairly recently it was doubted that such an infinity existed. However, there is now no question. These infinite sequences lack a name so far and are dependent upon the notation meant to express them. Elsewhere in this encyclopedia the term "compacted sets" has been used. Such series cannot be created from a single notational base. Pure notation can only create infinite dense or discrete sets. The Universal Decimal Classification utilizes a compacted notation employing structural devices which must be considered different from the Arabic numbers. Granting that the decimal point in the Dewey Decimal Classification is an ornament of no significance in the definition of the type of notation, the decimal point in the Universal Decimal Classification is an essential feature that permits the extension of subjects into new disciplines; in addition, the other structural signals, marks of punctuation, accomplish provisions of infinite change of the classification while the basic system remains intact.

In place of these marks of punctuation, which have the deficiency of not yet having acquired an inherent order, we may substitute letters of the alphabet but not Arabic numbers. Arabic numbers would create ambiguity, but letters of the alphabet do not. If in place of the decimal point, Dewey had used a letter of the alphabet, he would have created an infinite compacted set much larger than the infinity of his dense set. It can easily be shown that compacted sets cannot be put into one-to-one relationship with a dense set. There are always more numbers in the compacted set. Mixed notation always provides for greater infinities than pure notation.

When these possibilities of structure are arranged in fixed and limited order, a faceted classification, like that of Ranganathan, results. The faceted classification determines certain fields and requires that these fields be filled, if only with an indication that nothing is contained when the number creates an inapplicable semantic context for a given item. Faceted classifications have the advantage of providing access by any of the facets to any of the arrangements possible.

In all these kinds of notation, it must be observed that the notation provides for semantic contexts that may not be labeled because of deficiencies of natural language. This can happen in a sequence that potentially outruns the present, so that in numbers providing for chronological events, the creation of empty classes provides for events in the future which have yet to occur, let alone be named. Often in hierarchical notation a class is created that cannot be named and can only be labeled by a list of the contents of the class. Thus a class containing the subsections of rabbits, alphabets, geometrical patterns, and life expectancy of life forms would have no name, although such a class is entirely possible. In the Dewey Decimal Classification such hierarchies are abundant and are simply named by including the labels of the subjects contained (e.g., Philosophy, Psychology, and the Occult).

The potentiality of associations in the Universal Decimal Classification is so great that what can be constructed will probably never be named. The notation escapes the limits of language, which is always finite in the number of words provided though not in the number of arrangements possible. In designing classification systems, faceted classifications tend to be favored because the limits of association may be attuned to a given subject matter without constricting it, and the number of arrangements is much greater than the material to be classified requires. In expanding classification systems, it is necessary to avoid ambiguity so that the possibilities are somewhat limited by the previously determined notation. Even so, expansion is possible by moving further along the scale of infinities, from the small discrete set to the dense set, and from a dense set to an impacted set. Although the rule of construction may require a pure notation, that is, not include both alphabetic and numeric characters, number-like series can be included, such as marks of punctuation, that will seem to maintain the purity of the graphemic base without restricting the further expansion of the notational system. The Library of Congress Classification is expanded by adding a dense feature—a decimal point which changes the sequences from a discrete set to a dense set—and by the potential of adding, or at least enumerating all the possibilities of the sequential notation as it is elaborated. Having up to three letters before four numbers that can be further subdivided by a decimal point and additional numbers beside two series of letter–number combinations, the total potential is incalculable—hence infinite—although the precise number of possibilities can be summed up for the sequential, or discrete, elements of the notation.

The purpose of notation in library classification is to provide an artificial language that will accommodate the semantic contexts needed for systematic arrangement. Natural classification always relates to the informational contents of the items to be classified, and these follow patterns of communication so far only dimly understood. A very fruitful field of investigation will compare the possibilities of natural classification with the requirements of communication within the world community and the changing understanding of what constitutes knowledge. While other kinds of notational patterns appear to be possible, they do not seem to be of much use in natural classification. Only one of these has been investigated to any extent, and this was found to be unwarranted by the informational contents of materials. This type of notation contains a negative feature, so that certain aspects of a class will be considered but not others—something like subtraction, the opposite of what is meant by an ampersand. Apparently semantic contexts can be labeled for what they contain, but only the labels can be changed to show what they do not cover. A kind of contradiction of terms is established that is not only unnecessary but undesirable. What was investigated, then, was not a different kind of infinite series but the operations possible within the series.

Semantic Contents

In the design of a natural classification, the notation becomes an artificial language that in large measure determines what labels will be given the semantic

Natural Classification

contexts created by elaborating the rules of the notation. These rules are very like those of the grammars of natural languages and even more like the rules of the languages usually called artificial, such as Esperanto, in that they are perfectly regular, without the exceptions imposed by tradition and the uneven changes characteristic of the history of a given natural language. However, the natural language used as labels of sematic contexts bears with it all the peculiarities of a history and a grammar that is more often irregular and filled with exceptions than totally predictable.

This explanation may seem to be exiguous, but no other accounts for the fact that natural classifications are meant to provide access to the contents of information sources; these usually employ natural language as a medium of communication and if one or two terms sufficed to indicate the contents, there would be little reason for using more to express the subject matter. An author could write some small group of terms and express his omniscence adequately with marvellous economy. However, information sources are not the pronouncements of oracles. Very often they are exploratory, more important for the manner in which something is investigated than all the conclusions the author (or authors) reach. The notation creates an artificial language capable of expressing distinctions that often go beyond the natural language of the information source and, in any case, provide access to subject matter that the user of a library needs.

Natural classifications are at once independent of and constrained by natural language. The labels of semantic contexts are meaningless if they veer from the pattern of a given natural language, however irregular and imperfectly explained. The labels of semantic contexts, while incapable of precisely translating the term created by the notation, must nevertheless adhere strictly to the grammatical and idiomatic usage of the language employed. This has been missed quite often in the design of classification schemes, especially those in English, and accounts for the shabby indexing of some schedules in the Library of Congress Classification and some editions of the Dewey Decimal Classification. The semantic contexts must remain the same in the schedules and in the index, and the labels used to indicate these contexts, to provide a natural language key to them, must be identical in schedule and in index if the user of the scheme is not to be misled by the index, or frustrated by it, and perplexed by the schedules. The variance has been noted by several and analyzed in detail for the Library of Congress Classification (*10*). The most outstanding failure was the 17th edition of the Dewey Decimal Classification, which had to be recalled. The index was nearly unusable for the very reason that the schedules of the Library of Congress Classification differ in the quality of the indexing.

Because of the belief that subject headings differ entirely from classification terminology, many years elapsed before it was observed that the classification scheme should contain its own subject headings and that these should adhere to the established patterns of morphology of a natural language. Natural classifications for specialized fields have at times accomplished this, though no scheme has fulfilled what are the primary rules for such a unified approach to subject access. It has long been known that an index to a classified catalog or to a chain-indexed catalog is essential for the user and that this index may contain many terms that refer to the same term of the notation. All but one of these would be unused headings in a subject heading list when any of them may be ideal for a particular user. All can be included as the labels of a given semantic context, the one serving as index term that is most easily located, next to the notation, and the others serving as *see* references to the index term but including the notation that applies to the semantic context indicated. No change of form is possible if the natural classification is to be computerized in any way. The slightest difference between the term used in the schedules and the term used in the index will create intolerable problems for the computer and for any program meant to relieve the designer of the classification of much drudgery. Human beings can make assumptions that the computer cannot be programmed to accomplish, so that schedule terms and index terms may differ in some degree before the user is frustrated. It is not desirable to impose on the user's facility with the natural language employed, in any case, and it is disastrous if some future computerization is foreseen.

The semantic context, then, is established by an index term and such other terms as are necessary because they are synonymous with the semantic boundary established by the term of the notation. This feature of natural classification plus the ease by which the notation can create empty classes prevents any intense destruction of the classification through semantic lag. Semantic lag is a feature of natural language that cannot be avoided, although measures can be taken so that the changes required do not alter the structure of the natural classification. Because the classification system eliminates the necessity for a complicated interweaving of subject headings through *see also* references, changes in the access to the classification scheme can be made readily. If computerized, new terms may be added, incorrect terms rearranged, and obsolete terms dropped as desired. This flexibility was available to libraries that used book catalogs, simply because each edition was *sui generis* so far as a subject classification was concerned. The computer has made the flexibility available again, but only if the terminology of the natural language is semantically controlled by the notation.

This can be explained by four features of semantics that can be observed wherever it is employed. First, there is semantic weight or semantic value. As the contexts in which a given word (or phrase) may be used increase, its value or weight decreases. The decrease in value may be as drastic as that observed in English syntactical words, sometimes called function words, that literally have no meaning save what is imparted by all of the contexts where they can be used. These are empty words, so far as semantic value is concerned. Other words are empty, even though not syntactical markers, because they exist only to fulfill requirements of the nominal structure. A term like "economic conditions" contains a prop word, "conditions" that has no meaning save that imparted by the adjective, "economic." It is required because the nominal structure will not allow for words with adjectival endings used as substantives without further change. The obverse of this is also observable in semantic color. A semantically valuable word tends to color all the other terms used with it to the extent that some may take on a new meaning simply by close association. Such a term as "creative activities in seat work" is dominated by the term "seat" with its reference to the human anatomy, even in extension. Although seat work is understood by teachers in the United

States, the chances are that other professionals and other users of English will tend to gain an understanding of the term because of the word seat. Extensive semantic color can create ambiguities of meaning to the extent that a term is meaningless unless a wider context is shown.

This is achieved by semantic limitation. In natural language, the meaning of the word is both intensional and extensional, that is, there is some inherent meaning, even for syntactic markers, but this is finally governed by the contexts in which the term can be used. Prop words characteristically have little semantic weight, but such meaning as may be conveyed is finally determined simply by their position with meaningful adjectives. The phrase so created is in turn limited by the wider context in which it is employed. Because language is always in a state of flux, especially where semantics is concerned, semantic limitation provides for exact usage of new terms needed as the variety of words increases. Semantic limitation both accounts for and ameliorates the fourth of the observable features of semantics, semantic lag. As new terms are created, they are used vaguely and interchangeably with other terms meant to express the same thing. However, contexts are created that finally control the terminology, making one term preferable and another wrong.

However, semantic lag is not simply a lack of precise terminology, but also change of value of terms. What has been a term without many referents becomes the center of an array of terms, and even the grammar of a natural language may be affected. This is especially noticeable at present, because technological and scientific advances—the increase of knowledge which is the ultimate purpose of all education—generally require a rearrangement of language. The American language, in Mencken's concept, is made up of new words and new uses of words that are scarcely predictable (11). A natural classification, then, must provide not only empty classes but new arrangements if it is not to become obsolete and unusable. How rapidly this can occur is evident in the history of the Lamont Classification, designed for the undergraduate library at Harvard University (12). In less than 20 years, the classification became totally unusable and had to be replaced. What has affected classification schemes most has been semantic lag, requiring new editions of the Dewey Decimal Classification and new schedules of the Library of Congress Classification. Other natural classifications have been even more drastically revised, for instance mathematics, and it is now possible to see how the depth of indexing may be reflected in a classification (13).

A natural classification may be general in nature, attempting to provide a subject organization for all the material in a general research library, as do the Library of Congress Classification and the Universal Decimal Classification. It may also be highly specific, like the classification designed for the National Library of Medicine, but following the pattern of the Library of Congress Classification in making provision for general classification within the special area. The question is really concerned with what the classification is supposed to arrange. The more specific the material, the greater the necessity for a highly detailed classification scheme. A moment's reflection will make this proposition seem eminently reasonable. A book is composed of the substance of many articles and may be given more general classification than each of the component parts. Articles have to be classified much more closely if the subject contents of the work is to be made accessible in any meaningful fashion.

Putting all this together, we can come to some immediate conclusions about existing natural classification schemes and about the design of classification or the emendation of existing schemes. We can, in fact, prescribe how natural classification can be used to make a single, unified approach to the subject contents of works. We can, in fact, make some judgments about how a natural classification should be used, first by the classifier and then by the user. The ultimate test of any natural classification is in its use, in the successful provision of access to the subject contents of the works classified.

At the outset it is necessary to note that the actual material can be arranged in any manner that suits the regulations of a library. Material in closed stacks to which the user has no access is best arranged according to an artificial or accidental classification that will most economically utilize the space available. If this is done, then the catalog of the library must provide for an approach based on natural classification, whether a classified catalog, a chain index, or classified subject headings. The methods now employed, following Cutter's prescriptions, have been shown to be unworkable in virtually every detail (14).

Material in open stacks will use the natural classification first for the purpose of providing location symbols, so that the library becomes a kind of vast encyclopedia. This does not make the subject approach any less desirable, although it will generally be not so heavily used. Nevertheless, a classified approach to the contents of the works is necessary in some form other than the arrangement of the material itself. For many libraries, the only economical method of providing a classified approach is through classified subject headings. Otherwise, an unthinkable task of creating afresh the subject catalog of the library, when it may contain millions of items, is required. Libraries that have closed, or will close, their giant card catalogs can begin with a subject catalog in classified array, something more than a shelf list, without attempting to address the problem of the old catalog.

The Design of a Natural Classification Scheme

The first step is obviously an awareness of the material to be classified as represented in the information sources available at the time the natural classification scheme is contemplated. Quite often in a general library, a decision is reached to amplify or augment the natural classification scheme already in use. This is rarely necessary if the Universal Decimal Classification is employed because, of the three general classification systems discussed, it is the most flexible and most easily employed without the need for any local tinkering. A deficiency has been the lack of a fixed order for the marks of punctuation which provide the associative features of the classification. Many libraries using the classification have gone on the comfortable assumption that all these were not necessary, but as the library grows in size, the need for close classification is more sharply felt.

Another consideration is the expense of classifying material when the work is done at some national or regional center, often without cost to the library. Cataloging in Publication, the project of the Library of Congress to include the portions of the catalog entry that cannot be obtained from the work of technical assistants or library assistants, makes the work of classification simple in a general library containing mostly books in English, and possibly French, German, Spanish, and Italian. Although Cataloging in Publication is not so far a universal approach to the problem of centralized cataloging, its use is spreading, and in the case of the more frequently used European languages, the Library of Congress provides the classification of such books in its card service. Whatever the desirability of a special classification scheme, the librarians in a general library, for instance a medium-size public or college library, must weigh the cost of close classification against the economies that centralized cataloging ensures.

Most locally designed classification schemes have been made for highly specialized collections with a clientele that is both sophisticated and limited. Special libraries that contain almost no material in about half the classes of a general classification are faced with a different evaluation of cost. Is it better to create a new scheme or to use one someone else created or to alter an available general scheme to make it more highly specialized? The question can be answered only by considering the way the users of the library are best served. In special libraries, the librarian takes on most of the effort left to the user in a general library. The librarian must find material for the user, and the classification scheme can greatly reduce the amount of effort this requires. Locally provided classification then becomes an economical way of organizing access to the material.

Supposing that the decision is made to create a natural classification scheme for the highly specialized material that must be fully analyzed if the library is to achieve the maximum degree of usefulness, the librarian's investigation of the material available will seek to discover how the authors organize their own works, what are the major classes and how they are organized. This utilizes the observed fact that natural classification bears a close relationship to the use of natural language for expository purposes. A disorganized work is very hard for the user to employ as a source of information.

This examination may be quite impressionistic at first, but at some point it will be found desirable to make definite notes, if not a sketch of the classification as found in the sources. This sketch will do much to clarify what kind of notational scheme will at once be sufficiently hospitable and economical. While an associative system provides greatest flexibility, it also incurs great difficulties of definition and usage. Faceted schemes are more desirable if the number of needed associations can be strictly limited. A purely hierarchical notation will often suffice—if not, associations of subject matter will be needed, and where possible, often within the associative or faceted scheme, both hierarchical and sequential arrangements are useful. Precise rules for the use of these notational devices are exceedingly abstruse and must be related to the practicalities of the particular situation in which they are to be used.

Having decided upon the nature of the scheme, the system of notation to be employed, and the major classes which constitute the facets or the primary classes of a hierarchy, the task next to be addressed is the choice of terminology. The form is governed mostly by the peculiarities of the natural language used to express these terms, so that rules of form of schedule terms, hence subject headings, and index terms, must be derived from a profound understanding of the nominal structure of the language in which the terms are expressed. Some cautionary words about English seem to be in order because the traditions of subject analysis have created unnecessary problems.

Inverted terms that put a modifier after the head of a construction are likely to incur problems of structural ambiguity. The use of prepositions to express headings that are constructed by the classifier where no natural language term seems adequate are likely to mystify users. Marks of punctuation should be used to show the rather vague relationships between words that English prepositions represent. Unfortunately, the use of one preposition or another is so little governed by fixed rules that any true analysis of style over a period of centuries will show the wavering of taste and preferences by leading authors of the times. English prepositions serve as syntactical markers with a slender infusion of semantic value. Thus we distinguish between things lying on the box and in the box, but the distinction between arriving on time and in time cannot be explained in terms of semantic value.

Wherever possible the classification is made up of terminology drawn directly from the information sources in an order of preference for the simplest clear expression of meaning that can be found. In English this may be a single noun, but often cases of modification must be investigated, including nouns as modifiers and heads of construction. The injunction against inverted terms derives from the inability of the language to produce in written form the aural signals by which different semantic values are indicated. While "criminal statistics" is distinctly and irrevocably ambiguous in written form, when spoken aloud by a native speaker of the language, a difference is immediately understood by native listeners, who know whether the statistics are criminal or the criminal has statistics into which he fits.

The term which is placed next to the notation is the index term. All *see* references in the index must refer to this term, even though the term from which a *see* reference is made ought to include the classification number. This introduces a flexibility of arrangement which, along with a hospitable notation, can preserve the scheme from deterioration as knowledge progresses. A natural classification is rather like those ancient dwellings in Europe or Asia which have been altered as time and technology demanded, always comfortable and convenient by the standards of any given period. New terms as required may be added and terms dropped, so long as the index term remains the same, without any further attention to the structure of the classification. If the index term is changed, then the changes within the index may be effected simply and efficiently.

This is the primary reason why the classification of terminology is a necessity, along with the observed fact that the human mind remembers terminology by associations of meaning rather than by the inherent order of the alphabet. Further, the term that best suits can be indicated by the structure of the notation which brings terminology into close relationship by semantic value. Semantic lag can affect a classification so drastically that it falls completely out-of-date and must be discarded, with attendant vast cost of reclassifying all the existing materials organized by the worthless scheme.

A further fact is that the techniques recommended here are admirably suited to computerization, not only for the material to be organized into an information retrieval scheme but also the scheme itself. By classifying the subject access to the information sources, the advantages of a classified system may be enjoyed although all access to the information sources is by means of search routines using whatever computer equipment is available. What makes a classified card catalog, or a chain index in card form, especially responsive to users is the arrangement of subject headings in classified order. These may be attached to the information sources and to the cards that represent them, or they may not. What is important is not the cards nor the sources but the access to them, and this is equal so long as the terms are classified in the first place and an adequate index to the classification is provided.

Conclusion

Natural classification is of ancient origins but of modern application, like natural language itself, on which and from which natural classification is based. Attempts to make the language serve by employing an inherent order of arrangement will fail as the size and complexity of the file of information sources grow. Access becomes more difficult as the user is faced with a large number of terms, not all of which he should be expected to know. The novice in a given field is primarily served by the subject access to material. The expert is more likely to rely on titles, perhaps, but especially on the names of other experts. Since in every field save his own, the expert is a novice, and the number of beginners in a field of knowledge greatly exceeds the number of experts, organization of material to provide maximum access at minimum cost demands the rather elaborate work of constructing and using a natural classification as the guide to all subject access. The preliminary work is slow and exacting, but it is ultimately a remarkably efficient way to save the time of the user of an information file and equally the organizer of the file, if he is sensitive to user needs and capacities.

The object of providing subject access is to ensure recall of material with a high degree of relevance for the amount of material obtained. No studies have confirmed that classified material will provide subject access with greater efficiency than other methods. In effect, now, some studies would be trivial, the complicated work of confirming the obvious; but Ebrami's preliminary study (15) in a language-free environment at least confirms the major propositions. The history of natural classification has done the rest, especially if the problems of subject headings are combined with those of existing natural language schemes where a notation may observably play a crucial role in the flexibility, usefulness, and responsiveness of a scheme.

Natural classification is, furthermore, especially adaptable to the technology of organization that would reduce the enormous labors of file systems and subject catalogs. The computer can deal especially well with a classification scheme, because many of the search routines can be developed within the notation, increasing the access to the material without complicating the methods by which the file is searched. Further experimentation along these lines will doubtless lead to exact statements of procedures. Although, as Maurice Tauber once said to a group of his students, "A lot of time and money are wasted on classification," even more money is wasted when subject access is not classified. At some point the entire scheme will break down. A poignant example of this can be found in the two National Aerospace Authority subject access thesauri. The slight differences of form were sufficient to make material organized by the first unsearchable by the second, even though it was meant to reduce the labor of searching and to increase the recall and relevance of material obtained. If the terms had been classified in the second place, these minute distinctions of form would have mattered not at all. In fact, there would never have been a need for a second thesaurus at all, as Manheimer's revealing study shows (16). Her analysis of the second thesaurus, which began as a comparison of technique of arrangement, ended as an analysis of the form of heading because of emendations that were not understood to have been crucial to the subject access of material.

A leading figure in the development of information science as a discipline, who need not be named here, once remarked to the present writer that subject headings need not be classified to provide access to material. That is true. In fact, the information sources need not be organized along subject lines at all if there are only a few of them, so that complete review of what is available takes but a short time. However, for a scheme that must keep pace with the change in the information sources, implying not only growth but alteration in the direction and reporting of research, a natural classification becomes the only efficient method of organization. We have learned this just in time to preserve computerized systems from the perils and final collapse of theory regarding the dictionary catalog and the use of subject headings.

REFERENCES

1. Ernest Cushing Richardson, *Classification, Theoretical and Practical: Together With an Appendix Containing an Essay Towards a Bibliographical History of Systems of Classification,* 3rd ed., H. W. Wilson, New York, 1930.
2. Saad M. Ibrahim, "Evaluation of the Medical Subject Headings of the National Library of Medicine as an Adequate Bibliographic Search Tool in the Field of Ophthalmology," Dissertation, University of Pittsburgh, Graduate School of Library and Information Sciences, 1973.
3. Martha L. Manheimer, *The Applicability of the NASA Thesaurus to the File of Documents Indexed Prior to Its Publication,* University of Pittsburgh, Pittsburgh, 1969.
4. George Martin Sinkankas, "An Investigation and Comparison of Three Associative Systems in a General Subject Heading List," Dissertation, University of Pittsburgh, Graduate School of Library and Information Sciences, 1974.
5. John Phillip Immroth, *Analysis of Vocabulary Control in Library of Congress Classification and Subject Headings,* Libraries Unlimited, Littleton, Colorado, 1971.
6. Noam Chomsky, *Syntactic Structures,* Mouton, The Hague, 1962.
7. Peter Mark Roget, *Thesaurus of English Words and Phrases, Classified and Arranged So As To Facilitate the Expression of Ideas and Assist in Literary Composition,* Longman, Brown, Green, and Longmans, London, 1852.
8. Anthony Thompson, *Vocabularium Bibliothecarii, English, French, German,* revised and enlarged edition, UNESCO, Paris, 1953.
9. Jay E. Daily, "Classification and Categorization," in *Encyclopedia of Library and Information Science,* Vol. 5 (A. Kent and H. Lancour, eds.), Dekker, New York, 1971, pp. 43–141.
10. Ref. 5.

11. H. L. Mencken, *The American Language: An Inquiry Into the Development of English in the United States,* abridged edition, Knopf, New York, 1963.
12. Martha L. Manheimer, "Lamont Library Classification Scheme," in *Encyclopedia of Library and Information Science,* Vol. 14 (A. Kent, H. Lancour, and J. E. Daily, eds.), Dekker, New York, 1975, pp. 34–37.
13. Barbara Kirsch Schaefer, "Classification of the Literature of Mathematics: A Comparative Analysis of the American Mathematical Society and the Library of Congress Schemes," Dissertation, University of Pittsburgh, Graduate School of Library and Information Sciences, 1972.
14. James G. Williams, Martha L. Manheimer, and Jay E. Daily, *Classified Library of Congress Subject Headings,* Dekker, New York, 1972.
15. Hooshang Ebrami, *Catchword Indexing, Subject Headings and Chain Indexing; The Formulation of Rules for Subject Analysis in Farsi,* University of Pittsburgh, Pittsburgh, 1970.
16. Ref. *3.*

20

Clumps, Theory of

Karen Sparck Jones / The University of Cambridge, Cambridge, England

Research in automatic classification for information retrieval, such as that associated with the theory of clumps, presents many interesting problems. This is because it lies at the intersection of four areas of investigation: it is linked with the study of classification theory in general, with information retrieval, with linguistic research into the nature of conceptual or semantic classifications and their use in discourse analysis, and with the development of programming techniques for handling a certain class of problem.

Broadly speaking, we may be primarily interested for retrieval purposes either in forming a keyword or term* classification, which can be used to characterize the documents in a collection as an aid to retrieval, or in forming a document classification. The two are clearly linked because both depend on the same information about the distribution of words in documents; thus the thesaurus class descriptions of the different documents in a collection, where these classes are derived from facts about the occurrences of the words in the documents, also classify the documents; and document classes, which depend on the same facts, also lead to vocabulary classes. The same grouping techniques can, moreover, obviously be used to generate either form of classification, since a general-purpose classification procedure can be applied to any data satisfying given formal requirements; and if we start with a document-term incidence array, we can clearly use it either way round. At the same time, there are important differences between what may be called primary and secondary classifications; for example, if we have overlapping classes of terms, these will generate exclusive classes of documents with the same

---

From Jones, Karen Sparck. *Clumps, Theory of.* ENCYCLOPEDIA OF LIBRARY AND INFORMATION SCIENCE. Vol. 5. Edited by Allen Kent and Harold Lancour. Assistant Editor, William Z. Nasri. New York, Marcel Dekker, Inc., c1971. pp. 208–223.

   * A term represents a set of morphologically related keywords. In the present context they can be regarded as having the same status as keywords, both being the initial items to be classified.

term class descriptions, and vice versa. The empirical reasons for taking one classification or the other as primary may also be quite different; thus a document classification may be required as a device for partitioning a collection, to reduce the amount of effort involved in searching, where a keyword or term classification is required as a device for providing characterizations for all the documents in a collection. Research on the theory of clumps was associated with the construction of keyword classifications that could be used as components of indexing languages, and though the techniques themselves were intended to be quite general, the classification of words will be taken as their usual application in the discussion that follows.

The argument for the use of a keyword classification itself is quite straightforward, and it will be familiar to anyone who has worked in information retrieval. Essentially, if we accept that the base mode of characterizing a document or request is by a simple keyword or term list, a keyword thesaurus is intended as a normalization device that permits matches between requests and documents that do not actually contain the same words. Or, to look at the situation from another point of view, we can say that in forming a keyword classification, we are setting up a list of descriptors, since the keywords of which it is composed, and which automatically lead to the assignment of classes to documents, can be equated with the kind of scope notes referring to keywords that justify the assignment of descriptors to documents. The fact that a keyword classification is a vocabulary normalization device then means, if we refer to a useful distinction, that it primarily appears to be a recall-promoting device as opposed to a precision device, to widen the scope of request-document matches, rather than to restrict them. But it must be emphasized than any classification that is not exclusive, and that permits a term to appear in more than one class, can in principle function as a precision-promoting device. This is because the different class assignments of a word may represent its different senses or contextual affiliations. In using word classes instead of words, therefore, we may be able to effect sense or use discriminations, through matching on one class for a word and not another, which are impossible if we use the word alone. It must further be accepted that the class-mates of a word, even in an exclusive classification, extend a request or document description, and it is generally accepted that the longer the list of words characterizing either, the more precise the specification they jointly provide. The relationship between these two aspects of a keyword classification is nevertheless a complex one, given that it depends not only on the nature of the classification itself, but on the characteristics of the initial word lists from which it is derived, and it is not at all easy to see how a classification may be designed to achieve a particular effect; but the fact that we have alternative possibilities, when we consider the way a classification may function as an indexing device, must be borne in mind.

But even if we do have some ideas about the possible retrieval functions of a keyword thesaurus, this does not assist us very much when we attempt to construct such a thesaurus automatically; and it is quite obvious that the replacement of single terms by groups of mutually substitutible terms with a wider range of matches will not necessarily improve retrieval performance as a whole: we may very well retrieve more relevant documents, but only at the cost of retrieving more nonrelevant ones also. Thus at this point it is important to distinguish two quite different problems; one is whether we can obtain a better retrieval performance with a keyword classification than we can with keywords alone, and the other is whether we can construct such a classification automatically. There are great difficulties in experimental work in automatic keyword classification, just because it may be far from easy to attribute the results of an experiment to the character of the classification used, or to the fact that an automatic procedure was used to generate it. For example, if we think that synonym groups are of value, and we find that a given set of synonym classes does not do well, this may be either because synonym groups are in fact not what are required, or because the automatic classification technique that was used does not generate good synonym groups (where it is of course assumed that these can be set up manually). A further problem arises under the first head because we have to consider not only the character of the classification itself, but how it is used as a component of an indexing language, and indeed as part of a retrieval system as a whole. The same classification may have different effects if it is used to characterize a request in different ways, for instance if it is associated with a structured representation or not, and equally, if the actual mode of searching with it varies. Under the second heading, moreover, we have to take into account both the character of the information on which the grouping is based, and the actual classification procedure that is applied to it, where the latter in turn may involve some compromises between what is required by the underlying classification theory and what is practicable from a computing point of view. In addition, quite apart from all these difficulties, there is the general problem of establishing a satisfactory experimental methodology in information retrieval research. The use of automatically constructed classifications is still a subject for investigation, and the inherent problems to be dealt with are compounded by the more serious ones associated with the characterization of information retrieval systems as wholes and the development of adequate retrieval performance measures. The present context is not, however, the place to go into these questions, as long as their relevance is borne in mind, and it is accepted that the application of automatic grouping procedures in information retrieval is still a matter of experiment. It is true that automatically obtained thesauri may be of great assistance in practice even now, for example as aids for anyone setting up a list of descriptors manually; but this obviously does not represent a full commitment to such a thesaurus, and the fact that work in this field is really still experimental must be emphasized.

With this background, we can now go into the specific question of automatic keyword classification in more detail, and in particular into the chain of argument on which any attempt to construct such a classification is based. This is that whatever means are used for grouping words when a thesaurus is constructed manually (or intellectually), the only sufficiently accessible, and easily manipulated, information about words that can be used if a thesaurus is to be constructed automatically, is that contained in notes of the occurrences of the words concerned in a document collection. We do not, however, use distributional information simply because it is the only available substitute for the human being's knowledge of word meanings. Distributional information has positive merits of its own. It can be maintained, that is, that the words which occur in a document are necessarily indicative of its content; and that while we may say that the characterization of a document for retrieval purposes should indicate its conceptual content, and that the relationship between this and the words constituting its text is not a straightforward one, the two are sufficiently close for us to be able to regard the words contained in a document text as a reasonably reliable indication of its conceptual content. (Its syntactic structure also plays a part, of course, but this is explicitly excluded here.) But what, then, is achieved by the use of a classification? The answer is quite obvious, namely, that if we accept that the words of a document text are reasonably representative of its conceptual content, we have also to allow for the fact that in natural language the same concept may be represented by different words, and that different concepts may be represented by sets of words that have items in common. The object of a classification is then to bring together those different words that represent the same or related concepts or topics, in order to maximize word matching in retrieval; for it follows from the general idea of verbal representativeness, if it may be so called, that the more two descriptions match, the more likely they are to represent the same concept or topic. If we have a request description and a document description, the more words they share, the more likely the document is to be relevant to the request; a document possessing all the ten terms of a request, that is, has a much better chance of being relevant to the request than a document containing only one of them. For instance, if we take a particular request associated with a test collection of 200 aeronautical documents as an example, we find that for the seven given request terms we get

Documents matching on any — term(s)	Relevant documents retrieved	Nonrelevant documents retrieved
1	0	48
2	1	54
3	4	27
4	1	11
5	2	10
6	4	2
7	0	0

The relevant documents retrieved thus constitute 67% of the total at level 6, while they constitute 8% at level 4, and only 2% at level 2. (From here we can of course proceed to the familiar precision ratio for each of the selected levels, which is 67%, 33%, and 12%.)

This statement about the correlation between the extent to which documents match requests and their probable relevance to requests constitutes what may be called the Relevance Hypothesis of information retrieval; it is generally supported by the results in terms of relevant and nonrelevant documents retrieved that different matching levels give, for virtually any indexing language, and it is what we have to work with. At the same time, it is well known that what makes a document relevant to a request is inordinately difficult, if not impossible, to define: if it wasn't satisfactory retrieval would presumably be mainly an economic problem; the fundamental problem of retrieval is that we do not have any precise information about the relevance relation between documents and requests that we can use to direct the formation of document and request specifications and the mode of searching. We can only assume that correlation in vocabulary has something to do with relevance, because given judgments about relevance can to some extent be interpreted to support this assumption, and proceed from here. But it is difficult to extract very much in the way of concrete suggestions as to exactly how request document vocabulary matching is to be optimized from the crude fact that the more matching items there are, the more likely the document is to be relevant.

Our starting position is therefore that a classification, in providing sets of substitutes for terms, makes it possible to amplify a request, and hence makes it more precise, so that in principle in matching against documents, which have themselves been treated in the same way, we are more selective. If we have a specific request containing terms *a*, *b,* and *c,* for example, and we have three corresponding classes of terms, say *apq, brs,* and *atuv,* the fact that *p* and *q* are allowed as alternatives for *a* may mean that we can retrieve a document containing only two of the request terms, namely *b* and *c,* at a higher matching level, because the document also contains *p*, though it lacks *a*; and the chance of the document being relevant to the request is therefore improved by its matching at a higher level. The same effect may be achieved by *q*, and equally by the substitutes for *b* and *c.*

We now come to the basis of the classification. This again is familiar, for automatic keyword classification depends on what may be called the Co-occurrence Hypothesis, to the effect that classes consisting of words with a tendency to co-occur in documents will permit satisfactory substitutions, i.e., ones that promote the retrieval of relevant documents. This follows from the earlier remarks about the use of distributional information in general: for if two words co-occur in a document, they can to some extent be regarded as alternative representatives of its conceptual content or topic, and if they co-occur in every document in which either occurs, they can be presumed to have a very strong topic connection. For example, in the aeronautical collection referred to earlier the words "hub" and "shroud" occur and co-occur four times; and they indeed have a strong topic connection which can be conveniently illustrated by the fact that the title of one of the documents concerned is "A Rapid Approximate Method for the Design of Hub Shroud Profiles of Centrifugal Impellers of Given Blade Shapes." From the retrieval point of view, moreover, terms that always co-occur can be regarded as intersubstitutible in the sense that the same documents will be retrieved irrespective of which is used in a request; though it must be emphasized that the terms need not have the same or even a similar meaning, as we can see from "hub" and "shroud." Of course there is no justification for putting two words that always co-occur in the same class, because matching on either as simple keywords will be wholly effective. But given the empirical fact that words connected with, or representative of, a given topic do not always co-occur, and indeed cannot be expected to co-occur in any collection not consisting of identical documents, we can then be interested in the tendency of words to co-occur, and can group those words that tend to co-occur as members of the same class. In *this* case, classification does more for us than keyword matching, because it enables us to retrieve a document containing one term in answer to a request containing another that we could not retrieve directly by a keyword search with the latter, where the presumption is nevertheless that the latter could very easily have occurred in the same document as the former, because of their general tendency to co-occur. This is the reason for assuming that the document containing the first term is relevant to a request containing the second. Thus if we take our previous example, we might well group "impeller" with "hub" and "shroud" because it co-occurs relatively frequently with them, and this would then enable us to retrieve two documents not containing "hub" or "shroud" that are nevertheless about the same subject, namely flowthrough impellers.

These two hypotheses must constitute the foundation for any attempt to construct a keyword classification for retrieval purposes. The usual difference between an intellectual and an automatic approach to the construction of such a classification is in the use made of distributional information in the strict sense, that is, information about the actual occurrences of the terms to be classified in the documents of the collection. The use of this information is, as we have seen, essential where automatic methods are concerned, because it is the kind of information that lends itself readily to machine processing, and is indeed the kind of information that can readily be provided automatically, if a wholly mechanized construction procedure is envisaged. Now it is true that the general argument in favor of using facts about the textual behavior of terms which was given earlier ultimately underlies any semantic classification of words, since the principles on which intellectual classification is usually based, such as restricting grouping to synonyms, or generically related items, in the end must refer to the way words are used in texts. The only justification we can ultimately give for the statement that two words are synonyms, or have synonymous senses, is that they are used in the same way in texts; we can, for example, say "big man" or "large man," "big house" or "large house," and "big book" or "large book" indifferently, and equally "bumpy surface" or "uneven surface" and "bumpy ride" or "uneven ride." At the same time, this reference to the way words are used in discourse is not usually explicit or systematic where manual classification is concerned, in the way in which it is, and indeed must be, in automatic classification: in an automatic classification grouping is based only on information about the occurrences of the words concerned in the document collection in question. This difference is important because it is reflected in the different preconceptions as to the linguistic character of the thesaurus that seem to be typical of manual and automatic classification respectively. Thus it is a common assumption in manual classification that thesaurus classes should consist of words linked by a single well-defined semantic relation, and in particular that they should consist of synonyms or near-synonyms (allowing for the fact that words may be treated as synonyms or synonyms within subject contexts that are not regarded as such from the point of view of the language as a whole). The explicit dependence on collocational relationships that characterizes automatic classification, on the other hand, at once suggests that it is not reasonable to suppose that words that are strongly connected in terms of their tendency to co-occur, and are hence likely to be grouped, will necessarily be synonyms or near-synonyms, though many classification procedures allow the grouping of items that do not usually co-occur but that co-occur with common items, which is true of synonyms. This contrast is apparent, for example, in the different characters of the classes in the manual and automatic thesauri that have been constructed for the aeronautical collection mentioned earlier. The manual thesaurus contains classes like

criterion parameter value factor requirement principle
diffusion joining merging exchange impinging
maximum complete extreme total

which consist, broadly speaking, of synonyms, while one automatic classification contains much more varied classes like

criterion cycles Lyapunov random
diffusion elimination hypervelocity peak
maximum hub impeller inlet shroud

The points discussed so far all became apparent at some stage or other in the research that has been associated with the theory of clumps and the subsequent extended work in automatic classification for retrieval purposes. This work represents the fullest investigation of the application of automatic classification techniques in information retrieval, and it is therefore of interest both in its own right, and as an example that serves to illustrate the characteristic problems that arise when any attempt is made to construct a retrieval thesaurus automatically.

The theory of clumps was first put forward in three papers—one by R. M. Needham and A. F. Parker-Rhodes, one by R. M. Needham, and one by A. F. Parker-Rhodes—in 1960–1961, and was further developed in R. M. Needham's doctoral thesis of 1961. The suggestions contained in these papers were a response to the difficulties that had previously arisen in the attempt to construct a lattice-type network of keywords which had been set up as an experimental information retrieval system at the Cambridge Language Research Unit, part of which is illustrated in Figure 1. The distinctive feature of this keyword network, and the character of the arguments used to proceed from it to a classification, influenced the approach to automatic classification that was adopted considerably, and they are therefore worth noticing here. Thus the network was based on the principle that

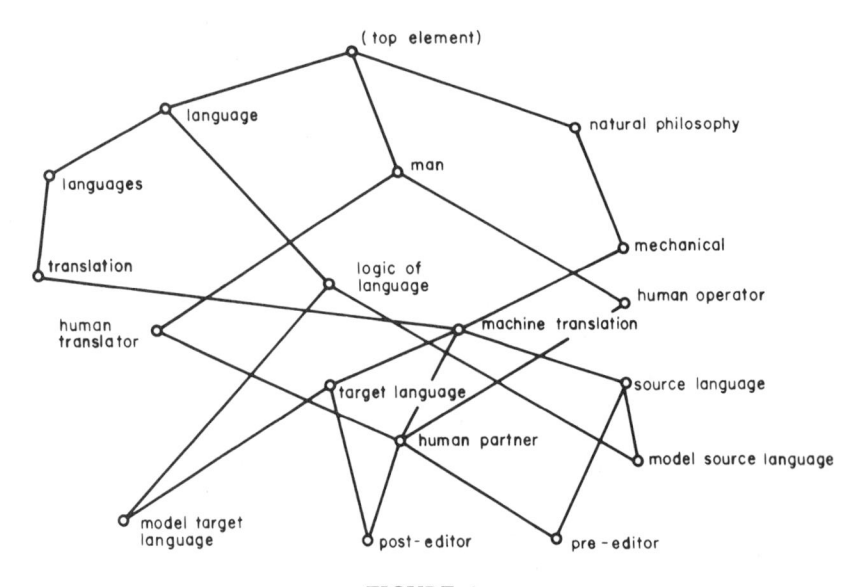

FIGURE 1.

term *a* is placed above, or includes, term *b* if a request containing *a* can be satisfied by a document containing *b*. This sometimes corresponded to the familiar generic relation, but by no means always. It was accepted, moreover, that an individual term could be subsumed under any number of proximate higher terms, which meant that the resulting structure as a whole was extremely irregular. In searching a "scale of relevance" procedure was followed in which given request terms were systematically replaced by their superiors, where any match on such a superior automatically involved a match on any other term below the latter. Unfortunately, the lattice was inordinately difficult to construct, once it included more than a few hundred terms; and it became apparent that the structure was in one sense more complex than was really required. A great deal of energy was expended on the precise placing of terms relative to one another, where these relations were to a considerable extent disregarded once the scale of relevance procedure had been entered. For the essential feature of the procedure was that in moving up from a given term *q* to its superior *p*, matches on any of *p* and its other subordinate terms, on all lower levels, were permitted. The set of terms dependent on a specific term was therefore being treated as a set of substitutible terms while their detailed relationships were disregarded. This then suggested the idea that sets of substitutible terms that would have the same effect in retrieval as the lattice might be established directly without any attempt to notice specific relations between them; and the argument that co-occurence information would provide a suitable base for setting up such groups of terms naturally followed.

This development is of interest because it exhibits both the relationship and distinction between the use of a network and that of a classification. The suggestion that an associative network of terms, or semantic map, should be used for literature searching has frequently been put forward, for example by Doyle (*1*) and Giuliano (*2*); and the idea of using the most rudimentary form of network, consisting simply of lists of terms that are directly associated with a given term, is often encountered too, and has been investigated by Salton and Lesk (*3*); clearly, combining all the lists for the terms in a vocabulary would generate a network. For example, take the following lists of items associated with given keywords for the aerodynamical collection:

Ablating	Average	Capacity	Copper	Homogeneous	Inconel	Shield	Teflon	Transpiration
Capacity Shield Teflon	Copper Homogeneous Inconel	Ablating Teflon	Average Homogeneous Inconel (etc.)	Average Copper Inconel (etc.)	Average Copper Homogeneous Teflon Transpiration	Ablating Capacity	Ablating Transpiration	Inconel Teflon

If we put these lists together we get Figure 2.

The important difference between these modes of organizing term relationships and that defined by a classification is that in the former the substitution of one term for another depends on the connection between them being explicit; to replace a given word by another requires a reference to the connection between them, if necessary via intermediate terms. Thus in the example we can only use

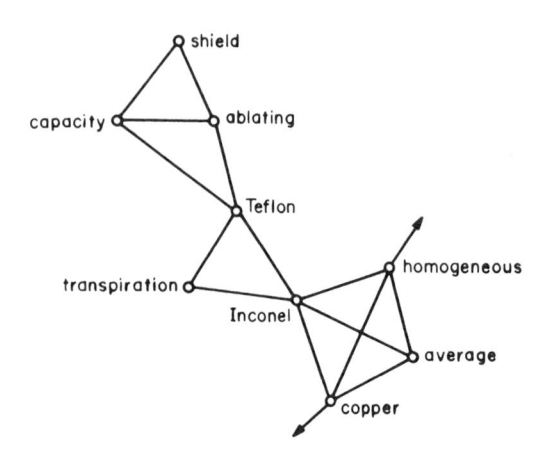

FIGURE 2.

"Teflon" to expand a request containing "shield" if we have followed the path from "shield" to "ablating" and from "ablating" to "Teflon." In a classification, on the other hand, if we have grouped "ablating," "capacity," "shield," and "Teflon" on the grounds of their being generally connected, we can substitute "Teflon" for "shield" without asking what the exact nature of the connection between them is. In general in a network the assumption is that only short journeys represent strong connections, and hence lead to worthwhile substitutions: thus we might proceed from "average" to "Teflon" but not further to "shield;" but it is clear that examining alternative routes between two terms to see whether any are acceptably short presents many problems, and the cumulative effect of several connections is not easily taken into account: this is clear in the example if we consider how we may reach "Teflon" from "average," or whether "shield" is strongly related to "Teflon" because the two are linked in more than one way. Following routes in a network also involves many purely practical difficulties. With a classification this detailed information about the precise pattern of connections between the members of a class is thrown away, but in return, a much more valuable gain in generality is achieved: for if we know that two items are members of the same class we can behave as if they are strongly connected, though the reason for their being put in the class may not be that this is already explicit, but rather that it is implicit in their position in the pattern of connections linking the members of the class as a whole. Of course we cannot obtain the classification without the initial connection network, but we abandon the detailed information it contains once the classification is completed, and this is in one sense a loss; but the more than compensating gain is in simplicity and the right to make assumptions about the relations between objects that we may not realize we can make if we confine ourselves to a network.

The other important point about the suggestion that the use of a lattice structure should be replaced by that of a classification is that it determined our views about the characteristic properties of the classification we were seeking. It led us to believe that from the linguistic point of view, the classification should not be confined to sets of synonyms and near-synonyms, or similarly narrowly related items: the relation on which the lattice was based meant that proximate terms in it could be semantically related in a great variety of ways; and this, when combined with the fact mentioned earlier that classes based on co-occurrences in only moderate amounts of text are unlikely to consist of systematically related items, meant that no attempt was made to place any semantic restrictions on the grouping procedure. It was on the contrary believed that the kind of topical relationships given by the lattice, and which were derived from co-occurrence information in the grouping process, are really appropriate to retrieval; and that while we may find it useful to take account of synonymy and similarly restricted relations, our classes as wholes should be topic classes which, though they can be described as semantically based, are not so in a very strong sense. Thus the words "burned," "composed," "equivalence," "ethylene," "exponent," "flame," "fuel," "methane," and "product' form a topic class, since they all appear in discussions of such topics as rocket propulsion, though they are clearly not all related to one another semantically in any other way. From what may be called the retrieval point of view, it was believed that the classification should be regarded primarily as a match-promoting as opposed to a match-restricting device, by comparison with keywords, with a view to improving recall; though it was intended that the fact that in the original network one term could be subsumed under several higher ones should be reflected in the classification by permitting a term to appear in more than one class, so that the classification could also be regarded as a precision device. Finally, since the classification was intended to replace the irregular set of relationships of the network, it was accepted that the conditions defining membership of a class should not be too restricted: for if two keywords could be treated as substitutible in the scale of relevance procedure without being directly connected, it was assumed that a class should be so defined as to allow the grouping of terms that were not directly connected. It was further recognized that it could not be expected that co-occurrence information should be wholly systematic, so that document connections based on it could not always be looked for; and this, when taken together with the view that overlaps between classes should be allowed and even encouraged, reinforced the belief that the type of classification that was required was one that permitted the multiple grouping of irregularly connected items. What was needed, in other words, was an approach to classification that on the one hand permitted a looser structure within a class than that represented by a definition that requires a connection between all the members of a class, and on the other permitted a more informal structure of the set of classes than that represented by a strict hierarchical ordering; the object was to set up a definition that did not depend on the notion of levels of grouping in the set of classes as a whole, but that did not on the other hand require either that the classes should be exclusive, or that they should be too tightly organized internally.

It must now be admitted that a satisfactory theory of classification of this kind has still not been developed: the theory of clumps represented a determined attempt to come to grips with the question, but it has not been pushed through to a successful conclusion. At that time (1958), the increasing capacity of computers stimulated interest in grouping and ordering algorithms of a much greater degree of complexity than were generally in use, with a view to their application to much larger quantities of material than could be properly processed by hand, in a variety of different areas; but it is clear that there was a great deal of confusion about the status of, and relations between, different methods of analyzing and arranging data that might be described as classification techniques, and about their propriety in particular circumstances. In information retrieval, a natural temptation was to apply techniques developed for other purposes, without sufficient attention being given to their real fitness for documentation: the attempt to apply factor analysis can be taken as an example. We are perhaps in a better position now to distinguish different types of technique; and it can be maintained that neither methods like factor analysis on the one hand, nor like multidimentional scaling on the other, should be described as classification techniques proper, though this in itself does not mean that they are inapplicable in the information retrieval content: that is an independent question. With regard to classification proper, we can broadly distinguish those techniques in which the notion of ordering among classes plays a part, whether this leads to a complete hierarchical structure or not, and those in which it does not. Whether there could ever be a global theory of classification which covered both, that is, which covered every form of processing we would call classification, is unclear, but the need for a well-constructed formal theory of classification, at least for each of the two forms of classification just described, is evident, where the criteria for such a theory are that it states the conditions, such as the preservation of continuity, that must be satisfied by any classification procedure, and relates different procedures to one another systematically. (Such a theory should of course include a component dealing with the prior notion of connection, resemblance, or similarity.)

The need for such a theory is evident as soon as we consider the problem of evaluating a given classification, which presents many difficulties that are particularly striking where automatic methods of generating classifications are concerned: in this case the fact that the computer acts as a black box, so that the actual grouping process is removed from human observation, means that we are not so easily lulled into the sense of security about the classification which is very natural if we are grouping by hand, and the need for confidence in the grouping algorithm is much more apparent. Essentially, for any classification of some data, we can ask not merely whether it is a good classification, but whether it is the best classification of the data; or, given several alternative classifications, we can ask which is the best of these, and again, whether it is the best obtainable; and in principle, if we have an adequate theory of classification, with an adequate supporting data theory, we should be able to answer these questions. However, it does not follow that the best classification on these internal grounds alone will work well when the classification is used for some purpose. For that a precise specification of the purpose itself, which can be used as a guide to the choice of classification procedure, is also required; and it is unfortunately true that in information retrieval, we cannot give a sufficiently precise specification of our purpose. We can therefore only evaluate any classification *post hoc,* by seeing how it works, and it will clearly not follow, even so, that we have the best classification for our purpose. The fact, moreover, that we have no general theory of classification to control the formation of the classifications which are then tested for their performance, and more particularly, that there is no theory covering procedures generating the nonordered classifications we have good reason for thinking are needed for information retrieval, means that we are in a far from strong position. We can only compare the retrieval performance of a given classification with that of unclassified terms, without much confidence either in its being the best classification available, or that the method which generated it is wholly reliable. At the same time, the importance of evaluating keyword classifications by their retrieval performance only, and not by their appearance (which may be very misleading), must be emphasized.

The work on the theory of clumps that will now be described in detail, though incomplete, is nevertheless of interest just because it represented a serious attempt not only to provide grouping procedures suited to its information retrieval application, but also to set up a theory of classification that was intended to cover those forms of classification that seem to be most intractable, though progress has been made in the area of ordered classification, for example by Jardine and Sibson (4).

The best way of presenting the main ideas of the theory of clumps itself is by considering it, initially, as a modification of simpler approaches to classification, as follows. We start with a connection or similarity matrix based on the given object-property (keyword — document) lists. There is no need here to go into the question of the definition of similarity, since the main emphasis was on what followed the computation of similarities, where it was assumed that well-chosen definitions of similarity would be used. The work on clumps was based largely on similarity matrices that were set up with the Tanimoto definition (5), where the similarity of two objects S_{ij} is defined in terms of the sum of their co-occurrences (shared properties), C_{ij}, and the sums of their occurrences (respective properties), O_i, O_j, so that $S_{ij} = C_{ij}/(O_i + O_j - C_{ij})$. For the present purpose it is sufficient to say that this definition has satisfactory theoretical properties, and to note a much more important fact about the use of a similarity matrix. This is that it must not be regarded only as a convenient simplification of the initial data. Its use is essential if we are interested, as we are, in polythetic classification, that is in finding groups of objects that do not depend on their all possessing the same property or set of properties, but only on each member sharing some properties with other members. The justification for this in the retrieval context is obvious: we clearly cannot expect that all the terms in a class should co-occur in one or more of the same documents (if only to allow for deficiencies in the initial keyword extraction). The use of similarity coefficients summarizes the information that we require about the fact that pairs of objects share properties while throwing away the unwanted information about which properties they share. For clearly, if we know that object i and object j are very similar, and that j and k are very similar, there must be some similarity between i and k representing some shared properties, and this is all we need.

Suppose, then, that we have a symmetric similarity matrix giving the connections between objects, which can conveniently be regarded for expository purposes as a binary matrix, indicating the presence or absence of connections. The identification of a class simulates the rearrangement of matrix rows and columns by bringing the objects concerned together; and we can first envisage a situation in which the result is a matrix in which the objects in a group are all connected with one another, without being connected to anything outside, which would be the case if the upper left quadrant in the matrix below represented the group, where each 1 or 0 stands for a quadrant filled with 1's or 0's:

1	0
0	1

But it will be evident from the earlier discussion that this is not the kind of classification we want, and it is also true that we have rather little chance of getting it in real life. So the first modification is to require, if not that all the objects in a class should have internal connections, at least that they should have no external ones, i.e., that if 0's are permitted among the 1's in the upper left quadrant, 1's are not permitted among the 0's in the upper right (and lower left) quadrant. But this suggestion is open to the opposite objection to the previous one: with the previous one, we would fail to obtain classes we would regard as acceptable, through the presence of an anomalous 0 in the upper left quadrant; whereas with this definition we would obtain classes which we would not regard as acceptable, since we would have a class if there were very few 1's in the upper left quadrant, as long as there were no 1's in the upper right quadrant. Both approaches fail to satisfy our views about what kinds of sets should be acceptable as classes.

We were thus led to consider the idea of defining a class in terms of its having stronger internal connections than external ones. The precise way in which this was done was by concentrating on the properties of the boundary between a clump and the rest of the universe of objects: we consider the extent to which a clump is separated from its surroundings, that is the relation between a clump and the remaining objects, rather than the internal character or content of the class itself, whether this is defined in terms of the presence of internal connections or absence of external ones. The notion on which this more sophisticated approach to the definition of a clump was based was that of a cohesion function, that is a function defining the strength of the connections across the boundary between a potential clump and its complement; the search for a clump then consists of an attempt to minimize the value of the function that is derived from an initial starting position like a random partition of the universe of objects. A successful minimization shows that the boundary associated with it represents a good demarcation line between a class and its complement.

Subsequent work was then concerned with the consequences of using different cohesion functions. If *Sab* is the sum of the similarities between all the members of a potential clump *a* and its complement *b*, and if *Saa* and *Sbb* are the sums of the similarities between the members of *a* and the members of *b* respectively, the first function to be tried was *Sab*/(*Saa* + *Sbb*). This arithmetic cohesion function was associated with the GR-clumps of the early literature. Unfortunately, the function is unsatisfactory from a practical point of view because the search for clumps necessitates a somewhat complex partitioning procedure. In general, clump-finding involves iterative scans of the universe of objects to see whether shifting objects from one side to the other of a given partition between a potential clump and its complement will lower the current value of the cohesion function; but with the function just given unseemly collapses of one side through the removal of all the objects to the other are liable to occur, and a complex procedure for resetting the partition to prevent this, by shifting those items in the strong side that are well-connected to the weak side to the weak side, is required, which is very tedious from a computational point of view. This first function was therefore replaced by the geometric cohesion function $Sab/(Saa \times Sbb)^{1/2}$, which can be combined with a wholly simple iterative scan in searching. But this function, like the previous one, suffers from the disadvantage that the relation between a clump and its complement is a symmetrical one: the complement of a clump must be a clump, and this is clearly undesirable; and more generally, these definitions suffer the defect that the fact that they involve balancing what may be called the internal coherence of a class against its external separateness, is not sufficiently indicated. The general objective of this whole approach is to maintain some sort of balance between these two, and it is desirable that this should be made explicit in the definition, if only so that the effect of changes in it can be easily studied. The third cohesion function that was investigated was therefore a nonsymmetrical one in which the emphasis was on the properties of a class in relation to the remainder of the universe, without anything being required of the latter, and one in which the distinction between the two components of the definition was more obvious. Thus if Na is the number of objects in a, the function is

$$\frac{Sab}{Saa} \times \frac{Na^2 - Na}{Saa}$$

A subsequent modification of this was designed to make it still easier to alter the relative weights of the internal connections between the members of a clump and their external connections.

This method of defining classes clearly involves subsidiary difficulties, for example those connected with the requirement that the set of classes obtained should exhaust the set of classes to be found in a given body of material, and those connected with the influence of the choice of starting positions on searches. No solution to the first problem could be found; and with respect to the second, single-element "seeds" were normally used to start a search, largely for practical reasons, though this has obvious limitations. For example, if we take a given element a as the starting point in a search for a class, we may fail to add b to it to enlarge the class because, though b is connected with a, it is more strongly connected with c, which is not a member; at the same time c may itself be strongly connected with a, but we cannot exploit this fact because c has not yet been put in the class; and when we come to consider c we do not put it in because it is connected with b, which is not a member, though c is connected with a. Clearly, we could get around this particular difficulty if we started with a and b; but the same problem arises on a larger scale even if we do start with pairs or n-tuples of well-connected elements, and the effort involved in doing this to avoid at least the striking defects of single starting elements is very large. At the time when the work on clumps was begun practical considerations were very important, and a considerable amount of effort went into the whole question of finding algorithms for identifying classes, and even more, on the computing characteristics of such algorithms. It is well known that a specific class definition need not lead to a search algorithm, and it may in practice be the case that even if such an algorithm does exist, it is not an economic proposition. From this point of view, the later cohesion functions were more satisfactory than the early ones, but clump-finding is still a time consuming process.

As far as experimental results go, it is difficult to say very much: the application of clumping techniques to data of quite different kinds, drawn from quite distinct areas of investigation, gave very varied results, some of them apparently quite satisfactory. In the retrieval application, Needham's earlier experiments were on too small a scale to be informative about the value of clumps found, as opposed to the feasibility of clump-finding; more recent experiments by the author, on the other hand, seem to show that clump classifications, unless they are derived from similarity matrices that are confined to strong connections only, do not work very well, compared with other types of classification; and restricting the similarity matrix this way is contrary to the spirit of the theory of clumps, which was specifically intended to pick up classes depending on the cumulative effects of many not very strong connections, as opposed to classes depending on strong connections only.

In conclusion, therefore, we can say that while the theory of clumps was not wholly satisfactory in itself, it has been of importance for other reasons. It was intended to be a theory of classification that explicated our intuitive idea of a class as a set of things that are somewhat loosely organized by family resemblances, where it was believed that this in particular is what is involved in the notion of conceptual classes of the kind that seemed to be appropriate to retrieval. More particularly, it was intended to be a theory of classification that was not naïve in the sense that it did not require perfect data, or depend on oversimple geometrical models of the kind that treats classes as footballs, for example. But unfortunately, this flight from the obvious went too far in the direction of the unobvious; clump classifications turn out to be too vaguely defined for it to be possible to prove anything really interesting about them. It appears to be the case that it is inordinately difficult, if not impossible, to set up a mathematics of clumps, so that all that can be done with a set of clumps is to look at them or use them as they stand.

The payoff from the theory of clumps has been in a rather different direction: it has stimulated research in automatic classification in a useful way, and has been followed by more intensive experiments on different modes of constructing retrieval thesauri from which it appears that some definite conclusions can be drawn about the value of keyword classifications, and about the classificatory principles on which they should be based.

REFERENCES

1. L. B. Doyle, "Semantic Road Maps for Literature Searchers," *J. ACM*, 8, 553–578 (1961).
2. V. E. Giuliano et al., *Automatic Message Retrieval,* Report No. EST-TDR-63-673, Arthur D. Little, Cambridge, Mass., 1963.
3. M. E. Lesk, "Word-Word Association in Document Retrieval Systems," *Amer. Doc.*, 20, 27–38 (1969).
4. N. Jardine and R. Sibson, "A Model for Taxonomy," *Math. Biosci.*, 2, 465–482 (1968).
5. T. T. Tanimoto, *An Elementary Mathematical Theory of Classification and Prediction,* IBM Corp., New York, 1958.

21

Dewey Decimal Classification

Martha L. Manheimer / University of Pennsylvania, Pittsburgh, Pennsylvania

Access to the scheme. There are two methods for finding a specific subject within the *DDC*, either through use of the summaries or through use of the index. There are three summaries: the first shows the class heading and number for the ten main classes; the second, for the 100 sub-classes; and the third, for the 1000 sub-subclasses. It is possible to go to the appropriate subclass by utilizing the summaries. A second method for access is through the index. In the index, there is an attempt to show the location of most subjects within the classes. For example, under "Soybeans" there are references to seven different classes in which books on soybeans might be classed depending upon the subject content of the book. There are also "see" references that direct the user from an unused term to the one used in the schedule and "see also" references that direct the user to related areas.

Standard Subdivisions. The Standard Subdivisions make it possible to specify more exactly either the form of the material being classed (i.e., -03 dictionaries; -05 serials) or to indicate something about the content of the book (i.e., -01 philosophy of the subject or -09 history of the subject). The range for the standard subdivisions may be specified within the schedules, as, for example, in the class "Philosophy and Related Disciplines" in which the standard subdivisions appear within the schedule as 101 through 109. These may be further extended by adding from Table 1.

    102   Miscellany of philosophy
    -0202 Outlines, from standard subdivisions, Table 1
    102.02 An outline of philosophy

Another way that the range of numbers to be used for the standard subdivisions is specified in the schedules appears in 361, "Social Problems and Social Welfare." In this class,

---

From Manheimer, Martha L. *Dewey Decimal Classification.* CATALOGING AND CLASSIFICATION: A WORKBOOK. 2nd Edition. New York, Marcel Dekker, Inc., c1980. pp. 104-105.

the standard subdivisions have been allocated the range .001 through .008. An outline in this class would therefore be

    361.00202   An outline—related to social problems

If there is no range assigned or implied, the standard subdivisions are used as they appear in Table 1, within the −01 through −09 range.

    549   Mineralogy
      −0202   Outline from Table 1
    549.0202   An outline of mineralogy

Other tables. The other tables may be used only when their use is directed either in the schedules or under a standard subdivision. When their use is directed, the user will always be provided with a base number to which the number from the table should be attached. For example, in 374.4, "Correspondence Schools and Instruction," the user is directed to add from Table 2, the area table, to the base number 374.4.

    374.4   Correspondence schools and instruction
      −73   United States from Table 2, the area table
    374.473   Correspondence schools in the United States

"Add to" directions. These directions are similar to those used for tables 2 through 7, except that instead of adding from a table, the user is given the base number and instructed to add from another part of the schedule. For example, in 359, "Sea (Naval) Forces and Warfare," the user is told to add the numbers following 355 in 355.1−355.2 to the base number 359:

    359   Sea (Naval) forces and warfare
  (355.1336)   Etiquette
    359.1336   Naval etiquette

In some cases, the "add to" directions provide for adding from the whole schedule or from a large part of the schedule. For example, under 016, "Bibliographies," it is possible by following the directions "add 100–900 to base number 016" to provide a class number for a bibliography on any subject:

    016   Bibliographies and catalogs of specific disciplines and subjects
      398   Folklore
    016.398   A bibliography of folklore

22

Techniques Used in Library of Congress Classification

Martha L. Manheimer / University of Pennsylvania, Pittsburgh, Pennsylvania

Book numbers. The LC call number usually consists of the class number followed by an alphabetizing code (the book number) for the author that permits all the works within any subclass to be arranged alphabetically within that class and enables the library to develop a unique call number for each book. The table issued by the Library of Congress for the development of book numbers follows below. It has been taken from *Cataloging Service Bulletin,* no. 3 (Winter, 1979)

Book Numbers

Book numbers consist of the initial letter of the main entry heading followed by an arabic number representing the second letter of the heading.

1. After the initial vowels
   for the second letter   b   d   l,m   n   p   r   s,t   u-y
   use number   2   3   4   5   6   7   8   9

2. After the initial letter S
   for the second letter   a   ch   e   h,i   m-p   t   u
   use number   2   3   4   5   6   7-8   9

3. After the initial letters QU
   for the third letter   a   e   i   o   r   y
   use number   3   4   5   6   7   9

   for names beginning Qa-Qt
   use 2-29

From Manheimer, Martha L. *Techniques Used in the Library of Congress Classification.* CATALOGING AND CLASSIFICATION: A WORKBOOK. 2nd Edition, New York, Marcel Dekker, Inc., c1980. pp. 79-82.

4 After other initial consonants
   for the second letter   a e i o r u y
   use number   3 4 5 6 7 8 9

5 When an additional number is preferred
   for the third letter   a-d e-h i-l m n-q r-t u-w x-z
   use number   2   3   4   5   6   7   8   9

For example, a book with an author named Johnson would be assigned the book number J6. The book numbers are decimal numbers and may be expanded in order to provide unique numbers for each author in the class. The following example illustrates how the books within the C author range might be assigned numbers within one subclass.

Catton	.C3	Cox	.C69
Cecil	.C4	Crain	.C7
Cheever	.C43	Crider	.C74
Cicco	.C5	Cronin	.C76
Clint	.C54	Cullen	.C8
Corson	.C6	Cyert	.C9

A-Z directions. This same technique, i.e., use of an alphabetic character followed by an arabic number, is used throughout the LC scheme to specify and subarrange in alphabetic order elements that would otherwise fall at random into a general class because the potential number of such elements and their names are unknown. When the names of some of the elements are known, they will often appear in the schedule with the appropriate book number, as in "General and Old World History," Class D.

```
       Second World War.
810    Other special topics, A-Z.
       .A6   Anarchism. Anarchists.
       .A65  Animals in the war.
       . . . . . . . . . . . . .
       .W7   Women's work
       .Y7   Young Men's Christian Association
             Young Women's Christian Association.
```

For example, a work on anarchists during the Second World War would be assigned the number

```
D810   for Second World War, Other special topics
.A6    for anarchists
```

Should another special topic appear, it could be provided for within this alphabetic array. Although it is not specified in the schedule above, a cutter (book) number for the author should be added to subarrange within the class and to provide a unique call number. The A-Z technique is used when book numbers have not been preassigned to topics. It is used frequently under a subject to subarrange by country, state or other political division. For example, in "Agriculture," Class S, the following appears.

```
S         Agriculture.
          Agricultural education.
             Agricultural extension work.
544          General and United States.
544.3        By state, A-W.
544.5        Other countries, A-Z.
```

Library of Congress Classification

A work on agricultural extension work in Canada would be assigned the number

>S544.5 for Agricultural extension work, Other countries
>C3 for Canada

Reserve cutter numbers. In some classes, a cutter number, or a range of cutter numbers, may be reserved for special purposes. Usually the objective is to indicate, and hold together, material in a particular format. For example, in the class "Plant Culture and Horticulture," Class SB, the following array appears:

>SB   Plant culture and horticulture.
>   Parks and public reservations.
>481   General works.
>   Including works on theory, regulation, . . .
>   .A1 Periodicals

A periodical entitled *Parks Monthly* would therefore be assigned the number

>SB481 for Parks and public reservations, general works
>.A1   indicating a periodical
>P3   for the title of the periodical

In another example from the same class, SB, the following array appears.

>SB   Plant culture and horticulture.
>   Landscape gardening.
>469   Periodicals and societies.
>469.4 Study and teaching.
>   .A2 A-Z, General works.
>   .A2-z, by country

All general works on the study of landscape gardening would be assigned the reserve cutter number .A2, and then assigned a book number for the name of the author, e.g., the book *A Beginning Text in Landscape Gardening* by Jones would be assigned the number

>SB469.4 Landscape gardening, Study and teaching
>.A2   a general work, not specifically for one country
>J6   for the author

In this instance the user has been directed to cutter for main entry by the A-Z following the .A2.

Reserve cutter number ranges. In some classes, a range of numbers has been reserved for a specific purpose. For example, in "Fish Culture and Fisheries," Class SH, the following array appears

>SH   Fish culture and fisheries
>   Documents
>11   United States
>   .A1-5, Federal
>   .A6-Z, State

This is a shelflisting device and there is no way to determine the sub-arrangement within .A1-5 without either recourse to the library's shelf-list or searching the *NUC* under appropriate headings in order to determine the arrangement at the Library of Congress.

Successive cutter (book) numbers. This is another technique for subarrangement and it is used to designate a subject subclass, indicate the form of the material, or signal further geographical subarrangement. In the class "Plant Culture and Horticulture," Class SB, the following table, utilizing successive cutter numbers appears.

SB	Plant culture and horticulture	
	Documents.	
	United States.	
19	Federal.	
21	State, A–Z	
	Under each:	
	State societies	
	(1)	Reports, proceedings, transactions (annual)
successive	(2)	Journals, Bulletins, etc. (weekly, monthly, quarterly)
cutter	(3)	Committee reports
numbers	(4)	Charters, constitutions, by-laws. By date. etc.

The *Bulletin* of the Horticultural Society of New York would be classed in SB21.N42. The N4 represents a New York horticultural society and the successive number "2" indicates a journal or bulletin.

Successive cutter numbers are also often used to provide for geographic subarrangement. In the class "Visual Arts," Class N, under Art schools, there is a provision for geographical subdivision.

N	Visual arts.	
	Art schools.	
	Special countries.	
331	Other American, A–Z.	
	Under each:	
successive	(1)	General works
cutter	(2)	By state, region, etc., A–Z
numbers	(3)	By city, town, etc., A–Z
	European	
332.A1A–Z	General works.	
.A2–Z	By country.	
	Divided like N331.	

A report from the Budapesti Pedagógusok would be assigned the number

N332	For European art schools
.H8	For Hungary
3	Signaling that further subdivision is by city
B8	For Budapest.

Double cutter numbers. This technique is used throughout the scheme and there are examples of its use above. It occurs most frequently when the first cutter number is used to indicate a subject, or is a reserve cutter number, and a second cutter number is added for the author. Usually no more than two cutter numbers are used in LC to develop the call number.

23

Classification, Theory of

A. Neelameghan / Indian Statistical Institute, Bangolore, India

Emergence of General Theory of Library Classification

SHELF ARRANGEMENT

The arrangement of books on shelves, as practiced in libraries for centuries, has been based on such characteristics as the size or the physical nature of the book. A location mark on the book facilitated its location and reshelving on the shelf. The catalog entry for each book carried this location mark.

ARRANGEMENT BY SUBJECT

Centuries of accumulated experience indicated that the dominant approach of readers was to the subjects embodied in books. By the latter half of the nineteenth century, librarians such as Melvil Dewey brought the arrangement of books by subject into library practice.

TRIAL AND ERROR METHOD

For a few decades thereafter, library work as a whole was largely a matter of trial and error and rule of thumb. Flair and experience helped the librarian whenever any difficulty arose.

From Neelameghan, A. *Classification, Theory of.* ENCYCLOPEDIA OF LIBRARY AND INFORMATION SCIENCE. Vol. 5. Edited by Allen Kent and Harold Lancour. Assistant Editor, William Z. Nasri. New York, Marcel Dekker, Inc., c1971. pp. 147-174.

BEGINNING OF THEORY OF LIBRARY CLASSIFICATION

In due course it was realized, though slowly at first, that library service should respond to and resonate with changes in pressure from the universe of subjects and reader requirements. It was also beginning to be realized that classification by subject should form the basis for efficient library service and, therefore, classification should also respond to this change. About this time, on the basis of a comparative study of the existing schemes for classification, Richardson, Sayers, and Bliss formulated some empirical principles. This may be taken as the first appearance of a theory of library classification. This theory was largely descriptive and empirical. It was not dynamic; that is, it had no inner drive for self-development.

FUNDAMENTAL LAWS OF LIBRARY SCIENCE

A unifying set of fundamental laws that could form the basis for the derivation of principles by deduction for library science as a whole was needed. The formulation of the five laws of library science by Ranganathan in 1928 and their publication in 1931 filled the need. This set the stage for developing a deeper and enduring general theory of library classification, with internal dynamism, as implications of the five laws.

DYNAMIC THEORY OF LIBRARY CLASSIFICATION

With the laws of library science as the basis, sets of postulates, canons, and principles for library classification could be formulated and explicitly stated. This facilitated examination of the rationale behind the various developments in the subject in the past, in the present, as well as the prediction of likely developments in the near future. The ideas which formed the basis of the theory and practice of library classification could be viewed in proper perspective in terms of the laws of library science on the one hand and the pressure from the universe of subjects and requirement of readers on the other.

HELPFULNESS OF GENERAL THEORY

A general theory of library classification can provide helpful guidelines for research and development in library classification at all levels, a standard to conform to and for evaluation of any existing practice or new development, and a system of control at each stage of work. Thus the development of the discipline of classification could conform to the scientific method. It would facilitate an orderly process of investigation, the exercise of analytical thinking, a critical approach to the study of the discipline, and open up the way for further development. In turn, it would reduce to a minimum the number of faulty steps in the investigation, and help to increase the consistency, stability, and reliability of the foundation of the theory and practice of library classification. Such a dynamic general theory of library classification was attempted by Ranganathan in his *Prolegomena to Library Classification* (1), first published in 1937. Since then, the general theory has been continuously developed and its versatility steadily increased.

TAKE-OFF FROM THE FIVE LAWS

The five Laws of library science are: (1) Books are for use; (2) Every reader his book; (3) Every book its reader; (4) Save the time of the reader and of the library staff; and (5) A library is a growing organism.

The term "use" in the statement of the laws denotes the use of the subjects expounded in a book. Therefore, library classification is, in essence, subject classification. If subjects are arranged alphabetically by their names, the books on a subject and on its subordinate and coordinate subjects will be scattered. This alphabetical scattering of subjects will increase the chance of the reader missing some of the subjects altogether. Further, much time will be lost even if a reader persists to get all that is relevant to his needs. Thus, Laws 2, 3, and 4 rule out an alphabetical arrangement of subjects. What should then be the arrangement? It should be the one that throws the subjects in the sequence of their mutual filiation. But there are several alternative ways of arranging subjects so as to respect this filiation. We are, therefore, obliged to choose one of the alternatives and use it consistently. Even after the choice of the sequence is made, it will be difficult to remember and be guided by the preferred sequence every time we have to arrange the subjects. To resolve this difficulty, we use a well-known method wherein each subject is represented by a unique ordinal number—called the class number. This fixes the position of the subject in the preferred sequence of filiation among the other subjects. The universe of subjects is ever throwing forth new subjects here, there, and everywhere. To meet the demands of Law 5, it is necessary to have guiding principles to accommodate the new subjects in the preferred filiatory sequence and to number them.

Planes of Work

THREE PLANES OF WORK

According to Ranganathan's general theory, library classification should be pursued in three distinctive planes: idea plane, verbal plane, and notational plane.

FUNCTION

The work in each of the planes has its own distinctive function. Delineating the structure of the universe of subjects, studying the interrelations among subjects, and fixing the preferred sequence of the subjects—past, present, and future—is the distinctive function of the idea plane. Naming each subject by a homonym-free, synonym-free term, single-worded or multiple-worded, is the distinctive function of the verbal plane. Implementing the findings of the idea plane is the distinctive function of the notational plane. Here, the work of the idea plane is paramount. This distinction of the functions was seized on by Ranganathan in 1950 and made the basis of his theory of library classification.

HELPFULNESS OF THE FUNCTIONAL DIVISION

This functional division of the work of classification into the three planes facilitates the work in each of the planes to proceed without being inhibited or hampered by the problems encountered in any of the other two planes. At the same time, there is proper coordination of the work done in all three planes. Thus, a holistic development of the theory and practice of classification is made convenient.

Classification Theory: Idea Plane

MAIN SUBJECT

It is generally found convenient to divide the universe of subjects, as a first step, into a few mutually exclusive and totally exhaustive set of main subjects. These are not too many in number. Therefore, most of the schemes succeed in arranging them on the basis of some principles, whether stated explicitly or not. The resulting sequence is more or less helpful in most cases. There is not much to choose between them. Therefore, we may take the main subjects and their sequence to be postulated by the scheme prescribing them. The presumption is that no main subject can be expressed in terms of the other main subjects in the schedule.

BASIC SUBJECT

It is generally found convenient to divide some of the main subjects, as a second step, into the following groups of mutually exclusive and totally exhaustive nonmain basic subjects. The illustrative examples are taken from *Colon Classification,* 7th edition, 1972 (2).

Kinds of Basic Subjects

A basic subject may be a main subject or a nonmain basic subject.

Nonmain Basic Subject

A nonmain basic subject may be one of the following five kinds:

1. *Canonical Basic Subject.* That is, a traditional division of a main subject, such as B1 Arithmetic, B2 Algebra, and B6 Geometry, in Mathematics; and R1 Logic, R2 Epistemology, R3 Metaphysics, and R5 Aesthetics, in R Philosophy.

2. *Specials Basic Subject.* That is, the subject of study restricted in some special manner, not amounting to any of the anteriorizing isolates or any other isolate ideas.

Examples:

L9C	Child Medicine
L9H	Female medicine
XX9B	Small industry

3. *Environmented Basic Subject.* That is, the entity in the study of a main subject being within extra-normal environment, such as those illustrated in the chapter on "DC Environmental Divisions" Ref. 2.

Examples:
    C9M42-2;62   Viscosity in low temperature ($=$ physics, low temperature, viscosity)
    L9UG6;3   High altitude physiology ($=$ medicine, high altitude, physiology)
    S9Y55   Psychology of a person amidst alien group environment ($=$ psychology, alien group)
    S9Y55;526   Fear in a person amidst alien group ($=$ psychology, alien group, fear)

4. *Systems Basic Subject.* That is, the subject of study expounded according to a particular school of thought other than what is currently popular, that is, currently favored system.

Examples:
    CN1   Quantum physics
    LB   Ayurvedic medicine
    SN1   Behavioristic psychology

5. *Compound Basic Subject.* That is, a basic subject formed by a combination of two or more of the above-mentioned four kinds of modes of derivation of a nonmain division of a basic subject from its main subject.

Examples:
    CN1-M42   Quantum physics of low temperature
    LB-9UA3-9C   Ayurvedic tropical child medicine
    XM2-9F   Private enterprise in socialistic economic system

"Basic subject" is the generic name used to denote either a main subject or any nonmain basic subject of the above five groups. The basic subjects having a single main subject are not large in number. Therefore, most schemes succeed in arranging them on the basis of some principles, whether explicitly stated or not. The resulting sequence is more or less helpful in most cases, and there is not much to choose between them. Therefore, we may take the basic subjects related to a single main subject and their sequence to be postulated by the scheme prescribing them.

TERMINOLOGY

In addition to the concept of main subject and of basic subject, the following terminology will be of help in further elucidation of the theory.
1. *Idea.* The product of thinking, reflecting, imagining, etc., obtained by intellect by integrating with the aid of logic, a selection from the apperception mass, and/or what is directly apprehended by intuition, and deposited in the memory.
2. *Subject.* An organized or systematized body of ideas whose extension and intension are likely to fall coherently within the field of interest and comfortably within the intellectual competence and the field of inevitable specialization of a normal person.

3. *Isolate Idea*. An idea or idea-complex fit to form a component of a subject, but not by itself fit to be deemed to be a subject. Example: "Bacteria" denotes an isolate idea. It is not, by itself, fit to be a subject. But it is fit to be a component of subjects, such as Biology of bacteria, and Diseases of human body caused by bacteria.

COMPOUND ISOLATE. An isolate idea in an isolate facet of a compound subject formed by combining two or more isolate ideas taken from one and the same schedule of isolates.

The following examples are taken from the schedule of organ isolates provided in colon classification to be used with the main subject "Medicine" to form compound subjects.

    163   Arm
    36   Artery
    36-163 Arteries of arms

The last example contains a compound isolate. The first two examples contain simple isolates.

SUBISOLATE. Each component of a compound isolate.

Special Component of Compound Isolate. An idea which is not by itself a subject or an isolate, but which can be used as a subcomponent to be attached to an isolate in order to form a compound isolate.

Examples:

    P,111-a Variants of English
    P,111-b English slang
    P,111-d English dialects

In these examples, a Variant, b Slang, and d Dialect are each a special component for a compound isolate, given in the schedules for P Linguistics.

    1-97 Pacific countries
    1-9B Eastern Hemisphere

In these examples, 97 Pacific and 9B East are each a special component for a compound isolate, given in the schedule of space isolates.

4. *Array and Chain*. The addition of a characteristic to a basic subject idea or an isolate idea leads to the addition of an array. The addition of an array implies the addition of a further subdivision of a basic subject or an isolate idea, as the case may be. Any isolate idea taken along with its succession of subisolates is also an isolate idea. The succession of the isolate ideas from the first to the last reached in this process is denoted by the term "chain of isolate ideas." A chain may similarly be formed in respect of basic subject idea. Example of a chain of isolate ideas: Asia, India, Mysore State, Bangalore District, and Bangalore form a chain of isolate ideas. Example of a chain of basic subject ideas: Mathematics, Algebra, and Determinants form a chain of basic subject ideas.

5. *Simple Subject.* Basic subject taken by itself. Examples: Geometry, Medicine, Metaphysics.

6. *Compound Subject.* A subject with a basic subject and one or more isolate ideas as components. Example: In the subject Absorption spectrum of electromagnetic radiation in radiation physics, "Electromagnetic radiation" and "Absorption spectrum" are each an isolate idea; "Radiation physics" is a basic subject.

7. *Facet.* Generic term to denote (1) the basic subject alone in a simple subject, and (2) either the basic subject component or the isolate component in a compound subject.

COMPOUND FACET. A facet having a compound basic subject or a compound isolate.

8. *Homogeneous Set of Compound Subjects.* The set of compound subjects going with a single basic subject.

9. *Modes of Formation of Subjects.* The following twelve modes of formation of subjects have been isolated thus far:

LAMINATION 1. In this mode, one or more isolate facets are laminated over a basic facet. This results in compound subjects.

LAMINATION 2. In this mode, two or more subfacets of a compound facet are laminated over one another.

LOOSE ASSEMBLAGE 1. In this mode, two or more subjects—simple or compound—are studied in their mutual relation. The relation may be a general one, or one of bias, or of comparison, or of difference, or of influence; or one subject may be used as the tool for studying the other subject. This is called "intersubject phase relation." This results in a complex subject.

LOOSE ASSEMBLAGE 2. In this mode, two or more isolates taken from one and the same schedule are brought into mutual relation. The relation may be of any of the kinds mentioned with reference to Loose Assemblage 1. This is called "intra-facet phase relation." This results in a complex isolate. A facet made of a complex isolate is called "complex facet of kind 1."

LOOSE ASSEMBLAGE 3. In this mode, two or more isolates taken from one and the same array of order higher than 1 in one and the same schedule are brought into mutual relation. The relation may be of any of the kinds mentioned with reference to Loose Assemblage 1. This is called "intra-array phase relation." This results in a complex array isolate. A facet made of complex array isolate is called "complex facet of kind 2."

FISSION. In this mode, an isolate or a basic subject—be it main or nonmain—is fissioned or split into subdivisions.

DISSECTION. This term is used to denote fission when we consider an array of divisions of an isolate or of a basic subject resulting from fission.

DENUDATION. This term is used to denote fission when we consider one and only one of the subdivisions of an isolate or of a basic subject resulting from fission.

FUSION. In this mode, two or more main subjects are fused together in such a way that each of them loses its individuality with respect to the schedules of isolates needed to form the compound subjects going with it. This results in "fused main subject." Fused main subjects have gained literary warrant within the last few decades. "GX Biochemistry" is an example.

DISTILLATION. In this mode, a pure discipline is evolved as a main subject, from its appearance-in-action in diverse compound subjects with different host basic subjects or occasionally even with host compound subjects. This results in a distilled main subject. Distilled main subjects have gained literary warrant within the last two decades. "8 Management" and "VT Pure discipline of archaeology" are examples.

PARTIAL COMPREHENSION. Several main subjects are sometimes treated integrally or disjunctively in one and the same book. A partial comprehension has meaning only with reference to the main subjects recognized and enumerated in the schedule.

Examples:

A	Natural Sciences
MZZ	Humanities
SZ	Social Sciences

SUBJECT BUNDLE. In this mode, a new kind of partial comprehension of subjects is formed. For convenience in organizing research, the preliminary results and the data, which are obtained in different basic subjects or compound subjects having different basic subjects involved in the study of some phenomenon or entity, are published in one and the same book disjunctively for further investigation and independent elaboration by the specialist in the respective subjects. Thus, accounts of different subjects are brought together out of exigency without any substantial integral account of them.

Examples:

AP	Ocean sciences
AS	Space sciences
AV	Defence sciences

Today, partial comprehension and subject bundle are the result of developments in book production rather than being intrinsic to subjects.

ARRANGING HOMOGENEOUS SET OF COMPOUND SUBJECTS

The number of subjects in the universe of a homogeneous set of compound subjects is far too large to be arranged helpfully and consistently without the aid of explicitly stated guiding principles, for such a universe is manifold multidimensional. Classifying it is equivalent to transforming its n-dimensional configuration into a one-dimensional or linear configuration. To change the figure of speech, it amounts to mapping an n-dimensional space on the one-dimensional space of a line. The difficult problem of "invariant" arises in such a transformation or mapping.

APUPA PATTERN

An arrangement of a homogeneous set of compound subjects in a sequence helpful to the majority of the readers and thus satisfying the laws of library science

Classification, Theory of

may be said to result in an APUPA pattern—that is, Alien-, Penumbral-, Umbral-, Penumbral-, Alien-subjects. For example, the sequence among the following subjects is deemed to be in an APUPA pattern: Physics, Electromagnetic radiation, Ultraviolet radiation, Spectroscopy of ultraviolet radiation, Electricity.

EVERYWHERE-APUPA-PATTERN

It is impossible to secure APUPA patterns everywhere in the entire range of the compound subjects. In other words, an everywhere-APUPA-pattern is not possible, for this requires keeping invariant every immediate-neighborhood-relation among all the subjects while mapping the n-dimensional universe of compound subjects in a line. A mathematical proof of this is possible, but it may be very involved. For our purpose, the following illustration will do.

Let the basic subject of a homogeneous set of compound subjects be represented by the center of a circle. Let the compound subjects be represented by points on the circumference of the circle. In this configuration, each of the points on the circumference has an immediate-neighborhood-relation with the center. Let us map the points in this two-dimensional space along a straight line, beginning at the center of the circle and stretching to the right. It is obvious that in this linear configuration only one of the points on the circumference can retain its immediate-neighborhood-relation with the center. The other points can have only immediate-neighborhood-relation of remove 2, remove 3, and so on, in succession.

CONSISTENCY OF PATTERN IN THE SEQUENCE OF COMPOUND SUBJECTS

Thus, in mapping the multidimensional universe of a homogeneous set of compound subjects on a line, the classificationist is obliged to keep invariant one and only one of the many immediate-neighborhood-relations found in an n-dimensional space. The question is what point should be given this privilege—that is, whose immediate-neighborhood-relation should be kept invariant, or, which point should be kept to be of remove 1. The choice may be left to conjecture by the classificationist. What point should be given the privilege of remove 2 may also be left to conjecture, and so on with remove 3, remove 4, etc. These conjectures may be based on the experience of the classificationist as to what is helpful to the majority of readers. This would mean too many conjectures to yield consistent results! The chance for consistency would become vanishingly small, for human experience and intellect have their limitations; and they vary from person to person and with the same person from context to context. It will rarely be possible for all to arrive by conjecture at one and the same pattern. It will be still more rarely possible for the same person to arrive at similar patterns in all the homogeneous sets of compound subjects. But consistency in the pattern of the sequence of the compound subjects in the context of all basic subjects would certainly be more helpful to all concerned—classificationist, classifier, and reader.

GENESIS OF GENERAL THEORY OF LIBRARY CLASSIFICATION

The need for a general theory of library classification to regulate work in the idea plane arises out of: (1) The difficulty of choosing a particular succession of immediate-neighborhood-relation of remove 1, remove 2, and so on; and (2) Securing the same pattern of arrangement in all the homogeneous sets of compound subjects among the very large number of subjects, irrespective of the basic subject. This is the problem in the phenomenal level. A general theory for this purpose was first developed by Ranganathan in 1950 and expounded a few months later at the Fifteenth Annual Conference of the Graduate Library School of the University of Chicago.

NEAR-SEMINAL LEVEL

Ranganathan's theory avoids working at the complicated phenomenal level of isolate ideas. It suggests a deep dive to a near-seminal level to reach something practicable.

FUNDAMENTAL CATEGORIES

Work in the near-seminal level disclosed the possibility of reducing to five types the large variety of the isolate facets presented by all the subjects in the universe of subjects taken as a whole. This gave rise to the postulate of fundamental categories. According to it: "There are five and only five fundamental categories"—personality, matter, energy, space, time (= PMEST). Manifestation of matter may be a material or a property or a method. Thus we speak of Matter (Material) isolate, Matter (Property) isolate, and Matter (Method) isolate. Each isolate facet is deemed to be a manifestation of one and only one of one or other of these five fundamental categories. Then followed the postulate of decreasing concreteness. According to it, the five fundamental categories fall in the sequence personality, matter, energy, space, time. Further, according to the postulate of basic facet, the basic facet of a compound subject should be put first.

ROUND

Further work in the classification of subjects of great intension led to the recognition of the cycle of recurrence of the manifestations of the fundamental categories in compound subjects. This led to the postulates of rounds for personality, matter, and energy.

Example. In the subject "Evaluation of the occupational method of preventing destitution among rural population," the isolate facets are Evaluation, Occupational method, Prevention, Destitution, and Rural people. The basic facet is "Sociology." The isolate facets "Evaluation" and "Prevention" are each deemed to be manifestation of energy. The isolate facet "Destitution" is deemed to be manifestation of matter. The isolate facets "Occupational method" and "Rural people" are each deemed to be manifestation of personality. A helpful arrangement of the basic subject and the isolate facets (see also the section on Principles for Facet Sequence below) would be:

> Sociology (BF). Rural people [P]. Destitution [M]. Prevention [E]. Occupational method [2M]. Evaluation [E].

The isolate facets "Rural people," "Destitution," and "Prevention" fall in Round 1. The isolate facets "Occupational Method" and "Evaluation" fall in Round 2. The resulting sequence of facets would be:

> Sociology (BF). Rural people [1P]. Destitution [1M]. Prevention [1E]. Occupational method [2M]. Evaluation [2E].

Here, [1P] denotes Round 1 of Personality facet, [2M] denotes Round 2 of Matter facet, [1E] denotes Round 1 of Energy facet, and so on. (BF) denotes basic facet.

LEVEL

It was also recognized that within one and the same round a manifestation of one and the same fundamental category may occur two or more times. This led to the postulates of level and of level cluster.
Example. In the subject "Mounting of wheel in a cycle," the isolate facets are "Mounting," "Wheel," and "Cycle." The basic facet is "Commodity production engineering." The isolate facet "Mounting" is deemed to be manifestation of Energy. The isolate facets "Cycle" and "Wheel" are each deemed to be manifestation of Personality. Both these isolates fall in Round 1. Viewed in relation to the isolate facet "Cycle," the isolate facet "Wheel" is considered to be a level.

CANONS

To secure a consistent and helpful pattern in the design of schemes for classification, canons for classification have been formulated by Richardson, Sayers, Bliss, and Ranganathan. Most schemes for classification generally conform to these canons in constructing the schedule. The canons of Ranganathan are more elaborate than those of the others. They provide guidelines for the choice of the different relevant characteristics and of their helpful succession for the formation of successive arrays in the schedules—each characteristic giving an array of its own.

PRINCIPLES FOR FACET SEQUENCE

A sequence of the isolate facets of a compound subject giving satisfaction to the intellect may be called the syntax of facets. The syntax of facets, based on the postulates and principles, is conjectured to give satisfaction to the majority of readers. Ranganathan has formulated five principles for securing such a syntax of facets. Of these, the Wall-Picture principle is the basic one, the others being derivable from it. This principle is stated as follows: "If two isolate facets A and B of a compound subject going with a basic subject are such that the concept behind B will not be operative unless the concept behind A is conceded, even as a mural is not possible unless the wall exists to draw upon, then the facet A should precede the facet B."

Example. In the subject, "Treatment of the diseases of the human ear," the concept behind "Disease" will not become operative unless the concept behind "Ear" is conceded. Therefore, these two isolate facets should be put in the sequence "Ear, disease." Similarly, the concept behind "Treatment" will not become operative unless the concept behind "Disease" is conceded. Therefore, these two isolate facets should be put in the sequence "Disease, treatment." Thus, the sequence of the basic facet and isolate facets in the subject will be "Medicine, ear, disease, treatment."

ABSOLUTE SYNTAX OF IDEAS

The sequence in which the isolate facets of a homogeneous set of compound subjects arrange themselves in the mind of the majority of readers may be called the absolute syntax of ideas. This may not coincide with the linguistic syntax—that is, the syntax of words—in all languages. It is conjectured that the syntax of facets is the same as the absolute syntax of ideas. It is further conjectured that the sequence of facets derived on the basis of the wall-picture principle generally parallels the absolute syntax of ideas.

PRINCIPLES FOR THE SEQUENCE OF ISOLATES IN AN ARRAY

The eligible isolates for use in the corresponding facets of the subjects of a homogeneous set are derived on the basis of a succession of characteristics. They form a schedule, and each of these characteristics corresponds to an array in the schedule. The isolates in each array have to be arranged in a helpful and consistent sequence. Different persons may think of different sequences; the sequence may even vary with one and the same person from time to time. Therefore, to remember the sequence once arrived at for the isolates in an array and to use it consistently may be difficult. Because of this, a comprehensive set of sixteen principles for arranging the isolates in an array in a sequence more or less helpful to the majority of readers has been formulated by Ranganathan. The principles are so arranged that if two of them give contradictory or unequivocal indication in the context of a given subject, the principle enumerated later is to be generally preferred. This guide line for the application of the principles is under further investigation.

REDUCTION OF WORK IN THE IDEA PLANE

Thus, the almost impossible task of enumerating and arranging a very large number of subjects—almost tending to infinity—in a helpful sequence in the universe of subjects is reduced by this theory to the enumeration and arrangement of a small number of (1) main subjects, (2) basic subjects going with some main subject or other, and (3) isolates in each array in the schedules of isolates. In these cases, arrangement in a helpful sequence can be determined by a few objective principles instead of by flair.

Classification, Theory of

OVER-ALL ADVANTAGE

There is also another over-all advantage of this theory. The design of a scheme for classification on the basis of the postulates, canons, and principles secures consistency in the pattern of the filiatory arrangement of the isolate facets in all compound subjects and also in the arrangement of all the subjects in the universe of subjects taken as a whole. While classifying a subject, it is not necessary to think of any of the other subjects. When the subjects are all classified according to the postulates, canons, and principles, all the subjects in the universe of subjects fall in a consistent helpful sequence. So long as this happens, we may accept the postulates, canons, and principles. Continued experience and research in the field may disclose cases not conforming to the current postulates, canons, and principles. Every care should be taken to eliminate any fault in declaring such cases as not in conformity with the postulates, canons, and principles; by carefully scrutinizing what is observed; and in making inferences from the postulates and principles. What survives these examinations are the true cases of nonconformity. A number of such true cases of nonconformity may accumulate. With these as the base, additional and/or new postulates and principles may be formulated. Thus, this cycle of collection of data from experience and the abstraction of postulates and principles will go on endlessly. This is in conformity with the spiral of scientific method. The dynamism of Ranganathan's general theory of library classification stems from this.

CONSEQUENCE OF THE UNIVERSE OF SUBJECTS TENDING TO INFINITY

As already stated in the section on Reduction of Work in the Idea Plane, the number of subjects in the universe of subjects tends to infinity. This implies the emergence of (1) new subjects; (2) new main subjects; (3) new basic subjects going with one or another of the main subjects; (4) new isolate ideas for inclusion in any of the schedules of isolate ideas; and (5) new schedule of isolate ideas to be added to the existing schedules of isolate ideas. All this implies the need (1) for extrapolating in any chain—be it a chain of basic subjects or of isolate ideas; (2) for interpolating in any chain—be it a chain of basic subjects or of isolate ideas; and (3) for interpolating or extrapolating of new schedules of isolate ideas among the already existing ones. Recognition of these implications is essential in any general theory of library classification.

TOWARD A FREELY-FACETED SCHEME

The recognition of the implications of the quality of the universe of subjects, mentioned in the preceding section, is a step toward the idea of a freely-faceted classification. This progress has been further helped by Ranganathan's classification theory which removes all residual rigidity by (1) recognizing that facets belong to compound subjects and not to the basic subjects as was implied by giving a facet formula of its own for each basic subject in the schedules; (2) clarifying the concepts about "whole entity" and "nonwhole entity"; and (3) developing the concept of "qualifier," now named "speciator." The latter may be explained as follows: In the subject "Production of gold nib," it is incorrect to take "nib" alone to be a manifestation of the fundamental category Personality and "gold" as of the fundamental category Matter (Material). On the other hand, "Gold nib" merely denotes a nib with certain specific characteristics—for example, gold nib as distinct from steel nib. "Gold" is a speciator of nib. Further, a commodity may have several speciators—for example, iridium-tipped gold nib. It will be necessary to mention both the speciators "iridium-tipped" and "gold" in the representation of the subject "Iridium-tipped gold nib." This representation is achieved by the formation of compound isolate by the combination of two or more isolates taken from the appropriate schedules. The theory found that the sequence of the component isolates could be generally determined on the basis of the principles for helpful sequence such as the wall-picture principle, or the principle of decreasing concreteness. This was a breakthrough in the general theory of library classification. It has led to a considerable amount of developmental and applied research in the design of schemes for the depth classification of compound subjects having different basic subjects.

ESSENTIALS OF A FREELY-FACETED CLASSIFICATION

A freely-faceted classification is a scheme for classification guided by explicitly stated postulates, canons, and principles for the three planes of work—idea plane, verbal plane, and notational plane—and involves the analysis of the subject into its facets in the idea plane, their transformation into kernel terms in the verbal plane using current standard terminology, their translation into kernel numbers in the notational plane according to a scheme for classification, and the synthesis of the kernel numbers into a class number. Such a scheme for classification can, with equal facility, coextensively classify a microsubject, such as that usually embodied in articles in periodicals, technical reports, and patents, as well as a macrosubject, such as that usually embodied in a whole book. This methodology, being based on postulates about the structure and development of the universe of subjects, theoretically admits of the addition of a large number of characteristics one after another in a large number of facets to be added one after another in the classification of the universe of subjects. Thus, it is fit to deal with the universe of subjects as a manifold multidimensional universe.

Classification Theory: Verbal Plane

NAME OF A SUBJECT

The number of basic subjects is comparatively small. A single-worded term is generally available for denoting many basic subjects, or many main subjects at least, but the number of compound subjects far exceeds the number of words available in a language. Therefore, multiworded terms are necessary to denote many of them. The constituents in a multiworded term denoting a compound subject normally correspond to its basic facet and isolate facets respectively. Such constituents are generally single-worded. Each of them may be called a fundamental constituent term. When there is a single word to denote a compound subject of two or more

Classification, Theory of

facets, it is called a derived composite term. It is sometimes helpful to denote a compound subject by a term made up of two or more fundamental constituent terms, even though a derived composite term is available to denote it.

Example: (1) The derived composite term "Pediatrics" may be denoted by the set of fundamental constituent terms "Medicine, child." (2) The derived composite term "The Bible" may be denoted by the set of fundamental constituent terms "Religion, Christianity, scripture." In the latter case, however, it is the usual practice to use the derived composite term "Bible."

NEED FOR STANDARD TERMINOLOGY

The problem in the verbal plane thus reduces itself to naming each of the isolates in the schedule of isolates contributing to the same kind of facet in all the compound subjects of a related set. Convenience of use requires standard terminology for naming each of the basic subjects, each of the isolate ideas—these two groups constituting the fundamental constituent term—and each of the compound subjects, when admissible. Scientists have learnt the helpfulness of using agreed standard terms in such cases. For different subjects, glossaries of standard terminology are being compiled by the standards bodies of different countries in conformity with the guiding principles laid down by the International Standards Organization through its Committee TC 37. The library profession will have to press its own requirements on the standards bodies in this matter.

CANON OF CONTEXT

Again, the limited number of words available in a language makes it necessary for one and the same word to be used to denote different isolate ideas going with different basic subjects. Thus, some standard isolate terms become homonymous. In the schedule of isolates, it is sufficient to use the homonymous term by itself, leaving the homonym to be resolved in the context of the basic subject with which it goes.

Example: In the schedule of isolates going with the basic subject "Education," it is sufficient to give the term "Child." It is not necessary to write "Child, education," or "Education, child." Similarly, in the schedule of isolates going with the basic subject "Psychology," it is sufficient to give the term "Child." It is not necessary to write "Child, psychology," or "Psychology, child." This is the canon of context. If this canon is followed by the classificationist and by the classifier, there will be economy in the schedule.

CANON OF ENUMERATION

A basic subject term need not be defined. Its denotation can be inferred by looking up the isolates in the schedules going with it. Similarly, the denotation of an isolate term can be inferred by looking up the isolates in the schedule given as subordinate to it. This amounts to definition by enumeration. In the theory of library classification, it is called the canon of enumeration. This is more economical than giving in the schedule itself a systematic definition for the basic subject term or the isolate term concerned.

CANON OF CURRENCY

The name of a subject or of an isolate idea may change from time to time. The term used to denote a compound subject as a whole, or a basic subject or an isolate idea in the schedule is to be the one in current use. This is the canon of currency.

SYNTAX OF MULTIWORDED TERM

When a compound subject is denoted by a multiworded term, the sequence in which the words are written requires attention. Ranganathan's general theory of library classification recommends the use of the nominative case, singular number for each of the constituent words; no help is taken from inflectional forms or apparatus words to indicate the syntax. Further, the theory recommends writing the constituent words in the same sequence as that of the facets themselves. The very sequence of the constituent words supplies the syntax, for this would conform to absolute syntax of ideas (see above).

Classification Theory: Notational Plane

NEED FOR A NOTATIONAL SYSTEM

Arrangement of subjects alphabetically by their respective names in a natural language will give, in general, a sequence totally different from the one preferred by the idea plane as filiatory and helpful. For example, the alphabetical sequence Agriculture, Algebra, Forestry, History, Mathematics, Political science is nonfiliatory and unhelpful. But the nonalphabetical sequence Mathematics, Algebra, Agriculture, Forestry, History, Political science is deemed to be more or less filiatory and helpful. To preserve the preferred nonalphabetical sequence of subjects, the representation of each subject by a distinct ordinal number is a necessity. Thus, the need arises for a notational system. The ordinal number representing a subject is denoted by the term "class number." The ordinal number representing an isolate idea is denoted by the term "isolate number." If a basic subject is not taken by itself as a subject, but is taken along with an isolate idea as a component of a compound subject, then the ordinal number representing the basic subject component is denoted by the term "basic subject number." So also we may speak of "main subject number."

ADVANTAGE OF CLASS NUMBER

Placing a book back in its appropriate place on the shelf can be done with the help of its class number mechanically and expeditiously—that is, without any thought or time being spent on its subject. The same is true of placing a new book in its appropriate place among old books. The same is also true in respect of the main entry for the book in the classified catalog.

CLASSIFICATORY LANGUAGE

The totality of the class numbers constructed according to a scheme for classification may be taken to constitute a classificatory language of ordinal numbers. It is an artificial language. Its creation and development is entirely in the hands of the classificationists; these form a very small group. Therefore, the listless drifting common in a natural language can be totally prevented, and should be, in this artificial language.

GRAMMAR OF CLASSIFICATORY LANGUAGE

According to Ranganathan's general theory of library classification, the principles governing the work of designing the classificatory language corresponds to the rules of grammar. This grammar would take the form of general rules or canons for the notational plane—that is, for the choice of digits (corresponding to the alphabet of a natural language), assembling the digits (corresponding to the morphology of sentences), and assigning meaning to each digit and to the combination of digits (corresponding to semasiology). The classifier should follow this grammar.

BASE OF NOTATION

By "base" of notation is meant the totality of distinct digits used in the scheme for classification. By "length of the base" is meant the number of distinct digits in the base. By "length of class number" or of an isolate number is meant the number of digits in it.

COMBINATION OF DIGITS

The number of subjects and of isolate ideas tends to infinity. But the length of the base available for use in a notational system is usually very short. Therefore, a class number or an isolate number will have to consist of a succession of digits written in the conventional way in arithmetic. If the base consists only of the ten Indo-Arabic numerals 0 to 9, and if we allow a succession of ten digits in a number, then the number of class numbers can be one billion. But the number of subjects and of isolate ideas is far in excess of this.

PHYSIOLOGY OF EYE AND PSYCHOLOGY OF MEMORY

A block of ten digits, as would occur in a class number of the kind mentioned in the preceding section, will be inconvenient to pick up in a single sweep of the eye; it is also difficult to carry it in memory even for a short while. The optimum number of digits comfortable to the physiology of eye and the psychology of memory is deemed to be three, and the maximum number is deemed to be six. Therefore, breaking a block of ten digits into subblocks of three digits or so each is helpful. This may be done, for example, by inserting a dot or leaving space, say, after each subblock.

INDICATOR DIGIT

Some additional purpose can also be served if the digits separating the sub-blocks are made meaningful. Here, the breaking of a subject into component facets in the idea plane gives a suggestion. For example, different separating digits can be used so as to indicate the nature of the facet immediately following it—that is, whether it is Personality, or Matter, or Energy, or Space, or Time. When a separating digit is used in this way, it is called an indicator digit. Incidentally, this method of representing in the class number the basic facet and each of the isolate facets fulfills the canon of expressiveness.

MIXED NOTATION

The longer the base, the shorter will be the average number of digits in a class number, or an isolate number. The digits used in a class number need not have cardinal values, since the class number is used only for arrangement and not for counting. Therefore, the digits used in the notational system need not consist only of numerals. It can also consist of the letters of an alphabet—say, Roman lower case or Roman capitals—or any one of the possible seven combinations of these three species. Obviously, taking a combination of all the three species will give the longest base and the smallest average length of class number. The ordinal values of the digits within a species may be according to the existing convention. The only additional prescription needed would then be to fix the relative ordinal values of the species themselves—say, whether the block of numerals should precede or succeed the block of Roman capitals. Using two or more species of digits in the base is said to satisfy the canon of mixed notation.

MNEMONIC USE OF DIGIT

One and the same digit will necessarily have to occur in two or more arrays in the schedule of isolates and of basic subjects. Naturally, this digit will have to represent different ideas in different schedules. Here is room for economy of thought. The ideas represented by a given digit in the different schedules may be made to be the same at the seminal level, or at least they may be made to be similar. The same can also be done with groups of digits within schedules. This is the canon of mnemonics.

EXTRAPOLATION IN ARRAY

The number of coordinate ideas based on a characteristic may be larger than the number of digits in the base of the notational system. In meeting such a situation, Ranganathan's theory uses sector notation. In sector notation, the last digit of a species of digits is made semantically empty but allowed to retain its ordinal value. Thus, 1, 2, . . . , 7, 8, 91, 92, . . . , 97, 98, 991, 992, . . . , 997, 998 form the first three sectors to represent twenty-four coordinate ideas, though the base consists only of the nine digits 1 to 9, both inclusive. The digits z, O, and Z are also used as sectorizing digits. In the notational plane, this is said to provide hospitality in array by extrapolation.

INTERPOLATION IN ARRAY

As the universe of subjects develops, a new main subject may emerge. The idea plane will ask for it to be interpolated between two main subjects already listed in the schedule. The class number of these two main subjects may each consist of single digits which are consecutive in the ordinal scale of the notational system. Therefore, no digit would be available to represent the new main subject. To meet the situation, Ranganathan's theory uses the concept of emptying digit. For example, let X be an emptying digit, and K a semantically rich digit. Then, in the class number KX, the digit K is emptied of its semantic value, though it is allowed to retain its ordinal value. Thus, the digit pair KX is taken to be coordinate with K and L. It has semantic value. Interpolation in any array in any of the schedules of the scheme can be done by using the emptying digit device. T, V, X and U, W, Y are used as emptying digits and empty-emptying digits, respectively. This conforms to the canon of hospitality in array by interpolation.

INTERPOLATION IN CHAIN

In decimal fraction notation, the addition of a digit to any isolate number would represent a subdivision of the original isolate idea. Thus a chain of a succession of digits can be formed to represent each of a succession of subordinate isolate ideas. This facilitates interpolation of new subordinate ideas in any chain. This conforms to the canon of hospitality in chain.

HOSPITALITY AMONG FACETS

The use of distinctive connecting digits for each of the fundamental categories, and sector notation makes it possible to receive new facets and rounds and levels of facets. This conforms to the canon of hospitality among facets. Conformity to this canon would make a scheme freely faceted. Nonconformity to this canon would make a scheme rigid even if it admits of facet analysis.

Future of the General Theory of Library Classification

IDEA PLANE

The general theory of library classification can never be completed with respect to the idea plane, for it will ever be growing. This is inevitable because the internal changes in the universe of subjects are continuous. In effect, the universe of subjects tends to become a continuum and infinite. New basic subjects emerge now and then by distillation from one isolate idea or another. For example, "Management" has now qualified to become a main subject although it was only an isolate idea till a few decades ago. A new main subject may emerge by the fusion of two or more main subjects. "Biophysics," "Bioengineering," and "Biochemistry" are examples of such fused main subjects. Subjects may be formed by modes other than the already listed modes of fission, denudation, lamination, loose-assemblage, and fusion. There is another direction in which the theory has to grow. A good deal more clarity has to be obtained in the identification of the fundamental category of which an isolate may be deemed a manifestation. There are still many dark regions here. Occasionally there may be need to modify existing postulates, canons, and principles. All these lead to a steady development in the general theory of library classification. We must also be prepared for moments of sudden mutation. Such a mutation may be precipitated by sudden eruptions in the universe of subjects quite unrelated to anything already known. It may also be forced by changes in man's mode of thinking, which cannot be anticipated now. This will, however, occur only very occasionally. When it does occur, we may have to burn our boat, as it were, and start again. Altogether a new general theory of library classification may have to be developed, but the slow small changes here, there, and everywhere in the existing theory will be a continuing feature.

VERBAL PLANE

Happenings in the verbal plane will have to be first met by the specialists in the different subject fields and linguists. After they have tidied up the new setup in the verbal plane and established a new or modified terminology, classification theory will have to absorb it in its own verbal plane.

NOTATIONAL PLANE

The versatility of the notational plane will have to be continuously improved and refined to enable it to keep pace with the demands of the idea plane. In the past the rigidity in the notational plane had not only failed to implement the findings in the idea plane, but at times it had also inhibited the proper functioning of the idea plane. Even today the versatility of the notational plane is still in a developing stage. Thus, even without any new happenings in the idea plane, growth in the theory of the notational plane is a necessity. But any mutation in the idea plane will produce violent repercussions in the notational plane also.

ILLUSTRATION

In *Prolegomena to Library Classification,* 2nd edition, 1957, a number of problems needing solution in the general theory of library classification in all the planes was listed. As each problem was solved, it brought to the surface other problems which had been hidden till then. Again, in the 3rd edition, 1967, the new problems awaiting pursuit have been listed. Their solution too may give rise to additional sets of problems. For example, a new problem arose as a result of solving the problem of extrapolation in array. It was the need for extrapolation at the beginning of an array. A solution to this problem was worked out in August 1969.

Putting Theory into Practice

CLASSIFYING IS TRANSLATING

According to the theory described above, classifying is equivalent to translating the name of the subject embodied in a book into its class number—that is, from

Classification, Theory of

a natural language to a classificatory language. We start with the title given on the title page of the book, the Raw Title. Seven successive steps are suggested by Ranganathan for carrying out the translation. These steps keep close to theory. To the beginner, translating will give insight into the art of classifying. After some experience classifying will be done by reflex action without the need to cover each step consciously.

EXPRESSIVE TITLE

In Step 1, the name of the subject is so expressed as to bring out each and every one of its facets. The ellipses are filled up. This may require a perusal of the book. Each of the derived composite terms, if any, is replaced by its fundamental constituent terms.

KERNEL TITLE

In Step 2, only the kernel terms denoting each of the kernel ideas are retained. The auxiliary and apparatus words and puffs are removed. Terms are separated from each other by a full stop.

ANALYZED TITLE

In Step 3, the basic subject term is labeled "(BF)." Each of the isolate terms is labeled by the abbreviation for the fundamental category of which it is deemed to be a manifestation, and the round and the level, such as "[1P1]" for Personality facet, Round 1, Level 1; "[1P2]" for Personality facet, Round 1, Level 2; "[1MM1]" for Matter (Method) facet, Round 1, Level 1; "[1MM2]" for Matter (Method) facet, Round 1, Level 2; "[1MMt1]" for Matter (Material) facet, Round 1, Level 1; "[1MP1]" for Matter (Property) facet, Round 1, Level 1; "[S1]" for Space facet, Level 1; "[S2]" for Space facet, Level 2, "[T1]" for Time facet, Level 1; and "[T2]" for Time facet, Level 2.

TRANSFORMED TITLE

In Step 4, the kernel terms along with their respective labels are rearranged according to the postulates for helpful sequence.

TITLE IN STANDARD TERMS

In Step 5, the kernel terms are replaced by their respective standard forms found in the schedules of the scheme for classification used, in case they are different.

TITLE IN KERNEL NUMBERS

In Step 6, the basic subject term and each of the isolate terms are replaced by their respective numbers found in the schedules of the scheme for classification used.

CLASS NUMBER

In Step 7, all the labels and full stops in the title in kernel numbers are removed, and the appropriate indicator digit or digit-group, if any, is prefixed to each of the isolate numbers.

EXAMPLE 1

Note. In this and the succeeding examples only titles that are more or less expressive of the subject of the book have been chosen. Imaginary and fanciful titles have been avoided.

0. *Raw Title:* High school education.

A perusal of the book shows that it gives a descriptive account of the state of high school education in Japan brought up to the 1950s. These ellipses are to be filled up. The derived composite term "High school education" should be replaced by the term "High school level of education" which makes explicit its fundamental constituent terms. Then we get:

1. *Expressive Title:* High school level of education in Japan brought up to the 1950s.

The auxiliary and apparatus words, and puffs are removed. The resulting kernel terms are separated from each other by a full stop. Then we get:

2. *Kernel Title:* High school level. Education. Japan. 1950s.

The basic subject term is labeled "(BF)." Each isolate term is labeled by the abbreviation for the fundamental category of which it is deemed to be a manifestation, and its round and its level. Then we get:

3. *Analyzed Title:* High school level [1P1]. Education (BF). Japan [S1]. 1950s [T1].

The kernel terms along with their respective labels are rearranged according to the Postulates for Helpful Sequence. Then we get:

4. *Transformed Title:* Education (BF). High school level [1P1]. Japan [S1]. 1950s [T1].

Each kernel term is replaced by its standard form found in the schedule of the scheme used for classification. Then we get:

5. *Title in Standard Terms:*
According to DC: Education (BF). Secondary education [1P1]. Japan and adjacent islands [S1]. 1950–1960 [T1].

Classification, Theory of

According to UDC: Education (BF). Secondary schools [1P1]. Japan [S1]. 195 [T1].
According to CC: Education (BF). Secondary [1P1]. Japan [S1]. 1950s [T1].

The basic subject term and each of the isolate terms are replaced by their respective numbers found in the schedules of the scheme for classification used. Then we get:

6. *Title in Kernel Numbers:*
According to DC: 37(BF). 3[1P1]. 52[S1]. 45[T1].
According to UDC: 37(BF). 35[1P1]. 520[S1]. 195[T1].
According to CC: T(BF). 2[1P1]. 42[S1]. N5[T1].

The label and full stop suffixed to each kernel term are removed. The appropriate indicator digit or group of such digits, if any, is prefixed to each of the kernel terms. Then we get:

7. *Class Number:*
In DC: 373.095 209 045

Note. This coextensive class number appears to be possible with DC. If the scheme does not allow it, then the Time isolate will not be respresented and the class number will be 373.095 2. In the succeeding examples the time isolate is represented in the DC number.
In UDC: 373.5(520)"195"
In CC: T,2.42'N5

EXAMPLE 2

0. *Raw Title:* Teaching techniques in high schools.

A perusal of this book shows that the only difference between its subject and that in Example 1 is the occurrence of the kernel idea "Teaching technique" in the former. Therefore, we get:

5. *Title in Standard Terms:*
According to DC: Education (BF). Secondary education [1P1]. Techniques [1MM1]. Japan and adjacent islands [S1]. 1950–1960 [T1].
According to UDC: Education (BF). Secondary schools [1P1]. Methods of instruction [1MM1]. Japan [S1]. 195 [T1].
According to CC: Education (BF). Secondary [1P1]. Teaching technique [1MM1]. Japan [S1]. 1950s [T1].

In DC only either "Secondary education" or "Techniques" can be represented in the class number. Then we get:

6. *Title in Kernel Numbers:*
According to DC: *Either* 37(BF). 3[1P1]. 52[S1]. 45[T1]. *or* 37(BF). 13028[1MM1]. 52[S1]. 45[T1].
According to UDC: 37(BF). 35[1P1]. 371.3[1MM1]. 520[S1]. 195[T1].
According to CC: T(BF). 2[1P1]. 3[1MM1]. 42[S1]. N5[T1].

7. *Class Number:*
In DC: *Either* 373.095 209 045 *or* 371.302 809 520 945
In UDC: 373.5:371.3(520)"195"
In CC: T,2;3.42'N5

Note. In the class numbers according to DC, either "High school" or "Teaching technique" cannot be represented.

EXAMPLE 3

0. *Raw Title:* Audio-visual teaching technique in high schools.

A perusal of this book shows that the only difference between its subject and that in Example 2 is the occurrence of the kernel idea "Audio-visual" in the former. Therefore, we get:

1. *Expressive Title:* Audio-visual teaching technique in high school level education in Japan in the 1950s.

2. *Kernel Title:* Audio-visual-teaching technique. High school level. Education. Japan. 1950s.
Note. (1) Since the isolate "Audio-visual teaching technique" has no single term to represent it, the two component terms are joined with a hyphen.
(2) The isolate "Audio-visual-teaching technique" is called a compound isolate. The indicator digit between sub-isolates of a compound isolate may be omitted in certain cases as prescribed by the scheme for classification used.
(3) This idea of compound isolate and other recent findings which are required largely in the design of schemes for depth classification, are not discussed in this short article. The results of recent investigations in this area are published in the quarterly *Library Science with a Slant to Documentation* and the volume of Papers and Proceedings of the Annual DRTC Seminars.

3. *Analyzed Title:* Audio-visual-teaching technique [1MM1]. High school level [1P1]. Education (BF). Japan [S1]. 1950s [T1].

4. *Transformed Title:* Education (BF). High school level [1P1]. Teaching technique-audio-visual [1MM1]. Japan [S1]. 1950s [T1].

Note. The change of sequence from "Audio-visual-teaching technique" to "Teaching technique-audio-visual" is determined by the wall-picture principle.

Classification, Theory of

5. *Title in Standard Terms:*
According to DC: Education (BF). Secondary education [1P1]. Technique-audio-visual materials for teaching [1MM1]. Japan and adjacent islands [S1]. 1950–1960 [T1].
According to UDC: Education (BF). Secondary schools [1P1]. Method of instruction-oral and visual method [1MM1]. Japan [S1]. 195 [T1].
According to CC: Education (BF). Secondary [1P1]. Teaching technique-audio-visual [1MM1]. Japan [S1]. 1950s [T1].

In DC only either "Secondary education" or "Audio-visual material for teaching" can be represented in the class number. Then we get:

6. *Title in Kernel Numbers:*
According to DC: *Either* 37(BF). 3[1P1]. 52[S1]. 45[T1]. *or* 37(BF). 133-[1MM1]. 52[S1]. 45[T1].
According to UDC: 37(BF). 35[1P1]. 371.33[1MM1] 520[S1]. 195[T1].
According to CC: T(BF). 2[1P1]. 31[1MM1]. 42[S1]. N5[T1].

Note. In colon classification the components of a compound isolate are connected by the indicator digit "-" (hyphen).

7. *Class Number:*
In DC: *Either* 373.095 209 045 *or* 371.330 952 090 45
In UDC: 373.5:371.33(520)"195"
In CC: T,2;31,42'N5

EXAMPLE 4

0. *Raw Title:* Technique of teaching carpentry in high schools.

A perusal of this book shows that the only difference between its subject and that in Example 3 is the occurrence of the kernel idea "Carpentry" and omission of the kernel idea "Audio-visual" in the former. Therefore, we get:

5. *Title in Standard Terms:*
According to UDC: Education (BF). Secondary schools [1P1]. Method of instruction-carpentry [1MM1]. Japan [S1]. 195 [T1].
According to CC: Education (BF). Secondary [1P1]. Teaching technique-carpentry [1MM1]. Japan [S1]. 1950s [T1].

Note. The sequence between the components "Teaching technique" and "Carpentry" in [1MM1] is determined by the wall-picture principle.
According to UDC: 37(BF). 35[1P1]. 371.3 694.2[1MM1]. 520[S1]. 195[T1].
According to CC: T(BF). 2[1P1]. 3(M2)[1MM1]. 42[S1]. N5[T1].

7. *Class Number:*
In UDC: 375.5:371.3:694.2(520)"195"
In CC: T,2;3(M2).42'N5

Note. The subject "Technique of teaching carpentry in high schools" is primarily of interest to one belonging to the profession of teaching. It has less interest, if at all, to one belonging to the craft of carpentry. Therefore, Law 2 of library science would prefer it to be taken along with the basic subject education. But DC takes it with the basic subject wood construction. Therefore, the class number for the subject according to DC will be 694.071 252 090 45.

EXAMPLE 5

0. *Raw Title:* Audio-visual technique in teaching carpentry in high schools.

Note. The 'Note' given at the end of Example 4 applies to this example also.

A perusal of the book shows that the only difference between its subject and that in Example 4 is the occurrence of the additional kernel idea "Audio-visual" in the former. Therefore, we get:

1. *Expressive Title:* Audio-visual teaching technique for carpentry in high school level education in Japan in the 1950s.

2. *Kernel Title:* Audio-visual-teaching technique-carpentry. High school. Education. Japan. 1950s.

Note. Since there is no single term for the compound isolate "Audio-visual teaching technique for carpentry," the component terms are joined by a hyphen.

3. *Analyzed Title:* Audio-visual-teaching technique-carpentry [1MM1]. High school [1P1]. Education (BF). Japan [S1]. 1950s [T1].

4. *Transformed Title:* Education (BF). High school level [1P1]. Teaching technique-carpentry-audio-visual [1MM1]. Japan [S1]. 1950s [T1].

Note. The change of sequence from "Audio-visual-teaching technique-carpentry" to "Teaching technique-carpentry-audio-visual" is determined by the wall-picture principle.

5. *Title in Standard Terms:*
According to UDC: Education (BF). Secondary schools [1P1]. Method of Instruction-carpentry-oral and visual method [1MM1]. Japan [S1]. 195[T1].
According to CC: Education (BF). Secondary [1P1]. Teaching technique-carpentry-audio-visual [1MM1]. Japan [S1]. 1950s [T1].

6. *Title in Kernel Numbers:*
According to UDC: 37(BF). 35[1P1]. 371.33 694.2[1MM1]. 520[S1]. 295[T1].
According to CC: T(BF). 2[1P1]. 3(M2)-31[1MM1]. 42[S1]. N5[T1].

7. *Class Number*
In UDC: 373.5:371.33:694.2(520)"195"
In CC: T,2;3(M2)-31.42'N5

Note. In DC the subject goes with the basic subject wood construction. Further, in its class number the isolate "Audio-visual" cannot be represented. Therefore, the class number for the subject, according to DC, will be 694.071 252 090 45.

Steps 1 to 4 involve essentially work in the idea plane. Step 5 involves work in the verbal plane. Steps 6 and 7 together form the translation steps. In Step 7, the synthesis of the basic facet number and the isolate number lies in the notational plane.

DIFFERENCE IN THE SCHEMES FOR CLASSIFICATION

It can be seen from the steps described above that the schemes for classification differ from each other essentially in the notational plane and occasionally in the standard terminology used in the verbal plane. This difference is reflected in Steps 5 to 7 of Examples 1 and 5.

OBSERVATION

The following differences may be seen in the design of the three schemes for classification:

1. DC is not designed to represent each and every subject and every facet of a compound subject in all cases—that is, it does not conform to the canon of expressiveness in all cases.
2. UDC and CC are each designed so as to conform to the canon of expressiveness in all cases.
3. DC and UDC use dummy digits such as a dot or a space in the class number to satisfy the comfort of the physiology of eye and the psychology of memory. CC totally avoids the use of such dummy digits and uses meaningful indicator digits to serve the same purpose.

REFERENCES

1. S. R. Ranganathan, *Prolegomena to Library Classification,* 3rd ed., Assist by M. A. Gopinath, Asia Publishing House, Bombay, 1967.
2. S. R. Ranganathan, *Colon Classification,* 7th ed., Asia Publishing House, Bombay, 1972.

24

Automatic Analysis

Mary Elizabeth Stevens* / National Bureau of Standards, Gaithersburg, Maryland

Next, then, we find the use of machine computational capabilities for the investigation of mathematical techniques for the classification or categorization of objects on the basis of sharings of common properties or attributes. Thus, referring back to the problems of automatic analysis as applied to character recognition operations, a class of upper-case E's can be identified by the machine on the basis of the property of having a relatively long, relatively vertical stroke plus the property of having three relatively parallel, short, horizontal strokes or blobs to the right. Hence, "E," "E," "E," "E," and other variants would all be grouped together as "the machine's idea of an E."

More commonly, a number of properties are determined for various objects for which groupings are sought and the presence or absence of each property for each object is recorded, for example, in a matrix such as in Table 3. Here, if we are aware of the properties of interest, it is clear that we can ask the machine to identify for us all the rows which have a positive mark in the columns having to do with the class of large, green, round objects—namely, cabbages and melons.

A more significant advantage of automatic analysis, however, is the capability of determining many classes whose common properties are not necessarily known in advance. In the above example, for instance, the machine could attempt to find classes of objects that have four properties in common (a class with no members), three properties in common (e.g., peas and cabbages, apples and oranges, basketballs and footballs, baseballs and golf balls, and lemons and limes. Then there are questions of what groups of seven or more members share at least one property (e.g., round objects) or of five or more members (such as medium-sized round fruit), and the like.

From Stevens, Mary Elizabeth. *Automatic Analysis*. ENCYCLOPEDIA OF LIBRARY AND INFORMATION SCIENCE. Vol. 2. Edited by Allen Kent and Harold Lancour. Assistant Editor, William Z. Nasri. New York, Marcel Dekker, Inc., c1969. pp. 167.
*Presently retired

TABLE 3

	Small	Medium	Large	Red	Orange	Yellow	Green	White	Brown	Round	Ovoid	Sports	Fruit	Vegetables
Apple		1		1						1			1	
Baseball		1						1		1		1		
Basketball			1						1	1		1		
Cabbage			1				1			1				1
Football			1						1		1	1		
Golf ball	1							1		1		1		
Lemon		1				1				1			1	
Lime		1					1			1			1	
Melon			1				1			1			1	
Navy bean	1							1			1			1
Orange		1			1					1			1	
Pea	1						1			1				1

ABSTRACTING

25

Abstracts and Abstracting

Charles L. Bernier / State University of New York at Buffalo, Buffalo, New York

Reasons for Abstracts

Abstracts are useful in at least nine ways:

1. Papers in science and technology are published in more than fifty languages. Most users of technical publications can read only a few languages, and abstracts in one language help them to select documents for translation. The user needs, at most, two languages; at best, he needs only one language.

2. The technical literature is too large for an individual to acquire or scan. There are estimated to be 35,000 or more technical periodicals. More than 200,000 papers are published per year, with some overlap, in each of the fields of chemistry, biology, and biomedicine. Abstracts facilitate the selection of papers to be read.

3. Informative abstracts substitute for the original literature in many cases.

4. The reading or scanning of abstracts for selection of data or for deciding to read the original articles saves time over that required for selection from original documents.

5. Abstracts are more convenient to arrange into related groups than is the original literature. Adjacent technical papers bound in journals may often be unrelated. The same abstract can be placed in several categories less expensively than can originals. Many articles and reports fall into several classes of useful classification systems. Classified abstracts in a published journal bring together guides into a large field of knowledge—one several to many times larger than the user can read.

From Bernier, Charles L. *Abstracts and Abstracting.* ENCYCLOPEDIA OF LIBRARY AND INFORMATION SCIENCE. Vol. 1. Edited by Allen Kent and Harold Lancour. Assistant Editor, William Z. Nasri. New York, Marcel Dekker, Inc., c1968. pp. 16-37.

6. Retrospective searches are greatly aided by classified, indexed abstracts. Search through reports or journals for any large field of knowledge is now impracticable.

7. By the use of abstracts, accuracy of selection of literature to be read or translated is increased over that of selection from titles or titles plus annotations. The additional information in the abstract increases the accuracy.

8. Abstracts facilitate indexing in two ways: (a) The abstract concentrates the indexable subjects so that indexing proceeds at two to four times the rate required for original documents. (b) Elimination of the language problem enables assignment of abstracts for indexing by subject only. This specialization improves both the quality and the rate of indexing, because the subject specialist is not also required to read another language.

9. The preparation of articles, bibliographies, reviews, and talks requires organization of the material used; so do acquisition and searching. Abstracts can be used to facilitate this organization. For this purpose they can be copied, cut, and pasted. Organized abstracts also facilitate the indexing of bibliographies and reviews.

Kinds of Abstracts

Abstracts can be classified in several different ways. Informative abstracts include salient data from the original. Indicative or descriptive abstracts indicate that such data and other information can be found in the original. For example (see Figure 1), an indicative abstract might have the sentence, "The octane number of benzene was determined and reported"; an informative abstract (see Figure 2) might read, in part, "The octane number of benzene is 100."

> Beneficial effects of reagents in solution on wet crushing of rock. S. K. Ghosh, C. C. Harris, and A. Jowett (Univ. Leeds, Engl.). Nature, 188, 1182 (1960).--
> Previous expts. of this nature were repeated. A rock was milled after treatment with electrolytes or water. The differences in crushing were determined, and surface area in relation to particle size was measured.

FIGURE 1. *Indicative abstract.*

> CA 55, 16309de (1961).
> Beneficial effects of reagents in solution on wet crushing of rock. S. K. Ghosh, C. C. Harris, and A. Jowett (Univ. Leeds, Engl.). Nature 188, 1182 (1960).--
> The expts. of Frangiskos and Smith (CA 52, 16808c) were repeated. Limestone was crushed in a drop-wt. mill after being treated with dil. NaOH and Na$_2$CO$_2$ at various concns. The samples treated with NaOH showed an increase in crushing over samples treated with 5.7–48.6% pure water. The samples treated with NaCo$_3$ showed an increase in crushing of 18.6–105%. Most of the new surface area produced is in the extremely fine sizes.

FIGURE 2. *Informative abstract from* Chemical Abstracts. (*Reproduced by permission of the Chemical Abstracts Service.*)

Abstracts and Abstracting

> The synthesis is described of purines and 8-azapurines substituted at the 9-position with ω-dialkylaminoalkyl groups. Some related ω-hydroxy- and ω-amino-alkyl-purines are included. Absorption spectra are recorded and discussed.

FIGURE 3. *Author abstract.*

Abstracts can also be classified by the kind of abstractor. Authors of documents are preparing more abstracts than in the past; more editors require abstracts with articles for publication. Author abstracts are prompt and are prepared by the person who knows most about the document. However, they do show undesirable variations in quality. It is difficult, if not impossible, to have all authors become experienced abstractors.

Sometimes authors write "pseudo abstracts" to meet deadlines for articles or for talks to be delivered.

Abstracts written by those actively working in subject fields have been called "subject-authority abstracts." Such abstracts have the advantage of being prepared by a person trained in abstracting and with comprehensive knowledge of a field. The inexperience of authors as abstractors is avoided. Owing to the fact that the abstractor prepares abstracts in addition to his regular work, promptness of abstracting may suffer. The quality of subject-authority abstracts, usually high, can be controlled by a central organization (see Figures 3 and 4).

Professional abstractors earn their living by abstracting. They accept assignments to abstract as they come along and may not have subject knowledge so extensive as that of the author or subject-authority abstractors. When they reject abstracting assignments, they lose income, and perhaps prestige. Their abstracts are usually prompt, easily controlled, and of variable quality. They may be the most expensive kind. Increased language coverage and promptness are the principal reasons for employing professional abstractors.

Large abstracting services customarily use the product of all three kinds of abstractors. Author abstracts are used for promptness. They are also used when the subject-authority abstractor agrees that they are adequate. Professional-abstractor abstracts are used to cover documents too numerous for the subject-authority abstractors available.

Abstractors

Subject-authority abstractors prepare abstracts for reasons that include the following:

1. Altruism; the thought of working for the common good powerfully inspires many of us. Abstractors believe that they can contribute to the welfare of mankind by assisting communication over the barriers of language and through the flood of documents. They realize that uncommunicated technical information represents waste and a slowing of progress toward a better world.

2. A realization of the importance of cooperation in providing guidance to the literature is another factor. The thought is, "If we all contribute what we are able,

Potential antipurines. III. Some 9-dialkylaminoalkyl purines and -8-azapurines. J. H. Lister and G. M. Timmis (Roy. Cancer Hosp., London). *J. Chem. Soc.* 1960, 327–31; cf. *C.A.* **53**, 10231g.—The synthesis was described of purines and 8-azapurines substituted at the 9-position with ω-dialkylaminoalkyl groups. Some related ω-hydroxy- and ω-aminoalkylpurines were included. Absorption spectra were recorded and discussed. 2,4-Dichloro-6-methyl-5-nitropyrimidine (Ia) (10 g.) in 150 ml. Et₂O treated overnight with 30 g. H₂N(CH₂)₃NEt₂ (I), and the Et₂O layer shaken with H₂O and evapd. gave 18 g. 2,4-bis(3-diethylaminopropylamino)-6-methyl-5-nitropyrimidine (II), yellow prisms, m. 37–9° (Et₂O). II (18 g.) hydrogenated over Raney Ni gave 14.5 g. 5-amino-2,4-bis(3-diethylaminopropylamino)-6-methylpyrimidine (III) as a low-melting wax; tripicrate m. 142° (alc.). III (14 g.) heated 0.5 hr. at 175–80° in 20 ml. HCONH₂ and 5 ml. HCl, the soln. treated with 10N NaOH, extd. with Et₂O, the ext. evapd., and the residue distd. gave 5 g. 9-(3-diethylaminopropyl)-2-(3-diethylaminopropylamino)-6-methylpurine, b₀.₄ 216–18°. The

following N:CH.N:CR.C(NO₂):CNH(CH₂)ₙX were similarly obtained (R, X, n, m.p., solvent, and % yield given): NH₂, NH₂, 2, 195–7°, H₂O, 88; NH₂, NMe₂, 3, 156–7°, H₂O, 63; NH₂, NEt₂, 3, 127–8°, alc., 98; NMe₂, NEt₂, 3, 174–6° (picrate), aq. alc., —; NH₂, OH, 2, 212–13°, H₂O, 92; NMe₂, OH, 2, 127°, alc., 88; NH₂, OH, 3, 175–6°, H₂O, 97. The

following N:CH.N:C(NR₂).C(NH₂):CNH(CH₂)ₙX were obtained (NR₂, X, n, m.p., solvent, and % yield given): NH₂, NH₂, 2. 270°, aq. ProH, —; NH₂, NMe₂, 3, 120–3°, EtOAc, 97; NH₂, NEt₂, 3, 123–5°, CCl₄, 76; NMe₂, NEt₂, 3, 85–8°, ligroine, —; NH₂, OH, 2, 127–8°, dioxane, 98; NMe₂, OH, 2, 119–20°, C₆H₆, 93; NH₂, OH, 3, 136–7°, dioxane, 99. The purines were recovered by adding concd. NaOH to the mixt.; other purines were obtained by similar addn. after evapn. and treatment with a little H₂O. The following (IV) were thus obtained, (R, X, n, m.p., solvent, and % yield given): NH₂, NH₂, 2, 219–21°, dioxane, —; NH₂, NMe₂, 3, 135–6°, C₆H₆, 57; NH₂, NEt₂, 3, 122–3°, EtOAc, 63; NMe₂, NEt₂, 3, — (b. 173–8°/0.8 mm.), —, 73; NH₂, OH, 2, 236–8°, HCONMe₂, 33; NMe₂, OH, 2, 135–6°, alc.-Et₂O, —; NMe₂, OAc, 2, 93–4°, C₆H₁₂, 58; NH₂, OH, 3, 194–8°, alc., 54; NH₂, Cl, 2, 203–5°, alc., —; NH₂, Cl, 3, 187–9°, MeOH, —. Ia (9.6 g.) in Et₂O treated dropwise with 12 g. I, after 1 hr. the soln. evapd., and an excess of alc. satd. with NH₃ added, the soln. refluxed 1 hr. (solvent gave a red oil when removed), and hydrogenated in alc. over Raney Ni gave 1.2 g. 2,5-diamino-4-(3-diethylaminopropylamino)-6-methylpyrimidine (V), b₇.₄ 123–5°, m. 123–5°. V — (1 g.) heated 0.5 hr. at 175° with 5 ml. HCONH₂ with 0.5 ml. HCl, cooled, and excess alc. picric acid added gave 2.15 g. picrate of 2-amino-9-(3-diethylaminopropyl)-6-methylpurine (VI), m. 208–10° (H₂O). VI was obtained by treating

[Structures: (IV) and (VII)]

the picrate with cold concd. NaOH and extg. with Et₂O, m. 53–4°. The appropriate triamine (1 g.) in 14 g. HC(OEt)₃ and 10 g. Ac₂O refluxed 1 hr., evapd., and the residue crystd. gave 6-dimethylamino-9-(2-acetoxyethyl)purine in 85% yield. This deriv. (0.25 g.) heated 25 min. at 40° in 4 ml. alc. and 5 ml. 2N NaOH, the whole evapd., the residue extd. with EtOAc, and the residual oil rubbed with Et₂O gave the 2-hydroxyethyl analog. 9-(2-Hydroxyethyl)adenine (0.85 g.) and 10 ml. SOCl₂ heated 0.5 hr., and the SOCl₂ removed gave 0.85 g. 9-(2-chloroethyl)adenine·HCl, yellow laths, m. 221–3°. The free base was obtained by treatment with Na₂CO₃. NaNO₂ (2.6 g.) in 15 ml. H₂O added to 5.5 g. 4,5-diamino-6-(3-dimethylaminopropylamino)pyrimidine in 50 ml. AcOH, the soln. brought to pH 7 by NH₄OH, and the ppt. collected, dried, and crystd. gave 3.9 g. 9-(3-dimethylaminopropyl)-8-azaadenine, m. 172–3° (Me₂CO). The following VII were similarly obtained (R, X, n, m.p., solvent, and % yield given): H, NEt₂, 3, 161–2°, Me₂CO, 99; Me, NEt₂, 3, —, — (b. 167–8°/0.1 mm.), —, 65; H, OH, 2, 253–4°, H₂O, 74; Me, OH, 2, 139–40°, C₆H₆, 54; H, OH, 3, 214–15°, H₂O, 69. The ultraviolet absorption max. of various of the above compds. were given at pH 2 or 7–12.

B. K. Wasson

FIGURE 4. *Subject-authority abstractor abstract. (Reproduced by permission of the Chemical Abstracts Service.)*

using the language ability we have and subjects we know best, then all of us will be able to keep up with what is going on better than if we do not cooperate in this way."

3. Many subject-authority abstractors list keeping up with the literature of their field in an especially effective way as one of the principal benefits of abstracting. The processes of reading, digesting, and condensing, in a uniform way, a part of the literature of their chosen fields are especially effective in making this literature of greater use to them. Requirements of the abstracting organization effectively help the abstractor to avoid technological obsolescence. Some abstractors make copies of their abstracts for their personal information systems.

4. Improvement in the ability to read, understand, condense, and evaluate are felt by abstractors to be important benefits of abstracting. The requirements of the abstracting organization promote this ability, and feedback to abstractors is often provided upon request.

5. Skill with foreign languages, often attained at considerable investment of time, is gradually lost if not put to use. Many abstractors report abstracting to be useful in helping them to keep up on their German, French, Russian, and the like.

6. Preparation of an excellent abstract gives a sense of worthwhile accomplishment—a piece of literary art has been produced; a valuable contribution has been made. This sense of accomplishment is strong among abstractors, especially those who have retired from active work. Abstracting enables them to continue making important contributions in their chosen field.

7. The prestige of working for a world-renowned abstracting organization and of having one's name carried in its publications is also motivating. Abstractors of good abstracting organizations are said to enjoy preference in employment and promotions.

8. Remuneration for abstracting is not a principal motivating factor, since many abstractors work for nothing. However, token recognition of service in this way helps to pay for reference works, supplies, and postage.

Motivations of author abstractors and professional abstractors are included in those listed above. The requirement of an abstract before the acceptance of an article or a talk is a motivating factor for author abstractors. For professional abstractors remuneration is the principal factor.

The recruitment of abstractors (usually subject-authority abstractors) is a necessary function of organizations publishing abstracts. Recruiters emphasize the above motivating factors. Professional societies are a common channel for recruitment. House organs can carry the appeals. Loyalty to a professional society or other organization is another motivating factor. The society or organization sponsoring an abstracting service is interested in its success and invests resources to promote or support the service.

Colleagues of an abstractor may take up abstracting. Campaigns for recruitment based on the concept of "each one reach one" have been successful. Sometimes the recruitment of colleagues follows unusual work loads or comes during planning for a vacation. Some abstractors, however, continue abstracting through vacations and trips.

Advertising in technical journals is used for recruitment. House organs of professional societies and especially of abstracting organizations may carry appeals for more abstractors. The motivating factors for abstracting are so effective that gift copies of the abstracting journal have not been used for recruitment.

Another method of recruitment that has not as yet been extensively used is the education of students and their guidance into abstracting. In the future this may become the method of choice. Learning to abstract and index is also important in establishing external memories (personal collections) that will become more necessary in our complex civilization.

Maintaining a staff of abstractors is of concern to abstracting–indexing organizations. One of the principal ways to hold subject-authority abstractors is through adequate communication with them. Among the most effective media are the house organs, e.g., *The Little CA* of *Chemical Abstracts* that effectively promotes the feeling of "belonging to the *CA* Family." Abstractors want to know about the organization for which they are working and about other abstractors. Meetings and dinners also bring a sense of belonging. Symposia on the organization and on documentation and information science are also useful. Prompt feedback of editorial changes in abstracts is interesting. Changes challenge abstractors to improve and show the way. Feedback shows interest in the abstractor and in the quality of his product. Another kind of communication useful in holding abstractors is justified praise. Encomiums for abstractors are appropriate. Another effective means of holding abstractors and their interest is insistence on standards of excellence. Also, many people, especially in science and engineering, enjoy working for the best organization. It is a challenge to stay on the team. Once an abstractor has been recruited and started into abstracting, he usually appreciates receiving additional work on a fairly regular schedule that he has helped to establish. Delayed assignments of additional work may make him apprehensive as to his ability as an abstractor and may cause him to wonder about the need for his services or about the competence of management in the abstracting organization. The schedule of assignments to a subject-authority abstractor can be made flexible enough to take care of vacations, special assignments of work from the place where the abstractor is employed and from the abstracting organization, and changes of interests. Remuneration, often as honoraria, is another way of holding abstractors. It does not seem to be a principal way, since some abstractors reject honoraria; also, many find that abstracting yields much less than the minimum wage.

Once a subject-authority of professional abstractor has been recruited, his training as an abstractor is the next step. Thousands of subject-authority abstractors have been trained through use of published instructions. The abstractor learns by reading, studying, and doing. *Directions for Abstractors of Chemical Abstracts* is an example of published instructions. Professional abstractors in organizations can be trained by coaching. The person assigned as coach goes over the work of the new abstractor, makes editorial changes, and discusses these changes with the new man. This feedback can be used with subject-authority abstractors functioning at a distance. First, abstracts are checked, edited, and copied; then they are returned to the abstractor with a covering letter to explain that the purpose of the feedback is not to find fault but to share improvements.

Rules for Abstracting

Organizations publishing abstracts have rules for abstracting to promote uniformity. Most of the rules are highly specific for the subject field abstracted. The

Abstracts and Abstracting

following rules are widespread and are used for both indicative and informative abstracts.

Material that is novel, emphasized by the author, or extensively reviewed needs to be represented in the abstract. Conversely, material that is old or well known to the reader of the abstract should be omitted. Bringing to the attention of the reader what he already knows, besides being irritating, wastes time. In general, subjects on which authors have invested effort should be saved in abstracts. Subjects copied by the author from earlier work can generally be omitted entirely from abstracts if the earlier work has already been abstracted. Reference to earlier abstracts of importance is useful.

The lengths of abstracts are extremely variable. For example, for an article entitled "Buchner or Büchner?," the body of the abstract might be the one word, "Büchner." If the original article is highly condensed, the abstract may approach it in length. If the article described were, for example, "Synthesis of Twenty New Chemical Compounds," it would seem unwise to condense the abstract by omission of reference to several of the compounds reported. Limitation of the length of an abstract to 150 words or to a certain part of a page may force the abstractor to generalize. For example, he may report classes of compounds studied rather than the names of the specific chemical compounds. Generalization makes work for the indexer, or for the index user if the indexer also generalizes: The indexer or user is made to seek specific items concealed by generalizations. Proper instructions for abstracting save space. The lengths of abstracts take care of themselves without rules specifying the number of words, pages, and so forth.

Of course, redundancy, repetition, and circumlocutions are avoided. This rule is more easily written than followed. The English language seems saturated with redundancy and circumlocutions. Examples of elimination of excess verbiage are omission of "The author reported that" and editing of "dust particles" to "dust" and of "owing to the fact that" to "owing to."

An example of the instructions provided to abstract editors as a guide to shortening abstracts is given in Table 1. Examples of edited abstracts are given in Figure 5.

Another important way in which abstracts are shortened is through the use of the abbreviations and symbols of certain fields. Abbreviations are defined in the introduction to the abstract publication or are limited to those in lists of abbreviations in dictionaries. In the field of chemistry, for example, the chemical elements can be symbolized to save space. Sometimes symbols become so commonly used, e.g., DNA and RNA, that it would seem strange to spell them out.

Abstracts should be clear and unambiguous. An excellent abstractor can often improve the clarity of the original document. The time of the user of the abstracts should not be wasted in solving unnecessary puzzles. The abstract should clearly help him to decide whether he wants to consult the original document; it can save him from finding it necessary to consult the original. If, after reading the abstract, the user is still uncertain as to whether he should consult the original, then the abstract has failed in one of its purposes. In answering the question, "Do I want the original?," the user should be able to say "yes" or "no," not "maybe."

Criticism is not normally a function of the abstractor, who is analogous to a reporter rather than to a commentator. One of the reasons for avoiding criticism —adverse or favorable—is that the authors of abstracted documents cannot be given space or time to reply. There is also cost and delay in linking criticism with

TABLE 1

Verbosese	Abstractese
It appears that	Apparently
On the basis of	From *or* by *or* because
As can be seen from formula I	Formula I shows
During the period of time that	While
The compounds exhibited activity	The compounds were active
The fact that the reaction did not succeed was due to	The reaction failed because of
Led to the production of	Gave
By means of	By *or* with
In order to	To
Owing to the fact that	Since *or* because
Proved to be	Was
The reaction of A and B, which is an exothermic process, is modified	The exothermic reaction of A and B is modified
The redn. having been completed	After redn.
With reference to	About
Serves the function of	Is
In a similar manner	Similarly
In a slow manner	Slowly
Takes place	Occurs
Used for fuel purposes	Used for fuel
In view of the fact that	Since
Was considered to be	Was
A yield of 80% of theoretical	A yield of 80%

Redundancy removal

Redundant	Unbelabored
0.5 N aq. NaOH soln.	0.5 N NaOH
At 30-mm pressure Hg	At 30 mm
Dark blue in color	Dark blue
Dust particles	Dust
Fewer in number	Fewer
Heterogeneous in character	Heterogeneous
An innumerable number of particles	Innumerable particles
The material was cooled at 0° in an ice bath for 1 hr	The material was put in an ice bath for 1 hr
For a period of 3 hr	For 3 hr
Previous history	History
At a temp. of 20°	At 20°
Throughout the entire expt.	During the expt.
Two equal halves	Halves

Deletion list

Investigation showed that
It was concluded (found, observed, shown, stated) that
It may be said that
The authors state that
The statement may be made that

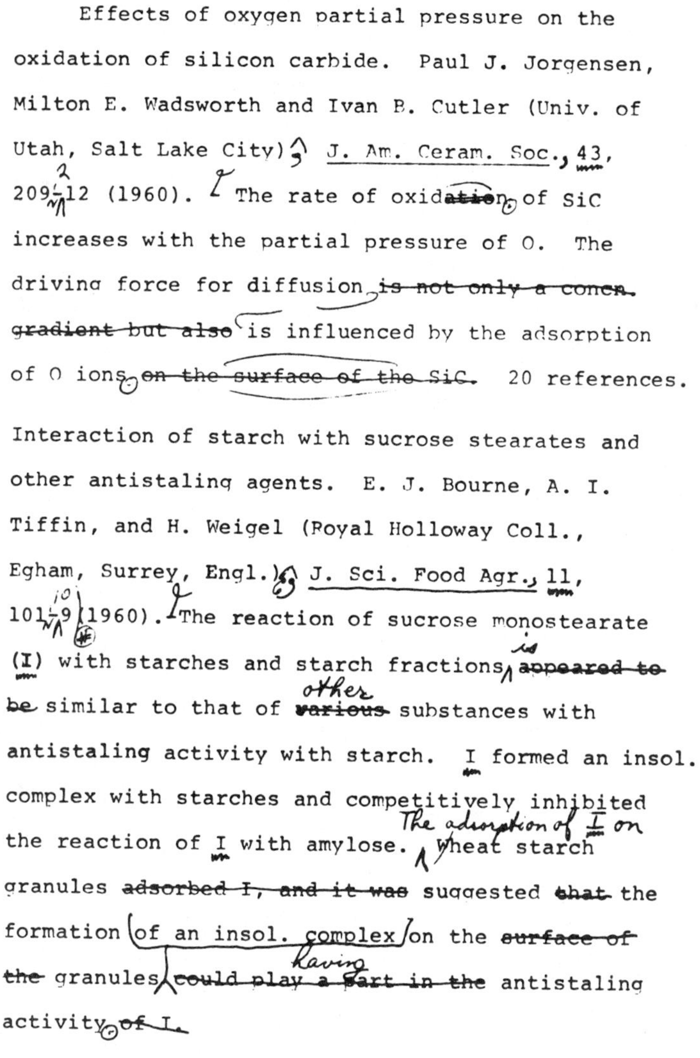

Abstracts and Abstracting

Effects of oxygen partial pressure on the oxidation of silicon carbide. Paul J. Jorgensen, Milton E. Wadsworth and Ivan B. Cutler (Univ. of Utah, Salt Lake City). J. Am. Ceram. Soc., 43, 209-12 (1960). The rate of oxidation of SiC increases with the partial pressure of O. The driving force for diffusion is influenced by the adsorption of O ions. 20 references.

Interaction of starch with sucrose stearates and other antistaling agents. E. J. Bourne, A. I. Tiffin, and H. Weigel (Royal Holloway Coll., Egham, Surrey, Engl.). J. Sci. Food Agr., 11, 101-9 (1960). The reaction of sucrose monostearate (I) with starches and starch fractions is similar to that of other substances with antistaling activity with starch. I formed an insol. complex with starches and competitively inhibited the reaction of I with amylose. The adsorption of I on wheat starch granules suggested the formation of an insol. complex on the granules having antistaling activity.

FIGURE 5. *Examples of edited abstracts.*

reply. Sometimes abstractors are unaware of their limitations as critics; new ideas, especially the radically new ones, have an aura of absurdity about them that may attract unmerited criticism. One of the safest forms of criticism, should any be permitted, is the use of quotation marks to indicate sentences or paragraphs for which the abstractor does not wish to take responsibility. Omission is another form of criticism.

A fairly common rule for abstracting is that abstracts be signed. This practice gives control during processing and publication, gives credit to the abstractor for his efforts, places responsibility for the abstract, and may give the user some idea of the quality of the abstract.

Published instructions for abstracting carry rules for format, organization desired, abbreviations permitted, content wanted, nomenclature allowed, and the like. Organizations producing abstracts may have instructions for their abstractors. Instructions greatly improve the quality of abstracts by standardizing the parts that can be made uniform. Users of abstracts may be disconcerted by unexplained and irregular variations in abstracts. They may waste time seeking reasons for such irregularities.

The application of instructions for abstracting can be made uniform by the return of the edited abstract to the abstractor. This has been mentioned. To avoid delay in use of the abstracts, copies of edited abstracts are sent to the abstractor. Relatively few abstractors in the field of science indulge in polemics with editors about changes. Many abstractors regularly request that all their abstracts be returned to them after publication. It may or may not be the policy of the abstracting organization to do this. However, feedback, at least to beginning abstractors, is necessary if the quality of the publication is to be maintained. Feedback to experienced abstractors, often with a suitable covering letter, is useful in correcting deviations from practice or for introducing new rules.

Assignment of Documents to Abstractors

It is necessary for an abstracting organization that covers a field of knowledge to make definite assignments to abstractors to avoid gaps and overlaps and to secure the best abstracting available.

Such assignment can be based on individual documents, e.g., technical articles or reports. A paper in a journal is assigned to the abstractor who is best suited to abstract it by reason of his technical and language backgrounds. Since the number of different languages multiplied by the number of specific subject fields gives a large product, it is usually necessary to approximate the subject field of the abstractor. It is usually necessary to meet the language of the abstractor exactly, for abstractors are usually reluctant to learn strange languages.

Assignment can be by journal. This is especially useful if the subject area of the journal is narrow. The abstractor can also be given the responsibility for the selection of articles from the journal according to explicit criteria. For example, one criterion might be that the article carry original research. Whole-journal assignment saves the time of the assigner; the cost of mailing (if the abstractor subscribes), the cost of subscription, and delays of assignment of individual documents.

Documents can be assigned by categories, e.g., those belonging to a series or from papers given at a symposium. There may be advantage in having one abstractor take care of all documents of a category.

In rare instances collaborative abstracting is desirable. The scope of a document may be broad. It may include two or more subject fields that are quite unrelated and that one abstractor has difficulty in handling.

In general, assignment is best when specialized. Specialization by language is nearly always necessary. An abstractor rarely rises to the challenge of a new language and abstracts from it just for the fun of doing so, e.g., the abstractor who learned Turkish so that he might help. Specialization by subject is also desirable.

Abstractors who do not know a subject field tend to make more errors than those who do know the field. The major errors are inadvertent omissions and unnecessary inclusions. Too frequently absurd errors creep past the abstractor who does not know the field. Assignment can be by class of document—as another form of specialization. For example, some abstractors may wish to handle patents, others papers, and still others both. The abstracting of patents differs considerably from the abstracting of papers. Specialization can also be geographical. For example, articles written in Japan can, perhaps, best be handled by Japanese abstractors organized as a group in Japan. They can have their own assignment organization and can function, to a large extent, autonomously. During wartime when sources of documents become blocked, it may become necessary to organize teams of abstractors in neutral countries.

Control of Assignments, Documents, and Abstracts

Techniques for control of documents coming into an abstracting organization have been well developed. There is automation of acquisition and circulation.

Assignments made to abstractors must be controlled, as mentioned, to avoid duplicate assignment and missed documents. One technique for control is the assignment card prepared on interleaf forms. Duplicates of the card sent to the abstractor serve as records in the assignment file, as author-index cards, and for other purposes. The record in the assignment file helps to prevent the overloading of abstractors, as well as to keep track of the assignment. Assignment files are arranged by name of abstractor, languages, and subjects covered. Mechanized assignment has been investigated by the Chemical Abstracts Service. In the system studied, language, subject, abstractor load, and abstractor availability were to be matched. Display of potential abstractors as names on a cathode-ray tube (CRT) screen was desired. Assignment then updated the computer record so that the CRT display would be affected if an abstractor became overloaded.

Editing of Abstracts

Nearly all abstracts, as they come in from abstractors, are unsuitable for publication. Deviations from rules occur. There are some omissions. A few serious errors in the references and in data occur. Many abbreviations are missed. Some abstracts have poor grammar and diction. The abstract may not be categorized or may be categorized incorrectly [see Figure 6(a) and (b)]. Cross references to other categories are frequently omitted. References to related abstracts may be needed. Punctuation can often be improved.

It has been found desirable to check the reference with the original document for correctness. Transposition of digits in a number is usually invisible to editors. Author names and sometimes names of journals are sources of trouble. Parts of the title may be omitted. The issue or series number of a journal may be needed.

The editor is responsible for everything not assigned to the preeditorial checker. Standardization of terminology and nomenclature to conform with rules given to

Synthesis of dimethyl ether of protoporphyrin--III.

T. R. Ovsepyan, R. P. Evstigneeva and N. A. Preobrazhenskii (Inst. Fine Chem. Technol., Moscow). Zh. Obshch. Khim. 36(5), 806-8 (1966) (Russ).

To 1.5 g. 2,4-dimethyl3-(2-diethylaminoethyl)-5-carbobenzoxypyrrole in AcOH was added to 50-60° 0.45 ml. SO_2Cl_2 in AcOH and after 0.5 hr. finally at reflux, gave after heating with added H_2O 3 hrs., and treatment with aq. NaOH, 62.4% 2,2'-[4,4'-dimethyl-3,3'-bis-(2-diethyl-aminoethyl)-5,5'-di-carbobenzoxy] dipyrrylemethane, m. 97-8° (aq.Me_2CO). This and 2,2'-[4,4'-dimethyl-3,3'-bis-(2-carbomethoxyethyl)-5,5'-di-formyl] dipyrrylmethane in AcOH in the presence of 57% HI in 0.5 hr. at 20°, gave after addn. of 3.5 g. NaOAc in AcOH and keeping the mixt. 1 day, 45.6% 1,4,5,8-tetramethyl-2,3-bis-(2-diethylamineothyl)-6,7-bis-(2-carbomethoxyethyl) porphyrin, m. 249-50° (MeOH-$CHCl_3$); dimethiodide, m. 269-70°, heated 3 hrs. and kept 10 hrs. at room temp. with MeOH and solid KOH, gave 81% di-Me ether of protoporphyrin-III, m. 270-2°. Absorption spectra reported.

(a)

Synthesis of dimethyl ether of protoporphyrin-III.

T. R. Ovsepyan, R. P. Evstigneeva, and N. A. Preobrazhenskii (Inst. Fine Chem. Technol., Moscow), Zh. Obshch. Khim., 36(5), 806-8 (1966) (Russ).

To 1.5 g. 2,4-dimethyl3-(2-diethylaminoethyl)-5-carbobenzoxypyrrole in AcOH was added at 50-60° 0.45 ml. SO_2Cl_2 in AcOH for 0.5 hr. at reflux, this gave, after heating with added H_2O 3 hrs. and treatment with aq. NaOH, 62.4% 2,2'-[4,4'-dimethyl-3,3'-bis-(2-diethyl-aminoethyl)-5,5'-di-carbobenzoxy] dipyrrylemethane, m.p. 97-8° (aq.Me_2CO). This and 2,2'-[4,4'-dimethyl-3,3'-bis-(2-carbomethoxyethyl)-5,5'-di-formyl] dipyrrylmethane in AcOH, in presence of 57% HI in 0.5 hr. at 20°, gave, after addn. of 3.5 g. NaOAc in AcOH, and keeping the mixt. 1 day, 45.6% 1,4,5,8-tetramethyl-2,3-bis-(2-diethylamineothyl)-6,7-bis-(2-carbomethoxyethyl) porphyrin, m.p. 249-50° (MeOH-$CHCl_3$); the dimethiodide, m.p. 269-70°, heated 3 hrs. and kept 10 hrs. at room temp. with MeOH and solid KOH, gave 81% di-Me ether of protoporphyrin-III, m.p. 270-2°. Absorption spectra reported.

(b)

FIGURE 6. (a) *Example of an abstract before editing;* (b) *example of an abstract after editing.*

Abstracts and Abstracting

abstractors may be required. Words or terms are abbreviated. Grammar defects, such as singular verbs with plural subjects, are eliminated. Diction is frequently improved. Consultation of the original document is sometimes necessary to resolve ambiguities and add missing information. Editors seemingly develop a sixth sense for the consultation of originals. The production of an abstract journal often seems to be a continuing fight against error. Much of the cost of production comes from preventing or eliminating errors that nobody could make—but did. There are errors in references, subjects selected or omitted, spelling, punctuation, format, symbols directing the printer, and so forth. Typewritten abstracts may be requested; the poorly legible longhand ones may be typed to avoid errors in editing and keyboarding. It is the primary responsibility of the editor to eliminate these errors and prepare the copy for the printer.

If abstracts for the printer are not retyped, so-called "penalty copy" may be involved. However, penalty copy may be less expensive than retyping and rechecking for error.

As mentioned, the editor sees to it that references are made to earlier abstracts and documents, to abstracts in the same issue, and to other categories of abstracts of interest to the one at hand. Cross references are made specifically from other categories to the abstract.

Abstracts can be categorized to aid in current awareness and browsing. The editor places or corrects the placing of abstracts into categories and can indicate subcategorization. Alternatively subcategorization can be delegated to another individual experienced in the subject field. This person also prepares the abstracts for shipment to the printer.

The printer may not be in the same location as the abstracting organization. The abstracting organization can be protected against loss by automatic microfilm cameras. Should a shipment be lost, the edited manuscript can be recreated from the microfilm. Abstracts in manuscript form, returned by the printer for checking and proofreading, are often stored for a few years to answer questions and to correct errors that may have been missed.

Shipment of abstracts to the printer may be periodical. A schedule of shipment, keyboarding, composing, proofchecking, proofreading, and printing times is established. Maintenance of schedules requires collaboration with the printer. Contingencies to be met include mail delays, strikes, and innovations by the publisher as well as the printer.

The printer normally supplies galley proof. This proof is first checked for those items that the proofreader cannot discover. Transposed digits are examples. Checking is carried out by comparison of the galley proof against the manuscript. Reference to the original document may be required. Proofreading comes next. The proofreader is responsible for everything else. Extensive editing on proof is costly and time consuming. It can be avoided by withdrawing the abstract and holding it for reprinting. The proofreader can refer to the original document. Often he may be the editor during another phase of the publication schedule. Such metamorphosis promotes good proofreading and editing. Feedback shows things to avoid in the future. Proofreader's marks are standardized. Special symbols may be developed to meet the needs of certain subject fields. Since proof changes are charged to the publisher, all changes are made with an eye on economies. Rules for proofreading can be developed and disseminated. Proofreaders are trained by coaching, as are editors. The coach goes over the work and shows the changes he has made to the new reader and discusses the changes.

Page proof is checked to determine if the changes on the galleys have been made correctly in type. Very few changes are made on page proof. This type of checking can be delegated to the printer to speed publication of the abstract journal.

The storage of abstracts on computer tape, aperture cards, microforms, or unpunched cards will include some of the processes described above which are mainly concerned with the publication of informative abstracts prepared by subject-authority abstractors.

Indexing

Classification and subclassification of abstracts into categories, while effective for current awareness, does not meet the needs of retrospective searching. As the issues of an abstract publication accumulate and as abstract cards accumulate in a tub file or drawers, searches become too long. Indexes take care of this problem. Author indexes published annually or in each issue of an abstract journal are especially effective in answering questions of recall in which reference to a remembered document or abstract is required. Also, since authors specialize, author indexes can be made to function roughly as subject indexes. Successful author indexes for issues of abstract journals can be prepared by the printer to speed publication. Keyword indexing of varying degrees of quality can also be prepared for such issues. Preparation of subject indexes of high quality is now too slow for publication in issues of abstract journals, although techniques for doing this are being developed (see Figures 7, 8, and 9). The general pattern for abstract publications is the

> **The reaction of halogen derivatives of acenaphthene with potassium amide in liquid ammonia.** A. I. Tochilkin and N. N. Vorozhtsov, Jr. *Probl. Organ. Sinteza, Akad. Nauk SSSR, Otd. Obshch. i Tekhn. Khim.* **1965**, 156–63(Russ). To 5.0 g. 5-bromoacenaphthene in 300 ml. liquid NH$_3$ a soln. of 1.64 g. K in 100 ml. NH$_3$ was added. The batch turned purple and finally greenish black. After 2 hrs. of stirring 3.4 g. NH$_4$NO$_3$ was added. NH$_3$ was driven off and the remainder extd. with C$_6$H$_6$. K was removed with dry HCl and the mixt. extd. with boiling H$_2$O, with C$_6$H$_6$, and with HCl (1:10). After alkalizing the exts. 0.74 g. of the aminoacenaphthene mixt. was obtained. The mixt. was extd. with hot petroleum ether to give 5-aminoacenaphthene, m. 86.5-7.5° (petroleum ether). The acetyl deriv., m. 178.5–9.5° (alc.), and the benzoyl deriv., m. 202–2.5° (dioxane), were prepd. After sepn. the C$_6$H$_6$ ext. was vacuum distd. and yielded 0.29 g. of acenaphthylene, m. 78–82°. The adduct with 1,3,5-trinitrobenzene m. 219–20°. The remainder, 1.97 g., was a hard, brown resin, m. 100–120°, and did not contain Br. After repeated dissolving in C$_6$H$_6$ and pptn. in petroleum ether 0.32 g. of a brown powder was sepd., m. 360°. The resin and the brown powder have the formula (C$_{12}$H$_8$)$_n$. Similar reactions were performed with F, Cl, Br, and I derivs. of acenaphthene in 3-, 4-, or 5-position and the ratio of KNH$_2$ to the halogen derivs. was varied from 1 to 4 per mole of the deriv. From the whole series of expts. the following conclusions were drawn: The reactions with the 3-, 4-, and 5-derivs. resulted basically in dehydrohalogenation (except the 5-fluoro deriv.) and in the formation of acenaphthylene and (C$_{12}$H$_8$)$_n$. Removal of halogen from the aromatic nucleus and H from an alkene group can be considered to be a new method for the formation of a double bond. A. P. Mueller

FIGURE 7. *Example of an abstract from* Chemical Abstracts. (*Reproduced by permission of the Chemical Abstracts Service.*)

Abstracts and Abstracting 437

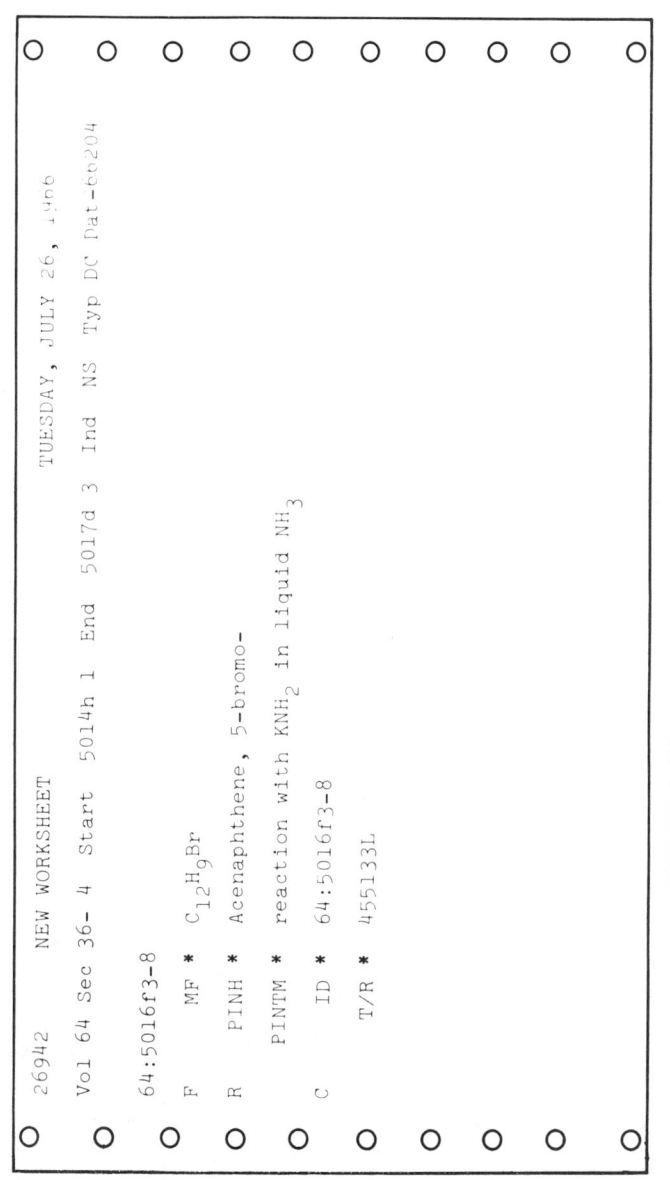

```
26942      NEW WORKSHEET                 TUESDAY, JULY 26, 1966
   Vol 64 Sec 36- 4 Start 5014h 1 End 5017d 3 Ind NS Typ DC Dat-66204

64:5016f3-8
   F    MF *  C12H9Br
   R    PINH * Acenaphthene, 5-bromo-
        PINTM * reaction with KNH2 in liquid NH3
   C    ID *  64:5016f3-8
        T/R * 45513L
```

FIGURE 8. *Work sheet for the abstract shown in Figure 7.*

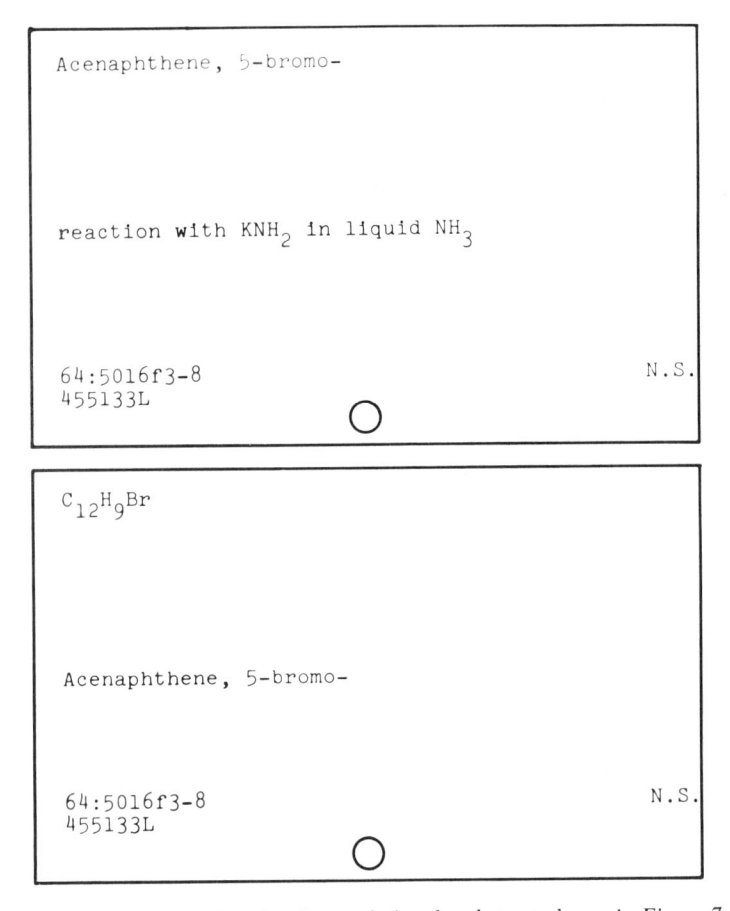

```
┌─────────────────────────────────────────────┐
│  Acenaphthene, 5-bromo-                     │
│                                             │
│                                             │
│  reaction with KNH₂ in liquid NH₃           │
│                                             │
│                                             │
│  64:5016f3-8                         N.S.   │
│  455133L                                    │
│                    ○                        │
└─────────────────────────────────────────────┘

┌─────────────────────────────────────────────┐
│  C₁₂H₉Br                                    │
│                                             │
│                                             │
│  Acenaphthene, 5-bromo-                     │
│                                             │
│                                             │
│  64:5016f3-8                         N.S.   │
│  455133L                                    │
│                    ○                        │
└─────────────────────────────────────────────┘
```

FIGURE 9. *Examples of index cards for the abstract shown in Figure 7.*

provision of (in addition to issue indexes) annual, semiannual, quinquennial, or decennial subject and author indexes of good quality—plus other specialized indexes such as formula, organic-ring, patent-number, taxonomy, and citation indexes.

Qualities of Abstracts

From the above description it is obvious that qualities of abstracts and their publications vary greatly. One of the more serious defects in abstract publications is the omission of abstracts clearly within the defined scope of the publication. Such losses come about through inadvertent omission of documents or journals. More frequently such omissions occur for economic reasons. The budget for the organization does not permit inclusion of all the documents and periodicals within its scope. Often entire classes of documents are omitted for security and other reasons. Examples are documents related to on-going research—work that is being carried on as these lines are read—and unpublished reports. Proprietary documents are omitted, as a rule, from a published abstract journal.

Besides omissions of abstracts, there are omissions from abstracts. Such omissions include subjects reported by authors, data from informative abstracts, references to other closely related abstracts or to original articles, complete references required to locate the original document unambiguously, or signature of the abstractor.

Reliability of abstracts, as indicated by consistency in following rules, is another measure of quality. Such reliability requires thorough knowledge of techniques.

Promptness in the publication of abstracts is often measured by the time elapsed between the appearance of the original article and of the abstract to it. The potential effects of delays in agriculture, medicine, and weaponry may be spectacular. In all fields delays cause economic loss. Delays may amount to several months to a year. Some organizations pride themselves on delays of only 1 month. Abstracts prepared from the page proof of articles in journals may appear before the articles. Abstracting from page proof is subject to the hazard of cancellation of the original article in proof.

The price of an abstracting journal is a quality factor too. High price limits access to the abstracts. Use is affected whether the journal is in a library a few doors down the hall or in a building 10 miles away. Issues and indexes should be on the desks of the users for greatest efficiency.

Indexes, or a lack of them, greatly affect the use of abstracts, especially for retrospective searching. Indexes, whether stored in a computer or in book form, increase the ease and effectiveness of access to abstracts. The most common indexes are to subjects and authors. In certain fields, such as chemistry, there may be other kinds, such as molecular-formula, organic-ring, and patent-number indexes, that are useful.

The authoritativeness of abstracts is another quality. It is related to the reputation of the abstract journal, which, in turn, is a product of the care with which abstracts are prepared, edited, checked, and printed. Abstractors recognized as authorities in the field also increase the authoritativeness of abstracts. Section editors, who oversee quality, lend authoritativeness.

The classification system (including subclassification) used for the abstracts is a factor in quality. The appropriateness of the system to current needs is relevant. Classification systems become obsolete if not given continuing attention. Changes that are too frequent may confuse the user and make the process of classifying abstracts more costly.

Categorization, the process of placing abstracts into the structure of the classification system adopted, is another factor affecting quality. Uniformity in categorization requires training and definition of the categories.

Perhaps the most frequently emphasized quality of abstracts is brevity. This factor can be measured by reediting the published abstracts and comparing lengths before and after. Abstracts that are too brief omit important information.

The formats of abstracts affect their usefulness. There is evidence to show that abstracts with a carefully selected lead-in sentence and with the reference to the original article at the end are preferred to abstracts starting with the title or other part of the reference. Other items of format, including a standard order for components of the body of the abstract, are also factors to be considered.

There is evidence to show that the kind of type face used affects the ease of reading and the legibility. Printing gives wide choice in this matter and computer outputs are beginning to have this variety also.

Printing, besides having the qualities of compactness and improved legibility over composition with all capitals or from typewriters, has intangible qualities.

Economics

The cost of classified, published, indexed abstracts varies considerably. The cost per abstract can be obtained by dividing the budget of the service, including research expenditures, by the number of different abstracts published. Values for *Chemical Abstracts,* for example, have ranged near $23–25, including research budgets.

Indexing costs may amount to more than half of the cost of publishing classified, indexed abstracts. For example, for *Chemical Abstracts,* indexing cost includes salaries of subject-authority indexers who have received extensive training in indexing.

The cost per abstract impression is obtained by dividing the cost per abstract by the circulation. For the above example, the cost per abstract impression has been near two-tenths of a cent.

The price of indexed abstracts is minute when compared with the cost of research and development that made the abstracts possible. The value of research and development (R&D) to the society in which we live is even greater than its cost. Such comparisons enable one to discuss the economics of abstracts in view of the total picture of R&D and its communication. It has been pointed out that R&D without communication of the results is not worth the investment. Indexed abstracts have turned out to be one of the more effective intermediaries in such communication for the reasons listed at the beginning of this article.

Problems of Abstracts

There are a number of problems in connection with abstracts that are unsolved or that do not have entirely satisfactory solutions.

One problem is concerned with bringing to the user only those abstracts of greatest potential concern to him. It is a problem in raising the relevance percentage. For example, it would take a chemist, reading at the rate of three research papers per hour, about 32 years to cover the original R&D papers published each year. It is obvious that most of the abstracts of the 97% of the papers that he would not have time to read need not be brought to his attention. How does one select from the 200,000 abstracts of chemical papers per year only those abstracts that should be brought to the attention of each chemist? Probably the chemist should be a party to this selection, since he, presumably, knows his interests and wants (if not his needs) better than anybody else. This seems to be a problem of repackaging and selective dissemination of abstracts.

Abstracts and Abstracting

The pricing of an abstract service for survival with quality, yet widest useful distribution, is a problem that remains unsolved. It is related to the problem of repackaging. Logically it would seem desirable to include most of the cost of an abstract service in the cost of research and development, in line with the belief that communication of research results is a part of research. However, the technique or will for doing this has not been established. The support of abstract services by their users is possible if the number of abstracts supplied to them is within their range of interests (the repackaging problem) and if there are enough users, which is a part of the pricing problem. Subsidy by societies, industry, government, and advertising has been tried.

Another serious problem is the delay between appearance of the original document and the indexed abstract. Delays affect health, safety, economics, and so forth. The life of an abstracting service is a continuing battle against delays.

Quality control for indexed abstracts is largely a problem of bringing understanding and an appreciation of quality. Many of the qualities of abstracts and indexes are invisible to the user, who is generally able to detect omission only of his own papers. Qualities other than omissions may be equally difficult to detect and appreciate. Quality control brings the continuing problem of justifying its expense to those who may not appreciate its necessity. Measures and measurements of the various quality factors are needed. Many of these factors exist independently of the users, although all of them affect the users.

The problems of inadequate coverage and limited distribution of service exist for several classes of information and documents. A complete, up-to-date inventory of on-going research is needed. Abstracts of descriptions of all work going on as these lines are read aid in avoiding duplication and in promoting earlier stimulation of new ideas. Classified (security) R&D presents another problem, as does proprietary R&D.

The stimulation of the effective use of abstracts by those who could benefit from their increased use is a problem that seems amenable to formal and continuing education. Techniques for effective use need improvement, additions, and development—as well as teaching. There is evidence that features built into existing abstract services are not known, appreciated, or used so effectively as they might be. Such features include translation services, access to original documents, cross references to related documents and abstracts, nomenclature information, lists of abbreviations, special indexes, and lists of periodicals abstracted.

Problems beyond Abstracts

The vast accumulating body of abstracts is searched repeatedly by different individuals for the same data and other information. Sometimes the same person repeats searches or parts of them. Better ways for sharing the results of searches are needed. One way is the evaluative (or critical) review; another way is tables of current data. Even more serious than loss of search time is loss of the critical evaluation that was invested in the searching and its product.

There are not enough evaluative reviews to cover adequately all fields of knowledge. Those who are knowledgeable in the fields do not have the time to write reviews. Annual evaluative reviews can help to save the time needed for repeated searches.

Current tables of critical data are also urgently needed to save repeated search and evaluation.

Perhaps the greatest problem of all is the development and maintenance of resources for information services. Such resources include financing, trained individuals, and facilities. Accurate understanding and presentation of the value of information services, including indexed abstracts, is required. Those who authorize resources may not have adequate, written justification for support or increase of such services. The solution to the problem of justifying communication of the results of R&D is, strangely, more difficult than justifying resources for R&D itself.

Major Abstracting Services

The major abstracting services, such as Chemical Abstracts Service, in the physical sciences have grown with the literature to fill a need that has not been filled in any other way. The National Federation of Science Abstracting and Indexing Services has compiled "A Guide to the World's Abstracting and Indexing Services in Science and Technology," Report No. 102, Washington, D.C., 1963. Another source is *Abstracting Services in Science, Technology, Medicine, Agriculture, Social Sciences, and Humanities,* International Federation for Documentation, 7 Hofweg, The Hague, Netherlands, FID372, August 1965.

The Future of Abstracts

In the light of the rapid development of information science, it is important to view the future of published, classified, indexed abstracts.

As adjuncts for abstracting services are systems for providing copies of the abstracts. The Rapid Selector was one of the first developments along this line. Saving the time of users spent in copying abstracts or parts of them is important. Copies of abstracts are useful in personal libraries, literature research, preparation of bibliographies, writing papers, and generating reviews. Another service as adjunct to abstracts is prompt supply of original documents or their translations upon request. Such originals can be supplied in microform as microfiche, Microcards, microfilm, microprint, and MiniPrint. Microforms enable the user to have in his desk a library of several thousand documents. It is technically feasible, although perhaps not economically easily justifiable, to place on his desk indexed abstracts to a somewhat larger set of documents than the subset in his desk. The user can have in his desk the hard copies of several hundred of the documents that he uses most.

Indexes have been used as substitutes for abstracts. Examples are *Index Medicus* and *Engineering Index*. Computer systems by which, in effect, tailor-made indexes are produced upon request are functional. Substitutes for abstracts may face the problem of the many languages in which documents are written; accurate selection;

Abstracts and Abstracting

need for translations, hard copy, and microforms; and functioning as a substitute for the original if the latter is unavailable promptly. One of the most interesting developments is the avoidance of abstracts altogether by use of an automated encyclopedia that is continually up to date from data supplied either from the originals or from the laboratory. Machine-assisted evaluation of the data would be a valuable adjunct to such a service.

Automation of abstracting has, except for a few studies, largely been a process of extracting. Usually sentences are extracted from the original. Practical systems for the automatic generation of abstracts identical with abstracts produced by subject-authority abstractors are for the future. Automatically produced extracts have not, in general, been considered to be the equivalents of abstracts produced in the usual way.

The problem posed by the increasing number of documents may be solved, if abstracts continue to be successful, by repacking them photographically into smaller categories of the major disciplines in such a way that each category is complete. Such repackaging does not seem to be especially formidable economically; the economics of distribution and indexing are not so favorable. The new techniques of computer-aided printing offer ways of repackaging indexes for the small categories, and even to repackaging the abstracts themselves. It does not seem too much to ask that someday every scientist, engineer, and scholar be supplied with a tailor-made (not ready-made) indexed abstract journal that follows his interests throughout his career and provides a guide to hard copy and microforms in his desk or files. Such an indexed abstract journal could be tailored to be somewhat broader than his current interests through citations, authors read, authors who read these authors, as well as subject interests. Proper feedback should keep the personal abstract journal tracking his career.

The question has been raised as to the manpower required to produce the ever-increasing number of abstracts. Since abstracts are prepared from documents whose number increases largely in proportion to the number of authors and since a certain percentage of authors are also willing to serve as abstractors, the continuing supply of human abstractors seems assured. The percentage of authors who have been willing to serve as abstractors seems to have remained fairly constant through the decades. However, the assurance of supply of abstractors should not prevent search for automated abstracting. As a result of this opinion, considerable effort has gone into automatic extracting and abstracting and into finding surrogates for abstracts. The use of authors to abstract their own documents has received continuing, enthusiastic support through the years. The success of a comprehensive program for producing author abstracts depends on insistence by all publishers, adequate instructions, and editing.

The economics of the publication of classified, indexed abstracts had been a serious concern of many organizations for years. Sources of support for published abstracts are users and authors, their organizations, professional societies, industry, government, and advertising. Combinations of these can be used. The users of abstracts may be able to charge part of the cost to their project or organization. Page charges levied on authors or their organizations would seem to require a clearinghouse that would place the cost of the communication of the results of R&D through indexed abstracts on the R&D budgets. Professional societies for very large disciplines have found that abstract publications cannot be supported by dues. Also, advertising has not provided adequate support, because those who use abstracts generally are not the ones who authorize the purchase of the items advertised.

The understandable concern for the cost of published abstracts has sometimes obscured proper concern for the relationship between the price of communication of the results of R&D, the cost of R&D, and the value of R&D to the society in which we live. The value of abstracts in the communication of the results of R&D has been established by the experience of the past century. The value of R&D to the society in which we live is perhaps one or two orders of magnitude greater than the cost of R&D. And the cost of R&D is about two to three orders of magnitude greater than the price of the best classified, indexed, published abstracts. For example, if the price of a published abstract is about $25, the cost of R&D behind the document abstracted may be about $25,000, and the value of R&D to the society around us could possibly be $250,000 or more. As an illustration, cures for the many kinds of cancer could lift a burden of about $11.2 billion a year from the United States. The importance of the proper concern for value–cost–price relationships lies in its aid to adequate support for communication of the results of R&D. When faced with the problem of adequate support for communication, some have argued that abstracts really do not help very much in the process of bringing the right information to the right person at the right time. If this is true, then abandonment of abstracts would seem the most judicious course.

Eventually one can picture the entering of processed or even raw data into a system that organizes it into an automated encyclopedia as current as the last quotation on the ticker tape. Such a system would eliminate not only abstracts but also papers and their authors by the conversion of the latter into more efficient human data processors.

26

Abstracting

Betty A. Mathis / The Ohio College Library Center, Columbus, Ohio

James E. Rush / James E. Rush Associates, Powell, Ohio

THE NATURE AND DEFINITION OF ABSTRACTING

Introduction

A discussion of the concepts "abstract" and "abstracting" is fraught with difficulty because the data upon which one must draw cover such a great span of time and because the concepts have until very recently been part of a venerable, empirical science. Thus, while the term "abstract" implies some kind of reduced form of a corpus of things, the nature of the reduction is poorly defined. And while the term "abstracting" implies a method of reduction, the known methods are all purely descriptive. Let us consider briefly the nature and significance of the traditional use of these terms.

The idea of abstraction pervades the whole of science, and the term suggests a transition from specific to general, from individual observations to class description. Thus molecular structural representation of chemical substances is an abstraction based on the detailed examination of many, but by no means all, individual chemical species. A description of some piece of research is an abstraction of the actual research. We might say therefore that an abstract is the quintessence of that from which it derives; that an abstract is a document shorn of detail. This notion is most often expressed by saying that an abstract is a condensed or abbreviated version of a document.[1]

From Mathis, Betty A. and James E. Rush. *Abstracting.* ENCYCLOPEDIA OF COMPUTER SCIENCE AND TECHNOLOGY. Vol. 1. Edited by Jack Belzer, Albert G. Holzman and Allen Kent. New York, Marcel Dekker, Inc., c1975. pp. 102-142.

[1] This is a very loose description and does not seem to be entirely compatible with the notion expressed in the preceding sentence. This point will be dealt with later when the term *abstract* is given a more formal definition.

When the term "abstract" is used alone it seems ambiguous. It may refer to the notion of an abstract property or expression ("World War II" is a concrete expression, while the word "war" is abstract). It may refer to title to real property (in this sense an abstract is a written, connected, chronological summary of the essential portions of all recorded documents and facts which can be discovered by a search of the public records of the jurisdiction within which the realty is located [1]). Or it may refer to a summary of the principal findings of the work reported in a paper [2]. We are concerned here with the last of these three senses of "abstract," but it should be obvious that the three senses are really quite similar in intent, the unity of purpose being the representation of the *essential* qualities of the thing(s) abstracted.

We will pick up this thread of reasoning again later, but first we wish to review briefly the history of abstracts and abstracting.

Historical Development of Abstracting

In tracing the development of information storage and retrieval, it is important to ask: What is the purpose of creating records of man's experience, of abstracting, indexing, consolidating, and distilling the contents of these records, of providing repositories for their housing and for central public access thereto? As Mellon [3] puts it,

> Very little advance in culture could be made, even by the greatest man of genius, if he were dependent for what knowledge he might acquire upon his own personal obervations. Indeed, it might be said that exceptional mental ability involves a power to absorb the ideas of others, and even that the most original people are those who are able to borrow most freely.

Without the availability, to present generations, of records of the experiences of those who came before, one would have no foundation upon which to build; one would have always to begin afresh. This sharing of experiences is at the heart of the need for and interest in personal communication of any sort. In fact, we can say that communication is the sharing of experiences. But most of us will never have the opportunity for personal communication with many of those individuals whose experiences we would most like to share (even if we knew of the existence of such individuals). However, records of the experiences of these individuals are, fortunately, made available to us and we can thus "commune" with persons long since dead or otherwise separated from us. This is the fundamental reason for the existence of libraries, of whatever form.

Concerted effort to bring scientific inquiry to an organized state seems to have had its genesis in the seventeenth century. According to some, Bacon [4] was most instrumental in bringing about this shaping and directing of human activity. As a result of Bacon's efforts to cause the establishment of research as a means of regenerating learning, and to found a college of research for the purpose of fostering the New Philosophy (the scientific method) and of providing for the publication of such discoveries which the research revealed, the Royal Society of London was eventually founded, and subsequently the whole fabric of European scientific societies was established.

Although the Royal Society was founded in 1662 and proceedings of its meetings were first published in 1665,[2] it was not until the nineteenth century, almost 200 years after the first serial publication appeared, that the collection of recorded data had grown to

---

[2] The *Philosophical Transactions*.

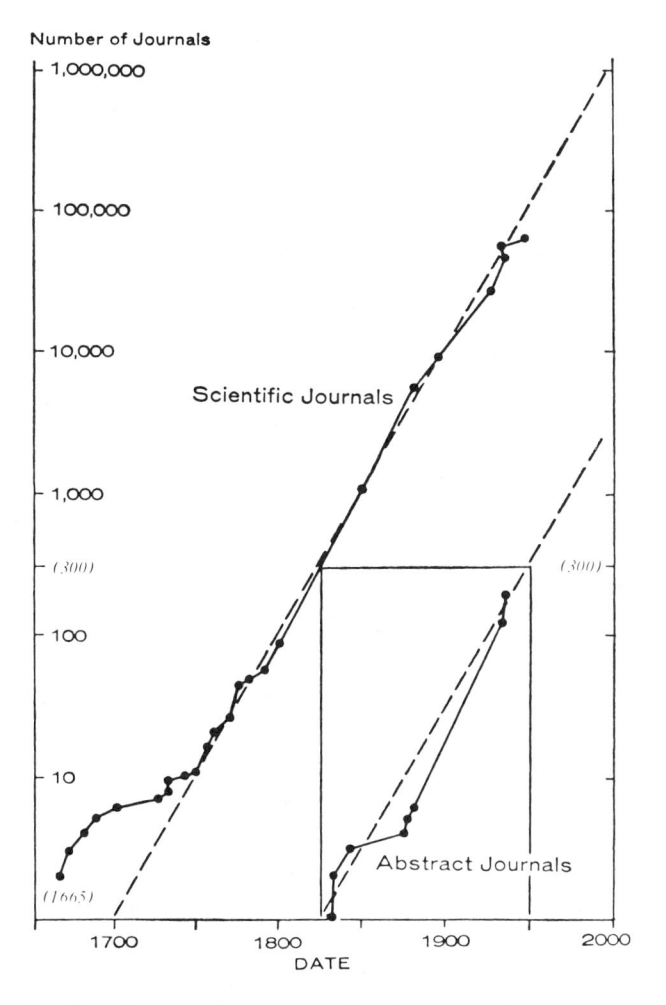

Fig. 1. Growth in primary and secondary literature. (Reproduced from *Science Since Babylon* [5] by permission of Yale University Press.)

proportions which made it desirable to collect and summarize this data on a regular basis. In 1821, Berzelius began his *Jahresberichte über die Fortschritte der physischen Wissenschaften*. Berzelius's effort had been preceded by a pharmaceutical "yearbook" which had been started in 1795[3] with a similar purpose. However, these publications were yearbooks in the sense of being annual summaries rather than more frequently appearing periodicals. As the number of articles increased, the need for more frequently published summaries or abstracts was felt. *Pharmaceutisches Centralblatt* was begun in 1830 to satisfy this need and, as Fig. 1 amply demonstrates, the trend toward more, more frequent, and more specialized abstracting publications has resulted in the concurrent appearance of a large number of them which presumably serve to make available

---

[3] *Berlinisches Jahrbuch für die Pharmacie und die damit verbunden Wissenschaften* (discontinued in 1840).

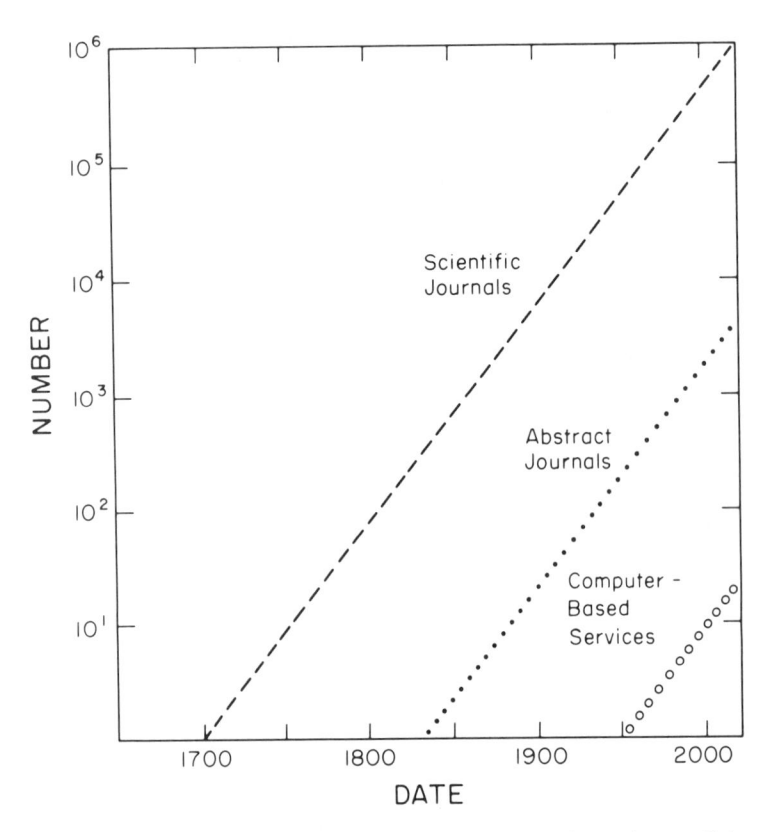

Fig. 2. Third level of experiential representation hypothesized to parallel the growth in primary and secondary literature (shown in Fig. 1).

the record of some portion of man's experience to modern scientists.[4] In fact, it is fashionable to illustrate the parallel growth of the primary journal literature and the secondary (abstract) journal literature by a means of a graph such as that of Fig. 1. The parallel is striking, but the figure raises the more interesting question: When the number of abstract journals becomes too large, what new representation of man's experience will assert itself, say around the year 1960? In other words, is there *now* a third level of experiential representation that is rising in importance and that will one day appear as a third "curve" on a graph such as that of Fig. 2?

Intensive Properties of Abstracts

A handbook for authors [6] admonishes an author to be aware of the "importance taken on by his abstract."

> The ideal abstract will state briefly the problem, or purpose of the research when that information is not adequately contained in the title, indicate the theoretical or experimental plan used, accurately summarize the principal findings, and point

---

[4] We realize that one must interpret this term very broadly if all those, whom we might better call students, are to be included in the ranks of those who have need of and use recorded knowledge.

out major conclusions. The author should keep in mind the purpose of the abstract, which is to allow the reader to determine what kind of information is in a given paper and to point out key features for use in indexing and eventual retrieval. It is never intended that the abstract substitute for the original article, but it must contain sufficient information to allow a reader to ascertain his interest. The abstract should provide adequate data for the generation of index entries concerning [both] the kind of information present and [the] key compounds [reported].

Chemical Abstracts Service's *Directions for Abstractors* [7] states that "*CA* publishes informative abstracts which contain the significant content of published works. . . . A *CA* informative abstract is a concise rendition of the significant content of a bibliographically cited paper or report which provides enough of the new information contained in the work with sufficient abbreviated details to enable a reader to determine if it is necessary to consult the complete work." This description of an "informative abstract" leaves a great deal to the discretion of the abstractor, but the publication also gives additional guidance on significant content:

> The following components are considered to be significant in the contents of an article and are included in *CA* informative abstracts:
> —The purpose and scope of the work, if it is not evident from the title.
> —New reactions, compounds, materials, techniques, procedures, apparatus, data, concepts, and theories.
> —New applications of established knowledge.
> —The results of the investigation.
> —The author's interpretation of the results and his conclusions derived from them.

Wyllys [8] has provided a more succinct, if not more precise, description of the term "abstract."

> An abstract is
> (a) a description of, or restatement of, the essential content of a document
> (b) which is phrased in complete sentences (except for bibliographic data)
> (c) and which usually has a length in the range from 50 to 500 words.

These descriptions of abstracts, although wanting in definitional precision, do provide a basis for the formulation of a definition. Thus, the abstract should consist of complete sentences rather than keywords or phrases, or association maps [9]. The abstract should (usually) be short, although the relation between the length of the article and its abstract is prescribed in many different ways [10]. The essential content of the article as reflected in the purpose of the work, the results and conclusions, new data, etc., should be included in the abstract. The problem with this last statement is that of determining what is the "essential content"; it is a problem central to all of language processing.

There are two ways of viewing an abstract, as a structural element to be formed and manipulated or as an intensive element. Most, if not all, current attempts at a definition of the term "abstract" mix these two views and consequently fail to provide a definition.

The following definition of an abstract [11], based upon structural considerations, provides a workable and useful basis for a better understanding of the abstracting process (but, as will be seen, it is incomplete in the form given here).

An abstract, A, is a set of sentences, s, such that

$$A = \{s | s \in D\}$$

where D is the document[5] abstracted, and such that certain transformations on the s are allowed: concatenation; truncation; phrase deletion; voice transformation; paraphrase; division; word deletion.

What does this definition do for us? First, it provides a more precise means of determining whether a document is an abstract than do earlier descriptions. Thus, one of its most important advantages is that it distinguishes abstracts from critical reviews[6] or other literary inventions of the abstractor. Second, it makes no mention of "content" or "meaning," notions which are difficult to deal with and which may vary with the *purpose* of an abstract. Thus, the definition distinguishes between what an abstract *is* and what an abstract *does*. Third, the definition allows for a certain stylistic freedom, but stylistic freedom does not encompass editorial comment (the latter is precluded by the definition). Finally, the definition is applicable to human, as well as to other, abstractors, thus permitting comparison of the abstracts produced by different abstracting systems.

It should be noted that the definition given above does not prescribe the length of an abstract. Length is a function of the purpose of an abstract and is therefore not of the essence of the concept "abstract." Abstract length is a variable under the control of the abstracting system rather than one whose values are dictated by the definition of the product of the system.

While the definition provided above is useful, it is really incomplete because the intension of an abstract is not provided for. Abstracts are usually placed into one or the other of two intensive classes: *informative* or *indicative*. An informative abstract is one characterized as containing some (or all) of the information contained in the original document. An indicative abstract is one which indicates that certain information is contained in the original document, but that information is not contained in the abstract.[7] Examples of informative and indicative abstracts are given in Fig. 3. Many variations on these two classes of abstract have been described [13]. In practice, most abstracts prove to be both informative and indicative, so it is perhaps less important to consider abstracts as belonging to one or the other of these classes than it is to consider the user population they are to serve.

To know the needs and desires of a system's user population is no easy accomplishment. But if we *assume* such knowledge for existing abstracting services, we can observe that *Chemical Abstracts*, for example, gives greater emphasis to current work in chemistry than to articles relating historical data (reviews, etc.) because articles of the first type are represented by informative abstracts while the latter type are represented by indicative abstracts. This observation leads to the inference that the users of *Chemical Abstracts* are, on the whole, more concerned with current work than with historical data.

These observations lead us to the conclusion that the purpose (which we have inferred from our examination of the products of various abstracting systems) of the abstract dictates the particular set of sentences which constitute the abstract. The purpose of an abstract is met by controlling the intension of the abstract, Thus, a chemical compound appearing in an abstract in *Index Chemicus* will almost invariably carry with it

---

[5] *Document*, as well as other fundamental terms, are defined in Ref. 12.

[6] An author of a critical review includes added interpretation and criticism of the article that he is reviewing.

[7] Hence an informative abstract is also indicative, but the inverse of this statement is not true.

(a)

35 0508 **Study of [the Corrosion-Resistance and Properties of] Two Aluminium Alloys Used by Japanese Builders of Liquefied-Natural-Gas Tanks and Tankers.** Walter Trüb. Schweiz. Aluminium Rundschau, Feb. 1969, 19, (1), 28-34 [in German and French].
Laboratory and ⅕th- and full-scale tests at +20 and −196 °C on Peraluman-460- and Unidur-100-type (Al—4.5% Mg—Mn and Al—4% Zn—Mg) alloys used in Japan for construction of tanks and tankers for storage and sea transport of liquefied gas are reported. Resistances of the structures to sea-water and stress corrosion, and to fatigue of welded and unwelded plates and sections, are compared, and UTS, YP, and extension data are plotted and tabulated.—J. R.

(b)

83-R. (French) METHODS OF CONTROL OF METALLIC COATINGS IN RELATION TO CORROSION PROTECTION. P. Morisset. Corrosion et Anticorrosion, v 10, no 9, Sept. 1962, p 281-285.

Determination of influence of adherence, thickness and structural uniformity of coating on corrosion resistance of Zn or Ni plated iron or steel components using atmospheric corrosion tests, or the TIM test using sulfur gas, saline solution and varying amounts of humidity. (R3, 1-54, L17b, Q10c; St, Ni, Zn)

Fig. 3. Examples of (a) informative and (b) indicative abstracts. (Reproduced from *Abstracting Scientific and Technical Literature* [9] by permission of the American Society for Metals.)

the intension of "newness," while a compound appearing in *Biological Abstracts* will most likely bear the intension of application in some biological system, regardless of its "newness." We see, therefore, that the structure of the abstract and the intension of the abstract are *not* independent, so the definition given earlier must be modified to account for the relationship between structure and intension.

Formal Definition of "Abstract"

Let us rephrase the definition of abstract given earlier, this time in the language of automata theory. The definition of an abstract can be given in terms of an automaton, *Ma*, denoted by [14]

$$Ma = (K, \Sigma, \Gamma, \delta, q_0, F)$$

where K is a finite set of states; Γ is a finite set of allowable input and output symbols: the original document, the abstract, and any additional data; Σ is the set of input symbols, i.e., the original document; δ is the next move function which is defined by machine configurations, selection rules, and transformations—this function also speci-

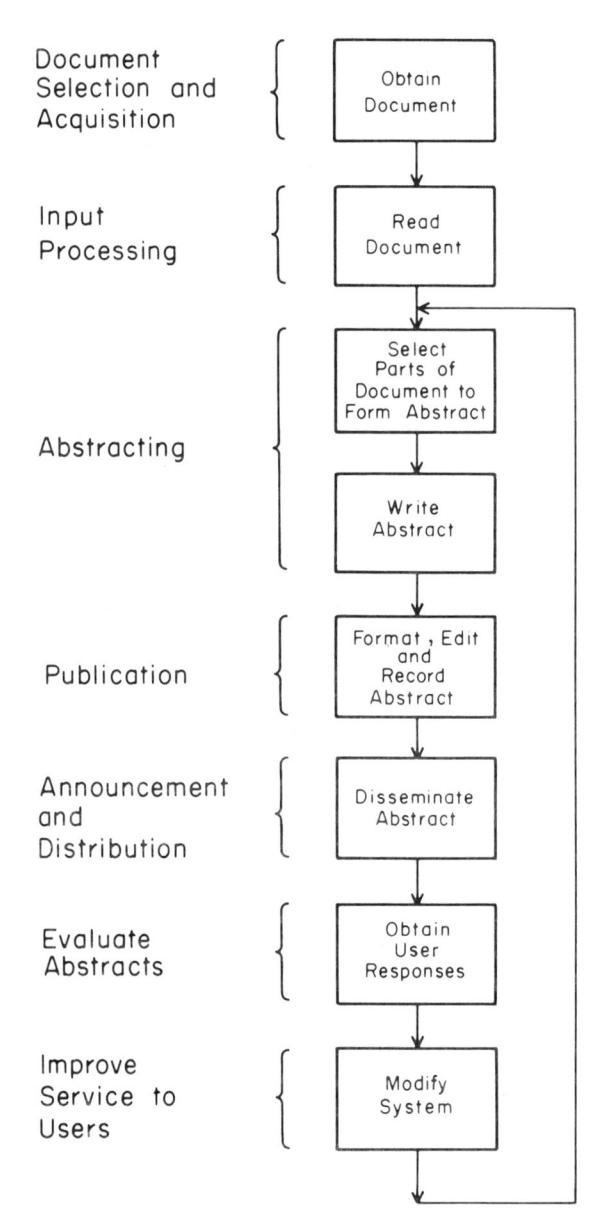

Fig. 4. Main components of an abstracting system.

fies the output of the automaton, the elements of the abstract; q_0 is the start state, which corresponds to the input of the title; F is the final state, which corresponds to the completion of the abstract.

Although the above definition of *abstract* may seem somewhat abstruse, it is really an operational definition. This definition provides the relationship between the abstract and the original document in terms of an abstracting algorithm. The set of states and associated mappings constitute an algorithm which is a realization of the intension of the machine. The machine can be given explicit definition for a particular abstracting system by specifying all the parameters necessary for operation of the automaton.

Based on the values of certain parameters, various types of abstracts can be defined. When the set of allowable input and output symbols, Γ, contains only the sentences of an original document, then the resultant abstract is a selection of sentences from the original, or an extract. When the set Γ contains additional symbols, such as alternative sentence structures and vocabulary items, which allow for the abstract to contain paraphrases of the original sentences, then an informative abstract is produced. When information about the original document is supplied by the abstracting system, i.e., when such information can serve as input to the automaton, then an indicative abstract is produced. Other types of abstracts that have been identified by authors, for example, critical abstracts, alerting abstracts, locative abstracts, and slanted abstracts, reflect the orientation of the information that is added to the set of allowable input symbols. By completely specifying all of the parameters in the formulation, an abstract will be completely defined and an algorithm for production of the abstract will also be available.

We have dealt at some length with the concept of an abstract, considering in particular: (1) what an abstract is, (2) the purpose of an abstract, and (3) to some extent how an abstract may be produced.

In the next section we consider the third point in greater detail. In general, an abstract is produced by an abstractor or an *abstracting system*. This latter term is more general (the former term seems to imply a human as the abstracting system) and can be applied with equal ease to humans or other kinds of machines which are capable of executing an abstracting algorithm. The main components of an abstracting system, and their interrelationships, are depicted in Fig. 4. In the sequel we will briefly consider human abstracting systems and then discuss computer-based systems.

METHODS OF PRODUCING ABSTRACTS

Human Abstracting Systems

Although automatic abstracting is a popular current topic, all operational abstracting systems are largely *human abstracting systems*. That is, the reading of the original document, selection of portions of it for the abstract, the writing of the abstract and, in many instances, its formatting and editing are processes performed by humans. The most important of these processes, from the viewpoint of the abstract user, is the selection of material from the original document for inclusion in the abstract. But this selection may be influenced considerably by the other processes.[8]

---

[8] A good deal of the discussion to follow is of necessity conjecture, but it should not be particularly difficult (however time consuming) to obtain data with which to affirm or deny the assertions made here. These studies would, of course, involve human subjects and unless the experiments were carefully designed and executed, the results would be of doubtful value.

The process of translation from one language to another, as carried out by human abstractors, may result in considerable variation in the size and quality of the abstract. Such variations depend largely upon the abstractor's facility with both the source language and the target language. Although no data are available to support this contention, it seems unlikely that an abstract prepared by an abstractor, whose facility with one of the languages is poor, will be of as good quality as that prepared by one fluent in that language. The fault is most serious when the source language is not well understood by the abstractor. Then the abstract may be well written but may not represent the content of the original document. On the other hand, when the target language is the source of difficulty the abstract will show this and the reader will be alerted to the possibility for error or misinterpretation on the part of the abstractor.

A second factor which influences the selection of material for the abstract is the abstractor's knowledge of the subject area of the document being abstracted. The abstractor who is expert in the subject area will likely produce an abstract which is shorter, more general, and which requires more knowledge on the part of the reader than an abstract produced by an abstractor whose knowledge of the subject area is marginal. On the other hand, the latter type of abstractor is perhaps less likely to get the main thrust of the document into his abstract than the subject expert. What is probably needed is an abstractor whose qualifications lie between the extremes of expertise and passing knowledge in a subject area. Again, there are no data to support these contentions, but the following quote lends some credence to them: "... the best way to get all of the new and significant information of a paper into an abstract, expressed in proper technical terms, is to obtain the spare-time abstracting service of someone actively interested and working in the specific field of chemistry into which a paper being abstracted fits" [15]. The suggestion is that it is better (and easier) to teach subject specialists to abstract than to attempt to teach abstractors a subject speciality.

Another factor which must influence selection of material for the abstract is the imposition of formatting and editorial responsibilities upon the abstractor. The more mechanical tasks the abstractor must perform, the greater is the likelihood that the quality of the abstract will suffer. Undoubtedly, Zipf's law of least effort [16] comes into play here.

Thus, it is suggested that a human abstractor who will produce the best abstracts is: expert in the subject area and is taught to prepare abstracts; fluent in both the source and target languages; subjected to as few purely mechanical tasks as possible. Although these are not the only factors which influence the quality of human-produced abstracts, they are probably the most influential. These and other factors are considered again later in connection with studies of abstractor consistency.

Operational Systems

Computer systems are presently being utilized in operational abstracting systems to speed up the production of abstract journals. The basic processes in the production of abstract publications can be defined in terms of the following five steps: (1) document selection and acquisition, (2) input processing, (3) abstracting, (4) publication, and (5) announcement and distribution (see Fig. 4).

The acquisition and selection of documents to be abstracted is essentially a manual operation at present. Most primary sources of information are received as hard copy and must be converted into machine-readable form for input to the computer system.

Abstracting

Current trends in information transfer suggest that increasing reliance will be placed in the exchange of information in machine-readable form. Through use of machine-readable records the process of producing secondary publications can become an integral part of other processes involved in information-transfer technologies. Publishers of primary journals, for instance, may be able to provide abstracting services with the machine-readable data used to typeset the original article.

Source-data preparation, or input processing, today is largely manual and consists basically of keyboarding punched paper tapes, punched cards, magnetic tapes, or disks. This input can then be edited using display-and-edit programs available through cathode-ray tube terminals. Increased use of optical character readers may also alleviate the need for transcription from hard copy to machine-readable form. Furthermore, the availability of primary sources in machine-readable form may eliminate the need for input processing in the foreseeable future.

Abstracting is currently a manual operation in all production environments. Subject experts who have been trained to write abstracts are employed. In order to meet the recognized need for qualified personnel to write abstracts, some journals now require that authors submit abstracts in addition to their articles. This is not a totally adequate solution because the author-generated abstracts are inconsistent with respect to style and coverage and do not, frequently, reflect the point of view of the abstracting service. Although research efforts appear promising, abstracts which are produced by computer cannot yet meet the demands of abstract journal publications. The abstracting operation itself will probably be the last to be fully automated in the production of abstracts.

Many abstract publications rely heavily on automatic data processing equipment for production of their journals. Secondary publications, such as *Index Chemicus*, *Biological Abstracts*, *Psychological Abstracts*, and *Index Medicus*, have pioneered in the use of computer-aided composition and typesetting. In most applications, the information handling capabilities of computers in printing have been used primarily for right-margin justification, hyphenation, and page composition or for instructing hot metal or photocomposition machines and teletransmission devices. Such modern typographic and printing tools as photocomposition, xerographic processes, and page composition will certainly continue to make printing faster, if not more economical [17].

Announcement and distribution of secondary services is being enhanced by the development and use of computer-based selective-dissemination-of-information systems. The selective dissemination of information to users is made on the basis of user profiles, each of which is a compilation of keywords reflecting a user's interests. The user is then presented with only those abstracts which have matched his profile. The goal of such systems is to present to the user only the abstracts which are of the greatest potential value to him.

Chemical Abstracts Service,[9] long a leader in improvements in abstract journal publication, recognized in the early 1960s that the traditional manual system for processing and publishing secondary chemical information was too slow, too expensive, too rigid, and too wasteful in its use of highly capable manpower to be effective in the face of the evergrowing volume of published information. A streamlined system was designed in which each primary document would be analyzed only once and the selected data

---

[9] Other services, such as *Physics Abstracts*, *Biological Abstracts*, and *Psychological Abstracts*, are also moving toward the development of sophisticated man–machine systems.

recorded only once in a form that could be used to produce a variety of information packages with overlapping content. The target system designed by the Chemical Abstracts Service for their operations combined human intellectual analysis and computer-based processing. The roles of the computer in the system are

1. to receive material derived by human intellectual analysis;
2. to support that analysis with machine aids and augment the information flow by retrieving related previous work;
3. to apply automated validation checks and trigger exception reviews by editorial staff;
4. to eliminate the necessity for manual bridging between processing steps;
5. to automate the ordering (sorting) and formatting of the information, both on a data-directed basis;
6. to control composition machinery; and
7. to provide computer-readable files.

This target system, which was initiated during the 1967–1968 period and will probably not be completed until the 1975–1976 period, represents a system which uses computer technology as an essential and integral component [18].

Selection and Consistency

Before any attempt is made to automate the process of abstracting, it is important to understand how humans produce abstracts. A number of studies have been reported which deal with the question: How does a human abstractor decide what material in the original document should be included in the abstract? A corollary question is: Does the abstractor display any consistency in the selection process: (a) within a document; (b) between documents; (c) through time for either (a) or (b)? In order to answer these questions, one needs to know

1. what constitutes a good abstract of a document (or what constitutes a good set of abstracts, if one allows for the possibility of several equally good, goal-directed abstracts);
2. what is the operational definition of an abstract used by a particular abstracting system, as embodied in the rules for abstracting prescribed (or described) by the system[10] and how does it contrast with the definition of a "good" abstract;
3. given answers to 1 and/or 2, what consistency does an abstractor display in following the rules of the abstracting system or in producing a good abstract (if the rules of the abstracting system seem, or are believed to be, at odds with the abstractor's understanding of what constitutes a good abstract).

These three questions can be studied alone or in pairs, as illustrated in Fig. 5. Only the last of these has been studied systematically, yet there is no clear answer to any of these questions, although some of the research which has been done at least suggests the direction further efforts should take. Such studies have a special significance for the development of automatic abstracting systems, as will be made clear subsequently.

---

[10] The directions for preparing author abstracts, as issued by a particular journal, constitute an operational definition (no matter how vague) of an abstract.

Abstracting

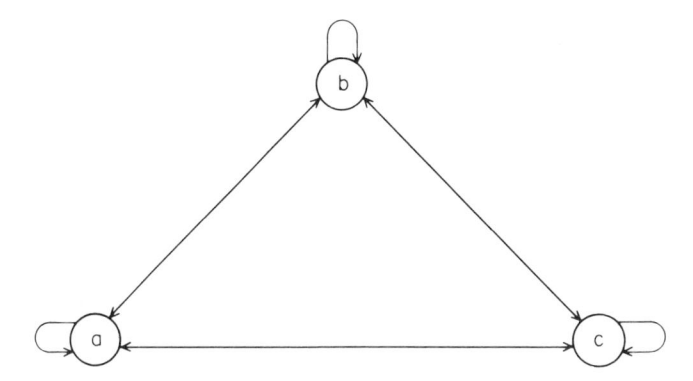

Fig. 5. Pairwise combinations of questions in the study of sentence selection and consistency of abstractors.

The most significant studies on selection and consistency are those of Rath, Resnick, and Savage [19–22] and of the TRW group headed by Edmundson and Wyllys [23, 24].

The main conclusions to be drawn from the Rath–Resnick–Savage studies is that human abstractors show poor consistency in selecting sentences for the abstract both between abstractors and with respect to time. In an initial study [21], these workers assigned six human abstractors the task of reading a set of ten articles from *Scientific American*, choosing the 20 most representative sentences from each article, and ranking these sentences in decreasing order of representativeness (measured against a background of those sentences already ranked). At the same time a computer program, similar to one developed by Luhn [25] (see the section entitled The Luhn Study), was used to also select and rank 20 sentences from each of the test articles. Five different methods of ranking sentences were used in the computer-based abstracting procedures.[11] One interesting point concerning *what* sentences were selected by human and computer was reported. It was found that the ten articles taken as a whole contained 37% "topic sentences" (after Baxendale [26]). Of these topic sentences, humans selected 47% and the computer selected 33%. It was also found that human-selected sentences came more often from the first half of the article, while the computer made more sentence selections from the latter half of the article.[12]

In a follow-up study, Resnick and Savage [27] showed that abstractors differed in their consistency in abstracting the same article at fairly widely separated points in time. Five subjects were asked to abstract six articles from *Scientific American*, as in the previous study [22]. Eight weeks later, they were asked to abstract the same six articles. Instructions included the admonition *not* to select sentences which had previously been selected unless the subjects felt the sentences were still representative, and to mark any currently selected sentence they believed they had previously selected. The accuracy of these identifications is indicated in Table 1. On average, these abstractors were able to

---

[11] It is important to note that the sample sizes used in this experiment are much too small to yield statistically valid results, although the data do support what one would feel, intuitively, was true. Nevertheless, the questions which this study attempted to answer remain open.

[12] This result may suggest that human abstractors get tired more readily than computers. Furthermore, the conditions under which the subject-set of human abstractors worked was probably a poor approximation of the (often harried) conditions under which the professional abstractor works.

TABLE 1

Mean Percentage of Responses of Five Subjects Making Selections of 20 "Representative" Sentences Two Months Apart from Each of Six Articles: During Second Selection Subjects were Asked to Indicate Whether or Not They Had Chosen Each Sentence Two Months Earlier [22]

	Sentence correctly identified	Sentence incorrectly identified
Sentence previously selected	42.5%	13.1%
Sentence not previously selected	21.7%	22.7%

correctly identify a currently selected sentence as one which had been selected previously 42.5% of the time (from Table 1 it is clear that they should have identified 65.2% of the currently selected sentences as ones previously selected—42.5% + 22.7%).[13]

Table 2 gives data on the consistency in sentence selection over time. It can be seen that there is greater variation among abstractors than between articles for a given abstractor.[14] One may conclude from these studies (keeping in mind the smallness of the samples) that human abstractors are modestly consistent in producing abstracts of a given document.

In another study of abstractor consistency, carried out by the TRW group [24], it was concluded that although human abstractors were not very consistent among themselves, the abstracts they produced were adequate (in terms of interabstractor consistency) to justify a study of the attributes of the sentences they extracted from the document.

The way in which the TRW group measured the consistency of human abstractors is of some interest. A correlation coefficient was devised which attempted to measure the similarity between two sets of sentences extracted from a given document, taking into account the sizes of the sentence sets relative to the original document and relative to each other. This measure can be expressed as

$$q_j = \frac{S_j}{L_j}$$

where L_j is the length of sentence T_j (number of text tokens) and

$$S_j = \sum_{\forall w_i \in T_j} P$$

and

$$P_i = \frac{N_{w_i}}{M_{w_i}}$$

where N is the number of text tokens of type w_i in the sentences extracted from a set of documents and M is the number of text tokens of type w_i in the document set ($M > N$).

---

[13] This result suggests that the subjects' memories functioned less well than their abstracting algorithms.

[14] It would be interesting to know the reason for the individual variations, which deviated widely from the average for a given abstractor. In Table 2 abstractors 2 and 4 (particularly 4) show between-article variations which are inconsistent with these variations for the other subjects.

TABLE 2

Percentage of Sentences Selected on Second Trial Which Were the Same as Those Selected on the First Trial [22]

	Articles					
Abstractor	A (%)	B (%)	C (%)	D (%)	E (%)	F (%)
1	60	55	45	45	40	40
2	45	50	75	80	45	60
3	60	65	55	70	55	50
4	45	55	55	55	40	15
5	80	70	70	60	55	80

q_j is the probability that a sentence will be extracted given N, M, L, and w_i. q_j can be derived from a consideration of the concept of inductive probability (developed by Carnap [28]) as follows [24].

Suppose two gamblers X and Y are told that a certain document has been extracted and that a particular sentence of that document has certain specified characteristics. These characteristics, together with all data available on past sentence selection by abstractors, are summarized in a proposition called the evidence, E. Let S be the hypothesis that the particular sentence has been extracted. Let the betting quotient, q, for a bet on S be the ratio

$$q = \frac{\text{stake offered for a bet on } S}{\text{total stake}}$$

Suppose the amount bet on S is q and the amount bet against S is $1 - q$. Then one can assume the existence of some q such that X would be equally willing to bet for or against S. Such a value of q is, as far as X is concerned, the psychologically fair betting quotient for S relative to the evidence, E, available. Another way of expressing the meaning of q is to say that q indicates the preference that X believes E confers on S. Y may be assumed also to accept either betting role for a q having the above value.

To determine whether q is indeed fair, a given document should be abstracted by a large number of abstractors.[15] If X and Y made a series of bets, X for S with quotient q and Y against S with quotient $1 - q$, then the total balance of wins and losses would be zero if the ratio of S_{true} to S_{false} is exactly q.

The TRW group [24] concluded that a representativeness score for a sentence under hypothesis S should incorporate:

1. the degree of evidential support that E confers on S;
2. the fair betting quotient for S relative to E;
3. an E-based estimate of the ratio

---

[15] Such a determination is always hindered, in practice, by the practical difficulties of carrying out a study involving large numbers of abstractors and/or large numbers of documents.

$$\frac{S_{\text{true}}}{S_{\text{false}}}$$

This measure is a general one because it permits the evidence (E) to be specified in any desired manner. Thus, although the TRW study used the measure as support for sentence selection based essentially on frequency criteria, any well-defined criteria may be used. The important point is that if the fair betting quotient q can be determined, then the selection criteria may be incorporated in a program for automatic abstracting.

In concluding this section, it is fair to say that little is known about how or why human abstractors choose from the original article what they include in the abstracts which they produce. Neither is it clear to what extent human abstractors are consistent in abstract production. Perhaps more importantly, especially since there is no concrete answer to the question of what constitutes a good abstract, questions relating to human selection and consistency may be irrelevant. It is just possible that the abstracts produced by humans are not good. If so, then it would be undesirable to try to emulate by computer the processes which humans use in abstracting, since such emulation would lead simply to a faster rate of production of consistently poor abstracts.[16] The major, unanswered question is: What makes an abstract a good one?

Computer-Based Abstracting Systems

We turn now to a discussion of abstracting systems in which the computer plays a central role. This discussion must, like that for human abstracting systems, be tempered by a lack of knowledge of whether the abstracts produced by such systems are "good." Happily, however, the questions of selection and of consistency of selection are easily dealt with. It is these two aspects of computer-based abstracting systems[17] that will be considered in greatest detail in this section.

There are eight[18] significant studies related to computer-based abstracting which have been described in the literature. These are

1. the Luhn study;
2. the ACSI-Matic study conducted by IBM;
3. the Oswald study;
4. word-association research;
5. the TRW studies conducted by Edmundson and Wyllys;
6. the Earl study;
7. the Rush study;
8. the Soviet study.

---

[16] A product easy to produce and difficult to sell.

[17] We prefer to call the process of abstracting by computer "computer-based abstracting," the abstracting system a "computer-based abstracting system," and the abstract produced by such a system a "computer-produced abstract," rather than to use the term *automatic* in place of *computer-based* as has commonly been done in the literature.

[18] To be sure, one could include other studies in this list, notably those of Baxendale [26] and of Climenson *et al.* [29], but we believe those listed to be representative of the various approaches taken to the production of abstracts by computer program, and that they are also of some historical importance.

Abstracting 461

Before we discuss these studies, it will be useful to describe the basic components of a computer-based abstracting system.

Basic System Components

A computer-based abstracting system (see Fig. 4) must: (a) read the document to be abstracted, (b) analyze the document, (c) apply a set of selection and/or transformation rules to produce the abstract, (d) format the resulting abstract, and (e) print the abstract.

Reading[19] the original document is perhaps as difficult a task as any subsequent processing steps the abstracting system must perform. A technical paper will commonly use many different characters in several different styles and in a half-dozen different fonts. The ordinary computer-system input devices are not capable of handling such a wide range of characters, nor are there optical readers (optical scanning devices) available which can do so economically.[20] One or both of two simple solutions to this problem are usually effected: (1) pre-edit the text, eliminating or altering those portions of the document which the input devices cannot handle; (2) use a scheme of flagging (coding) characters which cannot be read directly. Figures, tables, and other graphic materials will in all probability not find their way into the computer system at all. Pre-editing is most likely to be used, since the special text features which might otherwise be preserved are of questionable value in the actual abstracting process and since, until the use of optical printers becomes widespread, computer printers cannot economically (if at all) print the necessary range of characters.

Once the text has been read into computer memory, analysis of the input text is performed. The actual analytical methods used depend upon the particular abstracting system, so a discussion of this component will be deferred until the section entitled The Luhn Study.

Similarly, rules for selecting parts of the original document for inclusion in the abstract are considered under each of the specific studies which are discussed, beginning in the section on the Luhn Study.

Formatting the output of the abstracting process has not been particularly inspired. The usual methods include listing individual sentences or, occasionally, printing the abstract paragraphed as was the original document. Abstracts have never been noteworthy examples of literary work nor of the typographic art, so one should not criticize the output of computer-based abstracting systems too severely (although it does not seem unreasonable to hope that a little imagination might be applied to the formatting of computer-produced abstracts). No known computer-based abstracting system has utilized any output device other than the line printer.[21]

---

[19] Reading obviously involves seeing, and there are a variety of methods for recording data so that a computer can "see" (sense) it. These methods are beyond the scope of this work, but the reader is referred to Refs. 30 and 31 for details and further references.

[20] Except, perhaps, on a very large scale.

[21] Certain abstract journals are printed in a two-step process in the first of which an optical printer (COM, computer-onto-microfilm processor) is used. These publications do not, however, result from the compilation of computer-produced abstracts.

Exhibit 1

Source: The Scientific American, *Vol. 196, No. 2, 86-94, February, 1957*

Title: *Messengers of the Nervous System*

Author: *Amodeo S. Marrazzi*

Editor's Sub-heading: The internal communication of the body is mediated by chemicals as well as by nerve impulses. Study of their interaction has developed important leads to the understanding and therapy of mental illness.

Auto-Abstract*—Exhibit 1

It seems reasonable to credit the single-celled organisms also with a system of chemical communication by diffusion of stimulating substances through the cell, and these correspond to the chemical messengers (e.g., hormones) that carry stimuli from cell to cell in the more complex organisms. (7.0)**

Finally, in the vertebrate animals there are special glands (e.g., the adrenals) for producing chemical messengers, and the nervous and chemical communication systems are intertwined: for instance, release of adrenalin by the adrenal gland is subject to control both by nerve impulses and by chemicals brought to the gland by the blood. (6.4)

The experiments clearly demonstrated that acetylcholine (and related substances) and adrenalin (and its relatives) exert opposing actions which maintain a balanced regulation of the transmission of nerve impulses. (6.3)

It is reasonable to suppose that the tranquilizing drugs counteract the inhibitory effect of excessive adrenalin or serotonin or some related inhibitor in the human nervous system. (7.3)

Fig. 6. Example of an abstract produced by Luhn's system. (Reproduced from *IBM J. Res. Develop.* [25] by permission.)

Major Research Efforts in the Production of Abstracts

With this general view of the basic processes involved in computer-based abstracting, we turn to a discussion of specific studies which have lead to the implementation, at least experimentally, of computer-based abstracting systems.

The Luhn Study. Luhn is credited with having first suggested and demonstrated that abstracts could be produced via computers [25]. The procedures employed by Luhn for generating abstracts by computer were as follows.

1. The document to be abstracted was first punched into cards (texts which were used required no pre-editing) and then transferred to magnetic tape.

2. The text was then read, word by word. *Common words*[22] were deleted through table look-up. The remaining words, called *content words*, were associated with any punctuation that preceded or followed them, and their exact location in the original document was noted.

3. The content words were then sorted into alphabetical order.

4. Words of similar spelling were "consolidated" as follows. Successive pairs of word tokens[23] were compared letter-by-letter and at the first point of difference a count was

---

[22] Common words might well be called *nonsubstantive* words, since these are words that are considered to have no value in determining the significance of a portion (sentence, paragraph, etc.) of text. *Common* should not be confused with *function* in reference to word classification.

[23] A *word token* (sometimes *text token*) is a place-holder in a text. Each different word token is called a *word type* (or *text type*).

initiated of the number of nonmatches observed from that point to the end of the longer word token. If this count was less than seven (<7), the word tokens were taken to be of the same word type (i.e., to represent the same notion), otherwise the word tokens were taken to be distinct word types. The frequency of occurrence of each word type was then determined and word types occurring less frequently than some prescribed value were deleted. The remaining word types were considered to be "significant."

5. The significant word types were then sorted into location order.

6. Sentence representativeness was next determined. Sentences were divided into substrings, each of which was bounded by significant words separated by no more than four nonsignificant words. (Significant words separated from other significant words by more than four words were called "isolated" words and were not given further consideration.) For each substring, a representativeness value r_i was calculated according to the equation

$$r_i = \frac{p_i}{q_i}$$

where p_i is the number of representative tokens in the cluster and q_i is the total number of tokens in the cluster. The highest r_i for a sentence is taken as its representativeness of document content. Sentences having a value of r_i above a prescribed value (or else a predetermined number of sentences of highest r_i) were selected for inclusion in the abstract.

7. The abstract was then printed (as a set of sentences), formatted in paragraph style.

While the methods employed by Luhn for determining word and sentence significance have fallen somewhat into disrepute, the technique is clearly of historical importance. An example of an abstract produced by this method is given in Fig. 6. Additional examples of abstracts produced by this method, as well as data on word representativeness and word-token and word-type counts may be found in Luhn's papers [25, 32].

The ACSI-Matic Study. The ACSI-Matic study, conducted by IBM [33, 34] for the Army Department's Assistant Chief of Staff for Intelligence, was (and is) the only study which led to a computer-based abstracting system as part of an operational information system.

ACSI-Matic employed selection procedures analogous to those suggested by Luhn; the importance of this study lies in the rather novel variations imposed on Luhn's basic techniques. These modifications included:

a. elaboration of Luhn's sentence scoring technique;
b. special treatment of documents with an unusually large fraction of low-frequency words;
c. special treatment of documents with extraordinarily long sentences;
d. choice of sentences, once scored, to form a tentative abstract;
e. procedures to reduce redundancy among the sentences selected.

The ACSI-Matic scoring technique improved upon Luhn's treatment of the density of representative words in a sentence. To illustrate the technique, consider the sentence

$$N\ R\ N\ N\ R\ N\ N\ N\ R\ N\ N$$

where N is a nonrepresentative word (N-words) and R is a representative word (R-words). R-words were given a value of 1 and nonterminal sequences of N-words were given a value of $1/2^n$, where n is the number of N-words between successive R-words. Thus, the sentence above would be scored

$$1 + \frac{1}{4} + 1 + \frac{1}{8} + 1 = 3\frac{3}{8}$$

This procedure was applied to sentences of documents whose average sentence length was in the range 18 to 26 words.

When a document had an average sentence length greater than 26 words, each sentence score, computed as above, was divided by the square root of the number of words in the sentence to give a "corrected" score. The procedure slightly favored selection of longer sentences. On the other hand, when more than 10% of the sentences of a document exceeded 40 words in length, the unmodified scoring procedure was employed once again. Thus, the overall effect of these procedures was to give a slight preference for selection to sentences whose lengths were in the range 26–40 words (other things being equal).

The above scoring techniques were based on the assumption that words whose frequency exceeded the average word frequency within the document were "representative." This assumption was made when 48% to 56% of a document consisted of function words.[24] When the percent of function words in a document fell outside this range, special treatment of the document was effected. When there were more than 56% function words in a document, the list of potentially representative words was reduced by deleting all words whose frequency of occurrence was greater than 1% of the word-token count for the document.

If there was less than 48% of function words in a document and the document contained more than 35% of unit frequency words, those words were chosen as representative whose frequency of occurrence was less than or equal to the average word frequency for the document.

Once all sentences in a document had been scored, a set of sentences which were potentially members of the abstract were selected as follows [34]:

> The number of sentences in the document is divided by ten. If the quotient is more than 20, 20 is subtracted from the result and the remainder is divided by 32. The number of sentences in the abstract is this quotient plus 20. If the document has [fewer] than 200 sentences, the abstract has 10 percent of the total number of sentences.

The n sentences with highest scores were designated as "abstract sentences" and the $n/4$ sentences with the next highest scores were called "reserve sentences." Word-tokens were consolidated by a process analogous to Luhn's method following which the "abstract sentences" were examined for possible redundancy. Two sentences were con-

---

[24] Function words are those words not included in one of the classes: noun, verb, adjective, adverb. It is emphasized that there must be maintained a clear distinction between *function word* and *nonsubstantive* words.

sidered to be redundant if they contained a number of matching words which was greater than $\frac{1}{4}$ the total number of words compared in the two sentences. Highly redundant sentences were deleted and were replaced by sentences from the "reserve sentence" set. This process was continued until more redundant "abstract sentences" were found or until the set of "reserve sentences" was exhausted. The sentences that were in the set of "abstract sentences" at the end of this process constituted the computer-produced abstract.

The ACSI-Matic study thus employed several interesting criteria for selecting sentences from a document to form an abstract. The computational complexity of the algorithms necessary to perform the tasks outlined above is clearly considerable, and the selection criteria have not been validated.

The Oswald Study. The essential distinction of the Oswald study [23] is that he employed an *indexing* criterion in the selection of sentences to form an abstract. This indexing criterion was that groups of words, as well as single words, should be index entries. Consequently, Oswald chose sentences for an abstract that scored high in the number of "representative" word groupings they contained. Representativeness was determined in a manner similar to that employed by Luhn {25}.

Oswald's procedure involved the following steps [23].

1. Determine the count of the tokens of only those words which are significant in the context of the document.
2. Next, identify the highest frequency words and note words adjacent to them which had a frequency of occurrence greater than one. Such juxtaposed words formed "multiterms."
3. Identify those sentences which contain two or more multiterms, rank them in descending order of multiterms and select some number of the highest ranked sentences according to some prescribed criterion for the length of the abstract.

Since Oswald did not have a computer at his disposal, he was obliged to use human simulation of these procedures for his study. And when one considers that the identification of words "significant in the context of the document" entailed a subjective judgment, these procedures could not readily be implemented directly on a computer. Nevertheless, the study is significant for three reasons:

1. for its recognition of the relationship between an index and an abstract;
2. for its realization that an abstract represents, at least in part, an attempt to concentrate the essence of a document as much as possible;
3. for its recognition of the fact that word strings of length greater than 1 (multiterms) are important in determining sentence significance.

Word Association Research. The significance of word association studies is that they further emphasize the importance of word clusters (a fact already emphasized above) in conveying an author's intent. Doyle [35, 36], Bernier and Heumann [37], Quillian [38], and others have attempted to represent a measure of semantic information content (i.e., the measure of some textual structure's value in conveying an author's intent) through the use of special representations of language.

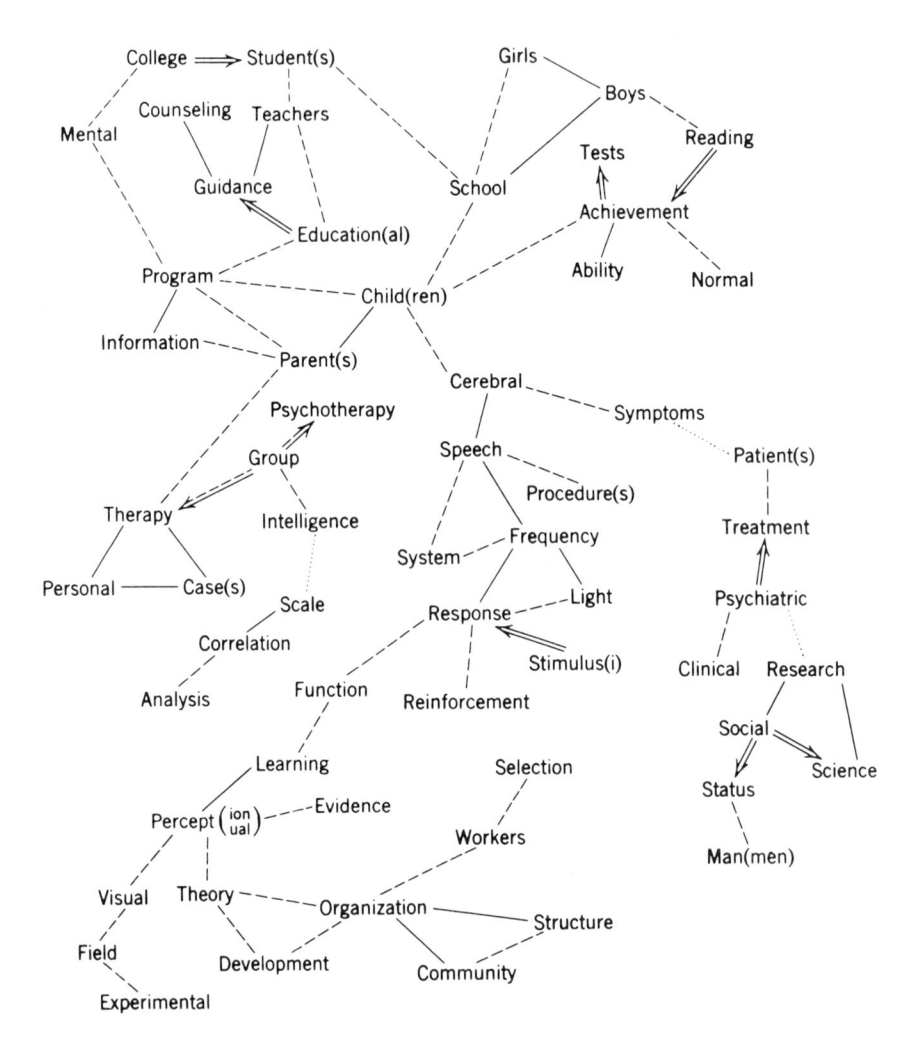

Fig. 7. Typical association map of Doyle, based on Pearson correlation coefficients. (Reproduced from Amer. Doc. [36] by permission of the American Society for Information Science.)

Doyle's *association map* concept is based upon statistical association criteria and a map could, therefore, be produced by computer program. The method for generating an association map involves the creation of an $n \times n$ correlation matrix ($n =$ number of keywords to be correlated), and the correlation of the matrix elements, by means of the Pearson correlation coefficient [36], for co-occurrence of keywords in individual documents.[25] A portion of a typical association map is shown in Fig. 7. Links between nodes (words) show the word associations. The numbers beside the links indicate the strength of the associations (i.e., the values of the Pearson correlation coefficient).

[25] In one experiment, Doyle [36] employed the document collection and corresponding index terms (keywords) already employed in another connection by Borko and Bernick [39].

Abstracting

Arrows indicate that word co-occurrence is due mainly to a two-word term; the arrows point to the second word of the term.

Doyle envisioned the use of an association map as an associatively organized index which would facilitate the operation of a combined man–machine searching system. But the association map derived from a single document represents a *telegraphic abstract* in which an attempt has been made to indicate term relations through statistical association.

Quillian's work is superficially similar to that of Doyle, but in the generation of what one might call "semantic maps" Quillian makes the associations intellectually rather than statistically. These semantic maps constitute a memory model which Quillian later employed in studies of human-like language behavior [38]. The significance of this work for abstracting lies in the strong emphasis on *relations* between words (concepts) rather than on the words alone. Although the details of this work cannot be treated here, the reader is referred to any of several good papers for this purpose [40–42].

In addition to the two works cited, Bernier and Heumann [37], and more recently Avramescu [43] and Fugmann *et al.* [44], have emphasized the importance of specifying both words and relations between words in indexes and abstracts. Nevertheless, there has been no concerted effort to use semantic structure as a basis for creating abstracts of original documents. But since abstracting is fundamentally a matter of semantic content abstraction, it is reasonable to expect that studies along the lines of the investigations mentioned here would be of value in the computer-based production of abstracts.

The TRW Study (Edmundson and Wyllys). The objectives of the TRW study in computer-based abstracting were twofold: the development, first, of an abstracting system to produce indicative abstracts, and second, of a research methodology which would permit new text and new abstracting criteria to be handled efficiently [24, 45–48]. The research methodology comprised a study of the abstracting behavior of humans, a general formulation of the abstracting problem and its relation to the problem of evaluation, a mathematical and logical study of the problem of evaluation, a mathematical and logical study of the problem of assigning numerical weights to sentences, and a set of abstracting experiments employing a cycle of implementation, testing, and improvement. The research concerned with the abstracting behavior of humans has already been discussed in the section entitled Selection and Consistency.

The evaluation of the quality of abstracts produced by any system is necessary in order to make improvements in that system. The TRW group considered five methods of evaluation [24].

1. Intuitive value judgement.
2. Creation of "ideal" abstracts to serve as standards of comparison.
3. Construction of college-type test questions on the document to be answered from abstracts by a sample population (evaluation of the summary function of an abstract).
4. Retrievability of the document via the abstract (evaluation of the retrieval function of an abstract).
5. Statistical correlations (applicable only to extracts).

Method 2 was implemented early in the research with the results giving an indication of how "human-like" the selection of sentences is. The method was not considered a final evaluation of abstracts, but only a rough indication of agreement with human selection of sentences. This method served primarily as a rejection test for abstracts which were little better than a random selection of sentences. Evaluation methods 4 and 5 were implemented later in the research to indicate areas of content improvement.

The TRW study developed a logical, mathematical method for the assignment of numerical weights to sentences. This study showed that there is considerable potential in a set of four methods of sentence selection which they called the Cue, Key, Title, and Location methods. These methods can be described, briefly, as follows [48].

The *Cue* method makes use of a list of words which are classified as bonus words (those that have a positive value, or weight, in sentence selection), stigma words (words that have a negative weight), and null words (those words which are irrelevant to sentence selection).

The *Key* method is based on the frequency of occurrence of words, and is similar in approach to the method used by Luhn in his pioneering study.

The *Title* method is based on a glossary of the words of the title and subtitles (excluding null words). Sentences containing words that also occur in the title are assigned a higher weight either than sentences which contain words that occur also in a subtitle, or sentences which have no such words (other things being equal).

The *Location* method is based on the hypothesis that certain headings precede important passages and that topic sentences occur early or late in a document or paragraph. This later was also Baxendale's hypothesis, resulting from observations made in her studies of automatic indexing [26]. These four methods are summarized in Table 3.

In the final system the relative weights among the four basic methods were parameterized in terms of the linear function

$$a_1 C + a_2 K + a_3 T + a_4 L$$

where a_1, a_2, a_3, and a_4 are the parameters (positive integers) for the Cue, Key, Title,

TABLE 3

Rationale of Four Basic Sentence Selection Methods Employed by Edmundson[a]

Linguistic sources of clues	Structural sources of clues	
	Body of document (text)	Skeleton of document (title, headings, format)
General characteristics of corpus	Cue method cue dictionary (995 words) (includes bonus, stigma, and null subdictionaries)	Location method heading dictionary (90 words) (location method also uses ordinal weights)
Specific characteristics of document	Key method key glossary	Title method title glossary

[a] Reproduced from *J. Ass. Comput. Mach.* [48] by permission.

Abstracting

and Location weights, respectively. The mean percentages of coselection of sentences from the ideal abstract and the test document for the most interesting methods are shown in Fig. 8, with the intervals encompassing the sample mean plus and minus one sample standard deviation. The Cue–Title–Location method is seen to have the highest mean coselection score, while the Key method in isolation is the poorer of the methods. On the basis of these data, it was decided to omit the Key method as a component in the preferred abstracting process. An example of an abstract produced by use of the combination of the Cue, Title, and Location methods in shown in Fig. 9.

The results of the research at TRW indicated that abstracts can be defined, indentified, and produced in a computer-based system. They concluded that future abstracting methods must take into account syntactic and semantic characteristics of the language and the text; they could not have relied simply upon gross statistical evidence. Edmundson concluded that the major task of any further research would be to indentify and define the differences between manual and computer-produced abstracts and to minimize these differences so that computer-produced abstracts can supplement, and perhaps compete with, traditional ones [48].

The Earl Study. The investigation of computer-based informative abstracting and extracting performed by Earl and her associates at Lockheed Missiles and Space Company has been aimed at basic research in English morphology, phonetics, and syntax [49–53]. This study, which has been supported by the Office of Naval Research since 1964, has dealt with basic linguistic research as a necessary prerequisite to the production of abstracts by computer.

During the first three years of the program, a word-data base was established. This data base along with a part-of-speech algorithm was used to provide an algorithmic determination of the parts of speech of written English words. The parts of speech were later used to determine if there existed any linguistic similarity between sentences that

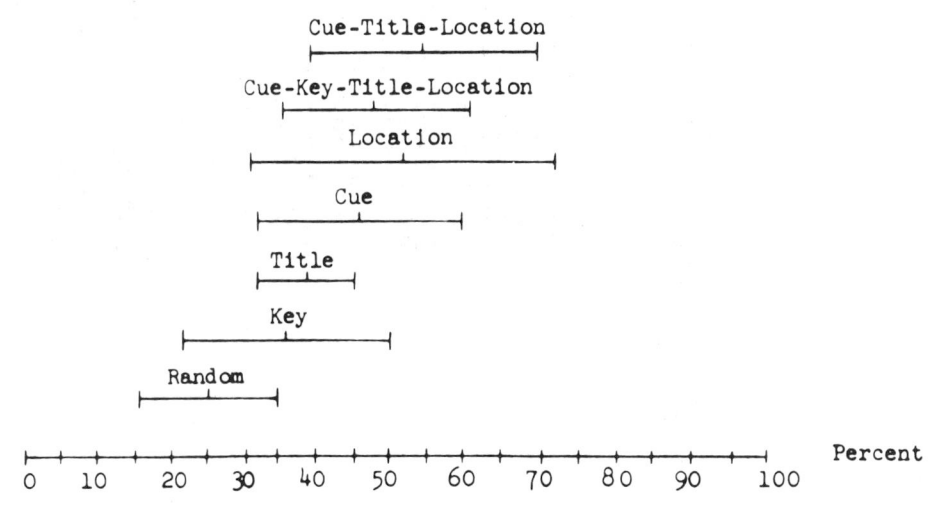

Fig. 8. Mean coselection scores obtained from the sentence selection methods employed by Edmundson. (Reproduced from *J. Ass. Comput. Mach.* [48] by permission.)

EVALUATION OF THE EFFECT OF DIMETHYLAMINE BORINE AND SEVERAL OTHER ADDITIVES ON COMBUSTION STABILITY CHARACTERISTICS OF VARIOUS HYDROCARBON TYPE FUELS IN PHILLIPS MICROBURNER (AD87730)
R. L. BRACE

ABSTRACT BASED ON CUE TITLE LOC. WTS.

1	0	SUMMARY
2	1	AT THE REQUEST OF THE NAVY BUREAU OF AERONAUTICS, PHILLIPS PETROLEUM COMPANY UNDERTOOK THE EVALUATION OF DIMETHYLAMINE BORINE AS AN ADDITIVE FOR IMPROVING THE COMBUSTION CHARACTERISTICS OF AVIATION GAS TURBINE TYPE FUELS.
2	2	BECAUSE OF THE SMALL AMOUNT (100 GRAMS) OF DIMETHYLAMINE BORINE RECEIVED FROM CALLERY CHEMICAL COMPANY, THIS EVALUATION HAS BEEN LIMITED TO THE MEASUREMENT OF ITS EFFECT ON THE FLASH-BACK CHARACTERISTICS OF THREE PURE HYDROCARBONS (TOLUENE, NORMAL HEPTANE AND BENZENE) IN THE PHILLIPS MICROBURNER.
3	2	PREVIOUS STUDIES IN PHILLIPS 2 INCH TURBOJET ENGINE TYPE COMBUSTOR HAD INDICATED THAT SUCH MATERIALS COULD SUBSTANTIALLY INCREASE THE MAXIMUM RATE OF HEAT RELEASE ATTAINABLE, ESPECIALLY WITH LOW PERFORMANCE FUELS SUCH AS THE ISO PARAFFIN TYPE HYDROCARBONS—PARTICULARLY WHEN OPERATING UNDER SEVERE CONDITIONS FOR COMBUSTION (I.E., HIGH AIR FLOW VELOCITY OR LOW COMBUSTION PRESSURE).
4	1	THE ASSUMPTION HAS BEEN MADE IN THIS FUEL EVALUATION THAT THE GREATER THE ALLOWABLE HEAT INPUT RATE FOR A GIVEN VELOCITY, THE GREATER THE DEGREE OF COMBUSTION STABILITY.
4	2	ON THIS BASIS, THE DATA INDICATE THAT ALL THE ADDITIVE MATERIALS TESTED CAUSED AN INCREASE IN STABILITY PERFORMANCE., A FUEL OF RELATIVELY LOW PERFORMANCE SUCH AS TOLUENE BEING BENEFITED TO A GREATER EXTENT THAN A HIGH PERFORMANCE FUEL SUCH AS NORMAL HEPTANE.
4	5	IN GENERAL, ADDITIVE CONCENTRATIONS OF ONE PER CENT BY WEIGHT IN THE SEVERAL PURE HYDROCARBONS WHICH NORMALLY DIFFERED QUITE WIDELY IN PERFORMANCE, PRODUCED UNIFORMLY SUPERIOR COMBUSTION STABILITY CHARACTERISTICS AS MEASURED USING THE PHILLIPS MICROBURNER.
3	0	I. INTRODUCTION
6	1	AT THE REQUEST OF THE NAVY BUREAU OF AERONAUTICS THE JET FUELS GROUP HAS EVALUATED THE EFFECTS OF THE ADDITION OF SMALL AMOUNTS OF DIMETHYLAMINEBORIN =S ON THE COMBUSTION STABILITY PERFORMANCE OF SEVERAL HYDROCARBON FUELS.
7	1	DUE TO THE SMALL QUANTITY OF THIS MATERIAL OBTAINED THE EVALUATION WAS CONDUCTED IN THE PHILLIPS MICROBURNER (MODEL 1A) WHICH IS A SLIGHTLY MODIFIED VERSION OF THE ORIGINAL PHILLIPS MICROBURNER (MODEL 1).
8	0	II. DESCRIPTION OF PHILLIPS MICROBURNER (MODEL 1A)

10	0	III. DESCRIPTION OF TEST APPARATUS
14	0	IV. DESCRIPTION OF TEST FUELS
17	0	V. TEST PROCEDURE
21	0	VI. RESULTS
25	0	VII. DISCUSSION
29	1	PREVIOUS WORK CONDUCTED IN THE PHILLIPS 2 INCH COMBUSTOR (REF. 2) INDICATED THAT SOME ADDITIVES CAUSED A SIGNIFICANT INCREASE IN THE PERFORMANCE OF A LOW RATING FUEL WHILE THESE SAME ADDITIVES DID NOT SUBSTANTIALLY EFFECT THE HIGHER RATING FUELS.
31	3	ALL FOUR ADDITIVES INDICATED THEIR ADDITION TO BE SUBJECT TO THE EFFECT OF DEMINISHING RESULTS UPON FURTHER ADDITION—THAT IS, THEIR EFFECT WAS NOT ESSENTIALLY A BLENDING EFFECT.
33	0	VIII. CONCLUSIONS
34	1	1. THE ADDITION OF DIMETHYLAMINE BORINE IN CONCENTRATIONS OF ONE PER CENT BY WEIGHT TO JET FUEL TYPE HYDROCARBONS RESULTED IN A UNIFORMLY HIGH LEVEL OF COMBUSTION STABILITY PERFORMANCE AS MEASURED BY PHILLIPS MICROBURNER.
35	1	2. THE ADDITION OF RELATIVELY LARGE AMOUNTS OF PROPYLENE OXIDE TO TOLUENE WERE NECESSARY TO PROVIDE SIGNIFICANT IMPROVEMENT IN STABILITY PERFORMANCE AS INDICATED BY INCREASES IN ALLOWABLE HEAT INPUT RATES.
36	1	3. THE ADDITION OF ADDITIVE CONCENTRATIONS (UP TO 1 PER CENT) OF AMYL NITRATE, CUMENE HYDROPEROXIDE, AND DIMETHYLAMINE BORINE ALL RESULTED IN IMPROVED STABILITY PERFORMANCE. THE GREATEST INCREASES WERE SHOWN WHEN BLENDED WITH A FUEL OF POOR PERFORMANCE CHARACTERISTICS—SUCH AS TOLUENE.
37	0	IX. RECOMMENDATIONS
38	1	BASED ON THE EVALUATION OF THE EFFECTS OF ADDITIVES ON THE FLASHBACK LIMITS OF THE ADDITIVE-FUEL BLENDS TESTED IN THE MICROBURNER (MODEL 1A) IT IS RECOMMENDED THAT DIMETHYLAMINE BORINE SHOULD BE FURTHER INVESTIGATED.
38	2	THIS FUTURE WORK SHOULD INCLUDE STUDY OF COMBUSTION STABILITY AND COMBUSTION EFFICIENCY EFFECTS IN THE PHILLIPS 2 INCH COMBUSTOR AND AN INVESTIGATION OF ITS INFLUENCE ON COMBUSTION CLEANLINESS.

Fig. 9. An abstract produced by use of the combination of the Cue, Title, and Location methods.

were used for abstracts. Also, during these years, it was demonstrated how an English–Russian phrase data base can be used to develop a technique for obtaining English indexes from untranslated Russian text.

During the third and fourth years of the project, experiments in the compilation of a "sentence dictionary" of syntactic types began and compilation of English syntactic word government tables was undertaken. The hypothesis which the sentence dictionary was used to support, states that if a large group of sentences, as representative of the language as possible, are processed, classified as "indexable" or "nonindexable," and assigned a syntactic structure, then when these structures are sorted, it will be found that like structures have like index classifications. The structures can be ordered into a "dictionary" of sentence types, each classified as indexable or nonindexable. When sentences from a document which is to be abstracted are matched against the sentence dictionary, those sentences which are indexable would be candidates for inclusion in the index or in the abstract. Table 4 shows the results of experiments designed to test this hypothesis.

Based on this data, it seemed clear that representing a sentence by part-of-speech strings made too fine a distinction between sentences. The sentences were then structured into phrases, to cause sentences of like phrase structure to be grouped. The phrase structure approach to syntactic patterns gave impetus to development of English syntactic word government tables. These word government tables contained entries which reflected the fact that a word's government pattern is often linked with its semantic meaning, that is, syntactic pattern is a clue to semantic meaning. Experiments were devised to test the applicability of the phrase to computer-based abstracting. The data obtained from these experiments is shown in Table 5 [51]. From these experiments, it

TABLE 4

Statistics of Part-of-Speech Patterns in Text [50]

Item	\multicolumn{4}{c}{Number of chapters in data base}
	3	6	8	9
1. Number of total patterns represented by more than one sentence	18	25	31	34
2. Number of total patterns represented by more than one sentence, with a consistent index code	14	15	21	23
3. Number of total duplicated patterns common to more than one article	3	6	8	12
4. Number of total duplicated patterns common to more than one article, with a consistent index code	2	3	4	5
5. Number of one-of-a-kind patterns	1198	2425	2822	3064
6. Number of total unique patterns	1216	2450	2853	3098
7. Ratio of the number of one-of-a-kind patterns to number of total unique patterns	0.985	0.989	0.989	0.992

TABLE 5

Comparison of Part-of-Speech and Phrase Patterns

Item	Part-of-speech patterns	Phrase patterns
1. Number of total patterns represented by more than one sentence	34	35
2. Number of total patterns represented by more than one sentence with a consistent index code	23	15
3. Number of total duplicated patterns common to more than one article	12	26
4. Number of total duplicated patterns common to more than one article, with a consistent index code	5	11
5. Number of one-of-a-kind patterns	3064	3026
6. Number of total unique patterns	3098	3061
7. Ratio of the number of one-of-a-kind patterns to number of total unique patterns	0.992	0.988

was concluded that both the part-of-speech and the phrase-pattern methods of syntactic classifications are inadequate to separate indexable from nonindexable sentences. The experimental results shown in Table 5 indicate that there are far too many unique patterns and that the consistency of index codes tends to decrease with the number of unique patterns. Based on these results, it was concluded that indexable and nonindexable sentences cannot be distinguished by structure alone.

During the fifth year of the project, Earl and associates developed a parsing program, initiated some extracting experiments on technical text, and experimented with automatic indexing of a medical book. In the sixth year, the sentence dictionary experiment was concluded, the extracting experiment was completed, a frequency-syntax method of indexing was conceived and tested, and the concept of English syntactic word government was expanded while compilation of the tables continued. During the seventh year, the scope of the parsing program was extended, preparatory to additional indexing experiments using syntax in conjunction with frequency counts or word government criteria. Also, during this period, some studies in describing and abstracting pictorial structures were undertaken. A critical review of the field was prepared and a series of experiments using human subjects to describe aerial terrain photographs was conducted.

While some interesting experimental data have been obtained by Earl *et al.*, it appears that they are no closer to a system for computer-based abstracting than when the study began.

The Rush Study. The approach taken by Rush, Salvador, and Zamora [11] to the creation of abstracts by computer is interesting in that it consists mainly of criteria for rejecting sentences [54]. In other studies the emphasis has been on criteria for selecting abstract-worthy sentences. In this study, all sentences of the original document that are not rejected are included in the abstract for that document. Some transformations are applied to the sentences of the extract, so this system is also of interest because it produces abstracts which more closely resemble abstracts that are prepared manually.

The automatic abstracting system developed by Rush, Salvador, and Zamora consists basically of a dictionary, called the Word Control List (WCL), and a set of rules for implementing certain functions specified for each WCL entry. This combination of rules and dictionary has been designed and implemented to accomplish the production of indicative abstracts which have been characterized as follows [11].

1. Their size is approximately 10% of the original document, and the use of arbitrary cut-off criteria is avoided.
2. They use the same technical terminology as in the document.
3. Except for actual results, they contain no numbers or cardinal expressions.
4. Unconventional or rare characters or abbreviations are excluded.
5. Preliminary remarks, equations, footnotes, references, quotations, tables, charts, figures, graphs, descriptive cataloging data and the like are not included.
6. Negative results, unless they are the sole results, are excluded.
7. They do not contain methodologies of data gathering, measurements, or preparation of samples, unless these are the purpose of the work.
8. No examples, explanations, speculative statements, opinions, or comparisons are included.

These are mainly things to be excluded from the abstract. On the positive side the abstract may include

9. Objectives of the work.
10. Methods used in the work (if they are the main purpose of the investigation).
11. Results and conclusions.

To automatically produce abstracts with these characteristics, various methods of sentence handling are used.

The exclusion of sentences from the abstract involves the deletion of words or strings of words which identify sentences giving historical data, results of previous work, examples, explanations, speculative material, and so on. Rush, Salvador, and Zamora claim that a few hundred word strings could serve to eliminate a high percentage of the sentences of a document. Such word strings were incorporated into the WCL.

The WCL consists of an alphabetically ordered set of words and phrases, which are referred to collectively as word strings. The entries in the WCL are treated as functions and each has two arguments: a semantic weight and a syntactic value. Each function returns a value which indicates whether the sentence is a candidate for retention or deletion. Such a dictionary organization makes it possible to change entries without necessitating any changes in the rest of the system.

The semantic weight of a WCL entry may be either positive or negative; it may cause the sentence to be retained or deleted. Most WCL entries have negative semantic weights, but the system allows a few notable exceptions. Some word strings have semantic clues which indicate that the sentence should be retained. For example, when the author of a document includes in a sentence a word string such as "this paper,"

Abstracting

"this study," or "present work," it is assumed that these phrases indicate that he is about to say what the document is all about. In addition, sentences which contain personal pronouns such as "we," "I," or "our," seem good candidates for retention. Also, sentences which contain significant title words and which do not contain word strings having strongly negative semantic weights are retained. These are the only instances in which a sentence is deliberately retained, although a small number of sentences of the document may be retained by default for inclusion in the abstract.

The semantic weights from the WCL are implemented using a set of rules. The rules are applied in a fixed order which provides a hierarchy among the various semantic weights. Once a word string has been identified and the semantic weight has indicated whether the sentence should be kept or deleted, its further processing is unnecessary. Flexibility was obtained by incorporating the rules in the program and supplying the semantic weights externally. Thus, the rules could be altered without the necessity for changing the WCL, and the WCL could be altered independently of the rules. (There are, however, a few exceptions to the general independence of rules and semantic weights which are implemented entirely within the program.)

Since the implementation of the semantic weights requires some syntactic information, a partial syntactic analysis of each sentence is performed. This analysis is carried out through use of the syntactic values associated with entries in the WCL, in conjunction with procedures implemented within the program. Principal use of the syntactic values is made in an analysis of the commas in a sentence. In order to utilize contextual inferences, three types of comma are distinguished [numerical commas (e.g., 3,462) are masked at input]: (1) commas which separate phrases, called "real" commas; (2) commas which separate the elements of a series, called "serial" commas; and (3) commas which set off dependent clauses, called "parenthetical" commas. Parenthetical commas cause the phrase or clause they isolate to be deleted. Serial commas are masked during processing to prevent their being confused with real commas, but are restored at output. Real commas delimit phrases or independent clauses and this information is used in impiementing some semantic rules and some transformations for restructuring sentences.

The abstracts obtained from this system appear to be of fair quality. An example of an abstract produced by this system is given in Fig. 10 and other examples may be found in Ref. 60. Further improvements and large-scale testing of the system are being planned. The results of research carried out so far indicate that abstracts can be produced automatically at costs comparable to the cost of those produced manually, although economic feasibility can only be accurately ascertained through large-scale testing. Abstracts produced by this system have generally been an 80 to 90% reduction of text without using the length of the abstract as a criterion in the abstracting algorithm and without any between-article modification of the WCL. According to the authors, the small size of the WCL (700 entries) is due, in large part, to the fact that it is possible to reject sentences by referring to a small list of frequently occurring words, whereas selection of sentences requires a long list of "desirable" words.

Rush, Salvador, and Zamora claim that one of the main advantages of their system is that its processing programs are text-independent. Abstracts of papers written in any language which is structurally similar to English could be obtained merely by substitution of the appropriate WCL. The system design also lends itself to a more formal characterization and such a formalization is being developed [55]. Another advantage

Together with the increasing shortage of qualified abstractors, the factors of time, cost and value have lent impetus to a trend toward the automatic generation of abstracts and indexes. This trend has caused increased emphasis to be placed on the abstract as the locus of data for automatic retrieval systems. This necessitates the creation of high quality abstracts. It is the purpose of this paper to report on the development of techniques for the automatic production of high quality abstracts from the full text of the original document. It is necessary to analyze the conditions under which various methods of sentence selection are successful, in order to develop criteria for selecting sentences to form an abstract. But clearly, an abstract can also be produced by rejecting sentences of the original which are irrelevant to the abstract. As will be seen, it is this point which is perhaps the most significant contribution of this paper. Methods of sentence selection and rejection are discussed. These include contextual inference, intersentence reference, frequency criteria, and coherency considerations. The automatic abstracting system we have developed consists basically of a dictionary, called the Word Control List, and of a set of rules for implementing certain functions specified for each WCL entry. The abstracts we have obtained so far are of sufficiently good quality to indicate that large-scale testing of the methods of the automatic abstracting system is warranted.†

Fig. 10. Example of an abstract produced by the system of Rush, Salvador, and Zamora. (Reproduced from *J. Amer. Soc. Inform. Sci.* [11] by permission.)

claimed for the system is that it is possible, through deliberate variation of the WCL, to produce abstracts which have a particular bias. Such user-directed, or tailor-made, abstracts should prove useful for many specialized information applications or services. This aspect of the system is also being investigated.

The Soviet Study. E. F. Skoroxod'ko is carrying on research in automatic abstracting at the Academy of Sciences of the Ukranian SSR in Kiev, USSR [56, 57]. His research is based on the assumption that only a method of automatic abstracting which adapts itself to a text can provide good and stable results. This assumption is based on the belief that a given text has individual characteristics and that the optimal selection criteria and abstracting procedure should be determined based on those characteristics.

The individual characteristics of a given text are defined by the form of a semantic network which represents the text. A semantic network is defined to be a graph where the nodes are associated with sentences and the arcs are associated with semantic relations between sentences. Two sentences, A and B, are said to be semantically related if (1) at least one noun occurs in both sentences A and B, or (2) sentence A contains a word "a" and sentence B contains a word "b" where "a" and "b" have been predefined as being semantically related, or (3) when words "a" and "b" in sentences A and B

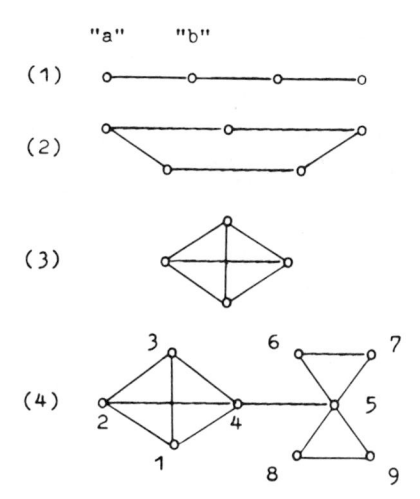

Fig. 11. Semantic structure types employed in the Soviet study: (1) chained, (2) ringed, (3) monolithic, and (4) piecewise. (Reproduced from *IFIP Congress 71* [57] by permission of North Holland Publishing Co.)

are related with respect to a given text. The graphs of the semantic structures can be identified in terms of four important types which are shown in Fig. 11. The selection of an appropriate abstracting procedure is based on the type of semantic structure.

The significance of each sentence is assumed to be directly proportional to the number of sentences which are semantically related to it. Thus, nodes in the graph which have the most incident arcs are defined to be the most significant. The sentence significance also depends upon the amount of change in the semantic network for that document when the node for that sentence is removed from the network. The general significance of a sentence is determined using the following formula:

$$F_i = N_i(M - M_i^H)$$

where F_i is the functional weight of a sentence in text; N_i is the number of arcs incident to a node associated with a given sentence (i.e., the number of sentences semantically related to a given sentence); M is the total number of nodes in a sentence network (i.e., the number of sentences in a text); M_i^H is the maximum number of nodes in any connected component of a network after removal of a node associated with a given sentence (i.e., the number of sentences in the longest connected fragment of text formed after the removal of a given sentence).

Based on this measure, Skoroxod'ko concludes that in the case of chained or ringed structure networks, it is impossible to form an adequate extract from sentences taken from the text since all sentences have approximately the same semantic value. Automatic abstracts can only be generated from texts where semantic relationships can be depicted as monolithic or piecewise structures.

Skoroxod'ko presents only one of the procedures developed for the adaptable process [56]. There are the following seven operations, with operations 6 and 7 being optional.

1. The determination of functional weights of all sentences in a text.
2. The compression of a text, i.e., the removal of sentences which have functional weights considerably less than the average functional weight of sentences throughout the text. Such sentences are generally examples, explanations, etc.
3. The segmentation of a text, i.e., its selection into segments which are relatively autonomous in semantic and informational aspects. A section begins with a sentence whose linear coefficient is less than a definite critical value.
4. The selection of one or more sentences with maximum functional weight in each segment. A set of such sentences forms an abstract of the text (extract).
5. The determination of functional weights of words in an abstract.
6. The removal of words with minimal functional weights from an abstract.
7. The translation of an abstract into an information retrieval language (if necessary for information retrieval).

The approach taken by Skoroxod'ko relies heavily on the co-occurrence of words in the text and the matching of words to synonym definitions in the dictionary. The quality of the abstracts would then appear to be greatly dependent on the construction of the dictionary, which is manually produced. Skoroxod'ko's publication [56] does not include any sample abstracts produced by this system or any mention of evaluation procedures. Thus, although the theory appears to be well developed, it is not possible to ascertain the practical effectiveness of this method.

Conclusion

In concluding our discussion of computer-based abstracting, it is noteworthy that no system so far developed has been brought to a stage of readiness for use in a production environment. The reasons for this, we believe, are twofold: excessive cost and rather poor quality of the product. In all fairness, however, we point out that the main concern of the designers of the various systems we have discussed (save, perhaps, for the ACSI-Matic system) was the testing of various ideas for computer-based abstracting. Efficiency, therefore, suffered; hence costs are not easily treated in a meaningful way.

On the other hand, the quality of abstracts produced can be treated, if not more meaningfully, at least more fairly. The problems which have plagued researchers in computer-based abstracting, as well as in all other areas of text processing, may all be thought of as language problems. That is to say, the problems are either of a semantic (interpretive) nature or of a syntactic (physical) nature. We shall close this section with a few remarks on semantics and syntax, particularly as they are related to computer-based abstracting, and on evaluation of computer-produced abstracts.

Syntax

It is difficult to effect a clear distinction between syntax and semantics, but we shall attempt such a distinction, nevertheless. What we include under the umbrella of syntax are morphology, spatial relationships, and other physical features of a string in a language which we shall call "sentence." What we are confronted with here are problems of recognition of physical objects by computer program.

Abstracting 479

One of the first problems to be dealt with is that of sentence recognition. In the absence of special pre-editing procedures, sentence identification by computer program is at present at best problematic. It is no good to say that a sentence begins with a capital letter and ends with a period, because Dr., Mr., No., and so on satisfy such a criterion. Adding the requirement that two spaces must follow the period is no help either. Errors are much too likely in such situations, and the fact remains that a string of words is a sentence or not regardless of the number of spaces between successive ones. How about other definitions? Say, for example, a sentence is any sequence of words that contains one and only one predicate (verb). Or, a sentence is any sequence of words that can be parsed successfully by some phrase-structure grammar. Even if we suppose that such definitions are adequate, they are computationally horrible, and both require foreknowledge of the grammatical classes to which the words belong.

Grammatical class determination is itself an ill-defined process [58]. The problem here is one of adequate definition of a class (for instance, what is a *noun*?) as well as adequate definition of the location or locations within a sentence that such a class can occupy. And of course, the identification, within a sentence, of phrases and clauses (a necessary condition for the proper functioning of the Rush, Salvador, and Zamora abstracting system, for instance) hinges upon the identification of sentence boundaries and of word classes within a sentence.

Syntactic considerations extend beyond sentence boundaries—not that they must, but the text which avoided the use of "extended syntax" would be tedious and boring, at best. But the techniques for dealing with intersentence relatedness and of producing abstracts in which the sets of sentences constitute smooth-flowing documents are nonexistent. To produce an abstract which does not have the appearance of a set of random thoughts is essential if computer-produced abstracts are ever to gain wide acceptance (regardless of their cost).

All these problems and more must be resolved before computer-produced abstracts of acceptable quality can be obtained. We suggest that one approach to solution of these problems is to stop attempting to emulate human behavior (which is not necessarily the "best" behavior) and to develop instead some concrete definitions upon which efficient and effective algorithms may be built.

Semantics

"'When I use a word,' Humpty Dumpty said, in rather a scornful tone, 'it means just what I choose it to mean—neither more nor less'." (See Ref. 59.)

Lewis Carroll, to use a popular turn of phrase, " said it all" in that one expressive passage. No word has any meaning save that imputed to it by someone. If the someone is an author, the imputation is called "intention"; on the part of the reader the imputation is called "interpretation." Much ado has been made of ambiguity of meaning. Great debate has raged over the "meaning" of sentences like

Flying planes can be dangerous.
The hungry dog turned on the spit.

Ambiguity arises as a consequence of two factors:

1. the multiplicity of intentions and/or interpretations which are associated with a language unit;
2. the inability of the reader to reduce (at least within some specified interval of time) the number of alternative interpretations to just one interpretation.

Ambiguity is not all bad. Humor could not do without it. And neither could most authors or readers, who find in ambiguity a harmless smokescreen behind which to hide incomplete knowledge of a subject. But ambiguity cannot be eliminated whatever its worth might be, because a given utterance in a language is interpreted, not *in vacuo*, but in the context of a rather complex environment and on the basis of experience. That is to say, interpretation is a purely individualistic thing. Thus, ambiguity can be removed only in the sense that when one interprets an utterance there remains no ambiguity, at that instant, for him. What is usually meant by ambiguity is that for a given utterance, ten readers (hearers) will give ten different interpretations of it. Nothing short of homocide will serve to remove that ambiguity.

We must leave resolution of ambiguity to the language teacher[26] and concentrate our linguistic endeavors upon the material we have to work with—text.

Evaluation

An unanswered question which has arisen frequently throughout this discussion of automatic abstracting is: How good are the abstracts that are produced by a particular abstracting system? Although we cannot offer a definitive answer to this question, we will try, here, to specify the requirements of an acceptable technique for the evaluation of abstracts.[27]

A major difficulty associated with the evaluation of abstracts and abstracting systems is that the purpose or goals of the product or system are not properly defined. Thus a system is built whose capabilities generally reflect the extent to which the system designer was able to perceive the purpose or goals of the system. As a consequence, the system may produce abstracts acceptable to the user or it may not.

An abstracting system, like any other system, is ultimately judged in the marketplace. If the products of the system are used to the extent that income offsets or exceeds the cost of operating the system, then the system is a success. Otherwise, it is a failure. To know the prospects for success or failure is the purpose of evaluation. Such prospects can unfortunately be known only imperfectly.

There are two distinguishable, but inseparable, areas of evaluation. The first concerns how well the system meets design criteria. These criteria may include such things as minimum acceptable composition of the abstracts produced; minimum and maximum average size of the abstracts; maximum acceptable cost per abstract; maximum allowable time to produce an abstract; maximum allowable preprocessing time; maximum allowable manual editing; maximum allowable recycling of abstracts. Evaluation of such factors is relatively easy, provided each has been adequately defined at the time

---

[26] Or perhaps, to age; since, as Oscar Wilde puts it, "The old believe everything; the middle aged suspect everything; the young know everything."

[27] A good point of departure in the study of evaluation techniques and results is King and Bryant [60]. See also Ref. 9.

of system design. When any of these factors is found to fall outside specified limits, then adjustments in the system are called for. Otherwise, the system may be said to be operating normally.

The second area of evaluation is concerned with user acceptance of the produce of the system. It is this area of evaluation that is most difficult to deal with, because the products of the system are likely to be used by many individuals with diverse interests. Two users may find the abstracts produced by a system acceptable for entirely different reasons. Thus, when the question is put: "What is right or wrong with the abstracts produced by our system?," many different answers may be received which are difficult to categorize as reflecting adequacy or inadequacy. Furthermore, even if an inadequacy is indicated, it may be difficult to determine its nature precisely enough to effect a change in the system which will correct the inadequacy. Not only may users of abstracts produced by a particular system find them acceptable for different reasons, but these users may also vary in their acceptability judgments with time. This is because the user's needs also change with time. It is for all of these reasons that abstracts cannot reliably be evaluated by means of user opinion surveys.

What is needed is a more objective, stable evaluation technique. Let us consider what such a technique entails. We assume that the abstracts produced by an abstracting system are used because the user has some (to him) reasonable expectation that he will be able thereby to satisfy his information need. But if an abstract can satisfy an information need, then it must contain information which is in some degree related to that required by the user. Thus, an abstracting system must produce abstracts which contain (or indicate) information that will satisfy a user's information need, and do so without undue delay or excessive cost to him. It is this basic criterion which the system designer must strive to meet. This means, in turn, that the identification of a well-defined class of user is required and that the intension of the abstracting system will be controlled by the nature of the user group. The intension of the abstracting system will determine the amount and value to the user of the information contained in the abstracts it produces. If the basic criterion is proved operationally to have been met, then the abstracts, and therefore the abstracting system, can be judged adequate. These requirements are difficult, if not impossible, to meet, and it is therefore not surprising that an adequate evaluation scheme has not been developed. Any scheme which is able to define, or approximate well, these parameters will certainly provide valuable direction for the future of automatic abstracting.

ACKNOWLEDGMENT

The authors wish to acknowledge the National Science Foundation for partial support of this work through Grant GN534.1 to the Computer and Information Science Research Center, The Ohio State University.

REFERENCES

1. Abstracting, *Encyclopaedia Britannica*, Vol. 1, Chicago, Ill., 1957, pp. 67–68.
2. B. Weil, Standards for writing abstracts, *J. Amer. Soc. Inform. Sci.* **21** (5), 351–357 (1970).

3. M. G. Mellon, *Chemical Publications; Their Nature and Use*, McGraw-Hill, New York, 1965.
4. F. Bacon, *Novum Organum*, 1620.
5. D. J. de Solla Price, *Science Since Babylon*, Yale University Press, New Haven, Conn., 1961.
6. American Chemical Society, *Handbook for Authors of Papers in the Journals of the American Chemical Society*, American Chemical Society Publication, Washington, D.C., 1967.
7. Chemical Abstracts Service, *Directions for Abstractors*, The Ohio State University, Columbus, Ohio, 1971 revision.
8. R. E. Wyllys, Extracting and abstracting by computer, in *Automated Language Processing* (H. Borko, ed.), Wiley, New York, 1968.
9. R. E. Maizell, J. F. Smith, and T. E. R. Singer, *Abstracting Scientific and Technical Literature*, Wiley-Interscience, New York, 1971.
10. H. Borko and S. Chatman, Criteria for acceptable abstracts: A survey of abstractors' instructions, *Amer. Doc.* **14** (2), 149–160 (1963).
11. J. E. Rush, R. Salvador, and A. Zamora, Automatic abstracting and indexing. II. Production of indicative abstracts by application of contextual inference and syntactic coherence criteria, *J. Amer. Soc. Inform. Sci.* **22** (4), 260–274 (1971).
12. B. C. Landry and J. E. Rush, Toward a theory of indexing, *J. Amer. Soc. Inform. Sci.* **21** (5), 358–367 (1970).
13. *A System of Abstracting and Indexing in the United States*, System Development Corporation, Falls Church, Va., 1966 (PB 174 249).
14. J. E. Hopcroft and J. D. Ullman, *Formal Languages and Their Relation to Automata*, Addison-Wesley, Reading, Mass., 1969.
15. E. J. Crane, ed., *The Production of Chemical Abstracts*, The American Chemical Society, Washington, D.C., 1959.
16. G. K. Zipf, *Human Behavior and the Principle of Least Effort*, Addison-Wesley, Cambridge, Mass., 1949.
17. F. B. Libaw, A new generalized model for information transfer: A systems approach, *Amer. Doc.* **20** (4), 381–384 (1970).
18. Chemical Abstracts Service, *Report on the Fourteenth Chemical Abstracts Service Open Forum*, American Chemical Society, Chicago, Ill., 1970.
19. A. Resnick, Relative effectiveness of document titles and abstracts for determining relevance of documents, *Science* **134** (3484), 1004–1006 (1961).
20. G. J. Rath, A. Resnick, and T. R. Savage, Comparisons of four types of lexical indicators of content, *Amer. Doc.* **12** (2), 126–130 (1961).
21. G. J. Rath, A. Resnick, and T. R. Savage, The formation of abstracts by the selection of sentences. Part I: Sentence selection by men and machines, *Amer. Doc.* **12** (2), 139–141 (1961).
22. A. Resnick, The formation of abstracts by the selection of sentences. Part II: The reliability of people in selecting sentences, *Amer. Doc.* **12** (2), 141–143 (1963).
23. H. P. Edmundson, V. A. Oswald, and R. E. Wyllys, *Automatic Indexing and Abstracting of the Contents of Documents*, Planning Research Corporation, Los Angeles, Calif., prepared for Rome Air Develop. Cen., Air Res. Develop. Command, Griffiss AFB, New York, 1959 (AD 231 606).
24. *Final Report on the Study for Automatic Abstracting*, Thompson Ramo Wooldridge, Inc., Canoga Park, Calif., 1961 (PB 166 532).
25. H. P. Luhn, The automatic creation of literature abstracts, *IBM J. Res. Develop.* **2** (2), 159–165 (1958).
26. P. B. Baxendale, Machine-made index for technical literature—An experiment, *IBM J. Res. Develop.* **2** (4), 354–361 (1958).
27. A. Resnick and T. R. Savage, The consistency of human judgments of relevance, *Amer. Doc.* **15** (2), 93–95 (1964).
28. R. Carnap, *Logical Foundations of Probability*, University of Chicago Press, Chicago, Ill., 1950.
29. W. D. Climenson, N. H. Hardwick, and S. N. Jacobson, Automatic syntax analysis in machine indexing and abstracting, *Amer. Doc.* **12** (2), 178–183 (1961).
30. *Special Report on Optical Character Recognition*, Auerbach Corporation, Philadelphia, Pa., 1971.
31. R. G. Casey and G. Nagy, Advances in pattern recognition, *Sci. Amer.* **224** (4), 56–71 (1971).

32. H. P. Luhn, *An Experiment in Auto-Abstracting*, Auto-Abstract of Area 5 Conference Papers, Int. Conf. Scientific Information, Washington, D.C., IBM Res. Cen., Yorktown Heights, N.Y., 1958.
33. IBM Corporation, Advanced Systems Development Div., *ACSI-Matic Auto-Abstracting Project, Final Rep.*, Vol. 1, Yorktown Heights, N.Y., 1960.
34. IBM Corporation, Advanced Systems Development Div., *ACSI-Matic Auto-Abstracting Project, Final Rep.*, Vol. 3, Yorktown Heights, N.Y., 1961.
35. L. B. Doyle, Semantic road maps for literature searchers, *J. Ass. Comput. Mach.* **8** (4), 553–578 (1961).
36. L. B. Doyle, Indexing and abstracting by association, *Amer. Doc.* **13** (4), 378–390 (1962).
37. C. L. Bernier and K. F. Heumann, Correlative indexes III. Semantic relations among semantemes—The technical thesaurus, *Amer. Doc.* **8** (3), 211–220 (1957).
38. M. R. Quillian, The teachable language comprehender: A simulation program and theory of language, *Commun. Ass. Comput. Mach.* **12** (8), 459–476 (1969).
39. H. Borko and M. Bernick, Automatic document classification, *J. Ass. Comput. Mach.* **19** (2), 151–162 (1963).
40. M. R. Quillian, *A Notation for Representing Conceptual Information; An Application to Semantics and Mechanical English Paraphrasing*, SP-1395, System Development Corporation, Santa Monica, Calif., 1963.
41. M. R. Quillian, Word concepts: A theory and simulation of some basic semantic capabilities, *Behavioral Sci.* **12** (5), 410–430 (1967).
42. M. R. Quillian, Semantic memory, in *Semantic Information Processing* (M. Minsky, ed.), M.I.T. Press, Cambridge, Mass., 1968.
43. A. Avramescu, Probabilistic criteria for the objective design of description languages, *J. Amer. Soc. Inform. Sci.* **22** (2), 85–95 (1971).
44. R. Fugmann, H. Nickelsen, I. Nickelsen, and J. H. Winter, TOSAR—A topological model for the representation of synthetic and analytical relations of concepts, *Angew. Chem. (Int. Ed. in English)* **9** (8), 589–595 (1970).
45. *Appendix "D"—Final Report on the Study for Automatic Abstracting*, Thompson Ramo Wooldridge, Inc., Canoga Park, Calif., 1961 (PB 166 533).
46. H. P. Edmundson and R. E. Wyllys, Automatic abstracting and indexing: Survey and recommendations, *Commun. Ass. Comput. Mach.* **4** (5), 226–235 (1961).
47. H. P. Edmundson, Problems in automatic abstracting, *Commun. Ass. Comput. Mach.* **7** (4), 259–263 (1964).
48. H. P. Edmundson, New methods in automatic extracting, *J. Ass. Comput. Mach.* **16** (2), 264–285 (1969).
49. L. L. Earl, *Automatic Indexing and Abstracting*, Annual Rep., Lockheed Missiles and Space Co., Palo Alto, Calif., 1967 (AD 659 057).
50. L. L. Earl and H. R. Robinson, *Automatic Informative Abstracting and Extracting*, Lockheed Missiles and Space Co., Palo Alto, Calif., 1968 (AD 667 473).
51. L. L. Earl and H. R. Robinson, *Automatic Informative Abstracting and Extracting*, Lockheed Missiles and Space Co., Palo Alto, Calif., 1970 (AD 867 656).
52. L. L. Earl, Experiments in automatic extracting and indexing, *Inform. Stor. Retrieval* **6** (4), 313–334 (1970).
53. L. L. Earl, O. Firschein, and M. A. Fischler, *Automatic Informative Abstracting and Extracting*, Annual Rep. Lockheed Missiles and Space Co., Palo Alto, Calif., 1971 (AD 721 066).
54. R. Salvador, *Automatic Abstracting and Indexing*, Computer and Inform. Sci. Res. Cen., The Ohio State University, Columbus, Ohio, 1969, Tech. Rep. Ser. (OSU-CISRC-TR-69-15).
55. Computer and Information Science Res. Cen., *Report to the National Science Foundation Office of Science Information Service on NSF Grant GN-534.1, July 1970 through June 1971*, Computer and Inform. Sci. Res. Cen., The Ohio State University, Columbus, Ohio, 1971.
56. E. F. Skoroxod'ko, Information retrieval system of the Ukranian Institute of Cybernetics, in *Proceedings of the International Congress on Scientific Information*, Moscow, 1968.
57. E. F. Skoroxod'ko, Adaptive method of automatic abstracting and indexing, *IFIP Congress* 71, *Ljubljana, Yugoslavia*, 1971, Booklet TA-6, 133–137.

58. S. J. Marvin, J. E. Rush, and C. E. Young, Grammatical class assignment using function words as a basis, in *Proceedings of the 7th Annual National Information Retrieval Colloquim*, Philadelphia, Pa., 1970.
59. L. Carroll, *Through the Looking Glass and What Alice Found There*, Macmillan, New York, 1916.
60. D. King and E. C. Bryant, *The Evaluation of Information Services and Products*, Information Resources Press, Washington, D.C., 1971.

EXTRACTING

27

Relevance Predictability in Information Retrieval Systems

Allen Kent, Jack Belzer,* Marvin Kurfeerst,† Eleanor D. Dym, Donald L. Shirey, and Anindya Bose‡ / University of Pittsburgh, Pittsburgh, Pennsylvania

An experiment is described which attempts to derive quantitative indicators regarding the potential relevance predictability of the intermediate stimuli used to represent documents in information retrieval systems. In effect, since the decision to peruse an entire document is often predicated upon the examination of one "level of processing" of the document (e.g., the citation and/or abstract), it became interesting to analyze the properties of what constitutes "relevance." However, prior to such an analysis, an even more elementary step had to be made, namely, to determine what portions of a document should be examined.

An evaluation of the ability of intermediate response products (IRPs), functioning as cues to the information content of full documents, to predict the relevance determination that would be subsequently made on these documents by motivated users of information retrieval systems, was made under controlled experimental conditions. The hypothesis that there might be other intermediate response products (selected extracts from the document, i.e., first paragraph, last paragraph, and the combination of first and last paragraph), that would be as representative of the full document as the traditional IRPs (citation and abstract) was tested systematically. The results showed that:

1. there is no significant difference among the several IRP treatment groups on the number of cue evaluations of relevancy which match the subsequent user relevancy decision on the document;
2. first and last paragraph combinations have consistently predicted relevancy to a higher degree than the other IRPs;
3. abstracts were undistinguished as predictors; and

From Kent, Allen, et al., "Relevance Predictability in Information Retrieval Systems," *Method. Inform. Med.*, 6, no. 2(April 1967) 45-51.
Supported by National Institutes of Health Grant FR-00202-01, FR-00202-02, and FR-00202-03.
*Presently retired
†Deceased
‡Presently at Kent State University, Kent State, Ohio

4. the apparent high predictability rating for citations was not substantive.

Some of these results are quite different than would be expected from previous work with unmotivated subjects.

VORAUSSAGBARKEIT DER RELEVANZ BEI INFORMATION-RETRIEVAL-SYSTEMEN

Es wird ein Experiment beschrieben, bei dem versucht wurde, quantitative Anhaltspunkte über die Vorbestimmbarkeit der Relevanzstärke von "intermediate stimuli" (das sind irgendweiche Repräsentationsformen eines Dokumentes anstelle des Gesamtdokumentes, z. B. Titel, Abstrakt, Extrakt) zu gewinnen. Da der Entschluß, ein Dokument vollständig durchzulesen, sich häufig auf die Durchsicht einer "Bearbeitungsstufe" des Dokumentes (z. B. ein Zitat oder eine Zusammenfassung) stützt, ist es interessant, die Eigenschaften zu untersuchen, die "Relevanz" ausmachen. Vor einer solchen Analyse mußte jedoch zunächst einmal geklärt werden, welche Teile eines Dokumentes daraufhin untersucht werden sollten.

Unter kontrollierten experimentellen Bedingungen wurde die Brauchbarkeit von Intermediärprodukten, die als Schlüssel zum Informationsgehalt des Gesamtdokumentes dienen, geprüft, um die Relevanzentscheidung, die nachfolgend von thematisch interessierten Benutzern des Systems nach Durchlesen des gesamten Dokuments getroffen wurde, vorauszusagen. Systematisch wurde dabei die Hypothese getestet, daß andere Intermediärprodukte (ausgewähte, Auszüge aus dem Dokument, wie z. B. erster und letzter Absatz der Arbeit oder die Kombination von beiden) möglicherweise genau so repräsentativ für den vollen Text sein könnten wie die traditionellen Zwischenprodukte (Zitat und Zusammenfassung).

Die Untersuchungsergebnisse zeigten:

1. es besteht kein wesentlicher Unterschied zwischen den verschiedenen Auswertungsgruppen hinsichtlich der Anzahl zutreffender Relevanzbewertungen im Vergleich zur nachfolgenden Relevanzentscheidung des Benutzers nach Durchlesen des gesamten Dokumentes;
2. die Kombination von erstem und letztem Absatz einer Arbeit liefert eine höhere Quote voraussagbarer Relevanz als die übrigen Zwischenprodukte;
3. Zusammenfassungen sind für die Relevanz-Voraussage nicht differenziert genug;
4. die anscheinend hohe Voraussagequote von Zitaten (Titelangaben) konnte nicht bestätigt werden.

Einige dieser Untersuchungsergebnisse weichen erheblich von den Resultaten früherer Arbeiten mit "unmotivierten" Versuchspersonen ab.

Introduction

The Knowledge Availability Systems Center of the University of Pittsburgh has been investigating the nature of the relevance judgments made by motivated users of information retrieval systems (4). A subproblem in the area of relevancy judgments, which has been investigated intensively and which is reported in this paper, is an evaluation of the predictive ability of Intermediate Response Products (IRPs)* which function as cues to the information content of documents. Do selected IRPs functioning as cues to documents have predictive ability for motivated users? Are there differences in the abilities of these IRP cues to predict the relevance of documents? Do these predictive abilities become stable as the sample size increases?

Previous research relating to relevance of responses from information retrieval systems is concerned with "user" studies, dealing mainly with habits and needs (1). In 1964, a paper by Hillman (3) discussed relevance in terms of "similarity-judgments" formed by users, but suggested difficulties in attempting to accommodate these in a formal theory. Accordingly, Hillman proposed to explain conceptual relatedness by describing what factors are relevant to similarity-judgments. However, no experimental methods were suggested for gathering data relating to these factors. The validity of comparative tests of information retrieval systems conducted in England has been questioned seriously by Taube and Swanson (7), partly because of the use of unmotivated subjects and questions which were not real. When motivated users were investigated by Tague (8), primary data were not available from them; rather, relevance judgments were obtained directly from system-oriented specialists who reviewed raw search output. In another experiment on relevance judgments, experts (in the subject matter of given questions) were used experimentally to judge the relevance of documents, but in terms of questions which did not necessarily relate to problems for which these experts were motivated to receive information at that time (6).

As a consequence, an experiment was designed, which considered as subjects only motivated users† of information systems. It was hypothesized that the results obtained would be quite different than would be expected from previous work with unmotivated subjects. Accordingly, the major thrust of this experiment was aimed at an evaluation of the ability of such motivated subjects to utilize various IRP cues in predicting relevance of documents.

To date, the two most common representations of a document, employed for the above purpose, have been the bibliographic citation and the abstract.

The rationale for employing *bibliographic citations* has been twofold: 1) the title of a document is assumed to be sufficiently informative to permit prediction of utility of the source document in terms of an existing interest or need; and 2) the citation is available quickly and inexpensively.

The rationale for employing *abstracts* has, also, been twofold, either a a substitute for the document (i.e., a condensation of the document's most salient features) or a predictor of the relevance of the document (i.e., a brief summation of what will be found). In either case, however, it has been assumed that the abstracts provide sufficient "relevance predictability" to warrant the costs of preparing and publishing them. And, furthermore, readers of abstracts have been conditioned to accept the premise that the abstract offers sufficient information to permit a decision to be made regarding the utility of reading the entire document.

---

*Intermediate Response Products (IRPs) are surrogates for full documents delivered as output by a system by which a user judges the desirability of obtaining the original.
†Motivated user is one who has a need and/or apparently sincere desire to obtain substantive information relating to a problem or interest of current or predicted future concern to him.

Bibliographic citations and/or abstracts, traditionally used as IRPs, are generally supplied in response to a question and function as a cue, which, it is hoped, will permit the user to predict whether the full document will be of interest and relevant to his information needs. Several additional IRPs, i.e., *document extracts,* are hypothesized to have the potential to predict relevancy, as well as the traditional IRP cues (citations and abstracts). These document extracts, which may be derived readily and unambiguously by clerical personnel, are the *first paragraph, last paragraph,* and a *combination of the first and last paragraphs* of the documents.

If experimental evidence would support the hypothesis, extracts, available immediately (contrasted with the typical delay necessary to abstract a document) could be substituted effectively without a resultant loss in the efficiency and effectiveness of the document retrieval system.

The basic premise has been that relevancy is not an inherent characteristic of a document but rather is a function of certain idiosyncratic variables of the user as he evaluates a particular document in relation to his own information need at that time. As a result, a document determined to be relevant by user X at time t_1 may not be relevant for the same user X at another time, t_2. If the information needs of individuals are not static, then evaluations made of IRPs and subsequently the documents associated with these IRPs are not unalterable, except in proximity to the time when the judgments were made. As the elapsed time interval between the user's statement of his inquiry and the presentation of information retrieved from a file in response to his inquiry increases, the probability that some of the retrieved information no longer meets his needs (which have changed in the same interval) increases. Time, with its concomitant change in information needs, seems to be an important variable in relevance judgments.

Since the decision to obtain a copy of the full document or to persue an entire document is generally predicated upon an examination of an IRP of the document, the differing potentials of IRPs to predict relevancy become a variable worth considering in the design of document retrieval systems.

On the basis of the content information that is included in the IRP, the user must infer all document content that is not included in the IRP. Now, ambiguity has been introduced, an ambiguity associated with information not included in the IRP that must be inferred about the full document. If the IRP had been the full document itself, there would have been no ambiguity about the document. However, as the IRP cues contain less than the full information content of the document, more of that information must be inferred. The more that must be inferred, the more the ambiguity and the less the ability to predict. Good predictive ability is predicated from certainty. As uncertainty increases monotonically to a maximum value, predictability decreases proportionately to a minimum.

Representativeness of an IRP is a characteristic related to predictability. The more faithful the representation, the greater the probability that the user will make the same decision about the content of a document in relation to his information needs after exposure to an IRP as he would have made if given the full document in response to his inquiry. In effect, testing predictability is testing representativeness. To the degree that an IRP cue reflects unambiguously the information content of the full document text, to that degree will an IRP cue be able to predict relevancy.

Method

Beginning with the hypothesis that an abstract may not offer the reader the best cue as to a document's content, other representations of a document were chosen to systematically test this hypothesis. The experiment was designed to answer the following question: Do extracts of a document (either singly or in combination) provide a motivated user of an information retrieval system with a means of selecting relevant documents at a higher level of probability than the traditionally-used representations of a document?

Selection of subjects—Initially, motivated users were solicited from the medical complex at the University of Pittsburgh. The primary criterion for sample inclusion was motivation, i.e., they were involved in an ongoing research activity and had a real need for literature in order to continue their investigation. Later, the sample was expanded to include other areas of academic interest[*] and other geographic areas[†].

Information retrieval system employed—Due to the nature of the underlying question being investigated, no specific information retrieval system was studied. Since the system itself was not under investigation, the focus was placed on the preliminary or intermediate output of systems by which a participant would decide whether to seek the entire document.

Selection of documents—After receipt of the inquiry from a motivated user, it was presented to a professional searcher who proceeded to search current literature (most recent five years) thoroughly but not exhaustively. An upper limit for search output of 25 documents and a lower limit of 10 documents was arbitrarily set. Approximately 10 percent of these were to be nonrelevant, as judged by the literature searcher.

Preparation of IRPs—Intermediate response products were identified for each document (including citation, first paragraph, last paragraph, and abstract); and, then, through a randomization process, an IRP was chosen from each document and prepared for presentation to the subject.

The intermediate response products, with their defining characteristics are as follows:

1. *citation*—the full bibliographic citations, i.e., author, title, journal, volume, number, date, and pagination;
2. *abstract including citation*—the abstract, whether from the article itself, or some other source (volume of abstracts) must be headed or clearly labelled "abstract" in order to be used;
3. *first paragraph including the citation*—the typographic first paragraph, unless it is an abstract, summary, or quotation from another source, in which case the paragraph immediately following is used;
4. *last paragraph including citation*—the typographic last paragraph unless it is

---

[*]Representing the areas of biology, chemistry, dentistry, education, health and welfare, psychology, and physics.
[†]University of California at Los Angeles; University of Missouri; Purdue University; Western Michigan University; Metropolitan Pittsburgh; Bethesda, Maryland; Hershey, Pennsylvania; New York City, New York; and Washington, District of Columbia.

part of a summary, abstract, conclusion, bibliography, appendix or acknowledgement, in which case the paragraph immediately preceding is used.
5. *First and last paragraphs including citation*—combination of 3 and 4 above and meeting the criteria defined for each. For every stimulus, the full bibliographic citation is an integral part of the stimulus, thus, approximating the "real-life" situation whereby an individual scanning a document has immediate access to its full citation.

The randomization process is conducted as follows. A table of two-digit random numbers had been generated for use in the randomization process. Initially, each document in a group of documents is assigned a two-digit random number that determines the order in which the documents will be arranged for the assignment of stimuli. Even though this actual assigning is an iterative process, it is, in effect, the same as a random assignment of stimuli since it assures that every document has an equal chance of being assigned a given stimulus. This randomization is necessary to determine which type of stimuli will be associated with which document in the sample.

Each inquiry must then have roughly the same number of each type of stimuli assigned to its documents. This is accomplished by first deciding what multiple of 5 is contained in the total number of documents. For example, if n = 17 documents, then the multiple of 5 is 3 (plus 2 extra), meaning that there should be 3 of each type of stimuli assigned to documents.

Of primary concern is the fact that many documents do not have available abstracts for use as stimuli. Therefore, documents with abstracts are assigned abstract stimuli in primary consideration of their scarcity; random assignment from this group is made to fulfill the needed number of abstract stimuli (i.e., in above example 3) and any excess documents with abstracts may then be randomly assigned to some other type of stimuli. A second consideration is the necessity, in the long run, of having approximately the same number of stimuli assigned to documents. The excess documents (i.e., in above example 2) are assigned a stimulus type from an "Excess Stimuli Check List"; and notation is made of the type of stimuli assigned to insure maintaining of equality of numbers*.

A second randomization is necessary to determine the sequence in which this corpus of documents will be presented to the inquirer. Again, the table of two-digit random numbers is employed for the assignments.

Presentation of cues and documents to subjects—The set of IRP cues (one from each document on a sheet) was arranged randomly, bound, and exposed one at a time to the participant for his evaluation of the potential document relevancy. This evaluation was on a "yes" "no" basis, i.e., did the cue from a document indicate that the entire document would be useful? After completing his evaluation of the cues, the participant was then given the full set of corresponding documents (randomly ordered) and asked, at his leisure, to provide his relevance judgment on each document.

Recording the data—The "yes" "no" relevancy evaluations of IRP cues were coded 1 and 0 respectively; and the subsequent "yes" "no" relevancy decisions on documents were, likewise, coded 1 and 0. Corresponding evaluations, i.e., 1-1 or 0-0, were re-

---

*The "Excess Stimuli Check List" is arranged with the stimuli types in successive order (i.e., Citation, Abstract, *First* paragraph, *Last* paragraph, and *First* and *Last* paragraph: C, A, F, L, FL, etc.) and checked off as availability permits.

corded as matches; and, non-corresponding evaluations, i.e., 1-0 or 0-1, were recorded as mis-matches.

Results

At the present time, data are available for analysis from 70 inquiries processed to completion. These 70 inquiries represent 1,114 documents that have been retrieved and presented to participants. Each participant has judged a set of documents, most of which are in direct response to his query. In addition, prior to viewing these documents, he has evaluated an IRP cue for each document. Table 1 gives a summary of the decisions made on these documents.

The data logically subdivided into four categories. Each of these categories has been given an identifying label. These labels are operationally defined to be as follows:

1. α match ($D_R C_R$)—occurs whenever the participant evaluates the IRP (stimulus or cue) to be relevant and then judges the full document (from which the IRP was extracted or abstracted) also to be relevant.
2. α mismatch ($D_R \bar{C}_R$)—occurs whenever the participant evaluates the IRP to be non-relevant, then, subsequently, judges the full document to be relevant.
3. β mismatch ($\bar{D}_R C_R$)—occurs whenever the participant evaluates the IRP to be relevant, but subsequently judges the full document to be non-relevant.
4. β match ($\bar{D}_R \bar{C}_R$)—occurs whenever the participant evaluates the IRP to be non-relevant, and then, subsequently, judges the full document to be also non-relevant.

A one-way analysis of variance using a fixed-effect model indicates that the data do not provide enough evidence to warrant the conclusion that differences in the mean proportion of cue-document matches, when effected by the type of IRP cue, truly exist among these treatment groups at the .05 level of confidence. Table 2 gives the summary data for this test.

Although the differences are not significant at the .05 level, the index ω^2 was computed to see if there is any degree of association between the type of IRP cue and the number of cue-document matches. A high degree of association would imply that signifi-

Table 1 Categorical Summarization of Decisions Made on Both IRP Cues and Documents by 70 Respondees. (D_R and C_R are Relevant Documents and Cues Respectively; $\bar{D}_R$ and $\bar{C}_R$ are Non-relevant Documents and Cues Respectively)

Decision	Type of IRP cue					
	Citation	Abstract	First paragraph	Last paragraph	First and last paragraph	Σ
D_R, C_R	112	113	110	106	121	562
$D_R, \bar{C}_R$	16	18	16	20	10	80
$\bar{D}_R, C_R$	55	39	43	38	31	206
$\bar{D}_R, \bar{C}_R$	44	43	55	61	63	266
Total documents judged	227	213	224	225	225	1,114

Table 2 Analysis of Variance of "Matches" on Document-cue Decisions Using Five (5) Independent IRPs

Source of variation	Sum of squares	df	Mean square	F
Between IRPs	2.01	4	.50	263
Within IRPs	2105.56	1109	.19	
Total	212.57	1113		

$F = 2.63$ with 4 and 1113 df, $p > .05$

cant differences may exist and that, by either increasing sample size or refining the experimental procedures, these differences may be uncovered.

An estimate of ω^2 using the summary data for the analysis of variance in Table 2 is .007 (2). This estimate implies a very weak statistical association. It does not seem likely that increasing sample size or refining the procedure will ever result in a significant difference.

Thus, curiosity regarding differential effects of the IRP cues on the number of document-cue matches was diminished by the lack of evidence supporting significant differences.

Next, probabilities for predicting relevance under specified conditions, e.g., the probability that a document will be judged relevant, given that its IPR cue has been evaluated as relevant, were computed. As this is akin to selection procedures, for example, predicting a student's course grade, given his diagnostic test score and information about the relative frequency of success of others having comparable test scores, conditional probabilities are appropriate. The basis for these conditional probabilities is Bayes' theorem (5). These probabilities have a simple relative frequency interpretation. The conditional probabilities are shown in Table 3.

The results recorded in Table 3 indicate that the conditional probabilities for this sample warrant further examination. Some examples are:

1. Given that the IRP cue is evaluated as relevant, the greatest probability that the associated document will subsequently be determined to be relevant, $p(D_R | C_R)$, occurs when the first and last paragraph of a document is used as the IRP.
2. One type of mismatch, $(D_R | \bar{C}_R)$, occurs when the cue is evaluated as non-relevant, but, subsequently, the document is determined to be relevant. This type of mismatch is least likely to occur when the first and last paragraph is used as a cue, and it is a great deal more likely to occur when the abstract is used.
3. The other type of mismatch, when the cue is evaluated as relevant, but the document is non-relevant, $(\bar{D}_R | C_R)$, occurs more frequently. It would seem that in cases where the IRP cue is obscure and there is a great deal of ambiguity, there is a tendency to evaluate the cue as relevant (it may necessitate the reading of additional non-relevant material, but this is often considered by information system users to be preferable to evaluating the IRP as non-relevant, thus losing the opportunity of reviewing the document, thereby missing potentially useful information). Once again, the IRP cue least likely to lead to this type of mismatch is the first and last paragraph combination.

Table 3 Simple and Conditional Probabilities for the Decisions Made on 1,114 Documents with Five Types of Cues by 70 Respondees

	Citation	Abstract	First paragraph	Last paragraph	First and last paragraph
Simple probabilities					
$p(D_R)$	.564	.615	.563	.560	.582
$p(\bar{D}_R)$	.436	.385	.437	.440	.418
$p(C_R)$	.736	.714	.683	.640	.676
$p(\bar{C}_R)$	.264	.286	.317	.360	.324
Conditional probabilities					
$p(C_R \mid D_R)$	.875	.863	.873	.841	.924
$p(C_R \mid \bar{D}_R)$	.555	.476	.439	.384	.330
$p(\bar{C}_R \mid D_R)$	.126	.137	.127	.159	.076
$p(\bar{C}_R \mid \bar{D}_R)$	.444	.524	.561	.616	.670
$p(D_R \mid C_R)$	.671	.744	.719	.736	.796
$p(D_R \mid \bar{C}_R)$	.267	.295	.225	.247	.137
$p(\bar{D}_R \mid C_R)$	.330	.257	.281	.264	.204
$p(\bar{D}_R \mid \bar{C}_R)$	.734	.705	.775	.753	.863
p (matching)	.687	.732	.737	.742	.818

4. The remaining match occurs when both the cue and the document are rated as non-relevant, $(\bar{D}_R \mid \bar{C}_R)$. This match is more likely to occur when the first and last paragraph IRP is used than for any other IRP.

Demonstrated in the foregoing examples, described by conditional probabilities, is an ability to increase the likelihood of being right about an event after having been given some prior information about it (contrast the conditional probabilities with the simple probabilities in Table 3).

Some other conditional probabilities of interest for this set of data are:

> Given a relevant document, the IRP cue that is least likely to be evaluated as relevant is a last paragraph, while the IRP cue with the greatest probability of being evaluated as relevant is the first and last paragraph.
> However, when given a non-relevant document, the first and last paragraph is still most likely to discern that it is non-relevant, while the citation is the IRP that is the poorest predictor of non-relevancy.

These conditional probabilities are graphically represented in Figure 1.

The differences in the probabilities of document-cue matches are fairly consistent, except for the citation. It appears to be a superior predictor for relevant documents, but, comparatively, a poor one for non-relevant documents. This is misleading, however; for the probabilities associated with citations are inflated on relevant documents and conversely attenuated on non-relevant documents. These extreme values are an artifact of the document-cue judgment process. As mentioned previously, when the cue is ambiguous, there is an optimistic tendency to judge it relevant; the more ambiguous the cue, the more of the information content of the document that must be inferred. Since the cue most frequently evaluated to be relevant was the citation and since over half the corresponding documents were also determined to be relevant (see the simple probabilities

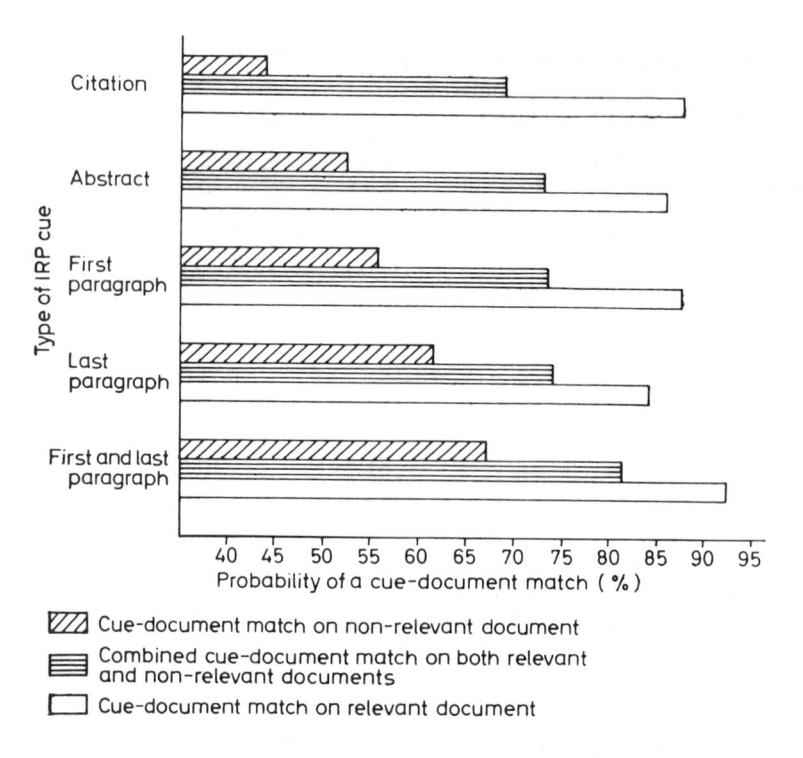

Figure 1 Probabilities of cue-document matches as a function of document state.

in Table 3, especially p (D_R) and p (C_R), the probability of a document being relevant and a cue being relevant, respectively), the probability of a match on a relevant document was greatly enhanced, while a match on a non-relevant document was depressed. This artifact was in operation with the other cues, also, but to a lesser extent as evidenced by the smaller differences between the probabilities on relevant and on non-relevant documents; in fact, an index of relevance predictability developed around these differences may result in being quite useful.

The bottom row of Table 3 shows the probability of the user's evaluation of the cue concurring with his judgment of the document. This is the probability of making the same "yes" "no" evaluation on both the IRP and full document. These percentages represent the probability of a user receiving, from a system, those documents most related to his information needs, at that moment, if he was presented only with that set of documents corresponding to those cues he had evaluated as relevant. This is the amount of assurance the user has that his judgment would have been the same, in judging the relevance of a document using an IRP as a cue, as it would have been had he read the full document before making his decision.

For example, the probability is .818 that the user would make the same judgment of a given document, having seen only the first and last paragraph combination as he would have made after seeing the full document. Similarly, a user would have been a little less sure (probability is .732), had he used an abstract, instead, as the IRP cue.

Figure 2 is a graphic portrayal of the stability of the IRPs as predictors of relevancy over an increasing number of inquiries.

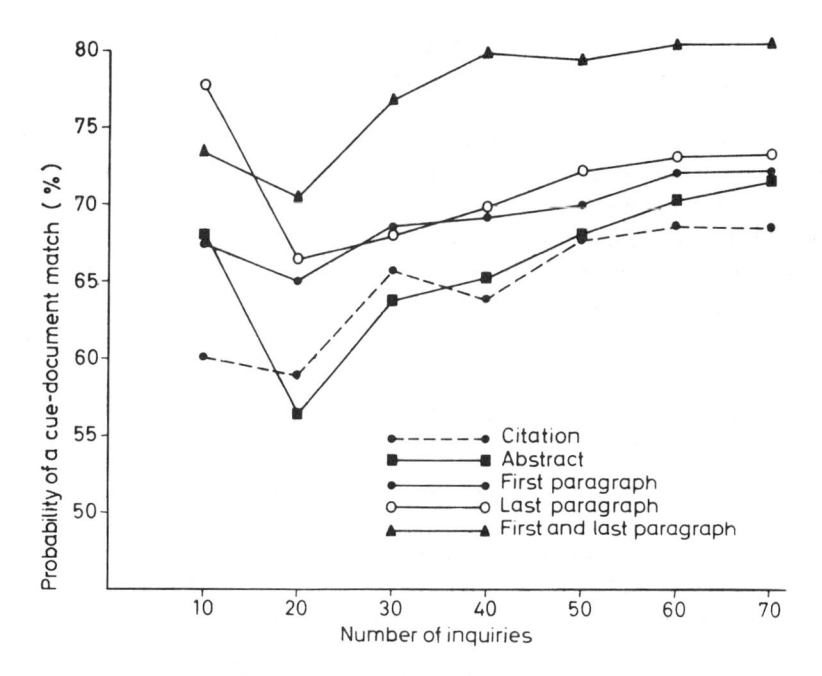

Figure 2 Stability of cue-document matches over inquiries.

The graph shows succinctly a general tendency to stabilize on the percent of document-cue matches as sample size increases. By extrapolating, it seems possible to hypothesize that the differences between the five types of IRP cues in predictive ability may become undifferentiable after additional inquiries are processed and the sample enlarged. Also, it can be seen that after ten inquiries (approximately thirty document-cue pairs of each type had been evaluated by the participants) that the first and last paragraph combination has consistently been the best predictor of a document's relevancy. And, conversely, it can be seen that the abstract's record has been poor and, at best, no better than the other cues, i.e., the extracts (citation, first paragraph, and last paragraph).

Summary

A controlled experiment was designed to systematically test the hypothesis that other IRP cues, in addition to the traditional citation and abstract, may predict the relevancy of documents for motivated users, as well as these conventional cues.

A one-way analysis of variance indicated that significant differences between the mean proportion of document-cue matches exist with a probability which is greater than five percent, and which is an unacceptable level; therefore, the hypothesis of no differences continues to be held. An estimate of the degree of associativity between the number of document-cue matches and the type of IRP employed, using the index ω^2 gives evidence that an increase in sample size or a change in procedures will never result in significant differences.

Conditional probabilities give some evidence that the first and last paragraph consistently predicted relevancy better, throughout this sample, than any other type of cue. The predictive ability on relevant documents was inflated to some degree on all cues, an artifact of document-cue evaluations when ambiguity was operating. The differences between the probabilities of a match on relevant documents and a match on non-relevant documents will give a rough estimate of the relative extent of this factor.

In conclusion, there is empirical evidence that extracts (particularly first and last paragraph combinations), functioning as cues to the information content of documents, serve as well as (in our opinion, better than) the traditional citation and abstract.

REFERENCES

1. Davis, R. A., and Bailey, C. A.: Bibliography of Use Studies. (Drexel Institute of Technology, Project No. 195, Graduate School of Library Sciences, March, 1964. 98 pp.).
2. Hayes, W.: Statistics for Psychologists. p. 382. (Holt, Rhinehart, and Winston, Inc., New York 1963).
3. Hillman, D. J.: The Notation of Relevance. Amer. Doc. *15*: 26-34, 1964.
4. Kent, A.: The Information Retrieval Game. In Kent, A. and Taulbee, O. E. (ed.), Electronic Information Handling, pp. 311-348. (Spartan Books, Inc., New York 1965).
5. Kullback, S.: Information Theory and Statistics. p. 84. (John Wiley & Sons, Inc., New York 1959).
6. Resnick, A., and Savage, T. R.: The Consistency of Human Judgments of Relevancy. Amer. Doc. *15*: 93-95, 1965.
7. Swanson, D. R.: The Evidence Underlying the Cranfield Results. Library quart. *35*: 1-20, 1965.
8. Tague, J.: Matching of Question and Answer Terminology in an Education Research File. Amer. Doc. *16*: 26-32, 1965.